WINDOWS NT SERVER
SURVIVAL GUIDE

Rick Sant'Angelo

Nadeem Chagtai

SAMS
PUBLISHING

201 West 103rd Street
Indianapolis, Indiana 46290

I dedicate this book to my daughter, Amber Fu-Juan, and the roughly 1.7 million other infant girls who are abandoned in China each year.

—*Rick Sant'Angelo*

I dedicate this book to my mother, Zakia Chagtai; she has been an inspiration and the guiding force in my life.

—*Nadeem Chagtai*

COPYRIGHT © 1996 BY SAMS PUBLISHING

FIRST EDITION

International Standard Book Number: 0-672-30860-6

Library of Congress Catalog Card Number: 95-72335

99 98 97 96   4 3 2 1

Interpretation of the printing code: the rightmost double-digit number is the year of the book's printing; the rightmost single-digit, the number of the book's printing. For example, a printing code of 96-1 shows that the first printing of the book occurred in 1996.

Composed in New Century Schoolbook and MCPdigital by Macmillan Computer Publishing

Printed in the United States of America

TRADEMARKS

PUBLISHER AND PRESIDENT	*Richard K. Swadley*
ACQUISITIONS MANAGER	*Greg Wiegand*
DEVELOPMENT MANAGER	*Dean Miller*
MANAGING EDITOR	*Cindy Morrow*
MARKETING MANAGER	*Gregg Bushyeager*

ACQUISITIONS EDITOR
Grace Buechlein

DEVELOPMENT EDITOR
Tony Amico

SOFTWARE DEVELOPMENT SPECIALIST
Steve Straiger

PRODUCTION EDITOR
Johnna L. VanHoose

COPY EDITORS
Margaret Berson, Kimberly Hannel, Charles A. Hutchinson, Kristine Simmons

EDITORIAL COORDINATOR
Bill Whitmer

TECHNICAL EDIT COORDINATOR
Lynette Quinn

FORMATTER
Frank Sinclair

EDITORIAL ASSISTANTS
Sharon Cox
Andi Richter
Rhonda Tinch-Mize

COVER DESIGNER
Dan Armstrong

BOOK DESIGNER
Alyssa Yesh

PRODUCTION TEAM SUPERVISOR
Brad Chinn

PRODUCTION
Carol Bowers
Georgiana Briggs
Jeanne Clark
Terrie Deemer
Cheryl Dietsch
Jason Hand
Mike Henry
Ayanna Lacey
Kevin Laseau
Paula Lowell
Nancy Price
Laura Robbins
Bobbi Satterfield
Todd Wente

Overview

Introduction   xxvii

PART I   INTRODUCTION TO NT SERVER

1   Overview of the Windows NT Server Product   3
2   NT Design   23
3   Building the Server   49
4   Microsoft's Protocol Support   73

PART II   INSTALLING AND CONFIGURING THE NOS

5   Selecting a LAN   99
6   Installing and Configuring the NT Server OS   125
7   Migration Procedures   153
8   Connecting the Client   177

PART III   SYSTEM ADMINISTRATION

9   Workgroups and Domains   209
10   Groups, Rights, and Permissions   257
11   Setting Up the User Environment   285
12   Controlling the User Environment   329
13   NT Printing Services   359
14   Managing the Network Registry   405
15   Administering Workgroup Applications   451
16   Gateway Service for NetWare (GSNW)   493

PART IV   APPLICATION SERVER ADD-ONS

17   Systems Management Server   507
18   Remote Access Server   529
19   SQL Server   551
20   SNA Server   577
21   Microsoft TCP/IP Services   595

PART V   OPTIMIZING PERFORMANCE, REDUCING DOWNTIME

22   Monitoring Tools and Techniques   623
23   Evaluating Performance Opportunities   643

24   Monitoring and Tuning Performance   661

25   LAN Capacity Allocation   695

26   Virtual LAN Capacity Allocation   715

27   Physical Security, Quick Recovery   725

PART VI TROUBLESHOOTING

28   Troubleshooting Overview   751

29   Server Hardware Troubleshooting   769

30   LAN Troubleshooting   785

31   File System and Disk Subsystem Problems   835

APPENDIX

A   NT Server 3.51 System Requirements   855

B   Where to Find Support and Updates   865

C   NT Quick Reference Guide   875

D   Logon Script Programming Guide   907

E   Glossary of Networking Terminology   917

      Index   945

Contents

PART I   INTRODUCTION TO NT SERVER

1   Overview of the Windows NT Server Product   **3**

LAN Manager Heritage 6

Similarities to OS/2 7

DOS Compatibility 7

Similarities to Windows 3.1 and Windows For Workgroups
(WFW) 3.11 8

Similarities to NetWare 8

Why Is Everyone So Excited about Windows NT? 9

   Simplified Learning 9

   Multiple Windows 9

   Multitasking 10

   Multi-user 10

   Fun and Enticing! 10

   System Administration 10

   Simple Migration with Native Support for Popular
     Protocol Stacks 11

   32-Bit Network Device Interface Specification (NDIS) Drivers 11

   Software Development 11

   Scalability 12

   BackOffice 13

   Hardware Status 14

   Technical Expertise 15

   Features 15

  Summary 21

2   NT Design   **23**

NT Server OS Architecture 25

   Compatibility 26

   Security 27

   Portability 28

   Scalability 30

   Distributed Computing 31

   Operating System Features 33

Centralized Control of Client Environment 43

   User Profiles Overview 43

   Logon Scripts 44

   Permissions 45

   System Environment Variables and Account Parameters 46

Summary 47

3   Building the Server   49

Terms Used In This Chapter 50

Server Hardware Compatibility Issues 54

Intel x86 Platform Specifics 54

   Choosing Hardware 55

Running Setup 67

   SMP Support for Multiprocessor Computers 68

RISC Platform Specifics 68

   OpenGL 69

   RISC-Based Server Installation Considerations 69

   Emergency Repair Disk For RISC 70

Keeping Up with Growth 70

4   Microsoft's Protocol Support   73

Protocols and LAN Data Communications Overview 76

   What Is a LAN? 76

   Virtual Circuits versus Physical Circuits.................................... 78

   How LANs Move Data from One Network Card to Another 78

   Segmentation and Reassembly of Messages 79

   Bridging 81

   Routing 82

   Switching Hubs 83

   Bridging versus Routing 84

Network Architecture 85

   The OSI Model 86

   NetBIOS 87

   NetBEUI (NetBIOS Extended User Interface) 87

   IPX/SPX 88

   Microsoft TCP/IP 89

   Network Device Interface Specification (NDIS)........................... 90

   Data Link Control (DLC) 91

   Server Message Block (SMB) 91

NT Server's Workstation Support 91

Supporting NetWare Clients 92

   Using IPXODI Client Support Drivers 92

   Using NDIS Drivers and IPX/SPX Compatible 94
    Transport (NWLink)

Changing Network Card Driver and Protocol Configurations 95

   Using Gateway Service for NetWare 96

Summary—Connecting NT to Any Network Client 96

Part II   Installing and Configuring the NOS

5 Selecting a LAN   **99**

   Preparing for an NT Server Installation 102

   Understanding LAN Technologies 102

      Bandwidth (Capacity) 103

      Ethernet or Token Ring and Usable Bandwidth 103

      The Case for Ethernet and Fast Ethernet 105

      The Case for Token Ring 106

      The Case for Fiber Distributed Data Interface
        (FDDI) and TP-DDI (FDDI on Twisted Pair) 107

      The Case for 100VG-AnyLAN 108

      The Case for Asynchronous Transfer Mode (ATM) 109

   Installing LAN Cabling 109

      Selecting the Correct Cabling and Layout 110

      Certifying Cabling 112

      Tips on Installing Twisted Pair Cabling (EIA/TIA 568) 113

      Tips on Installing 10Base-2 (Thinnet) Ethernet
        Cabling (IEEE 10Base-2) 116

      Optical Fiber 118

   Installing Network Cards 118

   What You Need to Know About Network Card Drivers 120

   Summary 122

6 Installing and Configuring the NT Server OS   **125**

   Obtaining the Latest Drivers 127

   Overview of Installation 129

      Overview of Setup for Windows NT 129

      Installation Support Checklist 130

   Running Setup to Install Windows NT 3.51 130
      (Server or Workstation)

      Before You Begin 131

      The Installation Procedure 131

   Unattended or Customized Setup 146

      Setup Mechanics 147

      How to Configure and Run an Unattended Setup 148

   Post-Installation Configuration 150

      Adding/Editing Devices in an NT Server or Workstation 151

   Summary 152

7 Migration Procedures   **153**

Conservative Migration Strategies 154
   Planning a Migration Strategy 155
The NetWare Migration Utility 157
   What Is Not Migrated 158
   How to Use the Migration Tool for NetWare 159
Upgrading from LAN Manager 2.*x* 170
   Migration Utilities..170
   Integrating LAN Manager 2.*x* and NT Servers 171
   Limitations of LAN Manager 2.*x* Servers on NT Networks 171
   Account Replication..172
   File Replication 172
Other NOSs 172
Migration from Minicomputers and UNIX Systems 173
Summary 175

8 Connecting the Client   **177**

Overview and Notes on
   Setting Up Clients 180
   Caveats and Networking Limitations of Microsoft
      Operating Systems 180
   The Network Client Administrator Utility 185
   Creating an MS-DOS Client Bootable Disk 186
   Make Installation Disk Sets for DOS, WFW, and
      LAN Manager Clients 188
MS-DOS Client Setup..189
Windows for Workgroups (WFW) 3.11 Clients 191
Windows 95 Clients 195
   Setting Up Network Services... 197
   Mapping a Drive Letter to a Share... 202
   Capturing a Printer...203
   Troubleshooting Tips 203
Windows NT Workstation Clients 204
Summary 204

PART III   SYSTEM ADMINISTRATION

9 Workgroups and Domains   **209**

Workgroups versus Domains 211
   Local versus Domain Logon 212
   Logon Security 213
   Universal Naming Convention (UNC) 214
   Access Permissions 214

The Concept of Domains 215

The Mechanics of User Accounts 216

Trust Relationships 216

Domain Rules 217

Trusting versus Trusted Domains 217

One-Way Trusts 218

Two-Way Trusts 218

Pass-through Authentication 219

The Four Basic Models for Building Domains 220

Setting Up Trust Relationships 221

Establishing a Route for Passing Validations 222

Domain Replication: PDCs and BDCs 225

Fault Tolerance 225

Managing Domain Controllers 226

Promoting a BDC to PDC 227

Optimizing Domain Synchronization 229

Directory Replication 233

NT Workstations in Domains 236

Reconfiguring Domains 236

Using Server Manager to Add a Computer to a Domain 237

Adding a Computer to a Domain During Installation 237

Workstation Joining a Domain 238

Recombining Split Domains 239

Changing Computer Names 241

Changing the Computer Name of an NT Server 241

Changing the Computer Name of an NT Workstation 242

Application Servers 243

Domain Behavior, Example: Setting Time 245

Browser 246

Determining Browser Roles 246

Disabling Browsing 248

Account Authentication 248

NT Server Security Account Manager (SAM) Database 248

MSV1_0 Authentication 249

Pass-Through Authentication 249

Permissions on Shared NTFS Directories 252

Summary 255

10 Groups, Rights, and Permissions   257

Implementing User Groups on an NT Network 258

Local versus Global Groups 259

Built-in Groups 261

Group Strategies 261
  Global Group Mechanics 263
  Local Group Mechanics 263
  Global Group Rules 264
  Groups As Members of Other Groups 265
Built-in Groups 266
  Built-in Local Groups 266
  Implementing Group Rights 268
  Built-in Global Groups 270
User Rights and Strategies 271
  User Rights Mechanics 271
  Managing Other Users' Rights 274
  File, Directory, and Printer Ownership 274
  Customizing Group Definitions 275
  Assigning Rights 276
  Security Administrator 277
  Strategies for Account Policy 278
File Access Permissions 279
  Editing Permissions 281
Planning Your Network Security 282
Summary 284

11   Setting Up the User Environment   285

Overview of Sharing Objects on the Network 287
  NT Services 288
  NT Server Objects and Object Mechanics 289
Making Network Directories (Shares) Available 293
  Universal Naming Convention (UNC) Share Names 294
  Creating a Share 294
  Eliminating a Share 295
Making Network Printers Available 296
  Access Permissions 298
Connecting Users to Shared Resources 298
  Connecting to Shared Directories (Shares) 298
  Disconnecting from a Shared Directory 300
Setting Up Groups 300
  Group Dynamics 300
  Viewing or Editing Rights Policies Defined for Groups 301
Setting Up Users 301
  NT User Account Information: 302
  Default User Accounts 303
  Initial User 303

Ownership 307
Group Assignments and Rights 307
Granting Users Rights to Access Resources 308
Global and Local User Accounts 309
Log on to a Remote Domain Where No Trust Exists 311
Monitoring and Auditing 313
Event Logs 314
Auditing and Monitoring Mechanics 318
Failed Logon Attempts 318
The Welcome (Logon) Dialog Box 319
Logon Mechanics 319
Logon Steps 321
The Authenticating Process 323
Summary of Initial and Server Logons 326
Where You Are Logging On 327
How To Automate Account Logons 327

12 Controlling The User Environment   329
User Profiles 331
Overview 332
Why Use Profiles 333
Profile Mechanics 334
How to Set Up Server-Based User Profiles 337
Re-establishing Network Connections 341
Logon Scripts 341
Reasons to Use Logon Scripts 342
The Mechanics of Logon Scripts 343
Logon Script Parameters 344
How to Set Up Logon Scripts 344
Using PUTINENV 345
System/User Environment Variables and Account Parameters 345
System Environment Variables 346
User Environment Variables 348
Changing User Environment Variables Using the 348
Control Panel
Other System Adjustments 349
Virtual Memory 349
Recovery 350
Tasking 351
Home Directories 351
Home Directory Permissions 353
The Replicator Service 354
Summary 357

13   **NT Printing Services**   **359**

Overview of Microsoft Network Printing 361
  Printing Concepts and Terminology 361
  Print Spooling Illustrated: the Components of
    Network Printing 363
  How NT Server Printing Works 365
Sharing and Using Network Printers 369
  Creating a Printer Share 369
  Connecting to a Printer Share 371
Administering Printers 371
  Separator Pages and Files 372
  Adding a Print File Name 374
  Setting Automatic Printing to File 374
  Disable Notification Boxes 375
  Clearing Print Jobs from JetDirect Queues After Printing......... 376
  Envelope Printing...376
  Remote Printer Administration 377
Printing Components 378
  Where to Find What You Are Looking for 378
  Registry Entries for Printing 378
  Client Applications 380
  The Print Router 384
  Print Processors and Data Types 384
  Print Providers 387
  Print Monitors 391
  Printer Drivers 392
  Printer Mini-Drivers 392
  Cross-Platform Printing 393
  Network Interface Printers (Network Card Installed
    in a Printer) 394
Printer Administration 395
  Printer Pools 395
  Printer Security 396
  Problems Related to Security.. 398
  TCP/IP Printing...399
Common Printing Problems 402
Summary... 403

14   **Managing the Network Registry**   **405**

Starting the Registry Editor 410
Using the Registry Editor for Configuration Management 411
  Viewing the Registry for a Remote Computer 411

Loading Hives from Another Computer 412
How to Unload a Hive from the Registry Editor 413
Saving and Restoring Keys 413
The Registry Structure 415
Hives and Files 415
The HKEY_LOCAL_MACHINE Key 417
The HKEY_CLASSES_ROOT Key 438
The HKEY_USERS Key 439
User Profiles for NT Workstations 439
Value Entries in Registry Subkeys 439
Referential Integrity of Registry Data 440
Key and Hive Recovery 441
Flushing Registry Data 441
Registry Size Limits 442
Network Settings 443
Maintaining Registry Security 449
Summary 449

15   Administering Workgroup Applications   451
Distributed Computing Environments 452
Installing Applications Locally or Centrally 452
Application Suites 453
Installing Applications Locally or Centrally 454
Network-Aware Applications 455
The Microsoft Office Suite 456
Considerations Before Installing MS Office 457
Before Starting Setup 459
Administrative Installation 459
Client Installation 460
Customizing Your Setup Script File 461
Distributing and Using a Script 463
Files Installed by Workstation Setup on Workstations 465
General Troubleshooting 467
The Novell PerfectOffice Suite 468
Network Installation 471
Services for Macintosh 472
Transparent File Sharing 472
The File and Print Server 473
Apple Networking Overview 474
Installing Services for Macintosh on an NT Server System 477
Problem Areas 487

Lotus Notes 488
    What Is Notes? 488
    Printing from Lotus Notes 490

16   Gateway Service for NetWare (GSNW)   493

Installing and Configuring GSNW 495
    Prerequisite NWLink IPX/SPX Protocol 495
    GSNW Installation 495
    GSNW Configuration 496
    NetWare Broadcasts.. 498
    GSNW Dependencies... 499
    GSNW Performance Issues 499
    GSNW File Security 500
    Controlling Access to Files 500
Accessing File Resources 501
    NetWare File Attributes 501
    NetWare File Locks 501
Accessing Printers 502
Running NetWare-Aware Utilities 502
Running NetWare-Aware Applications 503
File and Print Services for NetWare.. 504
Summary 504

PART IV   APPLICATION SERVER ADD-ONS

17   Systems Management Server   507

Introduction 508
    SMS Functions 508
    SMS Components 509
    SMS Structure 510
    System Requirements 511
    Installation 511
    Security 512
    Configuring SMS 513
    SMS Clients 515
    Inventory.. 517
    Audited Software 518
    Creating and Distributing Packages 519
    Program Group Control... 520
    Using Network Applications 521
    Installing Applications on Clients 522
    Notes on Installing Specific Applications 523
    Using SMS to Install Operating Systems on Clients................... 525

Automatically Configure Workstation
Logon Scripts 526
Network Monitoring 526
Summary 528

18   Remote Access Server   529

RAS Capabilities 530
Point-to-Point Protocol 532
SLIP 532
Internet Support 533
NetWare Networks 533
Software Data Compression 533
Data Encryption 533
RAS APIs 534
WAN Support for X.25 and Integrated Services 534
Digital Network (ISDN)
RAS Components 534
RAS User Interface 534
RAS Service Component 536
RAS Subsystem 536
NT RAS Installation and Configuration 538
RAS Requirements 538
Potential Conflicts 538
Joining a Domain as a RAS Client 539
RAS Integrated Domain Security 540
Challenge Handshake Authentication Protocol (CHAP) 540
Third-Party Firewall Protection 541
User Disconnection 541
Auditing 541
Restricted Network Access 541
Callback Security 542
How RAS Logon Security Works 542
RAS Configuration Files 542
Editing the Registry for RAS 543
Summary 550

19   SQL Server   551

SQL Server Networking Overview 553
Open Data Services 554
SQL Bridge 555
Installing SQL Server 555
Installing Utilities 557
Reinstallation 557

Configuring SQL Server for Named Pipes Clients 558

SQL Server Using SPX/IPX 559

SQL Server with TCP/IP Sockets Clients 561

Starting SQL Server 562

Devices and Databases 564

Backup and Recovery 565

Configuring Memory Usage 566

Other Configuration Issues 568

Efficient Index Design 568

Normalize Logical Database Design 569

Efficient Query Design 570

How to Find Bottlenecks 571

Administration 572

Starting SQL Server Remotely 572

Truncating Transaction Logs 573

SQL Server Registry Entries 574

Summary 575

20   SNA Server   577

SNA Server Features 578

Integration with NT Server 580

Capacities 581

System Requirements 581

Installation 582

Changing the Name of the SNA Server 584

Removing the SNA Server Administration Program 584

How to Start Up SNA Server 585

Backing Up the COM.CFG File 586

SNA Server Administration 586

SNA Server Clients 588

Windows-Based Clients 588

Special Settings for WFW Clients 589

TCP/IP Client 589

Configuring Windows 3.x TCP/IP Client 590

Using Third-Party Emulators 591

DOS Client Using IBM PC Support/400 592

Summary 593

21   Microsoft TCP/IP Services   595

Using NetBIOS to Advertise Available Services 598

NetBIOS Broadcast Storms 598

Administration Complexity When NetBIOS Is Layered
with Other Protocols 598

NetBIOS Is Not Routable 599

Using TCP/IP with NT 599

   Benefits of Using TCP/IP 599

   IP Tunneling 600

   WINS and LMHOSTS Limitations 600

   Browsing over TCP/IP 601

   NetBIOS Name Resolution over TCP/IP 601

NT's Native and Optional Routing Support 601

Installing the TCP/IP Protocol 602

Adding TCP/IP Support to an Installed NT Server 604

Dynamic Host Control Protocol (DHCP) 604

   Configuring DHCP Servers 605

   Creating DHCP Administrative Scopes 605

   Reserving Client IP addresses 606

   Active DHCP Client Leases 607

Windows Internet Name Services (WINS) 608

   Using WINS to Reduce NetBIOS Administration 608

   Installing a WINS Server 608

   Configuring a WINS Server 610

Windows NT Resource Kit WEB Server 611

   How to Install and Configure the NT Resource Kit WEB Server 612

   Removing the Gopher Server 614

   Configuring the Gopher Service 614

   Operating the Gopher Service 617

HTTP Server 617

   Installing HTTP Server 618

   HTTPS Configuration 618

Summary 620

PART V OPTIMIZING PERFORMANCE, REDUCING DOWNTIME

22 Monitoring Tools and Techniques   623

Monitoring Local Area Networks 624

   Cabling and Connectors 625

   Ethernet Cabling 626

   Monitoring Ethernet 627

   Token Ring 632

Monitoring the NT Server Operating System 634

   Event Viewer 634

   Dr. Watson for Windows NT 635

   Setting Up the Microsoft Windows NT Messages Database 637

Monitoring Server Usage 638

Monitoring Disk Subsystems 639
    Viewing Disk Partitions 639
    Checking the File System 640
    Disk Utilities to Check the Physical Disk Subsystem 641
Summary 641

23   Evaluating Performance Opportunities   643

Processor, Threads, and the Queue 644
Prioritizing Foreground Application Versus Server Performance .. 645
Interaction of SERVER Service with the Cache 646
Memory Optimization 647
    Pagefile and Virtual Memory 647
    Working Sets 648
    Paged and NonPaged Memory Pools 649
    The LargeSystemCache Subkey 651
    The Not_Enough_Quota Subkey 652
    VirtualLock() 652
Hard Disk Adapters 652
Cache Memory 653
    Physical Disk Drive Configurations 653
    SCSI Tagged Command Queuing 656
Server Network Cards 657
Truncate Event Logs 657
Disable BIOS Shadowing 658
Upgrading to RISC- and Multiprocessor-Based Computers 658
    Upgrading to a Multiprocessor Computer 658
    NT Resource Kit Upgrade Utility 659
Summary 659

24   Monitoring and Tuning Performance   661

Overview 662
Performance Monitor Internals 665
    Transaction 665
Counters 666
    Sample Counters 666
Performance Monitor Operations 667
    Security 667
    Uses of Performance Monitor 668
    Objects That Can Be Viewed 669
    Charting 670
    Logs 671
    Reports 672
    Alert 672
    Graphing Logged Data 673

How to Deal with Bottlenecks 673
   Processor Bottlenecks 674
   Disk Bottlenecks 675
   Memory Bottlenecks 676
   Cache Bottlenecks 677
   LAN Bottlenecks 679
Monitoring an Application 679
   Processor Queue Length 681
   Processor Time 682
   Service Requests 682
   Average Queue Time 682
Monitoring the Network 682
   Network Counters 683
Performance Tuning 685
   Server Tuning 685
   Tuning LAN Hardware 688
   Tuning the Workstation Service 689
   Tuning the Server Service 690
Miscellaneous Tuning 691
   Changing Default Spool Directory 691
   Shut Down Print Job Logging 692
   Setting Raw Read/Writes 693
Summary 694

25 LAN Capacity Allocation   695

What Is Bandwidth? 697
   Capacity, Not Speed 697
   Higher Bandwidth and Transmission Time 697
   Bandwidth Conclusion 698
   Theoretical Versus Usable Bandwidth ....:........................... 698
   Categorizing Bandwidth Needs 699
Monitoring Bandwidth 700
   Baselining 701
Bandwidth Solutions 701
Higher Capacity LANs 702
   Comparison of LAN Available Bandwidth and Bus
      Capacity in a Server 702
Internetworking Solutions—Segmenting LANs 704
   Internetwork Design 704
   Backbone LANs 704
   Bridges, Routers, and Brouters 705
   To Route or to Bridge; That Is the Question 707
   Mixing Bridges and Routers 708

Switching Hubs and Virtual LANs (VLANs) 708
  NT Multiple Network Adapters 709
Monitoring LAN Bandwidth 711
  Microsoft BackOffice System Management Server (SMS) 712
  W & G's Domino 712
  LANalyzer for Windows 713
Summary 714

26 Virtual LAN Capacity Allocation   715

Virtual LANs: The Automatic Solution 716
Switching Hub Benefits and Limitations 717
Planning 718
  Selecting the Best Hub for Your Network 718
  Switch Design 719
Joining Different Bandwidth Nodes 722
  Multiple Server Network Cards to a Single Switch 722
Summary 723

27 Physical Security, Quick Recovery   725

Backup and Restore 726
  Backup Devices and Software 726
  Backing Up Open Files 727
  Backup and Restoring the Registry 728
  Restoring NT System Volume 730
Rapid Recovery Procedures 731
  Reinstalling NT 732
  Emergency Repair Process 733
  Adjusting the BOOT.INI File After Reinstall 734
  Removing NT from the Boot Partition 736
  Virus Prevention, Detection, and Removal 737
  Recovering from Security Access Manager (SAM) Corruption ... 738
  Automatically Disconnecting Users 740
  Disk Space Alert 740
  Fault Tolerance 741
  NTFS Internal Tables 742
Disk Subsystem Fault Tolerance 742
  Sector Sparing (Hot Fix) 743
  Remirroring a Fault-Tolerant File System 743
Uninterruptible Power Supplies (UPSs) 747
  UPS Service Parameters 747
Summary 748

PART VI   TROUBLESHOOTING

28   Troubleshooting Overview   **751**

NT Server Hangs During Boot 752
Logon Script Problems... 753
Dropped Connections 754
JetDirect Printer Debugging 755
BrowseMaster Conflicts 757
Adjusting NWLink Packet Size 757
Dr. Watson 759
Enabling and Disabling Dr. Watson 759
Configuring Dr. Watson 759
Removing COM Ports 762
Removing Printers 762
Removing a Hewlett-Packard Network Printer Destination 762
Removing an AppleTalk Printer Destination............................ 763
Removing Control Panel Components 763
Disabling Printer Messages 764
Enabling/Disabling Shutdown Button 765
Changing the Domain for a Computer.................................... 765
Summary 767

29   Server Hardware Troubleshooting   **769**

How to Identify a Server Hardware Problem 770
Hardware Incompatibilities and Configuration Problems 771
Server Hardware Failure Signs 772
Testing a Server's Durability 774
Moving Data Storage to Another Server 774
Hot Online Backup Server 776
Frequent Server Replacement 776
Isolating the Offending Component 776
Reviewing the Event Log 777
Running the Diagnostics Utility 778
Control Panel's Device Applet...................................... 779
Dealing with Intermittent Problems 779
When the Server Cannot Boot 780
STOP Messages During Boot 781
Using the Windows NT Debugger 782
Working around a Failed Component 783
Replacing Suspected Components 783
Summary 784

30   LAN Troubleshooting   785

The Protocol Analysis Approach to Troubleshooting 787
    Which Protocol Analyzer to Use 788
    Troubleshooting by Layer 789
Troubleshooting the Physical Layer 791
    Cable Configuration, Testing, and Certification 792
    Coaxial Cable Problems 792
    Coaxial Cable 793
    Twisted Pair Cable, EIA/TIA 568 Cabling Specifications 795
    Split Pairs 801
    UTP Installation Tips 802
    Fiber Optic Cable 804
    Cable Troubleshooting Tools 804
The LAN Layer 807
    Ethernet Protocol Analysis 807
    Token Ring Analysis 819
Analyzing NetBIOS 826
Analyzing Transport Protocols.. 827
    NetBEUI 828
    Analyzing IPX/SPX in a Microsoft Network 828
    Analyzing TCP/IP in a Microsoft Network 829
Analyzing SMB 829
Summary 833

31   File System and Disk Subsystem Problems   835

Using the Emergency Repair Disk... 837
    Procedure for Using the Emergency Repair Disk 838
    Updating the Emergency Repair Disk 838
Running CHKDSK... 839
Backing Up and Restoring the Registry and the BOOT.INI File 840
    The BOOT.INI File 840
    The Registry and Configuration-Related Files 841
Managing RAID Disk Subsystems 841
RAID Levels 842
    RAID Level 0 842
    RAID Level 1 842
    RAID Level 2,3,4 844
    RAID Level 5 844
NT Fault Tolerance Design 845
    NTFT Behavior 845
    FTDISK.SYS Driver Details 846
    NTFT Volume Sector Sparing... 846

Sector Sparing Failures 847

FTDISK.SYS Error Handling 847

Support for RAID Hardware Devices 848

Fault Tolerance Recovery 848

Identifying When a Set Is Broken 849

Restoring the Computer to its Normal State 849

Recovering Orphans 850

RAID Performance 850

Summary 852

PART VII   APPENDIXES

A   NT Server 3.51 System Requirements   **855**

Hardware Requirements 856

Multiprocessing Requirements 856

NT Server/Workstation Features and Capacities 857

System Architecture 857

Network Interface Card Support 857

Client Workstation Network Card Support 858

Other Hardware Support 858

Protocol Support 858

Inter-Program Communication 859

File System Features 859

Performance Optimization Features 859

Security Features 860

NTFS Directory and File Permissions 860

User Rights 861

Security Auditing 861

Printing 861

Printer Alerts 862

Network Management 862

Performance Monitoring 862

Delegating Administration Responsibility 863

Alert Messages 863

Fault Tolerance 863

Backup Features 863

B   Where to Find Support and Updates   **865**

Before Calling Microsoft for Help 866

Microsoft Phone Numbers 866

Microsoft Solution Provider Network 867

FastTips 868

Bulletin Board Service: Microsoft Download Service (MSDL) 869

Standard Support 869
Priority Support 869
Premier Support and Premier Global Support 870
Electronic Services 870
Internet Services 871
Online Services 872

C   NT Quick Reference Guide   875

aclconv 876
append 876
at 877
cmd 878
compact 879
convert 879
diskperf 879
dosonly 880
echoconfig 880
forcedos 880
ipxroute 880
loadhigh 880
net accounts 881
net computer 881
net config 882
net config workstation 882
net continue 882
net file 883
net group 883
net helpmsg 884
net localgroup 885
net name 885
net pause 886
net print 887
net send 887
net session 888
net share 888
net start 889
net start alerter 889
net start browser 889
net start dhcp client 889
net start snmp 889
net statistics 890
net stop 890
net time 890

net use 890
net user 891
net view 892
ntcmdprompt 892
pentnt 893
print 893
start 893
switches 894
title 894
TCP/IP Utilities Reference 894
arp [-a inet_addr [-n [if_addr]] [-d inet_addr]
  [-s inet_addr ether-addr [if_addr]] 894
finger [-l] [User] @HOST [...] 895
ftp [-v] [-n] [-i] [-d] [-g] [Host] [-s:Filename] 895
hostname 899
ipconfig [/all | /renew [adapter] | /release [adapter]] 899
ipq [-Sserver | -Pprinter] [-l] 899
lpr [-Sserver | -Pprinter [-ooptions] [-cclass] [-jjobname]
  Filename 899
NBSTAT [-a Remotename] [-A IPaddress] [-c] [-n] [-R]
  [-r] [-S] [-s] [Interval] 900
netstat [-a] [-e] [n] [s] [-p Protocol] [-r] [Interval] 901
ping remote_computer [-t] [-a] [-n count] [-l length] [-f]
  [-i ttl] [-v tos] [-r count] [-s count] [[-j hostlink] |
  [-k hostlink]] [-w timeout] destination-list 901
rcp [-a] [-b] [-h] [-r] Source1 Source2 ... Destination 903
rexec Host [-l Username] [-n] Command 903
route [-f] [Command [Destination] [mask netmask]
  [gateway]] 904
rsh Host [-l Username] [-n] Command 904
telnet [Host [Port]] 905
tftp [-i] Host [get | put] Source [Destination] 905
tracert [-d] [-h maximumhops] [-j hostlist] [-w timeout]
  targetname 906
D Logon Script Programming Guide   907
Logon Scripts 908
Logon Script Path 909
Specifying Home Directory 909
Troubleshooting Logon Scripts 910
Writing Batch Files for NT 911
E Glossary of Networking Terminology   917
Index   945

Acknowlegements

I would like to thank my writing partner, Nadeem Chagtai, for his patience and hard work. Nadeem is one of the most knowledgeable software engineers I have ever met, and has tremendous depth of understanding in NT Server's internal mechanics.

Most importantly, a hearty thanks is due to the staff at Macmillan. These folks work long, highly productive hours to bring these books to us. I want to give special thanks to Grace Buechlein for putting up with me, Tony Amico for guiding the project, and Johnna VanHoose and her co-workers for making it make better sense to you, the reader.

—Rick Sant'Angelo

I learned a lot from Rick about writing style and getting a clear message across. I want to extend my appreciation to the team at Microsoft who developed NT Server. I also want to thank the staff at Macmillan, Grace, Johnna, and the copy editors on this project in particular.

—Nadeem Chagtai

Introduction

NT Server is a highly impressive and respectable NOS. This product is substantially different from Novell NetWare, offering a fresh approach to networking. The product is highly complex, but outwardly simple to pick up and start using. Today's networks are heterogeneous: many system administrators must manage Novell, Microsoft, and UNIX systems in a mixed-protocol environment. NT's multiple protocol options provide the means to integrate NT into an existing internetwork infrastructure. With Windows clients, an NT Server–based network is the most advanced solution to networking requirements. Many NetWare implementers are currently migrating to NT, and finding appeal in an all Microsoft solution.

NT is a powerful operating system able to handle print, file, and client/server applications for hundreds of users effectively. It is easy to learn and to manage, and the Windows graphical user interface and utilities provide the system administrator simple and effective tools for managing a network. The built-in Windows client management tools help the system administrator. NT Server's domain system provides the administrative superstructure for even the largest enterprise networks without the complexity of a directory services–based system.

NT's ability to scale up to more powerful hardware puts it at least on a par with market leader, Novell NetWare, and in some ways exceeds NetWare's power. NT Server stands as the premier application server platform without sacrificing server stability. As more NT Server–based applications come to market, NT will be used in even greater numbers to affect client/server solutions. NT's Internet solutions are a real bonus in today's global network arena.

But don't let NT's outward simplicity catch you unprepared. Your *Windows NT Server Survival Guide* is a system administrator's handbook to be kept at your side when challenging the network. This book was designed and written for you, the system administrator. You will find the depth and mechanics as well as the how-to's of effectively implementing and managing an NT Server–based network. A network does not need to be a "black box" to you—you can actually understand how it works. Use this book in good health as a tool for peaceful network coexistence.

How to Use this Book

This book is designed to be both a tutorial and a reference work. *Windows NT Server Survival Guide* is divided into seven parts:

- ◆ Introduction to NT Server
- ◆ Installing and Configuring the NOS
- ◆ System Administration

◆ Application Server Add-Ons

◆ Optimizing Performance, Reducing Downtime

◆ Troubleshooting

◆ Appendixes

The first part, "Introduction to NT Server," provides the foundation for the rest of the book. Each additional part addresses a significant subset of system administration needs. The appendixes provide a quick reference in easy-to-read format in order to find what you are looking for. The glossary discusses many words you will encounter here and in your Microsoft materials.

Note

Pay close attention to terminology in this book, as it provides the key to understanding what is discussed throughout. You will find consistent, precise use of terms throughout this book, something both Microsoft and Novell lack in their documentation and related materials. Please read the first few chapters before reading the rest of the book, to understand the mechanics and precise use of words discussed throughout.

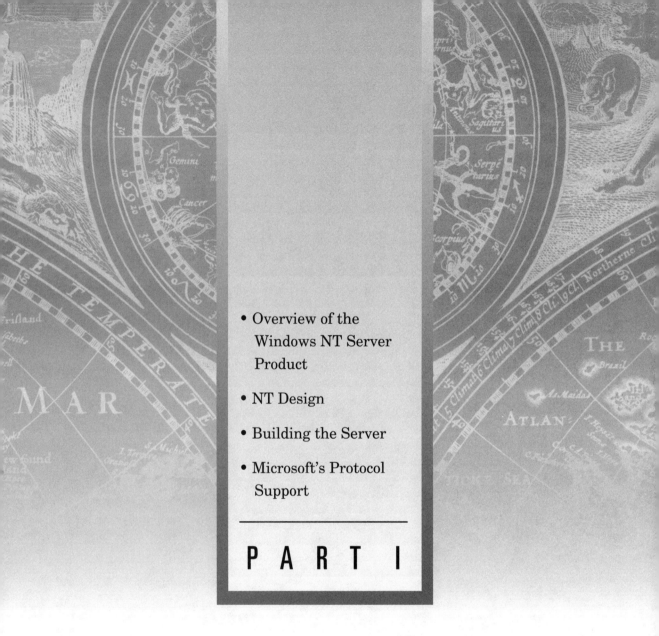

- Overview of the Windows NT Server Product

- NT Design

- Building the Server

- Microsoft's Protocol Support

PART I

Introduction to NT Server

- LAN Manager Heritage

- Similarities to OS/2

- DOS Compatibility

- Similarities to Windows 3.1 and Windows For Workgroups (WFW) 3.11

- Similarities to NetWare

- Why Is Everyone So Excited about Windows NT?

CHAPTER 1

Overview of the Windows NT Server Product

NT Server is an entirely new operating system that was developed from the Windows 3.x operating system. NT Server's kernel was heavily influenced by UNIX, NetWare, and Digital's VMS operating system, but incorporates advantages those operating systems lacked. NT Server differs from Windows NT Workstation in that it was designed to provide more robust networking features and was performance tuned for a server instead of a client.

NT Server is both an operating system (OS) and a network operating system (NOS). This differs from previous NOSes, such as LAN Manager, which ran on top of OS/2. NT Server is designed to be the optimal operating system for a server, not for a workstation. Although it shares this design feature with Novell NetWare, NT Server was designed not only to be a good server platform, but is also designed to run powerful 32-bit Windows server applications. NT's design and APIs provide many opportunities for developers to write software that can further client/server applications. This product makes the best application server platform for client/server software architecture.

With Windows NT, Windows 95, and Windows for Workgroups 3.11 as client operating systems, a Windows NT Server-based network has the performance, connectivity, and power to support today's networking demands. And every product is easy to learn and use.

This chapter discusses how NT Server evolved, and how it is similar to and different from other NOSes.

Before the emergence of LAN computing, mainframe and minicomputers were the power platforms of choice. Users were in virtual straightjackets; software was crude with fixed functions. Programs, menus, and input screens were controlled by programmers and MIS people. Those technologies may have been simple and crude, but they were very effective.

Ethernet ushered in a new age of distributed computing and the downsizing. Digital Intel and Xerox (DIX) championed Ethernet in the late 70s and IEEE furthered Ethernet standards in the early 80s. 3Com made the first PC boards in the early 80s. Ethernet's wide acceptance set the stage for Novell's success throughout the 80s. NetWare emerged in '83 and caught fire in '85 with NetWare 286. Novell produced Ethernet and ARCnet cards to drive the prices down and make the technology easier to install. These events set the stage for the advent of LAN computing and the wide acceptance of client/server computing strategies.

LAN development encouraged open system development, and designers created fascinating new multi-user network architectures. The industry lost much of the structured coherence and central control.The evolution of LANs spawned an era of downsized PC-based Network Operating Systems (NOSes), such as NetWare, using distributed computing strategies. System design was distributed to independent implementers, and virtually all systems have became heterogeneous.

Today, Windows NT takes LAN computing to a new level. Though NetWare has reigned supreme for the past decade, NT provides a more powerful server application platform that provides the platform for downsizing even bigger applications. NT's scalability, Windows interface, protection, and APIs have appealed to developers in a big way. This, coupled with ever more powerful Intel and RISC hardware, provides power previously requiring mainframes but includes a GUI that anyone can learn quickly. Transaction processing and other big system applications can now be downsized like never before!

More recently, Windows firmly established the Graphical User Interface (GUI) on common Intel desktop computers and added another level of complexity. The users complained about how their icons kept disappearing and that their printers didn't work at times. System administrators usually discovered that approximately fifty percent of help-desk time was spent fixing user's desktops and chasing down printer problems.

Although OS/2 LAN Manager and NetWare provided decent platforms for network computing, something had to be done about the lack of administrative support for Windows client desktops. Microsoft's answer to system administrators' complaints is Windows NT. NT's magic is that the Windows desktop is left intact, but desktops and printers can be controlled centrally, usually from the server itself using several Windows-based utilities. In this brave new world, administrators enjoy many of the benefits similar to centralized minicomputer or mainframe systems with distributed processing and autonomous GUI-based desktops. The best of both worlds is now at your fingertips.

NetWare system administrators quickly come to appreciate the benefits of an all-Windows network based on NT Server. It is far superior to the simple workgroup peer-to-peer approach available in Windows for Workgroups. It has the power of NetWare, and even more, it scales up to larger and larger hardware platforms in a spiral of file and print sharing power limited only by the implementer's budget.

NT Server makes an excellent platform for client/server software, such as SQL Server where programs are executed locally on PCs, while many of the software functions and processes are executed on the server itself.

In addition, Microsoft has packed NT with standard features you would usually have to purchase as separate software applications. NT's Internet connectivity and Remote Access Server are of great benefit and are included at no additional cost. Both of these features and many more are standard in NT and cost extra with NetWare.

Microsoft provides support for the most popular existing protocols. NWLink (Microsoft's version of Novell's IPX/SPX) networking protocol is supplemented by NetBEUI, native TCP/IP, transport-independent Windows Sockets, Clipbook, Network Dynamic Data Exchange (NetDDE), and Object Linking and Embedding version 2.0 (OLE 2.0). These make NT Server a very flexible and powerful NOS.

Other great features that make Windows NT very popular include:

◆ Simplified and more effective software system administration

◆ Easy-to-use GUI, especially when handling complex network management tasks

◆ A powerful platform for client/server applications such as SQL Server

◆ NetWare-compatible IPX/SPX routable protocol implementation supplementing Microsoft's native NetBEUI protocol

◆ TCP/IP support

◆ Remote Access Server (RAS) dial-in server support

◆ Transport-independent Windows Socket

◆ Clipbook

◆ Network Dynamic Data Exchange (NetDDE)

◆ Object Linking and Embedding version 2.0 (OLE 2.0)

◆ Built-in fault tolerant features such as RAID 1 and 5 support

◆ NT File System (NTFS) to equal NetWare's disk performance

◆ GUI server configuration and management utilities

◆ NT Server promises to be the 'magic glue' operating system that will allow the mixing and matching of heterogeneous applications under one umbrella environment. Most organizations are having to deal with this phenomenon of explosive growth in data and communication system complexity.

LAN MANAGER HERITAGE

NT Server evolved from Microsoft's previous NOS, LAN Manager, which ran on top of OS/2. This product used many of the same mechanisms as MS-Networks, the foundation of most peer-to-peer NOSes such as the IBM PC LAN Program, 3Com's 3Plus Share, LANtastic, NetWare Lite, and several others. NT Server, however, integrates the OS and NOS into a more powerful, robust, client/server NOS.

LAN Manager was not entirely successful. The product suffered from all the weaknesses of OS/2 1.x versions and did not truly measure up to the refined features and performance found in NetWare 3.x. Windows NT was redesigned to overcome these deficiencies.

Some of the objects retained from LAN Manager include: domains, groups, and the redirector at the client. Experienced LAN Manager administrators will find NT Server, domains, and user management quite familiar.

SIMILARITIES TO OS/2

OS/2 was Microsoft's first attempt at a kernel-level operating system since DOS, and as a result, many of the kernel internals are similar. Windows NT and OS/2 2.x share a common heritage in OS/2 1.x. However, Windows NT was designed with the following improvements:

- ◆ NT has an improved I/O request queue
- ◆ OS/2 cannot run 32-bit Windows for Workgroups (WFW) applications
- ◆ The NTFS file system is very similar to OS/2's HPFS, but HPFS does not have the extra file level security, small block allocation units, and fault tolerance built into NTFS
- ◆ OS/2 only runs on the Intel x86 platform (although IBM may soon release a PowerPC version)

Similarities between OS/2 and NT are significant mostly to software developers and people who already have insight into OS/2 internals.

DOS COMPATIBILITY

The "DOS box," or Virtual DOS Machine (VDM) in NT is a new, improved DOS. It actually registers in Microsoft Diagnostics as MS-DOS 7. The best thing about the NT VDM is that it is not DOS. Though the DOS VDM is a DOS 5.0-compatible environment, it is a 32-bit application called CMD.EXE. As a result, memory behavior is better, disk intensive DOS programs run faster, and programs are less prone to failure. Batch files can have a UNIX 'cron-like' feature that allows timed execution of programs.

NT does not allow program execution to control hardware; therefore DOS programs that directly access hardware cause NT's protection to halt the system. In this way, the NT VDM is better than the Windows 3.x VDM. Some stubborn DOS games that refuse to run under Windows 3.x do just fine in the NT VDM. TSRs (Terminate and Stay Resident programs) and can be loaded via AUTOEXEC.NT. Loadable device drivers can also be loaded via CONFIG.NT.

NT DOS box also has the capability to run 16-bit Windows applications from batch files. This feature, in conjunction with the timed execution feature, gives administrators the ability to automate many application-related tasks.

SIMILARITIES TO WINDOWS 3.1 AND WINDOWS FOR WORKGROUPS (WFW) 3.11

One's obvious reaction to the NT desktop is: "It looks exactly the same as Windows 3.x." It is the same: Windows 3.x programs look and feel exactly the same on NT as they do in their native environment.

NT owes a large part of its heritage to Windows 3.x. Almost the entire desktop is descended from Windows 3.x programs. The Program Manager, File Manager, and Control Panel are just a few examples. As a result of this relationship, *all* Windows 3.x applications run flawlessly on NT.

Adding an NT Server to a WFW network can be a shot in the arm for the WFW network for the following reasons:

◆ File access is much better

◆ Security is airtight

◆ Printing is managed much better

NT Server replaces the aged 16-bit MS-DOS operating system underlying Windows 3.x with a new high-performance 32-bit multi-tasking/multi-user operating system. Windows NT is designed to really exploit 32-bit hardware and applications.

SIMILARITIES TO NETWARE

NetWare has been the leading NOS product in over 60 percent of the market. Novell's intuition on developing features that the market came to appreciate is legendary. It only makes sense that a successful competing product would build on NetWare's success.

Microsoft's marketing plan is pointed at matching NetWare, virtually feature-by-feature, and to eclipse NetWare where feasible. Novell's strategy to use non-preemptive processing, IPX-routable protocol, and NetWare's built-in internal routers had made it quite popular. Microsoft's preemptive processing, IPX emulation, and built-in internal router matches NetWare, and allows it to coexist with NetWare. A NetWare client can access an appropriately configured NT Server with very little modification.

In order to capture a substantial portion of Novell's market share, Microsoft made it easy for NetWare integrators to switch. Microsoft added Gateway Services for NetWare where an NT Server can connect to a NetWare server and become the gateway between NT users and the NetWare server. Of course, eventually the system administrator would migrate files and users over the NT Server, but this product provides the vehicle for a smooth transition.

The following features were built into Windows NT Server in order to compete on an even footing with NetWare:

◆ NWLink IPX/SPX–compatible transport protocol providing support for combined NetWare-Microsoft networks. This allows the administrator to add connectivity to an NT server using existing client drivers.

◆ Gateway Services for NetWare that enables an NT Server to provide its clients with simultaneous access to a NetWare server.

◆ Native TCP/IP support.

In summary, NT Server is similar to and different from many other NOS products on the market today. However, it is far more evolved in several ways.

WHY IS EVERYONE SO EXCITED ABOUT WINDOWS NT?

The entire computer industry is "super-enthused" about Windows NT. It seems as though the promises and expectations that started in 1988 with the introduction of the IBM PS/2 and OS/2 have been fanned and have grown to explosive proportions. In many ways, OS/2 has already fulfilled those promises—UNIX has provided most of the promised functionality for over twenty years.

Windows NT is a multitasking and multi-user operating system with the now-familiar Windows Graphical User Interface (GUI), many slick utilities, and many new built-in features. Microsoft has built in many features and supporting facilities to capture a large proportion of the existing networking market. Several other important aspects have shown tremendous potential.

SIMPLIFIED LEARNING

Windows makes software complexities simpler to use and manage—it is ideal for "power users." Though Windows is less intimidating for new users who are first learning than text-based software, its true value is best epitomized by NT. This much complexity requires a user interface that permits quick access to menu selections that would otherwise be buried beneath many menu levels. In short, learning to navigate through the many complex tasks is simplified.

MULTIPLE WINDOWS

Multiple windows have many benefits. One major benefit is the ability to switch right from one active application function directly to another without exiting and loading the other application. A good example is a help desk. A user can go directly from logging a call (perhaps in a time and billing application) to a support library, and back to logging out the call with just a few keystrokes.

MULTITASKING

Multitasking is now a reality. You can have two modems: one to run a file transfer or fax in one window while you access the Internet on another. When a large database activity is running, you can check your electronic mail. Busy people who rely heavily on their computers as a personal productivity tool (power users) can truly be more productive.

MULTI-USER

Both NT Workstation and NT Server are multi-user. NT Workstation is peer-to-peer equipped for up to ten client connections. NT Server is designed for more powerful client/server applications with the capability of providing over 15,000 connections.

FUN AND ENTICING!

Windows NT is fun and enticing! People like to work with Windows. It makes an otherwise boring job more interesting and makes normal tasks more convenient and exciting. It's like the difference between a simple paper note and a cartoon-clad stick-on note. Why should your job be boring? Screen savers and games add to the many enticements that make this tool more interesting—as a result more people now use PCs as personal productivity tools.

NT Server also uses the Windows interface for management tasks on the server. This provides extensive system administration support at the server itself. Windows makes more difficult tasks easier to learn.

Note

Though the server can also be used *nondedicated* (as both a server and a client), this is not recommended. The power required to run software robs a server of server resources.

SYSTEM ADMINISTRATION

Many rich features to aid system administrators are built into Windows NT. While Windows 3.1 lacked many of these features, Windows NT's improvements have turned this area into a strength. Windows 3.1 was designed for standalone use, while NT is designed for network use. It has many new tools to manage users, their data, and their desktops.

Microsoft has a long way to go to provide really good system administration, especially in managing applications, but they have made a good start and are way ahead of Novell. Undoubtedly, the current tools and functionality will be improved, and new functionality will be implemented in future NT releases. Improvements will be forthcoming in new revisions, and third party developers will supplement Microsoft's efforts to make this product highly manageable.

SIMPLE MIGRATION WITH NATIVE SUPPORT FOR POPULAR PROTOCOL STACKS

Microsoft's native protocols, NetBIOS and NetBEUI, have proven to be effective, yet unpopular. Rather than fight the battle at this highly technical level, Microsoft opted to build native support for the other predominant protocols including TCP/IP and IPX/SPX. This not only provides simple migration from competing NOSes, but also enables:

◆ NT Servers to be available to TCP/IP and NetWare clients

◆ NT Workstations to access TCP/IP and NetWare hosts

◆ The use of routers (NetBIOS and NetBEUI are non-routable)

Multiple protocols can be configured at the same time, simplifying access to multiple hosts in a heterogeneous environment.

Microsoft has done everything possible to make it easy for you to integrate NT into existing networks. NT Server even includes Gateway Services for NetWare, a utility that provides NT clients simultaneous access to a NetWare server and its data. Migration tools are included to ease the transition from NetWare to NT.

32-BIT NETWORK DEVICE INTERFACE SPECIFICATION (NDIS) DRIVERS

NT (and Windows 95) is shipped with 32-bit drivers for most popular network cards. In many cases, you will find that the same network card can perform about twice as fast due to these drivers.

Microsoft's NDIS specifications allows a network network card developer to write drivers fully supporting the multiple protocols *at the same time*. This specification simplifies and standardizes driver development.

SOFTWARE DEVELOPMENT

Software developers are the most enthusiastic group of NT supporters—they are far past the point of objectivity. Microsoft's technical evangelists (this is actually a job title at Microsoft) have revved up interest among developers with the many advantages of developing in NT's 32-bit environment and using NT APIs. Truly, Windows NT is only one component of a vast system for developing the next generation of software.

SCALABILITY

Windows NT (both Workstation and Server) can currently run on Intel 386, 486, Pentium, Intel multiprocessor computers, as well as Digital's Alpha, MIPS, and IBM PowerPC RISC-based systems. In the future, NT promises to be ported to many other platforms, the next generation of desktop computers, and perhaps even mainframe servers.

Though this may be taken for granted by some younger computer professionals, many of us remember how it was just a few years ago. More often than not, an upgrade or movement to another platform meant reworking applications, sometimes completely overhauling them. For example, moving from a DOS or Windows 3.1 environment to a UNIX system required extensive modification even though the same Remote Procedure Calls (RPCs) and programming language was used.

Applications written for Windows NT do not need to be reworked when they are moved to another hardware platform. This means that applications can be scaled up without extra development effort. Software developers are able to leverage the functionality of a product making it available for small to very powerful systems.

A large part of Microsoft's effort is directed to developing powerful, simple, modular applications with many advantages. A partial but persuasive list of development tools and features includes:

◆ Object Linking and Embedding (OLE)
◆ Dynamic Data Exchange (DDE)
◆ Remote Procedure Calls (RPCs)
◆ High-performance database support
◆ Connection to hosts
◆ Store-and-forward messaging
◆ C2 and European E3 security certification
◆ Server Applications

NT Server makes an ideal platform for the server modules of client/server packages such as SQL Server and value-added applications such as an SNA gateway to an IBM mainframe. NT Server is designed to make these applications easy to install, manage, tune, and run.

NT also provides a preemptive processing environment where the operating system configuration can be adjusted to accommodate unusual software requirements.

BACKOFFICE

One of the reasons NetWare became popular was due to extensive server-based application support. You could link NetWare to IBM mainframes, Macintoshes, UNIX systems, remote users, various electronic mail packages, and install other applications on your server to provide extended functionality. Each package generally carried a hefty price tag based on the number of users.

BackOffice is a server software suite that includes the most strategically important server-based applications. BackOffice includes:

- NT Server
- SQL Server
- Microsoft Mail Server
- System Management Server
- SNA Gateway

Each BackOffice application is priced below comparable *NetWare Loadable Modules (NLMs)*. Currently, BackOffice is priced very aggressively. When compared to NetWare, along with similar server-based applications, the cost incentives for migrating to NT Server are extremely attractive. Without a doubt, Microsoft has thrown in all but the kitchen sink to persuade you to switch to NT.

FEATURES AND BENEFITS OF BACKOFFICE

The NT/BackOffice suite features:

1. Integrated directory and security model.

   Users get a single user login to network and server applications both locally and remotely.

   Reduces administrative overhead because administrators do not need to maintain separate user account databases for sharing resources and server applications.

2. Standard setup, installation, and configuration.

   Server and server applications all follow a similar setup process so the administrator does not have to learn different programs.

   The setup of the applications can be batch driven.

   GUI-based setup makes it easy to add additional connectivity and server services by simply pointing and clicking.

   Auto-detection of network protocols, network cards, and peripherals such as CD-ROM drives simplifies setup and lets you get applications up and running quickly.

Consistent and comprehensive help across all BackOffice component menus puts on-line help at your fingertips.

Automated client setup.

3. Similar systems management and administration.

Administrators can use a similar set of centralized management tools without needing to learn different tools across a variety of environments.

Administrators can centrally manage all shared resources and server applications through a single set of Windows-based management tools, both locally and remotely. This includes security management and auditing, event viewing and logging, performance and tuning, starting and stopping server services, and data backup.

4. Seamless integration with Windows and Microsoft Office.

Consistent development environment. The same Win32 and OLE component software technology is shared between the client, the server, and the server applications. This consistently lowers development, support, and training costs.

Published access to BackOffice services such as SQL Server through Open Database Connectivity (ODBC), Mail & Exchange through Messaging API (MAPI), SNA through the WOSA SNA APIs, System Management Server through DMI.

Best network performance for Windows-based clients.

5. Integrated networking.

Server applications can leverage the connectivity already included with NT Server; for example, IPX/SPX, TCP/IP, and dial-in support to access information no matter where it is located.

SQL Server has third-party gateway connectivity to Oracle, DB2, Informix, Ingres, Btrieve, VSAM, and IMS files.

Supports a variety of clients including Windows, MS-DOS, Macintosh, UNIX, and OS/2.

HARDWARE STATUS

PC architecture and hardware have progressed to the levels at which mainframes were just a couple of product generations ago. The hardware is now available to satisfy NT's appetite.

TECHNICAL EXPERTISE

Technical expertise is plentiful today. Integrators and in-house administrators built their knowledge and gained experience with NetWare. Novell announced in 1994 that over 50,000 technicians had attained Certified NetWare Engineer status. Microsoft capitalized on Novell's established network of service providers. Microsoft offered a quick and inexpensive path for Certified NetWare Engineers (CNEs) to become Microsoft Certified System Engineers.

Microsoft also found that existing Novell Authorized Technical Education Centers (NAECs) were more than willing to become Microsoft Solution Provider Authorized Technical Education Centers. Both of these factors removed the fear and uncertainty factor from integrating NT.

Finally, Microsoft's marketing efforts and licensing agreements have been extremely effective at getting the product into large accounts, even if only on a trial basis.

FEATURES

The following is a summary of NT Server's features:

- System Architecture
  Multi-user operating system
  Preemptive multitasking
  Processors—Intel, RISC: MIPS, DEC Alpha
  Symmetric multiprocessing up to 32 processors
  Maximum memory RAM up to 4GB
  Paged Virtual memory
  Dynamic memory cache
  Unlimited user connections
  Dynamic loading of services
  Memory protection
  Audit alerts
  Structured exception handling
  Micro kernel-based architecture
  Protected subsystems
  Hardware abstraction layer
  Unicode support
  Installable file systems

◆ Network Interface Card (NIC) support—Server

16-bit Ethernet support
32-bit Ethernet support
16-bit token ring support
32-bit token ring support
NDIS support
ODI support
Third party driver support
Multiple network cards
Client workstation NIC support:
16-bit Ethernet
32-bit Ethernet
16-bit token ring
32-bit token ring
NDIS
NetWare Open DataLink Interface (ODI)
NetWare shells and requesters (NETX and VLM)
Third party drivers

◆ Other hardware support

CD-ROM
SCSI adapters
Plotters
Scanners

◆ Protocol Support

Novell's Internetwork Packet eXchange (IPX)
IPX Dial-in
Packet Burst NetWare Core Protocol compatibility
Large Internetwork Packet compatibility
AppleTalk protocols
NetBIOS
NetBEUI
TCP/IP (native)
Open System Interconnect protocols (in the Software Development Kit)
DECNet (Digital)
IBM's Data Link Control
Internal routing
Remote access service for NetBIOS, TCP, IPX, TCP/IP (native)

◆ Inter-Program Communication

Named Pipes (client side)
Named Pipes (server side)
Sockets
Transport Library Interface
DEC compatible RPC
LU 6.2, LU 1, LU 0, LU 2, LU 3
HLLAPI
Local Procedure Calls (LPC)
Semaphores
Mutexs
Timers
Asynchronous Procedure Calls

◆ File System Features

Unlimited number of file locks
Unlimited number of file opens
Maximum file size—17 billion GB
Efficient sub-block allocation—512 bytes (NTFS only)
File compression (NTFS only)
Transaction-based file system
Support for DOS, Mac, OS/2
Support for NFS (third party)
Total disk storage 408 million TB
Up to 25 volumes per server
Unlimited physical drives per server
Maximum partition size—17000TB
Maximum volume size—17000TB
Disk quotas (third party)
High performance asynchronous I/O
Memory mapped file I/O
Length of filename—255 characters
Long filenames are made visible to DOS programs

◆ Performance Optimization Features

Dynamic cache up to 1GB per process
Elevator seeking
Read ahead caching
Background writes

Overlapped seeks
Split seeks
Directory hashing
File caching
Virtual memory
Returnable memory

◆ Security Features

Designed to meet U.S. C2 and European E3 security
Designed to meet B2 security (third party)
Single login to network
Single, secure logon, and optional background authentication
Single logon compatibility for MS client/server applications
Centralized security event auditing
Minimum password length restriction
Password encryption
Packet signing (secure authentication)
Password aging
Password history
Minimum time until password can be changed
Account lockout
Restrict login to specific workstation
Replaceable client login
Restrict login by time and day
Set account expiration date
Disconnect when access time expires
Rekey password verify
Configurable administrative rights
Security event alert
File system auditing

◆ Directory and File Rights

Read
Write
Execute
Delete
Grant
Ownership
List
Create

◆ User rights

Access workstation from network
Log on locally
Back up files and directories
Restore files and directories
Change the system time
Shut down the system locally
Force system shutdown remotely
Load and unload device drivers
Manage audit and security logs
Take ownership of files or other objects

◆ Security Auditing

Audit user security transactions
Audit user file transactions
Audit administrative transactions
Audit file-creation statistics
Audit volume statistics
Filter audit logs
Audit security policy changes
Audit restart or shutdown of system
Audit nondedicated server activity

◆ Printing

Remote printer port on Workstation
Peer print services
Assign priorities to print queue
Multiple queues to a single printer
Multiple queues on multiple printers
Multiple printers on one queue
Postscript supported
Unlimited shared printers per server
Cross-platform printing to OS/2, UNIX, NetWare, SNA
Remote queue management
Support for multiple forms
Network attached printer support
User notification of job completion
Operator notification of print problem

◆ Printer Alerts

Out-of-paper
Printer request deleted
Printer request completed
Printer offline
Paper jam

◆ Network Management

Command line utilities
GUI utilities
Remote administration, performance, and event monitoring
Asynch remote administration
Remote installation
Remote upgrade
Remote corrective service
Remote session security
Remote modem callback
Dynamic Host Configuration Protocol (DHCP) support for TCP/IP
Windows Internet Name Service (WINS) support for TCP/IP

◆ Performance Monitoring

View total percent CPU use
View total privileged CPU use
View total user CPU use
View logical disk use
View physical disk use
View cache utilization
View packets/bytes sent
View page/faults per second
View number of active processes
View number of active threads
View processor time by process
View processor time by thread
Log performance statistics
Graphical remote performance monitoring

◆ Delegating Administration Responsibility

Account operators
Backup operators
Directory administrator
Enterprise administrators
Print operators
Replication operators
Server operator

◆ Alert Messages

Volume is getting full
Volume is full
Error log is full
Connection slots depleted
Disk utilization above threshold

◆ Fault Tolerance

File system recovery log
Redundant directory structures
Directory verification during power-up
Read-after write verification
Hot-fix
Uninterruptable Power Supply (UPS) support
Disk duplexing
Disk mirroring
RAID 5
Server mirroring (third party)
Dynamic volume sets

◆ Backup features

Backup/restore of server disk with security attributes intact
Online backup of account files
Backup utility shipped with product
Workstation backup (for NT Workstation and WFW)
Automatic file replication service
Server job scheduling

SUMMARY

Microsoft has endeavored to produce the most advanced operating system at the lowest cost. NT promises to replace the vast majority of desktop and server operating systems. NT is ready for market, and the market is now ready for NT.

The stage is set for a battle of the titans over the next few years: NT Server versus NetWare. The outcome cannot be forecast because each firm holds cards that have not been played, and there are more cards to be dealt. One thing is certain, however: Microsoft can only gain, and Novell can only lose market share. It is just a matter of how much each will gain or lose.

Acceptance of NT is occurring at an increasing rate, and will continue to climb. As 32-bit NT applications become available, this product will really begin to gain acceptance. Now is the time to learn all you can about this product.

Tip

When you read this book, and as you use NT, pay close attention to details and try to understand the larger view of what is happening. Doing so will pay dividends in the future as related problems occur. Quite often a problem disappears and you simply move on. When learning a complex product like NT, you need to be cognizant of what happened, why, and how you fixed it, so you will be better prepared in the future.

If you understand mechanically what is going on in any system, you will be better prepared in the future to deal with the many complexities you will encounter.

- NT Server OS
  Architecture

- Centralized Control of
  Client Environment

CHAPTER 2

NT Design

Object   Any user- or resource-related network entity. Servers, users, printers, and groups are the most commonly used objects.

ACE   Access Control Entry. An entry in an Access Control List (ACL).

ACL   Access Control List. The part of a security descriptor that enumerates access protections and auditing attributes that are applied to an object.

NTFS   NT File System. NT's optional high performance file system.

UNICODE   A new ANSI 16-bit code for standard representation of international characters.

TDI   Transport Driver Interface.

CISC   Complex Instruction Set Computing.

IPC   Interprocess Communication.

OSF   Open Software Foundation.

DCE   Data Communication Exchange.

HP/UX   Hewlett-Packard UNIX.

LPC   Local Procedure Calls.

NetBIOS   The Network Basic Input/Output System standard, which was originally developed for IBM by Sytek in the early 80s.

SNA   IBM's Systems Network Architecture.

Btrieve   Trade name for LAN-based file management system.

NDIS   Network Device Interface Specification. Microsoft's specifications for interface between network card drivers and NOS transport protocols.

Redirector   A program that captures requests for resources made by the application and redirects these to the NOS.

WAN   Wide Area Network. A network carried on leased or dial-up telecommunications lines.

SAM   Security Account Manager. Database entries in NT's Registry for each user account.

VDM   Virtual Dos Machine. A DOS window. NT creates an independent DOS environment inside a resizable or full screen.

Portability   A software's capability to run on more than one hardware environment.

Scalability   A software's capability to run on small to large hardware platforms.

Fault Tolerance   A system's capability to keep operating even when parts of the system have failed.

This section covers the internal design of the NT Server NOS. This information can be useful for the administrator. The discussions that follow will help save the administrator considerable time in researching connectivity, performance, fault tolerance, and compatibility issues.

Most system administrators have worked with either Novell NetWare or peer-to-peer networks. The unique mix of centralized control and distributed processing provided by NT Server can prove to be unfamiliar for some. NT Server is a complicated product that maintains compatibility with many existing environments, has connectivity to many diverse environments, and has rich features. This chapter contains technical information needed for the administrator to understand and to act on important implementation and performance concepts presented in later chapters.

This chapter provides an overview of the NT Server operating system architecture as well as putting into perspective the impact of the operating system features on the overall networking environment. It also provides basic knowledge about the NT operating system and networking internals.

This chapter explores:

> NT Server Operating System (OS) Architecture
> Centralized Control of Client Environment

NT Server OS Architecture

Microsoft's design goals for NT were quite general in nature. NT Server shares its design with NT Workstation, which needs to have the capability to run desktop applications. In addition, NT Server is targeted for back-end or application service duty such as running SQL Server. The following is a brief description of the expressed design goals and an administrator's point of view.

◆ Software compatibility: Any new operating system has one thing going against it; applications designed for it will not be created for a while. Microsoft has designed NT Server with compatibility as a primary goal so that existing Windows applications will work until new NT 32-bit applications are delivered. Software compatibility, as distinct from hardware compatibility, has a much wider scope, so there are layers of sometimes extraneous technology that your installation may not need.

◆ Hardware compatibility: NT is the first and only operating system from Microsoft that can run on a variety of hardware platforms. NT contains a Hardware Abstraction Layer (HAL), which shifts the burden of compatibility to the hardware developer. This adds another dimension of complexity to the product that impacts all the platforms because the product must have an extra layer of abstraction between the software and the hardware.

◆ Security: Lack of a secure environment would automatically preclude using a NOS in many organizations, including government agencies where C-2 security is required. Corporations are becoming more security minded because of the added exposure due to internetworking and remote access. For the administrator, setting up security is an extra chore during the install process but is a powerful tool to control the network environment once in routine use.

◆ Portability: NT Server is one of the first network operating systems that can be moved from one hardware platform to another as more performance is required. NT's current release provides Hardware Abstraction Layers for the Intel X86 CISC processors as well as a few RISC processors.

◆ Scalability: The base NT Server operating system is Symmetrical Multi-Processing (SMP) equipped—it will run on a single or multiple processors with no modifications. This allows hardware upgrading flexibility without requiring changes to the operating system or any software.

◆ Client/server computing: NT was designed to provide a stable platform for applications designed with software components running on both the client and the server. The client and server modules communicate with one another to provide both centralized and distributed processing at the same time. NT Server has many features that make it an ideal operating system foundation for client/server applications.

◆ Reliability and robustness: Each new generation of operating systems must deal with more and more complex applications and at the same time be more reliable. Previous PC operating systems have lacked the power and have not been reliable enough to downsize mission-critical mainframe and minicomputer applications.

◆ Central control: Control of the client desktop is one of the most important features of NT Server. This gives administrators minicomputer-like control of the entire network including the NT Workstation desktops.

COMPATIBILITY

To make the NT compatible with existing PC environments, the familiar Windows interface is used. Support for File Allocation Table (FAT) and High Performance File System (HPFS) provides compatibility with MS-DOS and OS/2 file access. The designers have also included network connectivity to several existing networking environments and protocols. Compatibility cannot be theoretical; a product must be interoperable with existing systems to effectively integrate into today's existing multiprotocol environments.

The job of making NT interoperable was mind-boggling because the mix of existing network products in the PC marketplace is staggering. The administrator must take a conservative approach and should prove compatibility before putting certain product combinations into a production environment. For example, some MS-DOS character-based software packages do not run properly in an NT Workstation DOS Virtual Machine (VDM). Administrators need to carefully evaluate software limitations like this before integrating NT. Other more critical examples can be illustrated where further in-house evaluation of application behavior is called for.

Most compatibility information published by Microsoft targets the behavior of applications actually running on NT Server or Workstation. Comprehensive compatibility information is not yet available about the behavior of existing DOS and 16-bit Windows applications running on client workstations.

An additional perspective covered by this book describes the behavior of the NT Client Redirector, the workstation software that connects the client to an NT Server. Redirector parameters can be adjusted to improve compatibility with many distributed applications.

The Microsoft Redirector handles DOS software interrupt 13h (disk access) and software interrupt 21h (general-purpose) calls made by many existing applications differently than NetWare handles them. The majority of these differences have been ironed out during the short time that WFW has been deployed as an add-on to NetWare networks. Chapter 30, "LAN Troubleshooting" covers this topic in greater depth.

This book provides guidelines for compatibility conformance evaluation. Of special interest are: DOS, Windows on Windows (WOW), OS/2, and POSIX compatibility. Compatibility is important because you may prefer to use hardware that is not included in Microsoft's NT Hardware Compatibility List. The book suggests some rules-of-thumb in using "clone" components to build systems that will work reliably.

SECURITY

NT was designed with security that meets the requirements for C-2 U.S. government rating. This security model also provides a safe environment for critical application for corporate environments.

For administrators, security is a mixed bag—in many cases, security is of little concern, but in others high security is required. Many applications have internal security mechanisms that are difficult to configure so they mesh properly with the NOS security model. Before NetWare was popular and applications were "NetWare aware," administrators had to come up with "home cures" for dealing with security and concurrent use problems.

Dealing with security is not just a matter of establishing NT permissions and user rights. Integration of NOS security with security features built into software is the administrator's responsibility. Many network-aware applications are designed for NetWare networks and one of the difficult challenges administrators face is making the applications behave as well as they did on NetWare networks.

In many instances it is difficult to tell whether an application is malfunctioning because of a bug in the application itself, inadequate access to resources, improper security assignments, or time-outs due to network congestion.

Security in NT Server is pervasive. The security model includes components to control who accesses which objects (such as files and shared printers), which actions an individual can take on an object, and which events are audited.

NT Server creates *Access Control Entries (ACEs)* in a table called an *Access Control List (ACL)*. Each ACL is made up of ACEs specifying access or auditing permissions to that object for one user or group. There are three ACE types: two for discretionary access control and one for system security.

The discretionary ACEs are `AccessAllowed` and `AccessDenied`. Respectively, these explicitly grant and deny access to a user or group of users.

Note

There is an important distinction between a discretionary ACL that is empty (one that has no ACEs in it) and an object without any discretionary ACL. In the case of an empty discretionary ACL, no accesses are explicitly granted, so access is implicitly denied. For an object that has no ACL at all, there is no protection assigned to the object, so any access request is granted. The administrator needs to understand these default security assignments to prevent breaches once the server is put into use.

`SystemAudit` is a system security ACE that is used to keep a log of security events (such as who accesses which files) and to generate and log security audit messages. The impact of these internal control mechanisms on applications can be unpredictable because most existing applications are not specifically written for the NT environment.

PORTABILITY

NT Server can run on both RISC and CISC platforms. RISC computers, like the MIPS R4000, Digital Alpha AXP, and Motorola PowerPC processors, provide the administrator simple upgrade paths that were not available before NT. In some cases, applications running on RISC platforms can be downsized to less expensive CISC platforms. Organizations no longer have to rewrite or even rework their applications to move them between CISC and RISC platforms. Applications written for NT Servers and workstations do not need to be reworked at all to port to a different platform.

Figure 2.1.
Hardware Abstraction
Layer.

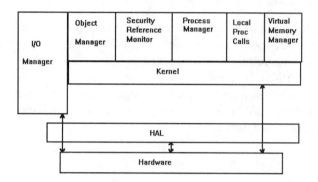

Portability is achieved via a mechanism called the *Hardware Abstraction Layer (HAL)*. HAL is a thin layer of software provided by the hardware manufacturer that hides, or abstracts, hardware differences from higher layers of the operating system. Thus, through the filter provided by HAL, different types of hardware all look alike to the operating system, removing the need to specifically tailor the operating system (and therefore applications) to the hardware with which it communicates.

NT does not allow applications to interact with hardware-related software elements, such as device drivers. This protects NT's portability and makes your operating system more reliable.

The goal for HAL is to provide routines that allow a single device driver to support the same device on all platforms. HAL allows a large number of variations in hardware platforms for a single processor architecture without requiring a separate version of the operating system for each one.

HAL routines are called from both the base operating system (including the executive kernel component) and from device drivers. For drivers, HAL provides the capability to support a wide variety of input/output (I/O) architectures instead of either being restricted to a single hardware model or needing extensive adaptation for each new hardware platform. HAL is also responsible for hiding the details of symmetric multiprocessing hardware from the rest of the operating system.

In NT's early stages portability was unproven. Digital Equipment Corporation has proven NT's portability on up to four Alpha processors for unprecedented power and reliability. It is basically up to the hardware vendors to provide hardware abstraction for their systems. As time goes on, NT Server's portability and compatibility with many vendors' computers will be established.

Your installation CD contains separate directories for installation on various hardware platforms. A greater variety of computer-processor platforms will be supported in future releases.

Many applications have become available to users with many different types of computers as a result of this portability. A Power PC from IBM or Apple can now run NT, Apple's System 7.5, and UNIX operating systems. This provides the ability to run 16-bit Windows applications, 32-bit applications written for NT or Macintosh System 7.5, Macintosh 16-bit applications, as well as UNIX applications. Administrators may have to manage applications previously available only on high-end RISC workstations.

SCALABILITY

NT Server takes full advantage of *symmetric multiprocessing (SMP)* hardware and can run on systems with up to 32 processors. This capability extends to NT Workstation as well as NT Server, so an organization's network can grow without being restricted by processing capability. The additional processors share in executing threads on a time slice basis. You can force a processor to stay with a thread to take advantage of the processor cache, which probably has thread specific data still in it.

Note

Intel has designed the capability to support SMP in the Pentium's architecture with up to four processors. Digital's AXP computers support up to four Alpha processors. However, Sequent, Pyramid, Tandem, and a few other minicomputer vendors have developed systems with support for up to 32 Pentium processors. Your NT applications can be scaled up to these platforms without having to change any of your applications or re-writing a single line of code.

Clustering technology, also called *failover*, is under development. Clustering mirrors data physically to another server or within the same server, thus preventing crashes. Clustering adds fault tolerance and improves performance.

Several difficult software problems must be solved to support server clustering, including the development of distributed lock managers to enable hardware vendors to turn servers into virtual mirrored pairs. Digital has already developed their first iteration of clustering on Intel Pentium processors, while AT&T, GIS, and Tandem Computers Inc. are currently developing clustering capability.

DISTRIBUTED COMPUTING

Distributed computing means that NT is designed with networking built into the base operating system. NT also allows for connectivity to a variety of host environments through its support of multiple transport protocols and high-level client/server facilities including named pipes, remote procedure calls (RPCs), and Windows Sockets.

A distributed computing application is one that has two parts—a front-end to run on the client computer and a back-end to run on the server. In distributed computing, the goal is to divide the computing task into two sections. The front-end requires minimal resources and runs on the client's workstation. The back-end requires large amounts of data, number crunching, or specialized hardware, and runs on the server. A connection between the client and the server at a process-to-process level allows data to flow in both directions between the client and server.

Microsoft Mail, Microsoft Schedule+, SQL Server, and SNA Server are examples of distributed applications.

For building distributed applications, Windows NT includes NetBIOS and Windows Sockets interfaces. In addition, Windows NT supports peer-to-peer named pipes, mailslots, and remote procedure calls. On Windows NT, for example, an electronic mail product could include a messaging service using named pipes and asynchronous communication that runs with any transport protocol or network card.

Of named pipes, mailslots, and RPC, RPC is the most portable mechanism. RPCs use other *interprocess communication (IPC)* mechanisms including named pipes and the NetBIOS and Windows Sockets interfaces to transfer functions and data between client and server computers. Figure 2.2 illustrates the relationship between the participants in an RPC sequence.

Much of the original design work for an RPC facility was developed by Sun Microsystems. This work was continued by the *Open Software Foundation (OSF)* as part of their overall *Data Communications Exchange (DCE)* standard. The Microsoft RPC facility is compatible with the OSF/DCE-standard RPC. It is important to note that Microsoft's implementation of the DCE standard is compatible and not compliant. Compliance in this case means starting with the OSF source code and building on it. The Microsoft RPC facility is completely interoperable with other DCE-based RPC systems such as the ones for HP's HPUX, Apple's UIX, and IBM's AIX systems.

2

NT DESIGN

Figure 2.2.
RPC components.

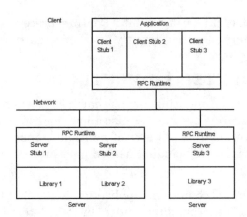

The RPC "mechanism" is unique because it uses the other IPC mechanisms to establish communications between the client and the server. RPC can use named pipes, NetBIOS, or Windows Sockets to communicate with remote systems. If the client and server are on the same computer, it can use the *Local Procedure Call (LPC)* facility to transfer information between processes and subsystems. This makes RPC the most flexible and portable of the Windows NT IPC mechanisms.

RPC is based on the concepts used for creating structured programs that can be viewed as having a "tree trunk" to which a series of "branches" can be attached. The tree trunk is the mainstream logic of the program, which should rarely change. The branches are the procedures the tree trunk calls on to do work or perform functions.

In traditional programs, these branches are statically linked. By using *Dynamic Link Libraries (DLLs)*, structured programs can dynamically link the branches. With DLLs, the procedure code and the tree trunk code are in different modules. The DLL can thus be modified or updated without changes to the tree trunk. RPC means that the tree trunk and the branches can exist on different computers, as shown in Figure 2.2.

Because of RPCs and HAL, software portability is assured. Applications written for NT Server–based modules, such as SQL Server, do not need to be reworked when scaled up or ported to other platforms. To migrate from single to multiple processors, or from CISC to RISC servers, you simply need to set up the new server, and move your applications to the new platform. Extensive changes to code should be eliminated if code was written for a server-based application.

Operating System Features

A NOS protects applications from damaging each other and the operating system. The NOS must schedule and manage the requests being made of the resources it controls. NT Server employs structured exception handling throughout its entire architecture. It includes a recoverable file system and provides protection through its built-in security and advanced memory management techniques.

NT Server is very different from the NetWare NOS in that it is designed to run server-based applications at the same time it is providing file and print services. Novell's *NetWare Loadable Module (NLM)* design allows server-based NLMs to run unprotected, almost as if they are part of the operating system rather than as applications. A misbehaved NLM can crash the server or dominate its processor. NT Server has much more protection and control in the server operating system to guard against server application problems that can affect the NOS.

The following discussions are presented here in the formal object-oriented nomenclature so that an administrator can relate to these terms when they appear in error messages, in the Event Log, and in product bulletins from Microsoft.

The Executive, which includes the Kernel and HAL, provides a set of common services that all environment subsystems can use. Each group of services is managed by one of the separate components of the Executive as shown in Figure 2.3.

Figure 2.3.
Local procedure calls.

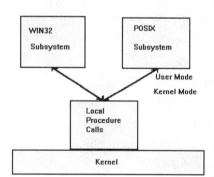

Object Manager

Objects are runtime instances of a particular object type that can be manipulated by an operating system process. Your applications communicate with objects, each of which points to a hardware or software resource on the target computer.

Object types include:

◆ system-defined data types
◆ a list of operations that can be performed on it (such as wait, create, or cancel)
◆ a set of object attributes

Object Manager is the part of the Windows NT Executive that provides uniform rules for retention, naming, and object security.

Before a process can manipulate a Windows NT object, it must first acquire a handle to the object. An object handle includes access control information and a pointer to the object itself. All object handles are created through the Object Manager.

Like other Windows NT components, the Object Manager is extensible so that new object types can be defined as technology grows and changes. An example of this is the ability to write one's own Performance Probe program and execute it at the mapped memory level that the NT Server Performance Monitor runs.

In addition, NT's Object Manager manages the global name space for Windows NT and tracks the creation and use of objects by internal operating system and software processes. This name space is used to access all named objects contained in the local computer environment. The object name space is modeled after a hierarchical file system where directory names in a path are separated by a backslash (\). Some of the objects that can have names include the following:

◆ Directory objects
◆ Object type objects
◆ Symbolic link objects
◆ Semaphore and event objects
◆ Process and thread objects
◆ Section and segment objects
◆ Port objects
◆ File objects

VIRTUAL MEMORY MANAGER

NT Server uses memory in many complex ways. Non-paged, cache, and virtual memory, as well as direct mapped memory are some of those ways. It provides applications with virtual memory. Virtual memory is the means by which NT Server allows applications to virtually have 4GB of linear address space. The virtual memory architecture for Windows NT is a demand-paged virtual memory system. It is based on a flat, linear address space accessed via 32-bit addresses.

Virtual memory refers to the fact that the operating system can actually allocate more memory than the computer physically contains. Each process is allocated a unique virtual address space, which is a set of addresses available for the process's threads to use. This virtual address space is divided into equal blocks, or pages. Every process is allocated its own virtual address space, which appears to be 4GB in size—2GB is reserved for program storage and 2GB is reserved for system storage. Few operating systems can see this much memory. MS OS/2 version 1.3, for example, can only see 16MB of physical memory.

Demand paging refers to a method by which data is moved by pages from physical memory to a temporary paging file on disk. As the data is needed by a process, it is paged back into physical memory.

The Virtual Memory Manager maps virtual addresses in the process's address space to physical pages in the computer's memory. In doing so, it hides the physical organization of memory from the process's threads. This ensures that the thread can access its process's memory as needed, but not the memory of other processes.

Because each process has a separate address space, a thread in one process cannot view or modify the memory of another process without the operting system's permission.

When a file is larger than the size of your available system RAM, the Virtual Memory Manager uses paging to move data between RAM and the hard disk. It accomplishes this by dividing all physical memory and virtual memory (the memory used by applications) into equal-sized blocks or pages (4K each). When a request is made to access data that is not in RAM, the Virtual Memory Manager swaps a page from RAM with the desired page from the paging file (a file on the hard disk used solely by the Virtual Memory Manager for extra data storage).

Page states are registered in a virtual page table. If a page is in RAM and is immediately available to its process (or program), it is marked as valid. Pages that have been moved to the paging file are marked as invalid. When a process tries to access an invalid page, the central processing unit (CPU) generates a page fault. The virtual memory manager traps page faults and retrieves pages from the paging file. If there is no room in RAM to store a new page, a valid page is moved out.

There are four policies used by the Virtual Memory Manager to determine how and when paging is performed:

◆ Demand Based

A demand-based paging algorithm is used to retrieve (or fetch) memory pages. The virtual memory manager waits until a process thread attempts to access an invalid page before loading the page into RAM. Because page faults and disk access are both somewhat slow, additional pages are loaded

along with the desired page in a process called *clustering*. The additional
pages are chosen according to their proximity to the desired page, the
theory being that the process may need information spanning several
consecutive pages. This reduces the number of page faults generated and
the amount of disk operations.

◆ Placement

Placement refers to the location at which a page is stored in RAM. The
Virtual Memory Manager chooses the first free page in RAM it finds.

◆ Replacement

If the placement policy fails because there are no free pages in RAM, the
replacement policy is used to determine which page will be moved from
RAM to the paging file. Each process has a group of valid pages in RAM;
these are called the *working set* (remember this term, it will be used often).
For simplicity, a first-in, first-out (FIFO) algorithm is used. When a page
replacement is required, the oldest page in the working set is moved to the
paging file to make room for the new page. Because the replacement
scheme is only applied to the working set of the current process, other
processes are guaranteed that their pages will not be replaced by other
processes.

◆ Mapped File I/O

If an application attempts to load a file that is larger than both the system
RAM and the paging file combined, the mapped file I/O services of the
virtual memory manager are used. Mapped file I/O enables the virtual
memory manager to map virtual memory addresses to a large file, inform
the application that the file is available, and then load only the pieces of the
file that the application actually intends to use. Because only portions of
the large file are loaded into memory (RAM or page file), this greatly
decreases file load time and system resource drainage. This is a very useful
service for database applications that often require access to huge files.

PROCESS MANAGER

The Process Manager is the component that tracks two types of objects—process
objects and thread objects. A process is defined as an address space, a set of objects
(resources) visible to the process, and a set of threads running in the context of the
process. A thread is the most basic schedulable entity in the system. It has its own
set of registers, its own Kernel stack, a thread environment block, and a user stack
in its process's address space.

The Process Manager is the Windows NT component that manages the creation and
deletion of processes. It provides a standard set of services for creating and using
threads and processes in the context of a particular subsystem environment. Beyond

that, the Process Manager does little to dictate rules about threads and processes. Instead, the Windows NT design allows for robust environment subsystems that can define specific rules about threads and processes.

The Process Manager does not impose any hierarchy or grouping rules for processes, nor does it enforce any parent/child relationships.

The Windows NT process model works in conjunction with the security model and the Virtual Memory Manager to provide interprocess protection. Each process is assigned a security access token called the primary token of the process. This token is used by the Windows NT access–validation routines when threads in the process reference protected objects.

The Process Manager participates in a message passing facility called *local procedure calls (LPC)*. Applications and environment subsystems have a client/server relationship. That is, the client (an application) makes calls to the environment server (a subsystem) to satisfy a request for some type of system service. To allow for a client/server relationship between applications and environment subsystems, NT Server provides a communication mechanism between them.

Applications communicate with environment subsystems by passing messages via the LPC facility. The message-passing process is hidden from the client applications by *function stubs* (nonexecutable placeholders used by calls from the server environment) provided in the form of special dynamic-link libraries (DLLs).

When an application makes an application program interface (API) call to an environment subsystem, the stub in the client (application) process packages the parameters for the call and sends them to a server (subsystem) process that implements the call. It is the LPC facility that allows the stub procedure to pass the data to the server process and wait for a response.

For example, consider how this process works in the Win32 subsystem. When a Win32 application is loaded to run, it is linked to a DLL that contains stubs for all of the functions in Win32 API. When the application calls a Win32 function (in this example, the `CreateWindow` Win32 function) the call is processed as follows:

1. The `CreateWindow()` stub function in the DLL is called by the client Win32 application.

2. The stub function constructs a message containing all the data needed to create a window and sends the message to the Win32 server process (that is, the Win32 subsystem).

3. The Win32 subsystem receives the message and calls the real `CreateWindow()` function. The window is created.

4. The Win32 subsystem sends a message containing the results of the `CreateWindow()` function back to the stub function in the DLL.

5. The stub function unpacks the server message from the subsystem and returns the results to the client Win32 application.

From the application's perspective, the `CreateWindow()` function in the DLL created the window. The application does not know that the work was actually performed by the Win32 server process (the Win32 subsystem), that a message was sent to make it happen, or even that the Win32 server process exists. It does not know that the subsystem called one or more Executive system servers to support its call to `CreateWindow`.

I/O MANAGER

The I/O Manager is the Windows NT Executive feature that manages all input and output for the operating system. A large part of the I/O Manager's role is to manage communications between drivers. The I/O Manager supports all file system drivers, hardware device drivers, and network drivers, and provides a heterogeneous environment for them. It provides a formal interface that all drivers can call. This uniform interface allows the I/O Manager to communicate with all drivers in the same way without any knowledge of how the devices they control actually work. The I/O Manager also includes driver support routines specifically designed for file system drivers, for hardware device drivers, and for network drivers.

The Windows NT I/O model uses a layered architecture that allows separate drivers to implement each logically distinct layer of I/O processing. For example, drivers in the lowest layer manipulate the computer's physical devices (called device drivers). Other drivers are then layered on top of the device drivers. These higher-level drivers do not know any details about the physical devices. With the help of the I/O Manager, higher-level drivers simply pass logical I/O requests down to the device drivers, which access the physical devices on their behalf. The Windows NT installable file systems and network Redirectors are examples of high-level drivers that work in this way.

This scheme allows easy replacement of file system drivers and device drivers. It allows multiple file systems and devices to be active at the same time while being addressed through a formal interface.

Drivers communicate with each other using data structures called I/O request packets. The drivers pass I/O request packets to each other via the I/O Manager, which delivers the packets to the appropriate target drivers using the drivers' standard services. The simplest way to perform an I/O operation is to synchronize the execution of applications with completion of the I/O operations they request. (This is known as synchronous I/O.) When such an application performs an I/O operation, the application's processing is blocked. When the I/O operation is complete, the application is allowed to continue processing.

One way that applications can optimize their performance is to perform asynchronous I/O, a method employed by many of the processes in Windows NT. When an application initiates an I/O operation, the I/O Manager accepts the request but doesn't block the application's execution while the I/O operation is being performed. Instead, the application is allowed to continue working. Most I/O devices are very slow in comparison to a computer's processor, so an application can do a lot of work while waiting to be notified that an I/O operation is complete.

When an environment subsystem issues an asynchronous I/O request, the I/O Manager returns to the environment subsystem immediately after putting the request in a queue without waiting for the device driver to complete its operations. Meanwhile, a separate thread from the I/O Manager runs requests from the queue in the most efficient order (not necessarily the order received). When each I/O request is finished, the I/O Manager notifies the process that requested the I/O.

While asynchronous I/O permits an application to use the computer's processor during I/O operations, it also makes it harder for the application to determine when I/O operations have been completed. Some applications provide a callback function that is called when the asynchronous I/O operation is completed. Other applications use synchronization objects, such as an event or the file handle, that the I/O system sets to the signaled state when the I/O operation is complete.

CACHE MANAGER

The I/O architecture includes the Cache Manager that handles caching for the entire I/O system. Caching is a method used by a file system to improve performance. For example, instead of reading and writing directly to the disk, frequently used files are temporarily stored in a cache in memory, and reads and writes to those files are performed in memory. Reading and writing to memory is much faster than reading and writing to disk.

The Cache Manager uses a file-mapping model that is closely integrated with the NT Server Virtual Memory Management. Cache Manager provides caching services to all file systems and network components under the control of the I/O Manager. Cache Manager can dynamically grow and shrink the size of the cache as the amount of available RAM varies. When a process opens a file already residing in the cache, Cache Manager simply copies data from the cache to the process's virtual address space, and vice versa, as reads and writes are performed.

Cache Manager offers services such as lazy write and lazy commit, which can improve overall file system performance. *Lazy write* is the ability to record changes in the file structure cache, which is quicker than recording them on disk; then later, when demand on the computer's central processing unit (CPU) is low, the Cache Manager writes the changes to the disk. *Lazy commit* is similar to lazy write. Instead of immediately marking a transaction as successfully completed, the committed information is cached and later written to the file system log as a background process.

FILE SYSTEM DRIVERS

In the Windows NT I/O architecture, file system drivers are managed by the I/O Manager. Windows NT supports multiple active file systems including existing file systems such as FAT. Windows NT supports FAT and HPFS file systems for backward compatibility with MS-DOS, Windows 3.x, and OS/2 1.x operating systems.

Windows NT also supports NTFS—a new file system designed for use with Windows NT. NTFS provides many features including file system security, Unicode support, recoverability, long filename support, and support for POSIX.

The Windows NT I/O architecture not only supports traditional file systems but has implemented its network Redirector and server as file system drivers. From the perspective of I/O Manager, there is no difference between accessing files stored on a remote networked computer and accessing those stored locally on a hard disk. In addition, Redirectors and servers can be loaded and unloaded dynamically just like any other driver, and multiple Redirectors and servers can coexist on the same computer.

HARDWARE DEVICE DRIVERS

Hardware device drivers are also components of the I/O architecture. All hardware device drivers (such as printer drivers, mouse drivers, and disk drivers) are written in the C programming language, are 32-bit addressable, and are multiprocessor-safe.

Device drivers access the hardware registers of the peripheral devices through support routines supplied by the Windows NT operating system. There is a set of these routines for every platform supported by Windows NT; because the routine names are the same for all platforms, device drivers for Windows NT are portable across different processor types.

Designers of device drivers are encouraged to create separate drivers for different devices, rather than monolithic drivers, and the design of I/O Manager makes it easy to do so. This allows more flexibility to customize device configurations on the computer and to layer device drivers and other drivers.

For example, the Intel 8042 (i8042) processor is an interface device—the keyboard and mouse communicate with the i8042 driver as well as with their own respective drivers. Three separate drivers are used (for the i8042, the keyboard, and the mouse) rather than one large monolithic driver. This makes it easier to change one component (exchanging the mouse for a different pointing device, for example).

NETWORK DRIVERS

A third type of driver implemented as a component in the I/O architecture are network device drivers. Windows NT includes integrated networking capabilities and support for distributed applications. As shown in Figure 2.4, networking is supported by a series of network drivers.

Figure 2.4.
Networking com-
ponents.

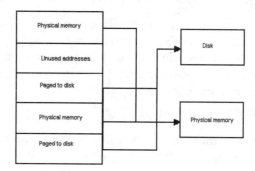

Redirectors and servers are implemented as file system drivers and run at or below a provider interface layer where NetBIOS and Windows Sockets reside.

Transport protocol drivers communicate with Redirectors and servers through a layer called the Transport Driver Interface (TDI). Windows NT includes a number of transports.

- ◆ Transmission Control Protocol/Internet Protocol (TCP/IP), which provides a popular, routable protocol for wide-area networks.
- ◆ NBF, a descendant of NetBIOS Extended User Interface (NetBEUI), which provides compatibility with existing LAN Manager, LAN Server, and MS-Net installations.
- ◆ Data Link Control (DLC), which provides an interface for access to IBM mainframes and IBM network-attached printers.
- ◆ NWLink, a Microsoft implementation of IPX/SPX, which provides connectivity with Novell NetWare.

At the bottom of the networking architecture is the network adapter card device driver. Windows NT currently supports device drivers written to the Network Device Interface Specification (NDIS) version 3.0. NDIS allows for a flexible environment of data exchange between transport protocols and network adapters.

NDIS 3.0 allows a single computer to have several network adapter cards installed in it. In turn, each network adapter card can support multiple transport protocols for access to multiple types of network servers.

FAULT TOLERANCE

The administrator needs to be well versed in the fault tolerant features of the NT Server environment. Many of these features take effect automatically; if the administrator does not take notice, these automatic actions can in fact cause catastrophic failures. For example, many administrators have had the DOS Recover program make a jumble of a local drive's directory structure.

The administrator cannot relinquish responsibility for the network's reliability. The operating system's automatic repairs need to be acknowledged and attended to. For example, if the file system is doing a lot of sector sparing, it's a sign of the disk subsystem's impending media failure. A disk replacement may be needed to prevent a system breakdown.

Reliability can be thought of in three distinct ways:

◆ **Uptime:** The availability of the server for file and print service resources residing on the server. Also included in this category are the applications actually running on the server, such as databases or communication services. Different operating system features make for less downtime. Statistics show that 70 percent of system failures can be attributed to disk and power failure. NT Server supports Redundant Arrays of Inexpensive Disks (RAID) features with standard SCSI disk adapters. RAID 1 can be configured for fault tolerant mirroring (or duplexing) of disk drives. RAID 5 can be configured with data striped over multiple drives for good performance, and a "parity" checksum on each drive that permits data reconstruction with no downtime. Interface to an Uninterruptible Power Service (UPS) is also included in the operating system.

◆ **Referential Integrity:** This is a new term used mostly in the context of database integrity. It can also apply to wordprocessing and spreadsheet files. More and more applications are becoming "docu-centric" which means that users need not concern themselves with which file a certain document is stored in or which spreadsheet file needs to be linked to a word-processing document. The application maintains linkages which are defined "visually" by the user by pointing and clicking. These clever linkages can come unglued if the file system at the server does not maintain referential integrity. The primary automatic repair mechanisms such as CHKDSK take effect at system boot time. That may mean that if the operating system has not been booted for some time, the inconsistencies are not detected by the operating system.

◆ **Concurrency Control:** NT Server provides file services to applications running at the server or at the client. One of the key features is file and record locking. DOS 3.1 was the first version of DOS to provide rudimentary file and record locking services via interrupt 21. Novell has implemented semaphores (A semaphore object grants a limited number of threads concurrent access to a shared resource, such as a buffer pool with limited entries; if more threads than the specified limit try to access the resource, they are automatically suspended until a resource becomes available. If these objects are given a name when they are created, they can be shared by multiple processes.) and sophisticated record and file locking mechanisms. NT Server's file management techniques, though they are not entirely new, are still different enough to merit the administrator's attention.

CENTRALIZED CONTROL OF CLIENT ENVIRONMENT

Previous Windows versions lacked tools a system administrator needed to manage and control network users and their Windows Desktops. NT has been updated to include many more tools to manage a centrally installed and controlled network.

Administrators need to control

◆ User Account Properties, Permissions, and Rights

◆ Applications installed on a server's drives for sharing

◆ Users' Windows Desktops and configuration files

NT networks are unique in that the security extends out to the client environment. For example, you can create a user's home directory on the user's local NTFS partition and still maintain airtight security.

This active security is expressed via User Profiles, Logon Scripts, Rights, and System Environment Variables/Account Parameters. The administrator needs to be very well versed in the use of these tools. Unfortunately, Logon Scripts, System Environment Variables/Account Parameters, and User Profiles do not work with WFW and Windows 3.1 clients. NT and Windows 95 clients take advantage of these NT Server features. Chapter 12, "Controlling the User Environment," shows detailed examples.

USER PROFILES OVERVIEW

A user profile stores the user's Windows desktop configuration. An administrator can use Profiles to create secure environments for a variety of jobs, store the profile centrally, and then assign the profile to users fitting that job description. For example, all bank tellers might have a Profile called TELLERS.MAN. When a user logs on with this profile, they get the centrally stored profile without changes they might have made locally. User Profiles apply to NT Workstation and Windows 95 client desktops.

Note for NetWare Administrators

NT User Profiles is a completely new concept and has no equivalent capability in NetWare.

The administrator can use Profiles to restrict users in the following areas:

- ◆ Creating Program Items and Groups.
- ◆ Changing the contents of Program Groups.
- ◆ Changing Program Item Properties (such as the application a program item starts).
- ◆ Running programs from the File menu in Program Manager.
- ◆ Making connections to network printers (other than those printers the Profile itself makes connections to).
- ◆ Ensuring structure so that several accounts will each have the same user environment. This can be done by either controlling the default environment or locking environment specifics.
- ◆ It may be desirable for an administrator to structure a network environment for the user. This could be necessary in a situation where security requires absolute or partial control, or if the users aren't familiar enough with computers and networks to be able to use the technology on their own. The solution is to use the User Profile utility to preconfigure the logon environment so that it provides Windows NT or Server users with a consistent, manageable set of network connections and program items.

LOGON SCRIPTS

Logon scripts provide the network administrator with a utility for creating standard logon procedures. Scripts can be personalized for individual users or standardized for several users. Typically, Logon scripts are used for making connections for network resources, and running special utilities and applications.

Note for NetWare Administrators

Logon scripts in NT are pretty much the same as Login scripts in NetWare, except drive mappings are not necessary in a Windows environment. Windows restores drive and printer connections unless configured otherwise.

◆ The Putinenv Utility can be used to copy parameters defined in the user's account on the NT Server to the client PC's DOS environment variables. These variables can be used in the Logon Script or by an application.

◆ Implementing Home Directories (directories for each user's private files).

◆ Logon scripts can be ordinary batch files.

◆ Logon scripts are batch files or executable files that run automatically when a user logs on at a workstation running either NT Workstation, Windows 95, or MS-DOS.

PERMISSIONS

NT Server enables administrators the ability to control access to directories by sharing them with the clients on the network. Permissions can restrict access for all users based on permissions placed on shared directories. This way, two levels of access control can apply. (The files have intrinsic permission attached to them by the NTFS file system.)

Note for NetWare Administrators

Permissions in NT are similar to a Rights Mask in NetWare that applies Access Rights to a directory or file. This feature is seldom used in a NetWare environment; instead, administrators generally rely on trustee assignments (rights to files and directories) applying to the user, not the files and/or directories.

Permissions can be set on shared directories (Shares) no matter what file system the shared directory is formatted with. These permissions are only effective when the directory is accessed across the network and apply to all files and subdirectories in the shared directory. If the shared directory is on an NTFS partition, the permissions set on the Share operate in addition to the NTFS Permissions and are the maximum permissions allowed.

2

NT DESIGN

It is possible to give permissions to users and/or groups of users. Each user or group listed can be given different access levels if desired. The following permissions can be applied to limit user access:

◆ **No Access:** This permission allows a connection to be made, but the directory cannot be accessed and the contents will not be listed. If the user is a member of any group with a No Access permission, No Access overrides any other permission(s) the user may have been granted individually, or as a member of other groups.

◆ **Read:** User may display subdirectory names and filenames, display the data and attributes of files, run program files, and access the directory's subdirectories.

◆ **Change:** This permission has all the access of Read, as well as the capability to create subdirectories and add files, change data in and append data to files, change file attributes, rename, and delete subdirectories and files.

◆ **Full Access:** This is essentially the same as Change, but also allows the Taking Ownership.

Note for NetWare Administrators

There is no specific concept of rights in NT Server as they are defined under NetWare. The user account permissions and the Share level/ NTFS File–level permissions are used to calculate the effective Rights, which are called ACEs as discussed in the section on Security earlier in this chapter.

SYSTEM ENVIRONMENT VARIABLES AND ACCOUNT PARAMETERS

System environment variables have information about the NT Server, such as a path to the TEMP directory at the NT Server. Account variables are pointers to the users' %HOMEDRIVE%, %HOMEPATH%, %HOMESHARE%, %OS%, %USERDOMAIN%, and more. The actual values for these reside in the SAM at the NT Server.

Note for NetWare Administrators

Similar variables are kept in the Bindery in NetWare 3.x and the Directory Services database in NetWare 4.x.

Summary

NT Server is a conglomeration of several technologies. Many of these technologies have been around for some time, and quite a bit of experience about them exists among the administrator community. With the formal release of the product, and Microsoft's stated intention of making NT Server the backbone of the BackOffice line, administrators must tackle the NT Server environment as a whole. NT Server does not come out of the box tuned to your specific needs. Even after you have initially tuned it, it constantly re-tunes itself and needs to be watched.

Many administrators have been handed down upper management's decision to make NT Server the organization's strategic computing platform and they have to manage the change. Many of these migrations have to be done in very limited timeframes and there may not be enough time for trial and error.

This book addresses NT networking from a practical point of view. Every administrator at one time or another has spent 45 minutes waiting for technical support on the phone. This book may not give you freedom from having to depend on technical support but it certainly helps with the obvious. It also helps you ask the right questions when you have to call for technical support. More and more frequently, technical support is not free-of-charge. If you know what questions to ask and if you can move the call along, you can save time and money.

2

NT Design

- Server Hardware Compatibility Issues

- Intel x86 Platform Specifics

- Running Setup

- RISC Platform Specifics

- Keeping Up with Growth

CHAPTER 3

Building the Server

TERMS USED IN THIS CHAPTER

Mbps Mega bits per second.

Mbytes/sec Megabytes per second (there are eight bits per byte).

SCSI Small Computer System Interface is an ANSI standard for SCSI I/O bus and bus adapters that can be used in most PC bus designs.

CPS Computer Profile Setup.

LAN An Ethernet, token ring, or other type of LAN that acts as a medium between computers.

NLM Netware Loadable Module.

HAL Hardware Abstraction Layer.

WFW Windows For Workgroups 3.11.

WAN Wide Area Network.

.INF FILE One of a set of files used by the Setup program, either during Windows NT installation or maintenance Setup, or both. An .INF file generally contains a script for Setup to follow, along with configuration data that ends up in the Registry.

PCI Peripheral Component Interface. A 32-bit and 64-bit bus-mastering bus design and specifications developed for standardized I/O adapters with up to 132 Mbytes/sec burst rate.

EISA Extended Industry Standard Architecture. An ANSI standard 32-bit bus design with a 33 Mbyte/sec burst rate for standardized I/O adapters.

MCA Microchannel Architecture. An IBM 32-bit bus-mastering bus design and specifications for standardized I/O adapters.

This chapter contains techniques for selecting hardware components for the whole network with emphasis on servers. Tracing hardware failures and incompatibilties is the hardest step in the NT Server implementation. The server hardware design especially must be analyzed on paper before any procurements should be made.

The NT Server NOS has special needs for memory, disk channel, and server network cards. NetWare has been so popular that hardware vendors have designed servers around what works best in a NetWare server. Some vendors even offer pre-configured servers (*superservers*) with NetWare installed. These systems require almost no tweaking to gain optimal performance. A network can have many bottlenecks, but most bottlenecks occur in the server. The server mainly provides disk storage and print services for user requests. NT Server's preemptive multi-threaded processing makes it quite different from other network operating systems. The processor is heavily utilized. The I/O path is also a significant area of concern.

The features discussed in this section were initially implemented by superserver developers. These designs were proprietary at one time and limited to a few vendors who had healthy research and development budgets.

Because these design features were standardized, many other developers followed the lead. Today, many choices are available at far lower prices without using proprietary hardware. It is no longer necessary to purchase a superserver to have superserver performance. A wide variety of hardware is available so you can assemble your own high-performance server; as a result, superserver prices tumbled. Today, the most important considerations in selecting server hardware include brand loyalty, dependability, support, warranty, and fault-tolerant features.

In selecting a server, you should focus on four areas:

◆ Processor
◆ Bus design
◆ Disk subsystem
◆ Server network cards

Most importantly, your server should be designed to service your specific needs for the present as well as the near future. Project your network's growth over the lifetime of the server (normally two to three years) and build the server to meet your highest projections.

Tip

For reliability, replace your server every two years. Most servers have a useful lifetime of several years; however, you should replace them more frequently. If you are in an environment in which new user workstations are acquired on a regular basis, consider giving the old server to a user and replacing it with a new server.

By updating, your maintenance costs are lower, and you can feel more secure knowing the new server is probably more dependable than an aging one. You can also project future demands more accurately because the foreseeable server lifetime is defined more accurately.

Some high-end, pre-configured NT servers (superservers) are appearing, but they always carry a premium price. The techniques discussed here can give the administrator insight into constructing powerful NT servers without incurring the additional cost associated with special NT superservers.

For server computers, disk drives, network cards, and their drivers present the greatest problems during installation. Traditionally, disk and network card drivers have been developed by the vendors (not by Microsoft or Novell) and become more stable with changes over a period of several years. At least for the time being, NT Server drivers should be carefully evaluated for stability. Microsoft includes certified drivers for most popular disk adapters and network cards on the NT CD in the\DRVLIB directory.

Tip

If you need to use \DRVLIB during over-the-network installation, copy the contents of this subdirectory from the CD to the NT Server hard disk and share it. The automatic share of \I386 created by NT Server does not include the \DRVLIB subdirectory.

Tip

It is useful to study the Microsoft Hardware Compatibility List available on CompuServe, Microsoft's FTP and Gopher Internet servers, or from Microsoft's Download Services at (206)-936-6735. To use this bulletin board

1. Call the above number

2. Enter your name and location

3. From the main menu, press F for File index

Select L to list the whole WNTDL list or E to examine a specific file.

This list is updated every two weeks. You do not need to restrict your choice of components on this list. A common practice in the computer industry is that a name-brand manufacturer buys components from suppliers who sell the same component as a generic version. For example, Gateway, Zeos, and some other manufacturers customarily use OEM (original equipment manufactured) motherboards from Micronics or Intel. BIOS chips are usually provided by a handful of manufacturers like AMI or Phoenix. If you wait six months after a new class of product comes to market you can be quite certain the bugs get worked out of the generic components far more quickly than name-brand products. You see, the products that get debugged quicker are those having wider sales audiences.

How can one figure out what hard disk controller or motherboard is used in a name-brand product (which happens to be on the compatibility list)?

Publications such as *PC Magazine* regularly review these products and provide the component information in great detail.

Tip

> If you want both the best performance and to conserve your installation time, buy the same components you see reviewed and have your hardware vendor build your system for you. This shouldn't cost much if anything at all. The alternative may be to spend dozens of hours and several technical support calls getting the product working.

When a product is new, usually the manufacturer has the responsibility for making it compatible with existing applications and other hardware and software environments. It still means that, in the final analysis, the administrator has the responsibility to make the product work. The administrator needs to know where to make adjustments so the product works correctly with the specific applications in the organization.

Also, when a new product comes to market, hardware vendors are the first to be involved in the alpha testing (the very first steps in testing a product, even prior to beta testing). Microsoft decided that NT Server should run on a number of hardware platforms and entered into agreements with the hardware vendors to co-develop the product. Once the alpha vendor's hardware has been proven compatible, the burden of hardware compatibility falls on the rest of the vendors to make their hardware compatible.

Many of the drivers shipped with NT were developed by Microsoft and have not been thoroughly tested. Microsoft has not formally instituted a hardware testing and certification program. However, Microsoft does provide vendors with a Hardware Compatibility Test (HCT) kit that allows them to test their own products and submit the test results to Microsoft. These test results are used by Microsoft to include the HCT tested products on the Hardware Compatibility List.

For mission-critical networks, warranty and support should be considered on par with performance. Cost savings are penny wise and dollar foolish if quality, warranty, and support does not backup the product. Higher cost is easily justified if a product is from a reliable vendor, performs well, and integrates without difficulty. Look for a lifetime warranty. Industry leaders give them and make network cards that are reasonably priced.

Some vendors provide support via distributors; others offer direct support. Generally, the network card developer can support their own products best, while distributors have many more products to support.

Some vendors provide after-hours support, while others restrict support to normal business hours. Downtime necessary for maintenance or upgrading should be scheduled in after-hours—lack of support can be counterproductive.

NT driver strategy is quite monolithic; there is a possibility that topics covered by this chapter are the different methods of installation and upgrading. Upgrading a production system is always a nerve-wracking operation; this chapter points out areas of impact (at least as of now, upgrading from NT 3.1 to 3.5 to 3.51 has been well documented).

This chapter discusses:

>   Server Hardware Compatibility Issues
>   Intel x86 Platform Specifics
>   Running SETUP
>   RISC Platform Specifics
>   System Sizing and Capacity Planning
>   Keeping Up with Growth

SERVER HARDWARE COMPATIBILITY ISSUES

Microsoft publishes an NT hardware–compatibility list which shows hardware that has been tested with NT Version 3.5. This list is updated frequently on the WINNT forum on CompuServe, and on Microsoft's FTP and Gopher Internet servers.

The accompanying NT CD has a SETUP.TXT file that shows additional installation information.

NT Server is a new product: hardware-related compatibility, performance, and reliability issues are more important during the infancy of a product. This section helps the administrator in putting together systems using these "tested" components. More importantly, this section also delves into techniques of conducting your own evaluation. Most administrators will not be able to put together cost-effective systems without resorting to the use of clone components. This chapter guides the administrator in recognizing incompatibilities and potential problem areas.

INTEL x86 PLATFORM SPECIFICS

x86-based computers account for the vast majority of NT Server platforms, at least for now. The discussion about the history of NT Server in Chapter 1, "Overview of the Windows NT Server Product," was presented not only for academic interest. One can extrapolate the knowledge gained on previous systems to apply it to NT Server. RISC computer vendors are quite pleased about this. They stand to inherit server positioning where they can eclipse the performance of installed Intel servers that clients outgrow.

NT is most directly related to OS/2 LAN Manager and WFW. The file system, memory management, and the NT Executive are inherited from OS/2; the server side networking technology is inherited from LAN Manager, and the client networking and desktop comes from WFW. This is why the Setup program looks very familiar, and it runs directly from the NT Server boot diskette. The complications start when you need to do the install from non-standard CD-ROMs, over the network, or from a shared server directory or CD-ROM. The last two options allow you to replicate the installation over the network to a large number of machines.

You can start with a standard ISA, EISA, PCI, or VLBUS machine. The hard disk does not need to be high-level formatted, but it does not need to have a partition defined before you can begin, and a standard VGA video is just fine.

So where do the NT specifics come into play? Setup is going to allow you to partition the disk drives, and to select a file system type. Setup also attempts to auto-sense devices including your server network cards. If you are prepared to answer some basic questions during the setup sequence, NT Server basically installs itself. The administrator should be aware that the default installation may not be suitable and NT Server will require further tuning.

CHOOSING HARDWARE

Increasingly powerful personal computers have two primary uses: as servers or as GUI workstations. These two applications are the most technically demanding and capture much of the attention of computer hardware designers. More importantly, they represent the largest PC market potential, so PC hardware developers tailor their efforts toward the requirements of servers and graphical workstations.

An appropriate processor for a server should have a good clock speed. The speed of a 486 or Pentium processor is required; unlike NetWare, the internal math coprocessor is used. A DX2 (double internal clock speed) also is used. A 66 MHz 486DX2 has an external clock speed of 33 MHz and a doubled internal clock speed. For the most part, doubling the internal clock speed does not help NetWare but does help NT Server.

In summary, competitive factors and pricing have made Pentium-based servers attractive. The Pentium's multithreading feature used in NT Server is an ideal server platform.

ERROR CHECKING AND CORRECTING (ECC) MEMORY

One of the more common problems that causes a server to crash is the incidence of parity errors (RAM chip failure). Because of NT Server's heavy use of file caching and preemptive processing, a simple parity error will crash a server.

This type of disability can be prevented by using ECC memory. ECC memory prevents a server crash due to a parity error. ECC memory is more expensive because you are actually purchasing more memory than you get to use. However, it is a bargain in a server, because one crash can have extensive repercussions.

32-Bit Features of EISA and PCI Local Bus

For networking purposes, the most important design feature of your computer is the bus design. EISA and PCI local bus have been designed to overcome the limitations of the standard ISA bus architecture. A 16-bit ISA bus theoretically can accommodate 5 Mbytes/sec. However, because every 16-bit word moved through the bus has an address byte, and because the bus can accommodate only a 16-bit data flow, your throughput will be limited to somewhat less than 1.5 million bytes per second. Currently, EISA has a theoretical limit of 33 Mbytes/sec (when using a 32-bit OS with all the 32-bit hardware features discussed in this section). Microchannel (MCA) is an IBM 32-bit bus with a 40 Mbyte/sec burst rate and is also quite acceptable for a server.

Potential throughput is only part of the story. EISA and MCA were designed for concurrent processing. Concurrency enables more than one process to occur at the same time on different processors sharing system memory and the interface bus. Factors that favor 32-bit bus and interface cards include:

◆ The 32-bit data path

◆ Bus mastering and concurrent processing

◆ Burst mode

◆ Streaming data mode

Both EISA and MCA enable multiple interface cards to move data at high rates with reduced conflict and restriction. ISA was not designed with this capability. An ISA bus can service only one device at a time. The interrupt controller stops (interrupts) each device to enable another device to control the bus. In ISA design, the CPU also must be interrupted to control the devices and move data. This is why a faster processor is so important in ISA design. In contrast, EISA devices rely less on the CPU because they use a process called *bus mastering*. Bus mastering devices offload some of the processing to a processor on the interface card. Although some ISA devices feature bus mastering design, the effectiveness is compromised by the limited bandwidth and interrupt-driven design of ISA.

Many EISA, MCA, and PCI local bus network cards and disk adapters have been designed to exploit the capabilities of advanced computer architectures. A PCI or EISA card can sport a 32-bit interface but not take advantage of bus mastering. Many bus mastering cards do not take advantage of the burst or streaming data modes. Tremendous differences exist in the sophistication—and therefore the performance—of 32-bit interface cards. In 1992, a host of new 32-bit EISA and PCI bus mastering interface products were introduced. Now, many disk adapters and network cards are available, and prices are more reasonable.

PCI, MCA, and EISA 32-bit bus mastering devices can take advantage of all four features previously mentioned.

32-BIT DATA PATH

NT Server uses a 32-bit word. It takes a 32-bit operating system, such as NT Server, to take advantage of moving data in 32-bit words. Moving 32-bit words also requires 32-bit processor architecture—hence, the requirement for a 486 DX or higher processor for NT Server.

It also takes a 32-bit NOS to take full advantage of 32-bit hardware—an ISA (16-bit bus interface) bus must break down every 32-bit word into two 16-bit portions for a trip across the bus. Each word (in this case, a 16-bit word) requires an address byte. Therefore, moving a 32-bit word across an ISA bus (or through an ISA interface card) requires four bus cycles. This is a tremendous restriction for a 32-bit NOS.

ISA cards cannot access the burst or streaming data modes of PCI, MCA, or EISA. Therefore, the use of 16-bit interface cards in a PCI or EISA bus can yield only a small portion of the benefits available from 32-bit bus design.

Note

In most EISA bus and PCI local buses, some of the slots do not include bus mastering. Make sure that you know which slots are and are not bus mastering slots in your server. Bus mastering and non–bus mastering slots look the same. See your computer owner's manual to make certain that you install bus mastering cards in the correct slots.

EXTENDED INDUSTRY STANDARD ARCHITECTURE (EISA)

EISA is a 32-bit bus designed for special EISA interface cards and bus mastering. You can use 16-bit ISA cards in an EISA slot, but there are a few caveats that apply:

◆ Use of older-design ISA cards in an EISA bus can steal bus cycles and affect the performance of EISA cards.

◆ ISA cards are driven by the CPU and therefore have a tendency to increase CPU usage.

◆ EISA configuration utilities cannot detect hardware configurations of ISA cards used in EISA buses and therefore may result in physical configuration conflicts. (MCA avoids this problem by not permitting ISA devices).

An ISA card installed in an EISA bus is not restricted by the limited bandwidth of an ISA bus and therefore can potentially perform a little better. The problem with using ISA cards is the conflict between multiple cards installed in the bus and the effect they have on processor utilization.

LOCAL BUS

The term *local bus* refers to a processor-direct (local to the processor) interface bus separated from the standard I/O bus. Two separate local bus designs have emerged: Video Electronics Standards Association's (VESA) *VL-bus* and Intel's *Peripheral Computer Interface* (PCI). These bus interfaces potentially enable transfer speeds more closely matched to processor speeds. These designs have the potential to interface disk adapters and network cards with even higher transfer rates and less conflict with devices residing on the ISA, PCI, or EISA bus. Computer designs currently incorporate local bus in addition to another I/O bus.

VL-bus was developed to facilitate rapid video updates for better GUI performance. The VESA standard has evolved further, but it lacks bus mastering capability. The number of devices on the local bus are also limited. Although many video cards have been developed for this bus, support for disk adapters is limited.

PCI was developed by Intel to facilitate video, disk, and network card interfaces. It has immense bandwidth: 132 Mbytes/sec—over four times the capacity of PCI or EISA. As soon as Intel announced the design, a standards committee was formed, and many vendors pledged to develop disk adapters and network cards based on this design. PCI includes support for up to 10 devices, 32-bit and 64-bit interface, bus mastering, burst mode, and streaming data mode. The most attractive feature of this local bus is the placing of the disk adapter and the network card on separate buses. PCI promises even more efficient use of multiple disk adapters and network cards by combining local bus and other buses in one computer.

Warning

Some VL-bus and PCI network cards and disk adapters have recently appeared on the market, but design flaws and driver bugs have caused numerous problems. Always select a reliable developer and look for drivers and I/O devices that are proven and listed on the Microsoft Hardware Compatibility List. It is also a good idea to wait until a product such as a PCI or VL-bus network card or disk adapter is mature and proven before depending on it. Flawed or defective hardware or drivers are often the cause of server crashes and integration difficulties.

BUS MASTERING AND CONCURRENT PROCESSING

Intelligent adapters can process I/O requests off-line and then use the arbitration controller for access to the bus. Caching on the intelligent adapter enables the flow of data to remain constant even though access to the bus is in cycles. In many cases, data flow can be accomplished without any CPU intervention. A bus master can take control of another bus master as a slave. The master and the slave can flow data (through the bus), eliminating the wait for the CPU to process data transfers.

Bus mastering not only reduces reliance on the CPU for I/O processing but makes more efficient use of the bus when combined with the burst and streaming data modes available to 32-bit bus mastering devices (as discussed in the following sections). Because I/O requests usually consist of transfers of many bytes from one device to another within the computer, these two features can enhance sequential data flow between devices.

BURST MODE

Normal I/O requests require one address byte for each data word to be moved through the bus. This costs two bus cycles and causes latency in access to the processor for addressing and to the bus for movement of each word. *Burst mode* defines eight additional direct-memory address paths for moving blocks of data. Each block of data is sent with one address byte. This increases the bandwidth available for data on the bus, reducing the percentage allocated for addressing. Burst mode also reduces the number of accesses to the CPU to address data transfers. Burst mode is designed for smaller blocks of random data.

STREAMING DATA MODE

Streaming data mode enables one address byte to be assigned to two words or blocks of words (if combined with burst mode). Streaming data mode effectively doubles data throughput. Streaming data mode is designed for more extensive sequential data transfers, which is the rule rather than the exception in a server. The combination of streaming data mode and burst mode can move up to eight times more data per address byte than normal nonburst transactions.

CONCLUSION: ISA VERSUS EISA AND PCI VERSUS VL-BUS

Many NT Servers manage only one disk drive, one server network card, and fewer than 20 users. If this is your configuration, an ISA computer may be an adequate choice for you. For a few bucks more, you can have the added features of EISA, MCA, or PCI. Both are comparable, and the performance differences between ISA and either EISA, or EISA with PCI slots are tremendous. MCA designs are offered only by IBM or a few vendors who license it, and unless your organization is a true-blue shop, MCA is not recommended because there is a limited choice of cards. VL-bus has limited support and also seems to be on its way out; PCI has a far higher bandwidth and seems to be the future bus design of choice.

Using an ISA device in an EISA server does not significantly improve the device's performance. Although the device may test slightly better under full capacity, you will probably never realize any improvement under normal circumstances. When using multiple network cards and disk adapters on your server, however, the difference is readily apparent in CPU usage.

Finally, match your EISA or PCI server to well-engineered, 32-bit bus mastering adapters. All 32-bit adapters are not created equal, so monitor your favorite LAN periodical for benchmark testing and reviews. Pay close attention to the device's effect on CPU usage—that is a critical measure of the effectiveness of 32-bit bus mastering device design.

Note

The 32-bit bus mastering adapter design is one of the most important features for powerful servers. The quality varies significantly from one adapter to another, so be sure that you carefully evaluate bus mastering adapters before you buy. Research current network card and SCSI adapter evaluations published in industry periodicals; they are generally far more objective than vendor claims or studies commissioned by vendors.

The first hitch you might experience is where Setup cannot properly auto-sense one or more hardware devices, such as a disk adapter or network card. At this point, you may simply bypass this step and elect to add the device later. Another possibility is that your installation will fail, crash the OS, and you will need to start Setup all over again. This problem can occur repeatedly during installation, with each episode taking up an hour or more of your time.

Tip

You should elect not to allow the Setup program to auto-sense devices during installation. For the sake of simplicity, you can add the device later, after your OS is installed, up and running.

If you pay close attention to screen messages during Setup, you may notice Setup testing various drivers to find the right one. It is possible to pause the screen during this process and make a note of some of them, and you can ask for those brands from your vendor.

Tip

You can pause the screen by pressing the Pause key and resume by pressing any other key.

CD-ROM SUPPORT

Non-SCSI CD-ROMs are the most troublesome to install under NT. By the way, IDE or ATA CD-ROM drives work just fine. The consensus among experienced administrators is that it is better to buy a new compatible CD-ROM for a server installation than to try to fiddle around with over-the-network installs, especially if the local machine happens to be the first NT Server being installed.

NETWORK CARD HARDWARE

One of the most important applications for bus mastering products involves multiple interface cards being installed in a server's bus. Normal traffic generated by one network card and one disk adapter is usually not a problem. However, when multiple network cards or multiple disk adapters are used in a server, bus traffic can become bottlenecked and CPU usage can run very high, causing an additional bottleneck at the CPU. PCI and EISA were designed specifically to alleviate this problem, but the computer and bus design provide only the capability for new performance levels. Your server's performance relies heavily on the design and use of 32-bit bus mastering adapters.

EISA design is a well-defined and widely used ANSI standard. The EISA standard has led to the wide availability of EISA bus mastering interface cards. Fewer MCA cards are available, but there is still a fair selection of MCA bus mastering cards. It pays to shop carefully for 32-bit disk adapters and network cards.

Well-engineered bus mastering uses both the burst mode and the streaming data mode to increase the flow of sequential data and reduce CPU intervention. The effectiveness of bus mastering varies widely, however. Most network card test suites presented in periodicals treat CPU usage as a major factor in choosing a 32-bit server disk adapter or network cards. Test results show that multiple cards working at full capacity affect CPU usage in varying degrees.

Network card drivers often cause problems, not only for NT, but for other operating systems such as NetWare and OS/2. Because drivers are a common problem, the best strategy for small networks is to use only the most popular network cards or

3

network cards compatible with a popular model network card, because they have stable, proven drivers. For example, the Novell NE200 network card and its drivers are stable and proven. You can purchase dozens of NE2000-compatible network cards from several vendors, and you can use the NE2000 drivers which are known to be stable. The NT drivers for NE2000 cards are known to work well.

Warning

Recent tests show that some bus mastering network cards are limited by CPU usage when two or three network cards are used in the server and operate at full capacity; others do not max out CPU usage even with four network cards running at full capacity. These tests isolate LAN I/O, bypassing physical read and write requests. When normal disk adapter traffic is factored into these tests, you can expect that a single disk adapter and three network cards can max out a PCI or EISA server in any case. Disk duplexing and the use of 100 Mbps network cards can push CPU usage to higher levels.

High-end proven network cards for EISA, MCA, and PCI bus are available; configuring them may require updated drivers.

Tip

If you have plenty of extra time on your hands, you can use trial and error during installation. You will learn a lot about compatibility; however, you will probably find that this approach can eat up hours of productivity.

It is a viable strategy to install and configure network card drivers from the Control Panel after the initial installation is finished.

Once the first NT Server is installed, other servers can be installed over the network. This procedure involves creating an MS-DOS client diskette, then booting the soon-to-be NT Server using this diskette. You can then access Setup on the first server's shared CD-ROM drive. It is a fairly cut-and-dry procedure. The most common cause of problems in this type of installation is getting the soon-to-be server connected as a client. For more information about this option, see Chapter 8, "Connecting the Client."

Tip

During installation of the soon-to-be NT Server as an MS-DOS client to another NT Server, it is best to use default settings on network card whenever possible, and to use major brand/model network cards. If you use settings other than the default settings, check your PROTOCOL.INI file. You may need to manually alter the settings in this file.

There is a tremendous amount of confusion about which network card is best for any given server. The answer is simple. If you decide to bite the bullet and buy the best you can find, just study the magazine reviews. One definite preference, however, is the use of 32-bit bus mastering network cards in a server.

If you are concerned about value, it may not be necessary to spend $300 to $500 or more for a bus mastering server network card. Many NT Servers have only one network card, one disk controller, and support fewer than 20 users. Under these circumstances, there is no reason to invest in an expensive server network card when an inexpensive 16-bit network card can deliver the level of performance needed. On the other hand, an extra few hundred dollars is well invested at this critical potential bottleneck point.

Due to the higher bandwidth of the PCI bus (132 Mbytes/sec), most motherboard designs can only support four PCI slots. Some vendors have started adding a secondary PCI bus, but there have been problems with these designs. There is a workaround for this situation. Many network card vendors offer quad cards (four Ethernet network cards on one board) that use up only one PCI slot.

HARD DISKS AND CONTROLLERS

SCSI disk adapters can totally saturate an ISA bus. EISA, MCA, and PCI provide higher bus capacity that makes higher disk I/O speeds feasible. Development of powerful 32-bit SCSI adapters has expanded the performance envelope. Therefore, developers have now extended the capabilities of disk subsystems. More importantly, bus mastering SCSI adapters enables NT Server's built-in split seek features to be activated without taxing CPU usage or interfering with concurrent network card transfers (as long as all devices are well-designed bus masters).

3

BUILDING THE SERVER

Older disk designs, including MFM, RLL, and ESDI, have become virtually obsolete. SCSI is actually a bus design—it combines a host adapter in the computer bus with intelligent embedded controllers on the disk. Each disk can read and write separately from the other bus devices.

As many as seven disk drives can be chained to a single SCSI host adapter. Other disk technologies rely on slave drives connected to a controller. Usually controllers can run two disk drives with only one operating at a time. Although ESDI and IDE adapters that can drive up to four disk drives have been developed, performance is still limited to running only one drive at a time.

SCSI is an ANSI standard that allows more than one intelligent disk drive to read and write at the same time and to share the SCSI bus. Original SCSI standards specify up to a 10 Mbytes/sec transfer rate through the SCSI bus. Many intelligent 32-bit bus mastering adapters can effectively reach the theoretical transfer rate by transferring data from more than one drive at the same time; ESDI and IDE drives are limited to the transfer rate of only one drive at a time.

Several SCSI host adapters can be installed in a single ISA, MCA, or EISA bus. Although the limited number of available interrupts usually restricts an ISA bus to four or five SCSI adapters, many more can be used with EISA, MCA, and PCI computers when using level-triggered (shared) interrupts.

SCSI adapters also affect CPU usage less than IDE and ESDI controllers because those designs rely mainly on the CPU for many I/O operations.

SCSI-2

SCSI-2, a new ANSI standard, requires both a SCSI-2 host adapter and disk drive(s) to be implemented to achieve SCSI-2 throughput. SCSI-2 adapters are usually backward-compatible with original SCSI drives. SCSI-2 standards include two new features that make it a far better value:

- ◆ **Fast SCSI** doubles the SCSI bus speed, effectively doubling the transfer rate ceiling to 10 Mbytes/sec. This feature requires nothing more than a SCSI-2 adapter and drive to be effective.

- ◆ **Command tag queuing** enables up to 256 commands to be downloaded to the intelligent disk controller from the host adapter for processing off-line. The original SCSI design requires an acknowledgment after each request before another request can be sent. This feature requires the disk driver to be engineered to take advantage of the process.

SCSI-2 also enables multiple types of devices to be connected to the same adapter at the same time. SCSI-1 supported all these types of devices, but they could not be operable at the same time. Theoretically, you can connect disk drives, CD-ROMs, optical drives, and tape drives to the same adapter using multiple drivers. This option definitely requires drivers to use command tag queuing; if they don't, disk performance suffers when slower devices are accessed. In current technology, this option is not practical.

Many SCSI adapters are available with excellent 32-bit bus master design and performance. 32-bit bus mastering SCSI adapters are essential components when requiring

- ◆ Heavy I/O processing at the server
- ◆ Multiple network cards in the server
- ◆ Disk duplexing (utilizes split seeks)
- ◆ Any server configuration that spikes CPU usage to 90 percent or higher (for example, server-based applications)

Hard disks (also called drives) are fairly easy to deal with as long as they are IDE or SCSI; it is strongly recommended that SCSI drives be used with NT Server. A crucial feature of NT Server is sector sparing (similar to hot-fix), which only works with SCSI drives.

The wild card in your server is not the disk itself but the disk controller. The complicated issues of hardware/software RAID, caching controllers, duplexing and mirroring are significant from the performance point of view.

NT Server supports caching disk controllers and drives only if one of the following is true:

- ◆ The controller has a driver that specifically supports caching (several of these exist: DPT and IBM SCSI Caching Adapter).
- ◆ Write-through is active (that is, write caching is disabled) either by setting it manually or by default when the computer starts.
- ◆ The entire cache option is off, either by setting it manually or by default when the computer starts.

Using a caching controller or drive in other situations risks loss of data if the computer is rebooted or a power failure occurs before the cache has flushed itself. You can minimize risk by waiting at least one minute (less if you know the maximum time the cache waits before flushing itself) after all system activity stops before rebooting. The disk activity light is a good indicator of how write caching is being done on your system. This applies to the initial NT Server installation as well as shutdown. Note that unexpected power failure at any time can potentially corrupt data on the disk, possibly to the extent that the disk becomes unreadable. Making the delay time that write data is cached before being flushed to disk as small as possible reduces this risk.

Tip

> Many clone systems have been shipped with generic local bus (VLBUS) or PCI bus (on dual bus only) IDE controllers, where you may get the `Boot NTLDR: I/O Error Reading Disk` error message. If one of these host adapters is used in the system, replace it with a normal IDE host adapter. If switching to a normal IDE interface corrects the problem, contact the manufacturer for further information about compatibility with NT Server. Also make sure that the interrupts are set properly if you are using a PCI bus computer.

Some of the controller card vendors actively providing NT Server–compatible products are Adaptec, Buslogic, and DPT, who have been the high-end controller vendors for the NetWare market. Compaq, Storage Technology, and Micropolis also offer pre-packaged RAID solutions. If you select a fault-tolerant strategy for your NT Server, want to get an initial install going, and want to come back to the fault tolerance issue later on, then the recommended method is to install the operating system and the paging file on a single hard disk.

NT Server needs a disk channel with both more speed and capacity. The interaction between the memory and hard disk is much more intense in NT Server than in NetWare. The throughput and fault tolerance of the disk channel are absolutely essential for an NT Server to deal with the load it will be subjected to.

Chapter 2, "NT Design," introduced the concept of fault tolerance through the use of RAID systems. The key point is that more spindles and more data paths mean better performance. NT has built-in support for the following disk configurations:

RAID 0 (Striping): Data is striped over more than one drive. Although this configuration provides top performance, it is fragile at best. The loss of one drive destroys all data because blocks of data are distributed over more than one drive. Volume information cannot be reconstructed if any drive in a stripe goes down.

RAID 1 (Mirroring/Duplexing): Mirroring duplicates data on one drive to the second drive in a mirror pair. Each disk write is echoed to the second drive in the pair, which at times reduces performance.

Duplexing varies from mirroring only in that each drive in a pair is connected to a separate disk adapter. In this configuration, two drivers handle the read/write requests, which allows the operating system to perform split seeks, resulting in additional performance over straight mirroring.

For example, a good strategy is to spread the PAGEFILE.SYS over more than one drive and not mirror them. The data and system drives should be mirrored. The data in paging files is usually discarded each time the system is rebooted. If a drive with a paging file fails during use, essential data may be lost, depending on how the application was designed and configured. Chapter 27, "Physical Security, Quick Recovery," covers this topic in much more detail.

RAID 5 (Striping with parity): This option provides the best of both worlds—data is written to multiple drives at the same time, as is the case in RAID 0, plus it provides fault tolerance by writing a checksum (called parity) on each of the participating drives.

RAID 5 is always configured with three or more drives. If any one drive fails, the other two drives can continue to operate without interruption of service. Parity information is used to reconstruct the data that is missing.

Implementing RAID 5 in hardware or software requires the following considerations:

- Overhead: Software RAID, at least theoretically, should impose overhead on memory and CPU usage. In anecdotal testing, this has not been confirmed. NT has been designed with new features such as multithreading, which reduces the impact of processor-based operations. More powerful server processors provide sufficient capacity to manage more features such as RAID 5.

- Obsolescence: The major argument in favor of software RAID is that it is upgradable with a simple software patch or new OS release. Hardware RAID subsystems become obsolete with new model improvements. Lack of support for outdated hardware often renders recently acquired hardware obsolete.

- Proprietary Layer: Hardware RAID requires a layer of proprietary functionality that creates dependence on a specific vendor. RAID hardware often uses proprietary adapters, embedded controllers, and disk drives. Of course, these products often come at a premium price and may be difficult to replace. The administrator also has an added burden of updating firmware (ROM chips) and proprietary drivers.

RUNNING SETUP

NT's Setup application walks you through the process of installing NT Server or any Windows OS. The following options are available to you:

- Setup can be customized to run unattended through the creation of an ascii configuration file.

- You can manually edit one or more of the .INF files.

- You can create a Distribution Share for future NT Servers and MS-DOS and WFW clients.

SMP Support for Multiprocessor Computers

Intel developed a four-Pentium processor system board that makes SMP easier for OS vendors to implement. In some working conditions you may need to install NT Server on a multiprocessor server.

Though Intel has made it simpler, some adjustments need to be made to implement SMP in NT. To take full advantage of the new processor, use the UpToMP utility included with the NT Resource Kit.

Note

Some recent server models are built with multiple processor sockets for future upgrades; others are not. To take advantage of NT's SMP features, you must have an Intel-based SMP equipped computer.

To use the utility you must know

Which disk drive your NT Server installation software is on (this can be a distribution share, a CD-ROM drive, or a floppy drive).

What type of processor is installed (this information should be included with the computer documentation).

Start UpToMP from the command line or by double-clicking the file in File Manager. Specify the drive with the installation software in the textbox provided, and choose your processor type (HAL) from the combobox. Then choose Continue.

RISC Platform Specifics

NT Server currently supports Digital, MIPS, and PowerPC Reduced Instruction Set Computing (RISC) processors. The primary advantages of RISC are graphics processing and scientific calculation. NT Workstation running on a RISC processor is able to perform on par with high-end UNIX CAD/CAM workstations.

Note

Using a RISC processor in a server may have limited value. For more information about the performance implications of porting to a RISC-based server platform, see Chapter 24, "Monitoring and Tuning Peformance."

OpenGL

NT supports the OpenGL standard software interface for producing two- and three-dimensional graphics originally developed by Silicon Graphics Incorporated. OpenGL under NT version 3.5 supports VGA 16-color mode, unlike other OPenGL implementations such as UNIX and X Windows, which require at least 256 colors. Therefore, the color resolution of OpenGL images runs in VGA 16-color mode will be lower than that experienced on other platforms, but will be comparable with 256 or more colors. In addition, VGA 16-color mode is not accelerated in any way, so it may be slower than running at higher resolutions.

RISC-Based Server Installation Considerations

Before you can run Setup on an Advanced RISC Computing (ARC) compatible RISC-based computer, you must read the vendor's instructions for starting programs from CD-ROM or disk. How you start Setup will depend on the type of RISC-based computer.

Once Setup is started, you simply follow the prompts on screen. If you already have NT 3.1 installed on a RISC-based computer, you can use the WINNT32.EXE to upgrade your existing operating system or install a new version.

Note

You cannot use WINNT.EXE on RISC-based computers.

The following is an example procedure for starting Setup, which may be typical of many RISC-based computers:

1. Insert the NT Server CD in the CD-ROM drive.
2. Restart the computer.
3. At the ARC screen, choose Run A Program from the menu.
4. At the prompt, type **CD:\SYSTEM\SETUPLDR** and press ENTER.
5. Follow the instructions on the screen.

These steps assume that your hard disk has already been initialized (low-level formatted), has one partition with hardware-specific files, and has a FAT partition of at least 2MB. On a RISC-based computer the SYSTEM partition contains the hidden files OSLOADER.EXE and HAL.DLL in the subdirectory \OS\WINNT. If the SYSTEM partition is large enough, it can also contain NT Server, or you may choose to use a separate partition. If your hard disk does not already include a SYSTEM partition, you will have to refer to the vendor's literature to learn how to create one.

EMERGENCY REPAIR DISK FOR RISC

The procedure to use the NT Server Emergency Repair Disk on a RISC-based computer is different from the procedure on an x86-based computer. On an x86-based system, the repair utility is run by booting from a startup disk that was created during the installation of NT Server. On a RISC-based computer, no startup disk is created, as the RISC-based computers do not automatically start from a floppy disk.

Use the following procedure to use the Emergency Repair Disk on a RISC-based computer:

1. Insert the NT Server CD-ROM into the CD-ROM drive and start your computer.
2. From the list of choices on the firmware menu, select Run A Program.
3. When you are prompted for the program to run, type the following and press Enter:

   CD:\MIPS\SETUPLDR
4. When the setup screen appears, type **R** to run the repair utility.
5. Insert the repair disk into drive A as prompted and continue to follow the instructions on the screen.

KEEPING UP WITH GROWTH

Even if your computer meets your needs today, you can be sure that at some point in the future it may prove insufficient. Newer software often uses more disk space and requires more processing power and RAM to get its job done. You will find, over time, that your hardware resources are not keeping up with your use of the system.

Managers like to have advance notice of upgrade requirements, along with plenty of documentation justifying the expenditure. NT Server includes tools for easily archiving the capacity planning data for your computer or network. See Chapter 25, "LAN Capacity Allocation," for information about how to collect data on a regular basis so you can predict your future requirements.

Monitoring your system on a regular basis also provides you with essential information for bottleneck detection. One of the topics covered in detail in this book is the equipment-dependent nature of performance counters. For example, the maximum transfer rate of a disk drive is dependent on many aspects of your system. No one can just provide you with a "good" number, but by having a record of your computer under normal operation, you can build an understanding of reasonable values for your counters. Then, if you make a change or something slows down, you have a baseline against which to compare your new situation. Without this baseline, the detection of bottlenecks is a guessing game.

You might think that capacity planning is something that only large information systems organizations need to do, but actually all of us change our work habits over time as we acquire new software. It can be fascinating to watch the computer system become taxed over time, but this fascination has its practical side. If you watch closely, you'll know exactly what to do to improve the performance of the system as the demands grow.

Chapter 24 provides many tips on how to stay one step ahead of system demands—for both NT Servers and NT Workstation computers. Capacity planning begins with keeping records of the performance of your system over time. These records can become so huge as to be practically useless if you're not careful. A significant part of capacity planning is thoughtful and organized record keeping. Once you have good records to sift through, you can get to the analysis of those records.

As a fringe benefit, the whole task of bottleneck detection is greatly simplified with even a little capacity planning. It's easier to see what's changed than to start from scratch to determine what's wrong. For example, when evaluating memory, non-paged pool bytes may have risen. Was it a recently acquired application that caused the rise, or was it adding TCP/IP to the network protocols? Just a little history is worth its weight in charts and trend graphs, which are included in NT's Performance Monitor.

- Protocols and LAN Data Communications Overview

- Network Architecture

- NT Server's Workstation Support

- Supporting NetWare Clients

- Changing Network Card Driver and Protocol Configurations

- Summary— Connecting NT to Any Network Client

CHAPTER 4

Microsoft's Protocol Support

LAN   An Ethernet, Token ring or other type of communication system that acts as a medium between computers.

Node   An intelligent device connected to a network; commonly a computer connected to a LAN.

Hub   An Ethernet LAN device sometimes called a wiring concentrator or multiport repeater that connects cable segments into a single LAN.

Protocol   Rules of communication between network peers; access protocols drive network card to network card communications on a LAN, network protocols provide routing information, transport protocols are used by the NOS to exchange data between computers.

Network architecture   The model of all components, software and hardware, incorporated into a network.

Frames   Protocol units that carry data from one network card to another over a LAN or WAN.

Packets   NOS protocol units that implement network, transport, and OS functions between computers.

Bridge   A device that connects two LANs that works at the frame (LAN) protocol layer. Bridges filter and forward frames from one LAN to another, disguising both LANs to appear as one LAN.

Router   A computer with software that moves NOS packets from one LAN to another LAN or WAN, acting at the network protocol layer.

Network Device Interface Specification (NDIS)   Microsoft's specifications for interface between network card drivers and NOS transport protocols.

One of NT's finest features is its capability to support several commonly used transport protocols. This allows you to install NT in a heterogeneous environment along with NetWare, LAN Manager, LAN Server, UNIX, TCP/IP-based NOSs, and various NetBIOS-based peer-to-peer networks and devices.

Most NOSs require the use of their own protocol stack—support for additional protocols is an add-on if available at all. Because NT is designed to co-exist within other NOS environments, the installer is presented with a plethora of protocol options, some of which baffle the most experienced network technicians. Though NetBEUI was previously Microsoft's required protocol, it is not even necessary to use NetBEUI at all with NT. You can use Novell's IPX/SPX or TCP/IP.

This multiple protocol feature may seem to add more complexity to your installation, but it actually simplifies implementation. Not only can you mix NT with other NOSs and servers, but you can install NT on an already functional LAN/WAN without having to change the protocols your are using. Once you gain some experience with a transport protocol option, you may decide that you like one better than the others.

Note for NetWare Administrators

NT allows you to install your servers and clients on top of existing NetWare ODI/MLID drivers and IPX/SPX protocols. Clients can access NT servers by adding the Windows client for NetWare in Control Panel. Because you have experience with this protocol and may have an existing NetWare installation, this feature can definitely shave hours off your installation and troubleshooting time. You can always change your protocol option in Windows Control Panel at a later date if you wish.

Microsoft's native transport protocol is NetBEUI. Though this protocol is a very good choice under many conditions, you may need to use another protocol to support such network capabilities as routing. NetBEUI is not routable, therefore a NetBEUI-based network must rely on bridges instead of routers to link LANs to other LANs or WANs. Routers require a routable protocol—to enable routing services with NT, you must select either IPX/SPX or TCP/IP protocol stacks when installing NT Server. If you use NetBEUI, servers and devices will be available to users only when they are connected to the same LAN the server or network device is connected to or when LANs are bridged together.

Microsoft has built multiple protocol stack support into all newer NOS implementations including NT Server, NT Workstation, Windows for Workgroups 3.11, and Windows 95.

This chapter discusses

- ◆ A brief overview of network protocols and data communications
- ◆ The NT network architecture model
- ◆ Microsoft's Network Device Interface Specification
- ◆ A discussion of each NT-supported protocol stack
- ◆ Supporting NetWare clients

4

PROTOCOLS AND LAN DATA COMMUNICATIONS OVERVIEW

Before discussing Microsoft's implementation of each protocol, this chapter first discusses how NT Server and other NOSs move data over a LAN. Though this discussion applies to NT Server and its clients running over a LAN, the description equally applies to any NOS and any type of LAN or WAN.

Tip

Understanding protocols truly helps the administrator—if you know what is going on inside the wires, you can figure out where problems occur, bottlenecks exist, and performance opportunities lie. If you understand what is going on inside the wires, you can fix anything. Moreover, if you have access to a protocol analyzer, you can locate the source of the vast majority of network problems from the codes contained in frame and packet headers.

WHAT IS A LAN?

The formal definition of a LAN (local area network) is a network of computers connected over a limited distance. However, today the LAN can be separated from the rest of the system—the LAN is the portion of the network that includes the network cards, cabling, and intermediate devices including repeaters and/or MAUs. Rules for LAN components are governed by IEEE (Institute of Electrical and Electronic Engineers) 802 specifications.

Note

In this book, the term *LAN* refers to an Ethernet, Token ring, or other type of local area network. The term *network* refers to the entire networked system of computers, LANs, WANs, protocols, NOS, and so on.

There are two primary distinguishing features between a LAN and any other type of computer network—multiple entry points and limited distances.

First, LANs have multiple entry points (nodes) sharing time on a single medium (usually cable). 10Base-T Ethernet cable (using unshielded twisted pair) is theoretically limited to 512 nodes. This differs significantly with other types of computer networks, such as wide area networks, where only two nodes (a single sender and a single receiver) communicate at any given time. Figure 4.1 illustrates a LAN versus a WAN.

Figure 4.1.
A LAN is a multipoint
medium.

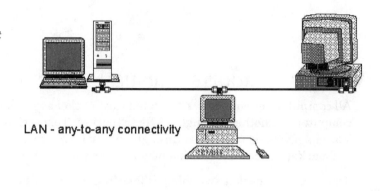

LAN - any-to-any connectivity

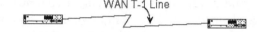

WAN T-1 Line

WAN - point-to-point connectivity

Second, cable lengths are severely limited according to the type of LAN and the type of cable being used. In any network, speed, distance, and type of cabling combine into specifications that allow high rates of data transfer with very low error rates. Ethernet and Token ring designers were able to pick two of the three factors mentioned. They chose high data transfer and low error rates, which meant limiting distances based on common cabling specifications.

A single Ethernet or Token ring LAN is usually limited to less than one mile from end to end when using common cabling. The use of optical fiber cabling extends distances, but still limits LAN distances to a single building or campus. In contrast, a wide area network (WAN) uses leased lines, such as a T-1, to connect point to point. Figure 4.2 illustrates cabling differences between a LAN and a WAN.

A LAN is therefore often used to link computers within a building or campus, thus the term "local area network." LAN cabling is installed and privately owned, unlike WAN lines which are generally leased from long distance carriers, such as AT&T, Sprint, MCI or Wiltel.

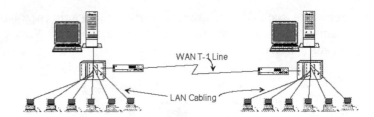

Figure 4.2.
LAN cabling versus
WAN lines.

VIRTUAL CIRCUITS VERSUS PHYSICAL CIRCUITS

All computer networks work the same way: packet switching moves data from one computer to another through LANs (Ethernet, Token ring, and so on) or WANs. Various protocols move data throughout a network, and are represented in frame and packet header information moving over your LAN.

The process of packet switching differs from other types of networks, such as the telephone network, in which a physical circuit is established at the outset of your call and maintained throughout a communication session. In a telephone network, when you make a call, switching equipment establishes a physical unbroken connection between the two parties.

In a computer network a logical connection is created between computers over a medium, like a LAN, where point-to-point or multipoint connections are established. At the beginning of a dialog, the sender and receiver exchange information establishing a virtual (logical) connection as shown in Figure 4.3. The data path in a computer network may switch routes during communications flow.

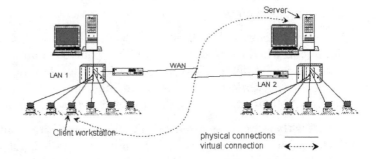

Figure 4.3.
A virtual connection
between client and
server.

HOW LANS MOVE DATA FROM ONE NETWORK CARD TO ANOTHER

LANs move data in units called frames. Each frame executes the functions of the LAN access protocol. A frame has both a header and a trailer; the header contains protocol information, while the trailer contains error checking.

There are four different Ethernet frame types, while Token ring has two basic data frame types and can have source-routing additions to the frame. Figure 4.4 shows the format of an Ethernet_802.2 frame type, and a Token ring data frame. Because frame fields are not always byte oriented, the length of each field is expressed in octets (sets of eight bits). Detailed information on LANs, LAN protocols, and frame fields is discussed in Chapter 30, "LAN Troubleshooting."

Figure 4.4.
Common Ethernet and
Token ring frames.

Ethernet 802.2 Frame

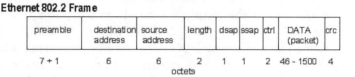

preamble	destination address	source address	length	dsap	ssap	ctrl	DATA (packet)	crc
7 + 1	6	6	2	1	1	2	46 - 1500	4

octets

Token Ring Data Frame

start delim	end delim	frame ctrl	dest addr	source addr	INFORMATION (packet)	frame chk seq	end delim	frame status
1	1	1	6	6	0-18000	4	1	1

octets

Each frame contains a source address and a destination address. Because each network card is identified with a unique address, these fields in the frame header provide the mechanism to transport the frame from the sender to the receiver, even though several nodes share the same medium. These addresses are often called *node addresses*, but are sometimes referred to as MAC addresses (as defined in IEEE's Medium Access Control specifications). A node address identifies each node as a unique physical entity on a LAN. Generally, the node address is the serial number of the network card. A portion of this address identifies the network card vendor as assigned by IEEE.

SEGMENTATION AND REASSEMBLY OF MESSAGES

Data does not flow over a computer network in steady unbroken data streams. All common LANs and WANs restrict the size of each data segment. Ethernet frames can carry no more than about 1500 bytes of data per frame (typically limited to 1024 bytes plus packet headers). Token ring frames can carry as much as 18,000 bytes (typically limited to about 4096 bytes plus packet headers). These restrictions allow multiple nodes to share a common medium with more equitable distribution of bandwidth. Therefore, each message must be divided into segments that fit into the type of frame.

When data needs to be sent from one computer to another, the data is first divided into messages. The message length depends on the operation; for example, when executing a 100KB program, the message size is 100KB.

The messages are sent in short portions, called segments. If the packet size is 1KB, the 100KB message must be divided into 100 1KB segments. Each segment is preceded by protocol information (packet header) and is then called a packet.

LANs move these packets from one network card to another by encapsulating each packet into a LAN frame. The packets are encapsulated into the frames by the network card driver. The frame differs from the packet in that access protocols control the frame's movement between network cards, while packets control movement of the data segments from computer to computer using a transport protocol, such as Novell's IPX, Microsoft's NetBEUI, or TCP/IP. The packets are formed and driven by NOS software and transport protocols, while the frames are driven by network card drivers and access protocols. Figure 4.5 illustrates how packets are encapsulated for transport over a LAN.

Figure 4.5.
Encapsulation of
packets into LAN
frames.

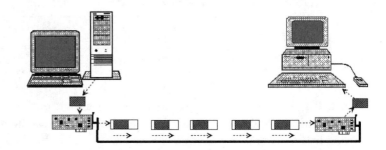

The complete transaction contains several steps. In each data transfer

1. The data transfer is divided into messages.
2. Each message is divided into data segments.
3. Each data segment is packetized (the data is appended with transport protocol information) and therefore becomes a packet.
4. Each packet is encapsulated into a LAN frame.
5. Each frame is transferred over the LAN.
6. Each frame is received, and the packet is extracted from the frame.
7. The packet header is read for protocol instructions.
8. The data segments are re-assembled into a message.
9. Generally an acknowledgment packet is returned indicating receipt of each packet; any missing packets are re-sent.

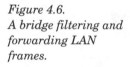

Note

The terms *packet* and *frame* represent two different protocol layers. Packets are protocol units generated and used by the NOS, while frames are LAN protocol units used between network cards. Packets are encapsulated into frames for movement over a LAN.

Though these terms are often used interchangeably, they are used more precisely in this book. Without the distinction between frames and packets, the whole process of delivering data over a LAN is seriously clouded.

This process of segmentation, encapsulation, transport, and reassembly occurs just as quickly as retrieving data from your local hard drive (provided the LAN is not congested). No matter which protocol stack you are using or what type of LAN is installed, the process occurs in much the same manner.

BRIDGING

LANs have serious limitations, namely in the form of limited capacity (bandwidth) and length of cabling. In order to overcome or reduce the impact of these limitations, devices called *bridges* are often introduced into the network. A bridge is one type of device that joins two separate physical LANs into a single, logical unit. A typical bridge is illustrated in Figure 4.6.

Figure 4.6.
A bridge filtering and forwarding LAN frames.

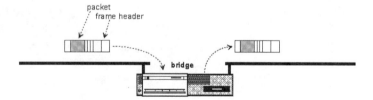

Bridges process LAN frames, copying only the frames that need to be forwarded to the other LAN segment. The bridge filters frames that do not need to be forwarded. A bridge can reduce traffic on each LAN, and can extend the length of your network by adding the lengths of two separate LANs.

Because a bridge works at the frame layer, data can be moved from one LAN to another without regard to what type of transport protocol is contained in the frame.

Bridges also are somewhat inflexible and have some serious limitations. Most types of bridges can only link LANs that are of the same type and use the same frame format.

Bridges are the preferred strategy for forming internetworks in an NT environment using NetBEUI protocol. Because NetBEUI is a nonroutable protocol, bridges must be used to make resources available regardless of where they are located. Both bridges and routers can link LANs and WANs into internetworks. However, when using a nonroutable protocol, routers cannot provide access to network resources (that is, servers, printers, communication servers) located on a remote LAN segment.

Whether you choose NetBEUI, IPX/SPX, or TCP/IP protocol stacks, bridging is an effective strategy for forming internetworks. However, you should also consider using routing (IPX/SPX or TCP/IP) as your internetwork strategy.

ROUTING

Routing accomplishes the same end result as bridging, but adds more robust networking features to the limited functionality of most bridges. Routers work at the packet layer instead of at the frame layer. Routers extract each packet from each frame, read the packet header protocol information, and forward or filter packets (not frames) based on the logical addressing contained in the packet header, as shown in Figure 4.7.

Figure 4.7.
A router processing
packets.

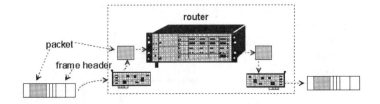

Routers require another protocol layer (packet header) between the transport protocol packet header and the LAN frame. In all routable protocols, logical addressing is contained in the routing packet header, which maps to a physical node address contained on a LAN connected to one of the network cards in the router. In a TCP/IP network, the IP packet header contains the logical address assigned each host (node). In a Novell IPX/SPX network, the IPX packet header contains network address and node address information the routers can use to route the packets to their ultimate destination.

Routers communicate with one another, building routing tables that map source and destination nodes to network card drivers. This allows the router to send each packet to a network card driver for encapsulation and delivery on that particular LAN. This process also allows the routers to discover changing path conditions, and allows them to dynamically re-route packets without disrupting communications. In addition, various routing protocol choices are available to change the way the routers make routing decisions.

Routable packets contain information about how many routers they have traversed (*hop count*). Routers cannot see bridges, therefore they sometimes make poor routing decisions when bridges are present. When a routable protocol packet traverses a bridge, no hop count is registered in the packet header.

Routers often include bridging functions to handle nonroutable protocols. These are sometimes called *brouters* or bridging-routers. These devices always check to see if a packet is routable before attempting to bridge a frame. They route routable protocols and bridge nonroutable protocols.

If you decide to use routing as an internetworking strategy, you will need to choose IPX/SPX or TCP/IP protocol stacks. Services provided over NetBEUI protocol are not available to nodes located on remote LAN segments (those nodes residing on LAN segments separated by a router).

SWITCHING HUBS

In an Ethernet LAN, a wiring concentrator, often called a *hub*, is a type of multiport repeater that joins several cabling segments together into a single LAN. A newer design for an Ethernet hub, called a *switching hub*, incorporates intelligent bridges between ports. In a switching hub each cabling segment can act as an individual LAN bridged with other cabling segments. This eliminates traffic from each local connection, reducing the need to share limited bandwidth among many users.

Switching hubs improves throughput by a factor of less than 100 percent. While this sounds impressive, remember that the cabling segment between the hub and the server still must share the bandwidth of the server's cabling segment.

A way to improve performance between a switching hub and a server is to install more than one network card between the switching hub and the server. NT automatically divides the load between the multiple network cards in the server. More discussion of optimizing the Ethernet environment is found in Chapter 23, "Evaluating Peformance Opportunities."

BRIDGING VERSUS ROUTING

Here are several points to consider about the issue of whether you should use bridges or routers in an NT network:

- ◆ Both bridges and routers are boundaries between LANs and WANs.
- ◆ They both segment LANs to reduce traffic on each LAN.
- ◆ They join LANs and WANs into internetworks.
- ◆ They can segment traffic to reduce the traffic on each LAN.

ADVANTAGES OF BRIDGING

Bridging is generally a simple, inexpensive solution to internetworking that

Is simple to install
Requires little or no configuration
Is usually inexpensive
Is available from many vendors

DISADVANTAGES OF BRIDGING

Bridges have some drawbacks, however. They generally

Are limited in configuration options
Lack flexibility to redefine paths
Lack filtering flexibility
Negatively impact routing information
Are limited to servicing same type of LANs only

ADVANTAGES OF ROUTING

Routers are quite flexible; they generally can

Join dissimilar LANs because they process packets after they have been extracted from their frames

Dynamically reconfigure according to more efficient paths and changing conditions

Often be configured to make routing decisions based on different factors, such as cost, time, number of hops over routers, and so on

Be used to filter packets based on data contained in the packet headers or even in the data segment

DISADVANTAGES OF ROUTING

Routers are sometimes not used because they

Are often more expensive than bridges

Cannot route nonroutable protocols (NetBIOS, NetBEUI, SNA)

Are often more difficult to configure and administer

Do not make good routing decisions when mixed with bridges, especially where redundant paths exist

Use logical addressing, which often increases system administration

In summary, to link departmental LANs into a campus-wide internetwork, you should select a strategy of either bridging or routing, but should not mix the two. Your choice should depend on the protocols to be used on your LANs. If you need to support products other than NT, your decision may need to be based on protocols supported by the other products. NT has the flexibility to support all major protocol stacks, so you do have options that can preclude poor internetwork configuration.

NETWORK ARCHITECTURE

Microsoft includes support for just about every protocol stack in common usage. NT must coexist with existing technologies. Novell held over 60 percent of the NOS market in 1994 and uses IPX/SPX routable protocols. TCP/IP networking, usually with UNIX, is widespread. Therefore, Microsoft's interests are best served in providing compatibility with competing protocols. Microsoft claims each protocol stack as native in an NT environment.

NT supports the following protocols:

NetBIOS
NetBEUI
Novell's IPX/SPX
TCP/IP
NDIS
DLC
SMB

The chart shown in Figure 4.8 charts the protocols supported in an NT Server network.

4

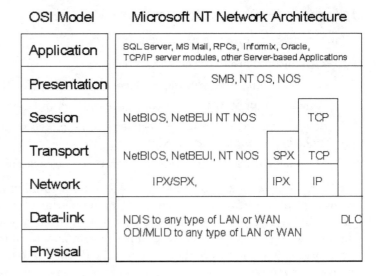

Figure 4.8.
Microsoft's Network
Protocol Chart versus
the OSI Model.

THE OSI MODEL

Networking protocol stacks are best described by the Open Systems Interconnect (OSI) Model, a product of International Standards Organization (ISO). This model was designed from other major protocol stacks and was intended to replace other proprietary protocol stacks. Though the OSI protocols themselves are not very popular, OSI has served as a standard model for protocol stacks. The OSI model provides a reference for other protocols.

In the OSI model, protocol functions are divided into seven layers and functions:

Application	Software-to-software communications
Presentation	OS function calls, fragmentation, reassembly of messages, and sequencing of message segments
Session	Creation and destruction of virtual connections
Transport	Guaranteed delivery of each packet (generally in the form of an acknowledgment packet)
Network	Routing and logical addressing
Data Link	Data framing, local delivery, and error control
Physical	Circuitry, connectors, and signal encoding

These layers are compared against other protocols for relational functionality. In this chapter, each protocol discussed is compared with corresponding OSI layer functionality.

Each protocol stack is discussed in the following section.

NETBIOS

This protocol, first developed by IBM and Sytek in the early 1980s, is still around, though not as predominant as it was at one time. Almost all peer-to-peer NOSs relied on NetBIOS to transport MS-DOS message segments to and from clients and servers.

NetBIOS is used in all Microsoft networks, including NT Server–based networks to advertise shared device names over the network. Every time a user accesses an application that looks for a shared network resource, a NetBIOS request goes out, and all computers sharing their devices respond by issuing a burst of NetBIOS broadcasts—one for each shared name. NetBIOS is also used to advertise workgroup and/or domain names as well as a few connection maintenance functions.

Today, far more robust protocols are used in networking; however, a few NetBIOS-based devices and applications are still in use. In many cases, IBM SNA gateways to mainframe systems use NetBIOS. Therefore, some organizations still need to provide NetBIOS services over their existing LANs. Generally, NetBIOS is supported in addition to another protocol.

NetBIOS is not routable: NetBIOS-based networks must rely on bridging as the primary strategy for internetworking. NetBIOS support is provided in NT Server, NT Workstation, Windows for Workgroups 3.11, and Windows 3.1.

NetBIOS support is available in WFW 3.11, Windows 95, and Windows NT Server and Workstation NOSs. In Microsoft's implementation, each NetBIOS packet must be transported by another transport protocol, either IPX/SPX, TCP/IP, or NetBEUI.

Note

When using routers in a Microsoft network, you must turn on the NetBIOS broadcast option in your routers. Generally, NetBIOS broadcasts are suppressed, in which case the broadcasts will not reach LANs on remote LAN segments (separated by a router).

NETBEUI (NETBIOS EXTENDED USER INTERFACE)

NetBEUI is the native protocol used in Microsoft's previous NOS—LAN Manager. It is Microsoft's intellectual property, and is used in IBM's LAN Server, which was originally derived from LAN Manager. This protocol is not routable, and therefore relies on bridges to form more complex internetworks.

You can use NetBEUI protocol alone in an entirely Microsoft-based network: no other network protocol is required. Windows for Workgroups 3.11, Windows 95, and NT Workstation all provide NetBEUI service. However, exclusive use of NetBEUI restricts clients from gaining access to NetWare and other NOSs, and resources located on a remote LAN (separated by routers) are not available to users on a local LAN.

NetBEUI is a most efficient protocol but limited in its ability to route and is quite broadcast intensive. It is recommended for smaller networks with perhaps 40–50 nodes or less all on one LAN segment.

IPX/SPX

Internetwork Packet Exchange (IPX) is Novell's routable datagram protocol and was originally derived from Xerox's Internetwork Datagram Protocol. This protocol carries other types of packets through routers, allowing the higher layer protocol to function as other transport protocols do. Sequenced Packet Exchange (SPX) was also derived from Xerox Network System protocols, and is a connection-oriented (acknowledged) transport protocol. SPX is used to move printing traffic over an internetwork. It is also used in a few miscellaneous functions, such as Novell's SAA Gateway server. SPX is rarely used anywhere else due to its high overhead. Because Novell holds about a 60 percent market share, IPX/SPX is used in the majority of PC networks.

In the late 80s, Novell and Apple Computer developed the Open Datalink Interface (ODI) specifications. These specifications support multiple network and transport protocols simultaneously through one network card driver. Within the specifications is the Multiple Link Interface Driver (MLID), which can support multiple LAN frame types. Network card vendors purchase the Novell's ODI software development kit and write their own MLID drivers.

Today, all current NetWare networks (3.12 and 4.x) use ODI drivers. Microsoft capitalized on Novell's open protocol architecture to develop multiprotocol support in NT, Windows for Workgroups 3.11, and Windows 95.

At some point, Microsoft realized that to make a networking product successful, it was going to have to coexist with the dominant networking protocols already in use. They also realized that they could not rely on Novell to provide the link. Microsoft had inherited the technology to support XNS protocols from 3Com's now-defunct 3+ Open NOS. Compatibility with Novell's protocols was just a step away, and Microsoft developed IPX/SPX emulation shipped with WFW 3.11. Microsoft's implementation of this protocol provides a convenient vehicle for introducing Windows into the many existing NetWare-based networks and internetworks.

Novell wasn't very cooperative in developing client links with NT, and took the stand that it would not support IPX in NT servers. Novell always expressed a commitment to support NT Workstation as a NetWare client, but dragged its feet for an extended period, finally introducing its NT Requester over one year behind schedule. In the meantime, Microsoft built its own IPX/SPX emulation and fully supports these protocols in NT Server and client workstations.

Routing is also a very important consideration in many accounts. Many NetWare and TCP/IP accounts demand routing support, and Microsoft's NetBEUI is not routable. The use of IPX/SPX protocols supplements or replaces NetBEUI and provides robust routing capability.

With IPX/SPX support, an NT client can connect with both NetWare and NT servers without having to unload and reload drivers. Even without NetWare, an NT network can provide routing with IPX by installing this protocol.

Microsoft did not stop there in its battle with Novell over market share. When the NT server supports IPX/SPX, the server can replace a NetWare server with very few modifications to the clients. Microsoft even has the Gateways Services for NetWare utility that allows an NT Server to connect NT users to a NetWare server. It also developed a NetWare migration utility that transfers user account information from a NetWare bindery to an NT Security Account Manager (SAM) database. These options are discussed in greater detail in Chapter 16, "Gateway Service for NetWare."

Not only is Microsoft's NWLink compatible with Novell's IPX/SPX protocols, it can be used to completely replace Microsoft protocols with very few limitations.

MICROSOFT TCP/IP

Opening the Internet to commercial use just a few years ago furthered TCP/IP's popularity. Since that time, many vendors have produced TCP/IP software to ease Internet integration.

Many vendors provide client TCP/IP software to run in Windows, DOS, OS/2, and other workstation environments. Microsoft developed its own TCP/IP client and server software and includes it with NT. TCP/IP can be used as an additional protocol stack, or it can replace other protocols as the only protocol stack used in an NT Server network. This feature has won support in universities and government agencies where well-established TCP/IP networks are in existence.

Microsoft's TCP/IP product provides:

> Server support as a TCP/IP host
>
> The use of IP as a routable protocol to carry SMB traffic

Internet access

Automatic IP address assignment (Dynamic Host Control Protocol)

Internet name services (Windows Internet Name Services)

A full compliment of TCP/IP client utilities and access

Along with features comes complexity. TCP/IP can be difficult and time consuming to configure, address, and administer. TCP/IP administrators require extensive training. More discussion of this topic is to be found in Chapter 21, "Microsoft's TCP/IP Services."

NETWORK DEVICE INTERFACE SPECIFICATION (NDIS)

Microsoft developed a standard for network card drivers called Network Device Interface Specification. This standard is used by Microsoft and all Microsoft-related vendors for all entities that need to connect to a LAN or WAN at the physical layer, and to a Microsoft supported protocol at the network or transport layer.

You can elect to use Novell ODI/MLID drivers instead of NDIS drivers. To use ODI drivers, you must load Microsoft's NWLink and ODIHLP, which allows ODI drivers to transport Microsoft traffic.

Note for NetWare Administrators

Microsoft's NDIS specifications provide exactly the same functionality of Novell's Open Datalink Interace (ODI) and Multiple Link Interface Driver (MLID) specifications.

You can use either NDIS or ODI drivers in newer Microsoft networks.

Several network vendors prefer to use NDIS for their own network card drivers. For example, Digital Equipment Corporation uses NDIS drivers in their OEM network cards, Pathworks (Digital's version of LAN Manager), and Windows NT. They also use NDIS for their own VMS, Ultrix, and OSF-1-based networks. Just about all network card vendors provide NDIS drivers for their network cards (for both LANs and WANs).

Microsoft also expanded NDIS to include the first 32-bit network card drivers for its 32-bit operating systems. NT Server, NT Workstation, and Windows 95 are all shipped with 32-bit NDIS drivers for just about every major network card. As you can imagine, these 32-bit drivers support greater performance over existing network cards.

DATA LINK CONTROL (DLC)

To support existing IBM SNA networks, Microsoft added support for DLC, IBM's protocol used in source routing bridges and other network devices. This allows Microsoft networks to act as an interface between 3270 workstations or PCs running 3270 terminal emulation and an IBM host.

SERVER MESSAGE BLOCK (SMB)

No matter which protocol stack is in use, Microsoft's proprietary SMB handles file and print requests. SMB is used in all Microsoft networks fulfilling the functions of the OSI presentation layer, but placed at the application layer as a software module. There is nothing you do to implement SMB, nor are there any configuration options for you to adjust. The use of SMB is a core part of networking with any Microsoft NOS and is installed by default any time any Microsoft NOS is installed.

SMB must be layered with a transport protocol to handle all the complexities of creating/destroying virtual connections, acknowledgments, and interface with the data link layer. Microsoft has implemented SMB as an application layer protocol, which enables porting to any Microsoft operating system. More detail on what SMB does and how to analyze SMB is contained in Chapter 30, "LAN Troubleshooting."

NT SERVER'S WORKSTATION SUPPORT

NT Server also supports several workstation operating systems. Of course, NT Workstation is the most preferred client, but you can connect the following clients to NT Server:

> NT Workstation
> Windows 95
> Windows for Workgroups 3.11 with MS-DOS 5.0 or higher
> Windows 3.1 with MS-DOS 5.0 or higher
> MS-DOS 5.0 or above
> Macintosh System 7–7.5

Figure 4.9.
Microsoft's supported
workstations.

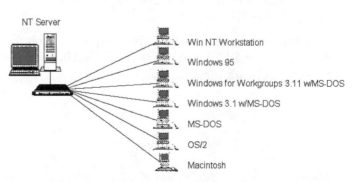

SUPPORTING NETWARE CLIENTS

Microsoft provides robust networking support for NetWare clients. There are three methods of providing simultaneous, transparent access to both NT and NetWare servers.

USING IPXODI CLIENT SUPPORT DRIVERS

DOS, Windows 3.x, and WFW configured as NetWare clients can be integrated with NT Server using their native NetWare ODI workstation software agents. The Windows Setup program installs a CONFIG.SYS driver (IFSHLP.SYS) and starts the Microsoft network redirector after loading the NetWare ODI driver stack.

Once you have NetWare ODI workstation drivers and shell/requester loaded, you can access a NetWare server. Once the NET START command has been run prior to starting Windows, you can access an NT host running the NWLink protocol.

Note for NetWare Administrators

To connect a Windows NT Workstation client to a NetWare 3 server, you should use NDIS drivers with NWLink and Microsoft's NetWare Requester for NT.

To connect a Windows NT Workstation client to a NetWare 4 Directory Services environment, you must use the Novell Requester for NT. You should check with NetWire, Novell's FTP site, or your NetWare Support Encyclopedia for the latest revision and any limitations the NT Requester may contain.

A Windows for Workgroups–NetWare client can add support for access to an NT Server by running Setup, or accessing the Network Setup icon. In either case, Setup will

> Edit your AUTOEXEC.BAT file
> Install software agents that are required
> Edit the .INI files

In Setup, select the IPXODI Driver Support option for EtherNet, Token ring, or ArcNet. Figure 4.10 illustrates how software layers interface the network card and Windows network services.

Figure 4.10.
NetWare Client
IPXODI Support Stack.

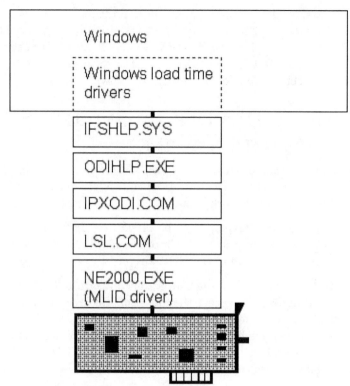

A typical NetWare ODI AUTOEXEC.BAT with Windows for Workgroups would look like this:

```
$echo off
path c:\windows;c:\dos;c:\nwclient
set NWLANGUAGE = ENGLISH
c:\wfw\net start
c:\nwclient\lsl.com
c:\nwclient\ne2000.com
c:\nwclient\ipxodi.com
c:\wfw\odihlp.exe
c:\nwclient\netx.exe
f:
login
win
```

Utilizing existing ODI support makes for an effective strategy in upgrading or migrating clients from NetWare to NT Servers. In this procedure, ODIHLP.EXE interfaces the native IPX/SPX protocol with the SMB protocol, which in turn provides communications with an NT Server.

Novell's ODI specifications allow multiple protocols to interface with a single network card driver. IPXODI.COM handles IPX and SPX packets, which are interfaced to the NetWare DOS Shell (NETX.EXE), or the NetWare DOS Requester (VLM.EXE). ODIHLP.EXE is loaded to interface IPXODI.COM to the Microsoft Redirector DLLs loaded during Windows loading.

USING NDIS DRIVERS AND IPX/SPX COMPATIBLE TRANSPORT (NWLINK)

Another option is to use Microsoft's NDIS drivers and NWLink, Microsoft's IPX/SPX emulator. In this case, the appropriate NDIS driver for your network card is selected through the Network Setup icon.

Microsoft has developed 32-bit NDIS drivers for most major network cards. These drivers provide substantial improvement in network card I/O. This alone is a major reason to migrate to the NDIS drivers.

In this type of installation, no drivers are loaded in your AUTOEXEC.BAT or AUTOEXEC.NT except the Microsoft Redirector. In a DOS/Windows 3.x or WFW installation, the NET START command is issued in your AUTOEXEC.BAT. When Windows is loaded, the appropriate drivers are loaded to support your network card drivers and various protocol options. Figure 4.11 illustrates the client files loaded to support this option.

Figure 4.11.
NetWare Client
Software Stack with
NWLink.

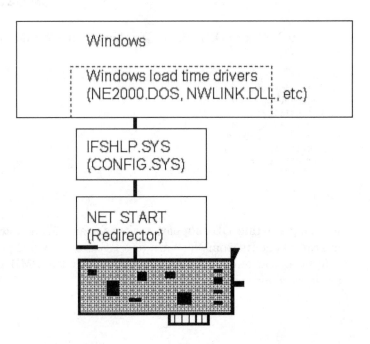

When you select an NDIS driver, the default protocol support includes:

> The NDIS network card driver for your network card
> Microsoft NetBEUI
> IPX/SPX Compatible Transport with NetBIOS (NWLink)

IPX/SPX Compatible Transport with NetBIOS is the default protocol used. It has the following features:

> Multiple Bindings—NWLink can be bound to multiple network adapters with multiple frame types.

> Frame Type Auto Detect—NWLink automatically detects during Setup which frame type is being used on the network and automatically selects that frame type. If there are multiple frame types detected, NWLink configures all frame types. If no frames are detected, it defaults to the 802.2 frame type.

> SPX II—NWLink supports Windows Sockets on the new Novell SPX II protocol. SPX II has been enhanced to support windowing and has the capability to set a maximum frame size.

> Direct Hosting over IPX—The NT Server (not the redirector) supports Direct Hosting technology. This allows WFW clients to communicate up to 20 percent faster than using NetBIOS over IPX with NT Servers.

CHANGING NETWORK CARD DRIVER AND PROTOCOL CONFIGURATIONS

If you wish to change ODI to NDIS drivers, it can be done through the Network icon in Windows' Control Panel. First add support for other protocol options, then remove support for the existing protocol. You will need to access the appropriate Windows' and/or vendor's driver disks, then reboot Windows.

Tip

If you have problems changing protocol options once Windows for Workgroups, Windows 95, or NT is installed, try the following procedure:

1. Remove the existing network card driver.

2. Reboot or exit Windows entirely.

3. Start Windows again, add the new driver and protocol options, and select the default protocol.

4. Reboot your workstation, or exit Windows and restart it.

USING GATEWAY SERVICE FOR NETWARE

Another popular option to support NetWare clients involves a gateway installed in an NT Server. In this option, the client is connected to the NT Server, and access to the NetWare server is provided by the Gateway Services for NetWare application loaded on your NT Server. In this approach, the NT Server forwards all communications for the NetWare server across its gateway, converting protocols in the process.

One advantage of this approach is that all connections between the NT clients and the NetWare server only take up one NetWare server connection. This may pay for itself in reducing the number of user licenses required on your NetWare server.

> ### Note
>
> In order for NT clients to access a NetWare server via Gateway Services for NetWare either the ODI or NWLink options must be used. Chapter 16, "Gateway Services for NetWare," covers this topic in greater detail.

SUMMARY—CONNECTING NT TO ANY NETWORK CLIENT

You can connect any popular desktop operating system to an NT Server over any type of LAN. NT can be integrated into existing networks using several protocol choices.

Microsoft has finally put it all together to make migration to NT Server feasible—perhaps even simple. NT Server can integrate with or replace other NOSs that are present on your system. NT is stable, performs well, and is ready for business. NT delivers on promises that have been made for several years. You can now leverage your existing resources and knowledge to include this product in your computing environment.

- Selecting a LAN

- Installing and
  Configuring the
  NT Server OS

- Migration Procedures

- Connecting the Client

PART II

Installing and Configuring
the NOS

- Preparing for an NT Server Installation

- Understanding LAN Technologies

- Installing LAN Cabling

- Installing Network Cards

- What You Need to Know About Network Card Drivers

CHAPTER 5

Selecting a LAN

LAN   An Ethernet, Token ring, or other type of communication system that acts as a medium between computers.

Node   An intelligent device connected to a network; commonly, a computer connected to a LAN.

Hub   An Ethernet LAN device, sometimes called a wiring concentrator or multiport repeater, that connects cable segments together into a single LAN.

Protocol   Rules of communication between network peers. Access protocols drive network card-to-network card communications on a LAN, network protocols provide routing information, and transport protocols are used by the NOS to exchange data between computers.

Network Architecture   The model of all components, software and hardware, incorporated into a network.

Frames   Protocol units that carry data from one network card to another over a LAN or WAN.

Packets   NOS protocol units that implement network, transport, and OS functions between computers.

Bridge   A device that connects two LANs together that works at the frame (LAN) protocol layer. Bridges filter and forward frames from one LAN to another, disguising both LANs to appear as one LAN.

Router   A computer with software that moves NOS packets from one LAN to another LAN or WAN, acting at the network protocol layer.

Network Device Interface Specification (NDIS)   Microsoft's specifications for interface between network card drivers and NOS transport protocols.

Note

In this book, the term "LAN" refers to an Ethernet, Token ring, or other type of local area network. The term "network" refers to the entire networked system of computers, LANs, WANs, protocols, NOS, and so on.

We stand on the frontier of a new era of computing. LANs have just lately evolved with sufficient bandwidth to support applications that were previously impractical to network. We know that 100-Mbps LANs can support document imaging and retrieval, full-motion video, multimedia, CAD/CAM, and so on. Processor power and storage capacity have gone up rapidly, while prices have dropped. With this availability, new applications will arise, and new applications will be downsized from mainframes.

High bandwidth (100 Mbps) LAN technology has been available in the form of FDDI (Fiber Distributed Data Interface) and TCNS (Thomas Conrad Network System, an Arcnet variant). More recently, we have seen the development of Fast Ethernet, 100VG-AnyLAN, and ATM LAN emulation products. However, nothing has as much potential to revolutionize the desktop as Fast Ethernet, because this product is priced where anyone who can afford a network can afford it.

But what of our existing technologies? Are existing Ethernet and Token ring LANs obsolete? Must we replace all our old network cards to improve network performance? Are more expensive, new 100-Mbps network cards our only alternative? The answer to these and many more such questions is "Maybe, maybe not." Most newer technology provides for interfacing older LAN technologies into higher capacity LANs by using switching hubs.

Clone 10-Mbps Ethernet network cards sell for as little as $35, major-brand network cards sell for around $100, and Ethernet hubs start at under $500. Token ring network cards have fallen to under $200, and MAUs start at under $500. FDDI, 100VG-AnyLAN, and ATM products are still far too expensive, but Fast Ethernet network cards retail for $250 from most major network card vendors. Still quite expensive are 100-Mbps hubs ($1,500 to $5,000) and switched hubs (100- and 10-Mbps ports bridged together) cost between $4,000 and $10,000. Due to economies of scale, however, we will see 100-Mbps switched hubs drop to the same prices as 10-Mbps hubs. Every Ethernet vendor is working hard to compete with better products at lower prices.

This chapter is about selecting the right fit for you, and how to implement a durable LAN. This chapter discusses the following topics:

◆ Preparing for an NT Server installation

◆ Understanding LAN technologies

◆ Installing LAN cabling

◆ Installing network cards

◆ Network card drivers

You will see exactly what goes on inside the wires of your LAN, how to select suitable LAN components for your current needs, how to provide an upgrade path for future needs, how to install and configure your network cards, and how to prepare your LAN for installing your NOS.

PREPARING FOR AN NT SERVER INSTALLATION

NT Server, like any other NOS, relies on a few key components for performance, proper communications, and durability. The LAN needs to be properly in place, configured, and working because your installation and network relies on this medium. After installing the LAN, the file server, and workstation hardware, you are then ready to install NT Server and client workstation software.

All networks communicate over a LAN. Your Ethernet, Token ring, or other type of LAN and cabling is a vitally important link between servers and clients. The performance and durability of the LAN installation is of the utmost importance. If the LAN fails due to a loose connector, damaged cable, malfunctioning network card or driver, your NOS cannot do its job. Without a reliable LAN, nothing works right.

Installing and configuring the NOS is designed to be simple and to go as smoothly as possible. In a perfect world, you would run the Windows Setup program and everything would go just fine. In a couple of hours you could log on to your new NT Server. But this is not a perfect world. Murphy's Law rules in this environment, so during installation you must make certain that each component is working properly before proceeding to the next step.

Many problems can occur during installation. As a matter of fact, most experienced network integrators will tell you that an installation that goes smoothly with no glitches is rare at best. NT, Windows 95, and Windows for Workgroup all have a Setup program that is a fine example of Murphy's Law. If anything goes wrong, it comes to a halt.

When Setup fails, it is generally due to one of the following problems:

◆ The LAN is not working due to cabling or configuration problems.
◆ Internal PC configuration conflicts between network cards and other components.
◆ Network card drivers that do not function properly.

Should you encounter any of these problems, you can elect not to install your network card driver during Setup, and then install it from a Control Panel or Network Setup icon after your OS is up and running.

UNDERSTANDING LAN TECHNOLOGIES

Selecting a LAN is not a serious issue today. You can hardly go wrong unless you select standard Arcnet or 4-Mbps Token ring. All other current LANs provide anywhere from 10-Mbps to 155-Mbps capacities, are reliable, and are relatively easy to install.

BANDWIDTH (CAPACITY)

The general impression non-engineers have about LAN bandwidth is that 100 Mbps is 10 times faster than 10 Mbps—this simply is not true. Bandwidth provides more *capacity*, and therefore *may* provide better performance, but only when capacity is restricted. Whether higher bandwidth results in better speed depends on how heavy your bandwidth utilization is.

Actually, electricity propagates on unshielded twisted pair wire at the rate of about 65 percent of the speed of light. This propagation rate (called the Nominal Velocity of Propagation) is fixed, regardless of whether fast signaling occurs. Bits are placed on the wire at a constant rate (that is, 10 or 100 Mbps). In short, speed is not an issue in this system.

Time on the wire is the real issue. Only one frame may exist on a single Ethernet LAN segment at any time. In order to share the cabling, network cards take turns on the cabling.

Because only one frame exists on the LAN at any time, faster signaling frees up more time for other nodes to use the cable. Therefore, when a 10-Mbps Ethernet LAN is at 60 percent utilization, the same traffic would only consume 6 percent of available bandwidth on a 100-Mbps LAN.

ETHERNET OR TOKEN RING AND USABLE BANDWIDTH

An age-old question lingers in the minds of network integrators: "Which is better, Ethernet or Token ring?" Most integrators have loyalties to one or the other, but it really amounts to two choices, and which is better is not generally the most important factor.

Few other types of LANs exist today, but more recently new LAN technologies have appeared. Today's race for improved bandwidth is due to two factors: More users and powerusers added to the LAN demand more bandwidth, and new applications such as image storage and retrieval, desktop publishing, and CAD/CAM now commonly use LANs to move data. In the past, these applications demanded more bandwidth than was available, but the advent of 100-Mbps LANs has opened a new world of possibilities.

LAN access protocols (how the network cards communicate) are classified as deterministic-oriented versus contention-oriented. Ethernet's CSMA/CD (Carrier Sense Multiple Access with Collision Detection) is contention-oriented. Contention means that each node must contend for its turn on the wire. Ethernet performance is limited because as the percentage of time the wire is occupied grows, the less chance there is of gaining immediate access to the wire. Delay in gaining access reduces performance. Collisions generated when two or more frames are put on the wire at the same time reduce available bandwidth and increase delay.

Typically an Ethernet LAN can only operate efficiently when up to 30–40 percent bandwidth is utilized. Above that level, an increasing proportion of bandwidth is occupied with re-transmissions and damaged frames. Though many performance reviews say otherwise, a typical installation cannot effectively support more than 70 percent bandwidth utilization. An industry standard for planning available bandwidth sets the higher threshold at 30 percent.

Token ring and FDDI's token-passing ring access protocols are deterministic. This means that each node takes turns based on the passing of a frame called a token. Because each node has an orderly method of taking turns, collisions are eliminated. Therefore a greater proportion of theoretical bandwidth is available.

Generally, a Token ring or FDDI LAN can accommodate up to 90–95 percent utilization before it levels off. Usually, a level of 60–70 percent indicates that you are approaching limited bandwidth, and you should plan not to exceed 60–70 percent under normal circumstances.

Bandwidth alone is only part of the picture. You must also consider what level of utilization is acceptable. When you factor these two considerations, you have a number representing usable bandwidth.

You can conceptualize available bandwidth by visualizing pipe. When you buy pipe, you often buy the pipe according to the outer diameter size. However, your capacity is limited by the inside diameter as shown in Figure 5.1.

Figure 5.1.
Pipe analogy to LAN
available bandwidth.

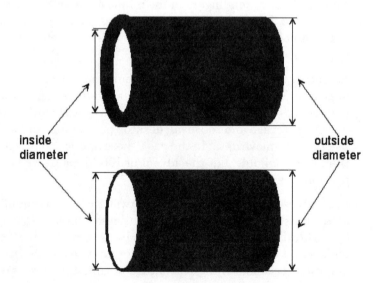

inside
diameter

outside
diameter

When you compare existing LAN technologies and their usable bandwidths, you find the results summarized in Table 5.1. A graph illustrating how much bandwidth is available on each type of LAN is shown in Figure 5.2.

TABLE 5.1. AVAILABLE BANDWIDTH FOR POPULAR LANs.

Type of LAN	Theoretical Bandwidth	Throughput	Available Bandwidth
Ethernet	10 Mbps	70%	7 Mbps
Token Ring	16	90	14.4
Fast Ethernet	100	60	60
FDDI	100	90	90
100VG	100	90	90
ATM	155	90	139.5

Figure 5.2.
Available versus
theoretical bandwidth
for popular LANs.

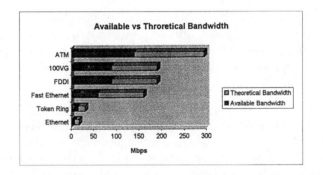

You must factor in cost to make an adequate decision. Don't forget to include all costs, network cards, hubs, cabling, cable installation, cable testers, protocol analyzers, and related labor. When all is said and done, you will definitely want FDDI or ATM, but management may not have the numbers in mind for your budget.

Tip

If you have champagne taste, but are on a beer budget, your only choice is Fast Ethernet.

THE CASE FOR ETHERNET AND FAST ETHERNET

Ethernet is a trusted environment for Digital, Hewlett-Packard, AT&T, and most other minicomputer and UNIX vendors. In almost all TCP/IP shops, Ethernet has been the overwhelming choice since the late 1970s. Most of these shops prefer Ethernet unless there is some compelling reason to choose otherwise. Ethernet conservatively accounts for well over 60 percent of all installations.

Fast Ethernet (100Base-X) is now on the market and is providing increased bandwidth at very low prices. Most major-brand Fast Ethernet 100Base-TX network cards using category 5 unshielded twisted pair retail for $258 and are expected to drop. Hubs have been quite expensive (over $3,000) but are dropping in price due to competition at the firmware layer (chip sets). Fast Ethernet hubs are expected to retail for under $1,000, and switching Ethernet hubs with 10- and 100-Mbps ports are expected to sell for under $2,000 in the near future.

You will not be able to use the entire bandwidth of 10 or 100 Mbps, as usable Ethernet throughput levels out at 60–90 percent utilization. Collisions, truncated frames, and other problems consume remaining bandwidth. When using a LAN monitor, we should be concerned about limited bandwidth any time utilization exceeds 30 percent of available bandwidth.

Higher levels of utilization are not possible in most Ethernet networks. Cabling problems may not affect throughput noticeably at lower utilization. However, higher levels of utilization are often restricted when cabling problems are present. A typical Ethernet LAN cannot accommodate more than 70–90 percent utilization levels, depending on cabling conditions.

This means that you only get to use 7–9 Mbps (875–1,000 Kbytes/sec) worth of the available 10-Mbps bandwidth. A jump to 100 Mbps allows you to use 70–90 percent of 100 Mbps. Though deterministic access methods, as used in Token ring and FDDI, allow a greater percentage of bandwidth to be used, 70 percent of 100 Mbps is adequate for just about any requirements you may have. When comparing the cost of Fast Ethernet to FDDI, the cost to performance ratio of Fast Ethernet is far more reasonable.

Ethernet's saving grace is price. It is by far the cheapest type of LAN available today. Though Ethernet's capacity is restricted when compared to Token ring, Ethernet is still more popular. Limited capacity can be handled with the use of LAN segmentation using switching hubs, bridges, routers, and multiple network cards in servers.

Because most Fast Ethernet network cards can automatically switch to either 10 or 100 Mbps, new purchases of Ethernet network cards will probably make 10-Mbps network cards obsolete, at least in the distribution channel.

THE CASE FOR TOKEN RING

Token ring accounts for about 30 percent of all network installations. Token ring was originally developed by IBM. Most large IBM mainframe accounts follow IBM's recommendations very closely, and IBM recommends IBM-brand Token ring components. As a result, over 70 percent of all Token ring installations are true blue IBM.

LAN vendors saw the potential in Token ring. Once 16-Mbps chipsets became available from IBM, Texas Instruments, and AMD, network card developers have flocked to build Token ring network cards and LAN product. Dozens of vendors in addition to IBM make Token-ring products today.

Token ring provides greater bandwidth than Ethernet in two important ways. First, 16-Mbps signaling provides 60 percent greater theoretical bandwidth than Ethernet. Second, Token ring's deterministic protocol provides greater usable bandwidth—it does not level out until utilization reaches over 90 percent of bandwidth. As an added benefit, the token-passing ring access protocol provides more equitable distribution of performance, and more error control. There are simply more and better problem indicators.

The token-passing ring access protocol carries a hefty patent royalty, however. This drives up the price of Token ring products. Each network card costs more because the royalty must be included in the manufacturer's cost, then marked up in the distribution channel.

THE CASE FOR FIBER DISTRIBUTED DATA INTERFACE (FDDI) AND TP-DDI (FDDI ON TWISTED PAIR)

FDDI was designed for optical fiber, but runs quite reliably on twisted pair. Bay Networks (formerly SynOptics) makes an unshielded twisted pair variety of FDDI for category 5 cabling. U-B Networks (formerly Ungermann-Bass) makes a variety of FDDI that requires shielded twisted pair. These two products are not interoperable, but the fact remains that copper wire is a perfectly acceptable medium for FDDI.

The previous discussions apply equally to FDDI and Token ring, except for one factor: cost. Because FDDI network cards generally contain two chipsets (Class A nodes), they carry twice the royalty. The royalty is based on selling price, and optical components incrementally increase the cost; therefore, the royalty is disproportionately higher than Token ring's royalty. Class A network cards retail for over $2,000, and Class B network cards are slightly more than half that much.

If you think the network cards are costly, FDDI switches that bridge between FDDI and other types of LANs generally cost over $10,000 and can range into the $30–40,000 range. This makes this type of LAN too expensive for local workstation connections. However, FDDI is generally used in a backbone for a few very good reasons.

1. High bandwidth availability (90 percent of 100 Mbps).

2. Fault tolerance. (Class A nodes provide fault tolerance from cable breaks. Other factors make it more reliable than any other type of LAN.)

3. Cost is generally less of a factor.

Note

Optical fiber cabling is no longer significantly more expensive than conventional copper wire. The cabling itself is slightly more expensive than category 5, but terminating and splicing has been the real killer. Several vendors now make cabling tools that reduce the price of implementing fiber. AMP makes a fiber optic splicing tool that sells for $500, while the microscope to test your cut sells for $1,500. Once you buy this set, the ends are only a few cents more than a standard RJ-45.

THE CASE FOR 100VG-ANYLAN

One of Fast Ethernet's downsides is its effective limitation to category 5 unshielded twisted pair. Because 10Base-T allows category 3 or 4 voice-grade cable in addition to category 5 data-grade cable, many existing cabling plants are category 3. When IEEE issued their 10Base-T specifications in the Fall of 1990, many organizations rewired their facilities. To upgrade those cable plants to category 5 would be exorbitantly expensive.

Fast Ethernet adds a 100Base-T4 standard that allows the use of category 3 cable but is limited to workgroups connected on a single hub only. Though switching hubs can overcome this limitation, many Ethernet developers championed a different variation of Ethernet called 100VG, or 100VG-AnyLAN. The following are characteristics of 100VG-AnyLAN:

1. It was developed to run reliably on category 3 cabling. Signals are split onto four pairs of wiring, each at 25 MHz instead of 100 MHz as is the case in 100Base-TX.

2. It incorporates a new access protocol, Demand Priority Access, which provides greater usable bandwidth when compared with Fast Ethernet.

3. It provides switching (bridging) between existing 10-Mbps Ethernet, 4- or 16-Mbps Token ring, and 100VG ports.

This new technology is better in every way than Fast Ethernet, except one: cost. The LAN equipment, like switching hubs, is simply more expensive.

This technology has been championed by Hewlett-Packard, AT&T, and IBM. IBM, however, pulled out of the 100VG-AnyLAN Forum, opting for ATM in their future plans. H-P and AT&T have disagreed on some minor issues that cast aspersions on the viability of the IEEE draft standards in place. These factors have hurt 100VG-AnyLAN's acceptance in the marketplace.

THE CASE FOR ASYNCHRONOUS TRANSFER MODE (ATM)

The entire networking industry is consumed with the idea that ATM is their future direction. Every leading network vendor has faith that someday ATM will replace all other high-capacity LANs, and WANs. However, that day is not here yet.

Current ATM products use LAN emulation. Instead of using the power of cell-switching technology to its fullest, current products run beneath various network protocols.

Future ATM networking will eliminate network and transport protocols (IPX/SPX, NetBEUI, TCP/IP, and so on). The technology is designed to segment a message into small cells (48 bytes plus a 5-byte header) directly from the application software to the network card. LANs and WANs will operate seamlessly.

Current LAN emulation products are available at 25-, 50-, 100-, and 155-Mbps bandwidths. ATM ultimately promises gigabit-per-second bandwidths on LANs, and major breakthroughs in WAN capacities.

The ATM Forum was formed to develop the standards. However, much of the communications equipment is being developed to theoretical specifications at this time. The products are not yet developed, so even though engineers know it is possible, much of the work is yet to be done. The ATM Forum estimates that products based on formal standards will be in production within a few years.

INSTALLING LAN CABLING

A recent industry survey concluded that well over half of all network disabilities were due to cabling and connector problems. A LAN installation consists of only a few components: cabling, hubs, and network cards.

Good-quality cabling is not enough. Cabling should be installed with full conformity to cabling standards and with rock-solid care for proper cabling conditions that will not degrade over the years. The relative cost and life expectancy of a cabling plant should be considered in the cable plant. This expenditure will be amortized over several years and allocated over many user workstations.

Each type of LAN has cabling standards that must be observed during installation. The Institute of Electrical and Electronic Engineers' (IEEE) 802 committee has established various workgroups to manage the standards for Ethernet, Fast Ethernet, Token ring, and 100VG LANs. The American National Standards Institute (ANSI) defines standards for FDDI. Every network card that is designed, built, and installed with conformity to these standards is assured of interoperability with competing products if these rules are observed.

When designing your cabling plant, a few important factors need to be considered:

1. Selecting the correct cabling and layout
2. Selecting a contractor or installing the cabling
3. Certifying the cabling
4. Securing the connections

SELECTING THE CORRECT CABLING AND LAYOUT

Though coaxial cable has been the traditional choice for Ethernet installations, 10Base-T (unshielded twisted pair) has become the overwhelming favorite since IEEE approved the 10Base-T standards in the Fall of 1990. Because 16-Mbps Token ring can now use either shielded twisted pair or category 5 unshielded twisted pair, most organizations have standardized on this lighter, more flexible choice in cabling.

Note

All the LAN types shown previously in Table 5.1 can run on category 5 unshielded twisted pair with up to 100 meters per cabling segment.

The most popular cabling and topology today includes category 5 configured into a star topology using hubs. This configuration provides many benefits, including:

◆ low-cost cabling
◆ flexibility with many LAN type options
◆ support of bandwidths up to 155 Mbps
◆ easy problem detection and diagnostics
◆ management via intelligent hubs

Ethernet depends on proper cabling conditions, and has little or no error control built into its access protocol. Cabling is a major problem in an Ethernet environment, mainly because integrators often do not understand how critical good cabling is, and how faulty cabling can whittle away at your available bandwidth.

When an Ethernet LAN has cabling problems, they are often intermittent. Usually the cabling problems surface when traffic is at high levels. At other times everything may work just fine. Because you often don't know how much traffic is present at any given moment, problems may seem to vanish and reappear for no apparent reason.

Note

A wiring concentrator with a simple collision indicator light is quite helpful in determining the cause of network bottlenecks.

Token ring has substantial error control, detection, and recovery built into its Medium Access Control. However, bad cabling can only touch off error recovery routines, such as beaconing or ring recovery. Some error recovery routines, like beaconing, can temporarily eliminate offending nodes; however, the process is sometimes devastating to all other nodes' performance.

To reduce the effect of cabling problems, you can use intelligent MAUs called Controlled Access Units (CAUs). These devices can diagnose many problems and remove offending nodes from the ring, preserving performance for all other nodes. CAUs help, but no network device can make bad cabling good, or make a node with defective cabling perform well.

IBM provides consulting on cable plant design, which is a valuable service. Token-ring cabling rules are quite complicated; allowable segment lengths and number of nodes depends on a combination of the type of cabling used and type of ring attachment devices (that is, MAUs or CAUs) to be used.

Accounts that use IBM's Token Ring expertise rarely experience cabling problems. Though Token ring has extensive error control and diagnostics in its access protocol, faulty cabling results in a plethora of error conditions.

Fast Ethernet requires category 5 unshielded twisted pair cabling or shielded twisted pair. The Electronic Industry Association's (EIA) 568 specifications provide guidelines for the type of cabling and connector pinouts. The later IEEE 100Base-X standards have revised restrictions from earlier 10Base-T on the number of repeaters in series.

Before laying out your cabling, check with your network card vendor for a cabling guide, or check with your cable supplier for an EIA/TIA specification guide.

In any LAN environment growth is inevitable. When integrators keep adding nodes to an existing LAN, cabling rule violations often occur. You are well advised to provide a good cabling layout diagram, and keep it up to date. Every time nodes are added, changes should be evaluated for potential cabling violations.

Category 5 is capable of handling virtually all types of LANs in common usage. Category 5 cabling supports

- ◆ 10-Mbps Ethernet (10Base-T)
- ◆ 4- or 16- Mbps Token ring
- ◆ 100-Mbps Ethernet
- ◆ 100-Mps copper wire variant of FDDI
- ◆ 100-Mbps TCNS (variety of Arcnet)
- ◆ 155-Mbps ATM
- ◆ 100-Mbps 100VG-AnyLAN

See Table 5.1 earlier in this chapter for a more comprehensive listing.

CERTIFYING CABLING

It is critical not only to install cabling with exacting conformance to cabling rules, but to make certain that the cable certifies according to specifications. Though cabling, connectors, and lengths may conform to cabling rules, your installed cabling segments may not provide adequate electrical characteristics. Connections, electro-magnetic interference, and other environmental factors can cause certification at the category 5 level to fail. Cable installers should be trained properly to avoid factors that can cause a cable certification to fail.

More factors than just cable type and length need to be considered when evaluating if cabling is acceptable. Cable segments are tested at various MHz levels. For the level you are to use, cable must be tested for noise, loss, attenuation, near-end crosstalk (NeXT), and appropriate pairing and pinout of wires.

Cable testers often have built-in certification that can tell you if your cabling is capable of performance in conformity to applicable specifications. Testers capable of certifying several types of LAN cabling range from $2,500 to $10,000. After all is said and done, your cabling needs to provide adequate characteristics to support heavy traffic levels.

You should always have your cabling certified by an independent, impartial tester. Like all contractors, cabling contractors should accept retention of a portion of their fees until certification proves the installation to be acceptable.

Tip

If you plan to implement 100-Mbps cabling, be sure to obtain a cable tester that is capable of testing cabling at 100 MHz, then test your cable at 100 MHz, not 10 MHz.

TIPS ON INSTALLING TWISTED PAIR CABLING (EIA/TIA 568)

Many rules need to be observed when installing your cable. Because the use of twisted pair wiring is so prevalent, the Electronics Industry Association (EIA) in conjunction with the Telecommunications Industry Association (TIA) have developed the EIA/TIA 568 standards. These rules apply to both shielded and unshielded twisted pair installations for many networks, as listed previously in Table 5.1.

Many installers are not aware of some of the more subtle, but important, rules about EIA/TIA 568. Here are some tips for installing your unshielded twisted pair:

♦ LAN cable should not be run in the same conduit or holes with other electrical wiring. It can be bundled only with other low voltage cables that are not sources of electromagnetic interference.

♦ Stay more than three feet away from fluorescent light-fixture ballasts and other sources of electromagnetic interference.

♦ Use EIA/TIA 568A (AT&T 258B) pinout on RJ-45s. This pinout is acceptable for Token ring, Ethernet, Fast Ethernet, FDDI on copper, and 100VG-AnyLAN. See Figure 5.3 for the EIA/TIA 568A pinout.

Figure 5.3.
EIA/TIA 568B pinout
for RJ-45.

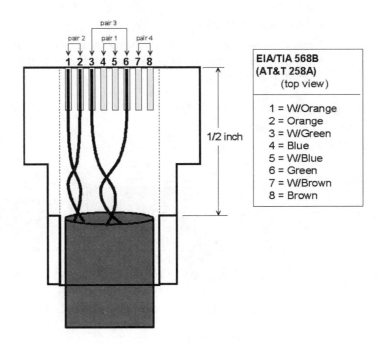

EIA/TIA 568B
(AT&T 258A)
(top view)

1 = W/Orange
2 = Orange
3 = W/Green
4 = Blue
5 = W/Blue
6 = Green
7 = W/Brown
8 = Brown

◆ Use no more than 90 meters for the horizontal cable run, and no more than 10 meters between the workstation and the wall jack and between the hub and the wiring block (see Figure 5.4).

Figure 5.4.
Horizontal and vertical
cable limitations.

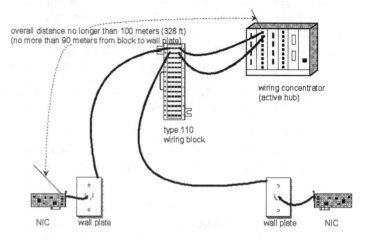

◆ Use all the same type of cabling and connectors, category 3, 4, or 5, throughout. For high-bandwidth applications, use only category 5–rated cabling and connectors.

◆ Fasten connectors carefully, peeling back only ½" of the wiring jacket. Be sure that the outer jacket is pinched tightly when crimping the RJ-45 as shown in Figure 5.5.

Figure 5.5.
Crimp RJ-45s onto the
cable jacket.

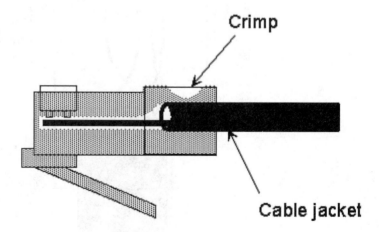

5

◆ Use stranded cabling in places where occasional bending occurs; solid core wire breaks easier when bent. Category 3, 4, and 5 and unshielded twisted pair can be obtained in either variety.

◆ Use the correct RJ-45 plug. There are two models, one for solid core, another for stranded wire (see Figure 5.6).

Figure 5.6.
Use the correct RJ-45
for stranded or solid
core.

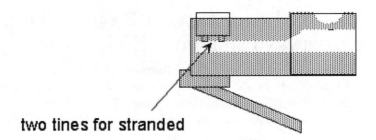

two tines for stranded

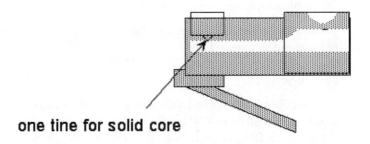

one tine for solid core

◆ Cabling segments should not exceed 90 meters (295 feet) from a type-110 wiring block to a wall jack.

No more than a total of 10 meters (33 feet) of cabling should be used between the wiring concentrator and wiring block and from the wall jack to the workstation network card.

Only category 5 wire should be used in all parts of your cabling, including the wall jack-to-workstation cable.

◆ Test all cabling segments before use, preferably before paying your contractor in full.

Tip

For more information on twisted pair cabling rules, contact your cabling supplier. Anixter provides a pocket reference guide on the EIA/TIA 568 standard at no cost. You can request one by contacting Anixter at (708) 677–2600.

TIPS ON INSTALLING 10BASE-2 (THINNET) ETHERNET CABLING (IEEE 10BASE-2)

A favorite choice for small Ethernet workgroups is Thinnet (sometimes called Cheapernet) RG-58 coaxial cable as defined in IEEE's 10Base-2 specifications. Before IEEE formalized their 10Base-T rules (September, 1990) for twisted pair, this was the most common medium used in Ethernet networks.

This type of cabling is preferred in small networks because no hub (wiring concentrator) is required. The linear bus topology employed in this scheme is very simple to install and inexpensive. However, it lacks many control features introduced by a hub, so it is not preferred in larger LANs.

10Base-2 uses BNC connectors, including cable plugs, t-connectors, 50-ohm terminators, and sleeves with RG-58 coaxial cable. This type of cabling is 50 ohms, thinner than normal TV coaxial cable (CATV-75 ohms), and can be used in stranded or solid core varieties.

Thinnet Ethernet is to be laid out in a linear bus topology. At each end of the cabling segment is a 50-ohm BNC terminator, and each network card is connected to the cable with a BNC t-connector, as shown in Figure 5.7.

Figure 5.7.
10Base-2 (Thin Ethernet) linear bus topology.

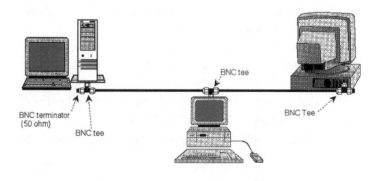

5

Warning

If your cabling breaks anywhere along a linear-bus cabling segment, no communications can be carried to any nodes on that cabling segment.

Cabling segments can be connected with *repeaters*. Repeaters simply repeat every bit from each cabling segment to every other cabling segment.

You can connect different cabling types through a hub, repeater, or external transceiver. Most hubs have multiple port types: RJ-45, BNC, and Attachment Unit Interface (AUI, also known as a *DIX*) to allow the use of different cabling types on isolated cabling segments.

Here are some tips on 10Base-2 installations:

◆ Only use RG-58 cabling, BNC connectors, and make sure your terminators are 50 ohms (75- and 93-ohm terminators look alike).

Warning

Many integrators seem to believe that standard TV coaxial cable (CATV, RG-59) is acceptable for Ethernet networks. Nothing can be farther from the truth.

Using the wrong type of cable may apparently work all right for a lightly loaded LAN, but the LAN will suffer from intermittent connectivity problems when bandwidth utilization climbs. Available bandwidth will also suffer.

Always use the correct components that conform to IEEE standards.

◆ Limit each cabling segment to no more than 185 meters (607 feet) from terminator to terminator.

◆ No more than 30 nodes are to be connected to each cabling segment.

Note

Managed devices, including intelligent hubs, protocol analyzers, and some types of repeaters, have network card chipsets and count as nodes.

◆ Connect each tee directly to the BNC port on your network card. *Never* use any cable between the t-connector and the network card.

OPTICAL FIBER

IEEE also drafted standards for the use of optical fiber cabling with Ethernet. The most secure with the longest distances are 10Base-F and 100Base-FX standards, with 1 kilometer per cabling segment.

Optical fiber has a reputation of being expensive and difficult to install. This is no longer true. The cable itself is about the same price as category 5 twisted pair. The most difficult part has been cutting and terminating optical fiber cabling.

Fiber termination previously required virtually clean-room conditions and extremely expensive tools to cut and terminate. Several cabling vendors have developed tools that are far less expensive than they used to be and easier to use for cutting, splicing, terminating, examining, and testing fiber cable.

Tip

AMP makes a complete fiber termination kit for under $500, and has a specially designed microscope for under $1,500 for examining the optical tip. You can find out more about AMP's LightCrimp XTC by contacting your local AMP dealer. Call AMP at (800) 522-6752.

Optical fiber can be used as a medium to connect two hubs or repeaters. Many more expensive hubs have optical ports, but you do not need to spend a fortune to use fiber between hubs. If your hub has an AUI (DIX) port, usually used for connection to Thicknet (10Base-5) cable, you can use it to connect a Fiber Optic Inter-Repeater Link (FOIRL) external transceiver (MAU). These devices are relatively inexpensive and allow you to use a fiber cabling segment of up to 1 kilometer between two such devices.

INSTALLING NETWORK CARDS

Installing network cards in your servers and workstations is one of the most challenging parts of installing a network. If a hardware conflict exists between your network card and other devices in your computer, you will not be able to communicate over the LAN.

Most network cards are 16-bit ISA interface cards, made to plug into an AT Classic Bus slot or EISA bus slot. When installing these devices, you must be sure to resolve conflicts in the following areas:

>   Base I/O address (port address)
>   Interrupt Request (IRQ)
>   Memory address for RAM buffering or on-board ROM
>   Direct Memory Address channel (DMA)

Configuration on these devices was done by setting switches and jumpers. However, newer network cards generally use software configuration. This is much easier to configure. Generally, the configuration software will not allow you to use a setting that conflicts with any other device in the computer.

Warning

If two devices share a common configuration option, your computer will lock up when both devices are activated at the same time. Generally this occurs while Windows is loading, but it could occur at any time the devices are activated.

Base I/O addresses identify each device connected to the bus with a unique hex number. This address is a bus address, and many such addresses are available.

Interrupt requests are more limited and usually present the biggest problem. There are only 15 IRQs, and many are already in use. Generally IRQ 10, 11, 12, 13, and 15 are available for interface cards. IRQ 5 is available if no LPT2 exists, and IRQ 3 is available if no COM2 exists. IRQ 2 and 9 are shared, and video normally uses this interrupt.

Warning

In a Windows environment, you should avoid the use of IRQ 2 or 9 if at all possible. If you must use IRQ 2 or 9, there are many "gotchas" that you will encounter. All of them may be resolved, but will require finding and reading several README files in various locations.

Memory addresses identify processor memory ranges where on-board RAM or ROM is to be found. In configuring a card to use a memory range, the specified location is referenced, and the memory on the board is located. If any other hardware or software device uses that range, the card will not function.

DMA channels allow ISA devices to perform a rudimentary type of bus mastering. Many sound, CD-ROM, scanner, and tape adapters use alternate DMAs so that byte transfers can occur between the device and RAM without interrupting the CPU. However, if two devices access the same DMA channel at one time, your computer will lock up. To be safe, avoid using DMA options on network cards if possible, and carefully eliminate DMA conflicts between devices before attempting any Windows installation.

EISA buses accommodate both EISA and ISA interface cards. EISA devices are all software configurable, and are configured through your computer's EISA Configuration Utility. This utility polls all known devices and prevents conflicts. However, most EISA Configuration Utilities cannot examine ISA devices and can still allow configuration conflicts.

Even in Microchannel Architecture buses, used in IBM PS/2 computers, where the use of ISA devices is not possible, you still must be careful to avoid conflicts between devices, especially IRQs and memory addresses.

Note

Hardware conflicts often do not affect MS-DOS operations, but cause NT and Windows 95 installations to stop dead in their tracks. The normal symptom is a computer lockup during installation or Windows load time.

To install and configure any version of Windows, especially NT or Windows 95, you must learn to master this problem and resolve these problems.

For more information about resolving hardware conflicts, look for a book on troubleshooting and upgrading PCs that is written to your level of understanding.

Tip

If you have a lockup problem during Windows NT or Windows 95 installation, do not allow the Setup program to auto-sense devices. Instead, install without any devices, and add the devices from your Control Panel after installation.

WHAT YOU NEED TO KNOW ABOUT NETWORK CARD DRIVERS

Drivers are a significant issue in the process of integrating NT Server and its clients. If the wrong driver is selected, or if a driver is not functional for any reason, Setup may crash, or everything will load okay, but you will not be able to connect to a server.

Wrong or bad drivers cause the integrator to spend many frustrating, non-productive hours during an installation. Even more frustrating is the fact that drivers may cause an NT or Windows 95 workstation to crash during OS loading, preventing you from fixing the problem.

In a protected-mode OS, such as NT, Windows 95, and OS/2, drivers run in a privileged memory space between the OS and the hardware layer. All other software enjoys the OS's memory protection. Driver failure in these environments spells certain disaster, and often disables the OS entirely.

In comparison to NetWare, NT is especially troublesome due to driver problems. NetWare drivers crash a server far less often, and let you know on the spot when a server or workstation driver cannot communicate with an network card. Because NetWare server drivers are loaded just like any other server-based module, they can be unloaded and reloaded without difficulty. An incorrectly configured driver fails to load, but does not crash the server. However, a driver with bugs can also crash a NetWare server.

Due to NT's memory protection, an NT server can install and load successfully, but communication will not be effective. This is one of the most difficult problems to troubleshoot during installation. On some occasions, you will even be able to connect to another computer but will not be able to access resources. This is one area where Microsoft engineers would be well advised to learn from Novell's experience.

Note

With Windows 3.1, WFW, NT, or Windows 95, a defective or incorrect driver may load, but will not connect you to your server. In other cases, Windows freezes during loading due to a bad network card driver. This usually happens with no error notification, and often with no way of knowing just why you cannot access a server.

NT and Windows 95 are especially sensitive to driver problems, and may freeze or halt your OS, and prevent you from even booting your computer. You may even need to use your Emergency Repair Disk, or product installation CD-ROM to fix the problem.

Network card drivers are written to specifications for a particular NOS. You must use the correct drivers for the correct OS, or you will not be successful in implementing your system. You may need to use one or more of the following drivers:

NDIS 2.0   used for WFW, and several other vendors' networks

NDIS 3.0   used for Microsoft NT and Windows 95, and several other vendors' networks

ODI/MLID   used for all Novell networks

Drivers are unique to each network card and are updated regularly. Some vendors provide a single driver for several models of their network cards, while at other times, each model may have a different driver.

Device drivers are provided in the box when you purchase your network card. You will find a disk in the box with your network card. That disk usually contains NDIS and ODI drivers for every major type of NOS. The drivers on that disk may be outdated, however, because a box may be several months old before you receive it.

Microsoft certifies drivers for use with their NOSs. However, due to the fact that networking hardware and software changes are so frequent, a device driver needs to be matched to the revision of OS and the model of network card that you are using.

Tip

> You may save yourself much time and frustration if you check with your network card vendor before installation to see if any more current network card drivers are available.
>
> Make sure the driver version you obtain works. You will be amazed at how many drivers contained on your Microsoft installation disks or with your network cards will not work with your version of NT or Windows 95. Even drivers that are certified may not be certified for a more recent release of NT or Windows 95.

For these very reasons, all reputable network card vendors provide one or more methods of making drivers accessible. Most have Bulletin Board Systems (BBSs), forums and libraries on CompuServe, and FTP servers on the Internet. It is in their best interest to see that you can obtain the latest driver revisions conveniently and efficiently.

SUMMARY

If you have read this chapter carefully, you know all you absolutely need to know about LANs. Armed with a good foundation of LAN basics, you can solve any problem you might encounter during installation of any Windows OS.

LANs are evolving very quickly. In the past, 10 Mbps was the benchmark of performance, a level of capacity that we all expected. Now the benchmark has increased tenfold. 100-Mbps Fast Ethernet is available to all at reasonable prices with no more complexity than 10-Mbps Ethernet.

Network cards, NOSs, and related standards change almost daily. An administrator must be aware of changes and how they impact their networks. Updating drivers not only impacts installation, but continues to be a major consideration in a system administrator's job. This will continue as long as network card vendors write their own drivers, which is not expected to change.

Though you may encounter finger pointing among technical support technicians, the buck stops with you. If the drivers don't work during your installation, you are stopped dead.

This chapter should help you resolve such problems through understanding of the mechanics of LAN technologies. In the future you may need to refer to this chapter to understand problems you may face in everyday business or the process of upgrading a network card or NOS version.

- Obtaining the Latest Drivers

- Overview of Installation

- Running Setup to Install Windows NT 3.51 (Server or Workstation)

- Unattended or Customized Setup

- Post-Installation Configuration

CHAPTER 6

Installing and Configuring the NT Server OS

Auto-detect (auto-sense)   NT and Windows 95 use this technique to discover hardware devices and to locate a driver to access each device during the Setup program.

CD-ROM   Compact Disc Read-Only Memory discs and drives provide over 600MB of disk storage on a single compact disc. Data is formatted in ISO 9660 standard format, and interpreted into various OS formats using CD Extensions.

Setup   This is the program you execute to install all Windows OSs.

SCSI   Small Computer Systems Interface is a computer bus standard developed by ANSI. SCSI adapters enable you to interface SCSI storage devices including disk drives, CD-ROMs, tape drives, and magneto-optical drives into a standard PC bus.

Unattended setup   Setup can run automatically when executed with the /U switch (for example, WINNT /U).

Answer file   A text file used in conjunction with an unattended setup that provides variables used to answer queries during Setup.

Note

In this book, the term *LAN* refers to an Ethernet, Token ring, or other type of local area network. The term *network* refers to the entire networked system of computers, LANs, WANs, protocols, NOS, and so on.

Note

Windows NT comes in both NT Server and NT Workstation versions. The two products have only minor differences that you will encounter during installation, but each difference has significant repercussions. This chapter discusses both product installations.

In this book the term *server* (not capitalized) is used to discuss either an NT Server or an NT Workstation server. Conversely, NT Server refers to the Windows NT Server product.

Two factors have changed that were designed to make installation easier but sometimes actually make the installation more difficult. First, Setup auto-senses hardware devices (such as video cards and network cards) to automatically locate the appropriate drivers and then load and configure them. Second, when you make a change to system configuration, such as changing network card drivers, any files that need to be replaced are normally updated.

When Setup auto-senses video cards, it can usually read the ROM on the video card and sense the appropriate driver, because most video cards have chip sets from just a few firmware developers. Auto-sensing network cards, however, is another matter. Quite often, this process causes Setup to crash. If there is no ROM message identifying the developer, NT simply attempts to load drivers until either one works, or the system locks up.

Plug-and-Play devices work better with NT as they are intended to, however, at this point in time, many devices are not Plug-and-Play compatible. The Plug-and-Play standard was developed by Microsoft and other industry developers to eliminate problems identifying devices and matching drivers. As time goes on, more and more devices will support this standard, and you will experience fewer device driver problems.

Obtaining the Latest Drivers

You should always obtain the latest disk driver, network card drivers, and other device drivers (for example, tape, CD-ROM, SCSI drivers, and so on). Microsoft provides drivers on your distribution CD-ROM, but these drivers might not be the latest revisions. In fact, many of them might not work with your device. Even worse, they might cause your installation to fail.

Drivers are a significant issue in the process of integrating NT Server and its clients. If you select the wrong driver, or if a driver is not functional for any reason, Setup might crash. Another possibility is that everything loads fine but you are not able to connect to a server.

Wrong or bad drivers cause the one doing the integration to spend many frustrating, nonproductive hours during an installation. Even more frustrating is the fact that drivers might cause an NT or Windows 95 workstation to crash during OS loading, preventing you from fixing the problem.

In a protected-mode OS, such as NT, Windows 95, and OS/2, drivers run in a privileged memory space between the OS and the hardware layer. All other software enjoys the OS's memory protection. Failure of a driver in these environments spells certain disaster, and often disables the OS entirely.

Note

With Windows 3.1, WFW, NT, or Windows 95, a defective or incorrect driver might load, but doesn't connect you to your server. In other cases, Windows freezes during load due to a bad network card driver. This usually happens with no error notification, and often with no way of knowing just why you cannot access a server.

NT and Windows 95 are especially sensitive to driver problems, and might freeze or halt your OS and prevent you from even booting your computer. If the situation is bad enough, you might need to use your Emergency Repair Disk or product-installation CD-ROM to fix the problem.

You can research and obtain the latest drivers from several sources, including

◆ The vendor's BBS

◆ The vendor's forum on CompuServe (if available)

◆ The vendor's FTP or Gopher servers on the Internet

◆ Microsoft's forum on CompuServe

Of course, your first and ultimate resource is the vendor's technical support. If you have a driver problem, you can bet that the vendor's technical-support personnel have had to deal with the problem already. If they seem surprised at your problem, you should check Microsoft's CompuServe forum for support (or to see if others have experienced the same problem).

Tip

You can save yourself much time and frustration if you check with your network card vendor before installation to see if any more current network card drivers are available.

Make sure the driver version you obtain works. You will be amazed at how many drivers contained on your Microsoft installation disks or with your network cards do not work with your version of NT or Windows 95. Even drivers that are certified might not be certified for a more recent release of NT or Windows 95.

OVERVIEW OF INSTALLATION

Installation for all Windows products employs the Setup program, which is generally named Setup.EXE. Windows NT uses another setup program named WINNT.EXE, which is located on your first disk or on your CD-ROM. Setup looks and runs pretty much the same way for every Windows version. Each Windows product has different Setup configurations, and you might need to start Setup from a different location.

OVERVIEW OF SETUP FOR WINDOWS NT

Installing a protected-mode OS such as NT can be tedious. Compatibility and device-driver problems can cause serious frustration and long hours without success.

These types of problems sometimes occur due to mistakes made during Setup, such as selecting incorrect options or configurations. Other times, your problem might stem from a defective or incorrect driver; or, if your device malfunctions, you get the same results.

After you have prepared your computer for installation, execute and run Setup following these steps:

<blockquote>

Step 1: Start Setup (WINNT.EXE)

Step 2: Enter path from which to install

Step 3: Remove Windows NT Server Setup boot disk and continue

Step 4: Read Welcome screen

Step 5: Select Express or Custom Setup

Step 6: Drive recognition

Step 7: Approve basic equipment options

Step 8: Select type of file system

Step 9: Select target directory

Step 10: Scan hard drive for corruption

Step 11: Enter name and company

Step 12: NT Server Security Role

Step 13: Enter licensing information

Step 14: Assign a computer name

Step 15: Select the language to be used

</blockquote>

Step 16: Select list of items to be set up

Step 17: Set up local printer

Step 18: Add network adapter

Step 19: Select protocols

Step 20: Edit network settings

Step 21: Configure domain or workgroup settings (choose one)

Step 22: Enter password

Step 23: Configure virtual memory

Step 24: Edit Date/Time information

Step 25: Detect and test video display

Step 26: Test processor

Step 27: Create Emergency Repair Disk

INSTALLATION SUPPORT CHECKLIST

Before you begin, you should make a checklist to be certain you have all of the items you will need during Setup. A sample checklist has been provided for you in Word 6 format on the CD-ROM that accompanies this book. Look for INSTCHK.DOC.

RUNNING SETUP TO INSTALL WINDOWS NT 3.51 (SERVER OR WORKSTATION)

This section is a step-by-step guide to help you during the installation of your NT operating system. Before you run Setup, review this section to see the options you need to consider. As you run Setup, keep this book open to the appropriate pages. You will find the tips, notes, and warnings helpful to explain the options you do not quite understand from screen messages.

Note

Your Setup program name for NT is WINNT.EXE for first-time installation. If you are upgrading from NT Advanced Server 3.1, you can use WINNT32.EXE.

BEFORE YOU BEGIN

Before beginning the installation procedure, go through this checklist to ensure you are prepared:

◆ Your local hard drive must be partitioned with MS-DOS 5.0 or higher and must be formatted and bootable. Install your CD-ROM drive as a DOS device, boot computer with DOS.

◆ Have three high-density, 3.5-inch, formatted, blank floppy disks ready (if you are using the default floppy installation).

◆ You need to have a minimum of 80MB of disk space to execute the installation. You should have several hundred megabytes of disk storage available, as NT will create a paging file several megabytes in size, plus you need storage space for applications, data, and so on. You need at least 12MB of RAM for NT Workstation, and 16MB of RAM for NT Server.

◆ You can install NT onto your target computer from a server's shared CD-ROM volume on any type of server, or from a shared volume on which the CD-ROM files directories has been copied. Simply share the server's CD-ROM drive, or copy the CD-ROM files onto a server's shared drive (about 260MB). Connect a client with MS-DOS, access the share, and start WINNT from the shared directory. For instructions on connecting an MS-DOS client, see Chapter 8, "Connecting the Client."

◆ You must install, configure, and test all disk storage devices, including disk drives, SCSI adapters, CD-ROM drives, and tape drives installed in your computer. Setup relies on real-mode drivers to be installed and working during Setup. If a device is not working before the installation, you cannot expect it to automatically start working during Setup.

Note

If your installation fails at any point, cold-boot your computer (turn it off and on, or use your reset button). Do not soft-boot your computer (by pressing Ctrl+Alt+Del).

THE INSTALLATION PROCEDURE

The following steps will help you install your NT Server or Workstation operating system. The procedures are the same except for obvious steps that NT Workstations do not need.

6

INSTALLING AND CONFIGURING

STEP 1: START SETUP (WINNT.EXE)

Change directories to \I386 (for Intel *x*86 servers) on your CD-ROM drive or shared volume. Execute WINNT.EXE. Enter the path where NT's WINNT.EXE is located.

There are several switches you can use. Switches are executed by adding them to your command. For example, to use the /B switch, execute WINNT /B. Your basic install options are

/T:*path_name* stores temporary installation files in *path_name* instead of on floppy disks. Use the local drive letter for *path_name*.

/B Floppyless operation. This option is very similar to /T: except that Setup selects a default drive and creates a default directory to store the working files.

Note

If you are installing from a shared CD-ROM or volume on a server, you should not use either of the above options. If you have difficulty loading your network card driver under NT, you will lose access to your shared files, and will not be able to complete your installation.

Tip

The /B option is faster, but if installation fails, you need to restart your installation from the beginning. When you restart Setup, it deletes all working files from the temporary directory. If this occurs, a basic install with three floppy disks will have been faster.

Tip

Type WINNT /? to see a help screen with a list and explanation of all switches that can be used.

STEP 2: PATH FROM WHICH TO INSTALL

Enter the path from which your installation starts. For all 486, Pentium, or Pentium Pro computers, it is the \I386 directory on your CD-ROM. There are other directories for RISC computers.

Unless you have specified the /B or /T option, Setup creates three floppy disks:

- Windows NT Server Setup Disk #3
- Windows NT Server Setup Disk #2
- Windows NT Server Setup Boot Disk (this is the #1 disk in the set)

Setup then copies your NT files to your hard drive. If an existing copy of Windows is found, Setup asks if you want to upgrade your existing Windows version (retaining all Program Manager icons and .INI settings). Alternatively, you may want to install a fresh copy of NT in a separate directory.

STEP 3: REMOVE WINDOWS NT SERVER SETUP BOOT DISK AND CONTINUE

When finished, Setup displays a screen letting you know that your computer will be restarted. It also instructs you to make certain the Windows NT Server Setup Boot Disk is in drive A: (if used), and to press Enter to continue.

If you have selected the floppyless installation method (/B or /T option), you are instructed to be certain that no disk is in drive A: before restarting your computer.

Note

If your computer will not boot from the floppy drive, check your advanced setup options stored in your computer's CMOS. Many newer BIOS chips can be configured to boot from C: before A:.

You then boot from drive A:. Setup reads the Windows NT Server Boot Disk, then prompts you to insert Windows NT Server Setup Disk #2.

Tip

When you install with the default option to use floppy disks, if you need to restart your installation for any reason you can reboot from the Windows NT Setup Boot Disk. You can start again from this point instead of starting over from the beginning.

Note

If you elected to use the WINNT /T or /B option discussed above, during boot a screen gives you the option to start Windows NT, boot into MS-DOS, or Installation/Upgrade. You should select Windows NT 3.51 Installation/Upgrade, or if you wait more that 30 seconds the system automatically defaults to this option. The NT operating system is initialized after any real-mode drivers needed are installed. Do not select MS-DOS at this point, as it terminates your installation.

If your computer locks up at this point, check your devices in your CONFIG.SYS. Check to see if the drivers are okay and that they are working properly.

If installation halts at this point, you need to start all over from the beginning. Setup then deletes all working files and reinstalls them.

STEP 4: WELCOME

You will see a Welcome to Setup character-based screen. It shows you the four following options:

To learn more about Windows NT Setup before continuing, press F1.
To setup Windows NT now, press Enter.
To repair a damaged Windows NT version 3.51 installation, press R.
To quit Setup without installing Windows NT, press F3.

You should press Enter to continue.

STEP 5: EXPRESS OR CUSTOM SETUP

You then have the option to select Express or Custom Setup.

Tip

Microsoft recommends the Express Setup, but experience has shown that you should select Custom Setup. If you select Express Setup, you might find the installation easier; then again, your computer might lock up. You might find that shortcuts do not save you any time because an Express Setup auto-senses devices, which often causes lockups. You will also find that default options, such as protocols, are selected automatically, and you might need to change them later on.

If you select Custom Setup, you can bypass the auto-sensing and add SCSI, CD-ROM, and network card drivers either manually without auto-sensing, or after the OS is installed and working. This is often the fastest and most efficient method of installation.

STEP 6: DRIVE RECOGNITION

Setup next locates and loads your disk driver if it can. Setup loads a viable disk driver, and your installation proceeds normally if possible.

Warning

> At this point, if your disk driver cannot be loaded you see no difference until the next time you need to access the disk drive. At that point, installation fails, and you need to restart Setup and scan for a mass storage device as discussed below.

Setup then asks you if you would like to scan for SCSI adapters, CD-ROM drives, or other disk controllers. This option provides support for

> Primary disk controllers where auto-sensing could not locate a driver
>
> Secondary SCSI adapters that have disk, tape, CD-ROM, or optical drives attached
>
> CD-ROM or tape drives that have proprietary controllers

Warning

> If this occurs, restart your installation, and be sure to scan for devices, or select S to select and install a driver supplied by your disk adapter vendor.

To load a storage device driver, press S. You will view a list of drivers. The Other option on this screen permits you to load a driver provided by the storage device vendor.

Setup displays a list of device drivers. The last selection is

```
Other (requires disk provided by a hardware manufacturer)
```

You can select this option to install a device driver provided by your hardware developer.

Note

> A very short list will be displayed. Press your up-arrow key to see more devices.

Tip

> If your SCSI adapter or CD-ROM vendor has provided a disk, and a Microsoft driver is also available, select the driver with the latest release date. If that driver causes a lockup, you should restart your installation by booting from your Windows NT Server Setup Boot Disk and then trying to using the other driver.

You can skip this option (thereby preventing a potential lockup) by pressing the Enter key.

Tip

> If your disk drive has been recognized, you can skip this step and elect to install your storage device after installation is completed by selecting your Setup applet. This option makes installation go faster and prevents lock ups due to mismatched driver detection.

If you are running an installation using floppy disks, Setup then instructs you to insert the disk labeled Windows NT Server Setup Disk #3.

Step 7: Basic Equipment Options

When you get past the previous step, Setup shows you a list of basic equipment it has detected, including your computer, keyboard, video card, keyboard language, and mouse or other type of pointing device. You can select No Changes to continue, or you can edit any of the options shown on the screen.

Tip

> If your computer locks up on you at this point, suspect one of the components listed in the previous paragraph. A common problem is a hardware conflict between two devices, such as a com port and a serial bus mouse card. Check your computer manual for special instructions concerning an NT Server installation.

Step 8: Type of File System

Select the type of file system to be installed in each partition on each disk drive. FAT (MS-DOS) is the default. NT can use this file system, its own NTFS, or OS/2's HPFS.

Tip

For best file-system performance and more efficient file storage, select NTFS. NTFS not only provides better physical read and write access, it also uses *small block allocation*, which stores data in a more compact manner. See Chapter 2, "NT Design," for more information about NTFS.

Note

If you select an NTFS file system, you will not be able to access that partition when you boot the server from DOS.

After you have converted a partition to NTFS, it cannot be restored as a FAT file system.

If you select NTFS, your default FAT file system will be converted to an NTFS file system after the installation has completed. Your computer will reboot; convert the file system and reboot again.

Note

You can convert your FAT file system to NTFS at some time in the future by running the CONVERT.EXE program after installation. This program is in your path when you boot into NT. See Chapter 23, "Evaluating Performance Opportunities," for information on this option.

STEP 9: SELECT TARGET DIRECTORY

Select the directory into which Windows NT files will be installed. If you have an existing Windows installation, you have the option of installing into that directory or another directory.

Installing into the same directory retains all current Windows desktop applets, options, and retains application entries in your .INI files.

Installing into a separate directory installs a fresh copy of NT with a default desktop.

Either option enables you to dual boot, either to Windows NT or to MS-DOS.

STEP 10: SCAN HARD DISK FOR CORRUPTION

Press Enter to allow Setup to scan your disk drives(s) for I/O errors. Skip this step by pressing Esc, as instructed on the screen.

Tip

If your disk drive is relatively new, skip this step; it just wastes time. If you are concerned about the durability of a disk drive, you should not use it in a server. You should always use the disk vendor's utilities to scan your drive surface if required.

You are instructed to remove any floppy disks and press Enter to continue.

The MS-DOS portion of Setup is complete. After your computer reboots, Windows NT starts up in its graphics mode.

During reboot, you will have the option to do one of the following:

◆ Start Windows NT Server
◆ Start Windows NT Server with VGA
◆ Start MS-DOS

Setup automatically selects Start Server. If the Windows Setup dialog box cannot be displayed, your video driver might be incorrect. You can reboot and select Windows NT Server with VGA to load a generic VGA driver that should work fine.

STEP 11: ENTER NAME AND COMPANY

Enter the system administrator or installer's name and company name at this point. Another screen pops up to verify that the information entered is correct before continuing.

STEP 12: NT SERVER SECURITY ROLE

If you are installing an NT Server, you are prompted to select whether the server is to be a Domain Controller (Primary or Backup) or a Server within a workgroup or domain controlled by another Domain Controller.

Microsoft networks were originally designed as peers in a workgroup environment. NT Server, however, was designed to take advantage of Microsoft's domain management features. When several servers are present in a larger organization, it is helpful to break the servers into divisions called *domains*. When your network is to contain a domain or multiple domains, use this option to select whether this server is to be a Primary Domain Controller (PDC) or Backup Domain Controller (BDC).

Each domain can only contain one PDC and can contain more than one BDC. If you select BDC, you need to enter a password to gain access to domain administration.

Each domain must have one Primary Domain Controller and should have at least one Backup Domain Controller for fault tolerance. If you are unsure about which option to choose, see Chapter 9, "Workgroups and Domains," for guidance. When in doubt, choose Domain Controller, not the default Server option.

Warning

Once you have selected Server in this screen, this NT Server can only be reconfigured as a Domain Controller by re-installing NT.

6

STEP 13: ENTERING LICENSING INFORMATION

At this point you are prompted to agree to the license terms. Once you agree and continue you will select whether your licensing is per server or per seat. In either case, each user is required to have an individual Client Access License. If you have a license-agreement arrangement with Microsoft, select per seat. All others should enter the number of Client Access Licenses in use at any given time.

STEP 14: ASSIGN A COMPUTER NAME

In any Microsoft network, each computer in a workgroup or domain must be assigned a name unique from all other network share names in the same workgroup or domain. Enter a descriptive name that identifies this computer. A convention should be applied that provides uniqueness, but retains identification that is consistent throughout an organization.

Note

Domain and workgroup names must be different from computer names.

STEP 15: SELECT LANGUAGE

Select from the list a language to be used on this computer's Windows screens.

STEP 16: SELECT LIST OF ITEMS TO BE SET UP

Like any Windows installations, you can elect which file groups to include in (or exclude from) your installation. You can select groups to include by clicking the box before each of the following options:

    ◆ Set up Only Windows Components You Select

    ◆ Set up Networks (shaded on NT Server because this step is mandatory)

    ◆ Set up Printers (locally connected printers only)

    ◆ Set up Applications on the Disk(s)

For each of these items, you can select the Files button to the right of the item, and select which files are to be included.

STEP 17: SET UP LOCAL PRINTER

Setup prompts you to select a printer for use as a local printer, to name the printer, and to select the printer port to which the printer device is attached.

If no local printer will be connected to this computer, you do not need to select a printer. To connect to a network printer, you may use Print Manager after the system has been installed.

STEP 18: ADD NETWORK ADAPTER

Setup continues to the Add Network Adapter dialog box. When you elect to continue, you are presented with a dialog box with options to "Continue" or "Do Not Detect." These options were provided because a large percentage of systems lock up when NT's auto-detect feature attempts to recognize your network card. If you have a "Plug and Play," a later model, or a more common network card, the auto-detect feature works just great. It locates the appropriate network card driver, loads the driver, and automatically detects the appropriate configuration options. If you have no reason to believe your network card cannot be auto-detected, select "Continue."

If your installation has previously failed at this point, or if you have any reason to believe that auto-detect will not be able to properly identify your network card, select "Do Not Detect." You will be permitted to select your network card driver from a list, and to configure it yourself.

Tip

The Do Not Detect option is certainly more conservative and permits you to install network card drivers that would otherwise lock up your system and cause your installation to fail.

For best results with auto-detection, select a network card that is "Plug and Play" compatible. NT and Windows 95 are the first operating systems to incorporate the "Plug and Play" standard into Setup.

If you have selected "Do Not Detect," you have the option to select the driver for the network card installed in this computer. Click the arrow next to the network card driver shown, and you will find a list of network card drivers. If you opt to continue, auto-detect selects the network card drive that should work.

Tip

When Setup is finished, and you cannot connect to other network resources, the network card drivers are most likely the cause. Just because a driver loads and seems to work does not mean it is working properly. Drivers can load and even allow you to log on, but may not allow you to access shared resources.

You should check with your network card manufacturer for the latest NDIS 3 drivers available (for NT 3.5*x*). Most network card manufacturers have online bulletin board systems (BBS), forums on CompuServe, and FTP servers on the Internet from which you can download the latest and greatest drivers.

After you have selected a driver, you will be prompted to configure the driver. Select the network card hardware settings. When you select OK, more files will be copied.

Tip

If you are installing from a server's shared CD-ROM or network volume, you must select the appropriate driver at this point or you will not be able to install the driver later on because you will not have access to your CD-ROM files.

To alleviate this problem, select the appropriate network card driver at this time, even if the network card is not installed or not configured properly. You will be able to reconfigure the hardware settings later on.

Next, you are prompted to select the bus. If you are using a PCI or PCMCIA device, be sure to select the appropriate bus. Setup defaults to ISA, which does not work if you have an alternative bus.

STEP 19: SELECT PROTOCOLS

Select the protocol stack(s) to be serviced by this network card. For small networks with only one LAN segment, NetBEUI should be your choice unless other protocol support is required. For compatibility with an exiting Novell NetWare installation, select NWLink. For compatibility with an existing TCP/IP installation or for future access to Internet services, select TCP/IP. For more information about network protocols, see Chapter 4, "Microsoft's Protocol Support."

STEP 20: NETWORK SETTINGS

If you have only one network card in your server, you can select OK and continue with your installation. In the Network Settings dialog box shown in Figure 6.1, you can perform several functions, now or after Setup is finished by selecting the Networks icon in Control Panel.

Figure 6.1.
The Network Settings
dialog box.

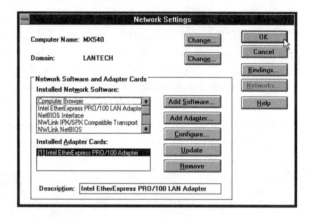

You can perform the following options from this screen:

♦ Add support for additional network cards (up to 16)

♦ Select protocol support for each network card separately

♦ View and edit Bindings (which protocols are bound to each network card)

The following protocols are supported for NT Server:

♦ NWLink IPX/SPX Compatible Transport

♦ TCP/IP Transport

♦ NetBEUI Transport

You may also select each software or hardware component and edit the configuration options. You should select the installed adapter, then select configuration to check each hardware configuration option.

Note for NetWare Administrators

NT Server includes support for NDIS drivers only. NT Workstation also includes support for Novell IPXODI Compatible drivers. If you select this option, NWLink is not selected.

The Protocol Configuration screen may appear in which case you need to select the frame type in use on your network. Both Ethernet and Token ring have various frame options. You should select the same frame type to be used on all computers that need to communicate with one another. You can select all frame types, but that is not optimal because it complicates the relationships between the network card driver and the various protocol options you have selected. For more information on frame types, see Chapter 5, "Selecting Your LAN," and Chapter 30, "LAN Troubleshooting."

STEP 21: DOMAIN OR WORKGROUP SETTINGS

The next screen you will see prompts you to enter the name of the workgroup or domain of which this server will be a member .

If you are installing an NT Server, be sure to select "domain" instead of the default "workgroup" option. Even a single NT Server should be configured as a domain. There is no downside and only benefits to gain from this configuration. For more information, see Chapter 9, "Workgroups and Domains."

Note

Although an NT Workstation can be configured as a member of a domain, they are not supported as Primary or Backup Domain Controllers. An NT Workstation can be used as a server, but will only support up to 10 concurrent clients.

If your network card driver and protocol options are configured correctly, Setup finds the domain or workgroup that you have entered. If a connectivity problem prohibits contact with other servers in a workgroup, or a domain controller in a domain, you are returned to the Domain/Workgroup Settings screen.

If your computer is to be a workgroup or domain server member, or a Primary Domain Controller, and it cannot communicate with other workgroup or domain controllers, simply select workgroup and proceed. You can change these options at a later date.

Note

> If your NT Server is to be a Backup Domain Controller (BDC), it must be able to contact an existing Primary Domain Controller (PDC) on the network. If you cannot contact a PDC, you must exit Setup and fix whatever problems caused your network card driver, or protocol options from loading and working properly.

If you have selected the domain option, you need to enter an existing domain user account name in the Create Computer Account in Domain box. If you can connect to a domain controller, and if the user account and password is valid in that domain, you receive a Welcome to <domainname> dialog box.

STEP 22: ENTER PASSWORD

Once these steps have been executed, Setup installs the desktop and options you requested previously.

You are then prompted to enter the Administrator's name and password. If you have elected to become a member of a domain, you should enter the password for the user account in the domain. Otherwise, the password you enter and confirm here becomes the password for a user account local to this server.

Warning

> It is imperative that you assign an administrator name and password at this point. Also, note that it is better to use the default name of *Administrator*. The reason for assigning a password right away is that if you forget to assign the password and another user assigns one by mistake and forgets the password, you will have to reinstall NT Server.
>
> It is also recommended that you use the Administrator user account for administering the network only, and not at any other time. This will reduce exposure to security breaches, viruses, and Trojan horse programs.

STEP 23: CONFIGURE VIRTUAL MEMORY

Windows uses disk space in the form of a Pagefile as a resource for temporarily storing data in RAM to the disk to make more space in RAM for active application code and data. Setup prompts default configurations for the drive letter and size of the Pagefile according to existing resources. You can change these options now or later if you prefer.

Tip

Place your Pagefile on an NTFS volume for best performance. Place your Pagefile on the boot partition for simple recovery in case your Registry becomes corrupted.

Setup then continues the installation by searching for program files to add to your desktop if you have opted to do so earlier.

STEP 24: DATE/TIME

The current date and time are taken from your computer's clock. Enter the date and time if the displayed information is incorrect. Then select the time zone where this server is. Time is synchronized across domains and workgroups.

STEP 25: DETECTED DISPLAY

In this step, Setup shows you a screen of test patterns to make certain that your video driver works properly. You must select Test before Setup enables you to proceed. If all is okay, you can continue Setup.

STEP 26: TEST PROCESSOR

Setup tests your processor to discover its type and to explore for known defects. If a Pentium processor with a floating-point defect is found, Setup prompts you to install a fix. Using a server for extensive graphical or scientific calculations is not recommended, as it robs your server of vital power needed to service clients. Unless your server is to be used for extensive graphical or math calculation, do not install the fix because it penalizes performance.

Note

Most integrators will not see this screen. It only presents itself if a Pentium processor with a known flaw is detected. If your Pentium processor is shown to be flawed, check with your computer vendor. You may be able to exchange the processor.

6

INSTALLING AND CONFIGURING

Setup next prompts you to create an Emergency Repair Disk if you agree. This disk may be vital to restoring your NT installation at a later date. If you skip this option, you can always make another Emergency Repair Disk (or update the old one) by running RDISK.EXE that is located in the \<winroot>\system32 directory.

At this point all configuration information is saved.

Tip

If your system crashes at this point, you must restart Setup and configure your hardware device drivers again, or eliminate hardware conflicts.

If you used the floppy-disk install method, you can restart your installation from the Windows NT Setup Boot Disk.

STEP 27: CREATE EMERGENCY REPAIR DISK

If the NT operating system, drivers, or file system become damaged, you can often repair the damage using the Emergency Repair Disk. To create this disk, follow the instructions on the screen. Insert a high-density, 3.5-inch disk into drive A: and select Yes.

At this point NT removes any temporary files and prompts you to reboot your computer so the NT operating system can start with all options installed.

RESTART COMPUTER, CONVERT FAT FILE SYSTEM TO NTFS

If you selected the NTFS option for one or more partition, NT converts the FAT file system to NTFS when you reboot. Your system again reboots to set security on your NTFS directory entries. If you did not elect to convert your FAT file system to NTFS, this step does not occur.

UNATTENDED OR CUSTOMIZED SETUP

You can customize your Setup procedure to automate NT installation. Microsoft calls this procedure an *unattended setup*. The unattended setup executes the NT Setup program (either WINNT.EXE or WINNT32.EXE) referencing answer files instead of querying for user input. You can still have Setup pause to wait for manual input where necessary. To execute an unattended Setup, you must create and/or edit the answer files, then execute Setup with the /U switch followed by the name of the answer file to be used (for example, WINNT /U:<answerfile>).

There are many reasons you might want to customize Setup, especially if you are installing several NT Servers and/or NT Workstations for a specific project, or to automate installations over an extended period of time. Most people who integrate and must install or upgrade an entire network of several hundred users and servers benefit from the unattended install. Not only can installations be performed quickly and efficiently, but installations can be delegated to less skilled technicians because complexities have been handled in the answer file.

Generally, system administrators who must install large numbers of servers and/ or workstations place a single copy of the installation files on a shared network drive, and then execute Setup from the network. Using the unattended setup from a network share can turn your network into an "NT factory."

SETUP MECHANICS

The unattended setup is one of the Setup program's options. Using an answer file when running Setup allows you to pre-configure the choices offered during setup. It works by simply using the file to input answers to Setup questions interactively.

Setup proceeds in stages, first starting with a text mode portion that asks the installer to specify the source and destination for the installation files. You have options to reformat and re-partition your local hard drive at this point. If your installation files are taken from a network share, Setup copies to your local hard drive a temporary file set consisting of the minimum files required to accomplish the installation.

Next, drivers for the Hardware Abstraction Layer (HAL) and device drivers for your computer's basic equipment are installed, such as the computer bus, hard drive, video, keyboard, mouse, and so on. After the first file copy has been accomplished as discussed above, Setup restarts your computer. The next phase initializes a graphical portion of Setup. Key components are installed at this point including File Manager, Program Manager, fonts, and compatibility files for DOS, earlier Windows versions, OS/2, and POSIX.

Finally, Setup proceeds by giving the installer choices as to which Windows components, printers, and other items are to be installed. Program Manager groups and application icons are installed in those groups. At this point, the computer's desktop, including program groups and their contents is assembled and installed.

You can regulate all these functions by editing statements in your answer file. You can make several answer files to handle common needs for groups of computers sharing a common hardware configuration. You can organize groups of default desktops for departmental groups. In short, you can pre-configure servers and workstations according to departmental needs. You can set basic answers to be unattended, while unique configuration options and minor adjustments can still be made or changed after installation.

6

INSTALLING AND CONFIGURING

HOW TO CONFIGURE AND RUN AN UNATTENDED SETUP

This section discusses a step-by-step procedure for making an "NT factory" server from which you can install dozens of computers over the LAN with the least amount of time and effort. The procedure requires:

A server with enough disk space to install NT Server (between 172 to 340MB) or NT Workstations (between 160 to 294MB)

A CD-ROM either on the server or installed on a computer as a shared volume

Your NT Server and/or NT Workstation distribution CD-ROM

A LAN that is not too busy (traffic generated by this procedure dominates LAN traffic)

Computers to be set up as NT Servers and NT Workstation fully assembled and tested, connected to the LAN, and logged on with sufficient permissions and rights to access the installation share

Current NT drivers for all devices to be installed, settings, configuration parameters, and so on (same as any installation)

STEP 1: A) USE THE SERVER'S SHARED CD-ROM TO RUN SETUP FROM, OR B) COPY THE NT CD-ROM ONTO A NETWORK DRIVE

1a) Use the server's CD-ROM as a shared device. If you have a CD-ROM that is sharable, this is the most direct method. If you do not have a sharable CD-ROM drive on your server, proceed to step 1b.

1b) Use XCOPY or File Manager to copy the CD-ROM to a server disk drive that is sharable. Omit the directories that are not required. The following directories and subdirectories at a minimum are required for a successful installation:

\I386, ALPHA, MIPS, or PPC (only the one for the computer hardware you are installing)

\DRVLIB

\SUPPORT

You may also copy the CLIENT directory structure if you are to install WFW or RAS clients from the server.

To use the XCOPY command, shell out to a DOS prompt on your server, and XCOPY each primary directory as follows:

```
XCOPY D:\I386 C:\i386 /S /E
```

This assumes that drive D: is the server CD-ROM drive, and C: is the local drive that is shareable. The /s switch creates and copies subdirectories, and the /e switch copies subdirectories that do not have files. This command creates the appropriate directories as necessary. Repeat this command for each directory to be copied.

STEP 2: CREATE A DISTRIBUTION SHARE FOR SETUP

Share the parent of the Setup directory. For example, if you have used XCOPY to copy the i386 directory to the C: drive on the server SERVER, use File Manager to share that drive as a network share. If you use the NET command from a DOS prompt, use the command: NET SHARE C:\ \\SERVER\CDRIVE. This shares C:\ as the name CDRIVE.

STEP 3: COPY THE UNATTEND.TXT FILE, THEN EDIT THE FILE AS NEEDED.

Copy the UNATTEND.TXT file from the CD-ROM accompanying this book, or from your NT Online Books to a directory of your choice. You can specify the directory and file name when you execute Setup as discussed in step 5 below.

Edit the file, changing the parameters to suit your needs. To help, the UNATTEND.TXT file (courtesy of Microsoft) is heavily remarked to make setting up your answer file easier.

STEP 4: CONNECT THE NETWORK DRIVE SHARE CONTAINING SETUP

Connect to the network drive that contains Setup and all the distribution files. Use File Manager, select Disk, Network Drive then locate the share, select a drive letter, and then map the drive letter to the share.

In the previous example where the root directory of SERVER's C: drive was shared as CDRIVE, select SERVER from the list of servers in File Manager, then select CDRIVE. If you are using the NET command from a DOS prompt (assuming you wish to use drive X: as the Setup share), use the command NET USE X: \\SERVER\CDRIVE.

STEP 5: EXECUTE SETUP WITH THE UNATTENDED SWITCH

Switch to the shared Setup drive letter (drive X: in the example above), and execute Setup using the /U switch, and designate the appropriate file location and destination. The following syntax applies for a new installation:

```
WINNT /U:<answer_filename> /T:<destination_drive> /S:<source>
```

The following syntax applies to an upgrade from NT 3.1:

```
WINNT32 /U:<answer_filename> /T:<destination_drive> /s:<source>
```

6

INSTALLING AND CONFIGURING

/U specifies that Setup should run in the unattended mode. When the switch is followed by a colon (:), the name and location of the answer file is specified.

/T: specifies the destination drive letter into which NT is installed (do not use a colon after the drive letter).

/S: specifies the source location of the Setup application. Here a drive letter and directory is provided (include the colon after the drive letter, and include the directory pathname—if the root, include the backslash).

For example, if drive X: is the location of the UNATTEND.TXT directory, and drive C: is the destination drive on which NT is to be installed, type the following command:

```
X:\I386\WINNT /U:C:\UNATTEND.TXT /T:C /S:X:\I386
```

For an upgrade from NT 3.1 to 3.51, type the command:

```
X:\I386\WINNT32 /U:C:\UNATTEND.TXT /T:C /S:X:\I386
```

In this example, the UNATTEND.TXT file is in the root of drive C:, NT is to be installed in drive C:, and the source for the Setup files is X:\I386.

STEP 6: RESTART THE COMPUTER AND VERIFY PROPER OPERATION AND CONNECTIVITY

Shutdown NT and restart your system. Make sure you can log on to the appropriate domain or workgroup and copy a few files back and forth to make sure that everything is working okay.

POST-INSTALLATION CONFIGURATION

After installation you might need to edit your device configurations. As recommended previously in this chapter and in other chapters, you might have installed NT or Windows 95 without installing some device drivers. This approach is used to overcome or to avoid a lockup during installation when selecting drivers.

To add or edit a device configuration, you can edit an icon from your Windows desktop. This is the most effective way to integrate products without suffering related complications in making the OS work.

Tip

> If Setup auto-senses a device and something is not just perfect, you not only experience a lockup, but your OS installation halts. You might find that reinstalling the OS without selecting the offending device is a less complicated method than attempting a full and complete installation from start to finish.
>
> During Setup you can decline the suggestion to auto-sense your devices and either configure them manually during installation, or install without them and install/configure them manually later.

ADDING/EDITING DEVICES IN AN NT SERVER OR WORKSTATION

You can add devices or edit device settings through Control Panel options, or in Windows NT Setup:

◆ To add a network card or to edit protocol options, select the Network icon in the Control Panel group. You see the same screen you saw during Setup, as shown previously in Figure 6.1. Setup automatically locates Microsoft drivers, and you have the option to reference a vendor's driver diskette.

◆ To add or remove a SCSI storage device or a CD-ROM (SCSI or non-SCSI), select Windows NT Setup, Options, and then Add/Remove SCSI Adapters to bring up the Select SCSI Adapter Option dialog box. (See Figure 6.2.) When you select Add, Setup automatically locates Microsoft drivers, and you have the option of selecting an existing driver or selecting a driver from a vendor's driver diskette.

Figure 6.2.
The Select SCSI
Adapter Option
dialog box.

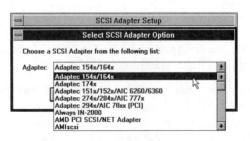

◆ To add or remove a tape drive, select Windows NT Setup, Options, and then Add/Remove Tape Devices to invoke the Select Tape Device Option dialog box. (See Figure 6.3.) When you select the Add button, Setup automatically locates Microsoft drivers, and you have the option to reference a vendor's driver diskette.

Figure 6.3.
The Select Tape Device
Option dialog box.

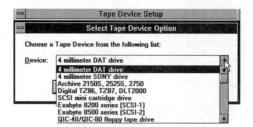

◆ To add or remove sound cards, select Control Panel, Drivers to bring up the Drivers dialog box. (See Figure 6.4.) Setup automatically locates Microsoft drivers, and you have the option to reference a vendor's driver diskette.

Figure 6.4.
The Drivers dialog box.

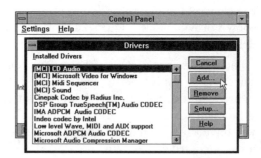

SUMMARY

Installation can go easy for you but only if you are lucky or if you follow some of the suggestions discussed in this chapter.

This chapter has provided tips and many notes about common pitfalls many experience during installation. You can pinpoint problems and fix them manually by installing the OS without some of your drivers and then adding them to a more solid platform—an OS that is installed and running already. You can automate Setup operation by editing one or more configuration files. Especially if you are in charge of installing or upgrading NT servers and clients, you should have found much help in this chapter.

- Conservative Migration Strategies

- The NetWare Migration Utility

- Upgrading from LAN Manager 2.*x*

- Other NOSs

- Migration from Minicomputers and UNIX Systems

CHAPTER 7

Migration Procedures

PDC   Primary Domain Controller. An NT server that contains the Security Account Manager database.

BDC   Backup Domain Controller. An NT server that contains the Security Account Manager database.

NWLink   Microsoft's implementation of IPX/SPX protocol.

Many NT Server installations replace existing NetWare, LAN Manager, LAN Server, and UNIX servers. Microsoft has provided tools for migrating from these other platforms. Two such tools, Migration Tool for NetWare and a toolset for migrating LAN Manager server to NT, are discussed in detail.

You'll find that several considerations need attention prior to and during your migration. Read this chapter while planning your migration; it discusses the following considerations:

◆ Conservative migration strategies

◆ The NetWare Migration Utility

◆ Upgrading From LAN Manager 2.x

◆ Migrating from other NOSs

CONSERVATIVE MIGRATION STRATEGIES

When making changes to a production system, you run the risk of interrupting other workers' productivity while your system is down. Two major surveys pegged the cost of downtime in a Fortune 1000 company at anywhere from $32,000 to $72,000 per hour. Even in the smallest company, interruption of normal work flow costs time and money.

If you are migrating any existing server to NT, you can effect a successful migration with a minimum amount of downtime. This strategy also retains your sanity. Under no circumstances, however, should you subject a mission-critical application to unnecessary downtime.

Here are several points to consider before starting your migration procedure:

◆ The impact of migration from one platform to another is almost always underestimated. Many organizations do not invest enough attention to planning for migration. As a result, the new system is blamed unfairly for problems that could have been prevented.

◆ The existing system should be kept operational until the NT Server–based system is fully operational and tested. Do not put yourself in a crisis situation by attempting to replace an existing production server. The cost of downtime is far too expensive in terms of lost productivity. The cost to your career might be irreversible.

◆ Set aside plenty of time for unforeseen difficulties. If your migration becomes messy, you must persevere in order to be successful. Many administrators have other duties that either are neglected or prevent a successful migration in a reasonable time because the administrator tries to maintain all of his or her duties.

◆ Make the migration a priority. If you have planned properly, it will not be urgent to complete the project. In many cases, people tend to do the easy tasks first and they put off the difficult tasks. A project like this can languish for a long time, which can cause added considerations and complications to come into play.

◆ Plan the new system carefully to make sure it has capacity above and beyond the existing system. Plan your system capacities for the useful life of your server, which should be at least two years. See Chapter 3, "Building the Server," for more information on this subject.

◆ It is important to work on preparing the new system during working hours so that technical support is available. For proper backup, however, you need to back up the existing system after hours to make sure that your backup contains the most recent updates.

◆ You should conduct the actual migration after hours or on weekends.

◆ Outsource where you must. You will find that many network integrators specialize in migrations. You can seek out a network integrator or Value Added Reseller (VAR) and get help in planning or conducting the migration.

◆ Back up, back up, and then back up again. Make sure you have reliable, current backups that are usable. You might find, for example, that your NetWare backups are not restorable on an NT system. After you repartition your existing server's disk drive, you will not be able to recover any data from it.

PLANNING A MIGRATION STRATEGY

Planning requires predicting upcoming situations and documenting detailed steps needed to deal with those situations. In addition, you will need to estimate the time and resources needed to finish the migration on schedule.

The following steps might apply to your specific circumstance; they are presented here as a general guideline:

1. Check your external resources. Many times an administrator doesn't realize that there might be a file-conversion issue or perhaps the application he wants to migrate is not compatible with NT Server. It makes a lot of sense to contact the manufacturer or find a consultant who has conducted similar migrations before starting your own.

2. Document the existing systems information in detail.

3. Make a copy of all menu, system, application, and batch files used by the existing system.

4. Make a hard copy of user accounts and group lists, trustee assignments, and rights masks. For NetWare, simple print-screens of SYSCON screens are quite adequate.

5. Make hard copies of login scripts.

6. There should be some printed documentation of the directory structure and contents of hard disks. In the case of peer-to-peer networks, you might have shared drives on many PCs.

7. A detailed cabling diagram is essential, even if you are changing to a new cable plant.

8. A profile of typical application tasks should be run and documented to be used for test cases on the new system. For example, if the primary application is an accounting system, you should run a set of financial reports. Later, after migration, you should run the same reports and make sure they match.

9. At least two tape backup sets, preferably different types of backups (DOS FAT with verify option) of the existing system, should be made before you proceed with the migration. Make sure the backup program is compatible with the NT Server system. Run a test restore on the NT Server before proceeding.

Note for NetWare Administrators

You *cannot* restore a NetWare file system to an NT drive. NetWare's directory listings and attributes are different from DOS FAT, HPFS, and NTFS listings. NetWare trustee assignments are also included in directory listings.

Use a workstation-based DOS tape-backup program to make your backups. Most NetWare backup software retains all of this information, and therefore cannot restore to a foreign file system.

Be sure you back up your NetWare volume with a DOS backup. This option might be available in your tape-backup software. Many NetWare server–based tape-backup systems offer DOS software that works with the tape hardware from a workstation. To implement this option, you need to move the tape unit to a workstation.

Your best option in upgrading from NetWare is to have the NetWare and NT Server online at the same time. Then you can use the NetWare NCOPY utility to copy the files from the NetWare server to the NT Server.

Note

If you plan to install your tape-backup drive on an NT Server, NT Workstation, or Windows 95 computer, make sure a certified and proven protected-mode (NT or 95 compatible) driver is available for your tape.

THE NETWARE MIGRATION UTILITY

The Migration Tool for NetWare (NWCONV.EXE) is a GUI-based utility that is included with NT Server version 3.5. Administrators can use the tool to copy users, groups, and files from bindery-based NetWare servers (versions 2.2 to 3.12) to an NT Server domain. Figure 7.1 shows the beginning screen for the Migration Tool for NetWare.

The NetWare Requester for NT is available with support for NDS. With it, you can log in to a NetWare 4 NDS tree; therefore you are not limited to bindery services (bindery emulation) in NetWare 4.

Note for NetWare Administrators

Use Admin to log in to NetWare 4.*x* and use Supervisor to log in on NetWare 3.*x* or older versions so you will have access to the greatest amount of security-related information possible.

Figure 7.1.
The Migration Tool for NetWare.

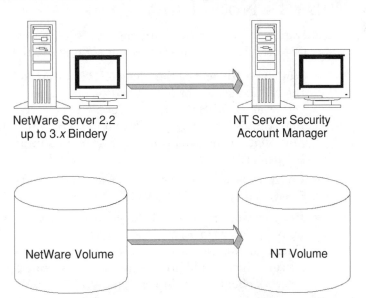

NetWare Server 2.2
up to 3.*x* Bindery

NT Server Security
Account Manager

NetWare Volume

NT Volume

You need to establish simultaneous reliable connections to the NetWare servers and NT Servers. You must therefore either use existing ODI client drivers with ODIHLP, or load the NWLink protocol with your NDIS drivers. This must be done independently of the installation of the Migration Tool for NetWare. For more information on these options, see Chapter 4, "Microsoft's Protocol Support," or Chapter 8, "Connecting the Client."

The steps to replace a NetWare server with an NT Server are as follows:

1. Using the Migration Tool for NetWare, transfer user accounts and the default settings used when transferring accounts.
2. Transfer the default NetWare groups to NT Server groups.
3. Transfer files and directories.
4. Transfer NetWare Trustee Assignments, Rights Masks, and file/directory attributes to NT Server File Access Permissions, Directory Rights, and file attributes.
5. Copy application and data files from your NetWare server to your NT Server.

Note for NetWare Administrators

You can simply copy most files from your NetWare server to your NT Server.

WHAT IS NOT MIGRATED

The Migration Tool for NetWare migrates files, users, and groups from NetWare servers to NT Servers; however, it will *not* migrate the following:

◆ **NetWare Directory Services (NDS) Related Information**   Currently, the NT Requester for NetWare does not support connection to a NetWare 4 server as an NDS client. Therefore, NDS objects and object-related information (that is, object properties and property values) cannot be migrated. Microsoft has pledged support for NDS in a future release of the NetWare Requester.

◆ **Login Scripts**   Windows NT logon scripts and profiles provide the same functionality as NetWare login scripts.

◆ **Printer Server/Queue Information**   As the administrator, you must set up NT printers to replace the NetWare print queues. You could use the Client for NetWare service to set up a print gateway to a NetWare print server, which would provide access to the same printers to both Microsoft network clients (NT Workstation, Win95, and WFW) and NetWare clients.

- ◆ **User-Defined Objects**   These objects do not exist in NT, and therefore cannot be transferred.
- ◆ **Workgroup/Usergroup Managers**   There is no equivalent to this type of object in NT Server and also cannot be transferred.
- ◆ By default, no NetWare users are added to the Administrators group in the NT Server domain. You can change this default, but even then only NetWare users with Supervisor rights are added to the Administrators group.

HOW TO USE THE MIGRATION TOOL FOR NETWARE

The Migration Tool for NetWare has many options that enable you to control migration. The following sections examine considerations you should take into account.

PLANNING YOUR MIGRATION

Before attempting the actual migration, you should spend some time planning how the NetWare users and files will be migrated, especially if the migration will involve more then one NetWare server.

In addition to the general guidelines presented in the section titled "Planning a Migration" earlier in this chapter, you should also consider the following issues:

- ◆ The administrator conducting the migration must be logged on as an Administrator of the NT domain to the NT Server that is running the Migration Tool. The administrator must also log on as user Supervisor on the NetWare server or have Supervisor rights on all NetWare servers to be migrated (user Admin for NetWare 4).
- ◆ Username conflicts can be a problem if not properly handled. Because the NetWare servers have separate bindery databases, there is a high probability that some users have accounts on more than one server, or have more than one user account on a single server or domain.

Note

Naming conflicts also exist with group, directory, and file names.

- ◆ Configure the Migration Tool for a trial migration before actually executing the migration. Files, users, and groups should be migrated during separate sessions. You should check the results of the previous session before proceeding with the next session. The Migration Tool records information about the migration in .LOG files. The administrator can then check these log files for information about potential trouble spots.

In the final analysis, the Migration Tool for NetWare is just a tool. It cannot solve problems that might be pre-existing in the NetWare or NT servers. Some of the problems may arise from extreme differences between the two user account environments.

Tip

> If you run into migration problems, you might find it more convenient to start with a fresh NT Server and build the new system without all the baggage that old systems collect. This might seem like more work, but after several failed migration attempts, it might be the path of least resistance.

In larger networks, where hundreds of user accounts may exist, it might be a foregone conclusion that the Migration Tool is the only practical way to migrate. In those circumstances, it is crucially important that the migration options be studied and tested very carefully. Several trial migrations should be conducted and the logs studied to make sure that your system is stable and complete before putting your NT Servers into production.

SETTING THE MIGRATION OPTIONS

You can set many migration options that help you to deal with the complexity of migrating several NetWare servers into one NT domain or to spread users to more than one domain. Figure 7.2 illustrates where migration options are set.

*Figure 7.2.
Setting migration
options.*

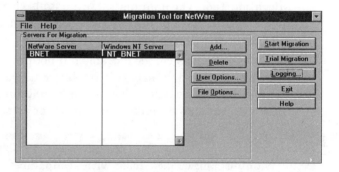

To select the servers for migration, select the existing NetWare servers and target NT Servers. You can set many migration options for this step. You can add one or more NetWare servers for migration, but it is not recommended. For each NetWare server picked, there must also be a target NT Server, however several NetWare servers can be migrated to the same NT Server. When the NT Server is selected, the domain the server belongs to is automatically selected.

Select the source and target servers as shown in Figures 7.3 through 7.8. The selected servers are listed under Servers for Migration.

Figure 7.3.
The Select Servers For
Migration dialog box.

Figure 7.4.
The Select NetWare
Server dialog box.

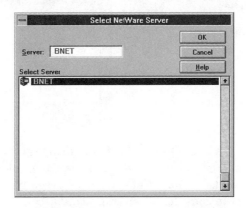

Figure 7.5.
The Select Windows NT
Server dialog box.

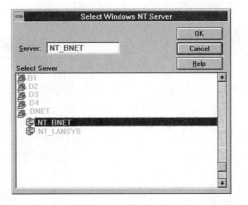

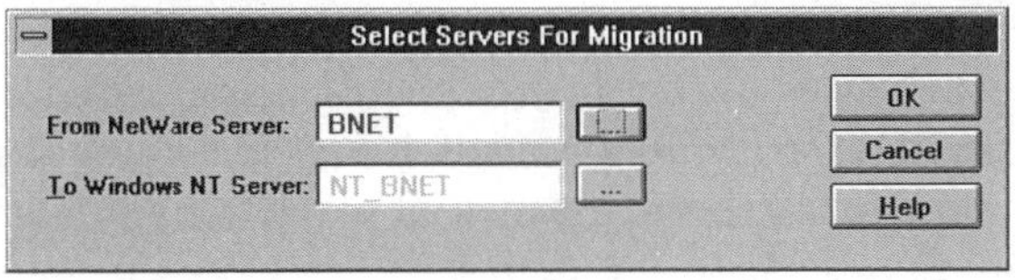

Figure 7.6.
The Select Servers for
Migration dialog box.

7

MIGRATION PROCEDURES

Figure 7.7.
The Enter Network
Credentials dialog box
with incorrect informa-
tion.

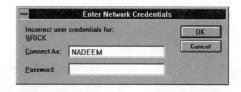

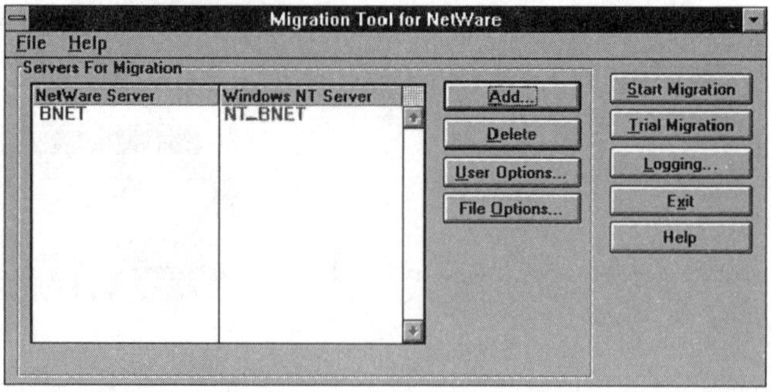

Figure 7.8.
The Migration Tool for
NetWare dialog box.

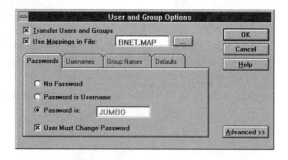

Click the User Options button to bring up the User and Group Options dialog box.
(See Figure 7.9.) Here you can change options that help control how users will be
migrated. Because NetWare user accounts are server specific, there are several
things to consider when migrating accounts from more than one server, such as
similar volume names, printer queues, and so on.

Figure 7.9.
The User and Group
Options dialog box.

Because NetWare passwords are encrypted, the Migration Tool cannot read user-
account passwords from the NetWare server's bindery. As the administrator, you
must choose how passwords should be migrated. By default, the account will be set
up so that the user is forced to change his or her password upon first logon. As shown
in Figure 7.9, there are several ways to handle passwords:

No Password   The account will be set up without a password.

Password is Username   The account will be set up with the password
set as the username.

Password is   The administrator can set up a constant password that will be assigned to all user accounts.

User Must Change Password   This option forces the user to change the password at the first logon.

Because NetWare 3 user accounts are server specific, any NetWare user accounts duplicated on multiple servers will become duplicate accounts in a single NT Server workgroup or domain when migrated. You need to choose one of the methods shown in Figure 7.10 for the Migration Tool to use to handle these conflicts.

Figure 7.10.
The Usernames tab of
the User and Group
Options dialog box.

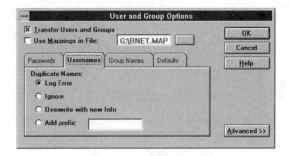

In this dialog box you can select from the following options:

Log Error   This choice adds an entry to the ERROR.LOG file if a duplicate name is found. Log files are created when a server is migrated; this is the default.

Ignore   This selection causes no action to be taken on conflicts; duplicates are ignored.

Overwrite with new info   This choice means that the new NetWare user-account information will overwrite NT account information. For example, if Rick already has a user account on the D1 domain and a user account named Rick was migrated, the NetWare account information would overwrite the NT account information. Any conflicts are recorded in the ERROR.LOG.

Add Prefix   This choice creates a new NT account when a conflict occurs with the specified prefix added to it. For example, an MG prefix can be added to each account to differentiate the migrated accounts from the original NT accounts.

There might be a group account on one NetWare server that has certain rights while another server has the same group name with different rights. You can choose a method to deal with this issue in the Group Names tab of the dialog box. (See Figure 7.11.)

Figure 7.11.
The Group Names tab
of the User and Group
Options dialog box.

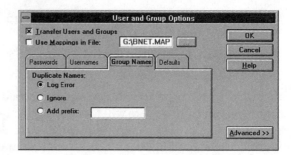

Note

Unlike the procedure for users, the option to overwrite with new information is not available for groups.

The tab offers the following options:

Log Error   Choose this option to add an entry to the ERROR.LOG file if a duplicate name is found.

Ignore   Choose this option if you want no action to be taken on conflicts.

Add Prefix   This option creates a new NT account when a conflict occurs with the specified prefix added.

The Defaults tab as shown in Figure 7.12 has the following options:

Figure 7.12.
The Defaults tab of the
User and Group
Options dialog box.

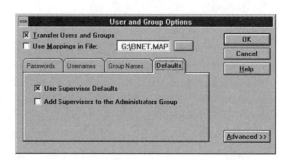

Use Supervisor Defaults   This option enables you to control whether NetWare account restrictions are to be migrated or if the NT account policy settings are to be used. Check the checkbox if NetWare account restrictions are to be migrated. The Migration Tool brings over the following account restrictions:

◆ Require Password
◆ Minimum Password Length

◆ Require Password Change

◆ Password Reuse

◆ Intruder Lockout

Add Supervisors to the Administrators Group   By default, groups
and users who have Supervisor, Workgroup Manager, and User Account
Manager rights are not added to the NT Administrators group. When you
select the Add Supervisors option, groups and users with Supervisor rights
are added to the Administrators group in the NT domain.

Use Mappings in File   This option enables you to create an ASCII file
containing a list of all the users and groups on the NetWare file server. The
administrator can edit the file and assign new names and/or passwords for
the users and groups to be mapped to when they are migrated to the
Windows NT domain. (See Figure 7.13.) The following is a sample mapping
file:

```
[RICK]
NewName=NT-RICK
Password=JUMBO
```

Figure 7.13.
Mapping file created
successfully.

Click the Advanced button to see more user and group options. (See Figure 7.14.)
The Advanced options enable you to transfer NetWare user accounts to a Trusted
Domain and are designed for companies that have implemented the Master Domain
model and want the user accounts added to the User Account domain and the files
to be migrated to the Files domain.

The dialog box now offers file options that enable you to control which files are
migrated and the location on the Windows NT server to which they are copied.

7

Figure 7.14.
Advanced User and
Group Options.

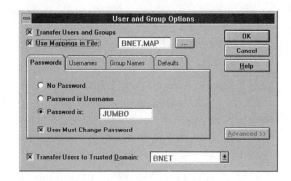

SELECTING WHICH FILES ARE TO BE MIGRATED

By default, all files except files with Hidden and System attributes are transferred to the selected NT Server. The \SYSTEM, \PUBLIC, \MAIL, \LOGIN, and \ETC directories on the NetWare SYS: volume are not transferred.

See Figures 7.15, 7.16, and 7.17 for File options.

Figure 7.15.
The File Options
dialog box.

Figure 7.16.
Transferring Hidden
files.

Figure 7.17.
Selecting files to
transfer.

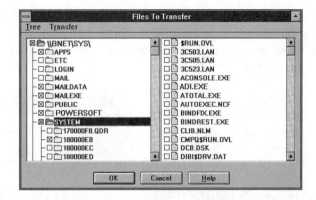

> ## Note
>
> These defaults can be changed by choosing the Files option and using the Transfer menu options.

You can also point to and put a checkmark by NetWare files to be transferred on the Files option. The Tree menu can be used to expand the branches of the directory tree.

Choosing the Modify option in the File Options dialog box brings up the Modify Destination dialog box. (See Figure 7.18.) This dialog box enables you to choose the share on the NT Server to which the NetWare files should be migrated. You can even create a new share for the files or have the files migrate to a subdirectory within the share.

Figure 7.18.
The Modify Destination
dialog box.

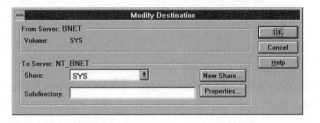

By default, the files are transferred to a new SYS directory on the NT Server volume, which is then automatically shared on the server with Share Permissions set to Full Control for Everyone.

You can select an alternate share from the Share list box; you can also use the Subdirectory option to have files transferred to a subdirectory under the share by typing in a path to the directory.

You can also create a new share for the NetWare files by choosing the New Share option. This brings up the New Share dialog box (see Figure 7.19), where you fill in a share name and path for the share. This share's permissions will be set to Full Control for Everyone.

Figure 7.19.
The New Share
dialog box.

To change the path for the share that is listed, choose the Properties... button in the Modify Destination dialog box. This brings up the Share Properties dialog box, which enables you to select the drive and directory to which the files will be migrated. (See Figure 7.20.)

Figure 7.20.
The Share Properties
dialog box.

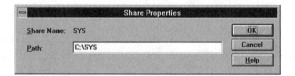

Note

Make sure the target is an NTFS partition. This way, the share created to contain the NetWare files is, by default, set to Full Access permissions for everybody. This is for the share only; all effective NetWare file permissions are applied to newly copied files on the NTFS volume.

SAVING AND RESTORING CONFIGURATIONS

You can save the configuration to a file for future use. The Restore Default Config... option under the File menu (see Figure 7.21) returns the Migration Tool to its defaults.

STARTING THE MIGRATION

The screen shown in Figure 7.22 shows how the migration is progressing.

As a last-minute check before running the migration, you need to make sure the following two conditions are met:

◆ All users are logged off the NetWare servers to be migrated and all files are closed.

◆ Sufficient file storage exists on the target NT server(s) to which files will be transferred.

Figure 7.21.
Saving and restoring
configuration.

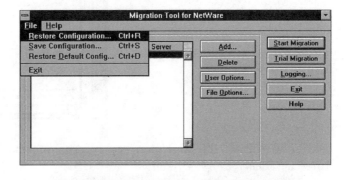

Figure 7.22.
Migration status.

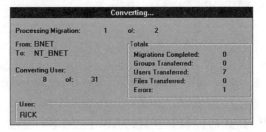

LOGGING

The Logging screen shown in Figure 7.23 enables you to set up certain logging options and view the log files.

Figure 7.23.
The Logging dialog
box.

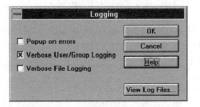

You have the following options in this dialog box:

Verbose options control the amount of information recorded in the log files during the migration.

View Log Files... button enables you to view the log files, as shown in Figure 7.24. These log files are stored in the \<winnt_root>\system32 directory.

*Figure 7.24.
Viewing the
LOGFILE.LOG
information.*

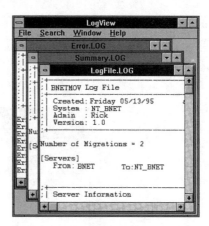

During migration, the Migration Tool records information about the migration in three log files:

◆ ERROR.LOG provides a list of any errors that occurred during the migration.

◆ SUMMARY.LOG provides statistics for the migration.

◆ LOGFILE.LOG provides a record of the migration that includes both what successfully transferred and what failed due to error.

UPGRADING FROM LAN MANAGER 2.*x*

With LAN Manager 2.*x*, a domain contains the Primary Domain Controller (PDC), backup, member, and standalone servers. This is similar to, but not the same as, an NT domain. LAN Manager 2.*x* domains are closer in design to WFW workgroups.

MIGRATION UTILITIES

This section covers several utilities that enable you to migrate from LAN Manager 2.*x*. These utilities make it easier to migrate from LAN Manager 2.*x*. In addition to the migration functions, some utilities back up the security information and others take these backup files and convert them to NT security format.

BACKACC is a LAN Manager 2.*x* utility that backs up the user-accounts database and network log file and creates a file containing the ACL information associated with the files and directories on LAN Manager 2.*x* OS/2-based HPFS volumes. This utility is run on LAN Manager 2.*x* before installing the NT Server over it. It is advisable to copy the backup file to a FAT volume on a computer other than the server being upgraded.

PORTUAS is an NT Server utility that merges a LAN Manager 2.x user-accounts database into an existing NT Server user-accounts database. You run this utility after the NT Server has been installed. Right after a LAN Manager 2.x server has been upgraded, the ACL backup file is then used to create the starting SAM (Security Access Manager) database for the newly upgraded NT Server.

The NT Server utility ACLCONV uses the ACL backup file created by BACKACC and creates equivalent file and directory permissions on newly created NTFS volumes. Another use for this utility is to merge more than one LAN Manager 2.x ACL backup file into a single NT Server. It is highly recommended that you perform a Registry backup before executing the ACLCONV.

CONVERT is an NT Server utility that converts FAT or HPFS volumes into NTFS volumes. Long filenames from HPFS are preserved.

INTEGRATING LAN MANAGER 2.x AND NT SERVERS

NT Workstation integrates with LAN Manager 2.x systems very well, but NT workstations are not capable of using the LAN Manager 2.x for logon authentication. You need an NT Server acting as a PDC, but NT Workstation users should have no problem using shared resources on either NT or LAN Manager servers. The NT Workstation users can also get messages from LAN Manager 2.x servers such as notification when a print job is completed.

You can add NT Servers to LAN Manager 2.x environments. In a domain situation, the NT Server must be the Primary Domain Controller. The LAN Manager 2.x servers can then receive security database changes and receive file replication from information from the NT Server. MS-DOS, Windows 3.x, WFW, and LAN Manager 2.x workstations can continue to log on to LAN Manager 2.x servers, and can log on simultaneously to NT Servers in the domain.

LIMITATIONS OF LAN MANAGER 2.x SERVERS ON NT NETWORKS

It is not recommended to use mixed networks for long-term situations, but interim use of mixed LAN Manager 2.x and NT networks can be quite effective if you keep the following limitations in mind:

◆ The LAN Manager 2.x cannot serve as a Domain Controller for an NT Server domain. An NT Server will not appear in a domain controlled by a LAN Manager 2.x Domain Controller.

◆ LAN Manager 2.x clients cannot allow logon from NT Servers. However, they can log on from OS/2, MS-DOS, and WFW clients.

◆ LAN Manager 2.x servers cannot provide pass-through authentication; thus they do not support trust relationships. Global groups and users from trusted domains are not available on a LAN Manager 2.x server. You can set up remote accounts for this scenario.

◆ LAN Manager 2.x servers cannot recognize NT Server local groups. The local group for an NT Server domain only applies to the NT Servers in that domain. Global groups defined in the LAN Manager 2.x domain can be used on the LAN Manager 2.x server only.

ACCOUNT REPLICATION

The user-account information is kept consistent across all the servers in a domain by the process of *repli2cation*. Replication copies security information from the PDC to BDCs to provide better performance (and fault tolerance if the PDC goes down).

An NT Server PDC can replicate to both NT BDCs and LAN Manager 2.x servers.

Note for NetWare Administrators

Account replication, as discussed in this section, is similar to replicas and partitioning in NetWare Directory Services.

FILE REPLICATION

The NT Server can replicate files to other NT Servers, NT workstations, and LAN Manager 2.x servers. Although LAN Manager 2.x servers can import replicated files, they cannot replicate files to an NT Server.

OTHER NOSs

You can convert WFW and other DOS-based peer-to-peer networks to NT Server in-place. The most direct route is to copy files from other servers to the NT Server(s). Another method is to create a DOS backup from your existing servers and restore the data to your NT Server(s).

As long as you have a good backup, you can proceed by running NT Setup on your main computer. In peer-to-peer networks, workstations usually do double duty as both a server and a client. Most installations use one main computer for centralized, shared data and have their application programs installed separately on each workstation. In the case of DOS-based networks, it is highly recommended that the workstations be upgraded to at least WFW.

To convert an existing peer-to-peer server, install NT Server, upgrade to WFW, and then upgrade WFW to NT Server. Retain your partition as a FAT partition until you have restored your backup and/or all files prove to be stable, then you can convert the partition to NTFS.

After the Setup is finished, you need to create user accounts. You should be able to connect to the NT Server and share the data files in the same way as you did when you were running the peer-to-peer network.

As pointed out in earlier sections, make sure that the application software is compatible with NT Server before going through all the tedious steps involved in migration. Some older, DOS-based programs have to be tweaked to work with peer-to-peer networks; you might need to do the same to get them working with NT Server. Chapter 31, "File System and Disk Subsystem Problems," covers typical file-incompatibility troubleshooting.

MIGRATION FROM MINICOMPUTERS AND UNIX SYSTEMS

IBM, H-P, and Digital minicomputers, as well as other systems running a proprietary operating system, are potential candidates for migration to NT Server. Microsoft, however, does not provide specific migration modules for these as it does for NetWare servers.

These systems can be migrated to NT Server successfully, and NT Server can, in many cases, provide equal or better functionality. If your organization is planning to migrate its current system to NT Server, you need to consider the following:

◆ Availability of Windows applications makes migration attractive. If you can find an application with features similar to or better than the original minicomputer application, a major goal of migration can be accomplished. Windows applications are generally easier to use, have more features, are less expensive, and can be executed on more computers.

In your previous environment, applications that fit your needs more than likely had a smaller user base and were probably character based. Client-server applications written for a proprietary OS are often underpowered compared to Windows GUI-based server applications, which are industrial-strength solutions.

◆ NT's strong Windows-based Network Management tools ease the transition from legacy systems (minicomputers and mainframes). Centralized computing systems routinely handle remote job entry, data entry screens are usually simple, and batch processing is commonly used. In a distributed computing environment, management is a bigger issue. NetWare with WFW left a lot to be desired in terms of performance, integration of the server and clients, and control of the desktop. Managing these facilities on a PC platform has been addressed very well by NT Server.

◆ Application Data Conversion is best outsourced to skilled ISDs (Independent Software Developers). Many network integrators have arsenals of utilities to offload and convert legacy data for migration to NT-based databases. Many application packages ranging from accounting, manufacturing, and distribution are available on the NT platform and integrators can populate the data files from the migrated data.

◆ Phased or incremental migration is possible. You do not have to move everything all at one time. In many cases, you can leave the existing system in place and extract and manipulate legacy data on an NT application server. Thus, NT Server provides added capability without disturbing the existing system.

These servers can be a means of conducting an incremental migration as the organization gradually gets excited about some of the slick new facilities. For example: System 3X, IBM System 36/38, or the even more recent AS/400 computer systems can be migrated by attaching NT Server using the SNA Server. The SNA Server acts as a gateway to an AS/400 or mainframe computer. Files can be transferred back and forth using the EBCDIC-to-ASCII conversion programs included as part of the IBM PC support software that is available on System 38 and AS/400 systems. Third-party vendors such as Wall Data and Attachmate also have software packages that enable interoperation between PCs and IBM minicomputers.

UNIX: Many integrators appreciate the portability, scalability, and compatibility of NT Server enough to want to migrate even UNIX installations to NT Server. The prime candidates are those sites where UNIX servers are already serving Windows clients. Many of these designs are convoluted and difficult to configure and maintain.

NT Server is also a good performer. It often requires far less hardware and a less-expensive (less-proprietary) platform to get the same performance out of NT Server–based applications. In these cases NT Server is a natural solution.

Note

There is a new class of products under development that can help in gradual migration from UNIX to NT Server. WinDD from Textronixs is such a product. You add an NT Server to the UNIX network. The NT Server enables you to run simultaneous sessions of Windows 3.*x* applications. The UNIX machines attach to the NT Server via a proprietary X Window implementation. Although it sounds complex, it is similar to a PC Remote control application because the applications run on the NT Server and the clients receive only screen redraws and keyboard refreshes.

SUMMARY

Microsoft has provided some tools to make migration simpler and more effective. Although there are many advantages and tools for migration, there is no substitute for good planning when migrating to a new platform.

Study your migration plans, test them when possible, and always provide enough time and testing before putting your new system into use. You should never put yourself into a potential position where your system is not available because of the infinite number of problems you might (and probably will) encounter during migration.

- Overview and Notes on Setting Up Clients

- MS-DOS Client Setup

- Windows for Workgroups (WFW) 3.11 Clients

- Windows 95 Clients

- Windows NT Workstation Clients

CHAPTER 8

Connecting the Client

Terminate-stay-resident (TSR)   A DOS program that is executed and remains in memory. Most DOS network drivers, protocols, and client files are loaded as TSRs.

Remote server   A server that is connected to a remote LAN segment.

LAN segment   A separate Ethernet, Token ring, or other type of LAN. LANs can be internetworked with bridges or routers, but an NT Server provides neither of these functions.

Peer-to-peer   Each workstation in a peer-to-peer NOS can share its own drives and printers, as well as access other servers' shared devices.

Internetwork   LAN segments are joined with bridges or routers to form internetworks.

Routing   A process by which network datagram packets (IPX, IP, and so on) are exchanged between logical LANs (see Chapter 4, "Microsoft's Protocol Support").

Bridging   A process by which network frames are filtered and forwarded from one LAN segment to another. When LANs are bridged together, they appear to be a single, logical LAN to routers and routable protocols. Also, a process where LAN frames (Ethernet, Token ring, etc.) are exchanged between (see Chapter 4).

Share   Shared disk drive or directory.

NTFS   NT File System, a type of partition and file system.

HPFS   This abbreviation stands for High Performance File System; it's a type of file system supported on OS/2 (and therefore LAN Manager) operating systems.

After you have accomplished installing an NT Server, your next job is the real killer: connecting your clients. Microsoft is doing everything possible to make your job easy, but many obstacles stand in the way of integrating various client workstations with a server.

Networking with Microsoft operating systems is a very complex operation. Microsoft considers its Setup programs to be user friendly and easy to understand. There are those who would disagree, especially when a driver does not seem to work properly or one of the many potential problems prevents effective sharing and using of resources on the network.

First is the issue of hardware conflicts. If your network adapter's hardware configuration conflicts with other devices in your computer, it will not work. Unfortunately, both hardware devices and software device drivers can conflict with your network adapter.

Statistically, cabling accounts for the vast majority of LAN connectivity problems. Poorly installed or incorrect cabling can either prevent your computers from communicating or, worse yet, can cause intermittent communications problems. See Chapter 25, "LAN Capacity Allocation," and Chapter 30, "LAN Troubleshooting," for details on how to design, monitor, and troubleshoot LAN cabling.

Note

In this book, the term "LAN" refers to an Ethernet, Token ring, or other type of local area network. The term "network" refers to the entire networked system of computers, LANs, WANs, protocols, NOS, and so on.

Fortunately, almost all network adapter vendors provide diagnostic utilities to verify that your network adapter is set up correctly and functioning without problems, and that the cabling is working. The biggest problem with these utilities is that so many people don't use them. When (not if) you encounter problems getting a client and a server to communicate, you most often find that physical connectivity and configuration are the culprits.

Tip

You can save yourself many frustrating hours if you just take a few moments to run your network adapter diagnostic utilities. Don't skip the test where two workstations exchange packets over the cabling, or at least verify minimally functional cabling with a loopback test.

Always make sure to have the latest drivers for your network adapters on hand. Drivers in the box might be months old before you get them. The drivers on your Windows distribution disks might be outdated or might not work as they should. Most network-adapter vendors have online services for downloading the latest drivers on BBSs, CompuServe, and/or the Internet. Read your network adapter instruction manual or call the network adapter manufacturer's technical-support line to gain access to the latest drivers.

For Windows 95 users, if you have problems getting your Windows 95 workstation connected to a server, try accessing your Network Troubleshooter in the Help facility. It asks you several questions and steps you through an excellent network-connectivity troubleshooting script. You can access it from the Help selection when you click your Start button.

8

CONNECTING THE CLIENT

This chapter discusses how to install the drivers for the most common types of clients. Along the way, many of the potential problems you might encounter in getting clients connected to your server are revealed.

OVERVIEW AND NOTES ON SETTING UP CLIENTS

All too many times equipment and software are purchased that do not accomplish what was intended. No network-product vendor warrants its product for fitness for your intended purpose. Resellers, consultants, and distributors are a little more responsible, but holding them accountable for your requirements is still difficult.

Tip

Find and use product-evaluation programs whenever possible. Most network distributors and larger resellers can provide a real-life evaluation unit for you to try out before you buy it. In many cases, you should simply ask for a return allowance along with your purchase if the product does not meet your needs. If you can withhold payment until the product is in and working, that is even better.

CAVEATS AND NETWORKING LIMITATIONS OF MICROSOFT OPERATING SYSTEMS

When you sign a contract, always beware of the fine print—you know, the stuff you won't find out about until a legal issue arises. Networking with NT has some similar fine print about which the marketing people did not tell you. These limitations can become really big problems later when you attempt to manage your installed base of various clients.

So it is with NOS products. You should understand what client limitations apply before you spend too much time setting up and configuring clients that cannot perform the functions you expected. Most major limitations you might encounter are discussed in the following section.

MS-DOS CLIENTS

You might need to set up a workstation as an MS-DOS client in order to install your client operating system. In other cases, you might find it more convenient to run the client installation from a server's shared disk or CD-ROM drive. Both of these procedures first require you to install a DOS client before you can even begin installing Windows for Workgroups (WFW), Windows 95, or NT Workstation.

NT Server has a Setup program so you can install MS-DOS or WFW clients from the server. NT Server also has the Network Client Administrator utility for setting up an MS-DOS boot disk, MS-DOS installation, and WFW installation disks.

The Microsoft MS-DOS client redirector and network adapter drivers take up a lot of RAM, however. Between 120KB to 180KB of conventional memory can be required to get connected to a server. Although much of this overhead can be loaded into Upper Memory Blocks, the size of the Microsoft terminate-stay-resident (TSR) programs seriously limits your ability to perform tasks connected to the network. Add CD-ROM and other drivers to this overhead and you might not even be able to run the WFW Setup utility.

In many cases it is handy for the system administrator to have an MS-DOS client boot disk on hand. For example, when a new computer is added to the network, and its operating system needs to be installed, it is handy to boot the workstation from DOS, run the DOS client redirector, and install from a server.

PEER-TO-PEER SERVICES

WFW, Windows 95, and NT Workstations are designed to be peer-to-peer computers. They can share their storage devices and printers as workgroup computers and can be client domain members, but cannot be domain controllers as NT Servers can. MS-DOS and Windows 3.1 clients cannot share devices, but they can participate as workgroup or domain clients. These are important distinctions to system administrators where multiple server networks are the rule. NT Server is designed to be configured within domains as client/server computers. For a complete discussion of the difference between workgroup and domain network configurations, see Chapter 9, "Workgroups and Domains."

Windows 95 and NT Workstations can participate fully in almost every aspect of peer-to-peer and client-server functionality. An NT Workstation can be a server for up to 10 clients, and can also be a client of other servers.

NT Servers can be used as client workstations, but this is not advised. The use of a server as a workstation is provided as a benefit, but robs a server of vital computing power needed to serve the I/O needs of many users. Using an NT as a client is a real bonus when it comes to accessing local resources, copying disks, or monitoring the network.

Peer-to-peer sharing has many advantages even in a client-server environment. Backups of each hard drive can be accomplished from one or just a few backup devices, and printers all over the network can be used by everyone. System administration is also simplified—you can edit CONFIG.SYS and AUTOEXEC.BAT files from your own workstation, or copy files to and from clients.

8

WORKGROUPS VERSUS DOMAINS

Default installation to a Microsoft network configures all computers and workgroup members—each computer sharing its devices is equal to and separate from all other computers. Domain configuration enables you to group servers together and manage user accounts that are domain-wide, and not specific to a server. This type of configuration solves administrative problems when users require access to more than one server.

MS-DOS and Windows 3.1 have very few network configuration options, and were designed to be workgroup clients. However, an NT Server can include these workstations as clients in their domains for the purposes of managing the groups to which they belong and granting access to resources.

WFW, Windows 95, and Windows NT workstations can become client members of domains. WFW has utilities that enable the client to select a logon domain. Windows 95 and NT Workstation add a few more network options. Although MS-DOS and Windows 3.1 clients can be domain members, they do not have utilities to properly manage domain membership. All Windows computers can be granted permissions and rights and be managed through group memberships.

Windows 95 and NT Workstations can be full-fledged members of domains; however, they cannot become either Primary or Secondary Domain Controllers (PDC/BDC)—only NT Servers can. This has significance in the fault tolerance of a client-server network. When a PDC goes down, a BDC keeps the rest of the network functional, and can even be configured as a PDC. Without this replication, the value of a client/server network would be sadly lacking.

REACHABILITY OVER REMOTE LAN SEGMENTS

A server that is connected to a remote LAN segment is called a *remote server*. When a server is located on a remote LAN segment from a client, that client is unable to connect to the remote server's shares or printer. In many cases, the client can see remote servers, shares, and printers in File Manager, Print Manager, Windows 95's Network Neighborhood, or elsewhere, but cannot access their server functions.

Note

In this book, the term LAN refers to an Ethernet, Token ring, or other type of local area network; it is not used synonymously with the term network. An NT Server can contain up to 16 network cards. This allows separate LANs to be interfaced to a single NT Server.

A remote LAN segment is a LAN that is separated from a local computer. Although multiple LANs might be interfaced to a single server, there is nothing in NT Server 3.51 as it is shipped to provide access from one LAN segment to the next. NetWare and most UNIX servers include an internal router that can provide internetwork communications, but NT lacks this service at this time. Microsoft has vowed to provide this service in a multi-protocol router add-on for NT Server in the near future. Check Microsoft's CompuServe forums or their FTP or Gopher servers on the Internet for the latest on this issue.

Figure 8.1 shows how computers become isolated when interfaced through an NT Server. In this figure, Main Server has two network cards, and therefore two LAN segments connected to it. Clients on both LAN Segment A and LAN Segment B can communicate directly with Main Server. Server B is located on LAN Segment A, and therefore can communicate directly with Client Fred. However, because Client George is located on LAN Segment B, and Server B is located on LAN Segment A, communications from Client George will not reach Server B because it is on a remote LAN Segment.

Figure 8.1.
Remote LAN Segment
limitations.

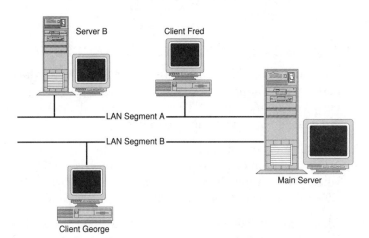

NT Servers can provide information about remote services because the information is stored in their Security Account Manager databases. For example, a Windows 95 or WFW client can see other clients in a domain or workgroup serviced in common by an NT Server (as Main Server is in Figure 8.1), but cannot access their resources if they are remotely located on a separate LAN segment.

A bridge or switched hub between network segments can resolve this problem; however, the full functionality of a router is not included in NT Server as it is in NetWare or many UNIX versions. So don't expect the same internetwork configuration to work in an NT Server–based network that will work for a NetWare- or TCP/IP-based network with routers.

Protocols are an integral part of internetworking. If routers connect LANs, only IPX/SPX and TCP/IP traffic is allowed to pass. NetBEUI and NetBIOS protocols are not routable, and because there is no internal router in an NT server, even the use of IPX/SPX or TCP/IP protocols does not accomplish internetworking.

Note

If you do use routers in your internetwork, make sure to turn on NetBIOS broadcasts. All Microsoft network computers, including NT Server and NT Workstation, use NetBIOS to advertise their network shared resources, regardless of which protocol option you have selected.

Most routers suppress NetBIOS broadcasts because they tend to cause "broadcast storms" on limited-capacity WANs in larger internetworks. However, if the NetBIOS broadcasts are not propagated over routers, computers on remote LAN segments will not be able to locate network resources even if routable protocols and routers are used.

FILENAME AND FILE SYSTEM ACCESS TO NTFS AND HPFS

NT Servers and NT Workstations can have NTFS partitions that provide better performance, support RAID configurations, and provide native long-filename support. You should select NTFS to provide the best file-system performance with the greatest file-storage density possible.

A few limitations do apply to an NTFS partition. All clients can access a server's NTFS partition over the network or from a local DOS session under NT. However, when you boot an NT Server or Workstation with DOS, you cannot access a local NTFS file system from the DOS operating system's command line.

Clients can utilize long filenames (up to 255 characters) on an NTFS server partition if their workstation operating system and software allow it. Windows 95 and NT clients can use long filenames on NTFS volumes without restrictions. MS-DOS clients see the same files with limited DOS filenames according to the conventions implemented in NT and Windows 95. Although a Windows 95 modified FAT partition can provide long-filename support, it is somewhat limited when compared against NTFS, and NTFS provides better performance.

Some of the security features in NT that enable access to files and directories (permissions) are only available in an NTFS partition. Log files showing updates to files can only be initialized on NTFS partitions.

NTFS uses a 512-byte block allocation unit for greater storage density. Extensive file and block indexing helps make up for the performance downside of using a small block allocation unit. This is a powerful incentive for switching to NTFS, especially on an NT Server.

NT drives can be partitioned into HPFS volumes for backward compatibility with OS/2 and LAN Manager computers. A server with an HPFS can be booted into OS/2 or NT, and can store and retrieve files on an HPFS partition.

THE NETWORK CLIENT ADMINISTRATOR UTILITY

The Network Client Administrator utility, located in the Network Administration program group, is designed to help system administrators set up new clients. The opening screen is shown in Figure 8.2.

Figure 8.2.
The Network Client
Administrator utility.

Setting up DOS, WFW, and OS/2 clients is simple with the help of this utility. It enables you to do the following:

◆ Create a bootable DOS client for a Microsoft network disk

◆ Install the DOS client software on your local hard drive

◆ Create a set of DOS clients for Microsoft network installation disks

◆ Create a set WFW installation disks

◆ Create and share a directory on your server from which WFW, DOS, and OS/2 clients can be installed

◆ Designate and share the CD-ROM's client-install directory

◆ Copy network administrative utilities to workstations

◆ View information about how to install diskless workstations

Note

Windows 95 and NT workstation clients must be installed from their original program CD-ROM or floppy disks.

CREATING AN MS-DOS CLIENT BOOTABLE DISK

You can use your Network Client Administrator to create a bootable DOS client disk that can be used to boot a workstation and connect it to a server. When this is done, you can continue your installation from the server or you can use this disk to provide access to the server.

To make a disk, select the Make Network Installation Startup Disk option in the screen shown in Figure 8.2.

You then see the Share Network Client Installation Files dialog box shown in Figure 8.3. This dialog box is used for two purposes: to designate the source installation files and to copy the files to the server drive, possibly creating a share for future installations without using the CD-ROM.

The original source directory is on your NT Server installation CD-ROM in the \CLIENTS directory. If you are installing from the CD-ROM, select the Use Existing Path option and fill in the Path field with your CD-ROM's pathname (for example, D:\CLIENTS).

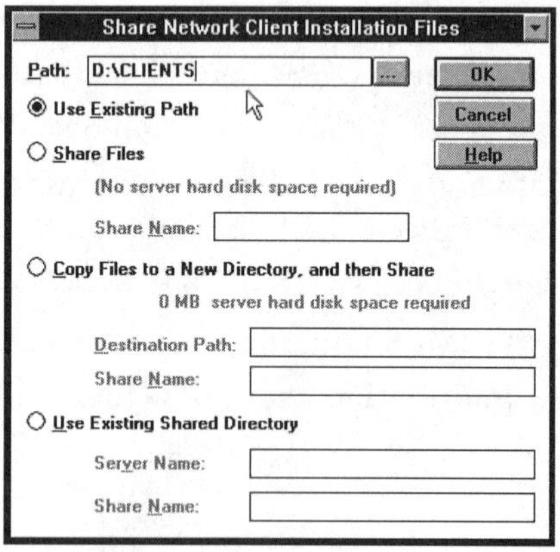

Figure 8.3.
The Share Network Client Installation Files dialog box.

If the \CLIENTS directory has been run previously and the files have already been installed, you can choose the Use Existing Shared Directory option to designate an existing directory as the source from which to draw the installation files.

Make sure that all other option radio buttons that do not apply are cleared. The following options are used as indicated below:

Share Files: This option creates a share as the future source directory.

Copy Files to New Directory and then Share: This option both copies the source files to a destination directory to be used as the source directory in future client installs and creates a share for future access.

Use Existing Shared Directory: By choosing this option you can create your client boot disk or installation disks from a share that already contains the source files.

After you have selected the appropriate selections, select OK.

In the the Target Workstation Configuration screen, shown in Figure 8.4, select Network Client v3.0 for MS-DOS and Windows. Then select the network adapter (network card) from the list.

Figure 8.4.
The Target Workstation
Configuration dialog
box.

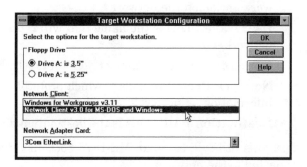

Note

If your network adapter is not listed, you cannot make a boot disk from this utility.

You might find that drivers selected from this list do not work with your network adapter even though the description seems to fit. This utility does not enable you to select a vendor-supplied driver from a floppy disk.

In those cases, you need to make an installation disk set from which to install your workstation.

When you click OK, the utility proceeds to the Network Startup Disk Configuration screen shown in Figure 8.5.

Figure 8.5.
The Network Startup
Disk Configuration
screen.

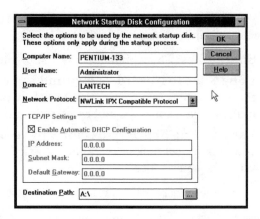

Fill in the name fields for this workstation. The fields shown in Figure 8.5 are

Computer Name: This is the name that will be used to represent the workstation on the network.

User Name: This is the name that will represent the user account on the network.

Domain: The server name or domain to which this user will logon.

Network Protocol: Selects which protocol stack to be used. (For more information on protocols, see Chapter 4.)

Destination Path: This is the destination disk for the installation files.

Next, this utility creates an MS-DOS boot disk with the files needed to get you connected to the network.

MAKE INSTALLATION DISK SETS FOR DOS, WFW, AND LAN MANAGER CLIENTS

You can use your Network Client Administrator to create a set of installation disks for all of the client types shown in Figure 8.6.

Figure 8.6.
The Make Installation
Disk Set screen.

To arrive at this screen, select Make Installation Disk Set from the Network Client Administrator main menu. Then fill in the Share Network Client Installation Files screen, shown in Figure 8.3, to indicate the source directory.

Your installation disk set will contain the Setup program you can run to install your client workstations.

MS-DOS CLIENT SETUP

To install a DOS client from the installation disks created in the previous section, run SETUP from disk #1.

In SETUP you designate the drive and directory to which you want to install your network files. The default directory is C:\MSCLIENT, as shown in Figure 8.7.

Figure 8.7.
The Setup for Microsoft Network Client v3.0 for MS-DOS screen.

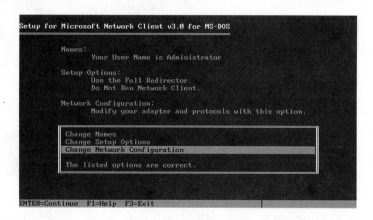

Select each option to be certain you know what Setup will do. The selections are very straightforward and understandable. Press F1 for context-sensitive help.

Select the first option to configure names for your workstation, user account, and workgroup or domain to which you wish to log on.

Select the second option to configure the Setup options.

Select the third option to configure your network adapter driver and protocol options.

Figure 8.8 shows part of the list of network adapter drivers provided with the NT 3.51 CD-ROM. Figure 8.9 shows the menu selection to edit the network adapter configuration. Be sure to select each of these options to at least view the selections.

Figure 8.8.
List of network adapter
drivers.

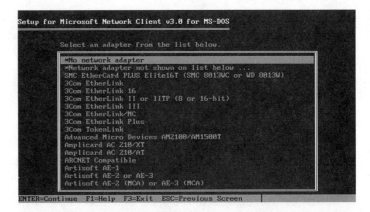

Figure 8.9.
Editing network
settings.

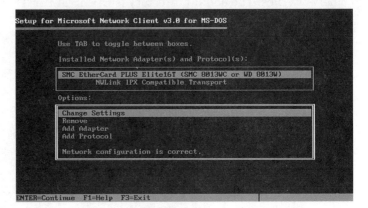

Pay particular attention to your network driver and its settings. If the resulting client software does not connect you to a server and your cabling and network adapter are working, chances are the driver is to blame. When drivers do not work, your drivers might load and your requester might start without errors, but you might not connect to a share.

Setup edits your CONFIG.SYS. When using NWLink, SETUP adds the following lines:

```
Lastdrive=Z
Device=c:\msclient\ifshlp.sys
```

Setup adds a few lines to the end of your AUTOEXEC.BAT. The following is an example used with the IPX/SPX protocol:

```
c:\msclient\net ititialize
c:\msclient\nwlink
c:\msclient\net start
```

Windows for Workgroups (WFW) 3.11 Clients

The major difference between Windows 3.1 and WFW 3.11 is networking. WFW includes peer-to-peer components, a new Network Setup icon, and a few applications for workgroup interaction. WFW's Setup program refined some of Windows 3.1's missing ingredients. It was a significant step toward integrating networking at a level close to the client operating system.

During Setup, or afterward, you encounter the Network Setup utility as shown in Figure 8.10. You can access the Network Setup icon through the Main program group by choosing Windows Setup, Options, and then Change Network Settings.

Note

If network support was not selected during installation, the Network program group is not included in your desktop and can be accessed as described above. After you add network support after installation as discussed in this section, the network program group is added to your desktop.

Figure 8.10.
The Network Setup
screen.

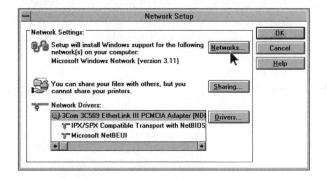

You work with this same screen during Setup, or afterward. It does not matter if you install network components during Setup or afterward; Setup doesn't take any additional steps automatically. The options you must select and configure are as follows:

Networks: This option is used to install client support for various NOSs. You must select Install Microsoft Windows Network to connect to an NT Server or any other Windows network servers. (See Figure 8.11.)

8

Note

To change your logon settings after you have completed your setup, select the Microsoft Windows Network icon in Control Panel. There are more options you can set in that utility. This icon is not present until a network has been set up.

Figure 8.11.
The Networks screen
for selecting client
support.

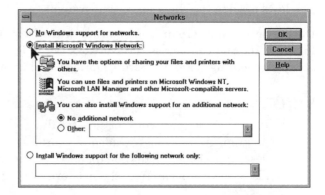

Sharing: Select which peer services you would like to offer in addition to being a client. You can share your local disks and storage devices as a server, and you can share locally attached printer(s) as network printer(s). If you select no boxes, you will be a client but will not be a server. (See Figure 8.12.)

Figure 8.12.
The Sharing screen.

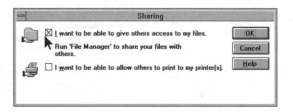

Network Drivers: Select Add Adapter and search the listing shown in Figure 8.14 for the driver that matches your adapter. If your network adapter is not listed, or if you have a later driver from your network adapter vendor, select Unlisted or Updated Network Adapter. When you select this option, you will be prompted to insert a disk with your network adapter driver in drive A:.

Figure 8.13.
The Network Drivers
screen.

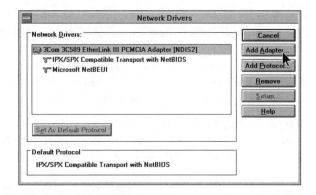

Figure 8.14.
The Add Network
Adapter screen.

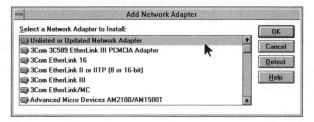

You can select the Detect option if you are adventurous. Quite often, the Detect option will cause your system to lock up. If this occurs, you will need to reboot, and select the driver instead of Detect.

Note

You should always obtain the latest driver from your vendor. Network adapter vendors generally have driver download support available on a BBS, on a CompuServe forum, or on an FTP server on the Internet. Check with your network adapter vendor's technical support for the latest driver files.

Note

In order for your driver file to be read, you must specify the disk and directory where the driver is found. This directory must have an NDIS 2 driver, an OEMSETUP.INF file, and the driver file which has a .SYS extension. Many vendors provide a disk with client and server drivers for several NOSs. You will find the driver in a directory shown for NDIS, WFW, or NDIS2. NDIS 3 drivers are used for NT and may not be used with WFW.

8

After you have selected your driver and selected OK, select OK from the Network Drivers screen shown previously in Figure 8.13. Your network adapter driver software will provide selection options that must correspond to your network adapter's hardware settings. If you have a software-configurable network adapter, generally only the port (base I/O) address is required, but this depends on your network adapter driver, and selections differ for different vendors' drivers.

Depending on your Sharing support, your driver will probably select both Microsoft NetBEUI and IPX/SPX Compatible Transport with NetBIOS. You can add support for various options shown in Figure 8.15.

Figure 8.15.
The Add Network
Protocol screen.

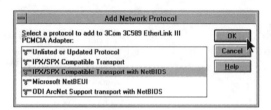

The options available are:

IPX/SPX Compatible Transport: This option selects the Microsoft IPX compatible driver (NWLink) to be used with NDIS drivers. This option does not include NetBIOS support which is required if you have configured the Network option to support sharing of storage devices or printers. IPX support is required for NetWare support.

IPX/SPX Compatible Transport with NetBIOS: Same as above with support for Microsoft peer-to-peer services or other products that require NetBIOS support.

Microsoft NetBEUI: This protocol is the only protocol required when you have an all-Microsoft network (access to NetWare servers or services is not required).

ODI ArcNet Support with NetBIOS: This option is selected only for NDIS 2 ArcNet drivers.

Note for NetWare Administrators

To support simultaneous access to Microsoft and NetWare networks, you can either select an NDIS driver with IPX/SPX Compatible Transport (NWLink), or you can use your NetWare ODI drivers. If you use the latter option, you must select the appropriate IPXODI Support Driver from the Add Adapter screen instead of selecting a listed (NDIS) driver.

If you use the Microsoft client for NetWare, you cannot access NetWare 4 in the NDS mode. To enable this option, you must obtain the NetWare Client Requester for NT from Novell (available on Novell's CompuServe forum, their FTP server on the Internet, or from the NetWare Support Encyclopedia Professional Version CD-ROM. If you use this product, you also need to install Novell's ODI drivers instead of Microsoft's NDIS drivers (included in the kit).

Once you have finalized your selections and selected OK, you need to reboot your computer and restart WFW before the changes can be effective. For more information and clarification on protocol support, see Chapter 4.

Note

WFW does not include native support for TCP/IP like NT Server and Workstation does. You may purchase a third-party Windows TCP/IP software to add TCP/IP support.

Setup will edit your CONFIG.SYS. Depending on the protocol options, Setup adds lines to your CONFIG.SYS. The following lines were added where NDIS drivers are loaded:

```
Lastdrive=Z
Device=c:\msclient\ifshlp.sys
```

Setup adds a few lines to the end of your AUTOEXEC.BAT. The following is an example used with the IPX/SPX protocol:

```
c:\msclient\net start
```

This line must come before Windows is loaded.

WINDOWS 95 CLIENTS

Windows 95 replaces WFW, and has many added network configuration options. Windows 95 was designed to be a good peer-to-peer operating system but also to be a good NT Server client and member of a domain. This is why Windows 95 and NT Workstation are the preferred client operating systems in an NT Server–based network.

To configure your network options, you work with the Network utility shown in Figure 8.16, found in Control Panel, or presented to you during Setup.

Figure 8.16.
The Network utility in
Windows 95.

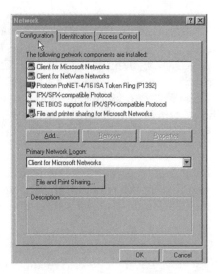

Note

If Windows 95 was installed before network support was added, you need to access the Add/Remove Programs Properties utility in Control Panel (accessible from the Start button menu, Settings, or from your desktop's My Computer icon). Select Windows Setup from the tabs at the top of the screen, then select Microsoft Network from the list. You must have your Windows 95 installation disks or CD-ROM available so the appropriate files can be installed. All appropriate icons and options will be installed automatically.

Tip

Windows 95 provides support for Plug and Play (PNP). If your network adapter supports PNP, it is physically configured during setup, and you can simply select your network adapter driver from a list in the Network utility.

If you have not purchased a network adapter yet, and you plan to use Windows 95, look for a major brand network adapter with PNP. You will find that physical installation and Windows 95 Setup smoother and more efficiently. Physical configuration difficulties account for the vast majority of problems users have in installing network services.

SETTING UP NETWORK SERVICES

Notice at the top of the Network utility screen shown in Figure 8.16 there are three file folder tabs for the following three functions:

Configuration: This option allows you to select a driver or protocol option, then configure it.

Identification: This is used to configure your Microsoft client software name and logon options.

Access Control: If you share drives and/or printers, this option allows new options to enable password control of access to your shared devices or user-level access to allow access based on user groups.

Select Configuration from the Network utility main screen, then Add, then Adapter as shown in Figure 8.17. You then see the Select Network adapters screen shown in Figure 8.18.

Figure 8.17.
The Select Network
Component Type
screen.

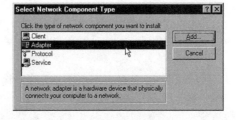

Figure 8.18.
The Select Network
adapters screen.

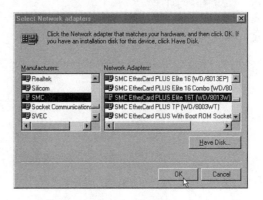

Select an adapter, then select OK. If you are upgrading from a previous Windows version, or if you already have NetWare ODI drivers installed, you can select one of the two options on the right side of the screen. To add a new driver, select from the list on the left side of the screen, and to select a driver from a floppy disk, select Have Disk in the lower right area of the screen.

Note

Windows 95 can use 16-bit NDIS 2 (real mode) drivers that are used with WFW, but it is best to obtain newer 32-bit drivers written for Windows 95. Contact your network adapter vendor's technical support line, BBS, CompuServe forum, or FTP server on the Internet for updated drivers.

When you select the driver and select OK, this utility adds the driver with default configuration for the driver hardware settings and protocol options. You are returned to the Network utility main screen.

Note

At this point, you must select the adapter and edit its properties to be certain that all options have been configured properly.

Click on your adapter driver listed on the Network utility main screen as shown previously in Figure 8.16, then select the Properties button. You can edit the following options:

◆ **Driver Type**: Select from the following options as shown in Figure 8.19.

Figure 8.19.
The Driver Type screen.

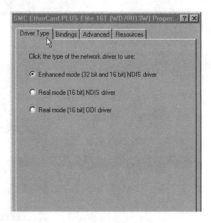

Enhanced mode (32-bit and 16-bit) NDIS driver for drivers (written for Windows 95)

Real Mode (16-bit) NDIS drivers

Real Mode (16-bit) ODI drivers

◆ **Bindings**: Edit the protocol options associated with your adapter driver as shown in Figure 8.20.

Note

There have been many technical problems with new NDIS 32-bit drivers. If you cannot get connected after you finish setting up and reboot, try switching to a Real Mode driver. These drivers do not perform as well, but are more stable.

Figure 8.20.
The Bindings screen.

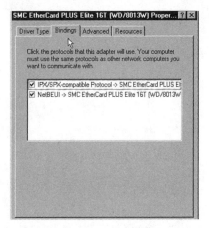

To delete an unneeded protocol, click on the corresponding option box and clear the checkmark. To add another protocol return to the main Network utility screen as shown previously in Figure 8.16, select Add, click on Protocol, then Add. You can then select the protocol support you would like to bind to this adapter driver.

Note

You can add support for TCP/IP (an option not included in WFW) by selecting Microsoft from the list of protocols. You can also select native support for NFS-Unix systems, and several other vendor protocol options that haven't been available in Windows products before. Check out the options in the Select Network Protocol screen to see your selections. See the WFW Setup section above in this chapter for more detail, and refer to Chapter 4. You can also select Have Disk if you have protocol-support from a third-party protocol-support vendor (such as a TCP/IP product other than Microsoft's).

◆ **Advanced**: Modify any advanced configuration options from your network adapter vendor as shown in Figure 8.21.

Figure 8.21.
Advanced network
adapter configurations
options.

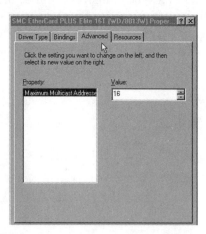

Note

The options shown in this screen are specific to your network adapter driver; there are no standard options specified by the network adapter driver developer. The values you see are default values that should be left alone unless your network adapter is configured differently from its default. Do not change these options unless you are certain you should. Read your network adapter installation guide or contact your network adapter vendor's technical support line if you are uncertain.

◆ **Resources**: Select the physical hardware configuration settings for your network adapter as shown in Figure 8.22. These options vary from vendor to vendor and model to model as they are functions of the network adapter driver. Select OK to save your configuration and return to the Network utilities main screen.

Select your Primary Network Logon options from the Network utilities main screen as shown in Figure 8.23. The options available will vary depending on which network client support options have been selected.

Select the File and Print Sharing button in the lower part of the Network utilities main screen, then select whether you would like to share local storage devices, and/or share locally attached printers as network printers, as shown in Figure 8.24.

Figure 8.22.
Resource settings
options.

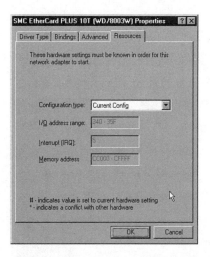

Tip

Selections in this screen must correspond with the settings you have physically configured to your network adapter. You must have resolved any conflicts with other devices, and you should have run your network adapter diagnostics program to made certain that your network adapter and cabling are working properly. Changing options in this screen does not reconfigure your network adapter; you must either run a network adapter setup utility or physically change the switch and jumper settings to physically reconfigure your network adapter.

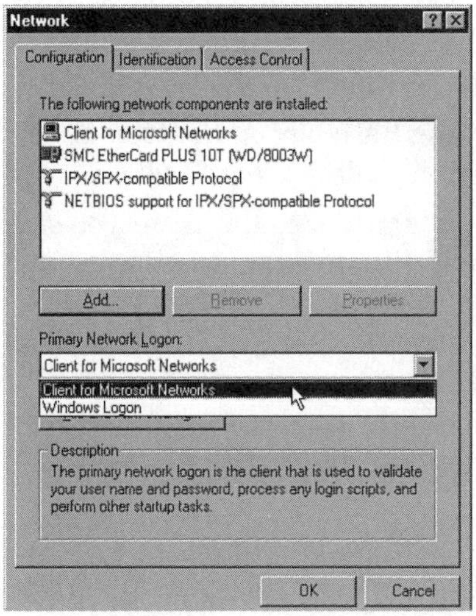

Figure 8.23.
The Network utility
main screen, selecting
Primary Network
Logon options.

Figure 8.24.
Selecting File and Print
Sharing options.

You have now completed setting up and configuring your network options. Once you select OK from the Network utilities main menu, you will need to reboot your computer for the changes to take effect.

MAPPING A DRIVE LETTER TO A SHARE

After you have successfully connected to an NT Server, you must establish your network connections. When you establish your network connections, you can check a configuration box that configures Windows 95 to automatically restore connections during Windows loading.

To connect to a Share on the network (now called a *Mapping* in Windows 95):

1. Use the Network Neighborhood utility to search for the Share you wish to map to.

2. Select the Path box on the toolbar as shown in Figure 8.25. If the toolbar is not visible, select View, Toolbar.

3. Click the Path box, and then type or select the path to the resource as shown in Figure 8.26. A password may be required for access to the resource.

Figure 8.25.
The Network Neighbor-
hood Search screen.

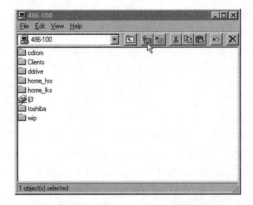

Figure 8.26.
Selecting the Network
Share and assigning a
drive mapping.

CAPTURING A PRINTER

Windows 95 now uses the term *capture* to refer to redirecting print output to a network printer. After you have installed your server and client, you can gain access to network printers through Printer in Control Panel (accessible from My Computer or Settings on the Start button menu).

Simply Add Printer, and a Wizard walks you through steps making it simple to browse your network neighborhood and to capture your printer.

More discussion of creating Shares and network printers is discussed in Part Three of this book, "System Administration."

TROUBLESHOOTING TIPS

1. If your system locks up during reboot do not warm boot (Ctl+Alt+Del); cold boot (turn off, then turn on or reset) your system. A defective or improperly configured adapter or adapter driver can sometimes cause this problem. If given an option, select Safe Restart during boot to get Windows 95 running again. This prevents drivers from loading and therefore usually prevents lock up. Once Windows 95 is up, select the Network utility from Control Panel to reconfigure the suspected component driver.

8

2. If Windows 95 runs, but you do not have connection to network services, attempt to determine whether the network adapter is physically working, or if your software setup is not correct. First check your network adapter diagnostics to make certain that the network adapter is working without conflicts. If such a test is available, run a test between two network adapters to see if the cabling is good. If the LAN checks out okay, check your adapter configuraton options in the Network utility. If those settings are correct, check the protocol options, then the Workgroup or Domain settings.

3. First attempt to get connected with an existing server you know is working before troubleshooting other connections. If you cannot connect, attempt to connect two Windows 95 and/or WFW computers set up to share their devices. If you can get two peer-to-peer computers connected, resolve Workgroup or Domain problems, or Group rights and permissions, to get clients connected.

4. Verify that you have selected the appropriate Identification options in the Network utilities main screen. You must enter the appropriate Workgroup or Domain in order to log on to an existing NT Server.

5. Run the Network Troubleshooter (new with Windows 95) from Help on your Start button's main menu (lower left-hand corner of your screen at all times). This script asks you questions, selecting additional questions based on your answers. It is an excellent guide for finding and resolving most network problems.

WINDOWS NT WORKSTATION CLIENTS

Installing an NT Workstation client is the same as installing a server. See Chapter 6, "Installing and Configuring the NT Server OS."

SUMMARY

An NT Server-based network has far more complexity than other networks. Windows NT Workstation, Windows 95, and WFW 3.11 clients are recommended good network neighbors; however, it looks like Windows 95 has the most features, support, and control of any client. NT Workstation has the added ability to be included as a server member of an NT domain, and WFW has adequate but aging networking configuration options. Windows 3.1 and MS-DOS clients can connect to an NT Server but lack many network configuration options.

You can install a network during Setup of any Windows product, but adding network support after installation is simple with any Windows product.

If you have a problem getting connected to a server after setting up your network options, the problem is most likely a physical network adapter configuration problem, cabling, or network software setup in that order. You should always run the network adapter diagnostics program and test your LAN to make sure the physical layer components are connected before chasing other potential problems. Windows 95 has a Network Troubleshooter help script that can walk you through a hierarchical question tree for helping you determine where the problem lies.

This chapter concludes the section on Installing and Configuring the NOS. Once your server has been installed as discussed in Chapter 5, "Selecting a LAN," and clients are connected, you are ready to set up your system administration.

8

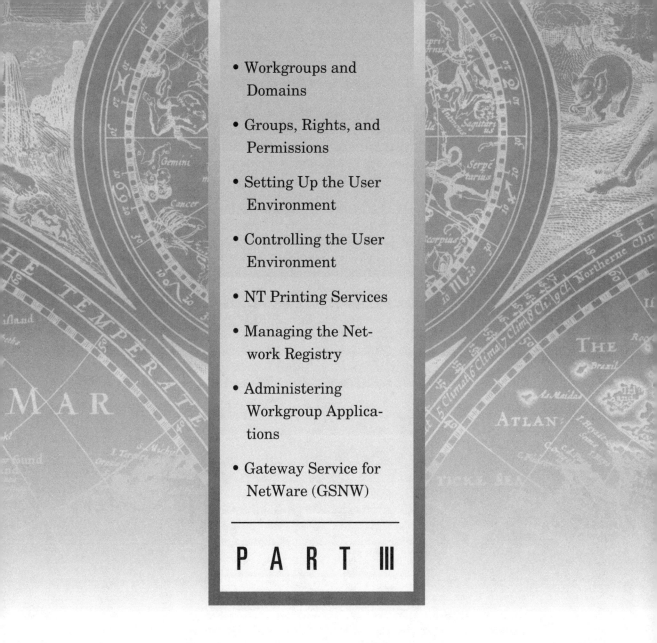

- Workgroups and Domains

- Groups, Rights, and Permissions

- Setting Up the User Environment

- Controlling the User Environment

- NT Printing Services

- Managing the Network Registry

- Administering Workgroup Applications

- Gateway Service for NetWare (GSNW)

PART III

System Administration

- Workgroups versus Domains

- Trust Relationships

- Domain Replication: PDCs and BDCs

- Optimizing Domain Synchronization

- Directory Replication

- Reconfiguring Domains

- Application Servers

- Domain Behavior, Example: Setting Time

- Browser

- Account Authentication

CHAPTER 9

Workgroups and Domains

LSA   Local Security Authority

RPC   Remote Procedure Calls

ACL   Access Control Lists

SNA   IBM's System Network Architecture

IPC$ Interprocess Control resource

RSA   RSA company encryption algorithm

SAM   Security Accounts Manager

UAS   LAN Manager User Account System

PORTUAS   A LAN Manager to NT account conversion utility

WINS   Windows Internet Name Service

LMHOSTS   IP Addresses versus computer names cross-reference file

Domains   A grouping of file servers, computers, and user accounts

security account database   The database containing user and resource account information used to control logons and resource access. In NT, this is the SAM.

trust relationship   A relationship between domains where one domain is accessible from another domain

resources   Printers, disks, and any other physical devices that are shared on the network

resource domain   The domain in which a resource is physically located

user domain   The domain in which the user is defined

local domain   The domain local to a resource or user

foreign domain   A domain other than the user's local domain

Universal Naming Convention (UNC)   The name and path assigned to a resource includes the server to which it belongs

WFW, Windows 95, and NT Workstations configured in a peer-to-peer arrangement are effectively managed in small workgroups with very little complexity. Though clients are subsidiary to servers in a workgroup environment, the servers are all peers.

However, NT Server's domain options provide another level of managing servers, user groupings, and interdomain access. Domains are the preferred strategy in managing an NT Server–based network even when only one or a few servers are present.

Note

Under virtually all circumstances, NT Server–based networks should be configured into domains instead of workgroups. The main reason for this recommendation is that the tools included in NT Server are designed for domain administration. Everywhere you look, the concept of domains is pervasive. If you try to use a workgroup instead of domains, you will be fighting this design strategy.

Warning

During Setup, configure your server as a domain member. One of the crazy things about NT is that during Setup, Workgroup is the default configuration. Once you have installed your server as a workgroup server, reconfiguration as a domain server may require reinstalling NT Server.

WORKGROUPS VERSUS DOMAINS

A workgroup is a group of peers in which access among computers is enabled, but no client/server strategy is defined—users are free to access other users' resources and vice versa with few restrictions. Workgroups are appropriate in small peer-to-peer networks where little or no centralized control of network administration is necessary, and access to resources within the workgroup should be widely available. The only existing controls include logon security to the workgroup, and/or access permission to the shared resource existing within the workgroup.

There are only advantages of a domain-based network configuration—there are no downsides. It is simply a better way to manage a network. Domains simply have more tools if you choose to use them. Workgroup configuration is an outdated configuration that has been around since 1983. Domain tools and features have evolved over years with LAN Manager, and more options have been added with NT Server.

In a client/server network, many of the domain tools help administrators with growth problems. In a large organization, domain management is a tool to centralize user access and administration into several smaller departmental or divisional units. Even in the smallest network there are some additional benefits, but at the very least a domain is equivalent to a workgroup. Managing a domain is no more difficult than managing a workgroup. There is no reason not to use domain management.

In larger client/server networks, servers are not peers of clients, they are special computers that are the repositories for data, applications, and centralized control of the network. In larger networks where more than one server exists, a method of organizing and dividing users and resources is needed. Servers are grouped into domains, which generally equate to a department, division, or some other separate portion of the organization.

Domains can be applied in a similar manner as workgroups, but additionally can control access to resources in and outside the local (working) domain. This distinction provides more flexibility, and more bulk administrative privileges where access between domains is necessary.

LOCAL VERSUS DOMAIN LOGON

WFW, Windows 95, and Windows NT Workstation computers simply appear on the network as peer servers. The logon is to the local server. When you run Setup for WFW, Windows 95, or NT Workstation, the user account is created locally on the computer you are installing—the user account and the computer are the same entity included in the workgroup. No user account is created in a centralized database as it is in NT Server.

You can define user accounts in an NT Server or NT Workstation used as a server. Permission to log on to the domain can therefore be controlled by the NT Server's Security Account Manager (SAM) database. This database is a centralized repository for user account information, group memberships, and object information controlling the user that is defined within the domain, as opposed to within a computer.

Multiple domains can represent multiple departments. In most cases resources and users reside within the same domain; however, NT's domain model allows controlled access to resources outside of a domain where necessary.

When access outside of a domain is required, domains become containers for resources and users: users in one domain access resources in another. Throughout this chapter you will see domains referred to as the *resource domain* or the *user domain* where users seek to access resources that are external to their own domain. Another way of referring to these entities is the *local domain* and the *foreign domain*.

LOGON SECURITY

In NT, a user account can be created by the administrator or a member of the administrator group with User Manager for Domains (or User Manager in NT Workstation). When the user account is created in User Manager, NT assigns a Security Identification (SID). The SID is the primary reference for the user object. The user name is simply one of the many values that are associated with the user account. Other values include the account password, group memberships, and initialization information including home directory and logon script.

When the user account is created, the SID and other values are placed into SAM, which resides in one or more domain controllers in the default domain. NT Workstation servers each have resident SAMs.

In an NT workgroup environment, the user logs on to a server and is aware of all servers on the network that are defined within the same workgroup. In this respect, workgroups and domains without trusts work the same way: a user logs on to a workgroup or onto a domain.

When the user logs on to a workgroup, each server responds to the logon by reporting its presence. When a server isn't up, persistent connections fail during Windows loading. Missing servers' resources do not appear in File Manager's Disk, Connect Network Drive... screen.

When a user logs on to a domain, however, the Primary or Backup Domain Controller authenticates the logon against the information stored in its master database (SAM). Upon logon, the Domain Controller provides a list of all servers in the domain whether they happen to be up at that moment or not. Regardless of whether the servers are up, it looks like they are until a user attempts to access a missing resource. At that point, a dialog box will inform the user that the server is not currently available.

In a workgroup environment, you should be aware that user accounts, logons, and resource connections are controlled locally from your computer. In WFW this information is stored in the COMPUTER.PWL file. In NT Workstations, the information is stored in the local SAM database. However, in domains, all user account, logon, and connection information is stored in the PDC's SAM database. Therefore, the logon is to a domain, and is controlled outside of your workstation.

In a workgroup environment, or in a domain environment lacking trust relationships, logon provides access only to servers within the domain or workgroup. As far as the client is concerned, either configuration has the same effect. However, the difference becomes meaningful when multiple domains exist, and trust relation-ships are established between those domains. The key difference is in the fact that in a domain the client is accessing resources that need not be tied to any specific peer workstation. In effect, domains help to make the resources more abstract.

UNIVERSAL NAMING CONVENTION (UNC)

The name and path assigned to a resource includes the server to which it belongs. When identifying any resource in any Microsoft network, you must use the UNC name. It is expressed as follows:

```
\\<SERVER>\<RESOURCE>
```

The server name is represented by <SERVER>, and is always preceded by a double backslash (\\). The Share name of the resource follows the server name with a single backslash delimiter.

ACCESS PERMISSIONS

Before a user can access a resource, it must be shared by the server in which it exists. Directories and printers on each server must be configured as Shares in File Manager and Print Manager respectively. At the time the Share is created on an NT Server or Workstation, the administrator selects the following permissions for all who access the Share:

> No access
> Full control
> Read
> Change

WFW and Windows 95 computers only allow

> Read-only
> Full
> Depends on password

Even though the user logs on to the domain that includes the resources, access to the resources is blocked by the access permissions. These permissions are absolute—user rights do not override them. Only the administrator or members of the administrator group can override local access permissions. For more information on permissions, see "Permissions On Shared NTFS Directories" later in this chapter, or see Chapter 10, "Groups, Rights, and Permissions."

Note for NetWare Administrators

NT's Share permissions are very similar to the Rights Mask in NetWare.

THE CONCEPT OF DOMAINS

A domain, simply stated, is a group of servers that is controlled by a Primary Domain Controller to behave as a single combined unit. It is important to understand this concept, or you will become very frustrated trying to manage your system. Domain users log on to a domain, not to a server. Administrators log on to a domain, and therefore manage resources and users within the domain. This simple understanding can alleviate the confusion most people experience when working with NT networks.

In an NT Server or NT Workstation, the user account is defined within the security account database (the SAM). A duplicate copy of the SAM is contained in all Domain Controllers within a domain. User-account logon and access is controlled by either a Primary or Secondary Domain Controller, whichever is more convenient.

Resources, however, are contained within servers, and user access to those servers and resources can still be controlled locally by the server, even though logon security controls primary access over the network. As with previous Windows versions, when the Share is created, the access permissions can be assigned and become the absolute mask.

Note for NetWare Administrators

Domain design is similar to the NetWare Directory Service (NDS) design in NetWare 4. However, NDS is more flexible and more complex.

NT's domains use trust relationships to handle the complexities of multiple levels. Even large organizations can be managed with domains, trust relationships and less complexity.

A domain is the NT Workstation security concept extended to cover a group of computers organized around a logical or common purpose. In a large company, for example, each department could create its own domain on the network. NT Server's user limit is currently 10,000 accounts per domain. Several reasons exist to use domain management instead of workgroup managment—there is virtually no reason not to use domains.

THE MECHANICS OF USER ACCOUNTS

User accounts are defined in the User Manager for Domains utility in the New User screen. To access this screen, select User Manager for Domains in your Administrative Tools program group, then select User, New User. An administrator must log on to a domain, then can add user accounts to the domain.

Because NT uses a SID and not a user name to validate resource requests, these accounts must be carefully maintained. For example, you cannot delete an account, add it back in, and expect the previous account properties to be restored. The main point to consider is that if a user account is deleted, it cannot be re-created and automatically reclaim its former access to resources.

For this reason, you should be careful not to name two objects within the same domain identical names. NT allows you to do this because identically named user accounts have different SIDs. Though each is recognized as a different account, access to resources becomes confusing because the share names are identical.

TRUST RELATIONSHIPS

Trust relationships allow users in one domain to access resources in another domain. Trust relationships add more dimensions to the domain model, and extend the domain model's capability to be more powerful, yet require less administration. NT introduced the concept of trust relationships to the domain model—previously, LAN Manager didn't have this powerful mechanism. Therefore, trust relationships can only be established between NT Server domains.

Trust relationships divide network objects into two categories: user accounts and resources. User accounts include users and user groups, while resources include objects such as file and print servers, workstations, and data sets.

Trusts allow users access to resources that exist in a foreign domain. By default, users in one domain do not have access to resources in another domain. When a user requires access to resources in a foreign domain, trust relationships can provide access to resources in that foreign domain. This enables access to the foreign domain without adding a duplicate user account in the foreign domain, even though the user does not exist in the same domain as the resource.

Trust relationships simplify system administration. In LAN Manager networks, access to multiple domains required separate user accounts in each domain, and users needed to log on to each domain separately. Trust relationships in NT alleviate this problem so the user can have a single logon, and the administrator can manage one user account instead of two. In many ways, a trust relationship can combine several domains into one managed unit. Once set up, up to 10,000 users can be managed through a single domain, which in turn can have access to several times as many resources.

9

DOMAIN RULES

In the following discussion of trust relationships, you must be aware of the basic design of resources, servers, and domains.

♦ Each resource is physically connected to, and therefore can only exist in, a single server.

♦ Each server can contain several resources.

♦ Each domain contains one or more NT Servers.

♦ Each server can only exist in one domain.

♦ Several domains can exist on the network.

TRUSTING VERSUS TRUSTED DOMAINS

Another distinction you must be aware of is the difference between *trusted* and *trusting* domains. In a very basic domain structure, the user domain is trusted, and the resource domain is trusting. This simply means that the resource domain trusts the user domain and its ability to control access to the resource domain's resources. Thus, the user domain is said to be trusted, and the resource domain is said to be trusting. The resource domain trusts that the user domain will control user permissions to its resources.

Figure 9.1 demonstrates the simple theoretical model of a trust relationship between two domains: domain A, the trusting domain that contains all resources; and domain B, the trusted domain that contains all user accounts.

Figure 9.1.
Trust relationship.

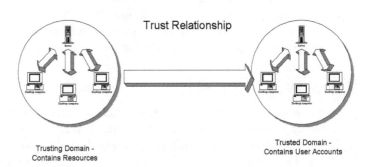

Trust Relationship

Trusting Domain -
Contains Resources

Trusted Domain -
Contains User Accounts

In the absence of a trust relationship, users in a domain do not have access to a foreign domain's resources. They only have access to resources if they exist within the same domain. In this example, domain A provides domain B full and complete access to all its resources, and trusts that domain B will control user access. The system administrator manages domain B to limit user access to resources in domain A. Therefore, domain A is said to be the *trusting domain*, whereas domain B is said to be the *trusted domain*.

This discussion starts with a simple one-to-one relationship between trusting and trusted domains. In most networks, you might have users in one domain accessing resources in another, and vice versa. These relationships are often on a many-to-one or many-to-many basis. More complex models are discussed after the basic one-to-one relationship is defined more fully.

It is also important to understand the difference between one-way and two-way trusts. The following simplified discussion should help you understand the mechanics of trust relationships.

ONE-WAY TRUSTS

The simplest trust relationship is a one-way trust relationship where one domain trusts the other: They do not trust each other, though they can be set up to do so.

Consider the theoretical simple model demonstrated previously in Figure 9.1 where a one-way trust relationship exists with only two domains: first is domain A, which contains all resources (and no users); second is domain B, which contains all users (and no resources). Domain B's primary job is to authenticate logons, user rights, and users' security policies based on the security account database and provide access to domain A's resources. Domain B trusts that the foreign domain A will control access to its local resources, so domain A is said to be the trusting domain, and domain B is said to be the trusted domain. This is a simple one-way trust.

The previous example is strictly theoretical. It is helpful to think of domains as either containing users or resources. However, each domain generally contains both users and resources, and the roles of each domain can be reversed when considering relationships between any users in one domain and resources in another. For the sake of simplicity, this example considers all the users to exist in one domain and their relationship to resources that exist exclusively in a foreign domain.

TWO-WAY TRUSTS

In a two-way trust, one domain trusts the other, and vice versa. The two-way trust is nothing more than two one-way trusts: domain A trusts domain B, and domain B trusts domain A. This allows users to log on from either domain and access resources in the user's own domain, or in the trusting domain.

In a two-way trust, each domain can have users that can access resources within their own domain as well as within foreign domains. In other words, both domains are trusted domains when considering user accounts, and both are trusting domains when considering resource accounts. However, a user account can have one set of rights and permissions within its own domain and perhaps a different set of rights in another domain.

PASS-THROUGH AUTHENTICATION

Users can log on to any trusted or trusting domain. During logon, the domain first checks its own database, then looks for any trust relationships for domains in which the user may exist. If a relationship is found, the logon is passed on to the account domain for authentication.

If the user attempts to log on to a trusted domain, the default domain processes the logon attempt and provides access to trusting domains. If the user attempts to logon to a trusting domain, the logon is passed on to the trusted domain for authentication before access is allowed to any trusting domains. If the user is not defined in either place, the logon is denied. In all cases, it is the functionality of the domains and not the physical connection that is important.

When a user logs on to a resource (trusting) domain, an access token containing the user's SID is passed on to the account (trusted) domain. Authentication of both the user's identity and password actually takes place within the account domain, hence the name pass-through authentication. This mechanism effectively allows a user to have an account in only one domain and yet access the entire network using trusted domains.

Note

One very important point to consider is that pass-through authentication is not transitive. That is, it can only be used where a direct trust relationship exists.

For example, if domain A trusts domain B, and domain B trusts domain C, then domain A does not automatically trust domain C. A user with an account in domain C who attempts to logon to domain A will not be authenticated because authentication can pass through to domain B, but will not be passed a second time to domain C. Trust relationships must be established between each pair of domains before pass-through authentication can occur between them.

This restriction has been specifically designed into the system so that an administrator cannot accidentally establish a circular trust relationship that was never intended.

Now that you have studied the basic mechanics of trust relationships, consider the four basic configurations that result.

THE FOUR BASIC MODELS FOR BUILDING DOMAINS

Four basic domain models can be created using trust relationship facilities. Each NT Server network, no matter how simple or how complex, originates from one of these four basic designs or models.

Single Domain Model   As the name implies, this configuration consists of only one domain. In this case, this single domain functions as both the account and resource domains.

Master Domain Model   This configuration consists of several domains, only one of which is the account domain. All user accounts reside within this domain. All other domains act as resource domains and trust the single "master" domain, as shown in Figure 9.2.

Figure 9.2.
Master Domain.

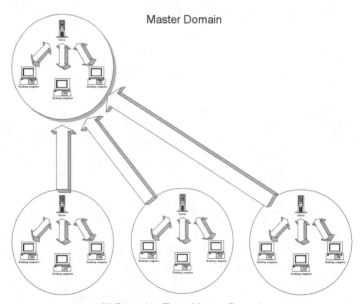

Master Domain

All Domains Trust Master Domain

Multiple Master Domain Model   In the Multiple Master domain model, there are several domains, each containing user accounts and resources. A complete trust relationship between these domains ensures that users may log on to any domain anywhere on the network. Once again, all other domains act as resource domains and trust some or all of the foreign master domains as shown in Figure 9.3.

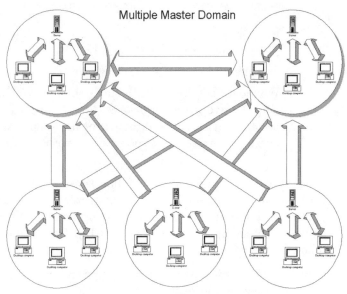

Figure 9.3. Multiple Master Domain.

Complete Trust Model   Finally, there is the complete trust model, which consists of several domains with each domain administered as a separate system. Each domain functions as a separate system; no single domain exerts any control over the other domains. Each domain functions as both account and resource domains, and each domain can control user access to resources in foreign domains through its own user-account properties, rights, and security policies.

SETTING UP TRUST RELATIONSHIPS

Two steps are needed to create a trust relationship. First, one domain must permit a second domain to trust it. Then the second domain can be configured to trust the first domain. Until the trust relationship has been established in the trusted domain, the administrator of one domain is not permitted to make changes like this to the other domain. Therefore these two steps often need to be performed by separate administrators, and must be accomplished in the proper sequence.

There are other ways to establish trust relationships. One way requires only that an identical user account with administrative privileges be created on both domains. This might be an option for network administrators who have identical passwords in each domain's administrative accounts, or, if this is not the case, the administrator must log on to each domain using the appropriate passwords to change their configurations while setting up the trust relationship.

Note

Keep in mind that creating duplicate accounts on different domains defeats the purpose of domain trust relationships, which is one of the key features of NT Server networks.

Whenever possible, create only one user account using trust relationships to give the account access in all authorized domains. If separate accounts exist, the administrator has double work in setting up users—each user must be setup in both domains.

To establish a trust relationship, follow these steps. Assume two domains: X and Y. First log on to domain X as administrator, or a user who is a member of the administrator group. X will be the trusting domain, and domain Y is to be the trusted domain. To set up the trust relationship from a single computer, perform the following steps:

1. Create identical user names and passwords on both domains with domain administrative rights.
2. Make sure you are logged on to domain X.
3. Make sure the title bar shows User Manager X. From User Manager for Domains, choose Select Domain from the User menu. Type Y. The title bar now shows User Manager Y.
4. From the Policy menu, choose Trust Relationship, then choose Add.
5. Enter the password for domain Y. Domain X should now be listed under Permitted to Trust this Domain. Close the Trust Relationship dialog box.
6. From the User menu, choose Select Domain and type X. The title bar should read User Manager X.
7. From the Policy menu, choose Trust Relationship. Add domain Y and use the same password you used above.
8. A dialog box appears notifying you, "Trust relationship with Y successfully established."

Each domain has a PDC. The trusting PDC needs a secure channel to pass validation requests to the trusted PDC. This requires that certain accounts be set up ahead of time to be used to create and maintain the secure channel.

Establishing a Route for Passing Validations

The following procedure is used in a trusted domain relationship to establish the route for passing validations. Similar accounts and procedures are used in the trust relationship between a PDC and a BDC, and between a PDC and a NT Workstation in the domain.

In the example shown in Figure 9.4, the trusted domain may be referred to as MASTER and the trusting domain is referred to as RESOURCE. The trusted domain, MASTER, contains the user account information. RESOURCE is the trusting domain; it trusts MASTER to validate user access to its resources.

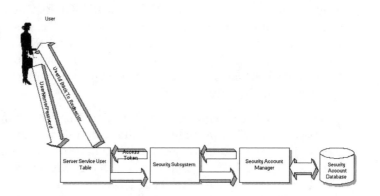

Figure 9.4.
Passing the LSA object
to the trusting domain
for validation.

On each domain controller in RESOURCE, the existence of the trust is represented by an LSA trusted domain object. It contains the name of the trusted domain and the domain security ID (SID). The LSA trusted domain object is replicated from the trusting domain PDC to each of the domain controllers in the trusting domain.

On each PDC in RESOURCE, a password is stored in an LSA secret object G$$<TrustedDomainName> (in this case, G$$MASTER). This object is stored in the registry key HKEY_Local_Machine\Security\Policy\Secrets. The LSA secret object for the trusted domain trust relationship is replicated from the trusting domain PDC to each of the trusting domain controllers.

On the PDC in MASTER, the password is stored in a SAM user account marked as INTERDOMAIN_TRUST_ACCOUNT (in this case, RESOURCE$). This can be viewed in the registry path SAM\SAM\Domains\Account\Users\Names HKEY_LOCAL_MACHINE subtree). This account is synchronized with the trusted domain PDC to each of the trusted domain BDCs.

These accounts are created when a trust is initially established. The administrator of the trusted domain, MASTER, uses User Manager to permit RESOURCE to trust MASTER's accounts. When the domain is added in the Permit to Trust dialog, a password is provided by the administrator. At this time, a hidden user account is created in the SAM for the trusting domain. The account contains the specified password (in this case, RESOURCE$).

The administrator of the trusting domain then establishes the trust. The administrator provides the password specified earlier. User Manager creates the LSA secret object. The server in RESOURCE attempts to set up a session with the PDC in

MASTER using the account RESOURCE$. The PDC controller in MASTER responds with the error `0xc0000198`, `Status_Nologon_Interdomain_Trust_Account` because the special Inter-Domain Trust Account cannot be used in a normal session logon. The session request fails because of this condition.

This error is informative to the PDC in the RESOURCE domain. Receiving this error indicates that the trust account exists and a trust is possible. Upon receiving that response, it establishes a null session and then uses RPC transactions to use remote API calls that establish the trusted domain relationship. A secure channel is set up later by the NetLogon service in the trust domain using the trust information that was stored by the user manager.

After the trust is established, the RESOURCE PDC changes the trusted domain object password. The procedure for this is detailed below. All PDCs in each domain receive the trust account objects through normal intra-domain synchronization of the SAM and the LSA databases. The PDCs in RESOURCE receive the LSA secret object during the update of the LSA database, and the PDCs in MASTER receive the account in the SAM update. With these objects, any PDC in the trusting domain can set up a secure channel to any PDC in the trusted domain.

Maintenance of these accounts consists of periodic password changes. Every seven days the PDC of the trusting domain changes the password of the trusted domain object. It does this by

1. Choosing a new password.
2. Setting the OldPassword field of the LSA secret object to the previous NewPassword field.
3. Setting the NewPassword field to the LSA secret object to the password chosen above. This allows the PDCs to always have a password that works in the event of a crash.
4. Remoting an `I_NetServerPasswordSet` RPC call to a PDC of the trusted domain asking it to set the password on the SAM user trust account to the value chosen in the first step. The trusting PDC remotes the RPC call to whatever trusted PDC it has the secure channel with. That computer passes the request through to the trusted PDC.
5. The password is now changed on both PDCs. Normal replication distributes the objects to the BDCs.

OK-NCA PDC of the trusted domain (MASTER) never initiates the password change; it is always initiated by the trusting domain PDC. It is possible, but not likely, that the trusting domain PDC will change the password without updating a PDC in the trusted domain.

Initiating the password change requires that the secure channel has been set up. It is remotely possible that the trusted side may have gone down at some point during the process and not received the updated password. For this reason, both the old and new passwords are kept in the LSA secret object on the trusting side.

The PDC in the trusting domain never changes to the new password until it has successfully authenticated the current password. This is called a secure channel. If authentication fails using the new password because the password is invalid, the trusting PDC tries the old password. If it authenticates successfully with the old password, it immediately (within 15 minutes) continues the password change algorithm with the steps above. It does not start over with the first step because that might lead to problems where role changes have occurred.

DOMAIN REPLICATION: PDCS AND BDCS

User access to resources within the domain is limited by the administrator's management. In order to provide this service over a domain, one (and only one) server in each domain must function as a Primary Domain Controller (PDC). At least one NT Server in the network must be configured as a PDC in order to create a domain.

Once a PDC is in charge of a domain, each user can have a single account that is recognized throughout the domain. The PDC server contains and provides the master database (SAM) of SIDs, equivalences, rights and permissions, logon scripts, and so on, against which all logons in the domain are authenticated.

When other NT Servers or NT Workstations are installed, Setup allows the installer to join the NT entity to an existing domain. NT Servers can either become server members of, or BDCs within, an exiting domain. NT Workstations can only become members of an existing domain. If no PDC is present at the time Setup checks, the NT entity cannot connect to an existing domain.

FAULT TOLERANCE

To eliminate any single point of failure in an NT Server domain, the PDC can be backed up by a BDC. The BDC contains a replicated copy of the master database (the PDC's SAM), and every change to the master is echoed (synchronized) to the BDC's replicated copy (local SAM). Even if the PDC is not running, the BDC authenticates user logons, and makes it look like all resources within the domain exist until a user attempts to access the missing resource. Then, of course, the resource cannot respond. Without this protection, a downed PDC would bring all user access down with it.

BDCs also provide additional performance. Instead of requiring one single PDC to authenticate all accesses to the security account database, the closest or less burdened BDC responds instead. This is very helpful when a Wide Area Network (WAN) or congested path is between a user and a PDC, or if a PDC is too busy to respond immediately.

Many aspects of NT security are controlled by the master database. Rights, permissions, and security policies, such as how long passwords remain valid, are applied uniformly over the domain by all servers in that domain.

Note for NetWare Administrators

A PDC is much the same as the master replica (root server) in a NetWare 4 NDS tree. A BDC is the same as a read-only replica, and there is no equivalent in NT to a read-write replica. The process of configuring and maintaining an NDS tree and an NT domain through replication is extremely similar, though the names are different.

Note

An NT Workstation can be used as a server, and can contain up to ten user accounts. The NT Workstation server can become a member of a domain, but cannot be configured as a PDC or a BDC.

An NT Workstation server and a Windows 95 computer that is a member of a domain derive the ability to recognize domain user accounts. Like any other server, they can also restrict permissions to local Shares and printers.

MANAGING DOMAIN CONTROLLERS

One of the significant duties of an NT system administrator is to ensure that the PDCs are backed up by BDCs and the domain is synchronized at all times. BDC computers are synchronized about every fifteen minutes, so there are times when the BDCs do not have current information. The Synchronize with Primary Domain Controller option in the Computer menu of User Manager for Domains should be run any time the administrator feels the BDC is out of synch with the PDC.

In order to provide uninterrupted access to domain servers, the administrator may need to reconfigure domain controllers as conditions require. Whenever a PDC is to be taken out of service for more than a few moments, another PDC should be appointed to take over. This process is called *promoting* the BDC.

9

PROMOTING A BDC TO PDC

If necessary, any BDC may be promoted to be the PDC at any time. The administrator should synchronize the domain before attempting this procedure because the BDC may have been out of synch for a variety of reasons and may not have the most recent account database information. If the PDC is active when you promote another server to be PDC, there is less risk of losing changes because the PDC synchronizes the BDC before abdicating its role.

BDCs stand ready to assist in authentication, and to be promoted to PDC when necessary. When the PDC is unavailable, no changes can be made to the domain's user account security database (SAM). Small changes to user account information, such as a user changing his or her password, can sneak by an administrator. Conservative management philosophy dictates that a PDC is online at all times.

Server Manager, in the Administrative Tools program group, is used to promote the new PDC. When a BDC is promoted, the existing PDC is automatically demoted to BDC (if needed it can be shut down now). This is the most common situation; basically you toggle the two NT Server roles.

Note

Any time a PDC is to be shut down, the administrator should first synchronize the domain. This procedure "seals the cracks" so that recent updates to the PDC's master database are sent to the BDC's replicated database without any exceptions.

In order to promote a BDC, the administrator must log on to the domain and access Server Manager (located in the Administrative Tools program group). Notice the title bar (at the top of the Server Manager window). The text in the title bar indicates the domain, workgroup, or server in which you are logged on. If logged on to another domain, the administrator can log on to the domain within Server Manager by selecting Computer, Domain. Once you are logged on to a domain as the Administrator, you can promote a BDC to PDC, select Computer, Promote to Primary Domain Controller as shown in Figure 9.5.

A BDC can only be promoted to a PDC if the Server Manager is focused on a domain. The focus is displayed on the title bar of the Server Manager window. The text on the title bar can have the following forms:

Server Manager - *<domain name>*

Server Manager - *<nt workgroup name>*

Server Manager - *<computer name>*

Figure 9.5.
Promotion of BDC to
PDC.

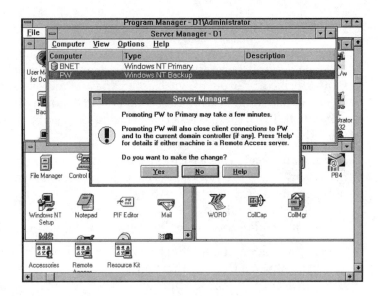

If you are logged on to a workgroup or an NT Workstation server, the Promote To Domain Controller, Synchronize With Domain Controller, Add To Domain, and Remove From Domain options on the Computer menu are unavailable (grayed). To use any of the domain functions, you must select a valid domain, where the PDC is up and running.

An example situation of two NT Servers wanting to be PDC could be the following:

When two different NT Servers in a domain think they are the PDC, the A domain controller is already running in this domain error message may appear in the Event Log.

It may be necessary to promote a BDC to PDC when the original PDC is offline. In the event that the original PDC is down for an extended period of time and will be unavailable during this process, it is necessary to promote the BDC without having the PDC online. This should only be done when the PDC is expected to be down for a long period of time because demotion of the original PDC to BDC will not occur. The error message Cannot find the Primary DC for Domain <domain name> occurs in Server Manager during promotion of a BDC to PDC when the original PDC is unavailable.

You can administer this domain, but certain domain-wide operations are disabled. Promoting the BDC to PDC should work properly at this point. When the original PDC is restarted, it attempts to also become the PDC, and two NT Server computers will both think they are PDCs for the same domain. As a result, the NetLogon service fails on the original PDC because a PDC already exists in the domain. Server Manager shows two PDCs for the domain. The original PDC has a transparent icon representing a domain controller while the current PDC has the correct colored domain controller icon.

To demote one of the PDCs follow these steps:

1. Stop the NetLogon service on the current PDC by typing:

   ```
   Net Stop NetLogon
   ```

2. Highlight the machine name of the original PDC and then select Demote To Server from the Computer menu. This changes the role of the original PDC to BDC.

3. Restart the NetLogon server by typing:

   ```
   Net Start NetLogon
   ```

4. The original PDC can be promoted to PDC in the second step. The current PDC needs to be demoted to a server immediately after this step.

The following rules apply to domain controllers:

◆ One server must be installed as a PDC to create a domain.

◆ A BDC cannot be installed without an existing PDC in an existing domain.

◆ NT Servers cannot be converted from a workgroup server to a domain controller, or from a domain controller to a workgroup server. In order to convert an NT Server from a workgroup server to a domain server (or vice versa), you must reinstall NT Server from scratch.

OPTIMIZING DOMAIN SYNCHRONIZATION

Security account database synchronization (auto-replication) updates all BDCs' replicated databases in the domain from the PDC's master database. This process occurs very efficiently: once Domain Controllers are synchronized, the PDC stores updates and relays the updates only periodically (every 15 minutes). This reduces the volume of data being exchanged to a minimum.

A full synchronization occurs when the PDC sends its entire security account database to all BDCs. This occurs on request (select Synchronize Entire Domain, under the Computer menu in Server Manager), or at times when the PDC determines that BDCs may be out of synch. This process is controlled by the server's NetLogon Service.

The NetLogon Service controls the security account database synchronization process. The NetLogon service can be paused on any NT Server including the PDC of a domain. This allows the computer to be available for other purposes. For example, one might pause the NetLogon service on the PDC of the domain to allow it to replicate more quickly to the BDCs.

Warning

You should pause the NetLogon service for only very brief periods, if at all. During the time the NetLogon service is paused, the PDC does not update any user information that may have changed, nor can NetLogon be the target of any pass-through authentication. Though an administrator may be careful not to update account information while NetLogon is paused, many changes may occur that the administrator does not have control over. For example, user password changes cannot be prevented.

Here are some factors to consider:

◆ NetLogon encrypts user account passwords, and password history as a user account is replicated from the PDC to each BDC.

◆ BDCs can control the load placed on the network due to Security account database synchronization. Each BDC has the ReplicationGovernor parameter in the Registry, which defines both the size of the data transferred on each call to the PDC, and the frequency of those calls.

Adjusting the ReplicationGovernor percentage works in two ways. First, it reduces the size of the buffer used on each call from the BDC to the PDC, ensuring that a single call does not consume the network bandwidth for too long. Second, it causes NetLogon to be disabled between calls, allowing other applications to access the network between calls to the PDC. The ReplicationGovernor value can be configured in the Registry to control the BDC under the following key:

`\HKEY_LOCAL_MACHINE \SYSTEM\CurrentControlSet\Services\Netlogon\Parameters`

◆ ReplicationGovernor—This value can be set from 0 to 100 (the default is 100), and defines in a percentage both the size of the data transferred on each call to the PDC and the frequency of those calls. For instance, setting the ReplicationGovernor value to 50% uses a 64K buffer rather than the full 128K buffer. In addition, the BDC only has a synchronization call outstanding on the network a maximum of 50 percent of the time.

Warning

You must not set the ReplicationGovernor too low, or synchronization may never be allowed to complete. A value of 0 causes NetLogon to *never* synchronize, and the security account database can become completely out of sync.

Note

This parameter must be set individually on each BDC. It is theoretically possible to have different replication rates at different times throughout the day. One could do this by adjusting the ReplicationGovernor parameter in the Registry and then restarting the NetLogon service from within an unattended scheduled batch file using the AT command.

◆ A full synchronization of the security account database is not necessary because the PDC keeps track of the synchronization level of each BDC, which allows the PDC to control the rate of partial synchronization. The PDC sends the security account database change mailslot message only to the BDCs in the domain that need the changes, instead of broadcasting to all or multicasting to BDCs.

These mailslot messages are sent in a polling fashion to 20 servers at a time, which prevents the BDCs from responding simultaneously. This helps to reduce network traffic and also ensures that the PDC does not become overloaded by the BDCs.

The values in Table 9.1 are expressed in seconds, and can be added to the Registry under the key described above.

TABLE 9.1. VALUES FOR THE *\HKEY_LOCAL_MACHINE \SYSTEM\CurrentControlSet\Services\Netlogon\ Parameters* KEY.

Value Name	Default	Minimum	Maximum
Pulse	300	60	3600
PulseConcurrency	20	1	500
PulseMaximum	7200	60	86400
PulseTimeout1	5	1	120
PulseTimeout2	300	60	3600
Randomize	1	0	120

Value Names:

Pulse   This defines the pulse frequency in seconds. All changes made to the security account database since the last pulse are accumulated. Then, after the Pulse time has expired, a pulse is sent to each BDC needing the changes; however, no pulse is sent to a BDC that is up to date.

PulseConcurrency   This defines the maximum number of simultaneous pulses the PDC sends to BDCs in the domain. NetLogon sends pulses to individual BDCs, which cause the BDCs to respond by requesting database changes that are pending. To control the maximum load these responses place on the PDC, the PDC will only have the number of pulses specified under PulseConcurrency waiting to be sent at one time. Increasing PulseConcurrency increases the load on the PDC, whereas decreasing PulseConcurrency increases the time it takes for a domain with a large number of BDCs to get a change to all of the BDCs.

PulseMaximum   This defines the maximum pulse frequency in seconds. Every BDC is sent at least one pulse at this frequency regardless of whether or not its security account database is up to date.

PulseTimeout1   This defines how long, in seconds, the PDC waits for an unresponsive BDC. When a BDC is sent a pulse, it must respond within this time period. If the BDC does not respond, it is considered to be unresponsive. An unresponsive BDC is not counted against the PulseConcurrency limit, thereby allowing the PDC to send a pulse to another BDC in the domain. If this number is too large, a domain with a large number of unresponsive BDCs will take a long time to complete a partial synchronization. If this number is too small, a slow BDC may be incorrectly assumed to be unresponsive. When the BDC finally does respond, it will receive a partial synchronization from the PDC, unduly increasing the load on the PDC.

PulseTimeout2   This defines how long, in seconds, a PDC waits for a BDC to complete partial synchronization. Even though a BDC initially responds to a pulse (as described for PulseTimeout1), it must continue making synchronization progress or the BDC is considered unresponsive.

Each time the BDC calls the PDC, the BDC is given another PulseTimeout2 seconds to be considered responsive. If this number is too large, a slow BDC (or one that has its ReplicationGovernor rate artificially governed) consumes one of the PulseConcurrency time slots. If this number is too small, the load on the PDC is unduly increased because of the large number of BDCs doing a partial sync. This parameter only affects cases where a BDC cannot retrieve all the changes to the security account database in a single RPC call. This only happens if a large number of changes are made to the database.

Randomize   This specifies the BDC back-off period, in seconds. When the BDC receives a pulse, it backs off between zero and the Randomize seconds before calling the PDC. Randomize should always be smaller than the PulseTimeout1. Consider that the time to synchronize a change to all the BDCs in a domain will be greater than: (Randomize/2) * NumberOfBdcsInDomain) / PulseConcurrency.

DIRECTORY REPLICATION

Directory replication is a great new feature that echoes updates to data files to two locations. It can be used to provide fault tolerance in case a drive goes down. Directory replicaton can also breathe more performance and more life into existing applications.

Fault tolerance is pretty simple. Each update to a data file is copied from a primary to a secondary directory, and therefore can be recorded on a separate storage device.

Faster file access for remote data files is really a bonus. You can configure an application with local access to data. Updates to the primary directory echo the update to the secondary directory, perhaps on the other side of a WAN. This way each system accesses data locally instead of waiting for a response from a limited-bandwidth WAN line or a congested bridge.

Directory replication can be used between NT Servers and NT Servers and between NT Servers and NT Workstations belonging to the same domain.

To establish directory replication, perform the following steps:

1. Before you can carry out directory replication, you need to set up the replication account and import/export computers. You will need to create a replication account called REPLUSER. For REPLUSER the following settings should be used:

   The Password Never Expires option is selected.

   The User Must Change Password At Next Logon option is cleared.

   The All logon hours are allowed should be checked.

   REPLUSER should be a member of the domain's Backup Operators, Domain Users, and Replicator groups.

   Assign the Log on as a Service right to the domain's Replicator group.

2. From the import computer

   Use the Services application from the Control Panel to configure the Directory Replicator Service so that it starts up automatically and logs on with the user account REPLUSER.

Log on to the workstation as Administrator.

Use User Manager to assign membership in the local Replicator group to \\<DomainName>\REPLUSER.

3. From the User Manager Policies menu, choose User Rights. The User Rights Policy dialog box appears. Select the Show Advanced User Rights option.

4. Assign the Log on as a Service right to the local Replicator group. Make sure you set the focus on your computer to find your local replicator group. (Select your computer name from the List Names From list box.)

5. Use the Services application from the Control Panel to configure the Directory Replicator Service so that it starts up automatically and logs on as \\<domain_name>\REPLUSER.

6. The following steps are performed on the export computer:

From File Manager on the export server, create the directories (at least two) that are to be exported. They should be created in the \WINNT\SYSTEM32\REPL\EXPORT directory on the drive where Server is installed.

Using Server Manager, double-click the export server's computer name. The Properties dialog box appears.

In the Properties dialog box, choose the Replication button. The Directory Replication dialog box appears. Select the Export Directories option button.

Choose the Add button at the bottom of the To List box. Add the computer names or domains to which the directories will be exported.

Choose the OK buttons in the Select Domain, Directory Replication, and Properties dialog boxes. The Replicator Service starts.

In the Server Manager window, double-click the name of the import computer.

In the Properties dialog box, choose the Replication button. The Directory Replication dialog box appears. Select the Import Directories option button.

Choose the Add button and add the export server computer name or domain from which the directories will be exported.

Choose the OK buttons in the Select Domain, Directory Replication, and Properties dialog boxes.

Periodically check the \WINNT\SYSTEM32\REPL\IMPORT directory on the import computer to see if the files have arrived from the export server.

7. The Directory Replicator service can be monitored from the export server.

On the export server, select Server Manager. Double-click the computer name of the export server in the Server Manager dialog box.

Choose the Replication button. The Directory Replication dialog box appears.

From the Directory Replication dialog box, choose the Manage button under the Export Directories option.

Stop a directory from being exported by selecting it and then choosing the Add Lock button. Add some files to the directory you selected and to another directory on the export server. Verify that the directory you selected has stopped exporting by viewing the appropriate directory structure on the import computer.

In the Server Manager dialog box, double-click the name of the import computer.

View the status of imported directories by choosing the Replication button from the Properties dialog box and then choosing the Manage button.

Perform the steps necessary to stop importing a directory by locking it. Confirm that the directory is no longer being imported by adding more files to both directories on the export server and viewing the import directory structure.

8. You can stop the Directory Replicator service and configure it so that it does not start automatically.

On the export server, double-click the export server name in Server Manager. The Properties dialog box appears.

Choose the Replication button. The Directory Replication dialog box appears.

Select the Do Not Export button, then choose the OK button.

From the Properties dialog box, choose the OK button.

From the Computer menu, choose Services. The Services dialog box appears.

Select Directory Replicator, and then choose Startup. The Directory Replicator Service dialog box appears.

Select the Manual button option, and then choose the OK button.

Choose Stop and then Yes to stop the Directory Replicator Service.

Choose Close to exit.

Double-click the import computer. The Properties dialog box appears.

Choose the Replication button. The Directory Replication dialog box appears.

Select Do Not Import option. Then choose the OK button.

From the Properties dialog box, choose the OK button.

From the Computer menu, choose Services. The Services dialog box appears.

Select Directory Replication, and then choose Startup. The Directory Replicator Service dialog box appears.

Select the Manual button option. Then choose the OK button.

Choose the Close button to exit.

NT WORKSTATIONS IN DOMAINS

Though NT Workstation servers cannot be assigned the role of PDC or BDC, they can be server members of a domain, freely sharing their drives and printers with domain users.

NT Workstation servers can have local user accounts that are not domain members. However, they gain the ability to recognize the domain user accounts. That is, users can log on to domain accounts at the NT Workstation. The users can remotely access the NT Workstation server using a domain account, and domain accounts can be listed as being granted permissions to files, and directories (and so on) on the NT Workstation servers and NT Servers in the domain.

NT Workstation's User Manager is called User Manager instead of User Manager for Domains. Call it what you will; it works the same way.

RECONFIGURING DOMAINS

Only NT Servers, NT Workstations, and LAN Manager servers can be added to an NT domain. WFW and Windows 95 users can become domain user members, but when they share their devices they are not part of the domain model.

There are three ways to add an NT Server or NT Workstation to an NT domain:

◆ Through the Server Manager

◆ During the initial Setup routine for the NT Server or NT Workstation

◆ By using the Networks option in the NT Control Panel

Note

Though it may appear that this option simply renames the domain, it does not—a domain cannot be renamed. This option changes the local computer configuration database to show which domain is the master for this computer.

USING SERVER MANAGER TO ADD A COMPUTER TO A DOMAIN

Follow these steps to use the Server Manager to add a computer to a domain as shown in Figure 9.6.

Figure 9.6.
Add Computer to
Domain.

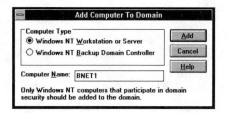

1. Log on as Administrator to any NT Server in the domain.

2. Run the Server Manager in the Administrative Tools group.

3. From the Computer menu, choose Add To Domain.

4. In the Add Computer to Domain dialog box, choose either the Server option to add an NT Server to the domain or the Workstation option to add a workstation to the domain.

5. Enter the name of the computer in the Computer Name edit control and choose Add. Then choose Close.

6. Log on to the newly-added computer and select the Networks icon in Control Panel. Make sure that the list of domains includes the newly specified domain.

ADDING A COMPUTER TO A DOMAIN DURING INSTALLATION

This is the procedure for adding a server to a domain during installation:

1. The Setup program includes a Network Configuration section to configure the NT Workstation computer to join a domain or join a workgroup.

2. If the NT Workstation computer needs to join a domain, enter the domain name. If an account for the computer does not already exist in the Server Manager, select an administrator name and password to create a new account for the computer in the domain.

3. After entering the domain name, administrator name, and administrator password (if required), Setup responds with the message `Welcome to the <DomainName> Domain` where `<DomainName>` is the new domain this computer has just joined. This message verifies that the NT Workstation computer was successfully added to the domain.

Tip

NT identifies each domain by its security identifier (SID), a unique number assigned to the domain. If an NT Server is moved from one domain to another, the new domain name and the original SID will not match. There is no way to replace the original SID without reinstalling NT Server. The procedure of joining different domains is to wait until Setup is finished. The only way an NT Server computer can join a different domain is if you reinstall Windows NT Server.

WORKSTATION JOINING A DOMAIN

When a workstation joins an NT domain or is re-joining a domain, it appears in computer browsers under the domain name it just joined. Domain computers are able to use and reference user accounts and global groups created in that domain. If the domain trusts other domains, the user accounts and global groups of those other trusted domains are also available for use on the workstation. Domain and trusted domain user accounts may be used to log on to the workstation or to allow remote connections to it. The trusting domain is referenced to grant permissions to use resources such as a shared directory or printer, and referenced to grant user rights on the workstation. The following actions take place:

◆ The workstation appears in the computer browser lists as being within the domain, just as it does when it belongs to a workgroup.

◆ The workstation can use accounts and global groups (but not local groups) from its domain and from any domain that its domain trusts. User accounts may be logged on to or used to remotely connect to the workstation; user accounts and global groups may be granted permissions to resources such as files, directories, and printers, and may also be granted user rights in the User Manager.

◆ NT Server adds the Domain Admins global group from the domain to the Administrators local group of the workstation, thus making it possible for domain administrators to administer the workstation remotely.

◆ By default, the Domain Users global group from the domain is added to the Users local group of the workstation, thus making it possible for any user in the domain to log on or connect to the workstation.

In the last two items, you just accept the default settings. These global groups may be removed from the respective local groups at any time by any administrator.

Joining a domain means that workstations that are members of a domain may still have their own local user accounts and local groups and are still subject only to local security policies. If a workstation doesn't belong to a domain, a local account must be maintained for every user that is to log on to or connect to the computer.

By default, the Guest account is enabled on NT Workstation, so that anybody can remotely connect to an NT Workstation computer as a guest. They will only gain access to items that grant access permissions or user rights to the Guest account, the Guests local group, or to the Everyone group. This is not the case with NT Server, however.

With NT Server, the Guest account is disabled by default. Any workstation in a domain can log on to the computer locally or connect to it remotely. Of course, all security protections are still in effect, so logging on or connecting to a workstation doesn't compromise protected information.

To make a workstation appear in the computer browser list along with other resources, all that is necessary is to add the computer to the workgroup. Note that a domain may be used as a workgroup by any NT Workstation or WFW computer without having any security implications whatsoever.

Computers that are members of a domain or that use a domain as a workgroup all appear in the Server Manager main window. To distinguish between computers that are members of a domain, filter the main window using the Show Domain Members Only option from the View menu.

Also, workstations in the main window that appear grayed-out are members of the domain that are currently not turned on or are not running the Server service. Normal workstations in the main window are currently on and running the Server service, but may not be members of the domain. A computer account must be created in the Server Manager using the Computer Add to Domain command in order for a workstation to be added to the domain.

Recombining Split Domains

You cannot split a domain or rename a domain by changing the domain name on servers or on some of the servers in a domain. Attempting to split a domain by renaming it on a subset of servers may seem to work fine at first, but several problems will arise later. Trust relationships do not work in this type of situation because the two domains share the same SID, and the SID has not been changed. When you rename the domain on a server, it simply changes the domain name in that server's configuration table, but the SID remains the same in that server and in other servers. Attempting to split a domain by renaming the domain in each computer simply assigns different names to the same domain, which in itself causes more problems.

Unfortunately, NT has no utility for editing domain configuration. NT Server must be reinstalled on the servers to be removed from the domain in order to be effective. Even under these circumstances you will find conflicting domain information on the remaining servers in the domain because each server has tables that remember domain members and continue to include the removed servers in various domain information.

Tip

The same procedure of reinstalling servers can be followed if you wish to redefine domains or workgroups. Part of the procedure includes deleting the computers from all places in which they appear.

WFW workstations will continue to report former domain members as included in the domain until you delete the password list (.PWL) files.

Recombination of two domains can be done as follows. The domain that remains is referred to as Domain X and the domain that is deleted is referred to as Domain Y.

1. Logon as Administrator of Domain X.
2. Create new accounts on Domain X to replace the accounts that will be lost when Domain Y is deleted.
3. Log on as Administrator of each domain that trusts Domain Y, and remove the trust assignment that makes them trust Domain X. This is accomplished in User Manager for Domains, Policies, Trust Relationships.
4. In Domain X and all trusting domains, change Access Control Lists (ACLs) to replace references to the accounts on Domain Y with references to the new accounts created on Domain X.
5. Remove all workstations on Domain Y first, then add those workstations to Domain X.
6. Promote a BDC in Domain Y to PDC, thereby demoting the original PDC to BDC.
7. In Domain X, remove all servers from Domain Y using Server Manager (if the former domain members are still listed as under Domain Y), and add them to Domain X. Make sure the domain name on all Domain Y servers have been changed to match the name of Domain X.

8. Start the servers that had been in Domain Y. Allow at least fifteen minuntes for replication from Domain X to take place, then check the event log of each server to make sure each server successfully imported the account databases from Domain X.

Note

If domains are split or combined by changing the domain name on servers, all trust relationships with other domains will be affected and will need to be deleted and rebuilt. This should be done before altering the domain configuration, or your attempts will fail. Each time a trust relationship is changed, the PDC is referenced. If the original PDC is no longer servicing the domain, your procedure will be unsuccessful.

CHANGING COMPUTER NAMES

One of the most frustrating problems for an administrator is the constant reorganization that occurs. Users are constantly being moved, users' needs change, and computers are frequently upgraded or reconfigured. In a single server network the problem is only that of managing hardware and connectivity configurations for workstations.

Multiserver networks such as you would usually find in an NT domain and NetWare 4.*x* Directory Services environment present far more complicated network management problems. This section deals with computer name changes as an essential step in the process of network reconfiguration.

On NT networks, you can do the following:

◆ Change the computer name of an NT Server in a domain.

◆ Change the computer name of an NT Workstation in a domain.

◆ Change the computer name of an NT server not in a domain.

CHANGING THE COMPUTER NAME OF AN NT SERVER

Because NT Server is C-2 security compliant, certain complications arise when you attempt to perform a simple task like changing a computer name. In NT Server domains, domain membership (whether as NT Workstation or NT Server) is represented by a special system and security (SAM) account in the domain, and an

LSA Secret Object on an NT Server or NT Workstation server.

Both the account and the LSA Secret Object contain a password that is used by the Netlogon services to set up a secure channel between the computers. Netlogon periodically changes the password (both in the Secret Object and for the account on the domain) to prevent the password from being discovered. This is a common procedure in mainframes, minicomputers, and networked computer systems in order to comply with C-2 requirements.

The account on the server is marked as a WORKSTATION TRUST ACCOUNT or SERVER TRUST ACCOUNT. These accounts cannot be used to log on interactively, nor can they be used to set up a connection by issuing the DOS NET USE command.

The LSA Secret Object is created by Setup during initial installation or when a workstation joins a domain. The initial password is the same as the computer name (in lowercase and truncated to 14 characters).

The SAM computer account is automatically created by Server Manager when a workstation or server is added to the domain (or by Setup when an administrative user name and password are specified). The password is the same as the computer name (in lowercase and truncated to 14 characters).

For Netlogon to start on an NT server or NT Workstation, the passwords on the Secret Object and on the account on the domain must be the same.

Changing the Computer Name of an NT Workstation

As discussed previously, you must follow the proper procedures when changing any object's relationship to a domain. The proper way to change the computer name of a workstation in a domain is as follows:

1. As Administrator of the domain, run Server Manager. Add a workstation with the new name.
2. Choose the Network icon in Control Panel, and select any other domain or workgroup.
3. Change the computer name.
4. Reboot the computer.
5. Choose the Network icon in Control Panel, and then rejoin the domain.
6. Reboot the computer.
7. On the Domain, run Server Manager and delete the old NT Workstation name.

Application Servers

NT Server clearly distinguishes itself as an effective application server. Application servers are special-purpose servers dedicated to tasks other than providing file and print services (that is, database services, SNA server duty, or mail server). This section refers to an application server as a Server (as opposed to NT Server).

NT Server makes provisions for duty as an application server. PDCs and BDCs dedicate system resources to the tasks associated with managing domain configuration. You can configure an NT Server so that it does not have to devote excessive resources processing domain configuration and access.

The Server allows you to mix and match security; accounts may be created in the local security database and assigned to local resources. Any of the domain accounts (and accounts from trusted domains) can be assigned to local resources if the Server is a member of a domain.

A Server is easier to move to a different domain than a BDC, which must be reinstalled in the new domain. You can change a Server's domain membership without having to reinstall. A Server has the following characteristics:

- ◆ Does not get a copy of the domain account database, but does have access to it.
- ◆ Does not process domain logons.
- ◆ Has the same built-in user groups as an NT Workstation (including Power Users).
- ◆ Can be configured as a member of a domain or workgroup.
- ◆ Can have local accounts defined in the Server's local account database (like an NT Workstation server). In User Manager at the server, local accounts are represented by the user or group name, for example: Administrators. Only local groups exist on a Server.

An Administrator can work with the local account database by choosing Select Domain from the User Manager for Domains User menu, then select or add the local computer name.

The server maintains a local account database, independent of the domain account database. When a server joins a domain, certain domain groups are added to groups in the server's local account database. For example, the Domain Admins group is added to the local Administrators group and the Domain Users group is added to the local Users group.

When a user requests access to a resource on the Server, the Server checks its local account database to validate the user. If the Server does not have an entry for the user or group, it makes a request to the PDC to validate the user account. If the account is validated, the Server allows the user access. The server has a trust relationship with the PDC.

The Server has access to all of the domain user information; a secure communication channel is established between the server and the PDC. All domain accounts are available to the Server's local Administrators for assigning permissions to local resources.

When you log on to a Server, you can either log on to the local server or to the domain (or any trusted domains). If you log on to the local server using a domain account, you are validated only if an identical account exists in the server's local account database.

By default, the server is set up so that all members of the domain Administrators group can administer the server. You can add additional accounts to the server's local Administrators group. These accounts can be local accounts, domain accounts, or accounts defined in any trusted domains.

By default, only the local Administrators group is given the right to log on locally to the server. Because the domain Administrators group is added to the local Administrators group by default, domain Administrators may log on locally. You can use User Manager at the server to assign the log on locally user right to other accounts.

To remotely administer the server, log on to a remote computer with an account that is a member of the server's local Administrators group. There is another restriction, if the user account exists both locally and in a domain then you need to remove the user account from the local database. If you do not do so, there can be a credentials conflict.

If you have trusts, you can assign permissions for a Server's resources to any of the users or groups in the trusted domains. None of the trusted domain groups are automatically added to local groups when the server joins the domain, so you'll need to set this up yourself.

If you have users in the trusted domains who need to administer the server, add their accounts to the local Administrators group. You can either add the individual user account (for example, DOMAIN2*UserAccount*>) or add the domain Administrators group (for example, DOMAIN2\DomainAdmins).

If the user should not be allowed access to any domain resources, but should have the right to administer the server, create the user account in the local account database of the server but do not create a domain account. At all times, the user must log on with the local computer name and not the domain computer.

Domain Behavior, Example: Setting Time

After all the theoretical discussion in the previous sections, this section shows the application of that theory in the form of a detailed example.

Even the simple act of setting the time on the network can become complicated if you do not understand local behavior and domain behavior. For example, when attempting to execute the command NET TIME /DOMAIN:EXDOMAIN /SET you may get a message saying the account is not known or the password is invalid. This can happen if you are logged on using the account name "Administrator", but the account is a different Administrator account than the one on the PDC. For example, if you are logged on as EXMACHINE\Administrator, and attempt NET TIME /DOMAIN:EXDOMAIN /SET, you get an error message because EXMACHINE\Administrator is not the same account as EXDOMAIN\Administrator.

The solution is to log off EXMACHINE, log back on as EXMACHINE\PowerUsr1, then execute the command. Note that a privilege is needed to set the time on a computer. In the previous example, the account, EXMACHINE\PowerUsr1, was used to remind us that power users have the needed privilege.

While logged on to a domain, doing a NET TIME without the /DOMAIN parameter, as mentioned above, probably will not yield the desired results. However, because you are logged on to a domain, you can use the command NET TIME /DOMAIN /SET.

The PDC of the domain you are logged on to responds to the command. In other words, if you are logged on to a domain, the /DOMAIN parameter is necessary, but the actual domain name can optionally be left to default to the domain you're currently participating in. If your computer is joined to the a domain, that domain will be the default domain for NET TIME /DOMAIN.

If you are trying to get the time from EXDOMAIN and have done a prior

```
NET USE \\EXDOMAIN\IPC$ /USER:<UserName>
```

where <UserName> can be either a legitimate user name or <DomainName>/<UserName> pair, or anything that will use the guest access, then NET TIME uses the existing connection to the IPC$ Share, using the different user name.

Note

IPC$ represents a connection to the server's InterProcess Communications shared resource. This is done by the client performing a NET USE command. Therefore, any client that can establish a connection to a server's IPC$ resource is capable of running a named pipe client application.

BROWSER

Client computers may at times need to retrieve lists of domains, as well as lists of NT Servers in those domains. The NT `NetServerEnum` API (in other words, Network Server Enumerate) returns information about domains and PDCs in those domains. A browser can be elected as a master browser, it then broadcasts a DomainAnnouncement datagram (packet) every minute for the first five minutes, and then broadcasts once every 15 minutes after that.

Master browsers on other domains receive these DomainAnnouncement datagrams and add the specified domain to the browse list. This is how every computer in the network is apprised of the presence of other computers within a domain.

DomainAnnouncement datagrams contain the name of the domain, the name of the domain master browser, and whether the master browser is an NT Server or NT Workstation. If the master browser is an NT Server, the datagram also specifies whether that browser exists within the domain's PDC.

If a domain has not announced itself for three consecutive announcement periods, the domain is removed from the browse list.

Note

> When making changes to a domain, your changes may not appear for as much as 45 minutes. Because announcements occur every 15 minutes, a domain might be down for as long as 45 minutes before it is removed from the browse list.

The domain master browser also adds to the list of domains the domains that have registered a NetBIOS address with the WINS. Checking against WINS ensures that the browser maintains a complete list of domain names in an environment with subnetworks.

DETERMINING BROWSER ROLES

At certain times in each domain or workgroup, it is necessary to force election of the master browser. The following procedure explains how the election works, and how to force an election. The term "election" is used here instead of selection because the process of election is a mutual agreement among browsers as to which is to be the master browser.

When an NT computer needs to force a master browser election, it notifies the other browsers on the system by broadcasting an election datagram. The election datagram contains the sending browser's election version and election criteria, as explained later in this section. The election version is a constant value that identifies the version of the browser election protocol.

When a browser receives an election datagram, the receiving browser examines the datagram and first compares the election version with its own. If the receiving browser has a higher election version than any other browser, it wins the election regardless of the election criteria. If the election versions are identical, the election criteria for both computers is compared.

The election criteria is a 4-byte, hexadecimal value. If there is a tie on the basis of election version, the tie is broken by selecting the higher value of the election criteria.

Once the criteria has been evaluated by the browsers:

◆ If the browser has a higher election criteria than the issuer of the election datagram, the browser issues its own election datagram and enters the *election in progress* state.

◆ If the browser does not have a higher election criteria than the issuer of the election datagram, the browser attempts to determine which computer is the new master browser.

Specific groups of bytes are masked and their values are set according to the following list:

Operating System Type:	0xFF000000
NT Server:	0x20000000
NT Workstation:	0x10000000
WFW:	0x01000000
Election Version:	0x00FFFF00
Per Version Criteria:	0x000000FF
Primary Domain Controller:	0x00000080
WINS client:	0x00000020
Preferred Master browser:	0x00000008
Running Master browser:	0x00000004
MaintainServerList=yes:	0x00000002
Running Backup Browser:	0x00000001

If there is still a tie, the browser that has been running longest is the winner. If there is still a tie, the browser wth the lowest alphanumeric value name wins. For example, a server named X becomes master browser instead of a server named Y.

When a browser receives an election confirmation datagram indicating that it has won the election, the browser enters the *running election* state. In the running election state, the browser sends an election request after a delay based on the browser's current browser role:

Master browsers delay for 200ms.
Backup browsers delay for 400ms.
All other browsers delay for 800ms.

The browser broadcasts up to four election datagrams. If, after four election datagrams, no other browser has responded with an election criteria that would win the election, the browser is confirmed as the master browser and begins its role. If the browser receives an election datagram indicating that another system should win the election, the browser demotes itself to backup browser. To avoid unnecessary network traffic, a browser that has lost an election does not broadcast any more election datagrams.

DISABLING BROWSING

When the Show Domain Members Only option on the View menu in Server Manager is selected, all the computers in the domain, except for the Master PDC, are displayed as unavailable (grayed out), though they are available to be selected and administered.

Enabling this option tells the Server Manager not to use the Browser when enumerating servers and show only the computers that have accounts in the domain. Without Browser information, the Server Manager cannot determine whether a given computer is running or has been shut down.

ACCOUNT AUTHENTICATION

Every time a user logs on, or changes domains, user access must be authenticated. The following discussion describes the method and procedures NT uses to authenticate user access in three stages.

◆ Passwords are stored in the SAM Database.

◆ MSV1_0 Authentication Package authenticates users in the default domain.

◆ Pass-through Authentication handles user authentication in a separate domain where a trust relationship exists.

NT SERVER SECURITY ACCOUNT MANAGER (SAM) DATABASE

User records are stored in the SAM database. Each user has two passwords associated with it: the LAN Manager-compatible password and the NT password. Each password is stored double-encrypted in the SAM database. The first encryption is a one-way function (OWF) version of the clear text generally considered to be non-decryptable. The second encryption is an encryption of the user's relative ID

(RID). The second encryption is decryptable by anyone with access to the double-encrypted password, the user's RID, and the algorithm. The second encryption is also used for adding another degree of randomness.

NT stores two variations of a password in SAM. The LAN Manager-compatible password in NT is 100 percent compatible with the password used by LAN Manager. The NT password is based on the Unicode character set, is case sensitive, and can be up to 128 characters long. The OWF version (called the NT OWF password) is computed using the RSA MD-4 encryption algorithm, which computes a 16-byte composite of a variable length string of clear text password bytes.

Any individual user account might be missing either the LAN Manager or NT password, even though NT makes every attempt to maintain both versions of the password. For example, if the user account was ported from a LAN Manager UAS database using PORTUAS (the LAN Manager conversion program) or if the password was changed by a LAN Manager or WFW client, only the LAN Manager version of the password exists.

Only the NT version of the password exists if the password is set or changed by an NT client, and no LAN Manager or WFW client has ever changed the password and used one that is longer than 14 characters or the characters cannot be represented in the OEM character set. All existing user interface limits do not allow NT passwords to exceed 14 characters. The implications of this are discussed in the following section.

MSV1_0 AUTHENTICATION

All user authentication in NT occurs using the LsaLogonUser API. LsaLogonUser actually authenticates users by calling an authentication package. The default authentication package that comes with NT is the MSV1_0 Authentication Package. The MSV Authentication Package uses the SAM database as its database of users, and it supports pass-through authentication of users in other domains by using the Netlogon service.

PASS-THROUGH AUTHENTICATION

NT networks authenticate logons at domain controllers that may not have the user account information. This occurs where a trust relationship exists, and the user information is stored in another domain. The procedure of pass-through authentication via the NetLogon service procedure handles such requests.

NetLogon's role is threefold.

◆ It selects the domain to which it passes the authentication request.
◆ It selects the NT Server within the domain.

◆ It passes the authentication request through to the appropriate NT Server (PDC or BDC).

Selecting the domain is straightforward. The domain name is passed to LsaLogonUser. The domain name is processed as follows:

1. If the domain name matches the name of the SAM database, the authentication is further processed on that computer. The name of the SAM database on an NT Workstation that is a member of a domain is considered to be the name of that NT computer. The name of the SAM database on an NT Server is the name of the domain. All logons to NT computers that are not members of a domain are processed locally.

2. If the domain name specified is trusted by this domain, the authentication request is passed through to the trusted domain. On NT Server, the list of trusted domains is readily available, so this comparison is trivial. On an NT Workstation, the request is always passed through to the PDC of the domain to which the workstation belongs, allowing the primary domain to determine if the specified domain is trusted.

3. If the domain name specified is not trusted by this domain, the authentication request is processed on the computer being connected to as if the domain name specified were that domain name. NetLogon does not differentiate between a nonexistent domain, an untrusted domain, and an incorrectly typed domain name.

WFW 3.11 and LAN Manager 2.2 clients do not specify the domain name, and therefore generate a NULL value for the domain name. An NT Workstation handles this NULL domain name by checking to see if the account exists locally. If so, the request is processed locally; otherwise, the request is passed to the workstation's domain PDC. NT Server then also checks if the account exists locally. If so, the request is processed locally; otherwise, the NT Server checks to see if a trusted domain has the account. This is done by sending a second-class mailslot message to each trusted domain.

Each trusted domain responds indicating whether it has the specified account. The request is passed through to the first domain that responds affirmatively. If no domain responds affirmatively, this NULL domain is treated as an untrusted domain (as previously described). If more than one domain responds affirmatively, only the first response is used.

NetLogon picks an NT Server in the domain by a process called *discovery*. An NT Workstation discovers the name of one of the NT Servers in its domain. An NT Server discovers the name of an NT Server in each trusted domain.

Note

The use of NULL domain names makes for an inefficient and sometimes inconclusive discovery process, especially when the user account is stored in two domains instead of just one. Clients passing NULL domain names should be upgraded to NT Workstation or Windows 95 so that any individual user will have only one account throughout the network.

Pass-through authentication is merely an I_NetLogonSamLogon API call over the secure channel discussed earlier. If the logon call is an interactive logon, NetLogon encrypts the OWF passwords with the secure channel session key before passing them to the NetLogon service. The session key encrypted OWF passwords are decrypted before they are passed to the bottom half of the MSV authentication package.

If the user account is in a trusted domain, the request must first be passed from the computer in the trusting domain to a PDC in its domain. The PDC then passes the request to a PDC in the trusted domain, which authenticates the user account information and then returns the user information by the reverse route.

Figure 9.7 shows the user Rick's logon request to access a Seattle domain computer and how authentication is passed through. Seattle trusts Los Angeles and the NetLogon service at Seattle sends the logon request for authentication back to the Los Angeles PDC that locates Rick's account and sends back an authentication reply.

NON-INTERACTIVE LOGONS

If an application does not prompt for your user name or password, connect to the server from the command line using:

```
NET USE \\<SERVER>\IPC$ /USER:<DOMAIN>\<USERNAME> <PASSWORD>
```

The account in the remote domain can be either a domain user account or a local user account. If the two domains will eventually be configured with a trust relationship, then the best choice is to temporarily create a local account for the user in the remote domain. This is done to limit the use of the account outside the domain in which it is defined.

Figure 9.7.
Pass-Through Authenti-
cation.

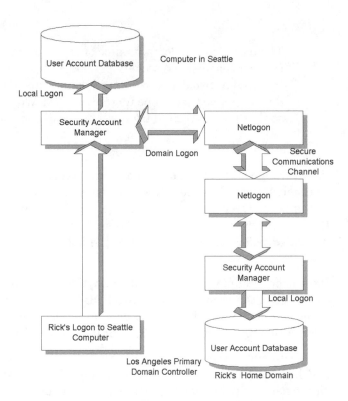

Local accounts are only recognized within the domain in which they are defined. It is undesirable to have multiple accounts for one person, so using a local account is one way to limit how widespread the account is referenced. This prevents domains that trust the remote domain from recognizing the account and using it in access control lists' ACLs.

Local accounts cannot be logged onto interactively. They are recognized only over the network, and therefore if the user needs interactive access, this type of account should not be used. Use a domain user account to create a single account for use in each cluster of trusting domains if the domains will never have a trust relationship.

PERMISSIONS ON SHARED NTFS DIRECTORIES

When sharing a directory on an NTFS volume, administrators should set permissions on the directory and its files and subdirectories. Share permissions are set in the process of sharing a directory.

Share permissions operate in addition to the individual file and directory permissions assigned to a user or group account. Share permissions serve as a maximum set of permissions for any file or subdirectory of the shared directory.

Note for NetWare Administrators

Share permissions placed on an NTFS directory work much the same way as a Rights Mask in a NetWare environment. File and directory permissions apply to the user or group, much the same way that Trustee Assignments do in a NetWare environment.

File permissions:

Read

Delete

Write

Change Permission

Execute

Take Ownership

No access

The following list shows two sets of abbreviations in parentheses. The first set of abbreviated individual permissions applies to the directory itself, and the second set of abbreviated individual permissions applies to new files subsequently created in the directory.

Directory Permissions:

Read (RX)(RX)	User can read files in the directory and run applications in the directory.
Change (RWXD)(RWXD)	User can read and add files and change the contents of current files.
Add (WX) (Not Specified)	A user with Add permission can create a file and after creating it, can read from or write to the file until closing it.
Add & Read (RWX) (RX)	Add enables a Windows NT user to add files to the directory but not to read the contents of current files or change them. Add & Read enables a user to add files to the directory and read current files, but not to change any files.
Full Control (All)(All)	User can read and change files, add new ones, change permissions for the directory and its files, and take ownership of the directory and its files.

No Access (None)(None)	Prevents a user from using the file or directory in any way. Usually, you can prevent a user from accessing a file or directory simply by not giving the user any permissions to it; however, you must use No Access permission to prevent a specific user from accessing a file while granting access to the file or directory to a group the user belongs to. For Windows NT, users cannot access the directory in any way, even if they have Full Control access through membership in a group.
List (RX)	User can only list the files and subdirectories in this directory and change to a subdirectory of this directory. User cannot access new files created in this directory.

For example, suppose at XYZ Corporation, the administrator grants the Engineers group Full Control for both the APPLICATIONS directory and its subdirectory TOOLS. Then the administrator shares the directory, and in the share permissions grants the Engineers group the Read Files/Directories permission.

When anyone from Engineers accesses the directory over the network, they will only be able to read it. The restriction set by the share permissions prevents anyone in the Engineers group from having full control, despite the Full Control permissions granted to anyone in the Engineers group for the directories themselves.

In the preceding example, if anyone in the Engineers group can log on locally at the workstation itself, they have Full Control to the two directories. The share permissions apply only when users access the share over the network.

Tip

Remember, it is recommended that administrators grant permissions only to groups, not individual users. Granting permissions only to groups makes the shared resource management much easier to maintain.

LOCAL FAT/HPFS SECURITY AND LOCAL NTFS SECURITY

NTFS improves on FAT and HPFS designs in many ways. From FAT, NTFS borrowed the "simplicity yields performance" philosophy. Performance increases when the number of disk transfers is minimized for common operations. From HPFS, NTFS borrowed techniques for speed and flexibility. For example, NTFS uses B-tree indexes in its directory listings similar to those used by HPFS to maximize performance.

NTFS supports both long and short (eight-plus-three) filenames for compatibility with MS-DOS, HPFS, and other networked clients including DOS/Windows, OS/2, UNIX/NFS, and AppleShare. NTFS also provides for multiple extended attributes and allows future applications to define other extended attributes. NTFS offers data security on fixed and removable hard disks, a feature important to corporate users and other power users.

For example, suppose user Rick has a removable hard disk. That hard disk is formatted as an NTFS volume and has security permissions that allow access only to Rick and to one other co-worker in his domain, Nancy. Nancy works at the company's branch office. Rick removes the disk from his computer and sends it to Nancy, who installs it in her computer. When she accesses the files on the disk, because Nancy's computer is in the same domain as Rick's, security mechanisms work the same for her as they do for Rick. This would not be so if the drive were installed in a server that is in another domain.

Note

When any volume on an NT Server contains an NTFS volume, be sure to shut down the system properly before removing a disk. If you do not, you may suffer severe file corruption.

In addition to these features, NTFS provides a recovery system that is more reliable than either FAT or HPFS. NTFS also meets POSIX requirements.

Summary

The following is a summary of domain authentication and validation rules:

◆ The PDC replicates the account database to the BDC.

◆ Account authentication for an NT Workstation belonging to a domain is executed in the domain PDC.

◆ If the domain PDC is busy or is remote (on the other end of a WAN), the BDC or a local PDC on trusted domains responds first.

◆ By default, a WFW client logs on to the PDC. After the account has been authenticated, that user can then access any resource on the domain within the range of permissions found in the user account profile.

◆ The user can utilize GUI tools such as File Manager or can issue a simple NET USE command for the resources located on an NT Server or NT Workstation in the domain.

◆ Users log on using a single user account and password even though the user may have different privileges defined in the SAM on the NT Server and for resources on an NT Workstation computer.

◆ Individual administrator level permissions are not given on any particular NT Server computer—they apply to the domain and all servers in the domain. That is, all NT Server computers in a domain are either PDCs or BDCs, and, as such, all administrator level permissions extend to the entire domain and not any specific NT Server.

◆ The user is granted privileges based on the user account profile in the domain database for domain wide access. However, each NT Workstation computer can be set up to give a user different privileges locally. For example, DOMAIN\USER may have administrator privileges on NT Workstation-1 but only user privileges on NT Workstation-2 (where NT Workstation-1 and NT Workstation-2 are workstations on the domain called DOMAIN). All NT Server and NT Workstation computers can set up Shares, to which privileges can be attached.

This chapter provides an overview of the key concepts and facilities of domains as they are implemented in NT Server. Included are the concepts of users, global and local groups, domains, trust relationships, and the various domain models available with NT Server. Together, these concepts provide the basic building blocks to provide a clear understanding of domain implementation.

The topics of reconfiguring domains and computer names, and authentication were discussed in technical detail because these topics present the most troublesome problems for administrators.

- Implementing User Groups on an NT Network

- Group Strategies

- Built-in Groups

- User Rights and Strategies

- File Access Permissions

- Planning Your Network Security

CHAPTER 10

Groups, Rights, and Permissions

User Group   A group of users who are given resource permissions and user rights based on common needs

Rights   Rights to perform specific tasks granted to a user or group

Permissions   File and directory access privileges given to users or groups

Workgroup   A group of computers networked together. In a workgroup, each computer that shares its resources also contains user accounts

Domain   A grouping of computers networked together that share a common security account database

System administration requires more than simply learning the utilities and tools provided in a NOS. It requires a good understanding of the utilities, tools, and strategies for using the tools, such as groups, in order to be effective. This chapter discusses the foundation tools used to manage an NT system which include:

◆ Groups for Users

◆ Rights to Use Resources

◆ Permissions to Access Shared Resources

These three tools work together to form the foundation for administering an NT-based network. The interaction between them combined with administrative strategies allows an administrator to secure a system to reduce unnecessary effort.

IMPLEMENTING USER GROUPS ON AN NT NETWORK

User groups are used to streamline user management. When a group is created, rights, permissions, and other user-related controls are applied to the groups—the user inherits these group attributes when he or she is made a member of the group. Though rights and permissions can be assigned directly to a user, grouping leverages time spent administering users.

Note for NetWare Administrators

The concept of user groups is the same in NT as it is in NetWare—groups are used to standardize access to various applications and data sets. NT, however, has more explicit options for controlling groups than NetWare. NetWare groups generally are created to restrict file/directory trustee assignments, while NT's rights control many more functions, such as the ability to access or manage a shared resource.

Generally, users in a department all access the same applications and data sets, while users in other departments share different data sets. Some data sets, such as electronic mail messaging, are shared globally. Wherever many users are employed, users are related in one or more ways. Groups need to be established according to working relationships in your organization.

Restrictions and permissions can be assigned to a group, then users who become members of the group inherit the group restrictions and permissions. Of course, for this strategy to be effective, groups need to be designed around unique working conditions and file access requirements.

Most networks have common administrative needs; NT Server's built-in groups should be used for this purpose. Requirements differ from organization to organization, so chances are that you need to create additional groups to handle your special requirements. Built-in groups, however, provide a good starting point to show you how group assignments work.

Local Versus Global Groups

Local groups are defined in each workgroup or domain, and group membership is limited to user accounts defined within a local workgroup or domain. Group access to resources is confined to local resources, so local groups are generally resource-oriented.

Global groups are not restricted to a single domain, and therefore they can contain members that may reside in the local domain or in a foreign domain. Global group users can only access resources that are local, so global groups are generally user-oriented.

Local groups make resources available. Resources such as drives, directories, and printers are physical objects residing in servers. Access to these resources may only be assigned to local groups, and cannot effectively be assigned to global groups. Rights to resources are therefore assigned to local groups, and users are generally assigned to either local and/or global groups.

Users only requiring access to resources defined within their default domain can become members of a local group. If the local group is provided access to local resources, the members of the local group have access to those local resources.

To provide local resource access to users of foreign domains, make the global group a member of the local group, and violà! Global group members have access to resources in the local domain, even though some of the users may exist in a foreign domain.

Figure 10.1 shows the direct relationship between the user MARY, who is a member of the group LOCAL. Because LOCAL has access to the printer LASER, MARY has access to LASER.

Figure 10.1.
Local group members
have access to local
resources.

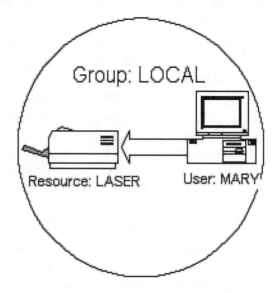

Figure 10.2 shows the indirect relationship that can exist between local resources and foreign domain users. In Figure 10.2, GEORGE is a member of the global group GLOBAL, which is a member of the local group LOCAL. Because LOCAL has access to LASER, and GLOBAL has access to LOCAL, and GEORGE is a member of GLOBAL, GEORGE has access to LASER.

Figure 10.2.
Global group members
have access to local
resources.

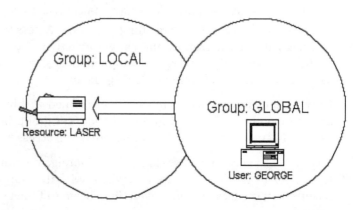

Built-in Groups

When you check User Manager for domains on a newly installed server, you see that several groups have already been established. These built-in groups give the system administrator a jump on managing users. Most basic user necessities are handled by the built-in groups, however, you can refine groups to grant exactly which rights and permissions should apply to your users.

Built-in groups include:

Administrators	Members can fully administer the domain.
Backup Operators	Members can bypass security to backup files.
Guests	Users are granted guest access to the computer/domain.
Powerusers	Members can share directories and printers.
Replicator	Supports file replication in a domain.
Users	Ordinary users.

Group Strategies

There is really no right or wrong way to do groups. There are simply many strategies—strategies that work for almost everyone, strategies that fit some organizations better than others, strategies that are effective, and some that are inefficient. The appropriate group strategies can leverage an administrator's time and can be highly efficient and effective. Good group strategies allow users just the right degree of freedom, yet protects resources from unnecessary exposure.

Groups are formed for various reasons. Some groups exist to grant common access to data, others provide common access to applications, and others are formed to provide members rights and permissions that allow them to discharge various duties. This section discusses various aspects of groups that will help you choose the right group policies and rights to fulfill your administrative objectives.

Before getting into the specifics of what groups do, it is helpful to understand the hidden mechanics of group configurations and definitions. It is very important to know whether group definitions are stored in the local security database or in a domain server's security database. If you do not get this distinction, the Microsoft method of distributing network account information causes serious confusion. This is especially so for administrators trained with NetWare which stores and controls user and group accounts quite differently.

In a workgroup configuration, group definitions are contained in a security account database that is local to each computer. Your computer, therefore, is the authority that allows or denies you access to other network computers, group accounts, and resources. This information is in each computer's local security account database. This applies to all Microsoft network computers sharing their disk storage or printers.

In a domain, however, one NT Server serves as the controller of the domain, and contains the group definitions for the entire domain. Therefore, when a user logs on to a domain, the authority that allows or denies access is the Domain Controller. This computer can be a Primary Domain Controller (PDC), or a Backup Domain Controller (BDC) which contains an exact duplicate of the PDC's SAM. The SAM is therefore the centralized master security account database for the entire domain. Logon, therefore, is to a domain instead of to a computer. More about domains and their mechanics is discussed in Chapter 9, "Workgroups and Domains."

It is important to be aware of your logon account and the authenticating object when administering an NT. In a workgroup environment, when you log on to a server computer that you are using, access is controlled locally. In a domain environment, you log on to a domain, and access is controlled by a domain controller. The domain controller can only be an NT Server—it cannot be an NT Workstation, Windows 95, WFW, or MS-DOS computer.

Groups work into the same security scheme; in a workgroup, each computer on the network that shares its devices has a local security database containing duplicate (hopefully) information about user and group accounts. In a domain, the NT domain controllers contain a master Security Account Manager (SAM) database containing the group information, so the user must log on to the domain, not the local computer, or to a workgroup in order to access groups defined within a domain. The Backup Domain Controllers (BDCs) have duplicate copies of the Primary Domain Controller's (PDC's) SAM in order to provide fault tolerant and quick user access to this information.

Note

If a PDC or BDC is not online when you log on, your local security account database allows you to log on. However, access to domain resources are not available. Because the local account user name and password are generally the same, when this occurs users are often confused about network access functionality.

As an administrator, you must be aware of the authenticating entity. If you are logged on to a local computer, you first need to log on to the domain you wish to manage. If you are not, your actions are limited to other than domain business.

Local groups provide a uniform set of user policies that include user account control requirements, and specific rights. Account control requirements include password and lockout restrictions, while users' rights are specifically descriptive of what the members of the group are allowed to do. For example, the Administrator group is granted the right to "Access this computer from the network," "Add workstations to the domain," and "Change the system time." These rights are only three of a list of 27 rights that are granted to the Administrators group. Explicit task-oriented rights are granted to a group to enable the members of the group to discharge their duties. Built-in NT Server local groups should be sufficient for most normal network management operations.

GLOBAL GROUP MECHANICS

Global groups exist within a domain. Rights and other user security policies can be assigned to global groups, and therefore extend to members of the group. Rights and user security policies can extend to

An entire domain
Servers and workstations in the domain
Trusting domains related to the domain

A global group can become a member of one or more local groups. A user account can become a member of a global group only if the user account exists within the same domain, within a server, or within a workstation existing within the working domain or a trusting domain.

LOCAL GROUP MECHANICS

A local group is local to a server or to a domain. These groups are the primary focus of resource management. Local groups are designed to do everything groups need to do when you have a workgroup or domain environment, or if you have one server or many. Rights to use servers within a domain can be controlled through assignment to a local group(s).

Any users defined within a domain or a trusted domain can be assigned to a global group or a local group. In a domain or workgroup environment, resources may only be assigned to a local group.

Another significant difference between a local and a global group is that the local group extends to trust*ed* domains, while the global group extends to trust*ing* domains. Because of this relationship, a local group can be used to extend access to local resources to members of the trusted domain. Local groups make their resources available to global group members, trusting that the global group will control user rights.

A global group can become a member of a local group. The members of the global group therefore have access to resources contained in the local group. A global group can hold membership in several local groups contained in multiple (trusting) domains.

Local groups work in the resident database where they were created. In NT Workstations, Windows 95, and WFW computers, this is the local computer account database, which limits the group definitions to the specific computer in which the group was defined. In an NT domain, local groups are defined within the domain master database, and can be used to grant user rights to resources local to server members of the domain.

Global Group Rules

Global groups cannot have local groups as members, nor can they have other global groups as members. Only users can become members of a global group.

Global groups are citizens of the entire network; they are not so directly tied to a specific domain. A global group appears within the local domain (the domain in which the global group was defined) with the group name only—no domain prefix is shown. In other domains, however, each global group has the domain prefix of the domain of origin.

In a single domain network, global group member access to foreign resources is not required. Even in this situation users should be placed into global groups and made members of local groups to ensure that resources on both NT workstations and NT Servers are equally available with a minimum of administration.

Global groups simplify administration. The global group is a means of assigning a number of users as a single unit to resource rights in the local or trusted domains.

Global groups exist for one purpose only; to contain members. Without local group memberships, global groups are powerless; they have no authority to perform any network functions. Their primary purpose is to provide a group that can be used either in remote domains or outside of a local domain's servers. In other words, a global group can be assigned rights or permissions to a resource on an NT Workstation by including a global group in a local group that has the desired permissions.

Note

A global group and a local group can both have the same name. Assigning permissions to one does not give them to the other. Separate permissions must be assigned.

By default, user accounts are global accounts. When a user account is created, it is automatically assigned to the global group "Domain local groups in a Domain."

A domain-local group can only be used in that domain. Further, only the NT Server computers in the group have the group in their database. That means that a domain-local group can only use resources on server computers in the domain, not on NT Workstations or other computers. This local group can contain user accounts from the local domain or any domain trusted by that domain. You can only grant permissions, however, to resources in the domain in which the group is defined.

GROUPS AS MEMBERS OF OTHER GROUPS

Groups can become members of other groups, just like users can. Local groups can have global groups as members as well as local users. Membership in a global group can therefore allow foreign users access to local group resources through local group memberships.

A local group can only be used in the domain where it was created, and the group can only possess rights to resources contained within the local domain. Group membership in a global group is therefore required in order to access resources outside of a user's default domain.

The relationship between global and local groups provides the basis for normal user and resource management within, and outside a domain. Domain groups are usually created with this simple relationship in mind: local groups contain rights to local resources, and global group members are granted access to resources defined within the local domain, and outside of other domains through global group membership in local groups.

By default, global groups are powerless in that they have no user rights associated with them. They must be assigned to a local group or to a user right.

Groups within a domain are employed most effectively when you

◆ Assign rights to resources to local groups

◆ Assign users to global groups

◆ Assign global groups to local groups

BUILT-IN GROUPS

When you install NT Server, you will find groups already defined and available for your use. These groups are provided to give you a head start on managing your network. Microsoft's intention is to provide a starting point for basic user and administrator functionality.

For many small organizations, built-in groups may fit all basic needs. In many other organizations the built-in groups prove somewhat helpful as examples of how local groups can be formed and configured. It is up to the system administrator to edit, add, and otherwise tailor group rights and policies to fit specific needs of the organization.

BUILT-IN LOCAL GROUPS

The following built-in local groups and group rights are available by default in your NT Server installation:

◆ **Administrators:** This group has the highest level of rights; members can:

Create, delete, and manage user accounts.

Create, delete, and manage global groups.

Create, delete, and manage local groups.

Create, delete, and manage Share directories and printers.

Create, delete, and manage resource permissions and user rights.

Install operating system files and programs.

◆ **Operators:** This local group and the Power Users group provide limited administrative capabilities. They have administrative authority only in limited areas.

◆ **Server Operators:** This group has the authority to keep network servers running. They can share and stop sharing a server's files and printers, lock or override a server's lock, and format the server's disks. They can also log on locally at the server, back up and restore server files, and shut down the server. They are limited, however, in that they do not have the authority to manage security on the server. This group does not exist on NT Workstation.

◆ **Replicator:** Maintains security through the Replicator service during file replication.

◆ **Backup Operators:** Allows backup/restore of files to a backup medium regardless of the permissions of the backup operator.

◆ **Power Users:** Combines user account and the ability to share resources. Can create non-administrator accounts.

♦ **Server Operators:** Allows operators to share resources at the server (printers and files), lock the server, back up and restore files, and shut down the server.

♦ **Account Operators:** Can modify and change user and group accounts. Certain accounts such as Administrators, Server, Account, Print, and Backup operators cannot be modified by a user with this privilege level.

♦ **Print Operators (in a workgroup):** Allows a permitted user account to manage printers and printer shares in the domain.

♦ **Network and Interactive Groups:** An interactive user accesses resources contained within the local computer. A user who accesses the same resources over the network is a network user. When accessing local resources, the user is a member of the Interactive group and has greater permissions than when the same user accesses the same resources over the network.

♦ **Everyone:** Automatically includes any user who accesses the computer. This includes guests and users from other domains, as well as interactive and network users.

The Everyone group provides access rights and permissions to files, directories, Share names (shared directories), printers, and registry keys to all users. Members of this group cannot add user accounts to the Everyone group. By default this group has Full Control rights to shared directories.

Note

> In most organizations, Administrators should modify or remove the Everyone group's Full Control permissions and add only permissions that are needed.

♦ **Print Operators (in a domain configuration this account has different rights):** Accounts in this group can share printers, stop sharing printers, and manage printers shared at NT Servers in the domain.

Note

> Only printers connected to a server that is a member of a domain can share printers with domain members.
>
> To access printers on a workgroup computer or server that is not a member of a domain, you must create a local group with rights to the printer, and assign a global group to the local group. Users who are members of the global group can then use the printers.

Warning

Print Operators can log on locally at servers and shut them down.

IMPLEMENTING GROUP RIGHTS

When assigning or changing group rights, use User Manager for Domains. Select Policies, User Rights... and you see the User Rights Policy as shown in Figure 10.3.

Figure 10.3.
Assigning rights
to a group.

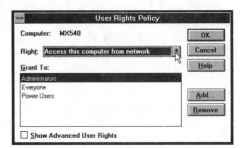

Assigning rights is not as logical as you might like. To assign a right to a group, select the right in this screen, then add or remove groups that have the right. This is the opposite of how you might think this tool should work, and is somewhat illogical, but you will get used to it once you have assigned or removed a few rights.

To help you know which rights map to which groups, use the cross references in Table 10.1. In the following list, groups are mapped into the table.

> A - Administrator
> B - Account operator
> C - Backup operator
> D - Everyone
> E - Guest
> F - Print operator
> G - Server operator
> H - Users

These local groups have the following rights shown in Table 10.1:

TABLE 10.1. BUILT-IN GROUP RIGHTS.

Default Rights	Local Group					
Back up files and directories	A	G	C			
Restore files and directories	A	G	C			
Log on locally	A	G	B	F	C	
Access from network	A	D				
Take ownership of files	A					
Manage audit & security file	A					
Change system time	A	G				
Shut down the server	A	G	B	F	C	D
Shut down the server remote	A	G				

The following abilities are allowed for built-in local groups as shown in Table 10.2:

TABLE 10.2. LOCAL BUILT-IN GROUP CAPABILITIES.

Capabilities	Local Group					
Share and stop share directory	A	G				
Share and stop share printer	A	G	F			
Create and manage accounts	A	B(1)				
Create and manage global group	A	B(1)				
Create and manage local groups	A	B(1)	H(2)			
Assign user rights		A				
Lock the server		A	G	D(3)		
Override locked server		A	G			
Format server disk		A	G			
Create common groups (desktop)	A	G				
Keep local profile		A	G	B	F	C

Note

Notes from Table 10.2:

1 Account operator (B) Cannot modify user accounts that are members of the Administrator, Operator, Administrators, or Domain Administrators groups.

2 User (H) Members have the ability to add local groups to an NT Server; they are not able to unless they have access to User Manager for Domains.

3 Everyone (G) Members can lock the NT Server only when logging on physically to the NT Server computer itself.

BUILT-IN GLOBAL GROUPS

In a domain configuration, the following global groups are built-in to your NT Server installation:

◆ **Domain Admins:** Users who have Administrator rights on all servers within the domain.

◆ **Domain Users:** Users who have domain-wide access to local groups.

◆ **Domain Guests:** Users who have more limited domain-wide access to local groups.

◆ **Auditor:** A special user who can audit all activity domain-wide, including changes to user accounts, rights, and permissions.

The Domain Admins global group is added to the Administrators local group on every NT Workstation added to the domain. This is so that administrators for the domain can also manage the domain's NT Workstations. Default Group permits access to the computer for people using the system infrequently. It also permits users without an account on a remote computer to access resources that have appropriate permissions.

Domain Users is the most prominent global group. It is provided to handle the bulk of users and their needs.

Note

There is a hidden, special group called Creator Owner. This group relates to the Owner attribute which only applies to NTFS volume directory listings.

The *Creator Owner* group includes the user account (or the Administrators group if the user is an administrator) that created or took ownership of a resource in an NTFS partition. Creator Owner permissions are assigned at the directory level. The owner of any directories or files created under this directory is given the permissions assigned to Creator Owner.

This local group can be used to manage assigned permissions to files and directories created in a public area on an NTFS partition. For example, you may assign Everyone Read access to the public directory while giving Creator Owner Full Control. Any user who creates files or subdirectories in this directory has Full Control over them.

USER RIGHTS AND STRATEGIES

System administration is like a game called "least privileges" where users seek all privileges and administrators seek to limit privileges to only what is necessary. The principle of least privileges should be adopted based on the idea that the users should have access to no more data than they need to discharge their duties.

As an administrator, you are responsible for data availability on your servers. Downtime and lost productivity due to loss of data is your responsibility, regardless of whether management has expressly included this in your job description. You should provide exactly the level of privileges to each user required to do his job efficiently, and no more.

You can prevent users from destroying data either intentionally or by mistake if you exercise the appropriate controls. Your system can be protected with a combination of user account controls as discussed previously: user rights and file permissions.

USER RIGHTS MECHANICS

User rights indicate specific tasks a user can perform. Rights are used to allow users to perform certain tasks. Rights are really kind of misnamed—they actually limit user activities.

You can select and combine many rights from the list of rights found in User Manager for Domains (shown in Figure 10.4). These rights apply to users and groups defined within NT Domains, NT Servers, and NT Workstations. User rights are manipulated in User Manager for Domains, Policies, User Rights.

Some basic security is required in all networks. In many peer-to-peer networks, such as for a WFW environment, it is assumed that users should have access to other users' resources with few, if any, restrictions. NT Server is a client-server NOS, where it is assumed that each server's resources are in high demand, and therefore high availability is required. To ensure that server resources remain available to all users as required, users should be restricted to only that which is necessary.

Figure 10.4.
User rights.

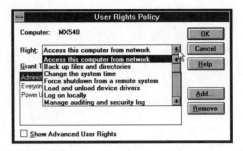

NT Server provides the User Manager for Domains tool for the express purpose of managing User Rights Policies and Permissions across workgroups or local groups. NT Workstation includes User Manager. You should select this icon to familiarize yourself with its options. You will find it in the Administrative Tools program group as shown in Figure 10.5.

Figure 10.5.
User Manager for
Domains applet in the
Administrative Tools
Program Group.

You can edit and adjust User Rights through User Manager for Domains, Policies, User Rights, then select the group you wish to manage (see Figure 10.6). Notice that Advanced User Rights are suppressed unless you check the box in the lower-left corner of the selection screen.

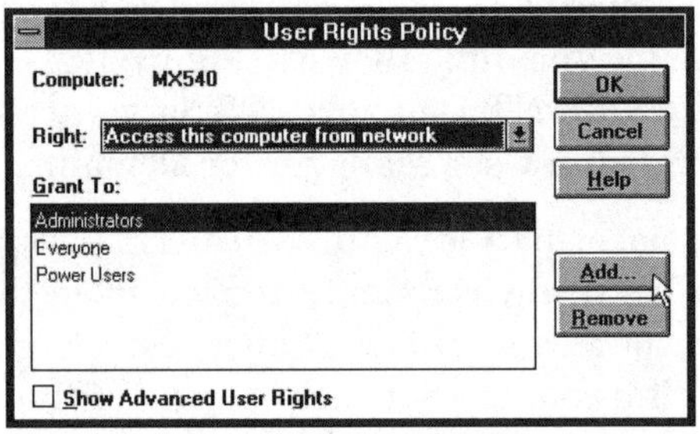

Figure 10.6.
Editing user group
rights.

Note

> When manipulating rights in NT, you must select the right, then select the group to which it should be assigned. This is backward from what you would expect, because several rights should apply to each group, and not the reverse.

The following User Rights are available to you:

Access this computer from the network
Back up files and directories
Force shutdown from a remote system
Load and unload device drivers
Log on locally
Manage auditing and security log
Restore files and directories
Shut down the system
Take ownership of files or other objects

There are several additional Advanced User Rights:

Act as part of the operating system
Add workstations to domain
Bypass traverse checking
Create a pagefile
Create a token object
Create permanent shared objects
Debug programs
Force shutdown from a remote system
Generate security audits
Increase quotas
Increase scheduling priority
Lock pages in memory
Log on as a batch job
Log on as a service
Log on locally
Manage auditing and security log
Modify firmware environment values
Profile single process
Profile system performance
Replace a process level token

In an NT domain, rights are granted and restricted at the domain level; if a group has a right in a domain, its members have that right on all servers within the domain (but not on NT Workstations participating in the domain). On each NT Workstation, rights granted apply only to that single computer.

Managing Other Users' Rights

As a member of the Administrators group, you have the ability to grant or revoke users' and global groups' rights. You cannot directly control other abilities; abilities are granted to some built-in local groups when NT Server is installed and cannot be changed. The only way for you to grant a user one of these built-in abilities is to make that user a member of the appropriate local group. For example, the only way to allow a person to create user accounts on an NT Server is to make that person a member of either the Administrators or Account Operators local group on the server.

Although you have the ability to grant and revoke local and global groups' and individual users' rights (using User Manager or User Manager for Domains), it is recommended that you do not do so, in most cases. This is because these groups have been carefully designed to provide all the administrative tasks required by most organizations. Instead, to give a user the ability to perform actions, put the user into the appropriate predefined local group.

There are also some advanced user rights, which you probably won't need to use so often. Many of these advanced rights are useful only to programmers writing applications to run on NT and should not be granted to any local group or user.

File, Directory, and Printer Ownership

Ownership of a resource provides a user with the right to restrict access to that resource. Files, directories, and printers are owned by the person who creates them. The owner is then the only one who can grant to other users permissions to these resources. Most files and directories are installed by administrators, who then provide permissions, generally to local groups.

Note

File and directory ownership is only available in NTFS volumes.

Ownership can be taken, but cannot be given. Members of the Administrators group have the right to Take Ownership; therefore the administrator can take ownership and then assign rights to other users if necessary. Ownership cannot be transferred to another user; the other user must take ownership in order to manipulate rights or permissions. This restriction prevents ownership from getting out of hand.

The Take Ownership right is pretty powerful, and therefore should be controlled carefully. To delegate administrative duties, an administrator may temporarily grant another user the right to Take Ownership. The administrator should then audit the user's activities to ensure that ownership is taken only of the resources specified by the administrator, then revoke the Take Ownership right as soon as the designated individual has finished that task.

Note for NetWare Administrators

File and directory ownership in NT is equivalent to the Access Control access right in NetWare. An individual who has Access Control rights can convey to other users access rights that he or she possesses.

NetWare's Print Server Operator is roughly equivalent to the owner of a printer in NT. The individual who is a print server operator can provide many of the same privileges to other users that the owner of a printer can convey in NT.

CUSTOMIZING GROUP DEFINITIONS

You can change the built-in abilities of the default local groups to be more in line with how your organization is set up. For example, suppose the administrator did not want anyone in the Power Users group to add user accounts to an NT Workstation's local account database. This can easily be achieved by securing the User Manager (MUSMGR.EXE) with permissions that do not allow Power Users to execute this application. In effect, what you have done is create a new local group with a different set of abilities.

Some organizations may find it necessary to modify the built-in local groups, though Microsoft recommends against it. For example, an administrator may want to restrict changing system time to members of the Administrators group only. Because this right is also granted by default to Power Users, the administrator can revoke this right from members of the Power Users group to accomplish this goal.

Tip

Microsoft recommends against changing built-in group definitions probably because they are concerned that changes to default group definitions will cause problems that are hard to support. This should not be a concern if you make only minor changes as discussed, and if you understand the consequences.

If you wish to retain the default built-in group definitions, you can copy a group, then make changes. Then you will not be changing the default group definition, you will be using a new definition based on the built-in group.

ASSIGNING RIGHTS

NT rights can be assigned to both users and groups. The following set of screens illustrates how the User Manager for Domains utility is used to regulate options available to an administrator (see Figures 10.7, 10.8, and 10.9). Figure 10.7 shows the New User, User Properties screen where the administrator sets the user's properties.

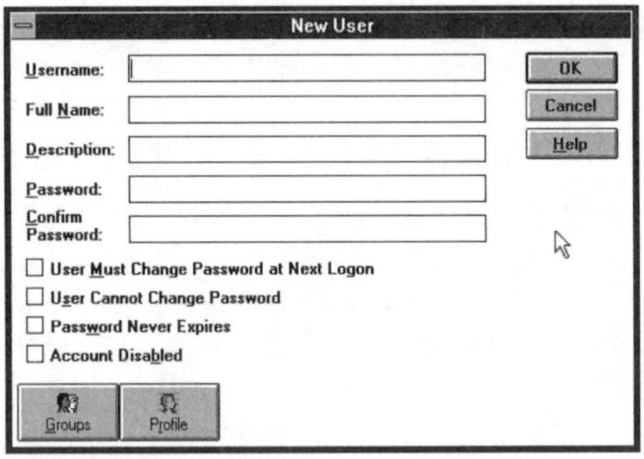

Figure 10.7.
The New User, User
Properties Screen.

Each individual NT computer controls user password and account policies for access to the computer. To set these restrictions, select Policies, Account... from the User Manager for Domains main menu bar as shown in Figure 10.8.

An administrator also has the ability to assign rights (privileges) to individual users or groups on a per-right basis. The previous figure showed the User Rights Policy screen in which rights are assigned to individual users or to groups.

These polices pertain uniformly to all servers in the domain instead of to a single computer in a domain environment. PDCs are synchronized to BDCs so all servers in a domain have duplicate information in their user accounts database.

Note

In order to allow domain users to access a workgroup, NT Server, or NT Workstation resources, you must assign a global group to a local group.

Figure 10.8.
User account policies.

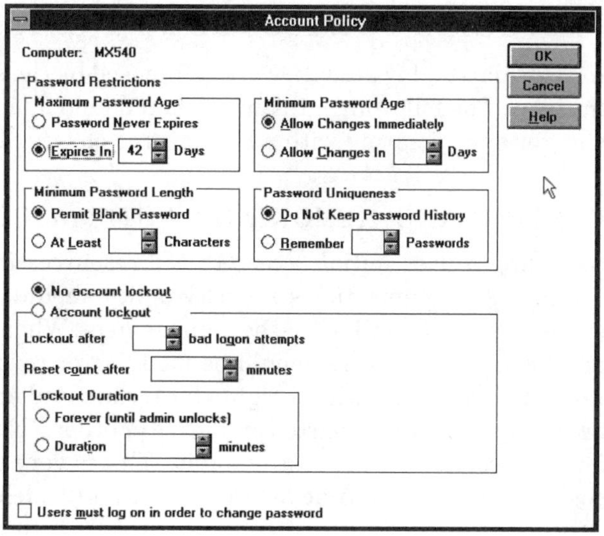

SECURITY ADMINISTRATOR

In any secure environment, no one user is allowed absolute authority and control. Instead, an auditor can be appointed, and the manager cannot hide actions from this individual.

The Security Administrator is the auditor account. In some networks the System Administrator may fulfill the duties of the Security Administrator, however, this account is provided so an external auditor can audit the administrators' actions.

Note

NT Server does not have a built-in account for the Security Administrator, but you should create one whenever there is a need to audit the administrator's actions.

When a Security Administrator account is created, the user to fulfill these duties should log on and immediately change the password and not divulge it to the administrator. To do so would compromise the ability of this user to audit the administrator.

Note for NetWare Administrators

The Security Administrator in NT is the equivalent to the Auditor account in NetWare 4.

STRATEGIES FOR ACCOUNT POLICY

A user's day-to-day activities are influenced by the security policy implemented at that site. The following guidelines should help administrators keep their environment or site operating with a high degree of security.

GRANTING AND REVOKING SYSTEM ACCESS

Assigning a user initial access to NT resources involves the creation of a user account. An organization's security policy should ensure that accounts are only created for people authorized by management. When a user terminates employment or transfers, this access should be modified or revoked. The main goal for timely revocation of system access rights for terminated employees is to prevent abuse of access rights by the departed employee or others. NT provides the ability to disable a user account without destroying it . This is very useful if an organization needs some administration time before the account is deleted properly.

PASSWORDS

A good password policy helps users protect their passwords from other individuals. This helps to reduce the probability of someone logging on with someone else's password and gaining access to data they are not authorized to access.

PASSWORD POLICY

Several policies need to be followed in order to secure password assignment and use. The following suggestions are a partial list of rules and are in no way complete. Your organization's policies should be formalized in writing and approved by management to be effective. Password security is specific to each organization, and may be required by outside agencies. For example, in government agencies, and for contractors who have government contracts, C-2 security may be required. In these cases, a list of password requirements must be followed.

When assigning user passwords, never distribute the user account name and password in the same communication. For example, if an administrator assigns a new user's account name and password in writing, the user logon name and password should be sent to the new user at different times.

The following list suggests rules for users. Users should follow these rules:

- ◆ Do not record your passwords, unless you store them in a secure place
- ◆ Do not divulge your passwords to anyone else
- ◆ Do not use obvious passwords such as your own name, spouse's, childrens' or pets' names.

PASSWORD ENFORCEMENT OPTIONS

The following facilities and features of NT will help to enforce a password policy and thus provide better protection for unauthorized use of passwords:

When a new account is created, you can require the user to change his or her password at the first logon. This ensures that no one else, including the administrator, knows the user's password.

Enforce a reasonable minimum password length (5 characters is generally okay). This increases the number of permutations needed to randomly or programmatically guess someone's password.

Set password uniqueness or history. This prevents users from changing back and forth between two or three favorite passwords. Administrators can specify the number of unique passwords that a user must have before that user can reuse a previous password.

Set maximum and minimum password age to make sure that users do not keep a password for too long. Over a period of time, other users may notice the user typing the password, or may in one way or another find out what the password is. Maximum password age requires the user to periodically change the password. Minimum password age prevents a user from immediately reverting back to his or her previous password.

FILE ACCESS PERMISSIONS

Access to files and directories is controlled by regulating permissions to a Share (shared directory). You can adjust permissions during creation of a Share, or at any later time. Multiple Shares usually can be created to the same server drives and directories so that each Share can have different Permissions.

NT Workstation and NT Servers allow you to provide share-level security. These permissions take precedence over any user account restrictions—a user might have rights to access a computer, but the local share permissions do not allow access.

NT Servers and NT Workstations allow

Full Control

No Access

Read (only)

Change

NT Servers and NT Workstations with NTFS file systems also have

> List
> Add
> Add & Read
> Special Directory Access...
> Special File Access...

NT permissions are adjusted through File Manager. Select a directory, select Security, Permissions, Share As..., Permissions, then adjust the Type of Access Field as shown in Figure 10.9.

Figure 10.9.
File and/or directory
access permissions
assignment in NT.

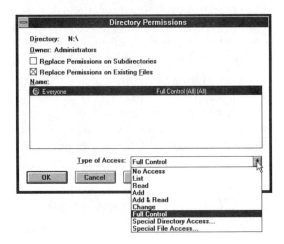

WFW computers can also share a directory in File Manager. When the Share is created, you have the option to provide the following permissions:

> Read-Only
> Full
> Depends on Password

These permissions have been updated and enhanced in NT and Windows 95. Windows 95 computers can be set up to provide share-level access control, or user-level access control. The former option works just like WFW. WFW and Windows 95 computers using share-level access allow the following permissions for a Share:

> Full Access
> Read-Only
> No Access
> Depends on Password

User-level access can take its control from a specified server or domain. You are allowed to specify an authority from which to draw permissions. You can specify a workgroup server or an NT domain to control user access.

Note

To implement user-level sharing you can select user-level access in Windows 95's Control Panel, Network, Access Control. Then you must also make the computer a member of the domain by using NT's User Manager for Domains from an NT domain server or domain controller. This step makes the resources on this computer available to local groups in the domain.

Don't forget, you also have to either log on locally, or to the domain in order to use the user account rights to access the Windows 95 computer.

This feature allows a Windows 95 client to be a full-fledged server member of a domain just like an NT Workstation or an NT Server that is not a domain controller. The user's access is restricted according to server or domain user account rights.

Whichever option you choose in Windows 95 can be implemented in Windows Explorer, File, Properties, Sharing. The options presented depend on whether you have chosen share-level or user-level access control. In WFW computers, access these options in File Manager when you share a directory. In NT computers, this can be done in User Manager or in File Manager.

EDITING PERMISSIONS

To edit Permissions, you can access the Permissions screen from Server Manager or from File Manager. Select a file or directory in File Manager, select the Security menu, Permissions..., you see the screen shown in Figure 10.10.

Figure 10.10.
Adjusting file access
permissions.

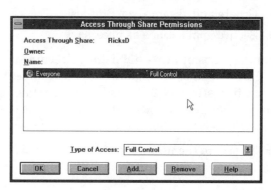

Note for NetWare Administrators

Permissions are similar to NetWare Access Rights, which are implemented as Trustee Assignments or Rights Masks.

NT Permissions map to NetWare Access Rights as follows:

No Access: No NetWare Access Rights

Read: Read, File Scan

Change: Read, File Scan, Write

Full Control: Read, File Scan, Write, Create, Erase, Modify (or Supervisory)

NT has no permission equivalent to NetWare Access Control. However, ownership of an NTFS file or directory provides similar control as previously discussed.

PLANNING YOUR NETWORK SECURITY

In very broad terms, the following is a set of implementation steps that an organization might follow in securing its NT environment. These implementation steps would be used in addition to an organization's own operational and security policies. Each step may involve several smaller steps to achieve the final results.

1. Create a plan
2. Select hardware
3. Install NT
4. Install any required applications
5. Add user accounts
6. Modify built-in local groups if necessary
7. Add global groups if necessary
8. Create and assign User Profiles
9. Secure applications as necessary

Planning is essential in establishing a secure and productive environment. You can use trial-and-error to establish the environment, however, you will find that this approach is stressful to the administrator and unproductive for the users. The following checklist of basic steps may be used as a guideline to jump-start the process. This is by no means an exhaustive list of issues that need to be considered.

◆ To secure the user desktop, apply permissions to profiles. This prevents users from changing their personal profiles.

◆ To prevent users from exiting to DOS, place the appropriate restrictions on CMD.EXE.

◆ To prevent users from accessing the floppy drive, place a physical lock on the floppy, or use a software lock like the NT Floppy Lock utility that is supplied in the NT Resource Kit.

◆ To deny access to specific applications, use File Manager, Security, Permissions… to apply restrictions to specific files.

◆ To establish auditing, clearly identify what needs to be audited. Enable auditing on all sensitive information. Apply auditing sparingly; audit logs can grow quite rapidly and auditing can be quite labor intensive.

◆ Establish appropriate logon security by first identifying the level of password protection required, then creating a password policy in User Manager. All users should be required to use a password and it should be changed frequently. Blank passwords should not be allowed.

◆ Physically secure NT Server computers. Open access to a server threatens the productivity and uptime of your entire network. Provide a safe, temperature and dust controlled area with limited access according to your organization's needs.

◆ Never allow users to leave workstations logged on and unattended. Train users to use the NT software workstation lock.

◆ If you install Remote Access Service (RAS), use the appropriate RAS security options and any third-party hardware options to prevent intruders.

◆ To exercise control over NT Workstations in the domain, make the Domain Administrators global group a member of the NT Workstations' Administrators local group.

◆ Install separate hard disk drives for the operating system and user data sets. If one drive fails the other will probably still be intact, reducing the time required to bring the system back into production.

◆ Do not share the system drive or directories. Do not expose a server's operating system to inadvertent or malicious potential deletion or tampering.

◆ Restrict access to system utilities. Install the Network Client Administrator utility only on administrators' desktops. There is no reason to expose your system to unnecessary risks.

◆ Display the Legal Notice warning screen on any NT computer requiring privileged access. You can display the Legal Notice during logon with a custom caption and message in a dialog box with an OK button by editing the following subkey in the registry.

To display the Legal Notice with your caption, use Registry Editor. Edit dHKEY_LOCAL_MACHINE\SOFTWARE\MICROSOFT\WINDOWSNT\ CURRENTVERSION\WINLOGON. Change the value entries `LegalNoticeCaption`: to whatever you would like the caption to display. The next value entry is `LegalNotice`:; enter your actual message after this parameter. First you must enter a value for the `LegalNotice` before a caption can be added.

◆ Provide users and administrators with network training. By far one of the most important aspects of securing any computer system is training users and administrators in access and use of the system. Several studies have shown that lack of training is a serious threat to security. Training needs to include all aspects of organizational security policy.

SUMMARY

This chapter contains the basic building blocks that you need to understand to manage an NT Server-based network. Though NT is almost as simple to manage as any other Windows-based operating system, the control and security of your system is based on your understanding of features buried in a few utilities.

In many cases, administrators find out that they could have prevented disasters only after the disaster has occurred. Every administrator should take the time to understand and implement security controls discussed in this chapter.

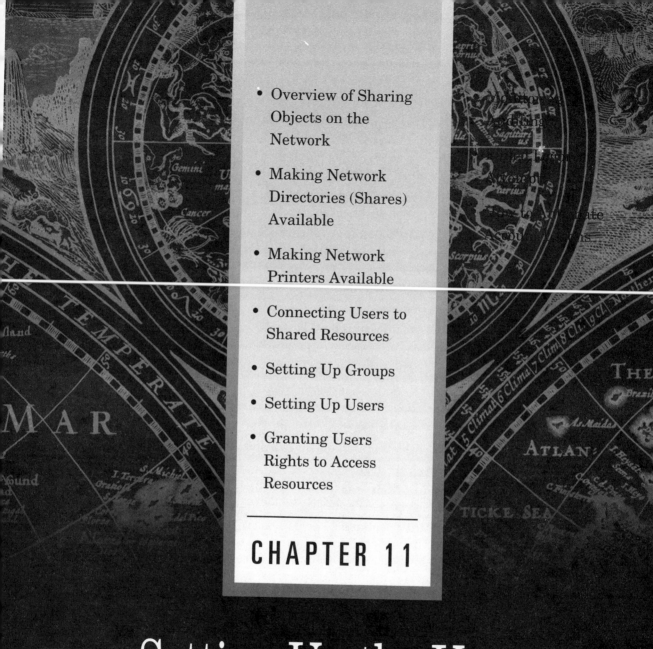

- Overview of Sharing Objects on the Network

- Making Network Directories (Shares) Available

- Making Network Printers Available

- Connecting Users to Shared Resources

- Setting Up Groups

- Setting Up Users

- Granting Users Rights to Access Resources

CHAPTER 11

Setting Up the User Environment

ACL   Access control list.

Access token   Uniquely identifies the user and the groups to which the user belongs.

Authentication   The process of checking a logon and password against information contained in the security account database.

Desktop   Windows background screen. This term is used to discuss elements in and on the desktop that can be changed by the user.

Domain   A group of servers working as one entity.

Domain controller   A PDC or BDC. These BDC computers service a domain by providing the Security Account Manager (SAM) database against which logons and connections are authenticated.

PDC   Primary Domain Controller.

BDC   Backup Domain Controller.

Local Groups   Groups local to a server or domain.

Global Groups   User-only groups that are used to provide access to local groups.

Rights   Rights allowed to users or groups to access network resources.

Permissions   Permissions to access shared directories and printers.

Mapping   A drive letter assignment to a shared directory.

Share   A shared directory or printer.

Security Account Manager (SAM)   Security account master database that resides in an NT Server or NT Workstation.

Security account database   The database of users, resources, other object IDs, and their related properties, such as names, passwords, and group memberships. In an NT computer, the security account database is SAM.

Security Identifier (SID)   A value assigned to each object created in the SAM or local security databases. All names and other properties are related to the SID.

Note

When you see the term *NT server* (lowercase s) it applies to both NT Server and NT Workstation computers functioning as a server. The term *NT Server* (capital S) refers to NT Server only, and not to NT Workstation computers.

You should already be familiar with the mechanics of global and local groups, built-in groups, rights, permissions, and most basic tools pertaining to the establishment of a user environment. If you are not familiar with these mechanics, please see Chapter 10, "Groups, Rights, and Permissions."

Note

> The key to NT system administration is understanding the foundation mechanics of the user environment. Chapter 10 discusses those mechanics. Although you may have worked a bit with NT in the past, it is extremely important that you understand the subtleties of groups, rights, and permissions. You should consider reading Chapter 10 so that when you apply them, you will understand fully how each of these tools works.

This chapter discusses the steps in setting up your network user environment in six steps:

1. Making network directories (Shares) available
2. Making network printers available
3. Setting up groups
4. Setting up users
5. Granting users with rights access to resources
6. Connecting users to shared resources

This chapter discusses additional controls and configuration to enhance the user's configurations. The next chapter, Chapter 12, "Controlling the User Environment," discusses setting up user profiles, logon scripts, system environment variables and parameters, home directories, and the replicator service. These features extend user account management once the account and use of resources have been established. This chapter explains the more basic procedures of setting up groups and users and establishing their connections.

Overview of Sharing Objects on the Network

All Microsoft networks work the same:

◆ Network resources are made available for users to access by establishing a Share name that represents the physical resource

◆ A relationship between the user and the Share name is established

◆ The user accesses and uses the resource via the Share name, even though the resource is located on a different computer

◆ Communications between the host computers are handled by one or more
protocols, rendering this process transparent to the user

Since Microsoft developed MS-Networks in the early 1980s just after the inception
of the IBM Personal Computer, this method of sharing and using resources has not
changed much. This product was based on IBM/Sytek's NetBIOS protocol.
MS-Networks was licensed by

IBM and marketed in the form of the IBM PC LAN Program

3Com and marketed in the form of the 3Com Ethershare, and later 3Plus
Share networking software

Novell and marketed in the form of NetWare Lite (later renamed Personal
NetWare)

Artisoft and marketed in the form of LANtastic

A host of other licensees that enhanced and resold the product under
various names, most of which are now defunct

When Microsoft and IBM later introduced OS/2, MS-Networks was used almost
intact in OS/2 LAN Manager, IBM LAN Server, and AT&T LAN Manager for UNIX
products. These products were based on NetBEUI protocol, an extension to the
original NetBIOS protocol.

Today, Windows for Workgroups, Windows 95, Windows NT Server, and Windows
NT Workstation are based on the latest iteration of MS-Networks, all of which
retain the mechanics of sharing and using Share names on the network. Microsoft
has re-engineered some of these products to run with other major protocols
including NetBEUI, TCP/IP, and Novell's IPX/SPX protocols.

Microsoft used to license this technology to other vendors, such as 3Com, IBM,
AT&T, and Novell. However, a few years ago Microsoft decided that the development, implementation, and marketing of the networking components should be
retained and driven by Microsoft and not licensees. WFW was the first iteration of
this philosophy, but NT is the first true implementation of Microsoft's broader plan
for developing robust networking services.

NT SERVICES

NT integrates the server operating system and networking software. NT Server is
designed differently from previous iterations of MS-Networks—the networking
components are not separated from the internal operating system components.
Networking APIs and mechanics are internal to NT, instead of interfaced from a
completely separate (and perhaps separately developed) software layer.

Features such as Dynamic Data Exchange, Object Linking and Embedding, Messaging API, and other features are built right into NT. This provides an excellent networking development platform which makes writing robust network applications simpler and more effective. Remote hosts can share data now with far less complexity than ever before. As a result, networked applications are easier to write, and far more sophisticated networked applications are more likely now than ever before.

Much of what Microsoft improved in later years has to do with NT's object-oriented design. Although networking has always used objects, NT as an operating system is far more object-oriented than previous Microsoft operating systems.

NT Server Objects and Object Mechanics

As discussed above, NT is object-oriented. This simply means that all processes and resources are represented by logical objects—they are not accessed physically. By placing an abstraction layer between all physical devices and the operating system, access between objects is controlled by the operating system and made more orderly than physical access can possibly be. Communications exist between processes occurring within the operating system, between user objects and internal processes, between user objects and resource objects, and between resource objects and processes. The whole scheme allows security, auditing, interfacing from applications, and many more interactions to occur safely and securely. The problem with applications or resources bringing the operating system to a halt is virtually eliminated.

Note for NetWare Administrators

NT is designed to be more stable than NetWare. One of the finest NT design features is the interaction between Intel's preemptive processing and NT's object-oriented designs. This design has virtually eliminated the occurrence of *Abends* to the operating system seen so commonly in NetWare servers.

In a NetWare environment, you cross your fingers every time you introduce a new server-based module (NLM, disk driver, or network adapter driver), hoping that it will not crash your server. Occasional hardware failures or conflicts can also bring your server down.

In an NT world, the server operating system is far less likely to go down through the fault of an offending application, or as the result of malfunctioning peripheral hardware.

Note

Virtually the only situations in which your server can lock up are when a hardware main board, internal power supply, or server hardware system fails, halting the processor—a process the operating system cannot possibly control.

If you do encounter a total system failure, you can examine the Event Viewer log to determine what caused the problem.

To prevent even these problems, base your server design on fault tolerance hardware and rapid recovery features built into your server. Examples include RAID 5 disk subsystems and Compaq's built-in server monitoring. If a Compaq server is so equipped, an internal monitoring interface card with its own processor and RAM remains running to record the events.

Your user account is a logical object representing you. The printer you seek to use is the logical object representing the printer port and printer attached to it, and the Share you wish to use is the object name representing the directory on another logical object, a volume. On it goes: even internal processing threads on the system are objects that are used to access the internal resources of your server. In the midst of all this is the NT Server operating system, the context for all objects. Every request to use an object is processed by the operating system, so communications are object-to-object.

You do not need to know all the internal API calls used to access these objects because you set up relationships between these objects and automate the links. These relationships are created in using the system administration utilities discussed in this chapter. The relationships are saved to files such as the Registry, so that you can reinitialize them each time the server comes up, and in some cases when you log on.

This process is no different from how networking operates in any other network environment, such as IBM's System Network Architecture (an IBM mainframe environment), a NetWare system, or a UNIX-TCP/IP environment. In any network environment the devices are physically separated, and therefore they require object-to-object communications, all controlled by the NOS, using protocols to communicate between operating systems spread out over the network.

To summarize, your job as a system administrator is to define some of the objects, create relationships between them, and make some of those relationships persistent (automatically re-established). At the same time, you can also place some restrictions (security) on the relationships between those objects.

SECURING OBJECTS

Security concerning objects consists of the following:

Tracking accesses and attempted accesses of objects. Because NT uses one mechanism for controlling access to all objects, it can keep a record of which users perform and attempt to perform what actions. The system administrator can control which objects are tracked and what types of actions and/or failed attempts are recorded.

Preventing monopolization of objects. In NT, each user has resource quotas regarding the resources he or she may use. Resources can be memory, disk space, processor time, and so forth. NT ensures that each user does not exceed the amount allowed. Resource quotas prevent a single user from taking over the computer, and they are enforced using the same security scheme used for controlling access to objects to and auditing objects. Each object has resource charges associated with it that are charged against the user's resource limit when the object is accessed.

IDENTIFYING WHAT EACH USER OR GROUP CAN DO TO AN OBJECT

The logon process allows users to log in and create an access token. The access token uniquely identifies the user and the groups to which that user belongs. NT compares that access token with the access control list in each object the user accesses.

Each object has associated with it a list of permissions for various users and groups called an access control list (ACL). The ACL has the entire list of access rights for that object.

The ACL is created when the object is created. The object's owner has discretionary control over which processes may access the object and what they may do. The owner may control this by modifying the object's ACL.

Each entry in the ACL contains a security ID (which can be either a user or group) and the permissions that are allowed or denied.

SECURITY CHECKS WHEN ACCESSING OBJECTS

Your access token and the object's ACL are used to decide whether to allow you to access the object.

The process of opening the handle is as follows:

1. The user program calls an operating system function to open the file. It specifies the filename and the type(s) of access it wants to the file (for

example, read, write, and/or execute). The type(s) of access the program requests are known as the requested access rights.

2. The object manager asks the security reference monitor to compare the process' access token with the object's ACL and determine whether the user should be granted the requested access right(s). If the requested access rights are granted, they are called granted access rights. Otherwise, the user's attempt to open the object fails.

3. The object manager charges the user for use of the object. If the user does not have sufficient memory remaining in his or her resource quota, the user's attempt to open the object fails.

4. The object manager passes a handle to the opened file back to the program. It also enters the handle and the granted access rights in the object table for that program.

The following example illustrates the opening of a file object:

A program run by user RICKS wants to open the file BILLS with READ access. Because RICKS is a member of the OFFICE group, and the READ access right is allowed for all members of OFFICE, the requested access right is granted. The object manager stores the granted access rights and the file's handle in the process' object table. The file's handle is then returned to the program (via the OpenFile function).

Once the program has opened the file BILLS, it can use the file's handle to read data from the file.

ACCESSING AN OBJECT

When a process needs to access an object the object manager does not have to re-check the object's ACL match with the process' access token. It just checks to see whether the action the process is attempting to perform is among the granted access rights associated with the object's handle. If the requested action is among the granted access rights, the access is permitted. If the action is not permitted, then it returns an error status.

The process running under the Security ID RICKS has already opened the BILLS file for read.

When the process performs a read request, the object manager looks up the handle in the process' object table to determine whether read access is among the handle's granted access rights. The handle is allowed to read, so the object manager allows the processing of the read request to continue.

ACLs are not checked for every access. NT checks the ACL only when a process opens an object. However, every access is checked against the granted access rights stored in the process' object table. This is much faster than checking the ACL for every access.

The granted access rights reflect the state of the object's security descriptor at the time the handle to the object is opened. Once the granted access rights are determined, the process retains the rights until it closes the object. If an object's security descriptor is changed either to be more restrictive or more permissive, the change does not affect the rights of the process to access the object using its existing open handles. The changes would not take effect until the object is re-opened.

Closing an Object

When a process does not need to access an open object, it calls a function to close the object. The object manager removes the handle and associated granted access rights from the process' object table. This ensures that the handle can no longer be used to access the object. The object manager also decrements the open handle count stored in the object. If the object is no longer needed by any process, the object may be destroyed or reused. If the system is still using the object, it is retained until the system is done using it. When the process is completed, all of its objects are automatically closed and therefore are properly cleaned up.

Making Network Directories (Shares) Available

Setting up your user environment starts with sharing directories for use by clients. In Microsoft networks, each resource that is to be used is given a name, called the Share name (sometimes Microsoft calls this a distribution Share). That Share name is made available to user-related objects. In a Microsoft network, you can assign a Share name to a directory, which then makes access to that directory (and therefore all subdirectories) available to users.

Prior to establishing the relationship between the user and the directory, the Share must be established and made available. This is the first logical step in setting up your users' environment. Without this step no server directories are available to clients.

In the process of creating the Share, you can restrict access permissions. If logon security allows a user to access a server, all Shares and network printers for that server are available to users. However, the permissions restrict the degree of access the user has to the Share. The mechanics of permissions are discussed in greater detail in Chapter 10.

UNIVERSAL NAMING CONVENTION (UNC) SHARE NAMES

Once the directory is shared, it is addressed by its formal Share name. The syntax for how the Share name is stated is called the Universal Naming Convention (UNC) name. The Share name is preceded by the server containing the Share. Like any object subordinate to another object, the Share name includes the name of the parent object. Because objects are contained in a hierarchical tree format, the Share name points at the specific object within the context in which it exists.

The server name, which is the top of the hierarchy, is preceded by double backslashes (\\). The UNC name is as follows:

`\\<Servername>\<Sharename>`

For example, the Share CDROM that was created on server SERVER_A would be assigned the UNC name: \\SERVER_A\CDROM.

File pathnames also follow the same convention. When pointing to a subdirectory, within a directory within a server's volume, the UNC name for the directory would be

`\\<Servername>\<driveletter>:\<directory>\<subdirectory>`

For example, the \APPS\WORD6 directory on the D: drive in server SERVER_A would be \\SERVER_A\D:\APPS\WORD6.

In some applications and utilities, you will see a Share name shown in UNC; in other cases, you will see the drive mapping letter substituted for the Share name. Microsoft and Windows developers are not as consistent about this convention as you might like, so you will sometimes be required to give a DOS pathname, and at other times you will be required to use a UNC pathname.

Tip

When naming a path in one of your NT administrative utilities, always use the UNC name. Sometimes you have the option of using the DOS pathname including the drive letter mapping that was assigned to the Share name. This name may not be recognized in various situations, whereas UNC is always recognized.

CREATING A SHARE

You can create Directory Shares in File Manager. Once you create a Share, it exists until you eliminate the Share in the Stops Sharing... selection in the Disk menu. Once you create the Share, it is listed in all computers that connect to the Share.

To create a Share, enter File Manager in your Main program group, select the disk from File Manager's list, point at the directory to be shared, then select Disk, Share As..., New Share to access this screen, as shown in Figure 11.1.

Figure 11.1.
File Manager's New
Share screen.

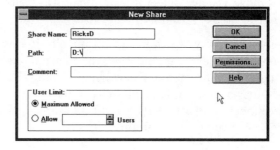

Notice in the lower left corner of the Shared Directory screen that you can restrict the number of users accessing this Share at one time. You can also adjust the directory access permissions.

Select the Permissions button and you will see the screen shown in Figure 11.2. This is where you can select the level of permissions allowed to users.

Figure 11.2.
The Access Through
Share Permissions
screen.

Once you select OK, the Share is available to domain and computer users to connect. See Chapter 10 or your Books Online (in your Main program group) for more details on permissions.

ELIMINATING A SHARE

Once a user connects to a Share, the Share is cached in the computer's local security account database. If for any reason the Share is no longer available or ceases to exist, the user still sees the Share on the list and at times suffers pauses as Shares are listed.

Always remove all references to a Share when the Share is eliminated or changed. To remove a Share, select File Manager, Disk, Stop Sharing... then select the Share from the Stop Sharing Directory list.

There are many occasions when an eliminated Share may be a problem. For example, if a server is renamed, the Share name will still list the old server name in the UNC Share name. You will need to stop sharing the Share, as discussed in the previous paragraph. Then at each computer connected to the Share, you must select Disconnect Network Drive from File Manager's Disk menu to remove the Share reference from that computer.

MAKING NETWORK PRINTERS AVAILABLE

Access to network printers is not available until you share them. Each printer is assigned a Share name just as a directory is. However, you will not see the printer called a Share; instead, it is simply called a network printer.

Printers are shared in Print Manager, which you can access in NT's Print Manager icon within the Main program group, or from the Printer icon within Control Panel. Either access method presents Print Manager's main screen as shown in Figure 11.3.

Figure 11.3.
The Connect to
Printer dialog box.

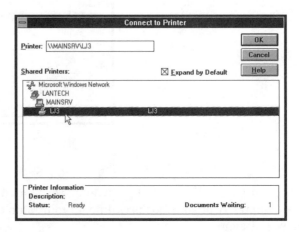

Once you have shared a network printer, users can connect to the network printer from their Print Managers, subject to the rights they have been granted and restrictions on group membership.

Print Manager can monitor jobs in the printer's queue. You can also change the default printer properties as shown in Figure 11.4.

Figure 11.4.
The Printer Properties
screen in Print Man-
ager.

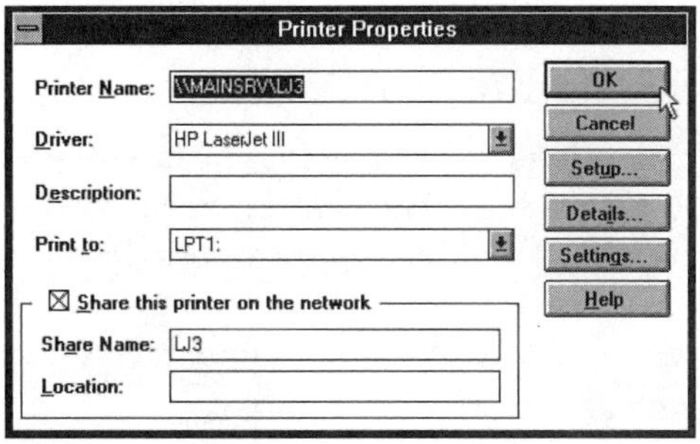

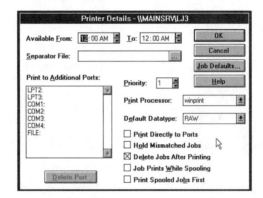

You can edit the printer Setup, Details, and Settings. The Setup button enables you to select features of your printer. The Details button shows the various options as shown in Figure 11.5.

Figure 11.5.
The Printer Details
screen.

The Settings button enables you to adjust the retry time period if the printer is offline or not available.

Note for NetWare Administrators

You will appreciate the print performance in NT printers. Once jobs enter the queue, they begin to print immediately. NetWare print jobs must finish printing to the queue before they begin printing.

As a member of the Users group (or Domain Users group, which is a member of the Users group), all users are members of the special group Everyone. The Everyone group has the right to "Access this computer from the network" and the right to "Print" to network printers. These rights allow all users to use the printers, but not to manage them.

ACCESS PERMISSIONS

When a printer is created, access permissions to use the printer can be assigned. In Print Manager, select the printer, Security, Permissions... to view the list of groups that have access and the type of access (lower right section) as shown in Figure 11.6.

Figure 11.6.
The Printer Permis-
sions screen.

CONNECTING USERS TO SHARED RESOURCES

In order for a user to access a resource, such as a shared directory (Share) or printer, the resource must first be shared as discussed previously. This section discusses how a logged-on user can access the Shares and printers that are already available.

To connect to a resource, the resource must be shared with permissions that allow users to use the resources in an appropriate manner. For example, if a Share was created with read-only permission, the user can connect but will not be able to update the files or directory entries in the Share. If No Access was permitted, the user cannot access the Share.

CONNECTING TO SHARED DIRECTORIES (SHARES)

To connect to a Share from a Windows computer, use File Manager from the client workstation and follow this procedure.

1. Select Disk, Connect Network Drive.... (You see the screen shown in Figure 11.7.)

Figure 11.7.
The Connect Network
Drive screen.

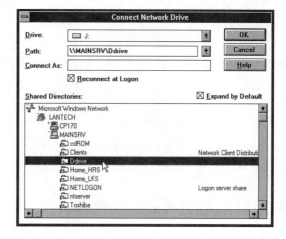

2. Select the drive letter in the Drive selection box.

3. Select the directory to be connected in the Shared Directories box. To locate a Share, you must click on the server that the Share exists within.

Note

All resources are listed under the server in which the resource is physically located. Each shared directory is located in a volume on a server. The list in this box shows the following levels:

The Microsoft Windows Network (globally all entities)

Domains and workgroups

Servers in those domains and workgroups

Shares in those servers

4. If the resource is located on a computer or in a domain where a different user account/password is required, enter the username in the Connect As field. This will cause an automatic logon as that user when the Share is accessed either during logon or when accessing the Share. You will be prompted for the password for that user in that computer or domain.

5. Select OK to save the connection. If the Reconnect at Logon box is checked, the connection is persistent (it will automatically be established during logon).

Note

A connection to a Share is sometimes called a *mapping* in Windows 95, elsewhere in Microsoft screens, and in other literature.

DISCONNECTING FROM A SHARED DIRECTORY

Disconnecting a Share stops automatic reconnection at logon. It will eliminate the path from all search boxes in applications. To disconnect a Share, use File Manager and follow this procedure:

1. Select Disk, Disconnect Network Drive....
2. Select the network mapping to be removed, then click on the OK button.

SETTING UP GROUPS

You may wish to set up new groups or use built-in groups. You should start with assignments to built-in groups. If this does not provide the exact mix of rights you wish to allocate, you can adjust the built-in group rights or add new groups.

GROUP DYNAMICS

In a domain environment, you will find local groups and global groups each represented by a different icon in User Manager. Rights to local domain resources can only be granted to local groups, whereas users are generally assigned to global groups. When you make a global group a member of a local group, the members of the global groups have access to the rights (and therefore resources) of the local groups as illustrated in Figure 11.8.

Figure 11.8.
Members of global groups have access to local domain resources via global group membership in local groups.

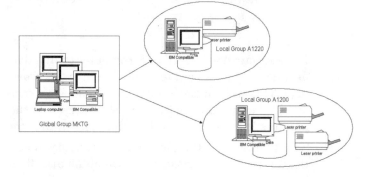

This arrangement is provided to allow inter-domain access. Only local groups can access resources local to the domain. Users in foreign domains can access resources in a local domain if they become members of global groups which in turn are members of local groups (global meaning not limited to a domain). This relationship is discussed in much greater depth in Chapter 10.

Viewing or Editing Rights Policies Defined for Groups

Use User Manager for Domains to view or edit the rights assigned to each group. The process of adding rights to a group is backward in NT—you select a right, then select to which group the right pertains. To view rights and a listing of which rights pertain to which groups, see User Manager, Policies, User Rights…, then select a right from the Rights box as shown in Figure 11.9. This screen shows you the groups possessing the selected right.

Figure 11.9.
The User Rights
Policy screen.

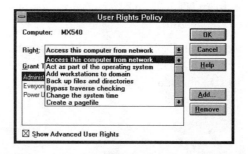

Note

For a list of rights pertaining to each group, see the section on Rights in Chapter 10.

Setting Up Users

User accounts are created and their properties defined in User Manager for Domains. To create a user account, select User Manager for Domains from the Administrative Tools program group. Then select User, New User… and enter user properties as shown in Figure 11.10.

11

Figure 11.10.
The New User Screen
in User Manager for
Domains.

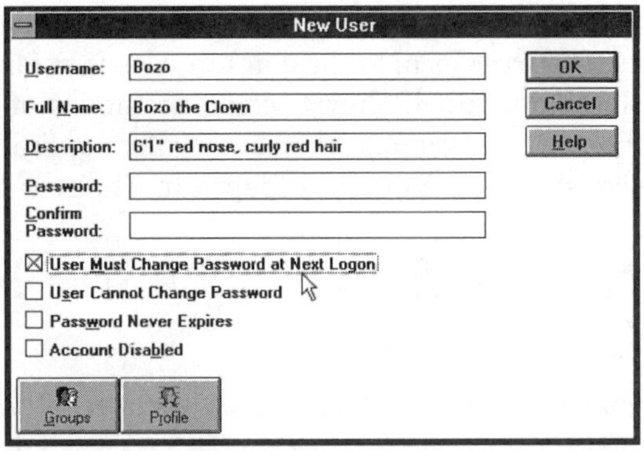

NT USER ACCOUNT INFORMATION:

An NT user account includes information about a user such as username, full name, password, and rights on the system. Each user needs one or more accounts in order to log on to an NT network. An account grants a user rights, defining how he or she may use the system.

The user is actually identified to the security account database in the form of the Security ID (SID). Names, descriptions, and other properties are associated with the Security ID. Therefore, two objects can have the same names and NT will distinguish between them.

Note

No Microsoft networking product allows you to create the same named object on the same server, but you can delete an object and re-create it with the same name. You cannot expect the old object's properties to be recognized, because they are related to a different object Security ID.

User account information is per computer in a workgroup environment, and per domain in a domain environment. In a peer-to-peer arrangement, each workgroup computer has duplicated information in its local security account database (hopefully). A domain configuration is recommended for all NT networks so that object information can be centralized on one server, as it should be in a larger, client-server network.

Default User Accounts

Three default accounts, Administrator, Guest, and an initial user (one you assign during installation), are created when NT is first installed. Each default account has specific rights on the system as follows:

Administrator

This account requires an initial password to be assigned during Setup. This account can later be renamed, but it cannot be deleted. The Administrator is by default a member of the Administrators, Domain Administrators, and Domain Users groups.

The Administrator has complete control over the entire network operation and security by virtue of its group assignments. The Administrator even has control over files owned by other users. Anyone who knows the Administrator account's username and password has complete control over the entire network.

Warning

If the Administrator password is forgotten or unknown, access to this account can only be restored by reinstalling NT or using the Emergency Repair Disk created during setup. To prevent the administrative account from becoming unusable or inactive, additional users can be assigned administrative privileges.

A user logged on to the Administrator account (or any member of the Administrators group) can perform the following tasks:

> Create, modify, or delete user accounts and groups
>
> Add or remove users from groups
>
> Assign special rights to groups
>
> Modify operating system software
>
> Install or upgrade application software and device drivers
>
> Format a fixed disk
>
> Set up the computer for remote administration on a network

Initial User

During installation an initial user account is created for the person installing NT. This account has the same group assignments and is for all purposes the Administrator, because it has the same rights and privileges.

11

Note

It is recommended that the name "Administrator" be used during installation instead of assigning another name. You can always add another administrator name later, and make the user a member of the Administrators group.

GUEST

This account is used by default for anyone using the system who does not have an Administrator or User account. Guest privileges give very limited access to the computer's resources. This account is often shared among many users for printer access or read-only access to Shares.

Guests are denied access to any private directories and files. The Administrator is responsible for setting up the directory and file security to restrict guest users from accessing private directories and files. If guest privileges are allowed on a system, the Administrator should set up a public directory to store files that are accessible to guests.

In some cases, an NT server may need to be restricted so that only specific users can access its Shares.

Note

To limit guest users from even limited resource usage, you can either disable the guest account or assign a password to the guest account.

HIDDEN ACCOUNTS

There are a few hidden accounts of which you should be aware, but you cannot really manage them. In an NTFS volume, these accounts can be assigned additional permissions, but in any environment, they still exist and have some default permissions that you cannot manipulate or even view.

Note

If you have shared both FAT and NTFS volumes, you can select each in File Manager, then select Security. Notice that the options in this menu are grayed out for a FAT volume. This is because Security Permissions, Auditing, and Ownership are only available on NTFS volumes.

These accounts are internal accounts the system or network uses to enable various functions. They are not managed via User Manager, cannot be added to any groups, or have any additional rights assigned to them.

Warning

These hidden accounts cannot be given additional permissions. You can remove file permissions from these accounts, but it is not recommended that you do so. You can prevent the operating system from having access to resources that are necessary to discharge various duties.

To see the hidden accounts, select File Manager, an NTFS volume, Security, Permissions..., and Add. You see the screen shown in Figure 11.11.

Figure 11.11.
The Add Users and Groups screen in File Manager showing hidden accounts.

Note that an NTFS volume can have additional file permissions (only available in this screen) that apply to the directory, regardless of logon privileges. The directory permissions that can be assigned here include

    No Access
    List
    Read
    Add
    Add & Read
    Change
    Full Control

The following hidden accounts are provided only in NT Server and NT Workstations with NTFS file systems:

CREATOR OWNER: This account is used to assign special privileges to the user who created or took ownership of the directory (or file). When you create a file or directory, your user account is allowed additional privileges that other users cannot have.

INTERACTIVE: This account allows users logged on locally to access this directory/file. Usually, interactive logons are ad hoc logons—the user logs on manually instead of automatically. If a user needs to log on only occasionally, such as a mobile user might, an interactive logon may be just the ticket. An interactive logon also has local connotations, although connections and mappings may differ depending upon whether the user logon is local or to a domain.

NETWORK: This account allows users logged on remotely to access this directory/file. This is the routine batch logon that is the most common way to log on to a network. Remote in this context means logging on to a server versus logging on locally to a workstation.

Replicator: This account enables directory replication. The system replicator uses this account to echo updates to an import directory, and/or to receive updates from an export directory.

SYSTEM: This account is used by the operating system and by services run by the operating system. There are many services and processes within NT that need to log on internally (for example, the SYSTEM account is used during an NT installation). Members of the Administrators group have the same file privileges, but the privileges are implemented differently.

Everyone (hidden local group): This special group is hidden like the above user accounts. It provides a minimum set of rights to enable all users to log on and use a server. All users are automatically members of this group.

Note

You can grant rights to all users in User Manager by giving the rights to the Everyone group. However, you should keep in mind that when you do, the rights assigned are the minimum set of rights for any users who log on to the domain in a domain environment, or any local computer logons in a workgroup environment.

It is not recommended to give additional rights to the Everyone group if you plan to restrict the Guest account to a minimum set of rights.

Ownership

File or directory ownership has significance only in NTFS volumes. Due to the permissions assigned to the hidden account CREATOR OWNER, the owner of the file/directory is the only one who can manage the file.

Unlike the security in traditional network operating systems such as NetWare, administrators do not automatically have access to every file on a server—if a file's permissions do not grant access to an administrator, the administrator cannot access the file. Every file on an NTFS volume has an owner, who can set permissions on the file. When a file is created, its creator becomes its owner. This means that confidential business files are protected from the administrator.

Group Assignments and Rights

Rights to local resources are granted by membership in a local group. Rights are always assigned to a group. Users become members of the groups and therefore inherit the group rights.

Note for NetWare Administrators

Rights in NT are approximately equivalent to trustee assignments in NetWare.

You cannot assign rights to resources directly to user accounts like you can assign trustee assignments directly to user accounts in NetWare. In NT, you must assign the rights to a group and make the user a member of the group for them to apply to the user.

If users from one domain need to access resources in a foreign domain, a trust relationship must be established. Then members of a global group (global to all domains and workgroups) must be assigned as members of local groups. More information about trust relationships and how to implement them is discussed in Chapter 9, "Workgroups and Domains."

When a user account is created within a domain, the user is automatically a member of the Domain Users group (or Users group in a workgroup environment). Because the Domain Users group is a member of the Users local group, all Domain Users have access to the Users group's rights. The Users group is a member of the Everyone special group, and therefore has the right to "Access this computer from the network." This right is limited by the file and directory access permissions assigned to the Share as discussed previously in this chapter.

Note

You can prevent Domain Users from gaining access to a particular server by removing the Domain Users global group from that computer's Users group.

You cannot withdraw the Domain Users group from the Users group on a domain controller (PDC or BDC).

You can refine users' rights by refining group rights. Each company or organization has unique requirements. Tailoring your users' needs is largely a matter of tailoring group rights. See Chapter 10 for more details.

GRANTING USERS RIGHTS TO ACCESS RESOURCES

NT needs only one logon, even for a mixed networking environment, because security in NT is set by user instead of by resource. Resource-based security requires a separate password for each resource accessed.

In NT, each user gets an account containing a unique SID in the security account database (SAM database). NT tracks permissions and user rights for the user. When a user logs on, the server's security process compares the logon information and references the SAM. If access is allowed, the Local Security Authority (LSA) creates a security access token for that user. Figure 11.12 shows a general view of the security components of NT.

Figure 11.12.
NT Account Overview.

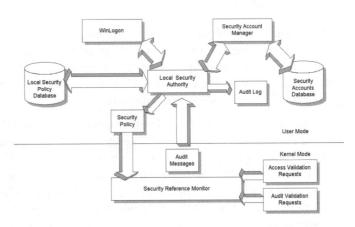

Note for NetWare Administrators

The SID is the same as the User_ID variable and bindery/NDS database entries in NetWare.

Note

A user who forgets his password cannot access resources via the Guest account using his own username. NT recognizes the username, and it compares the user's logon information only with the account information for that username. If the password does not match, no access is granted.

If the user logs on with a nonexistent username, he/she may be logged in as a Guest.

NT uses the Guest account to allow initial access to users with an unrecognized user account name, including users logging on from untrusted domains.

Warning

Do not change the user account properties for the Guest account. Because of NT's Guest configuration, anyone can log on to an NT server. If Guest privileges are changed, security in your system may be seriously impaired.

You can set up your network so that a user may have more than one account, one for access to the local computer or workgroup and the other as a domain user. The security account database used to authenticate a logon does not have to reside only at the user's local computer. Its location depends on whether the computer is in a workgroup or a domain and whether the user is logging on to the local computer, the home domain, or another domain. For convenience, the same name and password should be used in all places.

Global and Local User Accounts

There are two types of user accounts, global and local. Each type has significance when accessing resources in various network configurations and with various Windows networking products.

GLOBAL USER ACCOUNTS

Global user accounts are global to the network. Security account database information is replicated in servers or domain controllers and enables the user to log on remotely anywhere. The user information is replicated among domain controllers in a domain, and among servers in a workgroup.

LOCAL USER ACCOUNTS

The Local user account is contained in the local server's security account database. The user logs on to the network by logging on to the local computer. The following conditions apply:

Remote logons to other servers are authenticated at the remote server (NT Server or NT Workstation) or domain controller where either a separate local or global user account must exist.

A user may log on locally to a primary domain controller computer without a global logon. The user then only has access to local resources until logged on to a domain account.

A local user can use local resources without limitations; however, a remote logon to a remote server or domain controller can have more restrictions.

The local user participates in a domain but is available only by remote logon, and is authenticated only by user information available locally on the machine that is processing the logon. For example, a local user might be a member of a WFW, LAN Manager 2.x, or NetWare network. Local user accounts are available only within their domain; they cannot be authenticated through trust relationships.

A local account is defined only on the local computer running NT. If you set up NT so that your computer will not be a member of a domain, you are given the option to create a local account. This local account allows you to log on to your NT computer as a user account other than the built-in Guest or Administrator account. The local account created during Setup will be a member of the local Administrators group.

Logon accounts on the NT domain are maintained on the domain controller. The assumption during NT Setup is that if you choose to include your NT machine in an existing domain, you will most likely log on to that domain, and the logon will be validated by a remote server on the domain. Consequently, the need for creating a local account during NT Setup is less of an issue, because you should already have a valid user account on the domain that will allow you to log on to your NT computer. You can use User Manager to create local accounts after you have completed Setup.

LOG ON TO A REMOTE DOMAIN WHERE NO TRUST EXISTS

The term *local account* refers to an account that is local to the domain in which it is defined. The user account information is stored on the SAM in the PDC and replicated to all BDCs in the local domain. In order for you to access a server in a remote domain where no trust relationship exists, the remote domain must define another user account. The account in either domain can be a normal (global) user account, or a local user account.

To access a remote server or resource, your username and password in both the local and the remote domain should match. If the username and passwords differ, when connecting to remote resources you may run into software problems with applications that do not expect a logon interruption.

Note

Most Windows applications display a logon dialog box when the resource on the remote server or domain is accessed. If your application does not do this, you may be able to work around this problem.

Enter the remote server/domain user account name in the Connect As field of File Manager's Share Directory screen (in File Manager, select Disk, Share As... when creating the Share).

This option automatically sends the alternate username to the server where the other account exists at the time you attempt access to the resource. You may have to enter your password for the remote user account.

If your MS-DOS application does not prompt for the alternate username or password, you can connect to the server from the command line using the following net command:

```
NET USE <driveletter>: \\<server>\<share> /user:<domain>\<username> <password>
```

LOG ON TO A REMOTE DOMAIN WITH A LOCAL ACCOUNT

Local accounts are local to the domain in which they are defined. If access is required to a remote domain and a trust relationship has not been established, create local accounts in the remote domain and in each remote domain the user needs to access. Using local accounts in each remote domain denies access to remote domains where access is not required.

You cannot log on to local accounts interactively (manually); they are recognized only over the network. If the user needs interactive access, a local account will not be suitable.

The account in the remote domain can be either a global account or a local account. If you plan to create a trust relationship between the two domains, then you should create a temporary local account in the remote domain. This will limit the use of the account outside the domain in which it is defined.

Local accounts work only in the domain in which they are defined. It is not recommended to have multiple accounts for one user, so using a local account is a way to limit how much the account is referenced. Local accounts are recognized only over the network from a computer from another domain. If the user needs interactive access, a local account will not be suitable. Use a global user account to create a single account for use in each set of trusting domains if the domains will never have a trust relationship. If several domains trust each other, the account can be defined once in one of them and recognized in each.

It is not recommended to have multiple accounts for one user, so using a local account is a way to limit how widespread the account is referenced. This prevents trusting domains from recognizing the account and keeping the account in its ACLs.

Log on to Remote Domains with a Global Account

Global accounts make more sense when a user requires access to remote domains. A global user account can be recognized in all domains.

A global user account can be created in one domain and recognized in remote domains through the establishment of trust relationships. The global user account defined in the local domain will be recognized by trusting domains.

You can establish a trust relationship in User Manager for Domains. In this utility select Policies, Trust Relationships..., and you see the screen shown in Figure 11.13.

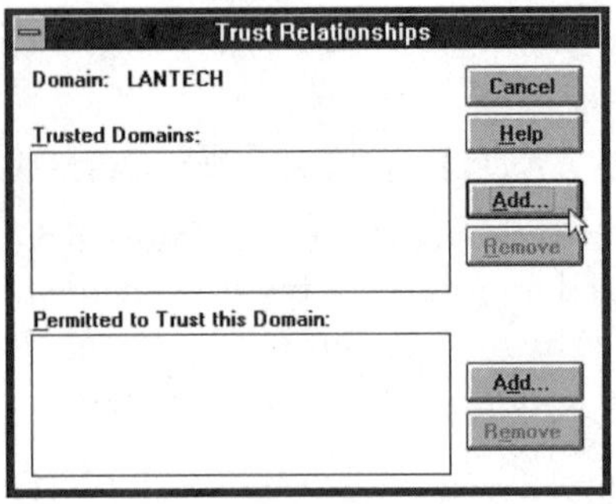

Figure 11.13.
The Trust Relation-
ships screen.

To establish a valid trust relationship, you must configure both domains. First, configure the local domain to permit the remote domain to trust. Then configure the remote domain to trust the local domain.

To establish the trust relationship:

1. Select User from User Manager for Domains main menu bar, choose Select Domain..., select the local domain, and log on as an Administrator (or member of the Administrators group). This will log you on to the local domain.

2. Select Policies, then Trust Relationships... as indicated in Figure 11.14.

Figure 11.14.
Trusting and trusted
domain configuration.

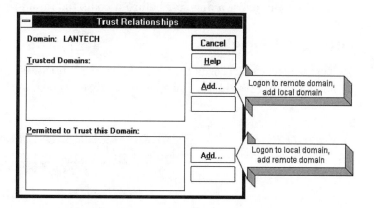

3. Click on the Add button in the Permitted to Trust This Domain box (lower box).

4. Return to the main menu bar, choose User, Select Domain, select the remote domain, and click on OK. Log on to the remote domain using the Administrator account on that domain (or member of the Administrators group).

5. Return to the main menu bar, select Policies, Trust Relationships..., and you see the screen shown in Figure 11.14.

6. Click on the Add button in the Trusted Domains box (upper box).

MONITORING AND AUDITING

Monitoring your servers is an important duty from the smallest to the largest installations. Indications of failures generally precede their occurrence, and monitoring a server helps locate problems before they disable your system. When problems occur, NT has built-in monitors that you can check to watch real-time activity and to see what went wrong after an event.

Auditing should be used in almost any company or organization to ensure that data is properly protected. It is the system administrator's responsibility to guard data regardless of whether this has been expressly communicated or not. A legal bailment is in effect for an employee to guard the employer's assets, and this includes data. In many cases, data is far more important than tangible equipment or even goodwill.

To establish appropriate levels of auditing, you should evaluate and implement NT's auditing services carefully. Too much auditing causes unnecessary entries in the audit logs, unnecessary reports, and soon ties up unreasonable amounts of disk space. Too little auditing results in not enough information being available. Good auditing can avert a disaster before it costs too much time and money.

EVENT LOGS

Event logs store records that may be viewed in the Windows NT Event Viewer as shown in Figure 11.15. Logs come in three types: system, security (audit), and application.

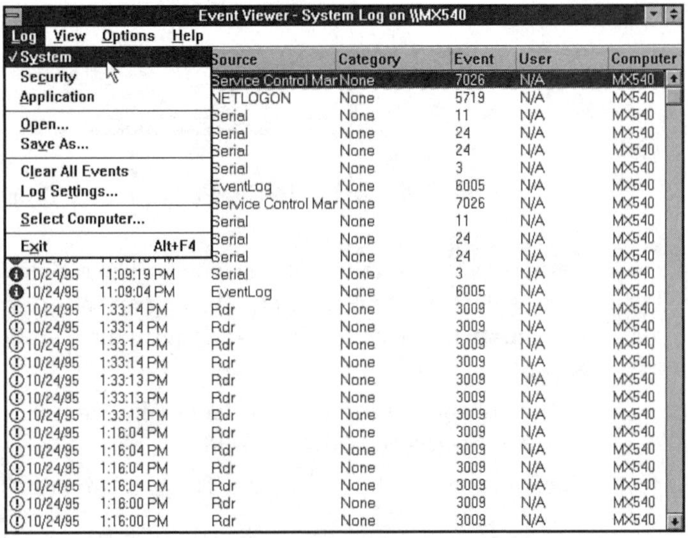

Figure 11.15.
Windows NT's Event
Viewer, Log menu.

◆ The system log contains errors, warnings, and messages generated during NT boot and afterwards by the NT operating system.

◆ The security log shows audit detail, as decided by the auditor, including invalid logon attempts and events related to access to objects as defined in User Manager, Policies.

◆ The application log shows errors, warnings, and messages generated by application software. What ends up in this log is totally up to the application developer who wrote the software issuing messages.

System Log

The need for system monitoring is obvious. If a device or driver malfunctions and users cannot log on or access their data, the system log is the first place the administrator will look to find the reason. It will contain error messages generated during boot or server operation indicating such failures and the processes affected.

Evaluation of system log messages is discussed in Chapter 22, "Monitoring Tools and Techniques," Chapter 27, "Physical Security, Quick Recovery," and Chapter 29, "Server Hardware Troubleshooting."

Security Log

The security log contains audit information concerning access to resources and changes in the SAM database. In most organizations, the system administrator or the administrative staff is responsible for auditing these events. However, in large organizations or in organizations in which secure information needs to be tracked, an independent auditor is responsible for duties related to auditing security-related information.

Many reasons exist for independent auditing. One of the most prevalent reasons is that public corporations' financial statements must be audited by outside CPA firms. In such cases, auditing should be established over financial records, and over administrative access and control of financial records. Many accounting firms now require a computer data audit to ensure that financial records have not been edited. In many other cases, the need to monitor the activities of the administrators is essential to guard data. The security log is an ideal tool for such tasks.

In order to discharge auditing duties, a group should be established for this purpose alone. No built-in group is established to perform the following advanced user rights:

◆ Generate security audits
◆ Manage auditing and security logs

To properly discharge auditing duties, you should create a global Auditors group, assign the Auditors group to a local group in each domain, and then assign the auditors to the global group. A global Auditors group makes more sense in a multidomain network, so that auditors can audit any domain. If you have only one domain, perhaps a local group would be more appropriate.

To create an Auditors group, use User Manager for Domains. First, create a global group called Auditors by selecting User and New Global Group. Then Select Policies, User Rights…, and choose the Show Advanced User Rights box in the lower left hand corner of the User Rights Policy screen (see Figure 11.16). Select each right individually from the Rights box listing, then Add the group to the selected right.

Figure 11.16.
The User Rights Policy
screen, for creating an
Auditors group.

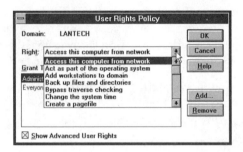

Note

When assigning rights to a group, as is the case in this procedure, you must select each right and assign it to the group. Even though it seems that the group should be selected and rights assigned to it, User Manager does not do it this way.

The Auditors global group must be assigned as a member to a local group in each domain to be audited (or in a computer in a workgroup configuration).

Only local groups can have access to local resources, but global groups can be assigned to local groups. Trust relationships can be established between domains to allow Auditors to audit systems in all trusting domains. In this manner, global group members (in this case Auditors) can access audit logs in foreign domains.

When an auditor other than the administrator is responsible for security, the auditor should seek to secure the audit log from the administrator's control in every way possible.

Note

To eliminate the possibility of an Administrator tampering with the audit logs, select the Manage auditing and security log right, and remove the Administrators group from this right.

Without having performed this step, any member of the Administrators group can edit, delete, or otherwise tamper with the security log.

Before you remove this right, be sure that you have already assigned the right to the Auditors group.

Warning

Although you may have taken these precautions to avoid allowing an Administrator from tampering with audit logs, any member of the Administrators group can add a group assignment back at any time, delete the audit log, or delete the volume on which it exists. Changes to the Rights Policies should be monitored to make sure this does not occur.

NT can log events related to system administration, the operating system, or software events. You can adjust what you would like to audit in User Manager by selecting Policies, Audit..., and editing the screen shown in Figure 11.17.

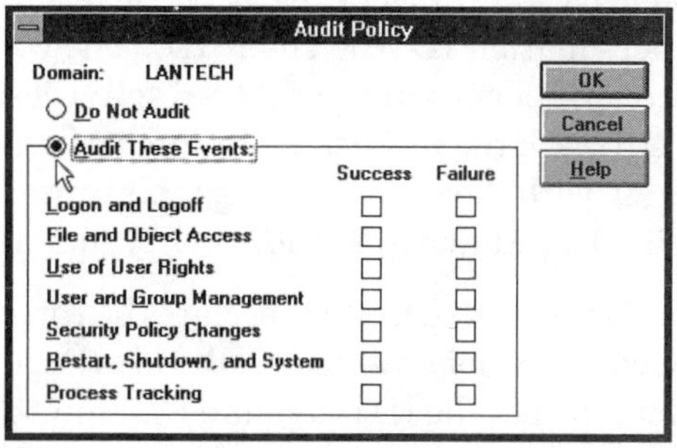

Figure 11.17.
The Audit Policy
screen.

```
┌─ Audit Policy ─────────────────────────────────┐
│ Domain:   LANTECH                      ┌──────────┐
│ ○ Do Not Audit                         │    OK    │
│ ◉ Audit These Events:                  ├──────────┤
│                        Success  Failure│  Cancel  │
│  Logon and Logoff         □       □    ├──────────┤
│  File and Object Access   □       □    │   Help   │
│  Use of User Rights       □       □    └──────────┘
│  User and Group Management □      □
│  Security Policy Changes  □       □
│  Restart, Shutdown, and System □  □
│  Process Tracking         □       □
└─────────────────────────────────────────────────┘
```

Note

Remember that more auditing is going to cost in performance. Even though each monitored event uses only a little CPU and disk time, heavy auditing can take its toll on performance when a server is very busy.

Adjust your auditing policies to the least amount necessary to accomplish your organizational goals on this subject.

APPLICATION LOG

The application log can help you hunt down problems in program execution, or it can collect usage information. Monitoring this log can help you keep a watchful eye on events related to system security, or determine the extent to which breaches could have occurred.

Some events will be written to an application log automatically, but it is the software developer's code that causes an event to be logged in the applications log. Therefore, how well the application log is used depends on the degree to which the programmer preferred to use this tool.

As NT applications mature, many of us hope that major software developers will use this tool to allow administrators to troubleshoot application execution.

AUDITING AND MONITORING MECHANICS

In NT, the user account does not always identify who is performing an operation. Therefore, tracking security can be a problem. Threads running in the operating system are identified with a Security ID; however, the thread can be impersonating another user, or it can be shared among various Security IDs. It would be misleading to log actions according to the Security ID in many cases.

NT's security auditing checks at two levels: the primary ID (the Security ID), and the impersonation ID (the client ID). The combination of these two IDs indicates exactly who is performing audit trail activities. A third level, the process ID, can also be used to track the process that is occurring. The process ID shows exactly what is happening with the process. To use this process, the administrator must turn on the option in User Manager's Audit Policy dialog box.

Handle IDs are also used to associate the thread with future events. Handle IDs are created when an object is accessed and are relinquished when an object is closed. At that time, the handle ID is available for another object to use it. By tracking handle IDs you can determine at exactly what point a failure occurs.

The access token has all these IDs associated with it. By auditing an access token, you can track the following information:

Group membership, security IDs, and properties

User rights and privileges and their properties

The User authentication ID, the ID that logon security tracks and authenticates

FAILED LOGON ATTEMPTS

The process of authentication can be confusing at times. When logon attempts fail, dicovering where the failure occurred is an important procedure in resolving the problem. This section exposes the hidden processes that occur during a logon.

THE WELCOME (LOGON) DIALOG BOX

When the Welcome Dialog Box appears and you can log on, you can specify to where you wish to log on. The From box indicates from which type of workstation you are logging on. Here you select or enter the name of the computer, workgroup, or domain to which you wish to log on. When you enter the username, the From The entity authenticates your logon.

Your choices are as follows:

If your workstation is a workgroup client, and you select the default workgroup name, the local computer authenticates your logon. Any time you attempt to access resources on another server, your account is authenticated by that computer's local security account database.

If you are a member of a domain, and you select a domain name in the From box, you will be authenticated by a domain controller in your local domain, and by domain controllers in any trusted domains.

If you are logging on as the local client on an NT Server, you may choose to log on to the local computer, the local domain, or a remote domain where a duplicate user account exists, or where the remote domain is trusting.

An NT Server local client can log on locally and be authenticated by the local computer security account database. But when you log on to the domain, the domain controller (or trusting remote domain controller) authenticates the logon.

At an NT Workstation participating in an NT Server domain, the security authority authenticates accounts using either the local SAM or the SAM of an NT Server in the local domain (or trusted domain).

At an NT Server that is a PDC, the logon is authenticated by the local SAM, which is also the domain SAM.

If the user attempting to log on exists in another domain, then the local domain controller passes through the authentication to a domain controller in the trusted domain. The From dialog box lists the domain and trusted domains of the NT Server.

After initial logon authentication, an access token is created and assigned to the user process created for the user by the Win32 subsystem.

LOGON MECHANICS

Here is the general progression of a logon:

1. The Welcome user logon screen appears asking you to log on. You are prompted to enter:

    ◆ a user account

    ◆ a computer, workgroup, or domain name

    ◆ a password

2. The username and password are authenticated by a security process in a local computer or a domain controller.

3. If the user information can be verified, a Security ID (SID) is issued and sent to the client redirector to identify the user. The SID's account information defines the user's relationship to the server's security process created in the local or remote computer.

4. An access token is issued to the computer's security process.

5. When initial local logon is accomplished first, an access token is issued for access to local resources only. If logon to a trusted domain is required, the logon request is also passed through to the remote domain controller.

6. In some cases, the request is passed through to a domain controller of a primary or a trusted domain. The authenticating server is determined according to a combination of the type of client configuration and the computer, workgroup, or domain name entered in the From box.

7. An access token is generated by the remote authenticating server's security process (in the case of a trusting domain, the access token is held at the trusted domain).

When a user attempts a session (remote) server logon for access to a computer, domain, or trusted domain, the remote computer's security process issues an access token used to provide access to resources defined within the authenticating computer, workgroup, or domain.

Every request is authenticated by mapping the SID against an access token. The access token is monitored by the authenticating server's security process for privileges, rights, and permissions.

The process of mapping a username to its privileges, rights, and permissions occurs as follows:

1. This user account name and password is compared to the information in the server's security account database. If login is secured, a SID is issued and sent to the client, where the SID is cached in the client redirector. The SID is used once an initial or session logon has been accomplished.

2. When a request is issued from a client, the SID is used to locate the server security process that represents the user.

3. The authenticating entity verifies the level of user rights and either issues an access token or denies access.

4. The access token is passed back to the Win32 WinLogon process.

5. WinLogon directs Win32 to create a new process for the user and attaches the access token to the process.

6. When any resources are accessed, the access token is used to gain access. If the access token does not have sufficient privileges to access a resource in the manner requested, access is denied.

7. If the request is for a remote resource, the request is passed to the remote server (or domain) containing the resource where a new logon process may occur.

Think of the access token as though it were an access card. Each time you encounter a door, you swipe the access card through a card reader. The door either opens or remains closed, according to the privileges recorded onto your access card.

The access token accompanies user requests for access, just as your access card accompanies you wherever you go. Every process initiated in the system carries the access token so that the operating system can check the card before providing any services. As mentioned earlier in this chapter, the access token contains the SID and group memberships to control which privileges the processes can attempt. Every time a user initiates a process, the access token is read to see if access requirements are equal to or greater than the requirements for the process.

Figure 11.18 illustrates this sequence.

Figure 11.18.
Logon steps.

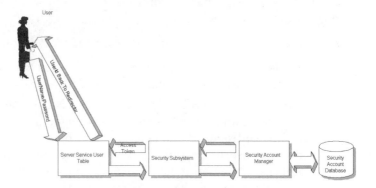

LOGON STEPS

Here are the steps your logon will follow:

INITIAL LOGON

Your initial logon is processed by the authenticating agent locally, in another workgroup server, or in a domain controller. The authenticating agency is determined by the type of user operating system, and whether you are logging on to a computer, workgroup, or domain according to the information entered in the From box.

The initial logon, therefore, generally controls only access to the local computer, until a remote Share or printer is accessed. During the local logon, the username, authenticating agent, and password are cached in the local redirector.

AFTER INITIAL LOGON

If access to a remote computer is required, every authenticating agent reads the locally cached username and password. Access to remote servers or domains are therefore either approved, or require another logon.

NT allows the user to override the cached username and password when accessing a remote server. This is done by specifying the remote username in File Manager, the Connect Network Drive, the Connect As option box, or by using the /user parameter with the DOS NET USE command.

VIEWING DOMAIN LOGONS FROM AN NT SERVER

The Server Service receives the logon request and creates a user process in the server's user table. During the logon process, the server issues a SID to the local redirector, and that SID identifies the user process. Whenever a request is made, the SMB protocol packet header contains the SID to identify which user process the request corresponds with.

A successful server logon at an NT server proceeds as follows:

1. The username, password, and computer name/domain name of the logged-on user are sent to the domain controller.

   If the server is an NT Workstation or an NT Server in a workgroup, the computer name is used as the workgroup/domain name since there is no domain controller. When accessing another workgroup computer, you use only your username and password. The computer must have a record in its local security account database matching your user information. The computer name, workgroup name, or domain name you enter is ignored, as it is not related to the logon process of a computer that is not a domain controller. In this case, the workgroup/domain name has no bearing on whether logon is permitted or not.

2. The NT server's security process checks the user SID and password against its local SAM database. If the entries match, the logon is permitted.

This process acts as an initial entry to the network, just as an initial logon acts as initial entry to the local computer.

If the logon request is for access to the NT server itself, the process ends. If any persistent connections are configured, requests are issued as Windows loads to the servers where the resources exist. The same process occurs at each of those computers, and access is granted or permitted according to whether the username and password in the request match the information in the computer's local security account database.

If the logon request is for a domain, the request is then passed on to any domain controller in the local domain and any trusted domains.

3. In some cases, the logon request is for an unknown authenticating server. Each of these requests is handled on a more specific basis depending upon the type of request, as discussed below. The authenticating security account database is researched to find a match; if none is found, the logon is denied.

THE AUTHENTICATING PROCESS

This section is about how a server's security process deals with account authentication.

IF A DOMAIN NAME IS SENT BUT NOT KNOWN AT THE REMOTE SERVER

If the receiver of the request is an NT Workstation configured in a workgroup:

The domain names are ignored since these computers always use their local SAM database for authentication.

If the receiver of the request is an NT Workstation that is a member of a domain:

The local security account database is checked. If no corresponding entry is allowed, the user is logged on with Guest account privileges. The domain controllers do not receive the request.

If the receiver of the request is an NT domain controller:

The server checks its domain SAM database. If the user account is not found there, the user is logged on with Guest privileges. The request is not passed on to trusted domains.

IF THE DOMAIN NAME IS NOT SPECIFIED

This may occur in LAN Manager 2.0 clients, LAN Manager 2.x, OS/2 clients, and the first release of WFW.

If the receiver is an NT Workstation configured as a domain member:

The server's security process checks its local SAM, the local domain controller, and domain controllers in trusted domains, in that order.

If the receiver is an NT Server:

The server's security process first checks its own domain controller, then trusted domain controllers (no local SAM is checked).

ONCE ACCESS IS AUTHORIZED

The access token is created and passed to the server process controlling the user process where a SID is assigned.

The SID is returned to the client's redirector, where it is cached for use with all client/server dialogs.

For each request, the SID is checked to locate the access token for authentication before the request is honored. Once the SID is referenced to the access token, the access token and the ACL are compared for assigned privileges, rights, and permissions.

LOGGING ON TO AN NT SERVER MEMBER OF A WORKGROUP

The username and password are compared against the local security account database. The From box specifies the computer name. The user cannot specify another workgroup or domain for logon. Because no NetLogon process is running in the workgroup NT Server, the pass-through authentication cannot occur. Therefore, there is no discovery of domain resources, or of the location of resources outside the workgroup. If access to another NT computer is attempted (persistent connection to a Share or printer), the request is handled as a logon request at the destination server. Logon proceeds as from any untrusted domain.

After authentication, the username and password are cached by the computer's redirector for use when connecting to remote resources.

LOGON TO A LOCAL DOMAIN

A logon from a domain member can be processed locally or at the domain controller, according to the user input in the From box of the logon Welcome dialog box.

If the logon request specifies a domain name in the From box, the request is passed on to any domain controllers in the local domain and in any trusted domains. The workstation connects to a domain with a workstation trust account.

In a logon request where trust relationships exist, the access token is kept in the primary domain controller's security process for use with access requests to trusting domains.

LOGON TO A TRUSTED DOMAIN

When the logon request comes from an NT computer that is domain member, but is not a domain controller:

The logon request is received by any NT Server and passed to a domain controller in the target trusted domain. Authentication is processed by the trusted domain's domain controller security process.

If the username is not recognized in the target domain controller, the logon is allowed and Guest account privileges are given.

Note

In domains, the logon defaults to a Guest account logon for members of remote domains only, and only if their usernames and passwords are not recognized in the remote domain controller's security account database.

If the Guest account is not available for any reason (for example, if the administrator has deleted this account), the logon attempt is denied.

When the logon request comes from an MS-DOS workstation:

The original logon request is authenticated at the local computer. At that time, the request is received by the remote domain controller. If the username and password entered originally match entries in the domain controller's SAM database, logon to the remote domain is allowed.

If the information provided by the original logon request does not match information in the domain controller's SAM database, the local redirector prompts you to enter a username and password for the remote domain or server. If using the NET VIEW command, your attempt fails because no additional user password information is requested.

When the logon dialog box appears, the From box provides the option of logon to each domain and each trusted domain permitted for this computer.

LOGON TO AN UNTRUSTED DOMAIN

When the logon request is issued to an NT computer, a logon to the local computer is attempted. If a valid user account exists there, a local logon occurs. If no local account is found, Guest privileges are provided, and the logon request passes through to the remote domain controller.

LOGON WITHOUT A DOMAIN NAME (WORKSTATIONS RUNNING WFW OR LAN MANAGER 2.0 ONLY)

When a logon does not contain an NT domain name, a local logon is attempted. If the username is not valid, an NT computer allows a Guest logon.

If the logon name is a valid domain user account, an NT computer will first authenticate locally, then pass the logon request to a domain controller.

If the username is not valid in the domain controller's SAM database, a Guest logon is permitted. If the username is valid, but the password is not, access is denied. Access is also denied if the Guest account is required but has been disabled. In this case, a password will be requested, but access will be denied no matter what password is entered.

When the logon request is for a trusted domain or a domain workstation, the authenticating entity is not obvious. In this case, the following attempts are made in this order:

The NT server checks its local SAM database.

A local domain controller checks its domain security account database.

Trusted domain controllers check their SAM databases. If all attempts fail, the user is logged on to the NT computer's Guest account locally (if possible).

SUMMARY OF INITIAL AND SERVER LOGONS

Local logons are usually executed smoothly. However, many factors often stand between the client and a successful global logon. Use this section to determine where and why logons may prove unsuccessful.

When following a logon, try to ascertain where the logon fails. You may have to enter different logon information, create new accounts or trust relationships, or do any number of things to resolve failed logon attempts.

WHERE YOU ARE LOGGING ON

When you log on, you either log on to the local computer, a server, or a domain. There are subtle, observable differences that let you know which authenticating entity verifies your user account and password. The differences depend on several factors.

NT WORKSTATION AS THE CLIENT

If you are logging on at an NT Workstation, the Welcome logon screen presents you with a From box—you can choose where you are logging on. In addition, an automatic logon using the Registry can log you on to a domain.

WFW CLIENT

The Network icon in the Control Panel enables you to establish startup sequences. If you want to disable the WFW Welcome Logon dialog box, you need to open the Startup Settings screen from the Startup button on the Microsoft Windows Network screen. The Logon At Startup checkbox should not be marked.

In addition, if you want to present the NT domain Welcome Logon dialog box, then you need to check the Logon to Windows NT or LAN Manager checkbox.

If you want an automatic logon to a domain, and do not want to display a successful logon notice, then you need to check the Don't Display Successful Logon checkbox.

HOW TO AUTOMATE ACCOUNT LOGONS

NT allows you to automate the logon process by storing your password and other pertinent information in the Registry database.

This is not recommended even in a secure environment, and it violates all rules of security. However, in a large number of organizations, passwords and security are ignored to some extent, and control over physical access to computers is the only security in use. In many organizations, passwords are routinely written on a stick-on note on the monitor with the ostensible permission of management, despite warnings to the contrary. In those cases, you might as well automate the logon and password entry function.

Another problem is that timing conflicts can occur. For example, if you have several network transports (protocols) loaded, logon may fail because a required protocol has not completed a background load in time. The autologin feature handles this problem nicely.

Warning

This feature allows other users to boot your computer and use your user account without appropriate password control.

Use the Registry Editor (REGEDT32.EXE) to add your logon information, as follows:

1. Start REGEDT32.EXE and locate the following Registry subkey:

   ```
   HKEY_LOCAL_MACHINE\SOFTWARE\Microsoft
   \Windows NT\CurrentVersion\Winlogon
   ```

2. Establish your domain name, account name, and password, using the values you would normally type when logging on. You should assign the following values:

   ```
   DefaultDomainName
   DefaultUserName
   DefaultPassword
   ```

Note

The DefaultPassword value may not exist. If it doesn't, from the Edit menu, choose Add Value. In the Value Name field, type:

`<DefaultPassword>` (without the <> marks).

Select REG_SZ for the Data Type. In the String field, type your password. Save your changes. Also, if no DefaultPassword string is specified, NT Server automatically changes the value of the AutoAdminLogon key from 1 (true) to 0 (false), thus disabling the AutoAdminLogon feature.

3. From the Edit menu, choose Add Value. Enter AutoAdminLogon in the Value Name field. Select REG_SZ for the Data Type. Enter 1 in the String field. Save your changes.
4. Exit REGEDT32.
5. Exit NT and turn off your computer.
6. Restart your computer and NT. You should be able to log on automatically.

Tip

If you take ownership of an object (a file, directory, Registry node, and so on) from an account that belongs to the Administrators group, the object is not actually owned by your specific account name, but by the Administrators group. This is the case to ease the burden of several administrators administering a single machine.

- User Profiles

- Logon Scripts

- System/User Environ-
  ment Variables and
  Account Parameters

- Home Directories

- The Replicator Service

CHAPTER 12

Controlling The User
Environment

Desktop   Windows' background screen. This term is used to discuss those elements in and on the desktop the user can change

Domain   A group of servers that work as one entity

Local Groups   Groups that are local to a server or domain

Global Groups   User-only groups that provide access to local groups

Rights   Rights allowed to users or groups to access network resources

Permissions   Permissions to access shared directories and printers

Mapping   A drive letter assignment to a shared directory

Share   A shared directory or printer

Security Account Manager (SAM)   The master security user account master database that resides in an NT Server or domain controller

Chapter 2, "NT Design," covered the design features of NT Server from a theoretical perspective. This chapter discusses the control of the user environment from a procedural standpoint.

Administrators should find the right balance in establishing control over a system. Consider that more control requires more discipline from the users, but too much control makes a network too rigid and difficult to use. On the other hand, a properly designed user environment offers users liberating conveniences to the users.

This chapter explains how to establish your users' groups, rights, and permissions. It shows how to use defaults and configurations to achieve your desired results when setting User Profiles, Logon Scripts, Rights, System Environment Variables, and User/Group Account Parameters.

Many configuration options are new in NT that were nonexistent in Windows for Workgroups (WFW). Administering an NT network generally requires more options—more control over user logons, user desktops, and other multi-user configurations. WFW is a peer-to-peer product that assumes users require simple and less extensive protection.

Prior to the release of Windows 95 these topics were moot, because the prevalent client base is Windows 3.x and WFW 3.11. Since the release of Windows 95, these topics have been at the top of the list of things to learn about NT Server. An NT Server is generally the central control point, while WFW, Windows 3.1, and Windows 95 are often clients.

Windows 95 and Windows NT Workstation were designed to be clients of an NT Server. Therefore, they have more user configuration options and integrate more fully with NT Servers. In the following sections, NT Workstation and Windows 95 are treated as equivalents. In many respects, Windows 95 is just as much in tune with NT Server as is NT Workstation.

Note

Many of these options are only available with NT Server, NT Workstation, and Windows 95. Previous Windows versions were not built with robust client/server network support, and therefore their users cannot take advantage of some of the features discussed in this chapter.

Look for notes like this one at the introduction of each section pertaining to each user configuration topic. Limitations of previous Windows versions are discussed throughout the chapter.

Microsoft hopes that the network configuration incentives provided in NT Workstation and Windows 95 will convince you to move your clients into these new client operating systems. You should look at each feature objectively to assess whether the cost of upgrading outweighs the missing features in your network.

This chapter explains how administrators control

◆ User profiles, configurations, and desktops

◆ User Account properties, permissions, and rights

◆ Access to applications installed on a server's drives for sharing

This is a *how-to* chapter that provides instruction on implementing these features on your network. Each subject is approached first conceptually, then procedurally.

USER PROFILES

Profiles are configuration files for users' desktops. In profile controls in previous Windows versions, each user's desktop was simply local—users' desktops were controlled totally at the users' computers. If you had checked Program Manager's Options, Save Settings on Exit, any changes to the desktop were saved on shutdown. There were few restrictions on what the user could and could not change. Also, Windows' designers assumed that each user always logged on to the same physical computer, so they designed Windows with the idea that the desktop was directly related to the workstation—if users logged on to another computer, they had to adjust to the other computer's desktop. Worse yet, if one user changed that desktop, another user just had to adapt.

NT Server changes all that. User profile options allow administrators to exercise control over users' desktops and many options pertaining to the desktop. If such control is not necessary, the administrator can allow Program Manager to work as it always has, and enable users to control exclusively their own desktops.

Note for NetWare Administrators

NT User Profiles are unique to NT Server and have no equivalent capability in NetWare.

You can accomplish the same type of control with Windows in a NetWare environment, but it requires third-party software.

OVERVIEW

There are two types of profiles—local and server-based. Local profiles are stored and updated locally at the workstation, whereas server-based profiles follow users wherever they log on. The server-based profiles can be mandatory (not changeable by the user), or the administrator can enable the user to update the desktop at will. These options provide an organization with far more control and flexibility. If the administrator or users do not want all this, local profiles work the same way users' desktops have worked since their inception.

The administrator can create user profiles to restrict users from

◆ Creating Program Items and Groups

◆ Changing the contents of Program Groups

◆ Changing Program Item Properties (such as the application a program item starts)

◆ Running programs from the File menu in Program Manager

◆ Creating persistent drive mappings (connecting to network drives)

◆ Making connections to network printers (printers other than those to which the Profile itself makes connections)

◆ Changing the desktop environment. The administrator can ensure structure to provide groups of users with the same user environment. He or she can accomplish this either by controlling the default environment or locking the environment specifics.

The administrator can configure the logon environment in advance to provide a consistent, manageable set of network connections, program groups, and program items. There are many incentives for such control, the foremost of which involves the installation of client workstations. The administrator can duplicate the desktop setup for a user, member of a group, or any departmental group. This feature has many security implications and reduces support time, especially if users are not familiar with Windows configuration options.

The alternative is to give users complete control over their desktops, which often causes a need for increased support and a loss in productivity. The use of user profiles to control users' desktops is a matter of strategy—the administrator can control user environments *or* enable users to control their own environments.

WHY USE PROFILES

To ensure consistency over time, the administrator uses profiles to prevent a user from changing the desktop appearance, Control Panel settings, system and user environment variables, and many other options.

The administrator uses profiles to restrict users from

> Creating new program items and groups
>
> Changing the contents of program groups
>
> Changing program item properties (such as the application a program item starts)
>
> Running programs from the File menu in Program Manager
>
> Automating connections to network drivers (mappings)
>
> Automating connections to network printers (other than those printers to which the profile itself makes connections)

All user-definable settings for File Manager are saved to either a local or server-based profile during shutdown. This includes everything the user changes, and the changes remain in the current state when the user selects Program Manager, Options, Save Settings On Exit. Among other saved changes, this includes

> All changes to Program Manager, File, and Properties, whether new or edited. This includes new icons and edited properties that affect the desktop's program group windows and program items.
>
> Network Connections selected in File Manager
>
> Printer Connections selected in Print Manager
>
> All user-definable, user-specific, and computer-specific Control Panel settings
>
> User Environment Variables defined in the System option of Control Panel
>
> Program groups added or deleted from the desktop
>
> All icons added or deleted from program groups on the desktop (and their properties)
>
> Application-specific configuration information for applications written specifically for Windows NT. Applications can be designed so that users resume where they left off, save or delete bookmarks, actuate security lockouts within an application, and save many other options to their user profiles.
>
> Help bookmarks placed in the Windows NT Help system

The administrator assigns profiles to individual users on the basis of group memberships, departments, or any other basis, in which case several accounts will have the same user environment. You can do this either by controlling the default environment or locking the environment specifics.

User profiles are used to preconfigure users' logon environments. They provide NT Server clients with a consistent, manageable set of network connections and program items.

By editing Control Panel's System settings in NT, the administrator also defines which variables in the local system and user environment to control:

> The workstation path
> The workstation's hardware driver configuration settings
> NT system settings
> SET environment variables saved to the environment space

Profile Mechanics

The administrator defines user profiles by creating a user profile configuration file containing settings for the user's Windows NT environment and local desktop.

If you want to assign profiles in User Manager for Domains, Users, and Properties..., select the Profiles button. The screen shown in Figure 12.1 appears. In this window, you can point to a user profile configuration file containing the options discussed in this chapter.

Figure 12.1.
User Environment
Profile in User Man-
ager for Domains.

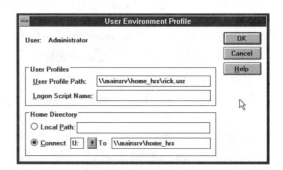

Profiles are stored in the same directory as the Registry. For NT Servers and Workstations, this is the \<winnt root>\SYSTEM32\CONFIG directory.

All user-definable options for Program Manager, personal program groups, their properties, and many settings are saved when the user shuts down his or her workstation (when Save Setting On Exit is checked), or when the user selects Save

Settings Now. Older Windows versions save this information in a desktop configuration file. NT and Windows 95 save this information to the Registry at the time of shutdown.

Note

Changes to the desktop are always saved when the user exits Windows, logs off, or when the system is shut down. Therefore, it is important for each user to exit Windows appropriately.

When using Windows 3.1 or Windows for Workgroups, user profile updates occur when the user exits Windows. Windows NT and Windows 95 save profile changes when the local computer is shut down. Although users can save profile changes during logoff and at Save Settings Now, they should always use the Shutdown option in NT's Program Manager, File menu, or from the Start button option in Windows 95.

Warning

Failure to shut down an NT or Windows 95 computer properly can cause serious damage to the system settings, resulting in failure to come up the next time.

For tips on recovering from such a system failure, see Chapter 27, "Physical Security, Quick Recovery."

Profiles are divided into two groups—server-based and local. They also come in three flavors—Local, Personal, and Mandatory.

LOCAL PROFILES

Local profiles are local to a computer and save the current settings of the local computer. They do not recognize different users; they change regardless of which username is logged on.

Local profiles are the only option available in Windows 3.1 and Windows for Workgroups. However, NT Server, NT Workstation, and Windows 95 can use either local or server-based profiles.

Local profiles for Windows and WFW computers are stored in one of many .INI files. It has always been challenging for administrators and users to locate and edit these options manually. Often, they have had few tools to manage these options automatically. In general, you must run or re-run setup programs for each application or for

Windows to change them effectively. In NT and Windows 95 computers, local profiles are stored with the local computer's Registry and are changed automatically whenever a change is made. In newer applications made for NT and Windows 95 even software installation, removal, and reconfiguration options are automatically stored from within the application.

There is nothing revolutionary about local profiles; you have been using them since you have been using Windows 3.1 or Windows for Workgroups. Simply stated, local profiles in NT or Windows 95 work just as Windows desktop settings have always worked, except that the information is stored in different configuration files.

Local profiles are stored every time the user shuts down the system or Windows. When an NT or Windows 95 user logs off, local profiles are updated. The changes are stored locally and are available locally (not remotely) from a server. Therefore, no matter who logs on at a workstation, the desktop for that computer is restored.

PERSONAL PROFILES

The first type of server-based profile is a personal profile. These profiles are called server-based because the profile information is stored in an NT Server's user account information directory along with the Registry. Local hardware/system settings are stored locally, but the server-based profile is referenced at the server for user-related information during Windows loading just before connections are re-established.

This type of server-based profile is called *personal* because it pertains to the individual user's logon account, not to the computer. The user personally controls this type of profile. When a user logs on, the personal profile follows the user. A personal profile restores the desktop and all Program Manager (or Windows 95 system settings) regardless of which computer the user logs on.

Several different users can log on to a computer. The computer's hardware/system settings are used, but the user settings are restored according to the user account name entered. Similarly, a user can log on to several different computers and each will bring up his or her personal profile settings. When the user logs on to a computer, its hardware/system settings are used, but the user's personal profile settings are restored.

In either case, the user can log on to any computer managed by an NT Server (or NT Workstation used as a server) and receive a personal desktop that includes the programs, program groups, and desktop settings pertaining to that user, not to the computer.

To configure personal profiles, run the User Profile Editor. Server-based profiles are managed at the server, and their configuration is accomplished differently in a domain or workgroup environment. In a workgroup, the user must connect with the specific server that contains the user account database. In a domain, a user logon can be serviced by any domain controller, and the appropriate personal profile will be located within the domain. When a user logs on to an NT Server locally, the local NT Server's account database contains the user profile.

Personal profile configuration files have .USR extensions and are stored in the same directory with the Registry (the \<winnt root>\SYSTEM32\CONFIG directory).

Mandatory Profiles

The second type of server-based profile is mandatory—the profile is assigned and may not be permanently changed. Mandatory profiles are the same as personal profiles in that they follow the user, not the computer; but when a mandatory profile is assigned, changes to the user's desktop during use are not saved. The next time the user logs on, the mandatory settings are restored rather than the settings left the last time the user logged off or shut the computer down.

Mandatory profile configuration files have .MAN extensions and are stored in the same directory with the Registry (the \<winnt root>\SYSTEM32\CONFIG directory).

Default Profiles

If no server-based profile exists, use a default user profile. The configuration placed in the USERDEF file is restored to the user desktop. If a user makes any changes to the desktop, a personal profile file is automatically created.

The administrator can change the default profile, thereby redefining the desktop for new users when they first log on.

The \<winnt root>\SYSTEM32\CONFIG\USERDEF file is where the default user profile is stored. This file has no extension and is created by the system during installation.

By editing the default user profile, the administrator reduces client workstation setup and installation time. A typical network client setup would involve installing Windows NT or Windows 95 locally (perhaps from a server's CD-ROM or shared drive/directory), and then the first time the user logs on, the default profile applies. The administrator can assign personal profiles to each user instead of reworking each user's desktop one by one.

How to Set Up Server-Based User Profiles

To effectively create user profiles, use the template approach. This process creates a template so that if you manage even a few users, you can *clone* future user templates with minor modifications. The procedure involves three steps.

1. Create a Working User Profile on the server
2. Create a template user
3. Create unique profiles for individual users

You can easily create future user profiles by replicating step three and using the template. The following sections explain each of these three steps individually and in detail.

Note

The following names are used in these instructions:

ProfTemp   The profile template user account

DomainA   The domain used in this example

ServerA   The server used in this example

STEP 1: CREATE A WORKING USER PROFILE ON THE SERVER

a. Create a profile template user account (for example, ProfTemp). Assign the user ProfTemp to the Administrators group. You will use this account to create the initial profile template.

b. Create a directory and Share where you want to save the user profiles. In File Manager, create C:\WINNT35\PROFILES, and in Share As..., assign the name Profiles.

c. Log off, then log on to ServerA as ProfTemp or the name you used for the template user account.

d. Configure the NT environment of your computer to be exactly as you want it for the user profile you are creating. The environment settings shown in Table 12.1 are saved.

TABLE 12.1. USER PROFILE SETTINGS.

Source	Parameters saved
Program Manager	All user-definable settings for Program Manager, including personal program groups and their properties, program items and their properties, and all settings saved by the Save Settings On Exit and Save Settings Now commands.
File Manager	All user-definable settings for File Manager, including network connections, and everything saved by the Save Settings On Exit command.

Source	Parameters saved
Command prompt	All user-definable settings for the command prompt, including fonts, colors, settings for the screen size buffer, and window position.
Print Manager	Network printer connections and all settings saved by the Save Settings On Exit command.
Control Panel	All settings for the Color, Mouse, Desktop, Cursor, Keyboard, International, and Sound options. For the System option, only the entries in the User Environment Variables box are saved. The other Control Panel options do not contain user-specific settings.
Accessories	All user-specific application settings affecting the user's NT configuration. These accessory applications include Calculator, Calendar, Cardfile, Clock, Notepad, Paintbrush, and Terminal.
Online Help	Any bookmarks placed in the Windows NT Help bookmarks system.

Note

To share common items (such as .BMP wallpaper files for your desktops), point to ServerA's Share to allow all users access.

e. Switch to Program Manager, choose Options, and choose Save Settings Now.

f. Run User Profile Editor from the Administrative Tools program group, then select the desired options shown in Figure 12.2.

g. From the User Profile Editor File menu, choose File, Save As.... Save the profile with a generic name (for example, UPROF.USR) and save it in the shared profiles directory (for example, \\ServerA\WINNT35 \PROFILES\UPROF.USR). If you want to use the profile as a mandatory profile, give it a name such as UPROF.MAN (\\ServerA\WINNT35 \PROFILES\UPROF.MAN).

Please note the following options in Figures 12.2:

In the first window, notice the option to allow this user to be *Permitted to use profile:* and the profiles you can select.

In the upper section of the screen, look at the available options for Program Manager Settings.

12

CONTROLLING THE USER ENVIRONMENT

Figure 12.2.
User Profile Editor
Desired Options.

In the middle section of the screen, see the Unlocked and Locked Program Groups option.

At the bottom of the User Profile Editor screen, see the window option *For Unlocked Groups, Allow User To:* and the options you can select.

At the very bottom of the screen, notice *Allow User to Connect / Remove Connections in Print Manager* and *Wait for Logon Script To Complete Before Starting Program Manager.*

As you can see, the Profile Editor allows you much control over user profile options.

STEP 2: CREATE A TEMPLATE USER

a. Log on to ServerA using your regular Administrator account.

b. Run User Manager for Domains, create a new user account (for example, ExampleUser), and assign the user the following profile:

\\ServerA\profiles\<username>.USR (substitute the user logon name for <username>).

Note

Use the filename <username>.MAN if you want the profile to be mandatory.

c. In User Profile Editor, open the template user profile D:\PROFILES \UPROF.USR (or .MAN).

d. Choose the Browse button next to *Permitted To Use Profile*. Permit the user to use the profile. For example, permit PWPDC\ExampleUser to use the profile. If you want everyone to use the same profile, you can permit Domain Users to use the profile. If you do this, ensure (with share or NTFS permissions) that users won't be able to save any modifications to the profile. If a user saves changes to his or her profile, the next person to log on gets the previous user's modified profile. For example, if User1 makes a change to the profile, and then User2 makes a change to the profile, the next time User1 logs on, his environment will look different than the way it did when he saved it.

e. From the User Profile Editor File menu, choose Save As File.

f. Save the file with a new name matching the username to which you just gave permission. For example, if you gave permission to GenUser, save the file as D:\profiles\GenUser.usr (or .man). If you permitted a group of users to use the profile, such as Domain Users, give it a name such as DOMUSR.USR (or .MAN).

STEP 3: CREATE UNIQUE PROFILES FOR INDIVIDUAL USERS

a. In User Manager for Domains, copy the template user to the new username. For example, copy GenUser to User1.

b. Repeat steps 2b through 2f to assign the proper user profile for each user you create. If you permitted Domain Users to use the profile, then all you have to do is make sure that the users have that profile specified.

RE-ESTABLISHING NETWORK CONNECTIONS

As indicated previously, the user's profile includes information regarding the connections to reestablish. To make a connection permanent, check the *Restore at Logon* checkbox when making the connection from File Manager.

Note

For an MS-DOS client not running Windows, make sure your NET USE statement includes the PERSISTENT switch as follows:

```
NET USE /PERSISTENT:YES
```

LOGON SCRIPTS

You can build logon scripts that execute during logon. Logon scripts are batch files and/or executable files that run automatically during logon for workstations running either Windows NT or MS-DOS/Windows. Any executable file, batch file, or MS-DOS internal command can be placed in the logon script. You might think of a logon script as the AUTOEXEC.BAT of the network.

Because MS-DOS-based computers cannot use server-based user profiles, logon scripts provide an alternate method of configuring the user environment when logging on to an NT Server. Typically, logon scripts are used to perform some (but not all) of the functions that a user profile provides, as discussed previously.

You can also use logon scripts to personalize an individual user's environment, or to standardize the environment for several users. You can assign a single logon script to all users, a different logon script to each user, or mix them. For example, a logon script can be used to run special utilities or applications, display a logon message, and to reset the path to include network shared directory. One such script may be shared among all users belonging to a certain group.

Note for NetWare Administrators

Logon scripts in NT are similar to Login Scripts in NetWare, except that drive mappings are not necessary because Windows restores drive and printer connections automatically (persistent connections).

Also, any batch or MS-DOS internal command will work in an NT logon script, which is not the case in a NetWare Login Script.

Unlike NetWare, a logon script occupies no overhead during its execution, and nothing can hook a logon script program in memory during execution. This means that you can execute Terminate Stay Resident (TSR) in memory software in a logon script.

Use logon scripts to

Copy parameters defined in the user's account on the NT Server to the client PC's MS-DOS environment variables (using the Putinenv Utility). You can use these variables in the logon script, or an application can use them.

Implement home directories (directories for each user's private files).

Automate MS-DOS batch, internal, or executable files to run automatically when a user logs on at any workstation including NT Workstation, Windows 95, or MS-DOS/Windows computers.

REASONS TO USE LOGON SCRIPTS

Although logon scripts aren't as powerful as user profiles, reasons to use them include the following:

◆ User profiles do not work on MS-DOS-based workstations (this includes Windows 3.1 and WFW 3.11 clients)

◆ You can manage only part of the user's environment

◆ You can automate network connections that are the same for the computer regardless of which user logs on

◆ You may want to use existing logon scripts, perhaps from a previous LAN Manager installation or converted from NetWare

◆ You can activate replication to any server (this allows accounts with logon scripts to be validated by any server)

◆ You can automate timed execution of applications such as virus scanning or backup software (by including the AT.EXE utility in the logon script)

THE MECHANICS OF LOGON SCRIPTS

During logon, a temporary network connection is made automatically to the SCRIPTS directory on the validating server. The connection is established using the last physical drive letter specified by the LASTDRIVE statement in CONFIG.SYS; the Netlogon Share to this directory is created by default. The user must at least have Read-only permissions to the SCRIPTS directory on the server. The Netlogon Share name must point to the SCRIPTS directory, which by default is located in \\<Server>\<winnt-root>\SYSTEM32\REPL\IMPORT\SCRIPTS.

When the user logs on, if the script exists in this directory it is downloaded and run without any further modifications. The script is always downloaded from the computer that validates a user's logon request, which is the first domain controller (PDC or BDC) to respond to the domain user's logon request.

To ensure that logon scripts always work for all user accounts in a domain, the administrator must make sure that all logon scripts are up to date on every Windows NT Server in that domain. You can use the Replicator service to accomplish this goal, as discussed in the note following.

When executing a script file, the local workstation runs a secondary MS-DOS command shell. When a logon script ends, the MS-DOS environment variables set during the script are lost. To make these variables permanently available, run the PUTINENV utility after logging on. The PUTINENV is included on the disk that accompanies this book, and is discussed later in this chapter.

LOGON SCRIPT PARAMETERS

NT has the following built-in logon script parameters:

Variable	Description
%HOMEDRIVE%	The user's local workstation drive letter connected to the user's home directory
%HOMEPATH%	Full pathname of the user's home directory
%HOMESHARE%	Share name containing the home directory
%OS%	The user's operating system
%PROCESSOR ARCHITECTURE%	The type of CPU in the user's workstation
%PROCESSOR LEVEL%	Indicates processor model (for example, 4=486)
%USERDOMAIN%	The user's domain
%USERNAME%	The user's name

HOW TO SET UP LOGON SCRIPTS

To create and assign a logon script, create and debug a logon script at a local workstation.

◆ Log on to a domain (not to a specific server).

◆ Copy the logon script into the SCRIPTS directory (as discussed in the previous section).

◆ Map a drive letter to the SCRIPTS directory.

Note

The administrator setting up the logon scripts can designate the pathname of the logon script file in the user's account, but the default directory is \\<Server>\<winnt-root>\SYSTEM32\REPL \IMPORT\SCRIPTS. If the default directory is used, no other modifications are necessary for the network to find the location of the logon scripts.

◆ To assign a logon script to a group, use the *Select Users* menu item in User Manager for Domains to select the users in the group. To set the actual script, go to User Properties Dialog and select the Profiles button. You can assign logon scripts to each member of the group individually, but this way you can assign a logon script to all group members at one time.

Tip

To ensure that logon scripts always work for users, you should ascertain that logon scripts for all user accounts in a domain exist on every Windows NT Server in the domain. Use the replicator service for this purpose—it maintains identical copies of your profile scripts on multiple servers.

To use the Replicator service with logon scripts, set up one of the domain's Windows NT Server servers as the export server, and all the other servers in the domain as import servers.

Using PUTINENV

PUTINENV, included on the disk accompanying this book, and available through CompuServe, the NT Resource Kit, and various other sources, is a utility that uses network API function calls to retrieve workstation variables. The variables are then set as MS-DOS environment variables and can be viewed from the MS-DOS prompt when you type **SET**. You can cull these variables from logon scripts or other batch files to provide customized settings. For example:

```
if %USERNAME%==GREGB net use lptl \\prntsvr\ljiii
```

PUTINENV is useful for standardizing logon scripts in MS-DOS machines.

Note

PUTINENV does not work on WFW 3.11 and Windows 3.x clients.

Note

PUTINENV is included on the disk accompanying this book.

System/User Environment Variables and Account Parameters

On an NT computer, Environment Variables are set for the computer (system) and the user. Both sets of variables are set in Control Panel's System icon as shown in Figure 12.4.

Figure 12.3.
System Screen in the
Control Panel.

System Environment Variables contain information about the NT Server, such as the path to the TEMP directory at the NT Server. SET parameters (placed into the DOS environment) pertaining to the user account logon are also manipulated in this same screen.

Account Variables are pointers to the key user directories, pathnames, domains, and operating system versions that NT needs to function properly. The actual values for these variables reside in the SAM at the NT Server.

When the user logs on, he or she encounters the following predefined environment variables and pieces of information:

◆ System environment variables

◆ User environment variables

◆ AUTOEXEC environment variables

◆ How environment variables are set

◆ How the path is built

◆ Changing user environment variables using control panel

SYSTEM ENVIRONMENT VARIABLES

System environment variables pertain to the computer itself—not the user. You can view them from Control Panel by choosing the System icon as shown in Figure 12.5. These variables are always set no matter who logs on, and they cannot be changed by any user.

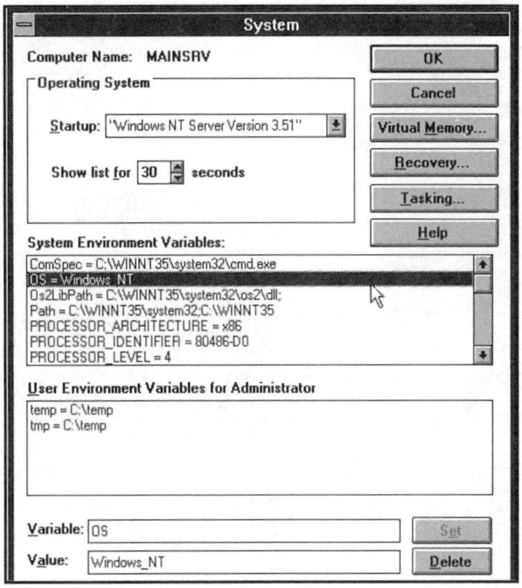

Figure 12.4.
The system environ-
ment variables in the
System screen.

A few additional predefined environment variables set when the user logs on do not appear in the System dialog box.

USERNAME

USERDOMAIN

NTVERSION

WINDIR

OS

PROCESSOR_ARCHITECTURE

values: x86, MIPS or ALPHA

PROCESSOR_LEVEL

values for x86: 3, 4, 5

values for MIPS: 3000, 4000

values for ALPHA: 21064

HOMEPATH

HOMEDRIVE

HOMESHARE

The following three environment variables are set based on the value of the home directory. The user's home directory is specified in User Manager (in Choose Profile and Properties). If the home directory uses universal naming conventions (UNC), then they will have the following values:

```
HOMESHARE=\\<server name>\<share name>
HOMEPATH=\<path>
HOMEDRIVE=<drive letter>:
```

If the home directory is a local path such as C:\NT, then they will look like this:

```
HOMEDRIVE=C:
HOMESHARE=
HOMEPATH=\NT
```

The environment variables listed are always present and may be used in logon scripts.

USER ENVIRONMENT VARIABLES

User environment variables pertain to user accounts rather than to computers. You can view them from Control Panel, as well.

The user may add, delete, or modify the environment variables in the User Environment Variables for the user field. These variables take precedence over system environment variables. The user path is appended to the system path.

All environment variables and the paths set in the AUTOEXEC.BAT file are used to create the Windows NT environment. Any paths in the AUTOEXEC.BAT file are appended to the system path.

Environment variables are set in the following order:

System variables
AUTOEXEC.BAT variables
User variables

The path is constructed from the system path, which can be viewed in the System Environment Variables field in the System dialog box. The user path is appended to the system path. Then the path from the AUTOEXEC.BAT file is appended.

Note

The environment variables LibPath and Os2LibPath are built the same way (system path + user path + AUTOEXEC.BAT path).

CHANGING USER ENVIRONMENT VARIABLES USING THE CONTROL PANEL

You can add, change, or delete user environment variables using the Control Panel. There is no need to reboot after making any of these changes, because the changes take effect immediately after exiting the System dialog box.

The next application you start uses the new settings. Any applications running before the changes were made will not recognize the changes.

Note

When you include the SUBST command in the AUTOEXEC.NT file in Windows NT, it does not execute. The AUTOEXEC.NT file only runs the 16-bit DOS binary command. The SUBST command is a Win32 binary command. To work around this problem, create a batch file including the SUBST command. Next, create a program item for the batch file in the Startup group of Program Manager. Include the SUBST command in a user's login script.

OTHER SYSTEM ADJUSTMENTS

You can adjust some of the most important system settings in Control Panel's System utility. You can adjust

Virtual Memory	pagefile drive location
	pagefile drive spanning information
	pagefile min/max current and allocated sizes
	Registry file current and maximum size
Recovery	actions to be taken when the system stops
Tasking	foreground/background response allocation

The following discussion should provide some guidance for adjusting these parameters.

VIRTUAL MEMORY

NT uses disk storage as if it were RAM in the form of virtual memory. The pagefile is the file space that Windows uses to swap memory contents to disk and back to RAM. Windows constantly optimizes allocation of memory between RAM and virtual memory.

You can adjust the size and location of your pagefile as shown in Figure 12.6. The default configuration that Setup yields is generally optimal, and cannot be improved except under unusual conditions. You may wish to adjust the pagefile size where CAD/CAM and complex graphics are concerned. However, you should not adjust it unless you observe error messages or poor performance.

For example, if you are running out of disk space, you may wish to reduce the size of your pagefile. However, this compromises performance and only buys you some time before the inevitable occurs—your disk becomes full. You are better off adding more disk storage.

12

CONTROLLING THE USER ENVIRONMENT

Figure 12.5.
Virtual Memory screen.

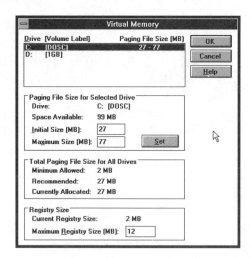

Tip

To reduce the effect of virtual memory page swapping, stripe your volumes over two or more drives. This RAID 0 configuration is an available configuration option in NT and improves physical read and write performance significantly.

RECOVERY

Recovery adjustments provide configurable options for action if a STOP occurs, bringing the NT operating system down. You have the following options:

Write an event to the system log
Write debugging information to (a specified path)
Overwrite existing file
Automatically reboot

You can select any box or any combination of boxes as you choose.

Note

The size of the pagefile must be greater than or equal to the size of the physical memory, and it must exist on the boot device in order for recovery to be enabled.

TASKING

The Tasking option allows you to adjust the foreground versus background processing priority. This enables you to tune your server for the demands you place on it.

More information on adjusting any of these parameters can be found in Chapter 23, "Evaluating Performance Opportunities."

HOME DIRECTORIES

A *home directory* is an excellent place to store a user logon script, especially in a domain environment where local disk space is at a premium, or when automatic backup of personal files is required. This way the user always gets the same logon script, even when logging on from a different computer.

When a user starts any Program Manager icon, the user's home directory is set as the default directory unless otherwise specified. Because many files end up in this directory by default, a home directory is a natural defensive tool system into which administrators shepherd the user's files.

In an NT Server or NT Workstation, the default home directory is a local directory, *<drive>*:\USERS\DEFAULT. You can add subdirectories to the \USERS directory for each user and assign this path as the user home directories. Another alternative is to assign a home directory for each group.

A home directory can be specified by using a common directory path or creating a unique share name for each user. The UNC path for a common directory includes the share name and the subdirectory—for example, \\SERVER \USERS\NADEEMC. Creating a unique Share name for each user's home directory requires more work for the network administrator, but it provides greater control and more convenience for the user. An example of a unique Share name path would be \\SERVER\NADEEMC.

Once you have assigned a home directory, install the logon script for the user or group in the home directory. To assign a home directory:

1. Select the User Manager for Domains icon from the Administrative Tools program group.
2. Select the user from the username list at the top of the screen, choose User, Properties..., and then select the Profile button in the lower-left corner of the User Properties screen. The window shown in Figure 12.6 appears.

12

Figure 12.6.
User Environment
properties.

3. In the Home Directory group box, enter the full pathname for the location of the home directory.

Note

If the home directory is located on a server instead of a local path, specify the entire pathname including the drive letter or UNC pathname—do not use the Share name. For example, F:\HOME\RICK, or \\SERVER\HOME\RICK.

Tip

If you assign the user Full Control permission to the home directory, don't forget to assign Full Control to members of the Administrator or Domain Administrators groups. Other users should have either No Access or List permission only in order to protect the directory for the user.

If your path points to a directory that does not exist, this utility creates the directory when you select OK.

The following rules apply to home directories:

1. A domain logon looks for a domain home directory first.
2. If no home directory exists, a logon looks for a local home directory.

3. If no home directory exists, NT Workstation or NT Server uses the \USERS\DEFAULT directory as the home and default directory in all Program Manager program item properties.

4. If no home directory exists, and no local \USERS\DEFAULT directory exists, then the \USERS directory is created in the root of the drive that contains the NT system files.

Tip

NT Server connects the user to the home directory specified in the domain user account only when the logon is from an NT, Windows 95, or WFW workstation.

MS-DOS workstations locate the home directory during logon by including the /HOME switch in the NET USE command as follows:

```
NET USE <drive>: /HOME
```

HOME DIRECTORY PERMISSIONS

If a user's home directory resides on an NTFS partition, appropriate permissions must be set. When the home directory is created, User Manager for Domains automatically applies permissions to allow the user Full Control of the home directory.

Warning

If the user's workstation locks up when the logon script should run, it may be because the user account has No Access to its home directory (typically the \USERS\DEFAULT subdirectory or any parent directory).

Make sure that each user has at least a read-only permission to his or her home directory.

If two or more accounts are selected and simultaneously given the same home directory, User Manager for Domains sets Full Control permissions on the directory for the special group Everyone.

Note

In NTFS volumes, if you remove the Full Access permission from the home directory from the Everyone group, users will not be able to access files including logon scripts in that directory. In this case, LOGON searches for the USERS\DEFAULT directory.

If you wish to remove Everyone rights from the home directories, don't forget to move your logon scripts to another directory, or to assign at least read-only permission to the directory where the logon script exists.

THE REPLICATOR SERVICE

NT has a replicator that can mirror directories from an NT Server's volume to another NT Server's or NT Workstation's volume. This is helpful for both performance and data security. You can realize increased performance when referencing data files over a Wide Area Network (WAN)—it is much faster to replicate the data on both sides of the WAN so that access to the database files is local, and all updates are replicated. If a disk drive or data file is corrupted, a replicated copy of your data directories is intact.

Replication occurs from an *export* computer to an *import* computer; that is, the export computer exports only updates to an import computer. The Replicator in the export NT Server catches the updates and echoes them to the import computer. Entire directory trees can be replicated, but it is more efficient to replicate only the needed portion.

Directory replication is used commonly for

> user logon accounts
> logon scripts
> user accounts
> databases

A classic example for using replication is a company that has a very large customer database, from which it draws accounting and marketing data. See Figure 12.7.

Company XYZ's customer database, CUSTOMER.DBF is replicated in Los Angeles and New York. When users in either Los Angeles or New York access the database, they receive information from their local server. When the users update data, the updates go only to the import computer, resulting in two identical local databases. In this example, data is always researched locally without the delay of accessing data over a potentially congested WAN link.

Figure 12.7.
A directory replication
example.

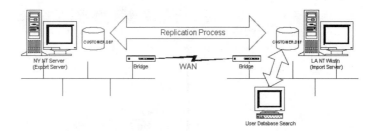

To establish replication, follow these steps on the computer from which files will be exported.

1. Create a domain user account in User Manager for the Replicator to use. Make the user a member of the Backup Operators group. Select Password Never Expires, and make sure there are no restrictions on the account that will prevent usage at any hour.

2. Place or locate the directory (and subdirectories) to be replicated on the export server. You have the choice of replicating a single directory, or many directories with subdirectories.

3. Select the Server Manager in your Administrative Tools program group. Select the Replication button. Click on the export server computer on your list, then Computer, Properties..., and the Replication button. The screen shown in Figure 12.8 appears.

Figure 12.8.
The Directory Replica-
tion screen in Server
Manager's Control
Panel server applet.

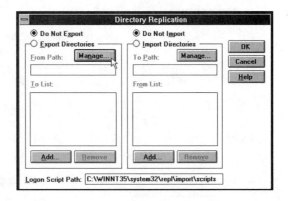

Note

You can also access the Directory Replication screen from the Server icon in Control Panel.

4. Select the Manage button under the Export Directories heading, and the screen shown in Figure 12.9 appears.

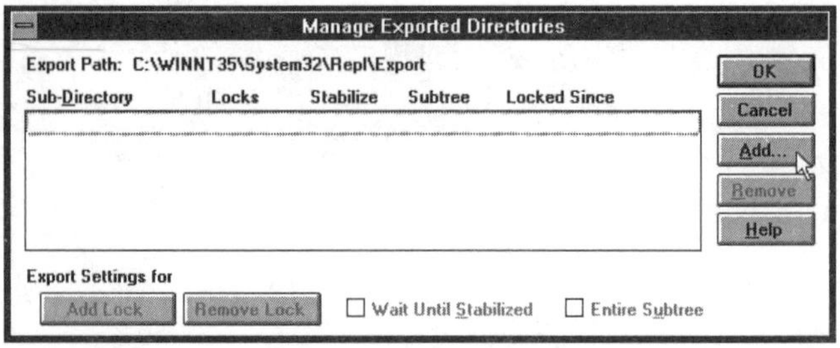

Figure 12.9.
The Manage Exported
Directories screen.

a. Select the Add button and enter the full pathname using the UNC pathname (*<server>**<drive>**<directory>**<subdirectory>*) or the Share name (*<server>**<Share>*) of the directory from which you wish to replicate.

Note

Do not use the Share name in this field. It is also recommended to use the UNC instead of drive letter pathname so that changes in drive letter mappings will not affect this process.

b. Select Entire Subtree to replicate subdirectories, as well.

c. Decide whether updates should be sent immediately or Wait Until Stabilized (the directory is stable when no updates have occurred for two minutes).

Tip

The Wait Until Stabilized option reduces the amount of traffic on a WAN. When first establishing a replication, you should select this option until the replication is stable.

5. Lock the directory using the Add Lock button. Make sure that the directories you wish to replicate are those to be used during this process.

6. If you want to replicate a logon script, see the Logon Script Path at the bottom of the screen.

On the computer from which files will be imported

1. Enter the Directory Replicator screen through Server Manager or the Server icon in Control Panel. Select the Replication button.

2. Select the Manage button under the Import Directories heading.

3. Select the Add button and enter the path of the directory to which you wish to replicate.

Note

You must first create the directory and any subdirectories to be imported on the import server. This utility will not create the directories into which you want to import.

    a. Enter the full pathname using the UNC (*<server>**<directory>* *<subdirectory>*)

To stop the export of a directory, log on to the export server, access the Directory Replication screen, apply a lock, and select the Remove button to remove the directory being replicated.

You can replicate a directory to another drive or directory on the same server or on another server for a type of online backup.

You can also enable users to access the import directory, which protects the export directory against updates or any damage from users.

Note

The import directory is read-only. Users accessing the import directory cannot update files; they must access the export directory to make read-write changes.

Summary

This chapter explains some of the most important features of managing your NT Server-based network. It is based on the assumption that you have chosen domain configuration instead of workgroups. If this is not so, it is recommended that you reinstall your NT Server so that it is domain based. If you do not, you will find that all domain-related features and options are not available to you. Many of these features are quite helpful, and should be available to you. There is not a downside to a domain configuration. See Chapter 9, "Workgroups and Domains" for more information.

In managing your system, it is helpful to try out some of the procedures discussed in this chapter before you need to use them. In the process, you learn how to get these features working for you quickly and effectively.

- Overview of Microsoft
  Network Printing

- Sharing and Using
  Network Printers

- Administering
  Printers

- Printing Components

- Printer Administra-
  tion

- Common Printing
  Problems

CHAPTER 13

NT Printing Services

Printer   The logical object to which print jobs are sent. The printer represents the print device (the physical printer itself).

Print Device   The actual physical printer, for example H-P LaserJet 4, or Epson FX-100. The print device includes the port on the computer, that is, LPT1 or COM1.

Spooler   The operating system process that directs print jobs and controls the mechanics of printing from the printer object to the print device.

Spooling   The process of sending the print job over the network to be printed on the print device.

Spool File   Print jobs are actually sent to a spool file where they are queued up to be printed. In other systems spool files are called queues. The spool files are controlled by the spooler.

Print Jobs   Each printing session submitted to the spooler is considered a print job. The spooler must modify print streams according to the designated job type. For example, one print job may require no modification whatsoever, while another requires a form feed.

Print Router   The device that accepts requests from clients, determines which spooler component should handle the request, and then sends the request to that component.

Rendering   Modifying or processing the print job to produce printed output. Most graphics print jobs require rendering to translate complex print codes into printed graphics.

Server   Any NT, WFW, Windows 95, or MS-DOS workstation configured as a computer that can share its printer. This computer becomes a server for the purposes of printing.

Workstation   Any Microsoft workstation can be a client that sends print output to a server that is sharing its printer(s).

Printer pools   A group of print devices represented by one printer object. Printing to the printer object sends the print job to the first available printer device.

VDM   Virtual DOS Machine. A DOS session running under Windows. An NT VDM differs from Windows 3.1 or WFW VDMs in that NT controls each VDM very tightly and does not allow DOS applications to access physical devices.

There are many excellent features to Microsoft printing, but the really great part of printing with any Windows operating system is the fact that print drivers are within Windows, and all applications use the same drivers. This factor has reduced the complexity of writing an application, using specific printer features, and controlling various aspects of printing. It also makes printing functionality uniform throughout all Windows applications.

This is not so in the MS-DOS world; each application has its own driver. Of course, MS-DOS is the one that is different—just about all other operating systems install the print drivers into the operating system, not in each application. MS-DOS was designed so each program could physically control hardware. This concept is the paragon of NT's stability—no software is allowed to control hardware; not even DOS applications running in a Virtual DOS Machine are allowed to have their way with hardware or device drivers.

Microsoft network printing is deceptively simple to set up and use. Behind the scenes, however, is a very complex set of functions and components. Again, understanding the mechanics of how this network function works holds all the keys to proper system administration of printing.

This chapter discusses

- ◆ Sharing and using network printers
- ◆ Administering printers
- ◆ Printer mechanics
- ◆ Printer administration
- ◆ Common printing problems

Overview of Microsoft Network Printing

If you understand the mechanics of printing in a Microsoft environment, you will be able to resolve any problems that occur. This section discusses concepts of print setup and operation, how print spooling works, and the mechanics of NT Server's print engine.

Printing Concepts and Terminology

NT Server offers numerous network printing features, including the ability to browse for available printers, direct connection to shared NT Server printers (local print drivers are not needed), and remote administration. To understand the screen selections available, you should first understand how Microsoft networking is object-oriented.

Selecting Printer Objects

When the word "printer" is used in Microsoft networking, most people have a misconception about what is meant. In all Microsoft networks, the printer is a logical object—a convenient representation of a print device that is the target of our print output. Our applications hand the print job to the printer object, and behind the scenes, a whole world of mechanics controls the flow of the print output until it ends up at a *print device*. Print device refers to the actual physical hardware device that produces printed output (usually called a printer).

The point is that when you print, you print to the printer object. The Microsoft network sends your print job to the physical print device through an elaborate process. The path and process your print job takes depends on the format of the print output, which Windows version you are running at your workstation (for example, Windows 3.1, WFW, Windows 95, NT), and which Windows version the print server is running.

Note

> Unless otherwise specified, this book always refers to the printer object as the printer, and the physical printer itself as the print device. The print device includes the printer port to which it is attached.

Printers are created, managed, and viewed using Print Manager. This utility is found in the Windows Main program group. Figure 13.1 shows Print Manager's main screen and menu bar. In this figure, the printer \\MAINSRV\LJ3 is on the screen.

Figure 13.1.
Print Manager main
screen.

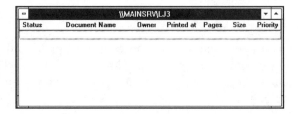

A physical port refers to a hardware connection to the local computer such as LPT1:, COM2:, and so on. A logical port refers to a network connection to a remote printing device. NT Server Print Manager enables you to set up a printer using either a physical port or logical port as the print destination. The logical port name is expressed in Universal Naming Convention (UNC) to point at the printer device and the computer to which it is physically attached. The syntax is as follows:

```
\\<servername>\<printername>
```

In NetWare and OS/2 environments, print jobs are directed to a queue, which in turn is directed to a printer. In Microsoft networking, including NT Server, the print job is sent to the printer object—not to a queue. An NT spool file is equivalent to a queue, and is generally involved in all print jobs, local printing, and network printing. However, the user never uses the spool file as an object; it is behind the scenes being controlled by the print spooler, so it is transparent to the user and administrator. Instead the print spooler uses the spool file. You can see jobs in the spool file by accessing Print Manager and selecting the printer. The jobs in the spool file are listed under the printer as shown in Figure 13.1.

Note for NetWare Administrators

Printing is handled quite differently in NT than it is in a NetWare environment. NetWare print output is always sent to a queue, then sent to a printer. A user redirects (captures) print output to a queue, and the print server directs the print job to go from the queue to the printer. The administrator must set up this configuration.

Microsoft networking conceals all the mechanics of printing in the *print spooler*, the software mechanism that handles printing. As far as the user interface is concerned, we simply print to the printer object and all the details are handled behind the scenes. This arrangement is simpler to understand and easier to administer than NetWare's systems of captures, queues, print servers, and printers.

You will also find that NT printing works faster. Your print job can begin printing immediately instead of finishing output to the queue before starting to print, as is the case in a NetWare environment.

NT printing is quite robust, and provides many options. Any NT Server, or any WFW, Windows 95, or NT Workstation client can be configured to share its printer on the network. You can form printer pools, where several physical printers are represented by one printer object. You can set up multiple printer objects that print to the same printer with different configurations. You can then establish print priorities of one printer over another. You can schedule one printer object to hold print jobs and print them at a later time. These are only a few configuration possibilities of printing on a Microsoft network.

PRINT SPOOLING ILLUSTRATED: THE COMPONENTS OF NETWORK PRINTING

The main components used to process jobs on an NT Server server are illustrated in Figure 13.2. The components are arranged from top to bottom, with the components on top using the services of the components below them. For example, print clients use the services of the print router, which in turn uses the services of a print provider, and so on.

Figure 13.2.
Components used to
process jobs on an NT
Server print server.

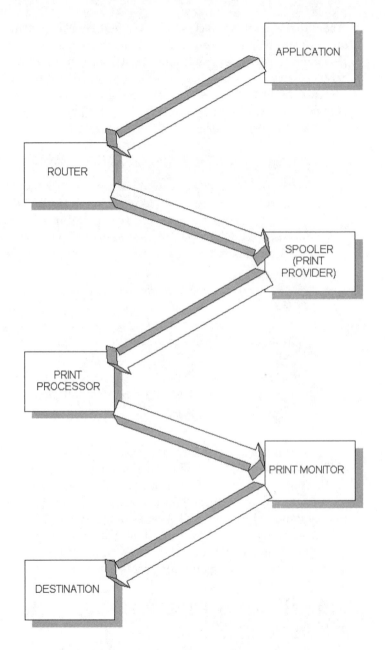

The components shown below the clients are collectively called the *spooler*.

Note

In NT Server 3.5x, the spooler components are implemented as a service, which you can stop and restart from the Services icon in Control Panel or from the command line in an MS-DOS client using the NET STOP SPOOLER and NET START SPOOLER commands.

The following list briefly explains each of the components in Figure 13.2. The following section discusses each component in more detail.

Clients are any applications that send jobs to the spooler. Clients include locally-run applications (both Windows applications and non-Windows-based applications), as well as applications running on other computers, which send print jobs over the network to an NT Server print server.

Print router is the device that accepts requests from clients, determines which spooler component should handle the request, and then sends the request to that component.

Local and remote print providers. The local print provider manages spool files and processes separator pages. It also determines the data type of each job and sends the job to the print processor responsible for that data type. The print provider then determines which print monitor is responsible for the output port. In addition to the local print provider, there are also remote print providers, which transfer jobs from the NT Server print server to MS-Network print servers or NetWare print servers.

Print processors are available to modify print jobs of different data types. There are several different types of print processors to handle different types of print jobs. When print processors are finished modifying the job, they give control back to the print provider; this is why this component is embedded within the print provider in Figure 13.1.

Print monitors are responsible for transmitting print jobs to different types of print devices. For instance, one print monitor sends jobs to local devices like parallel and serial ports, and other print monitors send jobs to different kinds of network interface printers.

HOW NT SERVER PRINTING WORKS

Microsoft network print jobs can take a few different paths depending on the type of client and the type of server. Figure 13.3 shows the normal flow a print job takes when spooling from an NT, WFW, or Windows 95 client to an NT Server.

Figure 13.3.
NT printing methods
flow chart.

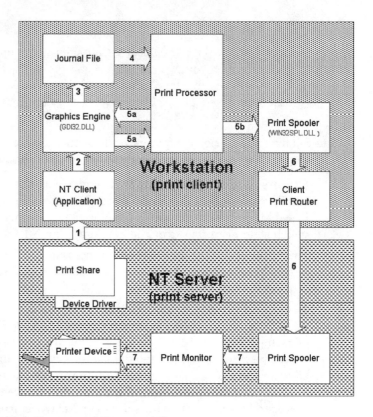

PRINTING TO AN NT SERVER PRINT SHARE FROM ANY WINDOWS-BASED CLIENT

As you read this section, refer to the flow chart in Figure 13.3 to follow a normal print job spooled to an NT Server:

1. The client workstation's redirector copies the Print Share's device driver into memory. This allows the application to communicate bi-directionally with the printer device.

2. The print job generates output to the Graphics Device Interface (GDI) engine (GDI32.DLL) using GDI commands. The GDI engine translates the GDI calls into Device Driver Interface (DDI) calls.

3. GDI calls are sent to a *journal file* (spool file).

4. When the printer device is ready to accept output, the spooler queries the journal file and directs output to one of the following output paths discussed in step 5, depending on the type of print job.

5a. If the print job is graphics-oriented, your software prepares output in raster, PostScript, or PCL. Therefore, the print job must be returned to the GDI engine for rendering. The graphics engine renders output in bitmap, PostScript language, or PCL and returns the print job to the print processor.

5b. If the print job was output in RAW data type (a simple text output document), or the print job has been rendered, the print job is sent to the spooler for remote delivery.

Note

Enhanced metafiles (EMFs) are spooled rather than sent as RAW printer data when printing from Windows–based applications, resulting in a quicker return to application time. After it is spooled, the EMF is interpreted in the background by the printer driver, and output is then sent to the printer. If the job is to be printed to a local printer port, it follows the same steps up to this point. At this point, however, the RAW or rendered print job is sent to the local port instead of the spooler.

6. The client print spooler sends the job to the server print spooler via the print router.

7. The print spooler sends the print job to the printer device. The job is monitored by the print monitor as the job is spooled.

Note

Windows 3.1 does not contain network software that allows printer sharing. Therefore, the process of redirecting the print output is controlled by a third-party NOS. In these cases, spooled output is simply captured and redirected by the NOS client software, and print server software is also part of the NOS. Each one may work a little differently.

PRINTING DOWN LEVEL FROM AN NT COMPUTER TO A NON-NT PRINT SERVER

The *down level* method of printing is used when printing from an NT Workstation client to a non-NT print Share, such as a WFW print Share (and device). It is called down level because you are printing to an older Windows version print server. This involves issuing spooler calls to create a spool file on a local disk or on an NT Server file Share, writing to it with regular file system calls, and then scheduling it for printing via another spooler call.

In this case, the workstation renders the output and the print spooler in the non-NT print server and sends the rendered or RAW output to a spool file on the print server's disk until the printer is ready to accept a print job.

All the steps the print job goes through are the same as in printing to an NT print server (refer to Figure 13.3), except for two differences:

1. The print job is not paused at the journal file (between steps 3 and 4).
2. The print job is saved to a spool file at the non-NT print server until the printer is ready, and there is no print monitor to monitor the print stream to the printer.

In a WFW or MS-DOS print server, the RAW or rendered output is spooled to a spool file on the disk until the printer is ready to accept it. API calls are used to create the spool file at the print server, and the print job is saved and read to or from the disk using standard file system function calls. When the printer device is ready, the print job is sent to the spooler for delivery to a local port or network print spooler via normal file system calls.

This is the method used by an NT Workstation printing to a redirected port rather than to a direct connection. NT Workstations can either print from their own ports or redirect (assign) a printer Share as the destination to which output should go. In this case, instead of the NT Workstation's local Print Manager spooling the printout, the spool files are located on the NT Server in

```
\<winnt root>\SYSTEM32\SPOOL\PRINTERS
```

PRINTING FROM WINDOWS APPLICATIONS

Windows applications follow the previous diagrams to render graphics output. They can therefore use Windows 3.x drivers in a WFW or Windows 3.1 environment, or they can use the driver installed on the NT or Windows 95 print server. Windows 95 or NT print drivers in those environments are recommended.

PRINTING FROM MS-DOS APPLICATIONS

MS-DOS applications each have their own print drivers, and therefore must render their own graphics output. In this case, RAW output is generated, bypasses the GDI engine, and is sent directly to the print processor for spooling.

Each driver is written by the application developer; therefore, they do not all work the same way. Typically, MS-DOS applications generate either ASCII or RAW output. When an MS-DOS application is running under Windows, Windows redirects the print output to the Print Share by redirecting parallel port output to a software interrupt.

A Windows application is much simpler to write because the software developer does not have to write any print drivers. Instead, they simply have to use GDI calls to generate their output. With the help of the printer driver, the GDI engine generates output that the print processor can use.

SHARING AND USING NETWORK PRINTERS

To use a network printer, a Print Share must first be created, then a client can use the Share. The processes of sharing and using a network printer are both accomplished in Print Manager, regardless of the Windows product used (WFW, Windows 95, or NT).

CREATING A PRINTER SHARE

In order to share a printer, the print device driver must have been installed. This is generally done in Setup; however, if your printer device driver has not been installed, or you are installing a new printer, you can install the driver through Control Panel, Printer, the same way you would install any local printer. On an NT Server, both the Control Panel and Printer Manager options bring you to the same screen. In other Windows products, the screens to install the drivers are outside of Print Manager.

When printing to an NT Server Print Share, the Printer Drivers are stored on the print server and it is not necessary to install a print driver at the client. This enables an administrator to be sure that everyone is using the same Printer Driver and to easily update the Printer Driver, because it is stored in a single, central location.

When printing to an NT Server Print Share, it is possible to install a Printer Driver locally. This can be done by creating a printer to print to a local port, which installs the Printer Driver locally. After the driver is installed, change the properties of the printer to the correct network Share. However, when a Printer Driver is installed locally, the local Printer Driver is *always* used, regardless of whether the NT Server print Share's driver has been updated.

Note

If client workstations of each type will be using the Printer Share, an NT Server must have the x86, MIPS, Power PC, and/or Alpha Printer Driver installed for each Printer Share. The reason for this is that an Alpha or MIPS computer cannot print using the x86 Printer Driver or vice versa.

You can automatically install a Printer Driver at a Windows 95 or NT Workstation client when connecting to a printer attached to a NetWare server, NT Server, or Windows 95 print server. As a result, Windows 95 Printer Drivers can be located on an NT Server or NetWare server.

In Windows 3.1, all interpretations of print API calls were handled by the Windows Printer Driver before the information was spooled to Print Manager. PostScript print jobs were not impacted by this process because the Printer Driver sends high-level, Page Description Language (PDL)–based information to the printer, rather than sending RAW image data that must be interpreted by the printer itself.

Windows 95 and NT improve the return to application time by spooling high-level command information generated by the GDI print API, called enhanced metafile.

Network printer devices are shared by using Print Manager at the computer sharing its printer (the print server). To create a Print Share on an NT computer, select Print Manager, Printer, Create Printer as shown in Figure 13.4.

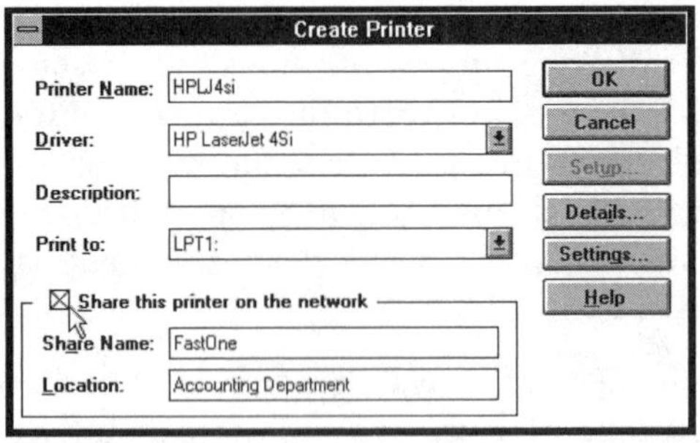

Figure 13.4.
Creating a Print Share
in NT's Print Manager.

The process for creating a Print Share on a WFW or Windows 95 workstation is similar. In both cases, you can share a printer in Print Manager.

Note

In WFW and Windows 95, you must select the Install the network in Setup option to allow printer sharing when installing the Microsoft networking software. This is usually an option that is queried during Setup. In both environments, if networking was not installed, adding a network adapter driver also provides an opportunity to select sharing of directories and printers (two separate options).

CONNECTING TO A PRINTER SHARE

Once network printers are shared, a client workstation can connect to the print Share using Print Manager. To connect to a Print Share, select Printer, Connect to Printer. NT Workstations and NT Servers will display the Connect to Printer screen shown in Figure 13.5.

Figure 13.5.
Print Manager's
Connect to Printer
screen.

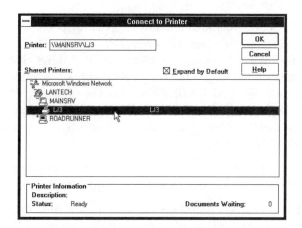

The Windows 3.x and WFW Connect to Printer screens are very similar. Windows 95 clients connect using Network Neighborhood or Print Manager in Control Panel. The process is also quite similar.

Note

In order to have the Print Manager options to connect to a network printer, your Microsoft networking software must be installed. This is usually done in Setup, but can be added later when you install a network adapter. To enable the option to use a network printer, you do not need to enable the options to share your directories or printers.

ADMINISTERING PRINTERS

Printers are managed in Print Manager. There are many printing functions that are managed at the client, and other options that are managed at the server.

Many aspects of managing your printers and print jobs are discussed in this section. There are many situations that can be handled if you know the capability exists.

SEPARATOR PAGES AND FILES

A Separator File may be selected through the Details button in Print Manager, under the Printer Properties dialog box. In this dialog box, there is a combobox labeled Separator File. In this combobox, the name of the Separator Page file may be directly entered, or click on the button to browse through the directories and select a file.

NT Server includes a default separator page, DEFAULT.SEP, for use with PCL-compatible printers. However, DEFAULT.SEP is not a file on disk, but rather built into Print Manager. Therefore, if DEFAULT.SEP is desired, the name must be typed in directly; DEFAULT.SEP cannot be chosen by clicking on the button to browse. DEFAULT.SEP contains the following codes: @N@4@I@4@D. NT Server also includes PSLANMAN.SEP, which is the equivalent of DEFAULT.SEP but is for use with PostScript printers. In addition, two other separator pages are included with NT Server.

> PCL.SEP switches a printer to PCL printing.
> PSCRIPT.SEP switches a printer to PostScript Printing.

The first character of the Separator Page file must always be the escape character. This character is used throughout the Separator Page file in ESCAPE CODES. The program replaces these escape codes with appropriate data to be sent directly to the printer.

Newlines are always sent as carriage-return/linefeed sequences. Therefore, it is important to make sure that the printer is not in a mode that will translate this to double-spaced lines.

Any text contained in the separator file that is not explicitly part of one of the escape commands is simply ignored (that is, not sent to the printer). For example, the sequence @Lthankyou @N hi @D would be translated to thankyou ricks08/06/92, where ricks is the username. The characters hi are removed; they are not considered part of the text sequence following the original @L.

By default, separator page files are kept in the currently logged-on user's home directory (by default this is c:\users\default).

CUSTOM SEPARATOR FILES

NT Server allows the specification of a separator page file to be printed at the start of each print job. Custom separator page files may be created using the following control codes:

1. Using a text editor such as Notepad, on the very first line type a single character, then press Enter. The character you have typed on the first line

13

defines the character to be used as the escape character. For example, the list below assumes that this character will be the at sign (@).

2. Enter the escape codes for the functions you want. Save the file with an .SEP extension in the NT Server SYSTEM32 subdirectory.

3. In Print Manager, select the printer with which you want to use the separator page file. Choose Properties from the Printer menu. In the resulting Printer Properties dialog box, select Details and specify the name of the desired separator page file in the Separator File field, and then choose OK.

The following are escape codes and their functions that can be used in a separator page file.

@N Prints the user name of the person that submitted the job.

@I Prints the job number.

@D Prints the date the job was printed. The representation of the date is the same as the Date Format in the International section in Control Panel.

@T Prints the time the job was printed. The representation of the time is the same as the Time Format in the International section in Control Panel.

@Lxxxx Prints all the characters (xxxx) following it until another escape code is encountered.

@Fpathname Prints the contents of the file specified by path, starting on an empty line. The contents of this file are copied directly to the printer without any processing.

@Hnn Sets a printer-specific control sequence, where *nn* is a hexadecimal ASCII code sent directly to the printer. To determine the specific numbers, see your printer manual.

@Wnn Sets the width of the separator page. The default width is 80; the maximum width is 256. Any printable characters beyond this width are truncated.

@U Turns off block character printing.

@B@S Prints text in single-width block characters until @U is encountered.

@E Ejects a page from the printer. Use this code to start a new separator page or to end the separator page file. If you get an extra blank separator page when you print, remove this code from your separator page file.

@n Skips n number of lines (from 0 through 9). Skipping 0 lines moves printing to the next line.

@B@M Prints text in double-width block characters until @U is encountered.

ADDING A PRINT FILE NAME

NT Server can be configured to print directly to a specified file without prompting for a filename. You can accomplish this by adding a value to the Registry. Once you add the value, you can configure an additional port from Print Manager.

To add the value, use the following procedure:

1. Start Registry Editor and locate the following Registry subkey:

   ```
   HKEY_LOCAL_MACHINE\SOFTWARE\Microsoft
   \NT Server\CurrentVersion\Ports
   ```

2. From the Edit menu, choose Add Value. In the Value Name field, type the full path and filename you would like to print to (c:\p1.fil for example). Select REG_SZ for the data type. Leave the String field Blank.

3. Save your changes and exit Registry Editor.

4. Exit NT Server and restart your computer.

5. Start Print Manager and select the correct printer.

6. Choose Properties from the Printer menu.

7. From Print To, select the filename you specified in Step 2.

SETTING AUTOMATIC PRINTING TO FILE

To enable automatic printing to a filename:

1. In the Print Manager window, choose Create Printer from the Printer menu.

2. In the Create Printer dialog box, type the printer name and description details in the Printer Name field, and then press Enter.

3. In the Print To dialog box, choose Network Printer, and then select the Local Port button.

4. In the Local Port box, type the 8.3 filename (include drive and path if necessary) that you wish the jobs to print to each time.

5. Choose the OK button. At this time, the Print Manager may need to install the printer driver software.

6. Changing the Print Setup in your applications to print to this newly created printer causes automatic printing to the filename that was supplied above.

Windows 3.1 supports automatic printing to a filename by modifying the WIN.INI file so that applications would print to the same filename. This disables the dialog box that prompts for a filename and writes to the same filename every time. For some applications, this behavior is desirable, especially for those applications that export data to other applications or databases.

NT Server contains all user-defined print information in the Registry and does not allow you to modify an .INI file to disable the pop-up messages prompting for a filename from the application.

Disable Notification Boxes

Under NT Server 3.5, it is possible to disable the Printing Notification network dialog boxes sent by the Spooler on a Print Server when a print job has been completed, there is an error, or if a job has been deleted.

Note

This setting applies globally to all the printers on a particular print server. It is not possible to set this option on a single printer basis.

To disable Printing Notification network dialog boxes, use Registry Editor as follows:

1. Start Registry Editor.
2. From the HKEY_LOCAL_MACHINE subtree, go to the following subkey:

   `\SYSTEM\CurrentControlSet\Control\Print\Providers`
3. From the Edit menu, choose Add Value.
4. In the Value Name field of the Add Value dialog box, type the following:

   `NetPopup`
5. Select REG_DWORD for the Data Type.
6. Choose OK.
7. In the Dword Editor dialog box, type **0** (zero) in the Data field.
8. Choose OK.
9. Exit Registry Editor.
10. Stop and restart the Spooler service from the Services portion of Control Panel so the new setting will take effect.

Note

If the print notification is turned off for the direct connected printer, via parallel and serial, error conditions will result in an error dialog box appearing on the server. While this error is displayed, printing will not resume to the printer even if the cause of the error is cleared from the printer. Someone will be required to log on to the server and choose Retry or Cancel in the error dialog box. This does not affect network-connected printers.

CLEARING PRINT JOBS FROM JETDIRECT QUEUES AFTER PRINTING

When you print to an NT Server server with the queue attached to a Hewlett-Packard (HP) JetDirect card, print jobs may not be removed from the print queue. The print job is sent to the print server, it prints, but the print job is not removed from the queue.

This behavior happens when Advanced Job Status is chosen in Print Manager. This option should be turned off in most printers. To check the setting of Advanced Job Status, do the following:

1. In the Print Manager window, choose Printer from the File menu.
2. Choose Properties.
3. From the Print To menu, choose Network Printer.
4. Select Hewlett-Packard Network Port, and then choose the Port option.

When the Advanced Job Status is chosen, the job is not removed from the print queue unless the printer supports bi-directional communication. The queue is waiting for confirmation from the printer that the job is complete. Most printers do not have the ability to send the confirmation.

The HP LaserJet 4 supports bi-directional communication. A LaserJet with the Windows Printing System also supports bi-directional communication, but the Windows Printing System is not supported under NT Server 3.5; therefore bi-directional printer communcations are not available with NT 3.5.

ENVELOPE PRINTING

When printing an envelope from Word 2 or 6 for Windows under NT Server to an HP LaserJet IIP or LaserJet IIIP, the printer displays the following message:

```
MP LOAD COM10
```

Even when you have an envelope loaded into the MP (manual feed) tray, pressing the Online button does not resume printing. You must press and hold down the Alt key while pressing the Form Feed/Continue key.

By default, NT Server does not select the manual feed tray for envelopes when printing on envelope-size paper from any Windows application.

Use the following steps to associate envelope size paper with the manual feed tray so that NT Server will know to select the manual feed tray when envelopes are printed:

1. Start NT Server Print Manager.
2. Bring the desired printer window to the front.
3. From the Printer menu, choose Properties.
4. Choose the Setup button.
5. Under the Source option, choose Manual Paper Feed.
6. Under the Name option, choose Envelope #10.
7. Choose OK.
8. Choose the OK button in the Properties window.

Through NT Server Print Manager, an administrator can assign paper sizes to specific paper bins on the printer. For instance, the administrator can specify that all letter-size pages printed come from the upper tray, no matter which tray the document is formatted for.

REMOTE PRINTER ADMINISTRATION

Although the "Microsoft NT Server System Guide" states that Print Manager can create, remove, and administer printers on remote servers, it has the following limitations in administering remote server print queues:

◆ The Print menu Connect To Printer option connects printers only on the local server, even when the focus is set to a remote server. If you want to create a NetWare printer that is shared through the Gateway service, you must create it at the local machine (because you must create a connection to the NetWare Print Share).

◆ When creating a printer on a remote server, Print Manager cannot choose a printer that is not physically connected to that remote server. When you attempt to create a remote printer, this error message appears: The parameter is incorrect.

◆ The Print menu Connect To Printer option under NT Server 3.5 can create a printer based on a port that is already defined on the remote server. If you choose Create Printer from the Print menu and attempt to connect to a port for DLC or LPR, this error message appears: Could not add port. The network request is not supported.

◆ This type of action requires the DLL, which is responsible for managing the port, to load. Loading the DLL across the network is not supported at this time.

PRINTING COMPONENTS

In many cases, print operations may seem illogical or random to you, and you may not be able to reason your way through. This section discusses components of the print process so you can locate and correct problems you may encounter.

WHERE TO FIND WHAT YOU ARE LOOKING FOR

By default, NT Server uses \<winnt root>\SYSTEM32\SPOOL to store some of the different components of the printing process. This subdirectory contains the following:

- \DRIVERS

Under this subdirectory are the subdirectories where any locally used printer drivers are stored. Intel drivers are in a \W32X86 subdirectory, MIPS drivers are in a \W32MIPS subdirectory, and Alpha drivers are in a \W32ALPHA subdirectory.

- \PRINTERS

This is the subdirectory in which all spool files are stored while a print job is spooling:

- \PRTPROCS

Once again, there is a separate subdirectory for each architecture (for example, Intel is in \W32X86). Under this subdirectory is the subdirectory in which the Print Processor is stored. Under the architecture-specific subdirectory, each Print Processor has its own subdirectory in which it is stored. On Intel-based machines WINPRINT.DLL is the default Print Processor and is stored in:

\<winnt root>\SYSTEM32\SPOOL\PRTPROCS\W32X86\WINPRINT\WINPRINT.DLL

The rest of the components involved in the NT Server printing process are located, by default, in the \<winnt root>\SYSTEM32 subdirectory.

REGISTRY ENTRIES FOR PRINTING

The most important entries regarding printing are located under

```
HKEY_LOCAL_MACHINE
    \SYSTEM
        \CurrentControlSet
            \Control
                \Print
```

As can be seen in the screen shown in Figure 13.6, below the Environments key are subkeys for each of the currently supported NT Server hardware platforms. Each of these keys contains the name of the directory in which the drivers for that platform are stored. Based on the information in the previous section, the NT Server x86 key has a Value of W32X86.

Figure 13.6.
*Environment Subkeys
in the Registry.*

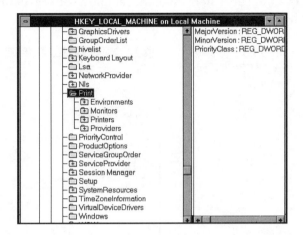

Under each of these are the subkeys Drivers and Print Processors. Each Drivers key contains subkeys for any and all locally, installed printer drivers for that platform. Under the key for each printer driver is the information regarding what files are being used as the components of that particular printer driver, as well as the version of the driver as shown in Figure 13.7.

Figure 13.7.
*The Registry printer
subkey.*

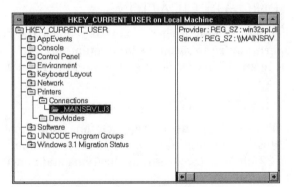

Under the Monitors key are subkeys for any installed print monitors. The Printers key consists of subkeys for any locally created printers (see the above information regarding the differences between created and connected printers). These subkeys contain all of the configuration information for the locally created printers on the system.

The other Registry entry dealing with printing is located in HKEY_CURRENT_USER\Printers. This key contains the name of the current default printer in Print Manager and a subkey, Connections, that lists any printers the system is currently connected to.

Figure 13.8
HKEY_CURRENT_USER
\Printers.

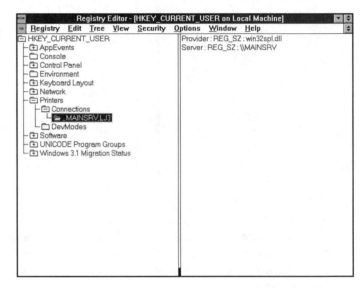

CLIENT APPLICATIONS

Clients are those applications that request the spooler's services. These include applications running on the local computer, workstations on the network that send jobs to an NT Server print server, and the Print Manager application.

LOCAL APPLICATIONS

Local print clients are any applications running on the local computer that send a print job while running on an NT Server-based computer. These include both 16-bit and 32-bit Windows-based applications and non-Windows-based applications.

WINDOWS-BASED APPLICATIONS

Windows-based applications are different from nearly all other printing clients, because they depend on the Graphics Device Interface (GDI) and the NT Server printer driver. These applications rely on NT Server to create their print jobs, whereas other printing clients rely on NT Server only to transfer their jobs to the appropriate print device.

The graphics engine (GDI32.DLL) is the printing component that provides WYSIWYG support across devices. The graphics engine communicates with Windows-based applications through the Graphics Device Interface (GDI) and with printer drivers through the Device Driver Interface (DDI).

When a Windows-based application prints, it describes the output it wants in a series of GDI commands. The graphics engine is responsible for translating these GDI commands into the DDI commands understood by components like printer drivers and print processors.

The graphics engine also communicates with the printer driver to find out what the printer's capabilities are. Then the graphics engine instructs the printer driver about which characters, fonts, locations, and point sizes to print and when.

The graphics engine can also query the printer driver about the fonts supported. Then, using that information, the graphics engine uses other DDI commands to specify the positioning of each character in the document by the print device. The graphics engine also uses DDI commands to define how the printer should draw and fill graphics, and how to manipulate and print bitmaps.

The graphics engine provides services to the printer driver, including compatibility with the environment subsystem (MS-DOS, OS/2, and so on), performance optimization, caching, client-server communications, and ANSI-to-Unicode conversion.

The graphics engine communicates with the spooler to determine which data type the graphics engine should spool. If the specified data type is RAW, the graphics engine calls the printer driver to render the DDI calls. If the data type is journal, the graphics engine writes a journal file and does not call the printer driver to render the DDI calls.

When the graphics engine passes the journal file to the spooler, spooling happens quickly because journal files are small and there is no wait for printer-specific rendering. (Rendering is done later as a background process.) Although journal files contain DDI calls rather than printer commands, they are device-dependent.

The graphics engine calls the printer driver and provides information about the type of printer needed and the data type used. In response, the printer driver provides the graphics engine with the printer's fully qualified path name for the printer and printer-setting information. This information is passed to the spooler.

Journal files differ from metafiles. NT Server does not spool metafiles because they are device-independent and thus do not translate reliably to an individual printer's page layout. Metafiles are pictures, not pages. In addition, metafiles often contain a list of acceptable font and color substitutions for a document. For WYSIWYG accuracy, such color and font substitutions are unacceptable. In contrast, use of journal files guarantees that NT Server provides true reproduction of spooled documents.

Journal files are concise and precise. They only contain calls that make a difference. For example, some applications add hundreds of unnecessary and/or redundant instructions for creating a graphic. The journal file includes only those necessary to draw that picture.

Journal files are tuned for a particular device; they are not device-independent. For example, a journal file created for a 150-DPI LaserJet printer cannot print on a 300-DPI LaserJet printer. A journal file is created to play back on a specific device and therefore is tuned for the device's specific coordinate space, color space, bits-per-pixel, fonts, and so on.

NON-WINDOWS-BASED APPLICATIONS

Non-Windows-based applications running on NT Server-based computers are not aware of the NT Server printing model; in particular, they are not aware of NT Server printer drivers, they cannot make use of them, and the NT Server driver does not get involved during the job's processing.

If you print from a non-Windows-based application, and the port it prints to is spooled, then the spooler components take control of the job, much like other clients' jobs. However, if the job is sent to a port that isn't spooled, the job goes directly to the device driver responsible for the port, for example, PARALLEL.SYS. A port is spooled if any printer defined in Print Manager prints to that port, or if you have issued a NET USE <portname> command in an NT Server command prompt.

REMOTE PRINT CLIENTS

Another type of print client is remote workstations that send print jobs over the network to an NT Server print server. The most interesting of these are clients running operating systems other than NT Server. This section concentrates on those clients: downlevel Microsoft Network clients, Macintosh clients, and UNIX clients.

The spooler on the NT Server print server does not care what kind of application the remote client is running. In most cases, the NT Server printer driver does not get involved in processing print jobs from remote non-Windows-NT clients. The two exceptions are when jobs sent from Macintosh clients to non-PostScript print devices and when jobs from UNIX or down level clients are sent to printers whose default data type has been set to TEXT.

DOWN LEVEL CLIENTS

Network computers running Windows for Workgroups, Windows 3.1, or MS-DOS are referred to as *down level clients*. Any down level client that can send a job to a

Windows for Workgroups print server or LAN Manager print server can also send jobs to an NT Server print server.

The NT Server service receives jobs from these clients and passes them to the spooler without alteration. Regardless of what kind of application created the print job on the down level client, the job is assigned the RAW data type when it reaches the spooler. In general, the printer driver installed on the NT Server print server does not get involved with processing jobs from down level clients.

MACINTOSH CLIENTS

Because NT Server Services for Macintosh is required for Macintosh clients to send print jobs to printers controlled by NT Server-based computers, Macintosh clients cannot print to printers controlled by NT Server Workstation computers. NT Servers running Services for Macintosh must make printers available to Macintosh clients.

Macintosh clients usually print using a PostScript driver, so their print jobs consist of PostScript commands. Jobs sent to PostScript print devices are assigned the RAW data type, and the NT Server printer driver does not help process the print job. Macintosh print jobs sent to non-PostScript print devices are assigned the Pscript1 data type, which causes NT Server server to convert the job from PostScript to the print device's native language. In this case, the NT Server printer driver is involved in processing the job.

UNIX PRINT JOBS

NT Server can also receive print jobs sent by UNIX systems. To enable this feature, you must first install the TCP/IP network protocol via the Network icon in the Control Panel window, and then install the TCP/IP Network Printing Support option. This procedure installs the LPD service (*daemon* in UNIX terminology), which enables NT Server to receive print jobs sent by UNIX computers. Once installed, you must start this service by using the Services icon in the Control Panel window or by typing the `net start lpdsvc` command at the command line. Jobs that reach the LPD service are assigned the RAW data type if they contain the l control command, or are assigned the TEXT data type if they contain the f control command.

PRINT MANAGER AS A CLIENT

Because Print Manager relies on the spooler components, it is also considered a client. Print Manager is a window to the spooler components, a user interface that lets you configure various options and manipulate print jobs as they are processed.

THE PRINT ROUTER

The print router researches and locates the destination print server from the printer Share name, then spools the print job to the destination. It consists of SPOOLSS.EXE, SPOOLSS.DLL, and WINSPOOL.DRV on WFW, Windows 95, and NT computers. These modules are responsible for sending print jobs to their client counterparts for delivery on a print server.

The receiving module at the print server is WINSPOOL.DRV. This module is actually a DLL but looks like a driver to the rest of the printing mechanisms. Once the print router and WINSPOOL.DRV establish communication, they work together transparently as if the print job were spooling to a local print device.

PRINT PROCESSORS AND DATA TYPES

Depending on the print job's data type, a print processor is selected to handle the job of making the application output ready for final print output. The job is then forwarded to the next step for delivery. This module can interpret journal and RAW data types, but other data types are sent to the GDI engine for rendering. The following print processors are used:

WINPRINT.DLL processes two data types, either of which require no rendering and can be forwarded for printing.

>   **RAW**   This type of data is sent straight to the local port or to the spooler for delivery to a print server. RAW data does not require rendering and therefore does not need to be processed by a print processor or the GDI engine.
>
>   **Journal**   This type of print job has already been rendered by the GDI engine or by the application itself. During rendering, the print job is saved to a journal file, thus the name of this data type.
>
>   The rendering process integrates the GDI and DDI (device driver interface) calls specific to the type of printer.

SFMPSPRT.DLL processes PostScript print jobs.

You can view the print processor used by each printer in Print Manager. Select the printer from the list in Print Manager, select Printer, Properties, details, then select the arrow bar for a list of Print Processors.

RENDERING

Print output provided by applications may require rendering to produce output that your printer can use. Rendering integrates printer-specific device driver interface (DDI) calls into the print job, and processes the data into data the printer can use

13

properly to print with. In some cases this requires rasterizing output into bitmaps, processing the output into PostScript language, outlining fonts, or integrating TrueType font information among other procedures.

WINDOWS PRINT PROCESSOR

Some applications produce RAW data type output that is ready for submission to the printer. Many applications render output that is ready for the specific printer.

Many applications simply send a text stream of ASCII characters, which may often contain characters that the printer cannot interpret properly. Many printer languages detect straight ASCII output and print it with default fonts and values, which often results in characters printing that should be used as commands. Applications can output in either "RAW [FF Auto]" and "RAW [FF Appended]" data types to handle printer-specific details.

PCL printers have problems knowing when to eject a page when printing straight ASCII output because printer-specific control codes are not present. Problems occur when:

> The page is full
>
> A form feed is sent
>
> A second print job arrives before the current one is finished
>
> A manual form feed occurs

When the output is categorized as one of the two types listed above, these problems are resolved.

If you configure the default data type in Print Manager as "RAW [FF Auto]" a form feed is sent at the end of every print job.

Note

> If you configure the default output type as "RAW [FF Auto]," you will have a double form feed (resulting in a separator page) when an application properly ends a print job with a form feed.

If you configure the default data type in Print Manager as "RAW [FF Auto]," a form feed is sent at the end of every print job, but only if the application has not sent a form feed.

The RAW [FF Auto] and RAW [FF Appended] data types are designed to work with HP printers. For many other printers, these data types may not print ASCII text as well. If you have problems with ASCII print output, configure your default data type as TEXT, and the GDI engine renders your output as required. The output is equivalent to opening the file with Notepad and printing.

In some cases, using the TEXT default data type causes output to printer control characters instead of using them to format graphics. In these cases, Windows generally partially renders the print job, and returns it to the application with the journal data type (NT JNL 1.000). These print jobs are sent to the NT Server's print processor (via the print router), and are rendered into final output on the NT server.

Applications using this method of producing final output allow the user to resume work faster because the print job prints faster, but it takes longer to print the job on the print server. This type of design is better for Windows-based applications that may need to produce large or complex graphics print jobs, saving the user time and spreading the processing over two different computers.

MACINTOSH PRINT PROCESSOR

When adding Macintoshes to your network, you install Services for Macintosh on your NT Server. This product includes the Macintosh print processor (SFMPSPRT.DLL), which can process PostScript print jobs. The data type an application puts out is PSCRIPT1. The Macintosh print processor can emulate a PostScript print engine and produce output for whatever type of printer you have, even if it is not a PostScript printer.

The Macintosh print processor (SFMPRINT.DLL) checks the print driver to see if a PostScript printer is available. If it is, the output is sent in PostScript language and labeled as RAW data type. This output is sent to the print device where the PostScript output is rendered.

If the print device is not a PostScript printer, SFMPRINT.DLL marks the output file as PSCRIPT1 data type. The print processor uses SFMPSPRT.DLL to render the print job into bitmaps which are sent a second time to the GDI engine for processing and output to the print device. In this process, SFMPSPRT's TrueImage raster image processor replicates the process usually performed at a PostScript print device itself. In conjunction with your printer driver, it can output to any type of printer that has a Windows driver.

Note

Even though your application and your printer can support special fonts, color printing, and higher than 300 DPI resolution, your print job can only print in black & white, 300 DPI. SFMPSPRT is limited to these capabilities. Any fonts used in a PostScript print job should be installed into the NT Server's desktop.

PRINT PROVIDERS

Local print providers handle print jobs that print to a local device, while remote print providers spool your job over the network to a print server.

LOCAL PRINT PROVIDER

The local print provider is LOCALSPL.DLL and works as shown in Figure 13.9. This software

Sends the print job to a spool file, then also makes a copy called the *shadow file*. For more information on these files, see the following section, "Spool Files and Shadow Files."

Passes control of the print job to the appropriate print processor. When the print processor is finished, it passes the print job back to LOCALSPL.DLL.

Adds a separator page wherever appropriate. For more information, see "Separator Pages," later in this chapter.

Passes control to the print monitor responsible for the destination printer port.

Figure 13.9.
The local print provider
(LOCALSPL.DLL).

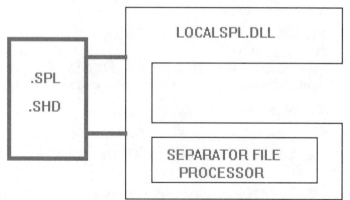

You can edit the print processor's functions in Print Manager. Select Printer Properties, Printer, Properties, Detail to arrive at the dialog box. The following options are configurable:

Print Directly to Port: The print job goes directly to the port; it is not spooled to the disk until a send data command is received.

Hold Mismatched Jobs: The spooler can hold the print jobs that pause when a requested feature is not present. For example, if an envelope is required and the manual feed option is selected, the print job pauses in the spooler until the envelope is inserted in the paper feed.

Delete Jobs after Printing: This option discards print jobs when finished printing. It is available in case print jobs are deleted before a good copy is printed.

Job Prints While Spooling: The print job starts printing to the print device before the job has finished writing to the spool file in its entirety.

Print Spooled Jobs First: Before printing the next print job, any jobs in the spooler are checked and processed first.

SPOOL FILES AND SHADOW FILES

For each spooled job, the local print provider creates two files:

The print job is saved to disk in the form of a spool file (.SPL extension).

The logistical information about the print job and the destination printer in the form of a shadow file.

If the print job is interrupted (for example, the print server is shut down), these two files are still in existence. The print job can be started again when the print server is brought up again.

The location of the spool and shadow files can be changed by manually editing the Registry. By default, these files are written to the file, \systemroot\SYSTEM32\SPOOL\PRINTERS. However, you can set a new default location or override the default location for each printer separately.

To edit the locations:

1. Start the Registry Editor (REGEDT32.EXE).
2. Edit the key: HKEY_LOCAL_MACHINE\SYSTEM\CurrentControlSet\ Control\Print\Printers.
3. Add a `DefaultSpoolDirectory` setting to the default spool directory for all print jobs.

Note

The change in the Registry takes effect after you stop and restart the spooler service. Generally this is done by downing the server, but it can be done in the Control Panel's Device icon.

To edit the location for a printer's spool and shadow files:

1. Start the Registry Editor (REGEDT32.EXE).

13

2. Locate the appropriate subkey for the print device.

3. Add a new SpoolDirectory setting, with the full pathname of the directory to contain the spool and shadow files.

REMOTE PRINT PROVIDERS

When an NT Server prints to another print server, remote print providers locate and direct output to the appropriate network printers. NT Server has two remote print providers.

◆ WIN32SPL.DLL spools print jobs to remote print servers.

◆ NWPROVAU.DLL spools print jobs to NetWare print servers.

PRINT OPTIONS FOR CLIENT SERVICE FOR NETWARE

The same options available in Novell's CAPTURE command are available for NT clients accessing NetWare queues. To set the CAPTURE switches, follow these steps:

1. In the Control Panel, select Client Service for NetWare, Print Options.

2. Select Add Form Feed to eject the page at the end of every print job, or No Form Feed if your applications always eject the last page of a print job.

3. Check Notify When Printed box if you would like each user to receive a message when his or her print job has been printed.

4. Check Print Banner if you would like a banner page to precede each print job.

Note

If your application ejects a page, this option causes a separator page to be ejected.

5. Select OK to save options and continue.

WINDOWS NETWORK PRINT PROVIDER

The Windows print provider, WIN32SPL.DLL, can spool print jobs to print servers running NT or other Windows versions. The print provider researches the specified print server from the printer Share name, and spools the print job to a down level redirector if the print server is a WFW or Windows 95 computer. It spools to the print router if the target server is an NT Server, NT Workstation, or the NetWare file server.

The functions provided by the Windows network print provider are illustrated in Figure 13.10.

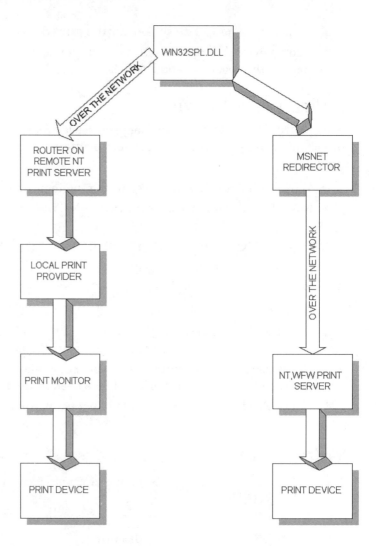

Figure 13.10.
The Windows network
print provider
(WIN32SPL.DLL).

NETWARE PRINT PROVIDER

The NetWare print provider, NWPROVAU.DLL, controls the print job when the print router sends the print job to a NetWare server. The print router then sends the print job to the NetWare workstation service, NWWKS.DLL, which in turn relays the job to the NetWare shell or requester, which in turn sends the job to the destination file server's queue as shown in Figure 13.11.

Figure 13.11.
NetWare print provider
interaction with
NetWare.

13

NT Printing Services

Print Monitors

The print monitor establishes bi-directional communications with the printer port. It listens to the data stream going to a port and port communications parameters.

Two print monitors are used in NT.

LOCALMON.DLL handles output for LPTx, COMx, FILE:, remote print Shares, and named pipes.

HPMON.DLL handles logical ports for HP Laserjet IIIsi and Laserjet IV printers and HP printers with printer interface cards installed.

The print monitor also

> Monitors and forwards printer error messages, such as out of paper.

> Monitors error recovery and restarts the print job when the problem has been resolved.

> Notifies the spooler that the job has printed so it can be deleted from the spooler.

You can add or install other print monitors if required. Other print monitors may become available in the future, or may be provided by application or printer developers to handle situations unique to their application or printer.

PRINTER DRIVERS

NT Server printer drivers generate a RAW data stream that makes up a document. The NT Server printing architecture requires every printer driver to be implemented as a pair of user mode dynamic link libraries (DLLs), as well as a printer-specific component. These three files consist of

> The printer graphics driver: This consists of the rendering/managing portion of the driver, which is always called from the GDI Server (GDISVR.DLL).

> The printer interface driver: This piece consists of the user interface/ configuration management portion of the printer driver, which is always called by the client side of the router (WINSPOOL.DRV).

> A configuration file (or mini-driver): This component is used by the other two pieces of the printer driver, as needed, to determine printer specific information.

NT Server supplies two printer graphics and printer interface driver combinations.

> Universal raster printer driver RASDD.DLL and RASDDUI.DLL.

> Universal Postscript printer driver PSCRIPT.DLL and PSCRPTUI.DLL. It is possible for other manufacturers to supply printer graphics and printer interface driver combinations. However, it is typically much easier to supply only a mini-driver.

PRINTER MINI-DRIVERS

Raster mini-drivers are actually DLLs. The NT Server raster printer driver can read most Windows 3.1 mini-driver DLLs (those that were created for UNIDRV.DLL) directly with minimal to no porting required. These DLLs contain printer-specific information, but do not contain executable code, except for a few rare instances, such as Toshiba and CItoh drivers.

PostScript mini-drivers are actually Adobe PostScript standard, PostScript printer description (PPD) files. A PPD file is a text file describing printer-specific information for a particular printer model and is available from the printer's manufacturer. Unlike Windows 3.*x*, the NT Server PostScript printer driver can directly interpret PPD files. Because PostScript printers ship with PPD files, when a new PostScript printer becomes available, it is ready for use with NT Server.

CROSS-PLATFORM PRINTING

An NT Server print server must have Intel x86, MIPS, and Alpha drivers installed if machines from different hardware platforms will be using it. Printer drivers are platform specific.

For example, if you are running an x86 machine and printing to a MIPS print server with only MIPS printer drivers, NT Server requests that you install an x86-based printer driver in order to complete the print job.

When a print job is issued from the client machine, a local printer driver is used if available. If no local printer driver is available, the x86 driver from the print server is used. The driver image is copied in memory to the local machine, which composes the journal file through GDI32.DLL. The journal file is then sent to the server spooler that manages the print job.

INSTALLING NON-NATIVE DRIVERS ON AN NT SERVER

Follow these steps to install non-native print drivers on your server.

1. From the non-native (to the print server) machine, log on with an account that has administrative privileges on the print server.
2. Start Print Manager and choose Server Viewer.
3. Select the server on which you want to install drivers.
4. Available printers are displayed. For each printer on which you want to install non-native drivers, do the following:

   Select the target printer.

   Choose Printer Properties, then OK.

You are prompted for the location of the printer drivers. The drivers can be on the local machine or the print server. Drivers are installed on the print server and are available to anyone connected to the print server (except when using different hardware platforms such as RISC and Intel).

NETWORK INTERFACE PRINTERS (NETWORK CARD INSTALLED IN A PRINTER)

Network interface printers are printers with network cards built-in or installed as an option. Currently, Hewlett-Packard makes the most common network interface printers. An NT Server print server can share and manage up to 255 HP network interface printers; by default Print Manager is configured to allow up to 64. To change this value, follow these steps:

1. In Print Manager, select an HP network interface printer and choose Printer, Properties.
2. Click on the Settings button.
3. At the bottom of the dialog box, click on Options.
4. Change the Link Stations Allocated value to the number of HP network interface printers that this system will manage.

To use an HP network interface printer, the Data Link Control (DLC) protocol must be installed. Installing this protocol can either be done during Setup, or later through the Network applet in Control Panel.

After setting up a network interface printer, it is necessary to run the printer's self-test mechanism to obtain the address of the network card in the printer. This card address is the address that should be selected from the list of available printer addresses when setting up the printer on an NT Server system.

The recommended method for using HP network interface printers with NT Server is to create a printer on an NT Server system and share it for all other users to connect to. This way every system will not potentially be trying to print to the actual HP network interface printing device. If this were to occur, only one system would be able to print to the printing device at a time, with no way for other users to view the status of the printing device. However, it is possible to configure a connection directly to an HP network interface printer to release the connection after completing the print job. This can be done by following the steps below:

1. In Print Manager, select an HP network interface printer and choose Printer, Properties.
2. Click on the Settings button.
3. At the bottom of the dialog box, click on Timers.
4. Set "Connection" to "Job Based."

When setting up an HP network interface printer on an NT Server print server, "Connection" should be set to "Continuous." This is so that no other system will be able to connect directly to the HP network interface printer and prevent jobs sent to the server from making it to the printing device.

PRINTER ADMINISTRATION

Many aspects of network printing require administration. The general categories that you need to manage include printer pools, print security, and printing in a TCP/IP environment.

PRINTER POOLS

A printer pool is created when two or more printers are represented by one Print Share. When a user prints to the Print Share, the print job may print on any one of the printers in the printer pool. This option is helpful for situations where a single printer cannot keep up with demand, or when printing needs to continue despite printer time-outs (that is, out of paper).

There is no way to specify which printer should service the print job when sending to a printer pool. All printers in a printing pool must use the same driver. For example, if a print job has been rendered for an HP LaserJet 4 and the target printer is a dot matrix printer, your print job will not print properly, if it can print at all.

You can mix the port types and communications parameters. For example, you can have a serial and a parallel printer together in the same pool.

The spooler sends to printers in a printer pool in the order in which they were added to the pool. For best performance, you should add the fastest printer or port first, then add printers according to speed.

HOW TO CREATE PRINTER POOLS

Keeping in mind that under NT Server, a printer is a software interface between an application and a printing device, and the instrument that prints is referred to as a printing device.

To create a printer pool:

1. From the Print Manager window, choose the Printers icon or the printer window for the printer you want to create a pool with.
2. From the Printer menu, choose Properties.
3. In the Printer Properties dialog box, choose the Details button.
4. In the Printer Details dialog box, select port names from the Print To Additional Ports dialog box that correspond to the ports where you have connected printers.

To add (or change) the port name:

1. In the Printer Properties dialog box, select Network Printer in the Print To dialog box.

2. In the Print Destinations dialog box, select Local Port.

3. Type the name of the port you want to add in the Enter A Port Name dialog box (this can include redirected ports to shared printers), and then choose the OK button. (This is when the administrator should assign unique, descriptive names.)

MANAGING A PRINTER POOL

After the printer pool is set up, it appears to the users as a single printing device. The owner of the printer pool should specify unique port names for each printing device because this is the only indicator to the user of which printing device a print job is being printed to.

A printer pool is most useful if all of the printing devices are in the same geographic location. If the user has to wander around from location to location to find a print job, a printer pool is probably not a good use of available resources. Because the user never knows which printing device in the pool will print a particular job, it does not make sense to have different types or models of printers pooled together. Even something as simple as a different default print tray or less RAM in one printing device in the pool may have adverse effects on a particular print job.

When you define a printer pool, it is best to define the fastest printing device first because the print spooler checks the available sources in the order they were created.

Note

NT Server imposes no limits on the number of print devices that can be in a printer pool.

PRINTER SECURITY

When sharing a printer, the default option is for all users to have full access to the printer. However, you can configure a Print Share to provide different levels of security access to different local groups.

A normal NT installation allows the following permissions to the following groups:

The Everyone group:	Print
Administrators and Power Users:	Full Control
Creator Owner:	Manage Documents
Print Operators:	Full Control
Server Operators:	Full Control

To change group security assignments, you can enter Print Manager, select the Print Share to be managed, select Security, Permissions. You can select a group, then select or edit the Type of Access granted to that group as shown in Figure 13.12.

Figure 13.12.
Selecting the Type of
Access for a group.

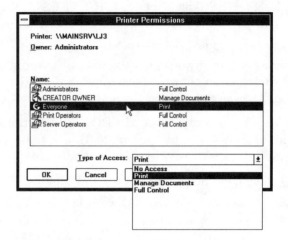

Table 13.1 shows the actions that the print permissions allow.

TABLE 13.1. ACTIONS PERTAINING TO PRINTER PERMISSIONS.

Action to be performed	No Access	Print	Manage Documents	Full Control
Print Documents		X	X	X
Control job settings for user's own documents		X	X	X
Pause, restart, and delete user's own documents		X	X	X
Control job settings for all documents			X	X
Pause, restart, move, and delete all documents			X	X
Share Printer				X
Change printer properties				X
Delete printer				X
Change printer permissions				X

PRINTING FROM MS-DOS APPLICATIONS

When using NT Server with an NTFS volume, users may have insufficient rights to print their jobs. If a user only has Read and Execute permissions to the WINNT\SYSTEM32\SPOOL\PRINTERS directory, you may not be able to print from an MS-DOS application or a command prompt (CMD.EXE).

When this problem occurs, the print job spools to the local print queue, but there is not any output. If you check the Event Viewer in the error (system) log, there will be entries listing the print job request, but with 0 pages printed. To remove the print jobs that won't print from the queue, shut down and restart NT Server.

To print correctly from MS-DOS applications and the command prompt, add either the Change or Full Control permissions to the WINNT\SYSTEM32\SPOOL\PRINTERS subdirectory by doing the following:

1. Log on as an Administrator and open the File Manager.
2. Select the \WINNT\SYSTEM32\SPOOL\PRINTERS directory.
3. From the Security menu, choose Permissions.
4. In the Directory Permissions dialog box, select the name of the desired User or Group and select the Change or Full Control permissions to this directory.

You should now be able to print correctly from MS-DOS applications and the command prompt.

PROBLEMS RELATED TO SECURITY

If an NT Server is sharing a printer that is redirected to an NT Server computer, down level client (like MS-DOS or WFW) print jobs get stuck in the NT Server print queue.

When an NT Server computer sends a down level print job, it sends the job as a null session. Null sessions are those where the user credentials are blank during the request to set up a session. Because the down level client may not have an account or because of a conflicting account on the second print server, down level jobs are sent as null sessions. Security is up to the first computer in this scenario. NT does not provide this support unless specifically configured to do so. This change was made in order to provide a higher default level of security.

This problem can be resolved by modifying the Registry on the NT computer to allow null sessions to the Print Share.

1. Start Registry Editor and locate the following Registry subkey in the HKEY_LOCAL_MACHINE subtree:

    \SYSTEM\CurrentControlSet\Services\LanmanServer\Parameters

2. Select the NullSessionShares value.

3. From the Edit menu, choose Multi String.

Note

Values will already exist and should not be replaced. If the values are accidentally deleted, just choose Cancel and try again.

4. Select the first blank line after the values that currently exist. (The lines above should not be highlighted.) Add the name of the Print Share on NT Server 3.5 you want to accept null sessions. This must be done for each share individually.

5. Choose OK and exit Registry Editor.

6. Either shut down and restart NT Server or from a command prompt type:

   `NET STOP SERVER` and press Enter. Then type: `NET START SERVER` and press Enter.

TCP/IP PRINTING

Any WFW, Windows 95, LAN Manager, or NT computer with TCP/IP installed can print to TCP/IP printers that are directly attached to the LAN or to a UNIX host. UNIX users may also print to an NT Server's printers.

To enable TCP/IP printing, at least one NT Server must have the Microsoft TCP/IP protocols, networking software, and TCP/IP printing installed and properly working. The NT Server with TCP/IP printing installed acts as a gateway between TCP/IP and other NT printing services.

Installing TCP/IP in itself is a challenge for administrators who did not install TCP/IP during original NT Setup. To effectively add TCP/IP to an existing NT Server, you must re-run the Setup program from the CD-ROM. To add TCP/IP, run WINNT with the /B switch from the CD-ROM. You must have at least 80 MB of free space on a FAT partition. You will re-install all operating system files, but if you are careful, you will not delete any data or configuration files. The process should take less than an hour.

Note

Though Microsoft documentation recommends using Control Panel's Network icon to update TCP/IP support, you will find that this procedure often does not work. Attempting to add TCP/IP after a server has been installed using the Control Panel, Network icon does not effectuate proper implementation of all required TCP/IP functions under NT 3.51.

One of many specific cases in which adding TCP/IP support does not work is when SQL Server is installed with TCP/IP networking enabled before TCP/IP is installed on the NT Server. This happens because SQL Server adds its own TCP/IP entries in the Registry which confuses Control Panel installation of TCP/IP into thinking that TCP/IP is already installed.

Warning

Remember to have the correct network adapter, SCSI host, and CD-ROM drivers available before attempting a reinstallation.

Before beginning the reinstallation, check your installed drivers for exact matches on the descriptions, file names, dates, and sizes. One of the worst problems you will encounter with NT is resolving driver problems. If you already have a working server, try to use the exact same drivers again. Many drivers shipped with NT 3.51 have serious problems, and many of these drivers have been updated by the developers.

CONFIGURING AN NT SERVER FOR TCP/IP PRINTING

The computer to which the printer is attached must have TCP/IP services installed. To configure an NT Server computer for TCP/IP printing:

1. During Setup, select TCP/IP in addition to any other protocols currently in use.

2. In the Network Settings dialog box, select TCP/IP Protocol And Related Components in the Network Software box, and then choose the Continue button.

Tip

Select Enable DHCP protocol unless you have assigned TCP/IP addresses integrated into an existing TCP/IP network. If you have an existing TCP/IP network, you must enter addressing information from your TCP/IP administrator before adding support for this protocol.

Note

If you have vendor supplied drivers, make sure you select the Have Disk option and copy the drivers from your floppy disk.

CREATING A TCP/IP PRINTER

Next, you must create a TCP/IP printer on this NT Server computer.

Create a Print Share the same way you would create a normal printer. You will need to enter the following information for a TCP/IP printer:

The printer's IP host address or DNS name. This is the IP address of the host to which the printer is attached. In the case of a printer interface card, an address or DNS name may have been assigned to the card.

Follow this procedure to create and set up a TCP/IP printer:

1. In Print Manager, select Create Printer.
2. Enter the Print Share name In the Printer Name box. This will be the Print Share name known to NT clients. You can use a different name from the TCP/IP name, but retaining the same name makes for better organization. You may have to follow instructions in your hardware installation guide for a printer interface card to define parameters for print queues, etc. For a direct-connect printer, see the hardware documentation to find the name by which the network printer identifies the print queue.
3. Select the appropriate driver.
4. Select Other in the Print To box; this displays the Print Destinations dialog box. Select the arrow bar and a list will be shown.
5. Select LPR Print Monitor, and then choose OK. The Add LPR Compatible Printer dialog box will appear.
6. In the Name Or Address Of Host Providing LPD box, type the DNS name or IP host address of the printer.

Note

NT 3.5x supports only UNIX LPD service; it does not support LPSCHED. You may need to obtain and install an LPD service on your TCP/IP host to enable NT-TCP/IP printing.

7. Type the host name of the printer in the Name Of Printer On That Machine box. This name is the assigned UNIX name, or the name assigned to the printer interface card during installation.

8. When the Create Printer dialog box reappears, select the Share This Printer On The Network option. The NT Server now becomes a host computer that will appear in UNIX utilities as if it were a UNIX printer host.

9. In the Create Printer dialog box, enter any other configuration information required, then select OK.

Once your TCP/IP printer has been properly defined and configured, it should appear to all UNIX users as any other TCP/IP printer. Both UNIX utilities and NT's Print Manager can be used to manage the printer, of course subject to Security Permissions as defined in Print Manager.

COMMON PRINTING PROBLEMS

Several common problems plague users and administrators. As is the case in most environments, a few problems account for the vast majority of time lost in troubleshooting. This section discusses various aspects of your printing environment you might check if printing problems occur.

NT PRINTING IS NOT INTERRUPT DRIVEN

Conflicting hardware interrupts is often a problem in any computer with more than one parallel port. Because NT is a fully multitasking preemptive processing environment, interrupt conflicts are not acceptable. NT is far more sensitive to interrupt conflicts than is a DOS-based printer host. This problem pertains to ISA, EISA, MCA, and PCI bus computers, since all need to use interrupts.

Note

When configuring EISA, MCA, and PCI slots, always use edge-triggered interrupts (meaning only one device per interrupt). If you choose to use level triggered to share a single interrupt between two interface cards, both must be compatible in how they share the level-triggered interrupt. As a result, this option is not recommended unless two identical cards share a trigger.

There is one exception to this rule: NT Server does not use a hardware interrupt request line (IRQs) for printing. The NT Server parallel port driver is thread-based, and the port is polled at background priority. This eliminates a number of potential hardware conflicts with other devices that use IRQ 7 or 5, the usual parallel port interrupts. This exception allows you to use IRQ 5 and 7 for other purposes, and prevents server crashes due to interrupt conflicts where they occur most often, IRQ 5 and 7.

However, this improvement sacrifices performance. Windows for Workgroups 3.11 print output is much faster than NT's and Windows 95 because Windows for Workgroups is interrupt driven.

Note

> Because NT Server does not use interrupts for printing, its printing is slower than WFW. Windows 95 has the same problem as NT Server. There is no relief in sight for this situation.

You can change the thread priority in the Registry to give more or less priority to print jobs. If you have an application that runs very slowly due to print spooling, you can reduce the thread priority of the port print function by adding the following registry entry:

```
HKEY_LOCAL_MACHINE
 \SYSTEM
   \CurrentControlSet
     \Control
       \Print
```

Add: Key: PortThreadPriority

```
Type:  REG_SZ
Value: Thread_Priority_Below_normal
```

Note

> If you boot OS/2 or MS-DOS, you still need to check for IRQ conflicts; the NT Server port driver will not be used. Under NT Server, a separate thread is used for each port to which a printer is attached. The spooler is called by any of these threads when they complete a job and is also called when a job is provided by an external thread.

Summary

This chapter is a comprehensive guide and reference work for printing. You should refer to this chapter whenever you have problems with printers or you try to figure out what occurs during a print job.

You will also find this chapter helpful in troubleshooting application problems where they relate to printing. Use it as a reference for future implementation issues.

- Starting the Registry Editor

- Using the Registry Editor for Configuration Management

- The Registry Structure

- Hives and Files

- The HKEY_LOCAL_ MACHINE Key

- The HKEY_CLASSES _ROOT Key

- The HKEY_USERS Key

- User Profiles for NT Workstations

- Referential Integrity of Registry Data

CHAPTER 14

Managing the Network Registry

Recognizer   Each time you start a computer running NT Server, an auto-detection software module called the Recognizer updates hardware-configuration data in the Registry.

SAM   (Security Accounts Manager) SAM is NT Server's and NT Workstation's security account database that includes user, group, and resource security information for a server or domain.

Registry   A database used by the operating system that contains computer hardware and software configuration data. When viewing data in the Registry with the Registry Editor, you see keys and subkeys in a hierarchical tree format on the left of the key window and values for the subkeys on the right of the key window.

Key   The first major division of the Registry. Each key is shown in the title bar of a separate Registry Editor window. A basic installation yields four predefined keys. You can add more keys for specific purposes as necessary.

Subtree   Registry keys are organized or broken down into subtrees, each containing other subtrees or subkeys. Keys are thus organized into a hierarchical tree format. Subtrees can also be subkeys, containing values as well as more subtrees or subkeys.

In Registry Editor key windows, subtrees's folders have a plus sign (+) if more entries are contained and a minus sign (-) when the subtree is expanded.

Subkey   A subkey is an entry under a key or subtree that contains a value. Each subkey represents an object and the value represents configuration parameters. A subtree entry can also be a subkey if it has a value associated with it.

In Registry Editor, subkeys have no plus or minus sign in their folders because they cannot be expanded. Values appear in the right side of the window according to which subkey is selected (highlighted).

Hive   A subtree of the Registry that has been saved as a file. Because the hive is a file, it can be copied or moved to other systems or edited with the Registry Editor utility.

NT Server has been designed as a multiplatform, scaleable operating system. Instead of a person having to hard code the operating-system configuration information, the information is retrieved from a database by the operating system itself. This database—called the *Registry*—is accessible to subsystems and applications as well.

The Registry is at the heart of your NT operating system. It is a repository of key software and hardware parameters with initial values and dynamic data that is updated by the various operating system and subsystem processes. Initially, the questions you answer in Setup configure the Registry keys, subkeys, and values. Later, as changes are made to the system, subkeys and related values are added or changed. Changes to the Registry are normally effected by changing your Windows desktop or via GUI-based administration tools such as the Control Panel. When applications are installed or configured, changes are made to the Registry via the WIN32 API. In some cases, applications change subkey values in the normal course of operation.

When changes are made to the Registry, the changes are saved in memory and then saved to disk when you shut down the operating system. This is why it is important to shut down the operating system properly before turning off your computer. You should never power down before receiving the dialog box indicating that it is safe to turn off the computer.

The Registry organizes keys and subkeys (hardware and software parameters) in hierarchical form so that administrators can manage the information in a logical and organized manner. The Registry Editor utility enables access to the Registry on local and remote computers.

You can use the Registry Editor utility (REGEDT32.EXE) to manually edit subkey values. This is necessary in some cases where a utility does not provide the option to change a value or when for any reason a configuration option cannot be changed through a utility. For example, under some conditions, the Ports Control Panel utility does not enable you to change or delete a communication port configuration. You can edit the Registry manually through the Registry Editor utility, bypassing the Control Panel. The Registry Editor is provided as a powerful tool for advanced system administrators who choose to force changes to specific operating system parameters.

14

MANAGING THE NETWORK REGISTRY

Warning

Editing subkeys and their values in the Registry can result in operating system failure. Where possible, it is advised that you make changes through the Control Panel and other configuration utilities, which results in automated changes to the Registry. It is advisable to restrict users from viewing or making changes through the Registry Editor utility. System administrators should fully understand subkeys and values before making changes and should exercise due caution in editing values.

See Chapter 28, "Troubleshooting Overview," for more details on how to deal with Registry disasters.

Registry data is used by the following utilities or processes:

Setup. Whenever you run the NT Setup program or other setup programs for applications or hardware, the Setup program adds new configuration data to the Registry. For example, new information is added when you install a new SCSI adapter or change the settings for your video display.

Recognizer. Each time you start a computer running NT Server, the NT auto detection utility updates hardware configuration data in the Registry. On x86-based computers, this is done by two programs: NTDETECT.COM and NT Kernel (NTOSKRNL.EXE). On RISC-based computers, this information is read from the ARC firmware.

NT Kernel. During startup, the NT Kernel reads information from the Registry, such as which device drivers to load and their load order. The NTOSKRNL.EXE program also sends information about itself to the Registry, such as its version number.

Device drivers. Device drivers update and receive load parameters and configuration data from the Registry. The data is similar to the DEVICE= lines in the CONFIG.SYS file under MS-DOS. A device driver must report system resources it uses, such as port addresses and hardware interrupts, so that they can be added or changed in the Registry. Applications and device drivers can read the information in the Registry and provide users with smart installation and configuration programs.

Administrative tools. The administrative tools in NT Server, such as those present in the Control Panel and in the Administrative Tools program group, can be used to modify configuration data. You also can use the Windows NT Diagnostics program (WINMSD.EXE) to view information stored in the Registry.

See Figure 14.1 for an illustration of how various NT Server components and applications use the Registry.

You can compare the Registry to the .INI files used under Windows 3.x and WFW. Each key in the Registry is analogous to a bracketed heading in an .INI file, and entries under the heading are similar to values in the Registry. INI files are no longer needed in NT because the Registry contains all information for all software configuration, as well as all information for hardware configuration. When installing or reconfiguring a 16-bit Windows application, you put information that would normally go into .INI files in the Registry. However, if .INI files exist, your applications still use them. For newer applications, the elimination of .INI files and automatic recording of configuration data in the Registry simplifies the administration of Windows applications.

Figure 14.1.
How Registry
information is used.

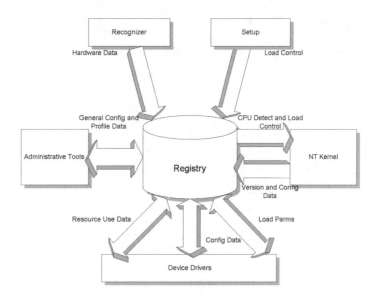

The Registry has more subkey levels, however, thus differentiating it from .INI files, which do not support nested headings. Registry values can also include executable code in addition to the string values, whereas .INI files cannot do so.

Another important distinction is that the Registry enables the storing of individual preferences for multiple users of the same computer by creating different keys for each user. This capability provides robust networking configuration for users. It is because of the Registry that different users can log on and receive different desktops and the same user can log on to different computers and receive the same desktop without affecting the hardware configuration of the computer.

Note

Please note that the previous discussion pertains to an NT Workstation acting as a client.

Each of the root key names begins with HKEY_; this prefix is also usable by software developers as a handle for programmatic access of Registry data. (A *handle* is a value used to uniquely identify a resource so that a program can access it.) The Registry contains the user profile for the user who is currently logged on, including environment variables, personal program groups, desktop settings, network connections, printers, and application preferences.

Also note that the four predefined keys are always shown in uppercase in the Registry Editor. Subkeys are expressed in upper- and lowercase according to the Windows API convention.

14

MANAGING THE NETWORK REGISTRY

Note

NT Server enables the continued use of .INI files for 16-bit Windows-based applications.

STARTING THE REGISTRY EDITOR

The Registry Editor application, REGEDT32.EXE, does not appear in any default program group in Program Manager, but you can run it in one of the following ways:

◆ Run the REGEDT32.EXE file from File Manager or Program Manager.

◆ Type the START REGEDT32 command at the command prompt.

◆ Click on the Windows NT Diagnostic icon and select Tools; then select Registry Editor.

◆ Add the Registry Editor icon to your desktop in Program Manager by selecting File, New, Browse and then locating REGEDT32.EXE in the <winnt-root>\system32 directory. You should add the Registry Editor utility to the Administrative Tools program group.

Note

If you plan to use the Registry Editor frequently, you can add the REGEDIT32.EXE icon to your desktop.

The first screen you see should be similar to Figure 14.2.

Figure 14.2.
The four predefined
keys of the Registry.

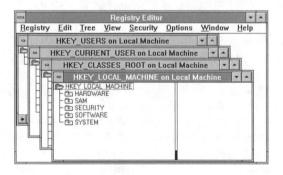

Using the Registry Editor for Configuration Management

You can use the Registry Editor to view and analyze Registry entries for the various components in NT. Learning to understand and view Registry keys, subkeys, and values is important for system administrators. The Registry contains all the answers to your configuration questions provided you understand where to locate the parameter and how to read its values. You can also use the Registry Editor to modify or add Registry entries.

It is recommended that, wherever possible, you make changes to the system configuration by using Control Panel or the applications in the Administrative Tools group in Program Manager or by running the Setup or configuration utility for your software applications. You should not edit the Registry through the Registry Editor except when absolutely necessary. Errors can be introduced by editing the values, but Control Panel or Setup place values into the proper places with correct syntax.

Viewing the Registry for a Remote Computer

You can use the Registry Editor to view and change the contents of another NT computer's Registry if the Server services on the remote computer are running. This way, you can provide troubleshooting or other support assistance over the telephone while you view settings on the other computer from your own workstation.

Note

Registry Editor's Auto Refresh option is not available when you are viewing the Registry from a remote computer. If Auto Refresh is on, manual refresh is disabled. Therefore, when you open a remote Registry, Registry Editor checks to see if Auto Refresh mode is on. If it is, Registry Editor displays the message Auto Refresh is not available for remote registries; Registry Editor will disable Auto Refresh mode.

You can work with a remote computer's Registry by choosing the Select Computer command in the Registry Editor menu and then selecting the computer whose Registry you want to access. Under an NT Server, the first name in this list represents the name of a domain. If no computer name appears after this domain name, double-click the domain name to view a list of the computers in that domain.

Two Registry windows appear for the remote computer, one for HKEY_USERS and one for HKEY_LOCAL_MACHINE. You can view or modify the information on keys for the remote computer if the access controls defined for the keys enable you to perform such operations. If you are logged on as a member of the Administrators group, you can perform actions on all keys.

LOADING HIVES FROM ANOTHER COMPUTER

You can use the Load Hive and Unload Hive commands in the Registry Editor to display and maintain another computer's Registry without viewing it remotely. You might want to do this to view specific values or to repair certain entries for a computer that is not configured properly or cannot connect to the network.

The hives that make up your computer's Registry are loaded automatically when you start the computer; you can view the contents of these hives in Registry Editor. If you want to view or change the contents of other hive files, you must use the Load Hive command to display its contents in Registry Editor. You use the Load Hive command in the following situations:

◆ To repair a hive on a computer that temporarily cannot run NT Server.

◆ To look at or repair hives for profiles of people who aren't currently logged on, either on the same computer or a remote computer.

◆ To create a custom LastKnownGood and other startup controls.

The Load Hive and Unload Hive commands affect only the Registry windows that display HKEY_USERS and HKEY_LOCAL_MACHINE. To use these commands, you must have Restore and Backup privileges, which you have if you are logged on as a member of the Administrators group. The Load Hive command is available only when HKEY_USERS or HKEY_LOCAL_MACHINE is selected. The Unload Hive command is available only when a subkey of one of these handles is selected. To load a hive into the Registry Editor, follow these steps:

1. Select the root in the HKEY_LOCAL_MACHINE or HKEY_USERS key.

2. From the Registry menu, choose the Load Hive command.

3. Use the File Name, Drives, and Directories boxes and the Network button of the Load Hive dialog box to select the file that contains the hive you want to load; then click the OK button.

Tip

If you are loading a hive located on a remote computer, the drive and path in the filename are relative to the remote computer. You can find the directory location and names of hives on a computer in the HKEY_LOCAL_MACHINE\SYSTEM\CurrentControlSet\Control\Hivelist subkey. This file must have been created with the Save Key command, or it must be one of the default hives. Under the FAT file system, the filename cannot have an extension. If you are unable to connect to another computer over the network, you can load a hive file that you copied to a floppy disk.

4. In the second Load Hive dialog box, type the name you want to use for the key where the hive will be loaded; then click the OK button. This name creates a new subkey in the Registry. You can specify any name using any characters and including blank spaces. You cannot load to an existing key; data from the loaded hive appears as a new subkey under HKEY_USERS or HKEY_LOCAL_MACHINE (whichever handle you selected before loading the hive). A loaded hive remains in the system until it is unloaded.

The Load Hive command creates a new hive in memory and uses the specified file as the backup hive file (FILENAME.LOG). The specified file is held open, but nothing is copied to the hive file unless the information in a subkey or value entry is changed. Likewise, the Unload Hive command does not copy or create anything; it merely unloads a loaded hive.

How to Unload a Hive from the Registry Editor

You need to select the key that represents a hive that you previously loaded, and then choose the Unload Hive command from the Registry menu. The selected key is removed from the window and is no longer actively available to the system or for editing in the Registry Editor. You cannot unload a hive that is currently loaded by the system or if it contains an open subkey.

Saving and Restoring Keys

The Save Key command enables you to save the information in a subtree (subkey and its subsidiary subkeys) into a *hive* file. This hive can then be used by the Restore and Load Key commands. Changes in the Registry are saved automatically, whether you make changes by using the Registry Editor or by changing settings in applications. The Save Key command is used specifically to save portions of the Registry as a hive file on disk.

Tip

Always back up subtree information into a hive before making changes. If your edits do not have the intended effect, restore the hive to prevent additional problems.

To use the Save Key command, you need Backup privileges, which you have if you are logged on as a member of the Administrators group. You can use the Save Key command on any Registry key; however, this command does not save volatile keys, which are destroyed when you shut down the system. For example, the

14

HKEY_LOCAL_MACHINE\Hardware key is volatile, so it is not saved as a hive file. If you want to view the Hardware hive for debugging, you can save it in a text file by choosing the Save Subtree As command from the Registry menu.

To save a subtree as a hive, follow these steps:

1. Select the subtree that you want to save as a hive file on a disk.

2. From the Registry menu, choose the Save Key command and then complete the filename information in the Save Key dialog box. Under the FAT file system, this filename cannot have an extension. If the key that you are saving is in the Registry of a remote computer, the drive and path that you specify for the filename are relative to the remote computer. The selected key is now saved as a file.

3. When you use the Load Hive command, you can select the filename for any files saved using the Save Key command. For example, as part of system maintenance, you might use the Save Key command to save a key as a file. When the key that you saved is ready to be returned to the system, you use the Restore command.

4. You can use the Restore or Restore Volatile command to make a hive file a part of the system configuration. These commands enable you to copy information in a hive file over a specified subtree. This information copied from the file overwrites the contents of the specified subtree, except for the subkey name. To use the Restore or Restore Volatile command, you need Restore privileges, which you have if you are logged on as a member of the Administrators group.

To restore a hive, follow these steps:

1. Select the subtree where you want to restore the hive.

2. From the Registry menu, choose the Restore command and then complete the filename information in the Restore Key dialog box to specify the hive you want to restore. Under the FAT file system, this filename cannot have an extension. If you are restoring a key on a remote computer, the drive and path of the filename are relative to the remote computer.

Note

If you want to add a key *temporarily* to a system, however, use the Restore Volatile command. If you use this command, the Registry makes a volatile copy that disappears when the system is restarted.

You cannot restore a hive that is open or that has subkeys with opened handles. This is why you cannot restore the SAM or SECURITY subtrees, because Windows NT always has handles open in these keys. Therefore, you use the Restore command only for special conditions, such as the restoration of user profiles on a damaged system.

The Registry Structure

The Registry is organized as a set of four predefined keys that contain per-computer and per-user databases. The per-computer information is about the specific computer's hardware and the software installed on it. The per-user information includes the information in user profiles such as desktop settings, individual preferences for certain software, and personal printer and network settings.

In the Registry, each individual subkey can contain data items (called *value entries*) and additional subkeys.

Note

In the Registry structure, keys are analogous to root directories, subtrees are analogous to subdirectories, and subkeys and their value entries are analogous to files.

Hives and Files

The Registry keys are subdivided into subkeys, which in turn have subkeys, which in turn can have more subkeys defined into many levels. Each subkey can have associated values. A tree consisting of a subkey and its lower subkeys is called a *subtree*. When a subtree is saved as a file it is called a *hive*. Each hive is contained in a single file and has an accompanying .LOG file. These files are in the <winnt-root>\system32\config directory. (See Figure 14.3.)

Figure 14.3.
Hives and files.

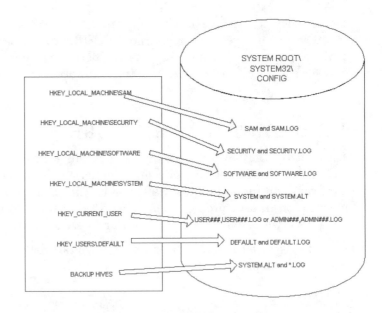

Table 14.1 shows the standard hives and associated log files for a computer running NT Server.

TABLE 14.1. HIVES AND ASSOCIATED LOG FILES.

Hive	Log File(s)
HKEY_LOCAL_MACHINE\SAM	SAM and SAM.LOG
HKEY_LOCAL_MACHINE\SECURITY	SECURITY and SECURITY.LOG
HKEY_LOCAL_MACHINE\SOFTWARE	SOFTWARE and SOFTWARE.LOG
HKEY_LOCAL_MACHINE\SYSTEM	SYSTEM and SYSTEM.ALT
HKEY_CURRENT_USER	USER### and USER###.LOG or ADMIN### and ADMIN###.LOG
HKEY_USERS\.DEFAULT	DEFAULT and DEFAULT.LOG

All hives are stored in the <winnt-root>\SYSTEM32\CONFIG subdirectory, which also includes SYSTEM.ALT and the .LOG files that are backup hive files. Hive files for user profiles can be stored in other locations as the system administrator chooses.

Figure 14.4 illustrates the interaction of the operating system with the four subtrees of the Registry.

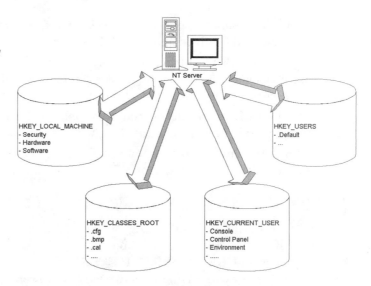

Figure 14.4.
The
HKEY_LOCAL_MACHINE
Key with some of its
subtrees expanded

THE HKEY_LOCAL_MACHINE KEY

This key contains the configuration data for the local computer. The information is used by applications, device drivers, and the NT Server operating system to determine the configuration of the local computer. HKEY_LOCAL_MACHINE contains five subkeys, one of which is expanded to show three subtrees under those subkeys. (See Figure 14.4.)

Note

You can read information in any of these keys, but you can only add or change information in the SOFTWARE and SYSTEM keys.

HKEY_LOCAL_MACHINE contains the following five subkeys, each of which contains an entire subtree:

HARDWARE   This subtree contains subkeys and values describing the physical hardware in the computer and show how the device drivers use that hardware. It also contains mappings and related data that link kernel-mode drivers with various user-mode code. All data in this subtree is deleted and re-created each time the system is started. The DESCRIPTION key describes the actual computer hardware. The DEVICEMAP key contains miscellaneous data in formats specific to particular classes of drivers. The RESOURCEMAP subkey describes which device drivers claim which hardware resources. The NT Diagnostics program (WINMSD.EXE) can report on the contents of the RESOURCEMAP subkey in an easy-to-read format.

SAM   This subtree contains the security information for user and group accounts and for the domains in NT Server.

SECURITY   This subtree contains subkeys and values containing the local security policy, such as specific user rights. This subtree is used only by the NT security subsystem.

SOFTWARE   This subtree contains subkeys and values for the local computer's installed software along with various configuration information.

SYSTEM   The subtree contains subkeys and values that control system startup, device-driver loading, NT services, and operating-system behavior.

Note

By convention, if conflicting values exist under both the HKEY_CURRENT_USER and HKEY_LOCAL_MACHINE keys, the values in HKEY_CURRENT_USER take precedence. However, values in this key can further extend (rather than replace) data in HKEY_LOCAL_MACHINE. Also, some items (such as device driver loading entries) are meaningless if they occur outside of HKEY_LOCAL_MACHINE.

THE HARDWARE SUBTREE

The HKEY_LOCAL_MACHINE\HARDWARE subtree contains the configuration data for the local computer. Figure 14.5 illustrates the layout of the HARDWARE subtree.

Figure 14.5.
The HARDWARE subtree.

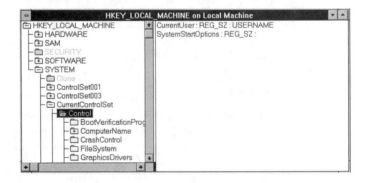

Note

You can read information in any subkey, but you can only add or change information in the SOFTWARE and SYSTEM subkeys. All information in HKEY_LOCAL_MACHINE\HARDWARE is *volatile*, which means that the settings are recorded each time the system is started and then discarded when the system is shut down. Applications and device drivers use this subtree to read information about the system components, store data directly into the DEVICEMAP subkey, and store data indirectly into the RESOURCEMAP subkey.

Tip

Do not try to edit the subkeys or values in HKEY_LOCAL_MACHINE\HARDWARE; much of the information appears in binary format, making it difficult to decipher. To view data about a computer's hardware in an easy-to-read format for troubleshooting, run Windows NT Diagnostics and choose the Devices button. Windows NT Diagnostics extracts the current information from the Registry and displays it in a more readable format.

The DESCRIPTION subkey under HKEY_LOCAL_MACHINE\HARDWARE displays configuration information derived from device firmware, the Recognizer (NTDETECT.COM), and the Executive itself, which manages the interface between the kernel and the environment subsystems.

Note

Network cards are not detected as part of startup but are instead detected during NT Setup or if you double-click the Network icon in Control Panel to install a new network card.

In some cases, network cards are software configurable. In these cases, hardware configuration changes can be automatically reflected without running Setup because the changes are contained in firmware on the network card. Even in the case of software configurable network cards, the appropriate base I/O address or slot number must be configured in Setup.

14

HKEY_LOCAL_MACHINE\HARDWARE\DESCRIPTION\System
\MultifunctionAdapter   This subkey contains several other subkeys, each
corresponding to specific bus adapters on the local computer. Each of these
subkeys describes a class (or type) of adapter, including adapters and
controllers for storage devices, display, keyboard, parallel ports, pointing
devices, serial ports, and SCSI adapters. The subkey's path describes the
type of component. The numbering for hardware components is 0-based,
which means that, for example, the first (or only) disk adapter appears
under the 0 subkey. The name of the MultifunctionAdapter subkey depends
on the bus type. For example, the subkey name for ISA and MCA buses
appears as MultifunctionAdapter. For EISA buses, the subkey name is
EisaAdapter, and for TurboChannel buses, the subkey name can be
TcAdapter.

For each detected hardware component, the optional Component Information and Configuration Data value entries store version and configuration
data in binary format. The Identifier entry contains the name of a component, if specified.

Figure 14.6.
The DESCRIPTION
subkey.

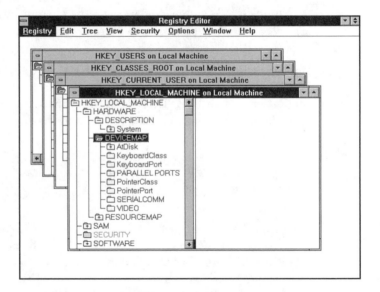

HKEY_LOCAL_MACHINE\HARDWARE\DEVICEMAP   Each Device
subkey contains one or more values to specify the location in the Registry
for specific driver information for that kind of component. Figure 14.7
shows an example of the PointerPort0 location for the serial port. Figure
14.8 shows an example of multiple SCSI adapters.

Figure 14.7.
The DEVICEMAP
subtree for a single
device.

Figure 14.8.
The DEVICEMAP
subkey for multiple
devices.

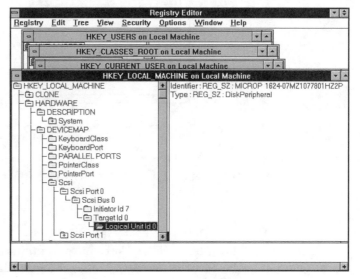

The RESOURCEMAP subtree under HKEY_LOCAL_MACHINE
\HARDWARE maps device drivers to resources that the drivers use. Each
RESOURCEMAP subkey contains data reported by the device driver about
I/O ports, I/O memory addresses, interrupts, DMA channels, and so on. The
data in the RESOURCEMAP subtree is volatile, so this subtree is re-
created each time you start NT Server. In the RESOURCEMAP subtree,
there are DeviceClass subtrees for each general class (or type) of device.
Each of these subtrees contains one or more DriverName subkeys with

values for each driver's configuration. For example, Sermouse is the DriverName subkey under the PointerPort DeviceClass subkey. The driver names in these subkeys match the services listed in HKEY_LOCAL_ MACHINE\SYSTEM\CurrentControlSet\Services. Figure 14.9 shows an example of serial port subkey highlighted on the left part of the window, and its associated values on the right.

Figure 14.9.
The RESOURCEMAP subtree

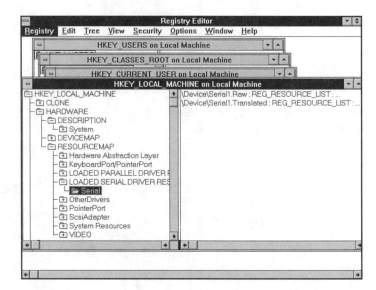

Tip

If you need to resolve resource conflicts, use Windows NT Diagnostics to view the data from these subkeys in an easy-to-read format.

THE SAM SUBTREE

The HKEY_LOCAL_MACHINE\SAM subtree contains the user and group account information in the Security Account Manager (SAM) database for the local computer. For a computer running NT Server domain controller, this subtree also contains security information for the entire domain. This information is what you see in User Manager for Domains; it also appears in the lists of users and groups when you use the Security menu commands in File Manager. This subtree is mapped to HKEY_LOCAL_MACHINE\SECURITY\SAM, so a change made in one of these subkeys automatically appears in the other. If you want to change user account, group account, or any user-related information, use User Manager for Domains. This will ensure that all affected subkeys and value changes are made appropriately.

Warning

The information in this database is in binary format and should not be changed using Registry Editor. Errors introduced into this database might prevent users from logging on to the network.

THE SECURITY SUBTREE

The HKEY_LOCAL_MACHINE\SECURITY subtree contains security information for the local computer, including user rights, password policy, and the membership of local groups, as set in User Manager. This information is not important for an NT Server computer.

THE SOFTWARE SUBTREE

The HKEY_LOCAL_MACHINE\SOFTWARE subtree contains specific configuration information about software installed on the local computer. Figure 14.10 shows the Registry Editor view of this subtree.

Figure 14.10.
The SOFTWARE
subtree.

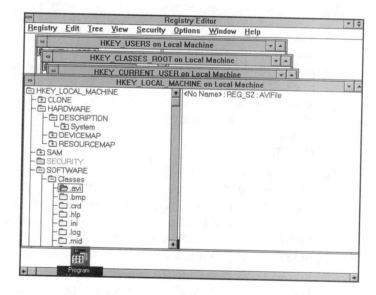

The entries under this subtree, which apply for all users using this specific computer, show what software is installed on the computer and also define file associations and OLE information.

The HKEY_CLASSES_ROOT handle is an alias for the subtree rooted at HKEY_LOCAL_MACHINE\SOFTWARE\Classes. This subtree contains, for example, the information you add by using the Associate command in File Manager, information added during installation for specific Windows-based applications, and information about applications installed on the NT desktop.

The HKEY_LOCAL_MACHINE\SOFTWARE subtree contains several subtrees, including Classes, Program Groups, and Secure, as well as various Description subkeys that might appear in the Registry.

HKEY_LOCAL_MACHINE\SOFTWARE\Microsoft and its subkey Windows NT\CurrentVersion are of particular interest. These subkeys contain information about software that supports services built into NT Server, as well as data about the version and type of the current release (multiprocessor versus uniprocessor).

For example, to check to be certain that your multiprocessor server is using the multiprocessor kernel instead of the uniprocessor kernel, see the value associated with the HKEY_LOCAL_MACHINE\SOFTWARE\Microsoft\Windows NT\CurrentVersion subkey.

THE SOFTWARE SUBTREES

Some of the SOFTWARE subtrees are very important to analyze. The following subtrees each contain the following:

◆ The Classes subtree contains subkeys that define types of documents, providing information on filename-extension associations and OLE information that can be used by Windows shell applications and OLE applications. (This subtree is not important for an NT Server computer because the actions performed locally at the NT Server are not the primary purpose of the computer.) Figure 14.11 shows an example of file extension association with an application. Figure 14.12 shows an example of a shell (the Cardfile applet).

◆ The Description subtree contain the names and version numbers of the software installed on the local computer. (Information about the configuration of these applications is stored on a per-user basis under HKEY_CURRENT_USER.) During installation, applications record this information in the following form: HKEY_LOCAL_MACHINE\SOFTWARE\<CompanyName>\<ProductName>\<Version>

Figure 14.13 shows an example of some entries under the HKEY_LOCAL_MACHINE\SOFTWARE\Microsoft subtree that contain entries for the DLC\CurrentVersion\NetRules software installed on the computer.

Figure 14.11.
SOFTWARE Classes
subkey example.

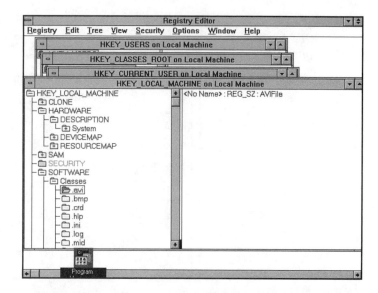

Figure 14.12.
SOFTWARE Classes
subkey example of a
shell.

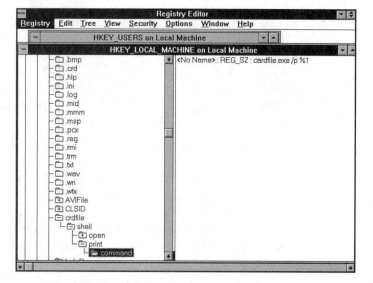

Figure 14.13.
The SOFTWARE
Description subkey.

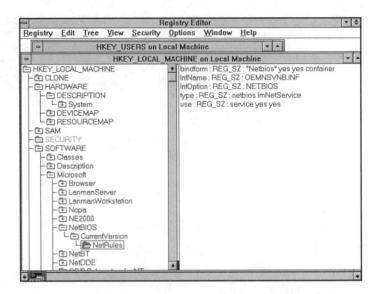

Note

The values associated with each subkey are added by the related application. The entries shown in brackets are only placeholders; for example, <CompanyName> can be Powersoft, Arcada, or any software developer company name. Do not edit entries in this subtree unless explicitly directed to do so by your software vendor.

The Program Groups subtree under HKEY_LOCAL_MACHINE \SOFTWARE contains the common program groups—that is, those used in common by all users of the local computer. (The program groups for an individual user can be viewed under HKEY_CURRENT_USER, and the default personal program groups can be viewed in HKEY_USERS\.DEFAULT.) Each subkey under the Program Groups subtree is the name of a common program group, and its value is expressed in binary data describing that program group. If you want to change the content of common program groups, use the menu commands or mouse clicks provided in Program Manager or the User Profile Editor.

The Secure subkey provides a convenient place for applications to store configuration information that should not be changed except by the application itself. Information in this subkey is hidden, but it can be viewed or changed in the Registry Editor by overriding the security—but it is not a good idea to do so. Usually, these values are best changed via APIs issued from the software application itself.

Note

> If you have a previous version of Windows (Windows 3.*x* or Windows for Workgroups) installed on your computer, you are permitted to migrate REG.DAT, Program Manager group (.GRP) files, and .INI files to the NT Registry when you first log on to NT Server. This may be important on an NT Server computer if a piece of shareable data needs to be migrated from a Windows for Workgroups shared drive to be shared from the NT Server.

THE SYSTEM SUBTREE STARTUP DATA

All startup-related data that must be stored (rather than computed during startup) is saved in the SYSTEM subtree. A complete copy of the data is also stored in the SYSTEM.ALT hive. Figure 14.14 shows the SYSTEM subtree.

Figure 14.14.
The SYSTEM subtree.

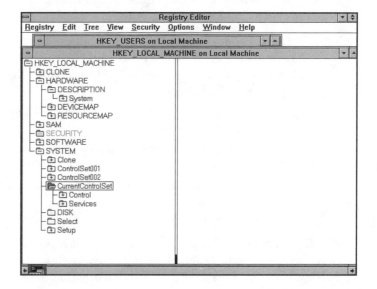

The data in the HKEY_LOCAL_MACHINE\SYSTEM subtree is organized into subtree control sets that contain a complete set of parameters for devices and services as described in this section.

The entries contained in the SYSTEM subtree are essential to starting the operating system. To ensure that the system will always start, a backup version is kept in the SYSTEM.ALT hive so that you can undo any configuration changes that did not have the intended effect.

All the entries required to control startup are gathered into subtrees called *control sets* in the Registry. Each control set has two parts: a Control subkey and a Services subkey. The Control subkey contains various data items used to control the system, including such things as the computer's network name and the subsystems to start.

The Services subtree contains a list of drivers, file systems, user-mode service programs, and virtual hardware subkeys. Its data controls the services (drivers, file systems, and so on) to be loaded and their load order. The data in the Services subtree also controls how the services call each other.

Multiple control sets are saved as subtrees of HKEY_LOCAL_MACHINE\SYSTEM under names such as ControlSet001, ControlSet002, and so on. Although as many as four control sets can exist, there are usually only two sets. This is similar to having multiple sets of CONFIG.SYS files under MS-DOS—a current one and a backup copy that is known to start the system correctly. However, in NT the work to create and maintain configuration backups is all done automatically by the system. The Select subkey contains the descriptions of how the control sets are used in four value entries:

◆ **Default**   This value specifies the number of the LastKnownGood control set (for example, 001 = ControlSet001) to be used at next system startup. An error during load or manual intervention by the user during boot can designate a different control set.

◆ **Current**   This value specifies the number of the control set currently used to start the system this time.

◆ **LastKnownGood**   This value specifies the number of the control set that was used last time the system started successfully.

◆ **Failed**   This value specifies the last control set used that failed to successfully start the system. You can examine this control set to learn why the replacement was required.

The CurrentControlSet subtree is not the root of an actual control set; rather, it is a symbolic link to the control set indicated by the value contained in the Current subkey. CurrentControlSet exists so that constant paths can be used to refer to keys in the currently used control set even though the name of that control set might change.

These multiple control sets are used to enable you to escape from various problems. Each time the system starts, the control set used to actually perform the startup is saved away (under Clone). If the startup is declared good, the old LastKnownGood control set is discarded and the Clone subtree is copied to replace it. Administrators can change how system startup is declared good, but usually it means no Severe or Critical errors (as reported in the OS Loader screen during boot) in starting services and at least one successful logon.

If system startup fails or if the user chooses LastKnownGood from the Configuration Recovery menu, the LastKnownGood control set is used to start the system instead of the Default control set. The Default set is reserved as Failed, and the LastKnownGood set is cloned to make a new LastKnownGood set. The LastKnownGood set becomes the new Default set. The effect of all of this is to undo all changes to configuration data stored in a control set since the last time a startup was declared good. (User-profile data is stored elsewhere and is therefore unaffected by this.)

Tip

> You can choose from among control sets on a computer by pressing the Spacebar immediately after selecting Windows NT at the Boot Loader prompt. A message asks if you want to choose to start the system using the current control set or the last known good configuration. To find out whether Default or LastKnownGood was used, look at the values in the Select subkey.

You can modify the information stored in these subkeys by choosing the Devices, Network, Server, and Services icons in Control Panel or by using Server Manager. If you need to modify the configuration in Registry Editor, make changes under the CurrentControlSet subkey.

THE CONTROL SUBTREE FOR ALL CONTROL SETS

The HKEY_LOCAL_MACHINE\SYSTEM\CurrentControlSet\Control subtree contains dozens of subkeys containing startup data for the system, including information about the subsystems to load, computer-dependent environment variables, the size and location of the paging files, and so on. Figure 14.15 shows the typical Control subkeys.

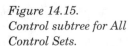

Figure 14.15.
Control subtree for All
Control Sets.

Following are descriptions of the contents of some typical subkeys for the Control subtree:

BootVerificationProgram   You can set this subkey's value to define a nonstandard mechanism to declare system startup as good.

ComputerName   This subtree contains the names of the default and active computers, stored in two subkeys: ComputerName and ActiveComputerName. The ComputerName value is normally set using the Network icon in Control Panel. If you log on using a different computer name, the ActiveComputerName will contain the current logon computer name. Normally, these two values will be identical.

GroupOrderList   This subkey specifies the order to load services for all groups that have services associated with them.

ServiceGroupOrder   This subkey specifies the order to load various groups of services. The loading order is specified within groups in the GroupOrderList subkey.

HiveList   This subkey contains the location of the hive files. This value should be maintained only by the system.

KeyboardLayout   This subkey contains the DLLs for the keyboard language used as the default layout, plus a subkey named DosKeybCodes that lists other available keyboard layouts. You should set the settings for keyboard layout using the International icon in Control Panel.

Lsa   The authentication package for the local security authority. This value should be maintained only by the system. Typing errors made here can prevent anyone from being able to log on to the computer.

NetworkProvider   This subtree contains two subkeys—Active and Order—that specify the network provider and the order in which to load providers. You should set the values for network providers by choosing the Network icon in Control Panel.

Nls   This subtree contains information on national language support in three subkeys: CodePage, Language, and OEMLocale. You should set your preferences about language and locale in NT Server using the International icon in Control Panel.

Print   This subkey contains information about the current printers and printing environment and also contains several subkeys:

Environments, which contains subkeys defining drivers and print processors for system hardware platforms such as Alpha, R4000, PowerPC, and x86.

Monitors, which can contain subkeys with data for specific network printing monitors.

Printers, which can contain subkeys describing printer parameters for each installed printer.

Providers, which can contain subkeys describing DLLs for network print services. You should use Print Manager to change printing parameters.

PriorityControl   This subkey contains the Win32 priority separation. This value should be set only by using the System icon in Control Panel.

ProductOptions   This subkey contains the product type, such as Winnt. These values should be maintained only by the system.

Session Manager   This subkey contains global variables used by Session Manager and contains several subkeys including the following:

DOS Devices, which defines the MS_DOS devices AUX, MAILSLOT, NUL, PIPE, PRN, and UNC.

Environment, which defines the ComSpec, Path, Os2LibPath, and WinDir variables. You can set user environment variables using the System icon in Control Panel. If you want to change or add to the computer's default path, or add default system environment variables, you must change the values in this subkey.

FileRenameOperations, which are used during startup to rename certain files so that they can be replaced. These values should be maintained only by the system.

KnownDLLs, which defines the directories and filenames for the Session Manager DLLs. These values should be maintained only by the system.

MemoryManagement, which defines paging options. You should define the paging file by using the System icon in Control Panel.

SubSystems, which defines information for the NT Server subsystems. These values should be maintained only by the system.

Setup   This subkey contains the hardware setup options. These values should be maintained only by the system. Users can make choices by running NT Setup.

TimeZoneInformation   This subkey contains the values for time zone information. You should set these by using the Date/Time icon in Control Panel.

VirtualDeviceDrivers   This subkey contains virtual device drivers and configuration values for them. These values should be maintained only by the system.

Windows   This subkey holds the paths for the NT directory and system directory. These values should be maintained only by the system.

WOW   This subkey contains the options for 16-bit Windows-based applications running under NT Server. These settings should be maintained only by the system.

THE SERVICES SUBTREE FOR ALL CONTROL SETS

The HKEY_LOCAL_MACHINE\SYSTEM\<ControlSet>\Services subtree lists dozens of subkeys. These subkeys contain driver information for all internal and external devices. (<ControlSet> refers to whichever control set is being viewed, as discussed previously.) The subkeys list all the kernel device drivers, file system drivers, and Win32 service drivers that can be loaded by the Boot Loader, the I/O Manager, and the Service Control Manager. This subkey also contains subkeys that are static descriptions of hardware to which drivers can be attached. Figure 14.16 shows some typical Services subkeys for an NT computer.

Entries appearing under the HKEY_LOCAL_MACHINE\HARDWARE \DEVICEMAP subkeys include values that refer to entries in the HKEY_LOCAL_MACHINE\SYSTEM\<ControlSet>\Services subkey in whatever control set you are viewing.

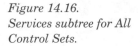

Figure 14.16.
Services subtree for All
Control Sets.

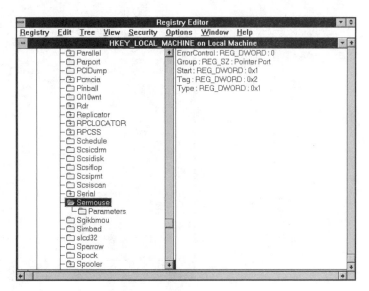

A related Services subkey named Sermouse defines values for the serial mouse driver. Rather than using Registry Editor to view this information, you can use NT Diagnostics and see it in an easy-to-read format. Run Windows NT Diagnostics and then choose the Drivers button and review details about a selected driver. You can choose the Devices icon in Control Panel to change startup and other information for a driver. For suggestions about how you can use this information for troubleshooting, see Chapter 28, "Troubleshooting Overview."

Each subkey includes several standard (but optional) entries as shown in the following example, where Alerter is the name of a service that appears in the HKEY_LOCAL_MACHINE\SYSTEM\<ControlSet>\Services subkey. You can see in Figure 14.17 that the value entries that control the behavior of a service include ErrorControl, Group, DependOnGroup, DependOnService, ImagePath, ObjectName, Start, and Type.

Some Services subkeys have one or more subkeys including Security, Linkage, or Parameters. These subkeys specify device configuration parameters for the device under which the subkey is defined.

The Linkage subkey specifies the binding options for the driver using the Bind and Export values. The OtherDependencies value appearing in the Linkage subkey for some services enables nodes to be loaded in an order related to other specific nodes with which they are closely associated. For example, the NBF transport depends on an NDIS driver. Therefore, to load the NBF protocol stack successfully, an NDIS network card driver must be loaded first. For details about loading order dependencies for network components, see the section titled *Dependency Handling for Network Components* later in this chapter.

Figure 14.17.
The Alerter Services
Control example.

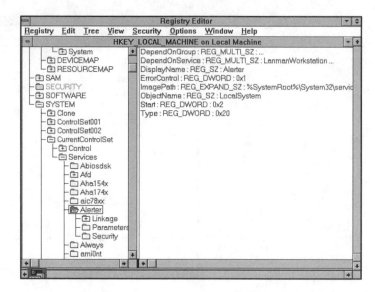

The Parameters subkey (optional for some Services subkeys such as an adapter entry) contains a set of values to be passed to the driver. These values vary for each device driver. Figure 14.17 shows the parameters for the serial mouse driver. The Security subkeys contain hidden information.

Figure 14.18.
Serial Mouse Param-
eters subkey.

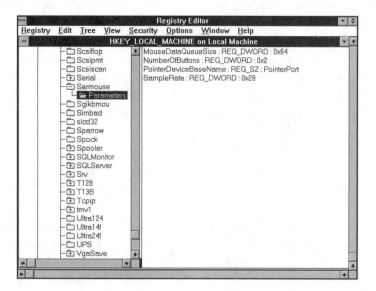

Because the entries in the Services subtree are Registry subkeys, you cannot make any assumptions about their order in an enumeration. Services can explicitly specify loading order in groups according to type. For example, the SCSI port driver can be loaded before any of the miniport drivers. The loading order is specified under the HKEY_LOCAL_MACHINE\SYSTEM\<ControlSet>\Control\ServiceGroupOrder subkey.

You can change the settings for the drivers that appear under the Services subkeys using the Devices, Network, or Services icon in Control Panel or, for network services, through the User Manager For Domains in NT Server. Table 14.1 lists the Services subkeys found in a control set.

TABLE 14.1. TYPICAL SERVICES SUBKEYS FOR AN NT SERVER COMPUTER.

Subkey	Description	Notes
ABIODISK	Primary disk	(1)
AHAxxx	Adaptec SCSI adapters	(1)
ALERTER	Alerter service for the workstation	(3)
ATDISK	Primary disk driver for non-SCSI hard disks	(1)
ATI	ATI video display	(1)
BEEP	Base sound driver	(1)
BROWSER	Browser used by Workstation and Server services	(3)
BUSLOGIC	BusLogic SCSI adapter	(1)
BUSMOUSE	Bus mouse pointer	(1)
CDAUDIO	Filter	(1)
CDFS	SCSI CD-ROM class file system driver	(1)
CDFS_REC	Recognizer for SCSI CD-ROM class file system	(1)
CIRRUS	Cirrus Logic video display	(1)
CLIPSRV	ClipBook (NetDDE service)	(3)
CPQARRAY	Compaq array driver	
DELL_DGX	Dell DGX video display	(1)
DISKPERF	Filter	(1)
DLC	DLC transport	(2)

continues

TABLE 14.1. CONTINUED

Subkey	Description	
DPTSCSI	DPT SCSI adapter	(1)
ET4000	Tseng ET4000 video display	(1)
EVENTLOG	Event log service	(3)
FASTFAT	FAT boot file system driver	(1)
FAT_REC	Recognizer for FAT boot file system	(1)
FD16_700	Future Domain MCS, TMC-7000ex, 800 SCSI cards	(1)
FLOPPY	Primary disk	(1)
FTDISK	Filter	(1)
HPFS_REC	Recognizer for HPFS boot file system	(1)
I8042PT	Keyboard driver	(1)
INPORT	Microsoft InPort Mouse pointer	(1)
JAZZGxxx	Video display	(1)
JZVXl484	Video display	(1)
KBDCLSS	Keyboard class driver	(1)
LANMANSERVER	Server service	(3)
LANMANWORKSTATION	Workstation service	(3)
MESSENGER	Messenger service for workstation	(3)
MOUCLASS	Mouse class driver	(1)
MUP	Network	(1)
NBF	NetBEUI transport protocol	(1, 2)
NCRxxx	NCR SCSI controllers and adapters	(1)
NETBIOS	NetBIOS transport interface	(1, 2)
NETDDE	Network DDE and Network DDE DSDM	(3)
NETDETECT	Network detection	(1)
NETLOGON	Network logon for workstation	(3)
NTFS	NTFS file system driver	(1)
NTFS_REC	Recognizer for NTFS file system	(1)
NULL	Base driver for null port	(1)
OLISCSI	Olivetti SCSI adapter	(1)
PARALLEL	Parallel port	(1)
PINBALL	HPFS file system driver	(1)

QVISION	Qvision video display driver	(1)
RAS	Remote Access Service	(3)
RDR	Network redirector	(1)
REPLICATOR	Directory replicator for workstation and server	(3)
RPCLOCATOR	RPC locator-name service provider	(3)
RPCSS	Remote Procedure Call (RPC) service	(3)
S3	S3 video display	(1)
SCHEDULE	Network schedule service	(3)
SCSIxxx	SCSI class devices, which do not require parameters in the Registry. The subkey can be SCSICDRM, SCSIDISK, SCSIFLIP, SCSIPRNT, and/or SCSISCAN.	
SERIAL	Serial port	(1)
SERMOUSE	Serial mouse	(1)
SGIKBMOU	Silicon Graphics keyboard and mouse driver	(1)
SGIREX	Silicon Graphics video display driver	(1)
SIMBAD	Filter	(1)
SPARROW	SCSI adapter	(1)
SPOCK	SCSI adapter	(3)
T128-T13B	Trantor SCSI adapters	(1)
TRIDENT	Trident video display	(1)
UBxxx	Ungermann-Bass NDIS drivers	(1, 3)
ULTRAxxx	UltraStore SCSI adapters	(1)
UPS	Uninterruptible power supply (UPS)	(3, 4)
V7VRAM	Video Seven VRAM video display	(1)
VGA	VGA video display	(1)
VIDEOPRT	Video display	(1)
WD33C93	Maynard SCSI adapter	(1)
WDVGA	Western Digital/Paradise video display	(1)
XGA	IBM XGA video display	(1)

14

MANAGING THE NETWORK REGISTRY

Note

The numbers in parentheses in the Notes (right-hand) column of the table mean the following:

1. Change settings for this driver using the Devices icon in Control Panel.

2. Change settings for this driver using the Network icon in Control Panel.

3. Change settings for this driver using the Services icon in Control Panel or using Server Manager in Windows NT Services.

4. Change settings for this driver using the UPS icon in Control Panel.

THE HKEY_LOCAL_MACHINE\SYSTEM \SETUP SUBKEY

The Setup subkey under HKEY_LOCAL_MACHINE\SYSTEM is used internally by NT Server for the Setup program. Do not change these value entries; these settings should be maintained only by the system.

THE HKEY_CLASSES_ROOT KEY

The HKEY_CLASSES_ROOT key contains data about file associations and OLE. As shown in Figure 14.19, this is the same data as in the Classes subkey under HKEY_LOCAL_MACHINE\SOFTWARE. This information is not important for NT Server.

Figure 14.19.
*The HKEY_CLASSES_*
ROOT key.

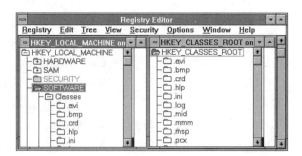

THE HKEY_USERS KEY

This key contains all actively loaded user profiles, including HKEY_CURRENT_USER (which always refers to a child of HKEY_USERS) and the default profile. An example is shown in Figure 14.20.

Figure 14.20.
The HKEY_CURRENT
_USER key.

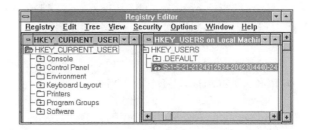

14

Note

Users who are accessing a server remotely do not have profiles under this key on the server; if they are on NT Workstation or Windows 95 computers, their profiles are loaded into the local Registry located on their own computers.

USER PROFILES FOR NT WORKSTATIONS

User-profile information is applicable only for NT Workstation or Windows 95-based personal profiles stored locally at the workstation. NT Server-based profiles are not kept in this part of the Registry; they are kept in the SAM. Each time a new user logs onto a computer, a new hive file is created for that user. Because each user profile is a separate hive, each profile is also a separate file.

Profile hives can be stored in other directories using Profile Manager on an NT Server. As the system administrator, you can copy a user profile as a file and view, repair, or copy entries using the Registry Editor from an NT Workstation client computer.

VALUE ENTRIES IN REGISTRY SUBKEYS

Registry data is maintained as value entries under the Registry subkeys. The Registry Editor displays data in two panes. The value entries in the right pane are associated with the selected subkey in the left pane.

A value entry has three parts: the name of the value, the data type of the value, and the value itself, which can be data of any length. A value entry cannot be larger than about 1MB. Values from 0 to 0x7fffffff are reserved for definition by the system, and applications are encouraged to use these types. Values from 0x80000000 to 0xffffffff are reserved for use by applications. The following are the data types currently defined and used by the system:

◆ REG_BINARY   Raw binary data. Most hardware-component information is stored as binary data, and can be displayed in Registry Editor in hexadecimal format or via the Windows NT Diagnostics program (WINMSD.EXE) in an easy-to-read format. The Registry value for a subkey might look like this:

```
Component Information : REG_BINARY : 00 00 00...
```

◆ REG_DWORD   A DWORD is a four-byte character. REG_DWORD data is represented by a four-byte DWORD. Many parameters for device drivers and services are of this type and can be displayed in the Registry Editor in binary, hex, or decimal format. For example, entries for service error controls are in this format:

```
ErrorControl :REG_DWORD : 0x1
```

◆ REG_EXPAND_SZ   An expandable data string, which is text that contains a variable to be replaced when called by an application. For example, for the following value, the string %SystemRoot% is replaced by the actual location of the directory containing the NT system files (normally shown as <winnt-root> in this book and other Microsoft documentation):

```
Prog: REG_EXPAND_SZ : %SystemRoot%\prog.exe
```

◆ REG_MULTI_SZ   A multiple string. Most values that contain lists or multiple values in readable text are of this type. Entries are separated by NULL characters. The following value entry specifies the binding rules for a network:

```
REG_MULTI_SZ : dlcDriver dlcDriver non non 50
```

◆ REG_SZ   A sequence of characters representing readable text. For example, a component's description is usually of this type:

```
DisplayName : REG_SZ : Messenger
```

REFERENTIAL INTEGRITY OF REGISTRY DATA

NT has some built-in mechanisms for protecting corruption in Registry values due to media breakdowns or other error conditions. The following discussion reviews some of the mechanics involved in keeping your Registry intact.

KEY AND HIVE RECOVERY

The Registry ensures the referential integrity of each key after each individual action. This means that any single change made to a value to set, delete, or save either works or doesn't work—even if the system goes down because of power failure, hardware failure, or software problems. For example, if an application sets values for two entries (x and y) and the system crashes while this change is being made, one of the following situations results:

You get a new value for entry x or entry y.

You get new values for both entries x and y.

You don't get a new value for either entry.

Because the Registry maintains referential integrity, you avoid the situation of getting a corrupted mix of old and new values for an entry. For example, you will not get a corrupted mix of old x and new x. In addition, the key containing entry x and entry y will have a size, time stamp, and other data that is consistent with what is actually there.

FLUSHING REGISTRY DATA

Data is only written to the Registry when a flush occurs. A *flush* writes data physically to the hard drive. This happens after changed data ages past a few seconds, or when an application forces a physical write request to the hard drive. The system performs the following flush process for all hives (except for the System hive):

1. All changed data is written to the hive's .LOG file along with a map of where it is in the hive, and then a flush is performed on the .LOG file. It is now certain that all changed data is written in the .LOG file.

2. The first sector of the hive file is marked to indicate that the file is in transition.

3. The changed data is written to the hive file.

4. The hive file is marked as completed.

Note

If the system crashes between steps 2 and 4, then the next time the hive is loaded at startup (unless it's a Profile hive that is loaded at logon), the system sees the mark left in step 2 and proceeds to recover the hive using the changes contained in .LOG file. So, the .LOG files are not used if the hive is not in transition. If the hive is in transition, it cannot be loaded without the .LOG file.

A different flush process is used for the System hive because it is an important element during system startup and is used too early during startup to be recovered as described in the previous flush process.

The SYSTEM.ALT file contains a copy of the data contained in the SYSTEM file. During the flush process, changes are marked, written, and then marked as done; the same flush process is then repeated for the SYSTEM.ALT file. If there is a power failure, hardware failure, or software problem during any point in the process, either the SYSTEM or SYSTEM.ALT file will contain the correct information. The system will first revert to the SYSTEM.ALT file if the SYSTEM file causes failure.

The SYSTEM.ALT file is not that different from any other .LOG file, except that at load time, rather than having to reapply the logged changes, the system just switches to SYSTEM.ALT. You do not need the SYSTEM.ALT file unless the System hive is in transition.

REGISTRY SIZE LIMITS

The amount of memory space used by Registry data is restricted by the Registry size limit, which is a quota for Registry space that prevents an application from filling the paged pool with Registry data. Registry size limits affect both the amount of paged pool the Registry can use and the amount of disk space.

Tip

> The Registry size limit can be manually adjusted by editing the value for the following subkey:
>
> ```
> HKEY_LOCAL_MACHINE\SYSTEM\CurrentControlSet\Control\RegistrySizeLimit
> ```
>
> The RegistrySizeLimit value must have a type of REG_DWORD and a data length of 4 bytes or it will be ignored. By default, the Registry size limit is 25 percent of the size of the paged pool, which is 32MB; so the default RegistrySizeLimit is 8MB (which is enough to support about 5,000 user accounts). Setting the PagedPoolSize value under the CurrentControlSet\Control\Session Manager\Memory Management subkey also affects the Registry size limit. The system ensures that the value for RegistrySizeLimit is at least 4MB and no greater than about 80 percent of the size of PagedPoolSize subkey.

The space controlled by RegistrySizeLimit includes the hive space, as well as some of the Registry's runtime structures. To ensure that the system will at least start and enable the administrator to edit the Registry if the RegistrySizeLimit is set incorrectly, quota checking is not turned on until after the first successful loading of a hive (that is, the loading of a user profile).

Warning

Despite the precautions taken by NT Server, you can reach the quota limit or you might run out of memory or disk space. You might get an NT Executive character-mode STOP message. It indicates that quota was returned to a process, but that process was not using the amount of quota being returned. You will end up with a locked-up server.

Try to restart and set the Recovery options in the System Control Panel or the /CRASHDEBUG system switch, or use the Emergency Repair Diskette to restore the system. Considerable damage can happen if this problem is not caught early. To catch this problem in time, you should use Performance Monitor logs to evaluate changes in the system's behavior on a regular basis.

NETWORK SETTINGS

When a network component is installed, various information is added to the Registry. Each network component is represented in two distinct areas of the Registry:

◆ Software registration keys for the component's driver and adapter card under HKEY_LOCAL_MACHINE\SOFTWARE

◆ Service registration keys for the component's driver and adapter under HKEY_LOCAL_MACHINE\SYSTEM

The following sections describe the general organization and content of the software and service registration information for network components and then conclude with information about bindings for network components and dependency handling.

NETWORK COMPONENT TYPES

The following are the network component types referenced in the software and service registration information for network components:

Adapter	A piece of hardware
Driver	A software component associated directly with a piece of hardware
Transport	A software component used by services
Service	A software component providing capability directly to user applications
Basic	A token used to represent a fundamental class name (that is, a class with no parent)

Each type of network component requires a subkey for both software and services. Therefore, the installation of a single network card usually results in the creation of four distinct subkeys in the Registry:

◆ The software-registration subkey for the driver is found in HKEY_LOCAL_MACHINE\SOFTWARE\Company\ProductName\Version. For example, the path for the driver for an Etherlink adapter is KEY_LOCAL_MACHINE\Software\Microsoft\Elinkii\CurrentVersion.

◆ The software-registration subkey for the network adapter card is found in HKEY_LOCAL_MACHINE\SOFTWARE\Microsoft\Windows NT\CurrentVersion\NetworkCards\netcard#.

◆ The service-registration subkey for the driver is found in HKEY_LOCAL_MACHINE\SYSTEM\CurrentControlSet\Services.

◆ The service-registration subkey for the network adapter card is found in HKEY_LOCAL_MACHINE\SYSTEM\CurrentControlSet\Services.

For example, you cannot configure an NT Server computer through the user interface to access two different IPX networks on two different network adapters, each with a different frame type. If you run Control Panel, choose Network, select each adapter, and assign a network address, the same network address is used for both network adapters. In order to provide the network address for each network card, you must modify the Windows NT Registry manually as follows:

1. Start Registry Editor (REGEDT32.EXE).

2. From the HKEY_LOCAL_MACHINE key, go to the following subkey:

   `SYSTEM\CurrentControlSet\Services\NwlnkIpx\NetConfig\<network card>`

   where `<network card>` is the network card you are configuring for a different IPX network.

3. Remove the NetworkNumber entry.

4. From the Edit menu, choose Add Value. Add the following:

   Value Name: NetworkNumber

   Data Type: REG_DWORD

   Data: <Network ID>

   Radix: Hex

5. If necessary, repeat steps 2 through 4 for each network adapter.

6. Quit the Registry.

7. Shut down and restart NT Server.

SOFTWARE-REGISTRATION INFORMATION FOR NETWORK COMPONENTS

Because installation of a network adapter card results in separate Registry entries for the driver and for the adapter, the Software subtree contains several subkeys to describe the network component.

For each network component, a special subtree named NetRules is created in the appropriate driver or adapter registration subkeys. The NetRules subkey identifies the network component as part of the network ensemble. For example, the standard software-registration entry for the Etherlink II driver appears under this path:

```
HKEY_LOCAL_MACHINE\SOFTWARE\Microsoft\Elinkii\CurrentVersion
```

The standard entries for the driver might include the following values:

```
Description = 3Com Etherlink II Adapter Driver
InstallDate = 0x2a4e01c5
...
RefCount = 0x1
ServiceName = Elnkii
SoftwareType = driver
Title = 3Com Etherlink II Adapter Driver
```

And under the Etherlink II driver's related NetRules subkey, these value entries might appear:

```
bindable = elnkiiDriver elnkiiAdapter non exclusive
bindform = "ElnkIISys" yes no container
class = REG_MULTI_SZ "elnkiiDriver basic"
Infname = OEMNADE2.INF
InfOption = ELNKII
type = elnkiiSys ndisDriver elnkiiDriver
use = driver
```

The Etherlink adapter is described in a NetworkCards subkey under this path:

```
HKEY_LOCAL_MACHINE\SOFTWARE\Microsoft\Windows
NT\CurrentVersion\NetworkCards\netcard#
```

The standard entries for the adapter might include these subkeys and values:

> Description = 3Com Etherlink II Adapter
> InstallDate = 0x2a4e01c5
> Manufacturer = Microsoft
> ProductName = Elnkii
> ServiceName = Elnkii02
> Title = [01] 3Com Etherlink II Adapter

Note

Drivers developed by Microsoft for other vendors' products are listed under the Microsoft subkey. If the driver was written by another developer, there will be a subtree with a different name, parallel to the Microsoft subtree discussed in the previous example.

These value entries might appear under the adapter's related NetRules subkey:

```
bindform = "Elnkii02" yes yes container
class = "elnkiiAdapter basic"
Infname = OEMNADE2.INF
InfOption = ELNKII
type = elnkii elnkiiAdapter
```

The information in the main entries for network adapters and drivers is maintained by the system and should not be changed.

SERVICE-REGISTRATION INFORMATION FOR NETWORK COMPONENTS

The HKEY_LOCAL_MACHINE\SYSTEM\CurrentControlSet\Services subkey is the service-registration area that contains the information used to load a network component into memory. These subkeys contain certain required information, such as the location of the executable file, the service type, and its start criteria.

Each network component's software-registration information (as described in the previous section) contains an entry named ServiceName, whose value is the name of the service corresponding to the network component. This name acts as a symbolic link to the CurrentControlSet\Services parameters.

Some network components are actually sets of services, each of which has its own subkey in the Services subtree. There is usually a "main" service, with the other services listed as its dependencies. For example, as shown in the previous section, the Etherlink driver's ServiceName is Elnkii, and this name would appear as a Services subtree that defines the location of the driver file, dependencies, and other startup information. The Elnkii subkey in turn contains other subkeys that define the parameters and linkage rules for the driver. The Etherlink adapter's ServiceName is Elnkii02, which also appears as a Services subkey that defines linkage rules for bindings plus physical parameters of the network card, such as its I/O address and interrupt request (IRQ) number, as specified in the Network dialog box in Control Panel.

BINDING FOR NETWORK COMPONENTS

For the networking software in a computer to operate properly, several different pieces of software must be loaded and their relationships with other components must be established. These relationships are often called *bindings*. To determine the complete set of optimal bindings among an ensemble of configured network components, the system checks the following information in the Registry:

- The set of network components to be configured
- The types of network components in this set
- The constraining parameters for the network components and their bindings
- The possible bindings that could occur
- The proper way to inform each network component about its bindings

During system startup, the CurrentControlSet\Services subtree is checked for binding information for each service. If any are found, a Linkage subkey is created and the values are stored. For example, the following string might appear in a value entry under the CurrentControlSet\Services\LanmanWorkstation\Linkage subkey:

```
Bind = \Device\Nbf_Elnkii01\Device\Nbf_Elnkii02
```

This entry describes the binding information used by the NT Redirector when two separate network cards are present. Each network card's symbolic name is suffixed with a network card index number. This name is joined to the name of the transport through which the network card is accessed. The names are generated by the system according to the constraints defined by the network component's rules.

Bindings have a usability requirement that means the binding must terminate at either an adapter (that is, a physical device) or at a logical endpoint, which is simply a software component that manages all further interconnection information internally. This requirement avoids loading software components that can never be of actual use. For example, a user might have a running network and then choose to remove the adapter card. Without the usability restriction, the bindings would still connect components and prepare them for loading even though the network was entirely unusable.

The following example uses NBF.SYS and SRV.SYS in an ensemble with two Etherlink II network cards and an IBM Token Ring card. First, in the CurrentControlSet\Services\Nbf\Linkage subkey are the following values:

```
Bind=    "\Device\ElnkII1"
         "\Device\ElnkII2"
         "\Device\IbmTok1"
Export=  "\Device\Nbf\ElnkII1"
```

14

MANAGING THE NETWORK REGISTRY

```
                   "\Device\Nbf\ElnkII2"
                   "\Device\Nbf\IbmTok1"
        Route=     "ElnkIISys ElnkII1"
                   "ElnkIISys ElnkII2"
                   "IbmtokSys IbmTok1"
```

Under the CurrentControlSet\Services\Srv\Linkage subkey, the following values might appear:

```
Bind  =  "\DeviCE\NBF\ELNKII1"
         "\DEVICE\NBF\ELNKII2"
         "\DEVICE\NBF\IBMTOK1"
EXPORT = "\DEVICE\SRV\NBF\ELNKII1"
         "\DEVICE\SRV\NBF\ELNKII2"
         "\DEVICE\SRV\NBF\IBMTOK1"
ROUTE =  "NBF ELNKIISYS ELNKII1"
         "NBF ELNKIISYS ELNKII2"
         "NBF IbmtokSys IbmTok1"
```

The names in the Bind and EXPORT entries are based upon the object names defined in the component's NetRules subkey; these entry values can therefore be different from the actual names of the services. The names in the ROUTE entry are the names of the Services subkeys comprising the full downward route through the bindings protocol.

When the system finishes computing the bindings for network components and the results are stored in the Registry, some network components might need to be informed of changes that have occurred. For example, TCP/IP needs to ask the user for an IP address for any network adapter that has been newly configured. If the NetRules subkey for a network component has a value entry named Review set to a nonzero value, the .INF file for the network component will be checked every time the bindings are changed.

DEPENDENCY HANDLING FOR NETWORK COMPONENTS

Services can be dependent upon other services or drivers, which can be dependent upon others, and so on. The system can establish three types of dependencies:

- ◆ Specific dependencies, which are represented by the names of the services upon which a service is dependent
- ◆ Group dependencies
- ◆ Static dependencies, which are required in all circumstances

A *specific dependency* is simply the name of a necessary service. By default, the system generates explicit names for all dependent services discovered during bindings generation. Specific dependencies are marked in the Registry as a value of the Use entry under the component's NetRules subkey. For example, assume the Workstation service is dependent on NBF. NBF is connected to two adapter cards and so is dependent upon their drivers. The system marks NBF as dependent upon the two network card drivers and marks the Workstation service as dependent upon the network card drivers and NBF.

Many times it happens that a service should be loaded if any member of a set of dependencies successfully loads. In the previous example, the Workstation service would fail to load if either of the network card drivers failed to initialize. Group dependencies are used to support this approach. Any service (driver, transport, or whatever) can identify itself as being a member of a service group. All NT Server network card drivers, for example, are treated as members of the group NDIS. Group dependencies are marked in the Registry as a value of the Use entry under the component's NetRules subkey. *Groups* are symbolic names listed in the CurrentControlSet\Control\GroupOrderList subkey.

A *static dependency* is a required service in all circumstances and is unrelated to how the system otherwise determines bindings. When the system computes dependencies, it discards any previously listed dependencies. To guarantee that a service is always configured to be dependent upon another service, the value entry OtherDependencies can be created under the component's Linkage subkey. OtherDependencies is a REG_MULTI_SZ value, so it can contain the names of as many services as needed.

MAINTAINING REGISTRY SECURITY

Windows NT enforces access control on Registry files, so it is difficult for users to accidentally or intentionally damage or delete hives on a running system. While the system is running, hive files are kept open by the system for exclusive access on all file systems. If the NT SystemRoot is not on an NTFS volume, the Registry files are vulnerable to tampering—specifically, users can remove hives for user profiles that aren't currently loaded. With NTFS, such tampering can be prevented. You should plan how to protect the Registry for each NT computer at your site. Do not allow users to log on as members of the Administrators group unless a specific individual has administrative duties. You might also choose not to put REGEDT32.EXE on workstations, because you can easily administer any workstation from a remote computer. You also can place access controls in File Manager on REGEDT32.EXE, limiting the rights of users to start this program.

SUMMARY

NT Server distinguishes itself by the openness of its architecture. The Registry is a vivid example of the degree of evaluation and control NT Server gives to the administrator. With openness comes vulnerability, however; so you have to be extremely cautious in viewing or making changes to the Registry.

- Installing Applications Locally or Centrally

- The Microsoft Office Suite

- The Novell PerfectOffice Suite

- Services for Macintosh

- Lotus Notes

CHAPTER 15

Administering Workgroup Applications

Share   This is the designation given to a directory that is shared as a network resource.

AppleTalk   This is the name of Apple Computer's network architecture and protocol stack.

AppleShare   This is the name of Apple Computer's file-sharing software (NOS).

LocalTalk   This is the name of Apple Computer's local area network that is built into all Macintosh computers. You can replace LocalTalk with EtherTalk or TokenTalk LAN.

PC-based networks use the *distributed processing model*, in which applications programs can be installed locally or at the file server. Although you can install applications at the server's disk drive, they are executed locally in the workstation. This is in contrast to a mainframe or minicomputer environment in which applications are both stored and executed centrally on the main CPU.

DISTRIBUTED COMPUTING ENVIRONMENTS

In a distributed environment, you access the file server's disk as though it were installed on your own computer. For example, drives A–C might be located in your local workstation, and drives F–Z might be on the file server. Where a file is located has no bearing on whether you can execute it, but it is more difficult to share files with good performance unless they are centralized on a server dedicated to this task.

Directories are configured as network *shares*, which makes them available to network users. The network users can access a share by assigning a DOS drive letter to the share. The *Network Operating System* (NOS) is responsible for the mechanics of making the drive available and accessing the drive from a workstation.

This process is accomplished by the combination of functions provided by the NOS, which includes a high-performance operating system and file system at the server, the LAN cabling and hardware, network adapter cards, and the redirector at the workstation.

INSTALLING APPLICATIONS LOCALLY OR CENTRALLY

Traditionally, Windows and Windows application software are installed locally, with the data residing on the server. This, however, is not the preferred configuration for a larger organization; most prefer to install all programs and data on one (or a few) centralized server(s).

APPLICATION SUITES

Almost every office has the same basic office-automation software needs, including

> word processing
>
> electronic spreadsheets
>
> databases
>
> electronic mail
>
> presentation graphics
>
> "workgroup" applications (that is, applications shared by a group of users, such as calendar and scheduling software)

These basic packages are often bundled together as a *suite*. Within the past two years it has become a common practice to use one suite of applications for basic user access on a network. Trying to support several competing products concurrently, such as WordPerfect, MS Word, and AMI Pro, has proven to be counterproductive for support personnel.

The system administrator sometimes has a say in selecting a suite of basic productivity software; other times he or she does not. In either case, the administrator is the one who faces the integration challenges inherent with the suite that is selected.

This chapter discusses the most common application suites used on networks today. Some of these products are robust with networking features and awareness; others involve many challenges when attempting to integrate them with dozens of users.

Other factors that you face as a system administrator are also addressed in this chapter. If you are integrating only Windows operating systems, including Windows for Workgroups (WFW), Windows 95, Windows NT Server, and Windows NT Workstation, your life is substantially easier than if you need to add Macintosh and OS/2 workstations and applications to your network. In the latter situation, after you handle the connectivity, file-system, and procedural differences you also have to deal with differences in applications on the different operating-system platforms.

NT Server uses the mountable file-system mechanism and can support FAT, NTFS, and HPFS. The NT file system (NTFS) is the best option for supporting all types of clients. It provides multistream file access that supports storing Macintosh resource forks and Finder information in the same file and also supports 31-character filenames, including an on-the-fly filename translation facility for all client types. These features increase performance and aid volume management. Using the NTFS

15

ADMINISTERING WORKGROUP APPLICATIONS

file system works well to support operating systems with long filenames and extended attributes. A FAT file system is limited in its capability to support Macintosh, UNIX, and OS/2 files, not to mention the performance and security considerations.

INSTALLING APPLICATIONS LOCALLY OR CENTRALLY

When it was introduced, Windows 3.x provided an option to install Windows centrally or locally. Since that time, it has become apparent that virtually all software developers expect to find the workstation operating system installed locally, including Windows. When Windows 3.1 or WFW is installed centrally, application-software installation is a nightmare. Each application expects to find Windows installed locally, and sometimes has to update or add Windows DLLs and other installation files. Administering a centrally installed shared copy of Windows on a network is a nightmare.

Although you can install WFW, Windows 95, NT Workstation, and NT Server from a server, the option to share a centrally installed copy is not available. This makes sense, because many desktop functions and utilities are not available if LAN connectivity fails somewhere. In addition, disk drives have become so cheap (in comparison with just a couple of years ago) that the cost of centralizing Windows is not a factor.

Centralized installation of software applications is a must in a larger organization. If you have dozens—perhaps hundreds—of users, installing a new version of a word processor can be a monumental task. In many larger organizations it is mandated that applications be installed centrally; therefore, you don't have the option of local installation. In these cases installing and maintaining centralized software applications is often defined as part of the system administrator's job, while installing and maintaining applications locally may be the user's responsibility or is done by the technical support staff.

One of the most compelling reasons to have a network is to centralize software and data storage. Some of the more attractive features of centralizing an installation include the capability to run the application from any workstation without having to do an entire installation. Another feature is the reduction of disk-space usage: an application that uses 50MB of disk space is multiplied by 1,000 users to require 50GB of disk storage when installed locally. When you have a large number of users, the storage requirements increase geometrically.

A well-designed network should enable you to administer applications centrally, without having to log on as a specific user and edit his or her settings manually. In many software packages, centralized storage is required because the software must be shared; cost is an incidental factor.

A new type of application called *workgroup* applications is emerging. These applications do not require that the data be centralized; they use automatic data-synchronization and -replication techniques. Lotus Notes is one of many such applications.

Some software suites have been engineered for centralized network installation, for some it was an afterthought, and others are just not designed for it at all. Some developers have simply fought the advent of local area networking, and refuse to live in this day and age. Installing such applications centrally can make a system administrator's job a nightmare.

The best idea is to select a single suite and stay with a one-vendor solution. (This applies to software applications, not necessarily to related resources.) You'll find that Microsoft Office works well on Microsoft and Novell networks, as does PerfectOffice. Consistency between applications is the most important consideration because the costs of training, administering, and supporting software applications far outweighs the license costs.

NETWORK-AWARE APPLICATIONS

Software developers are finally getting the idea of what *network-aware* means. In the past, applications were very clumsy to implement and use on a network, made little use of network security controls, and in some cases even conflicted with network configuration requirements. Some of the problems faced daily include developers not using network APIs which causes many of the following and other problems:

◆ Locked files

◆ Inappropriately configured record sharing/locking (that is, cannot read when record is open)

◆ Update conflicts

◆ Deadly embrace (computer lockup)

◆ Applications that cannot coexist with other applications

◆ Semaphore locks that become corrupted (which consequently limits the number of users)

◆ Copyright protection that complicates installation and use

- ♦ Excessively labor-intensive configuration options that cannot be automated
- ♦ Conflicts with various versions of redirectors, shells, and NOS versions
- ♦ Manual workarounds to correct network-installation problems
- ♦ Inadequate network configuration instructions
- ♦ Lack of choice to share/individualize software-configuration options
- ♦ Lack of technical support for NOS integration issues

These are just a few of the endless number of things software developers can overlook that should work properly in a network environment. In many cases, obscure bugs emerge that do not occur in a single-user environment. For example, programming language runtime interpreters and record managers behave differently on a local PC than they do on a NetWare or Microsoft network, and can work differently under a different version of a protocol. These are all problems that are difficult to troubleshoot, isolate, and resolve. In most cases, the administrator cannot resolve problems that are programmed at a very deep level.

Even Microsoft has been remiss in providing solutions to network-awareness problems. For example, when pulling up Word, a user might see a list of the last few documents opened by other users on the network instead of those he or she had opened—and there is no documentation that addresses this issue. The Microsoft Setup program for network workstations has only one small reference in the installation guide and a short NETWORKS.TXT readme file on one of the disks. If the administrator runs into a problem, even the support personnel are at a loss to address many of these issues.

Because many Windows applications take up such an obscene amount of disk storage space, sharing a single copy of a software application should not require tens of megabytes of disk space for each user. Another perplexing problem is when each application has a different data structure and is inflexible to the configuration needs of the administrator. For example, sometimes data files must reside in a subdirectory of an application or cannot reside on a different volume from the application.

Another problem administrators encounter is with running applications on the server as a local user. In many cases, applications dominate resources or do not release resources when they are finished with them. Some are very processor- or disk I/O–intensive and affect the server's performance.

THE MICROSOFT OFFICE SUITE

MS Office comes in three varieties: one for Windows/WFW, one for Windows 95, and one for Windows NT. Each is slightly different, but MS Office for Windows NT has more in common with all three than any other version. The following sections outline the steps to be taken to install and administer MS Office for Windows NT on an NT Server–based network.

CONSIDERATIONS BEFORE INSTALLING MS OFFICE

You should buy the correct version of MS Office for your workstations. MS Office for NT will only run on NT Servers and NT workstations. MS Office for Windows 95 will run on Windows 95, NT 3.51 Servers, and NT 3.51 workstations. MS Office for Windows will run on Windows 3.*x*, WFW, Windows 95, NT Server, and NT Workstation, but will not take advantage of the 32-bit operating system architecture in an NT or Windows 95 workstation. The Windows 95 and Windows NT versions, unlike the Windows version, are 32-bit applications that do take advantage of the features of a 32-bit environment.

Note

The following instructions apply to all MS Office versions, but focus on MS Office for NT. Notes are included throughout the procedure to point out the differences between versions during installation. You'll notice there are very few.

INSTALLATION METHODS

◆ **Individual workstation installations**   You can install each copy of MS Office individually on each workstation's local hard drive from the original distribution CD-ROM or floppy disks. This method of installation is not so bad when you are using a CD-ROM that is shared on the network, but is *very* labor intensive for floppy-disk installs. If you choose to use the disks, each installation will require more than 15 disk swaps.

Tip

When using this approach, the only way that makes sense is to use the CD-ROM installation. Installing from floppy disks is *very* labor intensive, because you must re-execute Setup manually and copy from each disk for each workstation.

◆ **Administrative install**   All files can be installed on the network server for installation to each workstation from one location. This eases installation labor time, but does not reduce the amount of disk space or time required to install all users.

Note

After you have performed an administrative installation, you can either install users as individual workstations or have them share a copy of MS Office, as discussed in the next section.

After your administrative installation, you can use a silent install (Setup /q) or use a Setup configuration file to install each workstation *silently*. This enables the administrator to set up each user individually from the Administrative install copy without stopping to ask configuration questions. Instead, all of the answers to configuration questions are included in the Setup script configuration file. Silent installation is discussed later in this chapter.

CLIENT INSTALLATION

After you have selected your method of installation, you must choose how you want to install the clients. You have the option of installing clients either with all files on the local hard drive or with a single shared directory plus unique user-configuration files for each user.

◆ **Sharing a single copy with unique user-configuration files**   You can install a single copy of MS Office on the file server that is shared by all users. A small amount of disk space is required for each user's individual configuration files, but the majority of the files are installed once and shared among all users. This requires more space on the server, but aggregately can cut down disk-storage requirements significantly. As the administrator, you can logon as a user with this method and upgrade or change his/her configuration with ease.

Depending on the version of MS Office you install, the shared directory will be about 35–105MB (depending on MS Office version), and each user should require less than 10MB of disk space.

◆ **Individual workstation installations**   This takes a significant amount of disk space. For each user, this disk space is replicated with no economies of scale. User configurations are not accessible to the administrator unless each computer is set up to share its disk storage. This approach is the most labor intensive because you have to replicate each installation in its entirety.

Depending on which version of MS Office and which components you install, 35–105MB of disk space is required for a minimum client installation.

Your decision on which way you want to install MS Office must be made at the outset and must be consistent throughout your administration. Each type of installation follows different rules and has various considerations. Using two (or all three) strategies can cost many hours of unproductive time and cause significant loss of productivity for users as well as administrators.

If you can't decide about how to install your MS Office suite, choose the administrative install option and then share a single copy with unique user-configuration files. This is the overwhelming choice of experienced system administrators in larger organizations, even for smaller networks.

BEFORE STARTING SETUP

Before you set up MS Office on a network file server, you must make certain that you have a working network and file sharing; also, the environment must be free to install without interruption. Check the following conditions:

◆ The network must be installed and working properly.

◆ You must be able to log on to the server and/or domain as user Administrator.

◆ All older copies of MS Office must be deleted.

◆ Make sure all users are logged off and are not using any MS Office application or directories.

◆ Make sure no virus software is running during the installation.

Note

In these instructions, "MS Office" is used to represent all MS Office software modules. Substitute the proper name of the module depending on which MS Office module you are installing. For example, if you are installing Word 6, replace MS Office with WINWORD.

ADMINISTRATIVE INSTALLATION

You perform this installation on the server from which you are going to install the workstations. Begin this installation by expanding all files on the installation disk(s) onto the server disk. Then create a share for the directory in which the raw files are stored and run workstation installations from that directory. This procedure is called an *administrative* installation and requires between 85 and 105MB of disk space (in the case of MS Office for Windows 95).

To execute an administrative installation, follow these steps:

1. Make sure the network is installed and working properly. Log on to the server and/or domain as user Administrator (or a member of the Administrator/Domain Admin group).

2. Map a network drive letter to the volume in which MS Office is to be installed.

3. Type SETUP /A.

4. When Setup has finished copying all the files to the MS Office directory, share the MS Office directory with a minimum of read, write, and delete/erase permissions.

You can use this share to install workstations for either of the client installation procedures outlined in the following section.

CLIENT INSTALLATION

Regardless of whether you install MS Office from a CD-ROM, floppy disks, or a shared administrator's copy on your server, the Setup program proceeds the same way. A minimum of 35MB of user disk space is required for each workstation.

NORMAL CLIENT INSTALLATION FROM THE SHARED ADMINISTRATOR'S COPY

This installation goes quite smoothly because no disk swaps are required. Follow these steps for this procedure:

1. Change to the drive letter that represents your shared administrative copy of MS Office.

2. Execute Setup.

3. Make the local hard drive the destination for your installation files.

4. Follow the prompts and choose one of the setup options: Typical, Laptop/Compact (Minimum), Workstation (use a single shared copy), or Complete/Custom. The following list shows the disk-space requirements for MS Office for the Windows 95 standard version (without Access; Professional Office contains Access which takes up about 25.5MB), which uses more space than the other two product offerings (including Access).

Type of installation	Space required
Compact	27.6MB (for each workstation)
Typical	56.1MB (for each workstation)

| Complete | 91.0MB (for each workstation) |
| Workstation | 107.0MB for the server plus 10MB for each workstation |

INSTALLING MS OFFICE SILENTLY

Setup can be run with the /q switch, which runs Setup *silently*; this means the switch performs an express installation of MS Office on the workstation without having to answer any prompts or choose any options. Setup installs MS Office in the default MS Office program directory, C:\MSOFFICE, and chooses all default values automatically.

INSTALLING MS OFFICE WITH A SETUP SCRIPT CONFIGURATION FILE

With this option, you can install each client with any options you choose without answering any questions during the install. You create or edit the SETUP.STF file to include all of the options you want. You specify this setup script as an option with the Setup command; it uses the script file to fill in all configuration options.

With a script, you can specify which components to install on the workstation and which to share over the network, as well as the directory locations for those components. You can also use this method to perform batch installations and can create different scripts for different groups of users, if needed.

UNINSTALLING AND REINSTALLING MS OFFICE

You can use Setup to remove MS Office from the server and from workstations, just as you can use it to install the suite.

After you have installed MS Office, it immediately displays the current configuration of MS Office on the local volume when you run Setup. You can choose the Remove All button to remove MS Office completely, or you can select individual components to add or remove. You can even completely uninstall if necessary. Sometimes it is just simpler to start all over, uninstalling, then reinstalling from scratch.

CUSTOMIZING YOUR SETUP SCRIPT FILE

You can define a setup script that can do the following:

◆ Perform a complete installation without input from the user.

◆ Control which type of installation (Typical, Complete/Custom, Laptop/Compact (Minimum), or Workstation) you want Setup to perform.

◆ Specify the directory in which to install MS Office.

◆ Ensure that all installations in a workgroup are the same.

Setup uses information in the file SETUP.STF to determine which files to install and where they should be copied. To control which type of installation Setup performs and to specify the directory where MS Office is installed, edit SETUP.STF to create a custom script that workstation users can run to install MS Office.

The Setup file, SETUP.STF, is a text file that you can edit using a text editor. The fields are delimited by tabs. It designates which options to install, where to install those options, and how to respond to current configurations and user input queries.

The Setup file has two basic sections:

◆ **Header Section**   The Header section is contained in the first 20 lines and is in a two-column format. This section contains information used by the Setup program such as the name and version of the application to be installed, text strings used in the Setup dialog box, and required System environmental conditions—you should not edit this part of the file.

◆ **Object Section**   The Object section of this file contains the sequence and options of the installation process as well as specific configuration information on a line-by-line, object-by-object basis. Each line consists of 13 columns and provides specific instructions for the Setup installation. The last three columns are reserved for use by the Setup program.

The Setup file is very detailed and precise. You must take care when editing the file to ensure its integrity.

Note

The following installation example uses MS Office for NT. Your version of MS Office might differ slightly.

To edit the information in SETUP.STF, follow these steps:

1. Copy the file SETUP.STF to a new name. Open the *copy* of SETUP.STF (not the original) with a text editor. It is easiest to work with this file in a spreadsheet application such as Microsoft Excel because it provides a second column with remark statements.

2. To specify the type of installation you want the script to perform, scroll through the table until you see the following list of installation options in the third column under the heading that reads

```
*** Main Setup Options ***
Typical
Complete/Custom
Laptop/Compact (Minimum)
Workstation
```

3. Type yes in the column labeled Install During Batch Mode to the left of the type of installation you want the script to perform. Type no next to the other options.

4. If you want the script to perform a Complete/Custom installation, scroll down until you see the following list of components in the third column under the heading

```
*** Custom Options ***
Microsoft MS Office
Graph, Equation, and WordArt
Proofing Tools
Converters and Filters
Online Help and Examples
Wizards, Templates, and Letters
Tools
Clip Art
```

You can select which components you want to install. Under several of the options, you can select a button to the right to select specific components within the group you want to install.

DISTRIBUTING AND USING A SCRIPT

After you create a Setup script, you can copy it to the file server or share from which you want users to install MS Office. You can also distribute it with Microsoft Mail or another application that can send items across a network so the users can use it to install their own applications.

Use one of the following methods to distribute the script:

◆ Copy SETUP.EXE and give the copy the same filename you gave the script but use the .EXE filename extension. Direct your users to run the copy of Setup (for example, NEWSETUP.EXE, not SETUP.EXE).

◆ To create one script for all users, rename the SETUP.STF file that comes with MS Office to something else, such as SETUP.OLD. Name the copy of the script that you edited SETUP.STF and save it in the same network directory as SETUP.EXE. Direct your users to run SETUP.EXE from the file server or the shared volume.

◆ To create different installation scripts for different groups of users, distribute the script with Microsoft Mail or another application as a Program Manager icon. The command line specifies the script and switches, as shown in Table 15.1.

15

ADMINISTERING WORKGROUP APPLICATIONS

TABLE 15.1. SETUP SWITCHES.

Switch	Description
/t tablename	Substitute the name of the new script for `tablename`.
/n username	Substitute a value for `username` to prevent Setup from prompting the user for a name. The name must be enclosed in quotation marks. To automatically register the workstation copy of MS Office with the workstation's existing username, type the quotation marks with no name (`"  "`). Setup uses the name specified in the Registry. This information is stored in HKEY_CURRENT_USER\ Software\Microsoft\MS Setup (Acme)\User Info.
/q	Causes Setup to run without any user interaction.
/q1	Causes Setup to run without any user interaction and skips the final Setup Complete dialog box.

For example, suppose you have installed MS Office in the MSOFFICE directory of a file server (where x designates the drive letter) and distribute a silent script that uses the MYSCRIPT.STF table file to a user named Bob Smith. The command line to run the script is as follows:

```
x:\MSOffice\setup.exe /t myscript.stf /n "Bob Smith" /q1
```

DISTRIBUTING A SCRIPT WITH MICROSOFT MAIL

If you use Microsoft Mail to distribute a script, create a new message and then choose Insert Object from the Edit menu. In the Object Type box, select Package and then click the OK button. From the Edit menu in Object Packager, choose Command Line. Type the full path to SETUP.EXE in the MSOFFICE directory of the file server or the shared directory. (If your network supports UNC pathnames, use that syntax. If not, your users must make the network connection themselves by using the same drive letter you specified before running Setup.) Type SETUP including switches and arguments as needed.

Installing MS Office on a network server does not modify the WINDOWS, WINDOWS\SYSTEM or WINDOWS\SYSTEM32 directories on the server's hard disk. From a workstation, Setup copies all files that are installed in these directories during a Complete setup to the MSOFFICE\SYSTEM32 directory on the server.

Setup copies the ADMIN.INF file to the MSOFFICE directory on the network server and renames the file MSOFFICE.INF. Also note that Setup does not create a

SETUP directory within the program directory, as it does for a Complete installation. All of the setup files are placed in the MSOFFICE program directory. In addition, Setup copies SETUP.INI to the network MSOFFICE program directory.

Setup stores a copy of all shared applications, converters, and graphics filters in the MSOFFICE\SHARED directory on the network server; this is the source for setting up local versions of these files on workstations. In addition, Setup creates the \MSAPPS directory structure for shared components (or updates the shared components if they already exist).

Note that you can update the shared components stored in the MSAPPS directory by subsequent application installations on the network server; you cannot do this for files in the MSOFFICE\SHARED directory.

FILES INSTALLED BY WORKSTATION SETUP ON WORKSTATIONS

The Workstation Setup option enables you to install a shared copy of MS Office and give each user private initialization files. This saves disk space on each workstation. Users' private initialization files can be located on the user local drive or on the server, perhaps in the user's HOME directory.

Note

When using the Workstation Setup option, when Setup asks you for the directory in which to install MS Office, specify the directory for the unique user files, not the master copy of MS Office.

MS Office for NT installs three types of files: system files, application files, and private initialization files. Setup must have write access to the following directories on the target workstation to set them up as discussed in these instructions:

MSOFFICE: No files

MSOFFICE\SETUP: SETUP.STF

MSOFFICE\STARTUP: No files

MSOFFICE\TEMPLATE: No files

WINDOWS, WINDOWS\SYSTEM, and WINDOWS\SYSTEM32: Like Complete Setup, Workstation Setup copies system files to the workstation's WINDOWS, WINDOWS\SYSTEM, and WINDOWS\SYSTEM32 directories.

WINDOWS\MSAPPS: If the network server does not specify that Workstation Setup should install local or shared versions of the tools in the server's MSAPPS subdirectories, Setup prompts the user to specify Local or Shared. If the user selects Local, Setup installs the MSAPPS files on the user's hard disk as in a workstation installation. If the user selects Shared, the files are not copied to the user's hard disk.

There are a few conditions that prevent the MSAPPS files from being shared from the server, even if the network server specifies Shared or the user specifies Shared during the workstation setup.

MSAPPS files may not be accessed when entries in the workstation's Registry file that reference the MSAPPS executable files in a location other than the shared drive and directory.

If MSAPPS executable files are found on a local drive, they are updated to the version being installed by Setup and are used by MS Office. However, MS Office does not use the shared copy of the MSAPPS files located on a shared drive. Note that these existing MSAPPS files can be on the user's local hard disk or on a network server's shared drive.

MSAPPS FILES NOT FOUND WHEN LOCATED IN A SUBDIRECTORY

MSAPPS files may not be accessed when MSAPPS executable files exist as subdirectories under the user's WINDOWS directory. Regardless of whether current Registry entries referencing this location exist, MSAPPS files will not be found when they exist in a subdirectory under the WINDOWS directory.

In either of these cases, a workaround is to use File Manager to rename the existing MSAPPS directory before executing the workstation setup. Regardless of whether the Registry entries remain, MS Office is installed to share the MSAPPS from the server. If other OLE server applications are installed in the renamed subdirectory, rename it back to MSAPPS after Setup is complete.

MSAPPS FILES NOT FOUND WHEN AN ADMINISTRATIVE INSTALL TARGETS A LOCAL HARD DRIVE

MSAPPS files may not be accessed when an administrative setup was run targeting a local hard drive instead of a server's shared drive. During a local administrative setup on an NT computer, you must enter the correct entries for the location of shared files manually. After you have made these manual entries and the administrative setup is complete, workstation setups from other workstations will work correctly. However, performing a workstation setup on the server computer produces errors because the server computer cannot confirm the specified network paths. In this situation you should respond by choosing Continue in response to each error message until Setup resumes the normal sequence.

An example of the appropriate manual entries is as follows: If an administrative setup is being performed to C:\APPS\MS\MSOFFICE, and C:\APPS is shared via the Windows File Manager as C:\APPS, edit the entries in the Network Server Confirmation dialog box as follows (assume the computer's network server name is BNET):

Network Server: \\BNET\APPS
Network Path: \MS\MSAPPS\

If you are unsure about the correct entry for Network Server, you can determine it from any workstation connected to the server. Start File Manager on the other workstation and establish a connection to the shared directory on the server computer. In the title bar of the File Manager window displaying that drive, the information following the hyphen is the correct entry for Network Server. The entry for Network Path is any additional directories in the path on the server that terminate with a final backslash, as shown.

MSAPPS FILES NOT FOUND WHEN ANY FACTOR PREVENTS THE USER FROM ACCESSING THE UPDATED MSAPPS FILES

There are many miscellaneous reasons that a user may not be able to access the MSAPPS files. Anything that prevents the user from correctly accessing the MSAPPS directory tree installed during the Administrative Setup can cause this problem. The most common reason for this is that the user does not have the correct network permissions to find or read the files.

Another factor that can prevent users from accessing the MSAPPS files is improper information in the application's Tools, Options screens. Troubleshooting these miscellaneous problems is often time consuming and goes on endlessly. If this is a problem, you might consider uninstalling, then reinstalling MS Office.

GENERAL TROUBLESHOOTING

You can resolve most Setup problems, regardless of their specific cause, using these general troubleshooting procedures.

- ◆ If you are using a video driver supplied with your computer, switch to the NT video driver for your video display type (such as VGA).
- ◆ Check the TEMP setting in your user environment variables. Make sure it points to a valid location on a drive with at least 6–8MB available disk

space. If the TEMP setting is invalid or missing, modify the environment variable using the System icon in Control Panel.

◆ Be sure the PATH statement in your AUTOEXEC.BAT file or the SET PATH statement in your CONFIG.SYS file does not contain more than 128 characters. The SHRRES32.DLL file used by MS Office does not support a PATH statement longer than 128 characters.

Note

NT computers can have a PATH statement longer than 128 characters. If you are running MS-DOS version 6.0 or 6.2, you can use a SET statement in your CONFIG.SYS file to set a PATH statement longer than 128 characters.

◆ Run a utility to diagnose and repair any hard disk problems on the drive where you want to install MS Office.

◆ If you have an older computer or interface card that has problems running effectively in the Turbo mode, turn it off, either by resetting the switch and restarting the computer or resetting the CMOS option.

THE NOVELL PERFECTOFFICE SUITE

Novell pulled together an office suite overnight when it acquired WordPerfect Corporation and Quattro Pro from Borland in 1995. Within a matter of a few weeks, the Novell people coordinated several WordPerfect products with Quattro Pro and a few other products to be a fully integrated suite.

PerfectOffice Professional has several modules that make it a complete groupware application suite. Their stated objective was to make the suite easy to install and administer on a network.

PerfectOffice Professional contains the following:

◆ WordPerfect for Windows v6.1

◆ Quattro Pro

◆ Presentations (presentation graphics, slide shows; similar to Microsoft's PowerPoint)

◆ InfoCentral (personal information manager: appointment book, phone numbers, to-do lists, and so on)

◆ Envoy (a tool to save graphics documents in a format anyone can view)

- Paradox (Borland's relational database and programming tool)
- AppWare (Novell's network-application development tools)
- GroupWise (e-mail integrated with calendaring and scheduling)

The following are reasons for selecting PerfectOffice over other suites.

- Network administration is easier due to the many tools provided to make application management more effective.
- Applications are better integrated. PerfectOffice integrates OLE 2.0 between all applications and integrates shared tools. Spell check and grammar checker work in all PerfectOffice applications.
- QuickTask macro tool makes it easier to automate regular tasks
- Envoy Electronic Publishing Software enables you to send a document in graphical format without requiring the receiver to use the same application to view it.
- InfoCentral, a personal-information manager, provides more personal productivity tools than other suites.
- 180 days of free technical support.

NETWORK ADMINISTRATION

PerfectOffice has an Administrator program group with utilities that help manage various applications globally. Several features provide administrators more control with less effort than do other suites.

The administrator program group provides utilities to manage the PerfectOffice applications and setup. After you as the administrator have changed the configuration options, future workstation installations yield the new default configuration options. This applies to hundreds of configuration options throughout several applications.

The toolbar, called the *Desktop Application Director* (DAD), can be configured by the administrator or users, and as the administrator you can decide what you will enable your users to change how applications and menus work.

BETTER APPLICATION INTEGRATION

PerfectOffice integrates OLE 2.0 between five applications: WordPerfect, QuattroPro, Paradox, Presentations, and InfoCentral. Spell checking, grammar checking, and intelligent find-and-replace work in all major modules, even in the e-mail and appointment book applications.

QUICKTASK SHORTCUTS

QuickTask enables you to create a list of frequent tasks and run them from a click on a single button on the QuickTask menu or from the DAD toolbar. This feature is similar to macros, but makes the process simpler to set up, runs outside of your applications, and provides a handy menu screen for all your daily QuickTask chores.

ENVOY ELECTRONIC PUBLISHING SOFTWARE

Envoy enables you to capture a document to a file, complete with graphics and fonts just the way it looks when it is printed. This enables you to send documents to anyone. You can send another user a graphics document created in an application that the receiver does not have (for example, a newsletter made in PageMaker can be viewed in its finished form even though the receiver does not have PageMaker). Using GroupWare (part of the Professional office suite), you can attach the document to an e-mail message and send it anywhere in the world.

INFOCENTRAL PERSONAL INFORMATION MANAGER

InfoCentral is a handy personal desktop set of productivity tools. It integrates with GroupWare, so much of what you accomplish in InfoCentral can be easily e-mailed and shared with workgroup users. It includes the following features:

- ◆ **InfoPad**   You can organize personal information with several category fields that enable you to view or look for information from several different aspects.
- ◆ **Calendar**   You can use this feature for appointments, important dates, notes, and so on.
- ◆ **Tasks**   This is a list of things to do, with information on priorities and hierarchical structure. The tasks are automatically integrated into the calendar.
- ◆ **Calls to Make**   You can list phone calls to be made, create entries that dial automatically, and use/save phone numbers in the mailing-list database.
- ◆ **Mailing List**   This is a personal database with fields for names, addresses, phone numbers, many other fields, and user-defined fields for use in InfoCentral applications. You can easily import and export data and extract mailing lists.

SUPPORT

Extensive online documentation is provided for all components, but free unlimited technical support is provided for 180 days by Novell's Applications Group. In addition, Novell has a free forum for support issues on NetWire, its support bulletin-board service on CompuServe. The company also has an FTP server on the Internet with many of the same services and access to downloads.

NETWORK INSTALLATION

Network installation requires up to 98MB (depending on the options you choose) for the shared program directories, plus 3MB for each client user. You can install all PerfectOffice 3.0 applications from your Professional PerfectOffice 3.0 for Windows CD-ROM. Here are the steps:

1. Log on as Administrator.
2. Insert the Professional PerfectOffice CD-ROM into your CD-ROM drive.
3. Choose Run from Windows Program Manager's File menu.
4. In the dialog box that appears, type

   `(drive letter):\POWIN30\SETUP (e.g. D:\POWIN30\SETUP)`
5. Click OK to begin installing PerfectOffice 3.0 for Windows.
6. Follow the directions and choices offered by the installation program.

Additional directories contain supplementary materials for WordPerfect 6.1: \PRINTER\README.TXT contains information about additional WordPerfect printer drivers, and \UTILITY\README.UTL contains information about WordPerfect 6.1 utilities.

The following procedure creates the Administrator's PerfectOffice program group. To install workstation clients and set up their applications, follow these steps:

1. Log on as the user you want to install.
2. Choose Run from Windows Program Manager's File menu.
3. In the dialog box that appears, type

   `(drive letter):\<perfofcdirectory>\SHARED\SETUP`

   (for example, `D:\OFFICE\SHARED\SETUP`).
4. Click OK to begin installing PerfectOffice 3.0 for Windows.
5. Follow the directions and choices offered by the installation program.

Follow these steps to install PerfectOffice online documentation from your distribution CD-ROM:

1. Insert the Professional PerfectOffice CD-ROM into your CD-ROM drive.
2. Select Run from the Windows Program Manager's File menu.
3. In the dialog box that appears, type

   `(drive letter):\DOCS\SETUP (e.g. D:\DOCS\SETUP)`

15

ADMINISTERING WORKGROUP APPLICATIONS

4. Click OK to start the file copy and installation.

5. Follow the directions and choices offered by the installation program.

This procedure creates a program group with online manuals for each application and for many other components.

SERVICES FOR MACINTOSH

Although many people think of Macintoshes existing in a corporate environment, system administrators are often surprised to find that they have to manage them when moving into a new job. Macintoshes are used extensively in universities, the printing and graphics industry, and various organizations where graphics and desktop publishing are required.

NT Server Services for Macintosh enables Macintoshes and PCs to share files and printers easily and inexpensively. NT includes a complete AppleTalk router, and up to 255 Macintosh users can connect to each NT Server in the same way as they do to an AppleShare volume. PC users can connect to the server as well, which enables the transfer of files between systems. A Macintosh user can print to a PostScript printer and to many non-PostScript printers. In addition, any PC user can print to a LaserWriter connected to a LocalTalk LAN.

TRANSPARENT FILE SHARING

To a Macintosh, an NT Server file server looks just like an AppleShare Filing Protocol (AFP) server. To a PC, the NT Server looks like any PC network server. The NT Server manages filenames, icons, and access permissions for both PC and Macintosh clients. Macs and PCs can use the same data files if the application provides this capability.

NT Server supports launching Macintosh applications from the NT Server. Services for Macintosh supports an unlimited number of simultaneous AFP connections to an NT server, and Macintosh sessions are integrated with NT sessions. The per-session memory overhead is approximately 15KB. When files are deleted, there are no orphaned Macintosh resource forks left to be cleaned up.

When using Services for Macintosh, it is recommended that you use the *NT file system* (NTFS) format, which provides multistream file access support, and stores resource forks and Finder information in the same file listings. NTFS also supports 31-character filenames, including an on-the-fly filename-translation facility for all client types.

In addition, you can require Macintosh users to use NT encryption when they log on to a server. The AFP server also supports both cleartext and encrypted passwords at logon time. You have the option of configuring the server to not accept cleartext passwords.

The File and Print Server

Services for Macintosh enables you to use any computer running NT Server, with its built-in networking, to a nondedicated, high-performance, AppleShare-emulation file and print server. You can create Macintosh-accessible volumes from File Manager: Services for Macintosh automatically creates a Public Files volume at installation time. NT file and directory permissions are automatically translated into corresponding Macintosh permissions.

Printer Sharing

Services for Macintosh not only gives Macintosh users access to printers on the NT Server domain, but also acts as a print spooler. This means that Macintosh users can get back to work before their documents have finished printing and without using valuable hard-disk space on their local computer for spooling. In addition, you can control the print queue for networked LaserWriter printers just as you can for any other printer attached to an NT Server domain.

A PC user can use these same print queues to print to any LaserWriter connected to the Macintosh network.

PostScript Printing

Services for Macintosh has a built in PostScript-compatible printing engine. With this engine, a Macintosh user can print to any printer connected to the NT Server domain as if it were a LaserWriter.

Integrated Administration

Administering and configuring the Services for Macintosh is integrated into NT Server; thus you only have to manage only one set of users and groups. You can create Macintosh-accessible volumes directly from File Manager and configure Services for Macintosh in the Control Panel. The system automatically translates NTFS file and directory permissions into corresponding Macintosh permissions. NT Server's challenge-handshake authentication mechanism uses the DES encryption standard. It is available to Macintosh users who have installed the Microsoft User Authentication Module (UAM) by dragging and dropping the UAM from an NT Server to the local system folder.

APPLE NETWORKING OVERVIEW

Macintosh networking includes the following network components:

LocalTalk
AppleShare
AppleTalk

LOCALTALK

LocalTalk is the Apple local area network that is built into every Macintosh computer. LocalTalk itself is built into a chip on the main computer system board; the part you install includes cables, connector components, and cable extenders. LocalTalk is usually used with a specialized cable using a bus or tree topology— usually one that supports a maximum of 32 devices at a bandwidth of 230Kbps using the CSMA/CA access protocol.

Because of LocalTalk's limitations, clients often turn to vendors other than Apple for AppleTalk cabling. Farallon's PhoneNet, for example, can handle 255 devices using common, flat phone wire.

APPLESHARE

This is the Apple fileserver software that provides file sharing using Apple Filing Protocol (AFP). The client-side AppleShare software is included with every copy of Finder and System Software version 6.0 or later. There is also an AppleShare print server, which is a server-based print spooler.

APPLETALK

Apple Computer's network architecture is called *AppleTalk*. It is actually a collection of protocols that map directly to the OSI model and are implemented and included in the Macintosh hardware (through a LocalTalk port) and operating-system software. The AppleTalk protocols support LocalTalk, EtherTalk (Ethernet), and TokenTalk (Token ring).

LocalTalk	32 Nodes	230.4 Kbps
EtherTalk	254 nodes	10 Mbps
TokenTalk	260 nodes	16/4 Mbps

LaserWriter printers can be directly connected to a Mac or connected over LocalTalk. The Apple LaserWriter has a built-in LocalTalk port and is designed to work with one or more Macs over LocalTalk with very little configuration. However, support for printers directly attached to an Ethernet or Token ring cabling system is not supported.

You can install a LocalTalk network adapter card on your server to support Macintoshes using their built-in LocalTalk networking. This option is not recommended, however, because LAN performance is substantially better with Ethernet or Token ring: LocalTalk is limited to 230Kbps bandwidth, while Ethernet is 10 Mbps and Token ring is 4 or 16 Mbps.

Not only is bandwidth severely limited, but integrating a LocalTalk network adapter card in an NT Server can be challenging. It is not necessary to add more complexity to your network than necessary, and you already have an Ethernet or Token ring card in your server, so why not use it for Macintoshes also?

PHASE I VERSUS PHASE II APPLETALK

There are two versions, or *phases*, of AppleTalk:

AppleTalk Phase I, as you might guess, was the first implementation of the product. It has the following characteristics regardless of whether it is used with LocalTalk, EtherTalk, or TokenTalk. However, Farralon PhoneNet has some extentions.

◆ A single LocalTalk LAN is limited to 32 nodes (Ethernet and Farralon PhoneNet limit is 254 addresses)

◆ Each LAN has its own network number and zone

◆ Each node on a network must belong to the same zone

◆ AppleTalk routable protocols support up to 16 hops

Apple created Phase II as a way of interconnecting to more popular protocols across networks incorporating *SubNetwork Access Protocol* (SNAP). The addressing under Phase II is now limited only by the type of LAN, not by LocalTalk addressing. Phase II is backward compatible to Phase I, but not vice versa.

Phase II LocalTalk has these characteristics:

◆ limited to a single network zone and a single network number

◆ supports 250 node addresses

Phase II Farralon PhoneNet, EtherTalk, and TokenTalk have these characteristics:

◆ Farralon PhoneNet limit of 16 million node addresses.

◆ Network number range

◆ 216 hops

◆ Up to 256 zones per user

◆ Zones can cross network numbers

◆ Implements spanning tree algorithm (802.1d) for bridges

Note

When installing Macintoshes on an Ethernet or Token ring network, you must make certain that the network card drivers in your server support AppleTalk protocols.

You must also select the appropriate frame types. All later-model Macintoshes use Phase II AppleTalk, which incorporates the Ethernet SNAP and Token ring SNAP frame types.

LOCALTALK LINK ACCESS PROTOCOL (LLAP)

Macintoshes on an AppleTalk network do not have fixed, assigned physical addresses. Instead, the *LocalTalk Link Access Protocol* (LLAP) implements a technique called *Dynamic Node ID assignment*. With this technique, node addresses are picked randomly when a node enters the network. LLAP broadcasts its choice; if no other node is using the address, the node address is accepted. The first Macintosh server picks a number in the same manner, but all other Macintosh servers are assigned a number by the primary server.

APPLETALK ADDRESS RESOLUTION PROTOCOL (AARP)

The *AppleTalk Address Resolution Protocol* (AARP) translates between the physical node addressing on LocalTalk, EtherTalk, and TokenTalk LANs and the logical network address and zones. Each node saves an Address Mapping Table in RAM to process various protocols and deliver them to the appropriate LAN segments.

APPLETALK ROUTING

Macintosh's *Datagram Delivery Protocol* (DDP) is processed by the Internetwork Routers to deliver data without having to create a virtual connection. Internetwork Routers examine the subnetwork address in the SNAP header, correlates it to an AppleTalk zone in its routing table, and forwards the DDP packet to the appropriate subnetwork (LAN segment).

HIGHER-LAYER PROTOCOLS

AppleTalk Transport Protocol (ATP), AppleTalk Echo Protocol (AEP), Name Binding Protocol (NBP), and AppleTalk Data Stream Protocol (ADSP) work together to set up and destroy virtual connections and to guarantee delivery of every DDP packet. *Apple Filing Protocol* (AFP) handles file system access; the *Printer Access Protocol* (PAP) processes print requests.

The AFP file structures resemble MS-DOS and NT directories, subdirectories, and files. However, the vocabulary used is slightly different:

Apple	NT
Volume	Share name/partition
Folder	Directory/subdirectory
File	File

Macintosh filenames can have up to 31 characters.

CHOOSER

The Chooser, which is available from the Macintosh Desk Accessory menu, provides a standard interface to help users select ports, printers, and network zones.

INSTALLING SERVICES FOR MACINTOSH ON AN NT SERVER SYSTEM

Services for Macintosh is on your distribution CD-ROM; you can install it by choosing the Networks icon in Control Panel. Click the Add Software button and select Services for Macintosh. The installation is fairly simple; follow the instructions offered by the install application.

INSTALLING NT SERVICES ON MACINTOSH WORKSTATIONS

Services for Macintosh also includes a Microsoft *authentication* component, which is an extension to AppleShare. NT authentication provides a more secure login session with an NT Server by sending an encrypted password rather than a cleartext password. Microsoft authentication also enables users to specify a domain when they log on, either to access accounts in multiple domains (by entering \domainname\username in the Name box) or to change their password.

You can install Microsoft authentication completely on all Macintosh workstations over the network by following these steps. Before you can successfully install authentication, you must be sure to have a properly installed EtherTalk LAN, and have AppleShare/AppleTalk software installed in your system folder. Refer to your Macintosh System 6 or System 7 manual for guidance.

1. From the Apple menu, select Chooser.
2. Select the AppleShare icon and the AppleTalk zone of the NT Server.
3. Select the NT Server and then choose either Registered User or Guest.
4. Select the Microsoft UAM Volume and then close the Chooser.

15

ADMINISTERING WORKGROUP APPLICATIONS

5. From the Macintosh desktop, double-click the Microsoft UAM Volume.

6. Select the AppleShare folder and drag it to the System Folder on the local hard drive.

After you have completed these steps, authentication is enabled and is required when a Macintosh user connects to the NT Server or domain.

Note

If the Macintosh is running System 7.1 or later and the cleartext and guest options are disabled at the server level, the user has only one choice: Microsoft authentication. Earlier systems show both choices: Microsoft authentication and cleartext passwords.

Note

The steps described in this section are a simplified version of the detailed installation instructions in the Services For Macintosh manual.

CREATING AFP VOLUMES

Creating a Macintosh-accessible volume is very similar to sharing a directory:

1. In File Manager, select the directory to use as a Macintosh volume.

2. From the toolbar buttons for the Services for Macintosh, or from the MacFile menu (both are added when Services for Macintosh is installed), select Create Volume.

The main differences between Create Volume dialog box and the Share As dialog box, which is used to share a directory, are the following items:

◆ **Volume Name**   This is the same as Share Name. However, the maximum number of volumes is 255 (this is an AppleTalk limitation), although the number that can be seen by Macintosh workstations is determined by the length of the volume names. Volume names can have a maximum of 27 characters and must all fit in a buffer in order to be displayed. The size of the buffer is determined by an underlying AppleTalk Protocol.

◆ **Password and Confirm Password**   Requires a user connecting from a Macintosh workstation to supply a password.

◆ **Volume Security**   This enables you to set the entire volume as read only and/or make the volume inaccessible to guests.

CONFIGURING VOLUMES

With NT Server, it is possible to share the same directory multiple times with different share names. It is also possible to share a subdirectory of a share with a totally different share name. For example, a user could share c:\apps as \\BNET\apps, \\BNET\test, and so on. Under NT Server, the user could also share c:\apps\123 as \\BNET\123.

But Services for Macintosh creates a Macintosh-accessible volume using different rules: It is not possible to configure one directory as two, or more, different volumes.

Therefore, after d:\temp has been made a Macintosh-accessible volume called "temp," it is not possible to create another Macintosh-accessible volume called "temp2" out of the d:\temp directory.

It is not possible to create a volume out of a subdirectory in a directory branch where there is already a Macintosh-accessible volume.

```
c:\temp
\docs
\files
\games
```

Based on this directory structure, if \temp\games is a Macintosh-accessible volume called "games," it will not be possible to create a volume out of \temp, \temp\docs, or \temp\files.

USING FILES

Within a directory that has been both shared and made a Macintosh-accessible volume, the following occurs:

◆ Non-Macintosh systems accessing the share see standard directories and files, which is how everything is actually stored.

◆ Macintosh workstations see what appear to be standard Macintosh files and folders, along with their respective icons.

When accessing the volume, Macintosh users can create files and folders with Macintosh filenames, which can be up to 31 characters and contain spaces and other characters. There are no limitations placed on the filenames because the volume is on an NTFS partition. Because Macintosh-accessible volumes are on NTFS drives, users accessing the shared drive on non-Macintosh systems that do not recognize long filenames see the NTFS-generated eight character with a three character extension (8.3) filename.

FILE EXTENSION–TYPE ASSOCIATIONS

With extension-type associations, both Macintosh and non-Macintosh versions of applications can easily work on the same data file should the data file format be consistent between the Mac and the non-Mac applications. When a file on the server has an extension associated with a Macintosh file type and file creator, the Macintosh Finder displays the appropriate icon for the file when a Macintosh user looks at the files on the server. In addition, if a Macintosh user chooses the file, the correct application starts up and opens the file.

HOW FILES ARE STORED

A file on a PC contains only data, but a Macintosh file consists of two forks:

◆ **Data fork**   This contains the actual file data itself.

◆ **Resource fork**   This contains operating-system information about the file such as menu, icon definitions, fonts, and so on.

NTFS files can have multiple data streams. This is why an NTFS partition is recommended for using Services for Macintosh.

When a Macintosh file is saved on the server, the two forks are saved as a single NTFS file. Each fork, however, is stored in a separate NTFS data stream. Users of non-Macintosh systems can access the file but cannot tell that it actually has two data streams; it appears as a normal data file.

Note

It is possible to create volumes on a CD-ROM drive using the CDFS (CD file system), but these volumes are read-only.

HOW FILENAMES ARE TRANSLATED

With Services for Macintosh, there are two kinds of filename translations:

◆ What Macintosh filenames look like to non-Macintosh users

◆ How longer NTFS filenames—those over 31 characters—are shortened for Macintosh users

Warning

When a Macintosh file is created on an NT Server, the server checks to ensure that it does not contain any characters considered illegal by NTFS. If any illegal characters are found, NT Server removes the illegal characters before passing the file to NTFS.

PRINTING TO AN APPLETALK PRINTER

When printing to an AppleTalk printer using Services for Macintosh, you can capture the printer. This way the NT Server administrator has full control over the captured printer.

It is recommended that you always capture the printer. However, if a source other than the print server will be sending jobs to the printer—such as Apple LaserShare, which provides print spooling for Macintosh workstations—the printer should not be captured. If a printer has not been captured, while one source is printing to the printer it will appear busy to any other system trying to print to the same printer.

Note

When a printer is created through Print Manager for an AppleTalk printer, the printer is automatically captured. To release the printer, go to Printer Properties and click the Settings button. You can then release the capture without deleting the printer.

NT PRINT SERVER FOR MACINTOSH

The Print Server for Macintosh is integrated into the NT Server Print Manager. Print Server for Macintosh can be started and stopped using the Services icon in Control Panel.

The print server provides Macintosh workstations with the capability to print to printing devices connected to the NT Server, including non-PostScript printing devices. The print server also enables non-Macintosh systems to print to AppleTalk PostScript printers that have been captured by an NT Server.

If a Macintosh workstation is printing to a non-PostScript print device, the NT Server Print Manager translates the print job into a format that the printing device can understand.

USING NT SERVER PRINTERS

To enable a Macintosh workstation to connect to an NT Server printer, permission must be given to the MacUser account. This account is created automatically when Services for Macintosh is installed on the system and is used by all Macintoshes when printing to a captured AppleTalk or NT Server printer. After the MacUser account has been given the proper permissions to enable printing, Macintosh users can connect to the printer as they would to any other printer.

15

ADMINISTERING WORKGROUP APPLICATIONS

USING APPLETALK PRINTERS

You should consider the following with regard to Macintosh print jobs.

- **Non-Macintosh systems**   For non-Macintosh systems to use an AppleTalk printer, the printing device must be PostScript compatible and use the LaserWriter driver. You must capture the printing device manually.

- **Macintosh workstations**   Macintosh systems should perform as they normally would, unless the printing device has been captured. If the printing device has been captured, Macintosh print jobs must be sent to the NT Server, which then sends the print job to the printing device.

NT PRINT SERVER FOR MACINTOSH INTERNALS

The print processor supplied with Services for Macintosh is SFMPSPRT.DLL. In Print Manager's Printer Details dialog box, this print processor appears as PSPRINT. Currently, SFMPSPRT.DLL only recognizes the PSCRIPT1 data type.

This is the component that translates a Macintosh PostScript print job into a print job that can be printed on any NT printer. You accomplish this translation by following these steps:

1. SFMPSPRT.DLL takes a Macintosh PostScript print job and converts it into a Windows bitmap.

2. The bitmap is passed to GDI, which uses the appropriate printer driver to convert the bitmap into the proper printer language.

The result of this conversion is that a Macintosh workstation can print to *any* printer supported by NT, using nothing more than the Macintosh LaserWriter driver.

PRINT MONITOR

The print monitor supplied with Services for Macintosh is SFMMON.DLL. This print monitor is responsible for sending print jobs to AppleTalk printers, and basically make AppleTalk printers work like another print device.

Because this print monitor is integrated into the NT Server Print Manager, users can browse for AppleTalk printers. This makes it easier to locate printers.

TRANSLATING PERMISSIONS

Services for Macintosh translates permissions so that those set by non-Macintosh users are translated into the equivalent Macintosh permission and vice versa. Permissions are translated based on the following table:

NT Server Permissions	Macintosh Permissions
Read	See Files and Folders
Write, Delete	Make Changes

> *Note*
>
> Permissions set on a Macintosh behave differently than NT permissions. From a Macintosh, a right assigned to "everyone" overrides any more restrictive rights set on the owner or a group. Under NT, rights assigned to "everyone" do not override a more restrictive right placed on a group or user. When a Macintosh is connected to an NT Server, the higher level of security in use takes precedence.

SETTING PERMISSIONS

When setting permissions, take the following factors into consideration.

◆ **From a Macintosh**   A folder's owner can set Macintosh permissions.

◆ **From an NT Server**   The folder's owner or a system administrator can set NT-type permissions. A system administrator can set Macintosh-type permissions by choosing Permissions from the MacFile menu in File Manager.

LOGONS

There are three possible ways a Macintosh user can log on to an NT Server running Services for Macintosh:

◆ As a guest.

◆ As a user with a cleartext password. This option allows logons without requiring a password.

◆ As a user with an encrypted password. Cleartext password protection is part of the AppleShare software on Macintoshes and does not provide any kind of password encryption. Passwords can be no more than eight characters. This option translates the cleartext password into an NT password using an encrypted password that can be up to 256 characters long.

You can set some security options through Server Manager for all Macintosh-accessible volumes on a server by following these steps:

1. Select the server running Services for Macintosh.

2. Select Properties from the MacFile menu and click on Attributes. The options that can be set include:

15

ADMINISTERING WORKGROUP APPLICATIONS

♦ **Server Name for AppleTalk Workstations**   This is the server name that Macintosh workstations see.

♦ **Login Message**   This is a message that Macintosh users see when they log on.

♦ **Allow Guests to Logon**   This option enables users who do not have a user account and password to log on.

♦ **Allow Workstations to save password**   This enables Macintosh users to save their password on their workstation so they are not always prompted for the password. This does, however, make the NT Server less secure.

♦ **Require NT Authentication**   Macintosh users must use the NT authentication to log on to the server.

♦ **Sessions**   This is the number of connections allowed.

♦ **Volume passwords**   Services for Macintosh also enables you to apply passwords to Macintosh-accessible volumes. When a password is placed on a Macintosh-accessible share, the Macintosh user has to supply the password to access the volume.

Note

The password only applies to Macintosh users accessing the volume. Non-Macintosh users do not have to supply a password.

CONFIGURING SERVICES FOR MACINTOSH

The following services must be configured when installing Services for Macintosh.

♦ **Network**   The list in this screen shows the network card drivers on the system. The adapter driver selected is the adapter to which the AppleTalk Protocol is bound.

♦ **Zone**   This is the zone in which the Macintosh-accessible volumes and NT Server printers appear through the Macintosh Chooser.

♦ **Enable Routing**   If this box is checked, the AppleTalk Protocol becomes a router. This means that if the AppleTalk Protocol is bound to more than one network adapter, the NT Server is seen by Macintoshes connected to all of the bound networks. If this box is not selected, the NT Server is seen only from the Macintoshes connected to the default network—that is, the one to which the AppleTalk Protocol is bound.

APPLETALK ROUTER CONFIGURATION

AppleTalk networking includes a couple variations on routers, all of which forward data from one LAN segment to another. Seed routers provide a unique additional service: they initialize and broadcast information about one or more physical networks that tells other routers where to send each packet of data. Each LAN segment must have at least one seed router, and it must be started first in the network to ensure that all other routers are initialized correctly.

A LocalTalk network can have more than one seed router, and in some cases multiple seed routers are recommended.

Multiple seed routers must have identical seeding information. If an NT Server seed router at startup detects another network seed router with different information, the first router's information is used to seed the network, and the second router is referenced in an "Invalid network range" event written in the NT Server event log.

There are three types of seeding information:

♦ A network number or range associated with each physical network. A network number is a unique identifier for an AppleTalk LAN segment (any number from 1 through 65,279) which routers use to send incoming data to the correct LAN segment. It is highly recommended that you plan your AppleTalk internetwork before adding NT.

♦ The zone list associated with each LAN segment. A zone is a logical grouping that allows the internetwork to be controlled in segments rather than as a single entity. NT domains are groups of users; AppleTalk zones are groups of machines. In LocalTalk networks, each LAN segment can be associated with only one zone. AppleTalk Phase II does not observe a strict relationship between zone names and network numbers, so two nodes in different zones can have the same network number.

♦ The default zone for the network, into which all AppleTalk devices fall if they do not specify otherwise. Each Macintosh client can select which zone to belong to.

The following summarizes AppleTalk router settings:

Seed this Network: *Seeding* the network means identifying zones on the network and determining network ranges.

Network Range: Setting the network range is an important part of seeding a network because all AppleTalk networks in an internetwork are assigned a range of numbers. Each workstation on the network is identified by one of these numbers, combined with a dynamically assigned AppleTalk node-identification number. Because of this, no two subnetworks (LAN segments) on an internetwork should have overlapping ranges.

The possible values for a network range are 1 to 65,279. If a range is specified that overlaps another range, an error message is given.

Zone Information: Setting zone information is also part of seeding a network. You can view the current list of zones, add and remove zones, and set the default zone. (The *default zone* is the zone in which all AppleTalk devices appear if a desired zone has not been specified for them.)

SERVICES FOR MACINTOSH REGISTRY KEYS

Following are the locations of all of the Registry entries for Services for Macintosh. The list below is not a detailed description of the Registry entries. It is only meant as a checklist. The valid values and their significance is described in the *NT Server Administrator's Guide - Services for Macintosh*.

```
\HKEY_LOCAL_MACHINE
    \SOFTWARE
        \Microsoft
            \SFM

\HKEY_LOCAL_MACHINE
    \SYSTEM
        \CurrentControlSet
            \Services
                \MacSvr
```

AppleTalk Keys:

```
\HKEY_LOCAL_MACHINE
    \SOFTWARE
        \Microsoft
            \AppleTalk

\HKEY_LOCAL_MACHINE
    \SYSTEM
        \CurrentControlSet
            \Services
                \AppleTalk
```

File Server for Macintosh Keys:

```
\HKEY_LOCAL_MACHINE
    \SOFTWARE
        \Microsoft
            \MacFile
```

```
\HKEY_LOCAL_MACHINE
    \SYSTEM
        \CurrentControlSet
            \Services
                \MacFile
```

Print Server for Macintosh Keys:

```
\HKEY_LOCAL_MACHINE
    \SOFTWARE
        \Microsoft
            \MacPrint
```

```
\HKEY_LOCAL_MACHINE
    \SYSTEM
        \CurrentControlSet
            \Control
                \Print
                    \Environments
                        \Windows NT x86
                            \Print Processors
                                \PSPRINT
```

```
\HKEY_LOCAL_MACHINE
    \SYSTEM
        \CurrentControlSet
            \Control
                \Print
                    \Monitors
                        \AppleTalkPrinters
```

```
\HKEY_LOCAL_MACHINE
    \SYSTEM
        \CurrentControlSet
            \Services
                \MacPrint
```

PROBLEM AREAS

When using the NT File Manager with Services for Macintosh, File Manager cannot access directories containing UNICODE characters that are not available in ANSI. Services for Macintosh maps the Macintosh character set to UNICODE when creating files and directories on an NTFS server. Because NT File Manager works with ANSI only, when you try to access one of these directories in File Manager, the search often does not recognize your characters and might sometimes revert to the root of the current drive.

The Win32 API functions support a maximum path length of 260 characters. Services for Macintosh enables you to create paths longer than 260 characters, but you cannot access them from the NT File Manager.

15

ADMINISTERING WORKGROUP APPLICATIONS

When using NT File Manager with a CD-ROM drive, note that CDs made for the Macintosh cannot be read by an NT computer. Macintosh uses the High Sierra format, whereas Microsoft uses ISO 9660 format.

LOTUS NOTES

Lotus Notes has taken the industry by storm, but its popularity was not attained overnight. Persistent visionary efforts have made Notes an industry phenomenon. IBM's recent acquisition of Lotus was the official stamp of approval for Notes to become a strategic component in everything from PC to legacy systems.

WHAT IS NOTES?

Notes popularity is a paradox. Although it is far and away the best known and most widely used groupware product, Lotus Notes remains a mystery to the vast majority of PC users. For geographically dispersed organizations interested in information collection and delivery and routing systems that can be quickly developed and implemented, Notes is a tool without equal.

So, what is Notes? An oversimplified answer: It is a database. Moreover, it is a distributed, multiuser database; it is an enterprise-wide filing system that everyone can access, even if geographically dispersed. The information is replicated in several places and can be accessed both over a LAN or WAN and via remote dial-up. It is a *multiformat* database, which means that different database templates are provided for tracking, reference, discussion, and information broadcasting. The end result is that Notes provides access to the equivalent of a filing cabinet in which each location (file folder) has automatically updated copies of everyone's files. This makes WAN links and various operating systems in a workgroup transparent and eliminates the boundaries within an organization.

You can use Notes for many tasks; it includes message transport (e-mail) and a programming language. All of this is built on top of an engine that enables Notes to operate over unlimited geographical areas in real time.

THE ENGINE

In a Notes installation, copies of the database are placed on geographically separate database servers—perhaps one in Chicago, another in Boston, and another in New York—that communicate via dial-up phone lines. Notes keeps all of these copies synchronized and up to date by carrying out periodic *replication*: At regular intervals, Notes compares these database copies, updating documents that have been added, deleted, or modified. Where it finds differences, the Notes engine automatically reconciles them, updating each outdated database as necessary. Because only changes are propagated, data transfer is kept to a minimum.

Users can keep their own local copies of individual databases. They can replicate these as needed by using their local file server, either across the LAN or by dial-up. A replicated event for a user can involve several events, such as sending and receiving mail messages, uploading a document to a tracking database, and adding comments to an ongoing discussion.

The net result is that every user on the system, whether at his or her desk or on the road with a laptop, has concurrent access to the same information.

THE NOTES OPERATING ENVIRONMENT

The hardware/software configuration of a typical Notes site is as follows: The Notes 3.3 Server software runs on a computer running NT Server (or NT Workstation). Typically, the client is a Windows 3.*x* or NT workstation connecting to the Notes Server through NetBIOS or NWNBLink and IP, respectively.

NWNBLink is a NetBIOS version 3 provider that runs in conjunction with NWLink and uses the Novell NetBIOS packet format to provide full compatibility with Novell's NetBIOS version 1 implementation. It provides support using NetBIOS for interoperating with other WFW- and NT-based computers, and with computers running Novell's NetBIOS driver. The use of NWNBLink provides application connectivity to NetBIOS-based environments such as Lotus Notes, without loading the Novell NETBIOS.EXE driver.

Users do not see any of this complexity; all they see are applications that are task-specific databases created by themselves or by third-party software developers.

Developers build applications using *forms* to input data into Notes databases. Notes forms can include a variety of special field formats such as radio buttons, check boxes, and small lookup tables called *choice lists*. You can link many of the 188 functions built into the Notes programming language directly into these controls.

The Notes engine takes care of moving documents and messages automatically among databases, on the same server, or at a server on the other side of the world. A key resource in this process is the Notes Name and Address Book, which contains entries for all of the databases in the network, including individual mailboxes.

On the surface Notes appears unimpressive, almost kludgy. Its interface is far from glamorous, its search and reporting features are primitive. Beneath the surface, however, it is powerful and robust.

The primary advantage of the NT Server version of Notes 3.3 is the ease of configuring the network component. In addition, Notes Server for NT was compiled as the first multitasking 32-bit application. The base code is still 16-bit, but it does benefit from the multithreaded NT environment. Notes Server for NT benefits from a multiprocessor system, especially Notes' Indexer function.

ADMINISTRATION REQUIRES NOTES SERVER SHUTDOWN

You have to bring the Notes Server down to conduct configuration changes, even to make changes to its local databases. This can be disruptive for the users only in terms of the freshness of the information—though users can still update documents and information, replication is suspended when the Notes Server is down.

Fortunately, you can perform some common administration tasks online. In fact, because the Notes Server installs as an NT service, you can conduct remote administration from a workstation.

PRINTING FROM LOTUS NOTES

Printer names should not have more than 32 characters. When you print from Lotus Notes in Windows NT to a printer with the printer name longer than 32 characters, the following error message appears:

```
Cannot access printer or printer driver(may be due to insufficient memory).
```

Lotus Notes maintains a 32-byte internal buffer size for filenames. Although the long filename of the printer is correctly reported, Notes accepts only the first 32 characters; therefore, it cannot locate the printer.

To correct this problem, either change the printer's name or connect to a printer with a printer name 32 characters or less.

RUNNING NOTES AS AN MS-DOS APPLICATION AND WITH OS/2

If you try to run the Lotus Notes application as an MS-DOS–based application, it fails because some "bound" applications, such as Lotus Notes, use PM APIs not supported by the OS/2 subsystem in NT.

To deal with this problem take one of the following courses of action:

1. Use a Windows Notes client, or
2. Disable the OS/2 subsystem.

Note

When you run the installation program for Lotus Notes version 2.1, the following error message is displayed:

```
Error ordinal not found INSTALL->PMWIN.246
```

The Lotus Notes 2.1 installation program is a bound application, containing both OS/2 Presentation Manager and MS-DOS versions in the same executable file. Windows NT, by default, attempts to run the OS/2 version. The error results because Windows NT does not support Presentation Manager code.

To install Lotus Notes 2.1, you can use the program FORCEDOS.EXE to force Windows NT to execute the MS-DOS–based portion of the installation program. To do so, use the following syntax:

```
forcedos install
```

Configuring NWLink to Work with Notes

This section deals with configuring a Lotus Notes client on an NT Server or NT Workstation computer using NWLink. In this case, the Lotus Notes server must communicate with the NT computer usingNovell's NetBIOS interface as the IPC mechanism.

Lotus Notes currently ships with two types of servers: a Windows server, which only uses NetBIOS; and an OS/2 server, which supports IPX/SPX and Novell's NetBIOS interface.

This section assumes that Notes server is loaded on an NT Server using NetBIOS configuration to communicate with its clients.

Note

All Microsoft network computers (including NT computers) use NetBIOS to advertise distribution shares and create virtual connections. However, when using NWLink, a Novell version of the NetBIOS interface is used, which can cause subtle communication problems when communicating with a computer using the Microsoft NetBIOS version. Unless you configure NWNBLink (IPX/SPX with NetBIOS), Notes cannot communicate effectively with NT.

For more information on protocol dynamics, see Chapter 30, "LAN Troubleshooting."

On computers with Windows 3.1 or MS-DOS, Lotus Notes clients need NETBIOS.EXE loaded in AUTOEXEC.BAT to communicate to the Lotus Notes server.

On computers running NT Workstation or NT Server, configure the Lotus Notes client using NWLink by doing the following:

1. In the Control Panel window, choose the Network icon, select Add Software, and then select the NWLink IPX/SPX Compatible Transport option. This also adds NWNBLink, which is an updated revision to Novell's NetBIOS implementation.

2. In the Control Panel window, choose the Network icon, select NetBIOS Interface, choose Configure, and then select the bindings that say

   ```
   "NWNBlink -> Streams" and change its Lana # to "0".
   ```

3. In the Control Panel window, choose the Network icon, select NWLink, choose Configure, and then select the appropriate IPX network number and LAN frame type.

4. Restart the computer after making these changes.

THE LOTUS NOTES CLIENT

On the Lotus Notes client, choose Network Port from the Options menu and make sure the Network Port is 0.

Note

The Lotus Notes client must be configured to use "Network Port #0 and NWNBLink -> Streams" binding must be at LANa #0 on the NT computer for this configuration to work.

With these changes, the Lotus Notes client can connect to the Lotus Notes server using NWLink transport.

- Installing and Configuring GSNW

- Accessing File Resources

- Accessing Printers

- Running NetWare-Aware Utilities

- Running NetWare-Aware Applications

- File and Print Services for NetWare

CHAPTER 16

Gateway Service for NetWare (GSNW)

TSR   Terminate and Stay Resident. These are quasi-multitasking programs common in the DOS environment.

DLC   Data Link Control. This protocol is primarily used to connect HP Jetdirect printers on NT networks.

LPR   Line Printer Remote. These are remote printers, usually UNIX based.

RIP   Router Information Protocol. This is a protocol used to communicate routing information between routers.

SAP   Service Advertising Protocol. This is a protocol Novell NetWare uses to advertise server services to routers and other servers.

SMB   Server Message Block. This is the highest level protocol used in a Microsoft network. SMB relays file read/write, print, and other connectivity information between clients and servers.

NCP   NetWare Core Protocol. This is Novell NetWare's highest level protocol that relays file read/write information between clients and servers.

Gateway Service for NetWare (GSNW) is included with NT Server and enables Microsoft network clients to access NetWare file servers without running the NetWare Shell or Requester. GSNW is designed for users who only occasionally need access to NetWare servers and would like to streamline the terminate-and-stay-resident-in-memory (TSR) driver files loaded locally. When a GSNW user logs in on a NetWare server, all NetWare services are available, just as if the client had logged into the NetWare server directly. GSNW includes all of the functionality of Client Service for NetWare.

Note

NetWare clients use Novell's Shell (NETX.EXE) or Requester (VLM.EXE). Microsoft collectively refers to these two components as the *NetWare redirector* or sometimes the *NetWare shell*.

You can use GSNW to

◆ Reduce or eliminate clients' use of IPX/SPX protocol on your network

◆ Ease the transition to TCP/IP

◆ Allow remote users access to NetWare servers via NT's *Remote Access Server* (RAS)

RAS (included with NT Server) enables WFW, DOS, and NT Workstation clients to securely dial into the network from remote locations and have access to all services as if they were connected directly to the LAN. RAS users can access NetWare servers via GSNW using PCAnywhere, Carbon Copy, or virtually any remote node or terminal-emulation software.

You can configure GSNW to start automatically as a service in the NT Server. This way GSNW service is available to authorized users as long as NT Server is running, and requires no special intervention after you have configured it. The connection established via GSNW looks like a single login to NetWare. That means that, for occasional use, you can have multiple users sharing one NetWare connection, and only one user login. It is possible to use GSNW to allow more user logins than your NetWare server license allows.

Note

> Though this option allows more user logins to a NetWare server than the server license permits, the authors make no representation that doing so conforms to your NetWare license agreement.

GSNW is also useful as a tool when migrating from NetWare to NT Server. GSNW enables a conservative, gradual migration to NT Server.

GSNW connects to the NetWare server, accesses the directory to be shared, and provides a Share for it just as if the directory were on the NT Server itself. Microsoft network clients (clients running one of the Microsoft redirectors) can access files on the NetWare server by connecting to the NetWare Share created on the NT Server.

INSTALLING AND CONFIGURING GSNW

The GSNW software is included on the NT Server CD-ROM and only requires certain prerequisites before you can install and use it. There are no hardware requirements as long as NWLink is already installed and running.

PREREQUISITE NWLINK IPX/SPX PROTOCOL

NWLink is a combination of Microsoft's emulation of Novell's IPX/SPX, and NetBIOS protocol implementations and is included with every NT Server. You can read about implementing these protocols in Chapter 8, "Connecting the Client."

GSNW INSTALLATION

GSNW is based on the Client Service for NetWare, as discussed in Chapter 8. The installation is very similar; you do it through the Network icon in Control Panel as shown in Figure 16.1. NWLink must be installed as the default protocol. It does not require any files from Novell.

Figure 16.1.
Installing Gateway
software.

The LAN frame type that NWLink uses must match the frame type in use on any NetWare servers that need to be accessed. Just as with Client Service for NetWare, NT Server users need to choose a preferred server before they can have seamless access to NetWare resources. After GSNW is installed and working, you must configure File Gateway through the GSNW application icon in Control Panel.

GSNW CONFIGURATION

As stated previously, GSNW works by assigning (redirecting) an NT Server drive letter to the NetWare server and then re-sharing that same drive letter. Microsoft networking clients can connect to the Share on the NT Server and access the files on the NetWare server. The preferred NetWare server needs to be designated as shown in Figure 16.2.

Note

Before you can set up GSNW, you must create a special NTGATEWAY group on the NetWare file server. All file access to the NetWare resource is done through a user account on the NetWare server. You can either create this user account for GSNW or use an existing one, but it *must* be a member of the NTGATEWAY group.

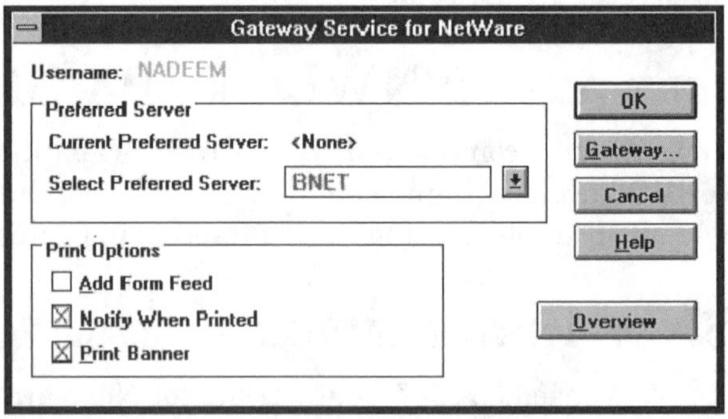

Figure 16.2.
Selecting the preferred
server for GSNW.

After you have set up the user account and group, you can configure GSNW. You do this through the Gateway... button in the GSNW application in Control Panel. The

Configure Gateway dialog box enables you to set up the drive mappings from the NT Server machine to the NetWare server(s). To set up GSNW, check the Enable Gateway box and add GSNW's user account and password that you created earlier. (See Figure 16.3.)

Warning

Remember that a GSNW user account *must* be a member of the NTGATEWAY group. In addition, you *must* enable Multiple Concurrent Connections in the user's Account Restrictions. You do this in SYSCON for NetWare 3, and in NETADMIN or NWAdmin in NetWare 4.

-or-

Set Limit Concurrent Connections to No for that user account using SYSCON, NETADMIN, or NWAdmin.

Tip

If you are unable to see all of the volumes on a NetWare 3 server, try running BINDFIX from the SYSTEM directory. BINDFIX is a NetWare utility used for maintaining the referential integrity of the bindery.

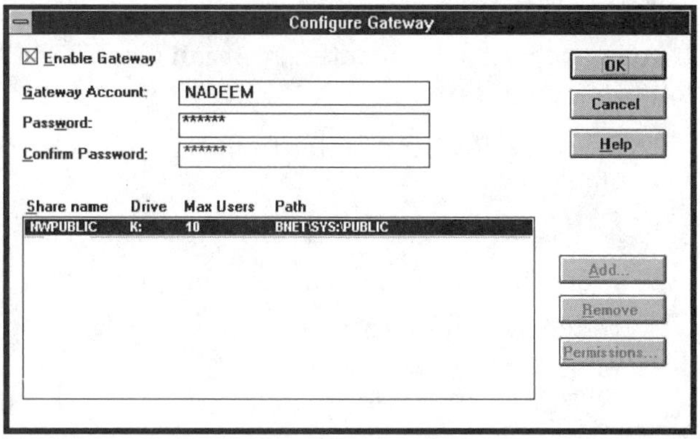

Figure 16.3.
Configuring GSNW.

After you have added this information, click the Add... button in the Configure Gateway dialog box to create the drive connection that will be shared by GSNW. (See Figure 16.4.) You must provide a Share name to be used by Microsoft network clients and a complete path to the NetWare directory. Gateway drive letters start at Z: and work backward. Figure 16.4 shows how to create a Share drive letter.

> ## *Note*
>
> By default, the User Limit selection is disabled. It is recommended that you impose a limit because GSNW was not designed for heavy use.

Figure 16.4.
Adding a shared drive.

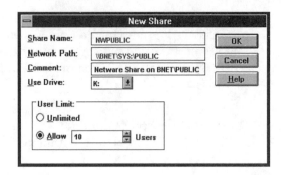

NETWARE BROADCASTS

NetWare servers broadcast *Router Information Protocol* (RIP) and *Service Advertising Protocol* (SAP) packets regularly to notify all other servers and routers of their IPX addresses and available services. Broadcasts from large numbers of NetWare file servers, communications servers, print servers, database servers, and routers can occupy excessive bandwidth and reduce client response time.

RIP and SAP broadcasts are required to keep routers updated in an IPX network. If you have no need for routers, you can disable the NetWare broadcasts using the following procedure:

1. Start the Registry Editor from NT Diagnostics and go to the following entry subkey:

   `HKEY_LOCAL_MACHINE\SYSTEM\CurrentControlSet\Services\NWCWorkstation\Parameters`

2. From the Edit menu, choose Add Value.

3. Enter the following values:

   ```
   Value Name: DisablePopup
   Data Type: REG_DWORD
   Value: 1
   ```

4. Exit the Registry Editor and restart NT Server.

Warning

Using the Registry Editor incorrectly can cause serious system-wide problems that might require you to reinstall your operating system to correct.

GSNW DEPENDENCIES

If service dependencies for the Server service are reset NT Server, the Share Name in the Configure Gateway dialog box for GSNW displays

```
*DELETED*
```

Resetting of the service dependencies happens when you run the Network option in Control Panel to configure your network. This option occasionally resets the service dependencies for the Server service.

Because the NT Server no longer depends on the GSNW service, it starts up before the GSNW service is loaded and hence does not create the shares it needs.

To correct this problem, do the following in the NT Server Registry:

1. Start the Registry Editor from NT Diagnostics.
2. Find the following key:

   ```
   HKEY_LOCAL_MACHINE\SYSTEM\CurrentControlSet\Services\LanmanServer
   ```

3. Verify the following entry is correct or add it if it is not present:

   ```
   Value Name: DependOnService
   Data Type: REG_MULTI_SZ
   Data: NwcWorkstation
   ```

4. Exit the Registry.
5. Shut down and restart NT Server.

GSNW PERFORMANCE ISSUES

When using the GSNW, you might experience slow performance and data throughput when using a NetWare server as a router.

NetWare servers can act as routers, linking NT clients using one frame type to NT Servers using a different frame type, but you pay the price in performance. NetWare internal routers can become sluggish when the NetWare file server is busy with other requests.

You should make sure that all of your NT clients are not using a NetWare router needlessly to access an NT Server. Configure all NT clients with the same LAN frame type whenever possible to prevent unnecessary traffic on the routers.

If you encounter this problem, do the following:

◆ Check the network protocol bindings and verify that the same frame type is bound to each client's NWLink IPX/SPX-compatible transport. Check to see that the same frame type is bound to the NIC driver in your NetWare server.

◆ Verify that the NWLink protocol is bound to the correct NIC in the NT Server running the GSNW.

GSNW FILE SECURITY

The Permissions option in the Configure Gateway dialog box enables you to assign permissions to users who have accounts on the NT Server or domain. These permissions are assigned to the Share on the NT Server, and the same permissions apply to all files and directories accessed through the Share. The default permission set for Gateway shares is Full Control for Everyone.

NetWare file or directory trustee assignments are assigned to the NetWare user account specified when GSNW is enabled. For example, if the SUPERVISOR account was used when GSNW was enabled, all NetWare trustee assignments are assigned to users who access files through GSNW. The only way to change these rights is to change the Share-level permissions for the NT Server–GSNW Share.

As the administrator, you must evaluate whether the NetWare Trustee Assignments are warranted. If they are, you can assign them to the NetWare user account in use by GSNW.

Microsoft networking clients use the *Server Message Block* (SMB) protocol to perform remote requests to Microsoft networking servers. Similarly, NetWare clients use *NetWare Core Protocol* (NCP) to communicate with NetWare servers. GSNW file gateway serves as a translator between the two protocols.

The GSNW enables the NetWare administrator to control which NT Servers can be gateways to the NetWare file server.

CONTROLLING ACCESS TO FILES

You can control file access at two levels:

◆ You can restrict access through GSNW by limiting which Microsoft networking users or groups have access to the NT Server or domain. You can also restrict access by setting Permissions on the use of the GSNW, and can use Share restrictions to control which NT clients and groups can access files through the GSNW.

◆ On the NetWare file server, you must create a special gateway group, NTGATEWAY as previously discussed. You can use NetWare Trustee Assignments to control access to NetWare volumes/files accordingly. (See Figure 16.5.)

Figure 16.5.
Access through Share.

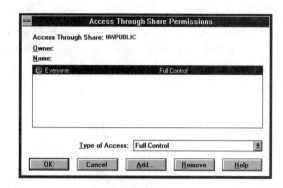

ACCESSING FILE RESOURCES

Users who access file resources via GSNW might not be familiar with NetWare file attributes and other limitations. You can prevent users from running into problems by making sure that trustee assignments and file attributes on the NetWare server are set properly.

NETWARE FILE ATTRIBUTES

If the NetWare Execute-only (X) file attribute is placed on an executable file, the following error message appears on all Microsoft network clients accessing the execute-only files through GSNW:

```
The system cannot find the file drive:\directory\executable_file
```

NetWare does not enable you to remove the Execute-only attribute from a file. To correct this problem, rename or remove the executable file and then reinstall the file or restore the file from a backup that was made prior to the time the Execute-only attribute was added.

NETWARE FILE LOCKS

GSNW might require you to increase the maximum number of file locks on your NetWare server. GSNW establishes a single session to a NetWare server, which it shares to multiple clients. If many client connections are made to GSNW, the number of file locks required on the NetWare server might surpass the default limit (250 per connection, including open files).

To increase the maximum number of file locks, you need to use the NetWare console SET command as follows:

```
Set Maximum File Locks Per Connection=n (where n is a value between 10 to 1000
```

> ## Tip
>
> Commands typed at the NetWare system console are not saved. To be sure the command is issued every time the server boots, you should include this SET command in the NetWare server's AUTOEXEC.NCF.

ACCESSING PRINTERS

Although the *Microsoft Windows NT System Guide* states that Print Manager can create, remove, and administer printers on remote servers, it has the following limitations related to administering remote server print queues:

◆ Choosing Connect To Printer from the Print menu connects printers only on the local server, even when the intent is to access remote servers. If you want to create a NetWare printer that is shared through GSNW service, you must create a printer capture at the local machine because you have to create a separate connection to the NetWare printer Share.

◆ When creating a printer on a remote server, Print Manager cannot choose a printer that is not physically connected to that remote server. When you attempt to create a remote printer, the following error message appears:

```
The parameter is incorrect
```

◆ The Connect To Printer option in the Print menu under Windows NT 3.5 can create a printer based on a port that is already defined on the remote server. If you choose Create Printer from the Print menu and attempt to connect to a port for DLC or LPR, the following error message appears:

```
Could not add port. The network request is not supported.
```

This type of action requires the DLL, which is responsible for managing the port, to load. Loading the DLL across the network is not supported at this time.

RUNNING NETWARE-AWARE UTILITIES

If a client computer is connected to a NetWare through GSNW's server connection, you can use any of the following NetWare system utilities:

CHKVOL   COLORPAL

DSPACE   FLAG

FLAGDIR	FCONSOLE
FILER	GRANT
LISTDIR	NCOPY
NDIR	PCONSOLE
PSC	PSTAT
RCONSOLE	REMOVE
REVOKE	RIGHTS
SECURITY	SEND
SETPASS	SETTS
SLIST	SYSCONTLIST
USERLIST	VOLINFO (If update interval = 5)
WHOAMI	SESSION (Search drive mapping is not supported because SESSION always maps as a root)

Running NetWare-Aware Applications

The NetWare system utilities and NetWare-aware applications use NetWare client application program interface (API) calls and NetWare Core Protocol. All Microsoft clients use the Server Message Block protocol for the same purpose, but Microsoft's SMB-based redirector cannot interpret NetWare API calls or NCP requests. Client Service for NetWare and GSNW convert NetWare API calls through NWRDR.SYS, but only for processes (not over routers).

The following is a partial list of applications that have been tested with GSNW:

Lotus Notes, SPX connectivity option

NetWare 3270 LAN Workstation for MS-DOS

NetWare 3270 LAN Workstation for Windows

Attachmate Extra! for MS-DOS to the NetWare SAA Gateway

Attachmate Extra! for MS-DOS to the Attachmate 3270 Gateway

Attachmate Extra! for Windows to the NetWare SAA Gateway

Attachmate Extra! for Windows to the Attachmate 3270 Gateway

DCA IRMA LAN for MS-DOS to Novell's SAA

Btrieve requester (BREQUEST.EXE)

Gupta SQLBase for NetWare systems

FILE AND PRINT SERVICES FOR NETWARE

In Chapter 4, "Microsoft's Protocol Support," you saw a reference to NT Server's emulation of NetWare 3.*x* file and print services. Following is a brief discussion of these new features of NT Server called File and Print Services for NetWare (FPSN).

FPSN makes it possible to add an NT Server to an existing NetWare network and have the existing clients access the NT Server without changing the login scripts or drive mappings.

The following NetWare utilities work:

> ATTACH
>
> LOGIN
>
> LOGOUT
>
> SETPASS
>
> MAP
>
> CAPTURE
>
> SLIST
>
> ENDCAP

When you install FPSN, a NetWare volume called SYSVOL: is created. Underneath it are created the following subdirectories: LOGIN, MAIL, PUBLIC, and SYSTEM.

SUMMARY

GSNW provides NT clients with seamless, concurrent connectivity to NetWare servers through a single user login on a NetWare server and is transparent to the client. You can use GSNW to reduce the complexity of protocol stacks loaded at the client workstation. As an added bonus, GSNW reduces NetWare license costs.

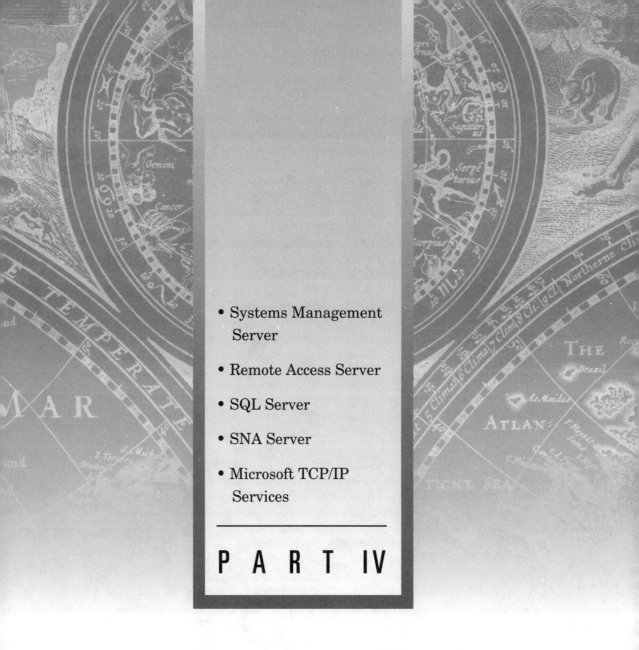

- Systems Management
  Server

- Remote Access Server

- SQL Server

- SNA Server

- Microsoft TCP/IP
  Services

PART IV

Application Server
Add-ons

- SMS Functions

- SMS Components

- SMS Structure

- System Requirements

- Configuring SMS

- SMS Clients

- Using Network
  Applications

- Installing Applica-
  tions on Clients

- Notes on Installing
  Specific Applications

- Using SMS to Install
  Operating Systems on
  Clients

- Automatically Config-
  ure Workstation
  Logon Scripts

- Network Monitoring

CHAPTER 17

Systems Management
Server

Auto-sense (Autodetect)   NT and Windows 95 use this technique to discover hardware devices and to locate a driver to access each device during the Setup program.

CD-ROM   Compact Disk Read-Only Memory disks and drives provide over 600MB of disk storage on one single compact disk. Data is formatted in ISO 9660 standard format and interpreted into various OS formats using CD Extensions.

Setup   You execute this program to install all Windows OSs.

SCSI   Small Computer Systems Interface is a computer bus standard developed by ANSI. SCSI adapters enable you to interface SCSI storage devices including disk drives, CD-ROMs, tape drives, and magneto-optical drives into a standard PC bus.

PDF   Package Definition Files.

SNMP   Simple Network Management Protocol.

PGC   Program Group Controller.

DHCP   Dynamic Host Configuration Protocol.

INTRODUCTION

The Systems Management Server allows central control of the client computers in the entire organization. The SMS is made up of several components, all of which work in unison. SMS is a powerful program, and it has to be installed and configured carefully; otherwise, it can cause problems by interfering with network functions.

SMS FUNCTIONS

You can use the SMS for the following functions:

- ◆ Installing software upgrades. Software upgrades require planning and monitoring and usually impose a burden on a support organization. You can use SMS for installing, testing, and monitoring risky changes to the network.

- ◆ Delivering and installing new off-the-shelf software. You can use SMS to install a standard tested configuration. You can determine optimum behavior without having to be at the workstation running the software.

- ◆ Resolving problems and technical queries. You can reduce the number of field visits required and improve the time it takes to resolve problems. You also can reduce the number of times users have to register and follow up on support issues. Your technicians can use inventory and configuration databases, remote diagnostics, and ultimately, remote control in resolving problems.

◆ Tracking software versions. You can exercise control over several versions of the same software installed on different computers on the network.

◆ Cleaning up virus infections. You can clean up viruses and install virus protection. You also can search for new virus strains.

◆ Managing assets. You can survey installed computer bases for asset management. You also can generate reports from local or centralized SMS databases.

◆ Saving install time. You can reduce the need for installing software by floppy disk and reduce installation time by installing from SMS. This way, you also can eliminate the need for backing up programs, thus reducing the time needed for backups because you need to back up data only.

◆ Installing during off-hours. Most client computers are not available during normal working hours for lengthy installations. You can install at a time more convenient for the users.

◆ Conserving software licenses. You can meter the actual use of enterprise software licenses.

SMS COMPONENTS

SMS is made up of several interdependent services and agents. Some of them run on the NT Server where SMS is installed, and some of them are roving agents. The following lists some of these components and their functions:

◆ Site servers. This server-based component is the place where the SMS database is stored in the form of SQL server-based tables. These tables contain system-inventory information for that site and any subsites in its hierarchy.

◆ SMS administrators. SMS Administrators enable you to manage the site server database. You also can administer remote site servers.

◆ NT sender service. This service updates inventory databases and sends updated information to client.

◆ SMS server agents. You can install SMS server agents remotely on client computers and site servers. They can send inventory information back to SMS and pick up software updates for installation at the clients.

◆ Automatic inventory. The SMS polls and collects data on hardware and software installed on clients in the entire enterprise. It can access hierarchical management domains and other organizational structures normally used to characterize networks. Hardware and software inventory tells you what you have and where it is. For instance, you can tell which client computers need updated printer drivers, which have enough memory and free disk space to run a new application, and how many copies of Word are actually installed throughout the network.

♦ Software distribution and management. SMS can conduct software distribution and installation through GUI utilities. Administrators can update software on clients and server computers in one step. SMS enables you to customize global installations or updates for each PC in the organization; it tracks certain parameters such as disk space on each computer. The software distribution and installation functions make it easy to upgrade clients most efficiently. SMS also makes it possible for you to centrally manage, install, and control applications that are run from file servers, and it enables users to run those applications from anywhere on the network.

♦ Remote management. Everything you can do locally, you can schedule or conduct remotely. Other maintenance activities—such as executing remote programs and scripts, updating configuration files, and removing program and data files—can also be done remotely.

♦ Diagnostics. PC and network diagnostic and other support tasks are facilitated by the centralized availability of client configuration information. Coupled with this capability is the capability to manipulate the client environment remotely. Network protocol analysis and performance monitoring allow the comparison of measured data against known good values stored in the central database. Network protocol analysis enables you to find bottlenecks anywhere on the network and manage network traffic to help users be their most productive.

♦ Network support. SMS supports NT Server, NetWare, LAN Manager, and PATHWORKS from Digital Equipment Corporation Client-System Options.

♦ OS support. SMS has support subsystems for MS-DOS, Windows 3.x, Windows for Workgroups (WFW) 3.11, OS/2, and System 7 clients.

♦ Wide-Area protocols. The SMS Server supports SNA, TCP/IP, X.25, ISDN, and Asynchronous communication.

♦ Standards. SMS is compatible with other industry-standard management tools with SNMP support, which is actually part of NT Server and NetView support supplied with SNA Server. This capability allows SMS to work with SNMP-based consoles such as DEC PolyCenter, Hewlett-Packard OpenView, IBM NetView/6000, and Network Managers NMC Vision, as well as IBM mainframe consoles.

SMS STRUCTURE

SMS structure has four levels of functionality:

♦ Level 1. A central SMS Server and an inventory database residing on SQL server.

◆ Level 2. The SMS site servers that are running on NT Servers. They can share the load of distribution to the logon servers and reduce the majority of network traffic generated on local subnets. Each also holds a local inventory database.

◆ Level 3. NT Servers providing logon authentication, or servers running NetWare or LAN Manager.

◆ Level 4. Client workstations.

Software and data are sent down these levels, and inventory data is sent back up these levels. SMS tools are available via each SMS site server.

SYSTEM REQUIREMENTS

SMS requires NT Server version 3.5 or later, SQL Server for NT 4.2 or later, 486/50 or higher processor with 32MB of memory, a CD-ROM drive, and network card.

INSTALLATION

The following is a checklist of what you must accomplish before Systems Management Server will install itself in the user logon scripts:

1. Configure and enable the Directory Replicator service for the domain being managed by SMS. SMS looks for a REPL$ share on the PDC. If the PDC or the share is not found, the Site Configuration Manager will not be able to copy the SMS logon support files to the \EXPORT\SCRIPTS directory.

2. Use the SMS Administrator to configure SMS Site properties as follows:

   In the Clients dialog box, select Automatically Configure Workstation Logon Scripts.

   In the Domains dialog box, select Use All Detected Servers for each domain that you want logon scripts enabled.

   At this point, SMS has been properly configured. It then configures the user logon scripts for each domain to include the SMSLS.BAT entry and copies the proper SMS support files to the REPL$ share during the next Site Configuration Manager watchdog cycle. This action occurs by default every 24 hours, but you can force it immediately by using one of the two following methods.

3. To force the watchdog cycle to occur immediately, use one of the following steps:

   Toggle the SMS Site property for Logon Scripts, changing it from its current state to the other state. This will toggle the site control file line PROP-ERTY <Logon Scripts><><><1> to 1 or 0. The Site Configuration Manager will read this line and immediately configure the logon scripts appropriately.

Use the SENDCODE utility, which is located on the SMS CD in the PSSTOOLS directory. At the SMS site server, open a DOS box and type in the following command line:

```
sendcode sms_site_config_manager 196
```

This command forces the Site Configuration Manager to perform its watchdog cycle immediately and configure the SMS logon scripts for all users in the domains that were enabled earlier.

SECURITY

SMS intervenes at very low levels, which means that the SMS service requires various administrator-type rights on each server it manages. SMS creates new shares and directories on each server in order and uses them for keeping its files.

SMS installs and starts the Inventory Agent service. SMS also installs the Package Command Manager. So that you have a successful installation and operation of these services, the SMS account needs to be able to log on as a service at each server.

If you have just one server site, the SMS service account needs to be a member of the Local Administrators group.

Note

If a NetWare domain is added, each NetWare server must have a supervisor-equivalent user account identical to the Windows NT SMS account.

If you add an NT domain to an existing site, you need to create a trusting relationship from the new domain to the domain already being managed by the SMS service account. After the trust relationship is active, add the SMS service account to the Local Administrators group in the new domain and give the account the right to log on as a service. Make sure that you use the full `<trusted domain>\<username>` syntax. This way, you ensure that the proper domain validates the account through the trust relationship.

When you're connecting sites together in a hierarchy, no administrative rights are required, and you do not have to create a trust relationship between the sites. The connection address for the respective sites must include the `<destination domain>\<username>` of the other site, and the account must have Change access to the SMS_SITE share.

CONFIGURING SMS

The SMS Server requires painstaking configuration to be effective. It also requires constant upkeep. Administrators have to think of configuring SMS as if they were configuring the entire network of server and workstations in one package.

SMS manages a good deal of information. The scope of this chapter does not allow a detailed treatment of all the screens and programs used when working with SMS.

CONTROLLING THE STARTUP GROUP

Most users need to have applications start up when Windows is loaded at the workstation. When SMS is in control, shared application startup requires that the Program Group Controller (PGC) must be executing first. Because PGC requires time to initialize, any SMS shared applications that are put in the Startup Group can fail to start.

Shared applications are started by APPSTART, which has dependency on APPCTL16.EXE or APPCTL32.EXE. The Windows program APPSTART checks for APPCTL16.EXE and fails to start any applications if APPCTL16.EXE is not running.

When an SMS-configured Windows 3.*x* client is started, the LOAD= line, in the WIN.INI file starts the SMS utility SMSRUN16.EXE or SMSRUN32.EXE. SMSRUN16.EXE starts APPCTL16.EXE. SMSRUN16.EXE uses the information in MS\SMS\BIN\SMSRUN16.INI. You can add other programs you want to be started by adding a line at the end of the [startup] section of the SMSRUN16.INI file.

On an NT Server, NT Workstation, and Windows 95 computer, the same information is stored in the Registry. To start an SMS application, insert a line that contains APPSTART and the Registry entry for that application. This line should be the same as the command line for the program item in Program Manager.

SMS uses CLI_DOS.EXE or CLI_NT.EXE to modify this file when changes are made to the SMS site properties. If this file is modified, you need to reinsert any changes you made to the SMSRUN16.INI file.

To start Excel as a shared application, you can use the following SMSRUN16.INI file:

```
[SMS Client]
Package Command Manager=c:\MS\SMS\bin\pcmwin16.exe
Program Group Control=c:\MS\SMS\bin\appctl16.exe
Remote Control=c:\MS\SMS\bin\wuser.exe
Help Desk Options=c:\MS\SMS\bin\editini.exe
MIF Entry=c:\MS\SMS\bin\mifwin.exe
SMS Client Help=c:\MS\SMS\bin\sm16.hlp
[startup]
```

```
load=c:\MS\SMS\bin\pcmwin16.exe
load=c:\MS\SMS\bin\appctl16.exe
load=c:\MS\SMS\bin\mifwin.exe /SMSLS
load=APPSTART.EXE msoffpro+excel
```

How to Apply Updates to SMS

SMS provides two utility programs, one for NT and another for WFW. Each is used in conjunction with a patch reader PATCHRDR.PDF file. This PDF contains package commands for both programs.

For updating NT, the files and the utility program PATCH.EXE are located in the PATCHES\NT subdirectory of the SMS CD. For the WFW update, the files and the utility program PATCH.EXE are located in the PATCHES\WFW subdirectory of the SMS CD.

To use the PDF, follow these steps:

1. Create a package source directory by creating an NT subdirectory and a WFW subdirectory under the package source directory.

2. Copy all the files from the PATCHES\NT and the PATCHES\WFW directories on the SMS CD-ROM to the NT and WFW subdirectories of the package source directory.

3. Create a package.

4. You need to import the PDF by choosing the Import button in Package Properties and then choosing PATCHRDR.PDF from the list.

5. Choose the Workstations button.

6. In the source directory box, type the path to the package source directory you created in the first step.

7. Select NT Patch of Redirector and choose the Properties button.

8. In the Command Line Properties dialog box, select both the Automated Command Line and System (Background) Task options.

9. Choose OK to close all the open dialog boxes.

10. Create one or more Run Command On Workstation jobs to run the appropriate package command on the appropriate computers.

You can run PATCH.EXE from the PATCHES\NT subdirectory of the SMS CD. Then you must reboot your computer. Rebooting causes the appropriate files (listed in the PATCHLST.000 file) to be updated. The files are updated only if the versions of these files on the SMS CD are newer than the versions already on your computer.

The SMSLS.INI File

The default SMSLS.INI file is placed in the SITE.SRV\MAINCFG.BOX directory on the SMS site server. If you want to use SMSLS.INI to map clients to domains, modify the SMSLS.INI. If you have enabled the Automatically Configure Workstation Logon Scripts option, the Site Configuration Manager copies the SMSLS.INI file from this location to the REPL$ share of SMS logon servers running NT Server. If you have not enabled the Automatically Configure Workstation Logon Scripts option, you need to copy the SMSLS.INI file manually to the NETLOGON shares of the SMS logon authenticating servers.

For computers running NT that are members of a domain, SETLS uses the domain as the workgroup if a WORKGROUP=DOMAIN mapping is specified in the SMSLS.INI file.

If the computer is in the SMSX domain and the SMSLS.INI file has SMSX = CENTRAL mapping for WORKGROUP, the computer running NT is added to the site in the CENTRAL domain. You can also use the [WIN.INI] section to map computers running NT to domains.

Configuring SMS for NetWare

You must make additional changes to the system login script when you use the Automatically Configure Workstation Logon Scripts option for NetWare 4.*x* servers. NetWare 4.*x* login scripts require an explicit mapping for accessing a volume.

After the Site Configuration Manager has configured the system login script on NetWare 4.*x* servers, you need to map a drive to the volume containing the SMS logon server LOGON.SRV.

The Site Configuration Manager adds the following lines to the system login script on NetWare 4.*x* and 3.*x* servers:

```
set SMS_LOGON="SMSVOL:smsroot\logon.srv"
INCLUDE %<SMS_LOGON>\SMSLS.SCR
set SMS_LOGON=
```

For NetWare 4.*x*, the SMS lines in the login script must have the following form:

```
map root X:= SMSVOL:smsroot\logon.srv
set SMS_LOGON="X:"
INCLUDE %<SMS_LOGON>\SMSLS.SCR
map rem X:
set SMS_LOGON=
```

SMS Clients

SMS clients can be any client. The following specifics apply to each type of client.

CLIENTS RUNNING DOS

SMS supports DOS clients running Microsoft Network Client for DOS version 3.0, which is provided on the SMS CD. It is recommended that you upgrade Windows 3.*x* clients to WFW 3.11 or Windows 95 to take advantage of SMS functions.

The Microsoft Network Client for MS-DOS version 3.0 has the following limitations:

◆ Remote troubleshooting utilities do not work on DOS clients using NWLINK. You can use remote troubleshooting utilities on DOS clients over NetBEUI or TCP/IP.

◆ SMS cannot read the network card ID (MAC/node address) on these clients for it to report this information in the SMS inventory.

CLIENTS RUNNING WFW

SMS clients running WFW need the latest version of the VREDIR.386 file. This file is included on the PATCHES\WFW directory on the SMS CD.

CLIENTS RUNNING WINDOWS 95

Windows 95 clients require no modifications to run the SMS client software.

MACINTOSH CLIENTS

The Apple Installer is required to install the appropriate SMS files to a Macintosh client. The Apple Installer is not supplied with SMS. After SMS Setup has been completed on a primary SMS site server, you need to install this file manually.

You must perform these steps before adding Macintosh clients to SMS and before adding any secondary sites that have Macintosh clients:

1. You need version 3.4 or later of the Apple Installer. The Installer ships with the System 7.1 or System 7.5 Macintosh operating system.

2. You also need an NT Server that has NT Services for Macintosh running on it. You need to create a Macintosh share using MacFile in the File Manager on an NTFS partition.

3. From a Macintosh computer, copy the Apple Installer file from the System 7 disk to the share volume.

4. Use the File Manager (or Explorer) to copy the file to the SITE.SRV\ MAINCFG.BOX\CLIENT.SRC\MAC.BIN directory.

If this site is a primary site with no secondary sites, the Installer file is copied automatically to the MAC.BIN directory in the logon share. If secondary sites do exist, then the Installer is not automatically copied to all sites. Then you need to change the date of the SYSTEM.MAP file in the SMS directory. Doing so causes all files to be updated, including secondary sites.

For Run Command On Workstation jobs targeted for Macintosh clients, the Despooler gives the package volume SMS_PKG*d* all permissions to Everyone. (*d* is the drive letter where the package is installed.)

When a package directory is shared as a Macintosh volume, the permissions set in the Access dialog box of the Setup Package For Workstations dialog box for a package are ignored. But the Despooler always sets the permissions for the package NT share to the permissions specified in the Access dialog box.

When the SMS client software is installed on a Macintosh client, the Installer always installs the Inventory Agent, Package Command Manager, and MIF Entry program (MIFMAC) on the client computer's local drive. The Installer also configures the computer to run the INVMAC program automatically during system startup. The INVMAC program automatically starts the Package Command Manager. The user must start the MIF Entry program manually.

You can use PDFs supplied with SMS to distribute packages to Macintosh clients. When you set up the package source directory for one of these applications, press the Command key while double-clicking the Setup icon. Continue pressing the Command key until the first dialog box appears.

In this dialog box, two options for installation on the client are offered. One option enables the user to install a complete version on his or her Macintosh client. The other option allows the user to install a version that runs from an NT share volume.

For Macintosh applications shared this way, all users run the application directly from the NT server with the package source directory.

Inventory

On clients running DOS, Windows 3.1, and WFW, the Inventory Agent always reports the protocol that it used to connect to the SMS logon server from which it is running. If information about other protocols is available to the Inventory Agent, it also reports these protocols.

For clients running WFW, you must run the SMSLS batch file or Inventory Agent using the Full or Enhanced Redirector. If you use the Basic Redirector, the Inventory Agent cannot report inventory and prompts you for an SMSID, or it terminates with an error that says your drive may be full. To solve this problem, start the workstation using the Full or Enhanced Redirector.

If you have clients that have both NetWare and NT networking capabilities, you should set up SMS to use only one of these network operating systems on these clients. Note that SMS supports only one network operating system at a time on a client.

To handle computers with duplicate SMSIDs, remove and reinstall SMS on the computers on which you want to create a new SMSID. If two or more clients have the same SMSID, you can generate a new SMSID for those computers by taking the following steps:

1. Remove SMS from the computers on which you want to create a new SMSID. You can remove SMS from a client by using the Client Setup program with the /R switch.

2. Add the computer back into the site. You can manually add a computer by running the SMSLS batch file from the SMS_SHR of an SMS logon server.

The Inventory Strategy When Network Is Slow setting takes effect when the next Logon Script Configuration Interval elapses. By default, this interval is 24 hours. You can confirm that the Site Configuration Manager has updated this setting at the site by looking in the Site Configuration Manager's trace log. Use NETSPEED.COM and NETSPEED.DAT.

If a computer running DOS or Windows has an inventory report that has no changes from the previous inventory, the Inventory Processor does not create a Delta-MIF to report the time of the inventory scan. Instead, the Inventory Processor waits for the inventory heartbeat period to elapse before it sends a Delta-MIF reporting no change and the scan time. By default, the heartbeat period is four days. This means that the Last Hardware Scan and Last Software Scan dates displayed in the Workstation Status section of the Personal Computer Properties window could be different from the date of the actual most recent scan by as much as the heartbeat period. If a change occurs in a computer's inventory, the Inventory Processor creates a Delta-MIF reporting the change and the scan time.

If the Inventory Data Loader sends a resync command to a client and no change has been made to the inventory, the client does not report a resync inventory until the inventory heartbeat period has elapsed, which is set at four days by default.

AUDITED SOFTWARE

If you want to customize the AUDIT.RUL file, you should rename the rule file. If you upgrade the site, SMS Setup overwrites the AUDIT.RUL file with the version on the SMS CD.

RUL2CFG.BAT needs to have one parameter. RUL2CFG.BAT requires only the package rule filename. The CFG file is not required because the AUDIT programs must always have a CFG file named AUDIT.CFG.

If you do not use the SMS Database Manager to remove the Audited Software group, the SMS site database will store the cumulative inventory for the Audited Software group. The SMS Database Manager DBCLEAN.EXE is provided so that you can remove the Audited Software group when you want to perform a software audit that contains only the latest audited software.

Before you create a job using the Audit package, you must run RUL2CFG.EXE to create the AUDIT.CFG file used for the software auditing package. You must take this step the first time you create a job with the package. If you make changes to the package rule file, you should also run RUL2CFG.EXE again to update the AUDIT.CFG file.

The RUL2CFG.BAT file puts the AUDIT.CFG files it creates into the PRIMSITE.SRV\AUDIT\PACKAGE\ x86.BIN directories (where x86 should be replaced with MIPS.BIN on a MIPS processor-based server). Also, package auditing using the RUL2CFG.BAT file in the default location (PRIMSITE.SRV\AUDIT) works only if the source directory for the package auditing is the PRIMSITE.SRV\AUDIT\PACKAGE directory.

For package inventory rules or the package rule file, do not enclose clauses containing OR operators in parentheses. Inventory rules and package rule files containing groupings (parentheses) around clauses containing an OR operator cannot be compiled by RUL2CFG.EXE—nor can they be processed by the Maintenance Manager.

The package rule file does not support an implicit AND clause before a set of OR clauses. The RUL2CFG.EXE compiler will not compile a package rule file containing an AND clause before a set of OR clauses. If you place the AND clause after the OR clauses, the RUL2CFG.EXE compiler will compile the CFG file successfully.

The package rule file (AUDIT.RUL) does not support an explicit AND operator. The RUL2CFG.EXE compiler will not compile a package rule file containing an explicit AND operator. If you use no operator between two files, an AND operator is implied. To combine file rules with AND operators, simply list them one after the other without an operator.

CREATING AND DISTRIBUTING PACKAGES

When you create a package, in the Workstation Command Line box you can type a path relative to the package source directory. For example, if the package source directory is C:\APPS, and the command line you want to run is C:\APPS\SETUP\SETUP.EXE, you can type `setup\setup.exe` in the Workstation Command Line box.

When you use either a Run Command On Workstation job or a Share Package On Server job for a package created using a PDF, clients that run the job may be rebooted when the job runs. Usually, a client reboots only the first time it receives a package created with a PDF. On some clients running Windows NT Workstation version 3.1, the reboot may damage data in files held open by other applications running at the same time. This problem happens only on clients running Windows NT Workstation version 3.1.

When you create a job to install a Microsoft application that has a PDF, you must copy the application's SMSPROXY directory to the package source directory. Copy the PRIMSITE.SRC\IMPORT.SRC*appname*\SMSPROXY directory (and its contents) to the package source directory you create for the application. You must perform this step when creating a package to either install the application on clients or to set up the application on a server as a shared application.

PROGRAM GROUP CONTROL

After you initially install SMS on the site server domain and add a client to the site server domain, you may see the following message when running Program Group Control:

```
Program Group Control: Could not open the application database due to a SMS
profile error.
```

If you add a client to the site by running the SMSLS batch file (or Client Setup) from a logon server with no servers in the [Servers] section, Program Group Control displays this message.

After you initially install SMS on the site server domain, you should ensure that all the logon servers are listed in the [Servers] section of the DOMAIN.INI file on the SMS_SHR share of each logon server in the site server domain. You can correct this error by running the SMSLS batch file or Client Setup again when one or more servers are listed in the [Servers] section of DOMAIN.INI.

When a computer running a network application logs on, the user may see the following message:

```
Failed to connect to SMS network server. Cannot determine which groups the users
belong to. Please contact your administrator.
```

This message means that the client cannot see any of the package servers that it is supposed to see. To correct this problem, follow these steps:

1. Check the SMSERROR.TXT file in the Windows directory on the client. This file may contain more specific information regarding the failure. You may find sufficient information here to correct the problem.

2. Check the [Servers] section of the SMS.INI file on the client. Set up a network connection to the SMS_SHR share of one of the servers listed in this section. Within the SMS_SHR share, change to the APPCTL.BOX\DATABASE directory and look for files with the .HAF and .HGF extensions. If you cannot find files with these extensions, the site

administrator may not have distributed a program group for the network applications to this site, or the client may not have the appropriate security credentials to see files in the share.

For shared network applications, SMS does not install program items in program groups other than the program groups SMS creates. If an application normally installs an icon in another program group (such as Startup), you can copy the necessary program item from an SMS program group to the other program group. For applications with program items in non-SMS program groups, you should also make sure the Drive Mode setting for the package properties is either Runs With UNC Name or Requires Specific Drive Letter.

After you upgrade the SMS software on an SMS logon server, all clients must run SMSLS.BAT (or the user must run his or her logon script, if that script runs SMSLS.BAT) before trying to run any shared applications made available by SMS.

USING NETWORK APPLICATIONS

If a user starts an application shared on SMS and then leaves it unattended, the application may fail if the server disconnects the client. To prevent this problem, you can turn off the autodisconnect feature on the distribution servers for shared applications.

If a client is configured to use some server applications made available by SMS that use the MSAPPS directory, and the client has applications (not using SMS) that also use MSAPPS installed directly on it, the locally installed applications will not function properly if a Remove Package From Server job is used to remove the MSAPPS directory from the server. In this case, the client's references to the MSAPPS directory will then point to the nonexistent server version.

You must check to see if your clients in a child site receive packages for shared applications from both their site and that site's parent site. If a client receives a package that uses MSAPPS from the client's site (a child site), a Registry key that refers to the MSAPPS distributed by the child site is created on the client. Later, if packages using MSAPPS are distributed from the parent site to the client, the MSAPPS Registry key is not changed, and still refers to the version from the child site.

If, after that, the administrator decides to make the original MSAPPS package (from the child site) unavailable, the privileges on the MSAPPS Registry entry are set to Deny. Any packages that refer to MSAPPS already distributed from the parent site will no longer work correctly. Also, any new packages installed will generate the following error:

```
MSAPPS is not installed. Would you like to continue anyway?
```

To solve the problem, be sure to delete any old program groups that include MSAPPS after they are no longer being used.

Shared applications made available by SMS cannot support shared documents. A user running an application shared by SMS cannot use documents shared by SMS with that shared application. For example, suppose you have installed Microsoft Word for network sharing. If you also make a package of Word documents for a Share Package On Server job, users of the shared Microsoft Word cannot use the shared documents. You can use the RSAPPCTL.EXE utility to fix any corruption or out-of-date problems with the database of shared applications. You may be directed to use this utility by an error message.

The RSAPPCTL.EXE utility is located in the PSSTOOLS\X86.BIN on the SMS CD.

Usage:

```
RSAPPCTL {/SELF}{/ALL}{/SITE:sitecode}{/SITESERVER:servername}
```

_/SELF	Resets database for this site (but not child sites)
_/ALL	Resets NAD for all child sites (but not this site)
_/SITE:sitecode	Resets NAD for the specified child site
_/SITESERVER:servername	Specifies this site's site server; needed only if RSAPPCTL is not being run on the site server

You can use both the /SELF and /ALL options to do a total reset of the local site and all child sites.

For Share Package On Server jobs that have target distribution servers running NT Server, the Despooler creates two shares when you specify a nested share name and path for the Share Name in the package's Setup Package For Sharing dialog box.

1. The Despooler uses the name at the beginning of the path to share that directory (using the directory name as the share name). For example, if you specify APPS\WIN\EXCEL, the Despooler shares the APPS directory as the APPS share.

2. The Despooler then shares the last directory in the path as an administrative share. Program Group Control uses this share to connect to the package server so that it can start a network application from that share. For example, if you specify APPS\WIN\EXCEL, the Despooler shares the EXCEL directory as the EXCEL$ share.

INSTALLING APPLICATIONS ON CLIENTS

When you use a PDF to create a job to install an application on workstations with a Run Command On Workstation job, you must copy the appropriate SMSPROXY directory to the package source directory before distributing the package to workstations. You can find the SMSPROXY directory in the PRIMSITE.SRC\ IMPORT.SRC*appname* directory. Copying the SMSPROXY directory to the package source directory is required for both Share Package On Server and Run Command On Workstation jobs.

If a computer is running a shared copy of an application, and you want to install a local copy of that application on that computer using a PDF, you must first remove the shared copy of the application. The deinstall program for a shared application is located in a subdirectory of the SMSPROXY directory. For example, the deinstallation program for Microsoft Word is MS\SMS\SMSPROXY\ WINWORD\DEINSTAL.EXE.

Notes on Installing Specific Applications

A few notes pertaining to basic Microsoft Office applications should be discussed. In the future, MS Office should integrate seamlessly with NT Server; however, older versions require some tweaking.

Microsoft Office

When you create the administrative installation of MSOffice version 4.2c or 4.3c, you may see a message stating

```
Setup cannot update the Proofing Tools in the shared location
because the lex formats are incompatible.
```

If you see this message, you can ignore it and continue with the installation. All components of Microsoft Office will work correctly.

Do not remove any program items from a Microsoft Office program group, either before or after the package has been distributed. For example, don't remove the PowerPoint program item from the Office program group. Otherwise, OLE functions and Registry entries will not work properly.

If you set up MSOffice version 4.3 or MS Access version 2.0 as shared applications, the package source directory for the application gives users both Read and Write permissions. This way, users can have the necessary write access to the MS Access file ACS200\WORKDIR\SYSTEM.MDA. These access permissions are set in the ACS200.PDF and OFP43_.PDF files. To protect other files in the package directory from being modified by clients, set the permissions to read-only on each distribution server after the package has been distributed.

When you set up Microsoft Office as a shared application, clients configured to use the shared copy of Microsoft Office cannot be configured to use separate shared copies of any of the Office applications. Do not assign a group the rights to use both a shared version of Microsoft Office and shared copies of any of the following individual applications:

- ◆ MS Word
- ◆ MS Excel
- ◆ MS PowerPoint
- ◆ MS Access

When you set up MSOffice as a shared application, you must set the program items for the MSAPPS applets within the Office package (such as Graph AutoConvert and MS Query) to use the same Drive Mode as the MSAPPS package. For example, if the MS Query program item in the MSAPPS package has Drive Mode: Runs With UNC Name, then the MS Query program item in the MSOffice package must also use the Drive Mode: Runs With UNC Name setting.

Note

If you choose to use a specified drive, you can specify different drives for the corresponding program items in the MSOffice package and the MSAPPS package.

Microsoft Word

When you set up MS Word version 6.0 as a shared application, it may produce an error when NT Workstation version 3.1 users exit the application. This problem does not occur on other types of clients.

Microsoft Access

If you set up MSOffice version 4.3 or MS Access version 2.0 as shared applications, the package source directory for the application gives users both Read and Write permissions. This way, users can have the necessary write access to the MS Access file ACS200\WORKDIR\SYSTEM.MDA. These access permissions are set in the ACS200.PDF and OFP43_.PDF files. To protect other files in the package directory from being modified by clients, set the permissions to read-only on each distribution server after the package has been distributed. For further information, see the MS Access README file.

Microsoft Works

When you use SMS to install MS Works on a server as a shared application, users cannot access the Works tutorial.

Using SMS to Install Operating Systems on Clients

When using SMS to install NT on a client previously running DOS, Windows, or WFW, you should take the following steps:

1. Copy the UNATTEND.SCR file from the LOGON.SRV\MSTEST directory to the package source directory.

2. Edit the UNATTEND.SCR file to make changes as needed for unattended installation of the operating system.

3. If the target clients run just DOS, and not Windows or WFW, you must also copy the DOSNTUPG.EXE, NAMECHGR.EXE, and AIDDOSNT.BAT files from LOGON.SRV\MSTEST to the package source directory.

Use the Windows NT Server Manager to add the computer name of the computer on which Windows NT is being installed to the domain. You can upgrade a group of computers from DOS, Windows, or Windows for Workgroups to Windows NT with a single job. When you do so, all computers being upgraded will use a single UNATTEND.SCR file. UNATTEND.SCR includes data about the operating system and network card type and card parameters. So, if you want the setup to be automated, then each job must target only computers with identical operating systems and network card setup data. You can query the SMS computer database to find computers with identical configurations. Computers targeted by a single upgrade job must also all join the same domain or workgroup, as this is specified in UNATTEND.SCR as well.

The default UNATTEND.SCR file (located in the LOGON.SRV\MSTEST directory) documents the settings you need to make in this file. Examine it if you want more information. You cannot use an automated setup to upgrade a NetWare client to WFW. You must perform each step in a NetWare upgrade manually.

On TCP/IP networks, when performing an automated upgrade of a client to Windows NT version 3.5 from a previous version of Windows NT, you must specify an upgrade script. Do so by modifying the command line for the Automated Upgrade for NT Client. In this command line, specify the upgrade script by adding a colon and the name of the script to the /U option at the end of the line. The following is an example of the command line after you make these changes:

```
NTENCAP /NTW WINNT32.EXE /U:NTUPGRAD.SCR
```

The upgrade script you specify must include the !UpgradeEnableDhcp setting, with either yes or no as the value. This setting indicates whether this client will have its TCP/IP address dynamically allocated by DHCP. The NTUPGRAD.SCR file in the LOGON.SRV\MSTEST is a sample script file you can use.

AUTOMATICALLY CONFIGURE WORKSTATION LOGON SCRIPTS

In NT domains, the Automatically Configure Workstation Logon Scripts option modifies only the logon scripts for user accounts that have no existing logon script or have a logon script with a file extension. For example, if a user has a logon script specified as USER.BAT, the Site Configuration Manager modifies the script to include the SMSLS batch file. If a user has a logon script as USER (instead of USER.BAT), the Site Configuration Manager does not modify the script. If you want to set up a user account so that the SMSLS batch file is not added to it, you can specify a logon script with no extension for that user.

NETWORK MONITORING

The network protocol analyzer function of SMS can run on any NT computer. The analyzer works as an agent which can remotely capture, filter, and replay network traffic. The results of the capture can be examined by the SMS administrator. You can decode and analyze the data with the help of the documentation included with SMS which provides a complete list of supported protocols.

The network monitor utility works as a software monitor. You can start the monitor from the PC Properties screen shown in Figure 17.3. You then configure the filter for monitoring all or selected traffic to and from the computer being monitored. After the network monitor program is started it can be treated just as a hardware monitor. You have to understand the mechanics of each kind of protocol you want to monitor.

For example, you could monitor the amount of NetBIOS broadcast activity to locate the source of broadcast storms. This information is useful for troubleshooting network problems in companies that have their network divided into multiple LAN segments, and the bridges or routers between the LAN segments are not configured to forward all network traffic, such as NetBIOS broadcasts.

Another example of activity you can monitor is a case where an SMS administrator connected to LAN segment A can use the Network Monitor utility to view the network activity on LAN segment B. This can be accomplished if the Network Monitoring Agent Service is running on an NT Server or NT Workstation computer on LAN segment B. An SMS administrator can also call into an NT RAS Server that has the Network Monitoring Agent Service started and view the network activity for troubleshooting purposes. The following steps are needed to set up the SMS Network Monitor utility so that it will use the Network Monitoring Agent Service on a remote NT computer:

1. From the Capture menu select Networks.
2. In the Network Information dialog box select Remote.

A screen pops up where you fill in \\<system_name> and check the Slow Link box if the connection to the system running the Network Monitoring Agent Service is via RAS.

INSTALLING AND STARTING THE NETWORK MONITOR SERVICE

The Network Monitoring Agent Service is a component that can be added by clicking the Add Software button in Control Panel Network. By default, this is *not* automatically installed. It does install the following files:

- ◆ BHNT.SYS   The main Network Monitor Driver, under \<winnt_root>\ system32\drivers.

- ◆ BHMON.DLL   This is used by Performance Monitor for the LAN Statistics counters.

- ◆ BHSUPP.DLL   This DLL contains helper functions for the service.

- ◆ NAL.DLL   This DLL is a network abstraction layer.

- ◆ NDIS30.DLL   This component is used to communicate with the NDIS 3 device drivers.

- ◆ RNAL.DLL   The RNAL.DLL (Remote Network Abstraction Layer) performs 99% of the work for the Network Monitor Agent service.

- ◆ NMAGENT.EXE   This is the component that is used to start and stop the service.

- ◆ BHCTRL.CPL   This is the Control Panel application that is added to allow a password to be set for the Network Monitoring Agent Service that must be supplied before the system can be used to monitor remote network activity.

- ◆ BHNETB.DLL   This component handles the NetBIOS communication for the service.

Once installed on a system, the Network Monitoring Agent Service can be started and stopped through Control Panel Services where it is listed as Network Monitoring Agent. The Network Monitoring Agent Service can also be started via the command line by using the following command: NET START NMAGENT.

The following network interface cards have been verified to work with Network Monitor. These network adapters support promiscuous mode.

3Com 3C503 EtherLink II[R] (Coax & TP)
3Com 3C503/16 EtherLink[R] II/16 (Coax & P)
3Com 3C507 EtherLink 16 (Coax & TP)
3Com 3C509 EtherLink III - ISA (Coax, TP and Combo)

3Com 3C579 EtherLink III Adapter - EISA (Coax & TP)
Novell/Eagle Technology NE2000
Novell/Eagle Technology NE3200
Xircom Corporate Series CreditCard Ethernet Adapter

SUMMARY

SMS is a very powerful and complicated piece of software. It requires meticulous planning, execution, and management. If your network needs this package, you have arrived.

Only a well-planned and properly functioning network can benefit or even continue to function when SMS is installed on it.

The fruits of the labor it might take to install and configure SMS on your network are many. You will save time, labor, and money.

- RAS Capabilities

- RAS Components

- NT RAS Installation and Configuration

- RAS Integrated Domain Security

CHAPTER 18

Remote Access Server

RAS   Remote Access Server.

MAC   Medium Access Control, the protocol layer of a LAN, WAN, or network service that lies between the hardware and transport layer protocol layers. A LAN driver is one example of a MAC layer component.

Gateway   A logical component that connects two dissimilar protocols. RAS uses a NetBIOS Gateway to link communications ports to the LAN as if the port were a network device. Other transport protocol stacks are supported between the serial port and the LAN transport protocol through RAS's gateway.

NT's Remote Access Server (RAS) is a dial-in/dial-out server software that enables users to dial in and log on to the NT Server. NT clients can use RAS to dial out to outside services, such as their Internet provider or a Bulletin Board System (BBS). After a connection is established, the user can access all network resources as if they were locally attached to the NT network.

This chapter discusses the functions of RAS and its client components. NT RAS security and firewall construction are also discussed because RAS can be a weak link. You also learn about the configuration of the NT RAS hardware and software and NT RAS administration so that you can take full advantage of the features of NT RAS services.

Network applications using the following protocols can access the NT RAS:

NetBIOS
IPC
Mailslots
Named Pipes
RPC
LAN Manager APIs
TCP/IP Utilities
Sockets

RAS can use Point-to-Point Protocol (PPP) or Serial Line Internet Protocol (SLIP) to frame and transport data over remote links. It can support client services using NetBIOS, NetBEUI, TCP/IP, or IPX during a RAS session. Applications using Windows Sockets, NetWare APIs, and NetBIOS can run remotely using PPP as the framing mechanism. The use of PPP and SLIP provides interoperability with other PPP- and SLIP-enabled products.

RAS CAPABILITIES

RAS provides the functionality outlined in Table 18.1.

TABLE 18.1. RAS FUNCTIONALITY.

OS	# of Port	Protocols	WAN Options
MS-DOS (RAS 1.1a)	1	NetBIOS	Async, X.25
WFW 3.11	1	NetBIOS	Async, X.25, ISDN
NT Workstation 3.1	1	NetBIOS	Async, X.25, ISDN
NT Server	2561	NetBIOS, IP, IPX	Async, X.25, ISDN
Windows 95	1	NetBIOS, IP, IPX	Async, X.25, ISDN

RAS also provides data encryption and compression, while providing security through various authentication procedures, as shown in Table 18.2.

TABLE 18.2. RAS ENCRYPTION, COMPRESSION, AND AUTHENTICATION.

OS	Encryption	Compression	Authentication
MS-DOS(RAS 1.1a)	No	Modem	MS Encrypt, Callback
WFW 3.11	No	Modem	MS Encrypt, Callback, Third Party
NT 3.5x	Yes	Modem, Software	MS Encrypt, Callback, Third Party
Windows 95	Yes	Modem, Software	MS Encrypt, Callback, Third Party

NT RAS implements the following RFCs:

> Requirements for PPP
> PPP
> PPP in HDLC
> PPP over ISDN
> PPP over X.25
> Internet support
> Multiprotocol routing via PPP support
> SLIP
> Van Jacobson TCP/IP header compression
> IP Control Protocol
> Authentication Protocols

18

REMOTE ACCESS SERVER

Integration with NetWare networks
IPXCP
LCP Extensions
NBFCP

POINT-TO-POINT PROTOCOL

Previous versions of RAS functioned as NetBIOS Gateways. Users would make their connections using NetBEUI/NetBIOS and then use other protocols from the server. This capability enabled users to share network resources in a multi-vendor LAN environment but limited them from running applications that relied on the presence of a protocol other than NetBEUI on the client side.

RAS 2.0 architecture continues to support the NetBIOS Gateway, but in addition it enables clients to load any layers of NetBEUI, IPX, and TCP/IP. Applications written to the Windows Sockets, NetBIOS, or IPX interface can now be run on an NT Workstation.

Multi-protocol routing is just one of the benefits of the Point-to-Point Protocol (PPP) in RAS. The Point-to-Point Protocol is a set of industry standard protocols that allow remote access solutions to interoperate in a multi-vendor network. PPP support in NT 3.5 means that workstations running Windows can dial into remote networks through any industry standard PPP server. It also enables an NT Server to receive calls from, and provide network access to, other vendors' remote access workstation software.

The NetBIOS Gateway function is used to support Lotus Notes users. Although Lotus Notes does offer dial-up connectivity, dial-up is limited to the Notes application only. RAS complements this connectivity by providing a low-cost, high-performance remote network connection for Notes users; this connection not only connects Notes, but it also offers file and print services and access to other network resources.

SLIP

SLIP, or Serial Line Internet Protocol, is an older communications standard found in UNIX environments. SLIP does not provide automatic negotiation of network configuration; it requires user intervention. It also does not support encrypted authentication. RAS supports SLIP on the client side so that the clients running NT Workstation can dial into an existing SLIP server. RAS does not provide a SLIP server in NT Server 3.5x.

INTERNET SUPPORT

RAS enables Windows NT and Windows 95 to provide complete services to the Internet. An NT Server-based computer can be configured as an Internet service provider, providing dial-up Internet connections to a client workstation running NT Workstation or Windows 95. A computer running NT Workstation can dial into an Internet-connected NT Server with RAS services enabled or to any one of a variety of industry-standard PPP or SLIP-based Internet servers. The RAS provides a pool of IP addresses that are reserved for static configuration during RAS installation. The IP addresses are automatically assigned to RAS clients using PPP when they dial in. If the administrator sets up the RAS to use a static pool of addresses, all clients dialing into a particular RAS are assigned the same network ID as RAS plus unique host IDs. (Of course, the network administrator must also reserve that range of static addresses on the DHCP server, if present, to make sure that those addresses are not assigned.)

RAS clients can connect to multiple TCP/IP networks that are logically joined (but physically separate) networks sharing the same address space. When it's using multiple connections, the RAS client can still use DNS and WINS for name resolution.

NETWARE NETWORKS

NT Server and RAS integrate into a NetWare network. The RAS clients can run IPX and/or NetBIOS, so all applications that work when directly connected to the network continue to work when remotely connected.

The RAS supports IPX routing, enabling remote clients to gain access to all NetWare resources via the RAS.

SOFTWARE DATA COMPRESSION

Software data compression in RAS increases throughput. Data is compressed by the RAS client, sent over the wire in a compressed format, and then decompressed by the NT RAS. In typical use, RAS software compression doubles effective throughput, except when data has already been compressed.

DATA ENCRYPTION

RAS provides encryption of the data being transferred. This capability is in addition to password encryption. Government agencies, law enforcement organizations, financial institutions, and others benefit from this feature. Microsoft RAS uses the RC4 encryption algorithm of RSA Data Security Inc.

RAS APIs

The RAS APIs are both 16-bit and 32-bit, which enables software developers to create custom, remote-enabled applications that can establish a remote connection, use network resources, and reconnect in the event of a communications link failure. Applications developed using the RAS API are compatible with Windows 95, Windows NT Workstation, NT Server, and Windows for Workgroups (WFW).

WAN SUPPORT FOR X.25 AND INTEGRATED SERVICES DIGITAL NETWORK (ISDN)

All remote clients can use an X.25 network by dialing an X.25 Packet Assembler/Dissembler (PAD). NT Server RAS computers have direct access via X.25 adapters, and NT Workstations have direct X.25 connectivity in addition to asynchronous access to X.25 PADs.

ISDN offers much faster communication speed than a standard telephone line. ISDN communicates at 64 to 128 kbps.

RAS COMPONENTS

RAS service is made up of three components:

RAS User Interface: This component is responsible for all user interaction and includes the Windows GUI and character interfaces.

RAS Service: This component is responsible for providing NetBIOS Gateway, router management, and authentication services.

RAS Subsystem: This component is responsible for providing connection management and integrating drivers for various media and device types.

RAS USER INTERFACE

The RAS user interface components are responsible for collecting and displaying RAS-related information to RAS users. Users are divided into two groups: RAS clients and RAS administrators. RAS clients call the RAS from a remote location, and RAS administrators are responsible for maintaining and monitoring the RAS itself.

In Windows NT RAS, much of the connection-management logic has been moved from the RAS client user interfaces into the RAS Manager (discussed in detail in the "RAS Subsystem" section later in this chapter). This isolates the RAS client user interfaces from most platform-dependent device and media behavior.

The RAS client user interfaces are Windows or character utilities that give the RAS user access to connection, disconnection, and status functionality.

The RAS client user interfaces create and maintain a "phone book," RASPHONE.PBK, containing user-defined connection entries. Each entry in RASPHONE.PBK consists of the connection parameters (such as phone numbers, PAD types, switch types, and so on) required to establish a particular connection. In addition to the basic RAS 1.*x* functionality, the Windows NT RAS client user interface provides optional modem feature support, enhanced X.25 support, and pre-/post-connect switch support.

The Windows NT RAS client user interface can implement a connection over one to four intermediate connections, such as a pre-connect switch to a modem to an X.25 PAD to a post-connect switch. In addition, a special "terminal" switch is provided (found under the Advanced Phone Book Entry dialog box, Switch button). This switch enables the user to interact directly with a pre- or post-connect device, such as a security box.

The RAS Character User Interface, RASDIAL.EXE, is very similar to the RAS 1.*x* RASDIAL utility. The main differences are as follows:

◆ An entry name is not necessary to delete a connection, unless more than one connection is active.

◆ The /DEVICE switch may be used to specify certain dial time parameters for batch operations.

◆ All new connection types supported by the graphical interface are supported, except for connections using interactive Terminal mode.

RAS Administration User Interface is an NT utility that enables administrators to monitor RAS clients on a domain and RAS ports on a specific server. From the RAS Admin utility, the administrator can disconnect and send messages to connected RAS clients, as well as start, stop, pause, and continue the Remote Access service on a RAS. In addition, the administrator can grant and/or revoke RAS permissions, including setting preset callback numbers on RAS.

The Windows NT RAS Admin utility allows RAS to be administered remotely (from the Server menu's Select Domain or Server option).

Note

Currently, no command-line RAS administration utility is available.

RAS SERVICE COMPONENT

The RAS Server component does the following:

- ◆ Provides NetBIOS Gateway services
- ◆ Manages routing tables
- ◆ Connects remote clients with the appropriate RAS services
- ◆ Provides authentication of remote clients
- ◆ Manages RAS connections

RAS Server has three functional areas:

> The RAS Supervisor
> The Authentication Service
> The NetBIOS Gateway

THE RAS SUPERVISOR

The RAS Supervisor starts the appropriate services according to the Registry configuration entries, checks the RAS endpoints, and answers incoming phone calls.

The RAS Supervisor is the local process that represents connected users, establishes channels for the Service Controller, and initiates services and user interface.

This service receives connection requests and initiates the requested services. When the call is terminated, the Supervisor closes out all services related to the endpoint and cleans up all remaining connection services.

THE AUTHENTICATION SERVICE

If the incoming call is a connection request, read and write APIs handle the transfer of data to the client connection. Once authentication occurs, APIs connect the client to the RAS endpoint.

THE NETBIOS GATEWAY

The NetBIOS Gateway forwards NetBIOS requests to the network. RAS makes all NetBIOS requests to the network on behalf of its clients.

RAS SUBSYSTEM

The RAS Subsystem handles connection management to the LAN via drivers. The following are components of the RAS Subsystem.

The RAS Manager is a user mode process that implements RAS APIs between the RAS services for the RAS Server and the RAS user interface to make RAS services available. RAS Manager arbitrates port usage between various applications and interfaces such as the RAS Gateway and the RAS user interface.

RASMAN.EXE is an NT service that owns handles to other entities (such as RASHub), ports and device-specific modules (such as MODEM.INF).

RASMAN and other processes attach to RASMAN.DLL, which contains the RASMAN API entry points.

Media DLLs control and communicate over various types of data connections such as ISDN, X.25, and so on. RAS Manager provides a logical interface between the endpoint and the media without media-specific knowledge. Even RAS Manager is media independent because of RAS Manager's abstraction.

Device DLLs provide the interface to devices such as modems, DSUs, switches, and so on. Device DLLs export APIs to enable communication with intermediate devices and interfaces with RASHub.

RASHUB

RASHub is a device driver that is NDIS 3.0 compliant and provides an interface between transport protocols and MACs. It acts as a switchboard to pass LAN frames between the LAN drivers and NetBEUI, NetBIOS, NWLink (IPX), or IP. RASHub looks like a normal NDIS network interface card driver. To the network interface card driver, RASHub looks like a transport protocol. After the bind occurs, RASHub becomes the RAS MAC, which becomes the point at which remote clients enter the network.

RASHub can interface with NDIS 3.0 network interface card drivers only. Only one binding is necessary, regardless of how many endpoints are being serviced.

RASHub exports the "Hub interface," which is a control interface. RAS Manager queries configuration data from RAS Manager through this interface. It provides a method which allows RAS Manager to determine the endpoints it will service, and which DLLs must be used to provide service to the endpoints.

THE ASYNCMAC

The AsyncMAC driver interfaces the RASHub to one or more serial ports. It is also an NDIS 3.0 driver that binds any network interface card drivers with serial port drivers. RAS Manager can therefore interface with both the Windows NT serial I/O interface and NDIS 3.0.

AsyncMAC converts data streams from the serial port to the NDIS interface, and it can implement compression/decompression algorithms.

WFW RAS

After you connect to a RAS under WFW, connections to other machines on the remote network are not possible.

The WFW RAS allows a point-to-point connection only. Therefore, the RAS client can use only resources local to the RAS. No other network access is provided. This product-security feature is implemented because WFW provides share-level, not user-level, security.

NT RAS INSTALLATION AND CONFIGURATION

You install NT RAS client and server software by opening the Control Panel and then choosing the Network icon. The RAS Setup utility is self-explanatory, and online help is available if needed. After RAS has been installed, the administrator must grant users permission to use RAS through the RAS Admin utility.

RAS REQUIREMENTS

The following is required to install RAS:

◆ One or more compatible modems

◆ An X.25 smart card, if using an X.25 network

◆ A multiport adapter card, if using more than two modems

Note

Hardware drivers required for multiport cards must be loaded and configured before you install NT RAS.

POTENTIAL CONFLICTS

You may be unable to access a serial port in a communication application while the NT server software is running. For example, if the RAS service is running, and you have configured RAS so that your modem on COM1 accepts RAS dial-in, the following error message appears if you attempt to use COM1 in Windows Terminal:

```
The selected COM port is either not supported or is being used by another device
Select another port
```

By writing a simple batch file, you can temporarily disable the RAS service so that you can use the COM port to dial out using another communications application.

Use the following batch file to stop the RAS service temporarily and run Windows Terminal or another communications application:

```
net stop remoteaccess
c:\winnt\ayatem32\terminal.exe
net start remoteaccess
```

Save the batch file and create an icon for it. The batch file disables the RAS service, making the port available for dial-out, and then it restarts the RAS service after you quit your communications application.

Note

Writing a batch file is not necessary if you dial out using the RAS client software. The RAS client temporarily disables the RAS service so that the port can be used for dialing out. Stopping the RAS service stops the service for all serial ports that have been configured to allow dial-in. If you have multiple ports configured for dial-in, you might want to reserve one of the ports for dial-out by not configuring it to allow RAS dial-in rather than disabling the RAS service. Only user accounts that have permission to start and stop a service can use this workaround.

JOINING A DOMAIN AS A RAS CLIENT

The following steps are required to use RAS as the network link when joining a domain. This capability is useful when a remote user does not have access to a WAN but can dial out and connect to the remote network through RAS. Creating a domain account for your NT RAS client enables you to be validated by a PDC on the NT network and to access domain resources using the same user account you use at the office.

1. If you haven't already done so, install Windows NT on your RAS client computer. Configure it as a member of a Workgroup, not a Domain.

2. Run Control Panel and choose Network.

3. Choose the Add Software button to install RAS.

4. Use RAS to connect to a RAS on the remote domain. This step requires that the RAS has granted dial-in permission for your account.

5. Create a computer account for your RAS client computer on the remote domain, as follows:

18

REMOTE ACCESS SERVER

Run Control Panel and choose Network.

Choose the Domain or Workgroup Change button.

Choose the Domain option button and type the name of the remote domain you want to join.

Select Create Computer Account in Domain.

Type the name of an Administrator user account and password in the domain you are joining.

If this procedure is successful, the following message appears:

Welcome to the *<domain name>* domain.

Shut down and restart Windows NT.

6. Attach to the network (using RAS) so that a domain list can be created, as follows:

Log on to Windows NT using a local user account.

Use RAS to connect to a RAS on the remote domain.

From the Program Manager's File menu, choose Logoff. The RAS connection is maintained.

Press Ctrl+Alt+Del to log on. The domain list is created through the RAS link.

Log on to the remote domain.

Note

After you have logged on to the remote domain once, your domain credentials are cached locally. Therefore, you do not have to repeat Step 5 when you log onto the remote domain again.

RAS INTEGRATED DOMAIN SECURITY

The RAS uses the same account database established on the NT PDC Server. Using the same database ensures that the user will have the same privileges and permissions that he or she would normally have if he or she were in the office. To use RAS, a user's account must have specific RAS permission as well as be a valid NT account.

CHALLENGE HANDSHAKE AUTHENTICATION PROTOCOL (CHAP)

The Challenge Handshake Authentication Protocol (CHAP) negotiates authentication by both servers and clients. It activates the highest level of secure encryption supported on either the client or the server. It also provides protection for passwords using a challenge-response mechanism in each response, negotiating one-way encryption from the "most-secure" to the "least-secure" environment.

CHAP can use various encryption algorithms, including DES and RSA Security Inc.'s MD5. DES encryption is used when both the client and the server are using RAS. Sessions between NT 3.5, WFW, and Windows 95 computers use DES. If a third-party application does not support encryption, RAS negotiates either SPAP or clear text authentication. MD5 is most often negotiated when a RAS client using PPP connects to a third-party remote access server.

Shiva LAN Rover uses Shiva Password Authentication Protocol (SPAP). A two-way (reversible) encryption mechanism is used when an NT 3.5x Workstation connects to a Shiva LAN Rover or when a Shiva client connects to an NT Server. SPAP is more secure than clear text but less secure than CHAP.

When a more secure authentication mechanism cannot be employed, Password Authentication Protocol (PAPI) is used to send clear text passwords. This method is used only when all other more secure authentication exchanges fail. Clear text passwords can be blocked, providing a high level of password security.

THIRD-PARTY FIREWALL PROTECTION

A firewall blocks users from accessing outsider resources and blocks outside users from accessing inside resources. You can connect an intermediary security host between clients and servers to provide additional security.

USER DISCONNECTION

The administrator can disconnect individual active users without disturbing other active users by using the RAS Admin utility.

AUDITING

RAS can save audit information on all remote connections if auditing is enabled. Auditing tracks usage including authentication, logons, and other usage-related options.

RESTRICTED NETWORK ACCESS

Users can be permitted to access resources on the network or can be restricted to RAS access only. The RAS client can use the RAS Gateway to access all loaded transport protocols, or you can limit access to one or more of the transports, provided sufficient permissions are assigned.

Callback Security

The RAS can call a client back at a preset number, a specified number, or not at all. The default is to call back at a preset number. It is recommended that you use this option for best security. Callbacks are made after authentication has cleared the client but prior to logon.

How RAS Logon Security Works

The following sequence occurs when a RAS call comes in:

1. The RAS challenges the incoming caller.
2. The client sends an encrypted response.
3. RAS compares the client account against its security account database locally or at a domain controller.
4. If the user account and password are valid, the RAS checks its RAS database for permission to proceed.
5. If access is permitted, the RAS provides a connection for the client.
6. If callback is enabled for the incoming client, the RAS calls the client back, and Steps 1 to 5 are repeated.
7. The client is then given a Welcome Logon screen. The user inputs his or her username, workgroup or domain, and the password. The domain controller or NT server authenticates the user and provides access to network resources.

RAS Configuration Files

The following RAS configuration files are located in the \<WINNT ROOT> \SYSTEM32\RAS subdirectory:

MODEM.INF
PAD.INF
SWITCH.INF
RASPHONE.PBK
SERIAL.INI

MODEM.INF

Modem definitions are stored in the MODEM.INF file including modem configuration parameters, setup strings, flow control, compression, speaker control, and so on. Most popular modems are supported, and you should not edit this file.

PAD.INF

The PAD.INF file contains configuration data for many X.25 Packet Assembler/ Dissemblers (PADs). Most popular PADs are supported, and you can add sections for PADs that are not supported. Other modifications are not advised.

SWITCH.INF

The SWITCH.INF file contains configuration data for intermediary devices. You can add sections for devices that are not supported. Other modifications are not advised.

RASPHONE.PBK

Data entered into the RAS Phone Book utility is stored in the RASPHONE.PBK file. You should not make manual changes to this file.

SERIAL.INI

The SERIAL.INI file contains configuration data for RAS communication ports and the devices connected to the ports. You can view or edit the configuration options by opening the Control Panel and choosing the Network icon. You should not manually edit this file.

EDITING THE REGISTRY FOR RAS

RAS's default values are okay for normal conditions. However, you may want to adjust some Registry values to provide better performance and security.

Note

The RAS default values use the REG_DWORD data type unless otherwise noted.

You can adjust the following categories in the Registry:

General Remote Access Parameters
NetBIOS Gateway Parameters
AsyncMac Parameters
RASHub Parameters

GENERAL REMOTE ACCESS PARAMETERS

You can adjust the Registry parameters shown in Table 18.3. You can find the entries under the following subkey:

```
SYSTEM\CurrentControlSet\Services\RemoteAccess\Parameters
```

TABLE 18.3. RAS REGISTRY PARAMETERS AND VALUES.

Parameter	Range	Default	Description
AuthenticateRetries	0–10	2	Sets the maximum number of unsuccessful retries at authentication.
AuthenticateTime	20–600 sec	120	Sets the maximum amount of time a user is allowed to finish authentication.
CallbackTime	2–12 sec	2	Sets the time interval the server waits before calling the client back; the client communicates the value of its own callback time when connecting to a Remote Access server. If the client does not communicate a callback time value (as with Remote Access 1.0 and 1.1 clients), the value of this parameter is used.
EnableAudit	0=disabled, 1=enabled	1	Enables or disables Remote Access auditing.

Parameter	Range	Default	Description
NetbiosGatewayEnabled	0=disabled, 1=enabled	1	Makes the server function like a NetBIOS gateway, enabling clients to access the LAN. If disabled, remote clients can access the files on the server in a point-to-point connection only.
NumRecvQueryIndications	1–32	3	Enables Remote Access clients to initiate simultaneous, multiple network connections.

NetBIOS Parameters

You can adjust the RAS NetBIOS Gateway in the Registry parameters shown in Table 18.4. You can find the entries under the following subkey:

```
SYSTEM\CurrentControlSet\Services\RemoteAccess\Parameters\NetbiosGateway\Parameters
```

TABLE 18.4. RAS REGISTRY NetBIOS GATEWAY PARAMETERS AND VALUES.

Parameter	Range	Default	Description
AutoDisconnect	0–60000 sec	1200	Number of seconds before an inactive connection is terminated. Setting this parameter to 0 disables it. It is recommended to set this parameter to 0 when using

continues

18

REMOTE ACCESS SERVER

Table 18.4. continued

Parameter	Range	Default	Description
			NetBIOS applications.
DisableMcastFwd	0=disabled, 1=enabled	1	Establishes WhenSessionTraffic priority over multicasts. Multicast datagrams are sent only when connection is dormant.
EnableBroadcast	0=disabled, 1=enabled	0	Controls whether broadcasts are forwarded to disconnect clients. See MulticastForwardRate.
MaxBcastDgBuffered	16–255	32	Configures number of gateway buffers for broadcast datagrams.
MaxDgBufferedPer	1–255	10	Configures the numbers of GroupName datagram broadcasts per group.
MaxDynMem	131072-4294967295	655350	Configures the amount of virtual memory allocated for NetBIOS buffers for each remote client session. (See Note 1, below.)
MaxNames	1–255	255	Configures the number of NetBIOS names per client.

18

Parameter	Range	Default	Description
			Each client session uses several NetBIOS names. Up to 255 names are allowed for all clients. A value of 3 normally supports up to 64 users.
MaxSessions	1-255	255	Configures the number of simultaneous NetBIOS sessions per user. (See Note 2, below.)
MultiCast	−1 to 4294967295 sec	5	Configures `ForwardRate` broadcast announcements for group names in a domain. −1—Disables forwarding; 0—Guarantees delivery of group name datagrams; and n—Forwards datagrams every n seconds. (See Note 3, below.)
RcvDgSubmitted	1–32	3	Configures the number of NetBIOS `PerGroupName` Receive Datagram commands that can be handled at one time. Reduce this number to the lowest level

continues

TABLE 18.4. CONTINUED

Parameter	Range	Default	Description
			possible. Each datagram uses 1500K of memory.
RemoteListen	0–2	1	Configures level of remote NCB_LISTENS. 0—Client cannot submit NCB_LISTEN; 1—Remote client can receive messages from LAN users and printers, and the client can submit NCB_LISTEN for NT aliases only (default, recommended); and 2—Enables all NCB_LISTENS for RAS clients' NetBIOS names. A value of 2 allows server applications to act as servers on the network. (See Note 4, below.)
SizWorkBufs	1024–65536	4500	Configures the work buffer size for SMB protocol.

Note

1. Because RAS synchronizes data flow between slower serial ports and faster LANs, buffers must be allocated to provide flow control. RAS minimizes memory usage by locking approximately 64K per client (minimum number of pages of memory). Virtual

memory is employed whenever more than 64K of memory is required.

2. Set NBF (network buffers size) to 3 (large) to remove the memory limitation for the gateway buffers when NetBEUI is used.

   A value of 2 limits the net buffer size to 300K, which is enough for about 64 normal connections. The Registry subkey for this parameter is

   `SYSTEM\CurrentControlSet\Services\Nbf\Parameters`

3. When many servers are in your domain, broadcasts may occupy an excessive amount of bandwidth on the remote (serial) connection. These broadcasts can be limited by filtering server announcements without compromising any connectivity or service. You can manipulate the `MultiCastForwardRate` parameter to filter server announcements by forwarding them at renamed intervals.

   An `EnableBroadcast` value of 0 disables forwarding of broadcasts. `MultiCastForwardRate` is disabled regardless of whether you set this parameter to 0 or –1 broadcasts. (See the `EnableBroadcast` parameter.)

4. `NCB_LISTEN` uses extensive system resources and affects performance. Set `RemoteListen` to a value of 2 so that all NetBIOS names will be handled for remote clients.

   A typical NT Server has about 5 NetBIOS names. The typical value for total NetBIOS names of an `NCB_LISTEN` value is therefore 5 times 64, or 320 (the maximum number of clients per RAS).

Async MAC Parameters

You can adjust Async MAC parameters in the Registry, as shown in Table 18.5. You can find the entries under the following subkey:

`SYSTEM\CurrentControlSet\Services\AsyncMacn\Parameters`

TABLE 18.5. RAS ASYNC MAC PARAMETERS.

Parameter	Range	Default	Description
FramesPerPort	2–20	3	Configures the number of outstanding frames per port.

continues

TABLE 18.5. CONTINUED

Parameter	Range	Default	Description
IrpStackSize	1–10	5	Configures the number of device driver stacks. The default is adequate, except when errors are noted.
MaxFrameSize	576–1514	1514	Configures the frame size. Use a smaller frame size when transmission data errors are detected.

RASHUB PARAMETERS

You can adjust RASHub parameters in the Registry, as shown in Table 18.6. You can find the entries under the following subkey:

SYSTEM\CurrentControlSet\Services\RasHub\Parameters

TABLE 18.6. RASHUB REGISTRY PARAMETERS.

Parameter	Description
NetworkAddress	Used for MAC local node addresses in place of the preconfigured IEEE universal address. When you're using local addresses, only the first 4 bytes are used. You can edit this parameter in the RasHub\Parameters subkey. Note that this parameter is the only one that uses the REG_SZ data type instead of the REG_DWORD data type.

SUMMARY

This chapter discusses various considerations in the setup, use, and configuration of RAS, which is a robust and respectable dial-in/dial-out server product that is included in NT at no additional cost. You install RAS by opening the Control Panel and then choosing the Network icon. Setup and installation are simple.

Via the RAS Gateway service, you can connect remote clients as if they were local to the LAN. Several protocols and other options are available.

- SQL Server Networking Overview

- Installing SQL Server

- Starting SQL Server

- Devices and Databases

- Configuring Memory Usage

- Other Configuration Issues

- Administration

- SQL Server Registry Entries

CHAPTER 19

SQL Server

The availability of SQL Server for NT is significant because it brings client/server computing to the masses. SQL Server running on the NT Server provides scalable transaction processing on a magnitude that has traditionally been available only in a mainframe environment. You can scale your SQL Server applications up to multiprocessor Intel Pentium computers or onto powerful RISC platforms.

SQL Server is also a significant product because it is the underlying database used by Microsoft add-on modules such as the SMS Server and Exchange Server. SQL Server has been around for a long time and is a sweet-tempered and elegant piece of software. On the other hand, SQL Server is a powerful program and can be difficult to manage if the administrator is not familiar with it.

The discussion of SQL Server is included in this book because network administrators often must manage SQL Server as part of their network administration duties. Traditionally, client/server databases were installed on UNIX computers and required a dedicated database administrator. SQL Server for NT breaks that mold, and as a result, more and more network administrators need help with it. SQL Server is an environment within an environment; for example, backing up and restoring databases are specific and different from the way spreadsheet files are backed up and restored. In the case of SQL Server for NT, the overlaps between NT Server functions and SQL Server functions are greater; for example, integrated security enables you to administer user accounts in only one place.

The following are the features of SQL Server for NT:

◆ The Symmetric Server architecture allows SQL Server to scale up to symmetric multiprocessor servers, with support for Intel and RISC computers. SQL Server dynamically balances the processor load across multiple CPUs and provides a preemptive multithreaded design for improved performance and reliability.

◆ NT provides preemptive scheduling, virtual paged memory management, symmetric multiprocessing, and asynchronous I/O, which is a strong foundation of a mission-critical database server platform. Integration with the NT operating system improves operational control and ease of use. Administrators can manage multiple SQL Servers across distributed networks using graphical tools for configuration, security, database administration, performance monitoring, event notification, and unattended backup.

◆ Unified logon security with NT security means that authorized users do not have to maintain separate SQL Server logon passwords and can bypass a separate logon process for SQL Server. Additionally, SQL Server applications can take advantage of NT security features, which include encrypted passwords, password aging, domain-wide user accounts, and Windows user administration.

◆ NT provides an ideal platform for building powerful 32-bit client/server applications for SQL Server. The SQL Server Programmer's Toolkit contains a 32-bit Win32 version of the DB-Library application programming interface.

◆ SQL Server is interoperable with SQL Server for OS/2, as well as with the Sybase SQL Server for the UNIX and VMS operating systems. Existing applications work unchanged. SQL Server operates across all corporate network environments, including Novell NetWare and TCP/IP LANs.

◆ Enterprise interoperability is network independence. SQL Server can support clients communicating over multiple heterogeneous networks simultaneously, with no need for additional integration products. SQL Server communicates on named pipes (over either NetBEUI or TCP/IP network protocols) with Windows, NT, DOS, and OS/2 clients. In addition, SQL Server can simultaneously support TCP/IP Sockets for communication with Macintosh, UNIX, or VMS clients, and SPX Sockets for communications in a Novell NetWare environment. It also supports DECnet Sockets, AppleTalk, and Banyan VINES. SQL Server leverages the power, ease of use, and scalability offered by the NT operating system to manage large databases for mission-critical applications.

SQL SERVER NETWORKING OVERVIEW

This section explores the various network transport protocol options that are available with SQL Server for NT and also details which configuration options to use with those protocols.

An interprocess communication (IPC) mechanism and a network transport protocol are different. An IPC is used to allow processes or threads to communicate with each other, either on the same computer or across a network. A network transport protocol is the mechanism responsible for carrying data over the network. IPC is independent of the network transport protocol. This way, for example, named pipes can be used over NetBEUI or TCP/IP.

Applications communicate with SQL Server using either DB_Library or ODBC calls. These API calls then communicate with the Net_Library, which abstracts the applications from the transport protocols. Several Net_Libraries can be loaded, depending on the type of IPC (such as named pipes or sockets) being used. Figure 19.1 shows the mechanism by which SQL Server communicates with clients and other SQL Servers.

For DOS clients, Net_Libraries are implemented as TSRs. For Windows 3.x, NT, and OS/2 clients, they are DLLs; this allows the concurrent use of multiple Net Libraries. The server Net_Libraries are also DLLs; this way SQL Server can

19

SQL SERVER

respond to clients on multiple connection types (such as sockets or named pipes) over multiple network transport protocols (such as NetBEUI, TCP/IP, or NWLink IPX/SPX). This capability also makes SQL Server accessible by many different clients.

Figure 19.1.
SQL Server
networking.

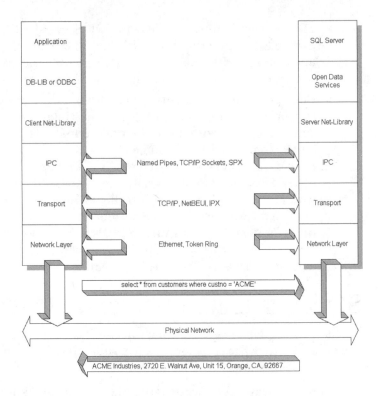

OPEN DATA SERVICES

Open Data Services is a server-side development platform that provides application services to work with the client-side APIs. Open Data Services provides multithreaded server applications to communicate with DB_Library or ODBC clients over the network. When the client requests data, Open Data Services passes the request to user-defined routines and then routes the reply back to the client over the network. To the client, the reply seems to be coming from SQL Server.

Open Data Services' server library can receive, parse, reformulate, and send TDS packets from many concurrent clients. It uses the multithreading facilities of NT to handle simultaneous requests in a fast, memory-efficient way.

On the NT platform, Open Data Services can load multiple server-side Net_Libraries concurrently. This way, applications based on Open Data Services can communicate natively with clients on different network protocols concurrently. It uses the same multithreaded architecture as SQL Server for NT.

SQL BRIDGE

SQL Bridge is a server application on Open Data Services technology. It acts as a protocol router. SQL Bridge uses the Net_Library architecture to support the IPC mechanisms used by SQL Server running on the OS/2, NT, UNIX, or VMS platforms. Each instance of SQL Bridge checks for TDS messages from clients using a particular IPC mechanism (named pipes, TCP/IP sockets) and then routes the TDS message to SQL Server using a different IPC mechanism. Results are received from SQL Server, translated to the client IPC protocol, and then sent to the client.

Using SQL Bridge in environments where communication is required between Windows and Sybase clients and servers can reduce cost and maintenance overhead, as well as free up resources on each client because loading multiple network protocols and Net_Libraries is not necessary. Because SQL Bridge uses the Net_Library architecture to support the various IPC mechanisms, you can configure and extend it.

The only function of SQL Bridge is to look for TDS messages coming in and to reroute them using a different IPC mechanism. Because it is optimized for SQL Server client/server communication, you should notice very little overhead when using SQL Bridge.

INSTALLING SQL SERVER

Installing SQL Server is the start of the overall configuration process and is relatively simple. SQL Server also enables you to update its setup easily without jeopardizing the integrity of user databases.

The purpose of the installation program is to expand SQL Server files on your hard disk and run procedures and utilities to autoconfigure SQL Server to match the resources available on your NT Server. SQL Server needs some databases, tables, and procedures for internal use; they are automatically created at installation time. The NT Server Registry entries are also created at this time.

At the end of the installation sequence, you will see the program group and icons for various SQL Server tools being created.

Follow these steps to install SQL Server:

1. In File Manager, select SETUP.EXE in the \I386 (or appropriate) directory of your SQL Server CD-ROM (there are different directories for RISC computers). The NT Options dialog box appears.

2. From the SQL Server for NT Options dialog box, select the Install SQL Server and Utilities option.

19

SQL SERVER

3. Choose the Continue button.

4. Follow the on-screen instructions.

Figures 19.2 and 19.3 show the initial steps needed to install SQL Server. See Figures 19.4 and 19.5 also.

Figure 19.2.
SQL Server installation
Welcome screen.

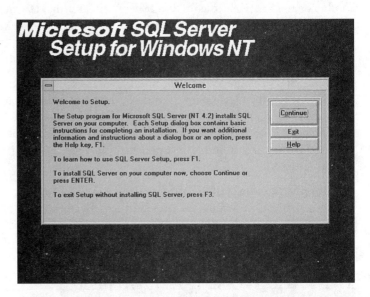

Figure 19.3.
SQL Server Setup-
Options.

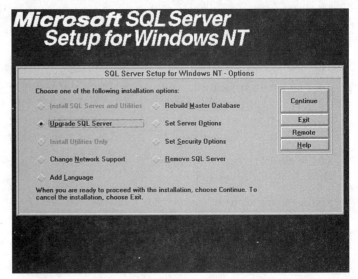

INSTALLING UTILITIES

SQL Server includes server as well as client utilities used for database and network tasks. The client utilities are automatically installed on the server, but you need to install the client utilities on remote computers. You can choose the Remote button on the SQL Server for NT Options dialog box, and you see the Remote Setup dialog box as shown in Figure 19.4.

Figure 19.4.
Remote utility installa-
tion.

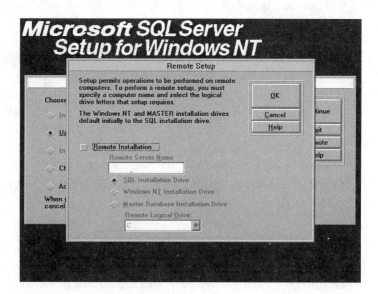

REINSTALLATION

If, for some reason, you have to reinstall NT Server, the registry may no longer have entries for SQL Server, and if you are using integrated security, you need to restore the usernames. The SQL Server Setup program includes an option that rebuilds the registry entries.

To re-register SQL Server, you need to make sure that the Setup program is in the NT Server's path. You add the path permanently by opening the Control Panel and then choosing the System icon. Or you can use the following commands to add the SQL Server directory to the path. Then you can run the Setup program to rebuild the Registry. The options to the Setup program are case sensitive and must be typed exactly as shown. Also, you must include a space on either side of the equal sign. This example assumes that SQL Server was installed on drive C:

```
set path=C:\SQL\DLL;%PATH%
cd \sql\binn
setup /t RegistryRebuild = On
```

19

SQL SERVER

At this point, you need to answer the questions exactly as you did during the initial installation. The Setup program reinserts all the entries into the registry but will not install or change any files.

If SQL Server was set up to use integrated security, you need to reenter all the users and groups that you had previously added by using the SQL Security Manager. The SQL Security Manager recognizes that the users already exist in SQL Server and will not modify it, but the Security Manager will add the necessary security entries to the NT Server.

Note

If you have to reinstall NT Server to change the domain, then you need to delete and reenter the users in SQL Server because the default domain name changes and will cause the username mapping to fail.

CONFIGURING SQL SERVER FOR NAMED PIPES CLIENTS

Named pipes is the default IPC mechanism, and NetBEUI is the default transport. You do not have to change the defaults if you are going to continue using NetBEUI. Even if you are using TCP/IP as your network transport protocol (instead of or in addition to NetBEUI), you can still use named pipes with SQL Server. The sockets IPC mechanism is not necessary for SQL Server to use TCP/IP as the network transport protocol. The named pipes IPC mechanism also works over SPX when you install the NWLink transport protocol.

Named pipes provide several advantages over sockets:

◆ No additional client Net-Libraries are needed.

◆ SQL Server integrated security is available only for named pipes clients.

◆ Named pipes clients require no additional configuration; sockets clients require a hard-coded TCP/IP address and port.

◆ Adjustable network packet size is available only for named pipe clients.

Note

If you want to use named pipes over TCP/IP, and you want to route to subnets, you can use the LMHOSTS file on NT Server.

CLIENT USING NAMED PIPES

The SQL Server client utilities are installed with named pipes support as the default Net_Library, so no configuration changes are needed on the clients after they are installed.

Note

> You can install the client utilities over the network if you already have a network connection in operation. You can run Setup from the CLIENT directory on the SQL Server for NT CD-ROM.

SQL SERVER USING SPX/IPX

NT Server includes the NWLink protocol (SPX/IPX), which provides communication between an NT Server computer and either another NT or Windows For Workgroups (WFW) client computer or a NetWare workstation. This capability allows SQL Server for NT to act as an application server in NetWare networks, and it accepts connections from DOS, Windows 3.*x*, NT Workstations, or OS/2 clients using IPX/SPX protocols. NT Workstation clients can connect to SQL Server using either named pipes or IPX/SPX over NWLink.

You can configure SQL Server for NWLink via the SQL Server Setup icon:

1. Confirm that NWLink is running.
2. Click the SQL Server Setup icon in the SQL Server for NT program group. The Options dialog box appears.
3. Select the Change Network Support option.
4. From the list of networks, select NWLink IPX/SPX, and then choose the OK button.
5. When prompted for the Novell Bindery Service Name (the default is the computer name of the server that contains the bindery), accept the default name or enter a different name. Then choose the Continue button.
6. Restart SQL Server.

CLIENT USING SPX/IPX

You also need to configure the client to use the proper Net_Library. You can use the Client Configuration Utility included with SQL Server for NT. You also can use the SQL Client Configuration Utility to set the network address of SQL Server, enabling you to make direct connections without accessing the Novell Bindery.

19

SQL SERVER

WFW CLIENTS ON NETWARE NETWORKS

When running NT/SQL Server in a NetWare network, you can use the Network Setup in WFW to install and configure several client options. When you choose the Networks button in Network Setup, you get these options:

◆ If you choose Windows support only for a Novell network (no Windows network support), you will be using Novell's IPX/SPX protocol (IPXODI.COM). This protocol supports SPX as the IPC mechanism to access SQL Server. Use the SQL Server Client Configuration Utility to set the default Net_Library to Novell IPX/SPX. This way, WFW clients can connect to SQL Server for NT using the native IPX/SPX protocol. For DOS applications, run DBMSSPX.EXE to load the Net_Library support.

◆ If you choose Windows network support with no additional network, you can still use an IPX network transport protocol to access SQL Server for NT. Choose the Drivers button to confirm that the IPX/SPX Compatible Transport with NetBIOS is loaded in place of, or in addition to, the other protocols. This IPX stack comes with WFW and is similar to NWLink on NT. It supports named pipes as an IPC mechanism, but it does not support the IPX/SPX Net_Library in Windows or DOS. Use the SQL Server Client Configuration Utility to set the default Net_Library to Named Pipes. For DOS applications, run DBNMPIPE.EXE to load the Net_Library support. This setup connects to a SQL Server for NT that is configured to use the NWLink protocol. It does not enable you to connect to a SQL Server running on OS/2 over IPX because the named pipes client in WFW is not designed to interoperate with the named pipes server provided in the Novell OS/2 Requester.

◆ If you choose Windows support for a Novell network in addition to support for Windows networks, then you can use either IPX/SPX or named pipes to communicate with SQL Server for NT. If you use named pipes as the Net_Library, you can connect to SQL Server for NT, but you cannot access a SQL Server running on an OS/2 server due to differences in the Novell named pipes implementation. Unless you need to access SQL Server on both OS/2 and NT, it is recommended that you use the named pipes Net_Library because features such as integrated logon security and adjustable network packet size are available only with named pipes.

The following is a sample of what is added to the WIN.INI for Windows clients communicating with SQL Server on a Novell network:

```
[SQLSERVER]
DSQUERY=DBMSSPX3
```

DOS clients require the same level of IPX that the Windows workstations do. DBMSSPX.EXE must be installed on the DOS computer. This TSR can be loaded either manually or from AUTOEXEC.BAT.

NT client workstations use NWLink, which is installed through the Network Control Panel. After installation, use the Client Configuration Utility to specify that the default network is Novell IPX/SPX. This, in turn, installs the required DBMSSPXN.DLL on the NT client side.

SQL SERVER WITH TCP/IP SOCKETS CLIENTS

To connect to SQL Server for NT from a client using a non-Windows version of TCP/IP (for example, from a UNIX, Macintosh, or other PC TCP/IP client), you must have the correct version of the sockets Open Client (available from Sybase). You need only the client-side Net_Library because the SQL Server for NT provides the server-side Net_Library for TCP/IP sockets. SQL Server for NT includes the Net-Libraries needed for WFW and NT Workstation clients to use standard Windows Sockets as the IPC mechanism across TCP/IP.

The Windows Sockets Net_Library is supported on WFW with TCP/IP for WFW and the Windows 3.1 environment (WOW) of NT version 3.1 and NT Server. The Windows Sockets Net_Library for NT is supported on the NT Workstation and NT Server. The TCP/IP socket Net_Library for DOS is supported for DOS applications running on WFW with TCP/IP for WFW, but it is not compatible with the DOS environment of NT.

To set up SQL Server to allow TCP/IP sockets clients to connect, use the SQL Server Setup program and follow these steps:

1. Confirm that TCP/IP is running.

Warning

If you try to install the TCP/IP connectivity for SQL Server without first installing the TCP/IP protocol on NT Server, you cannot install TCP/IP at all. Doing so may require an NT Server reinstall.

2. Start the setup by choosing the Setup icon in the SQL Server for NT program group. The Options dialog box then appears.
3. Select the Change Network Support option.
4. From the list of networks, select TCP/IP Sockets, and then choose the OK button.

19

SQL SERVER

5. When prompted for the TCP/IP port number, accept the default or enter a different port number. For versions earlier than version 4.21, the default TCP/IP port number is 3180. Beginning with version 4.21, the default port number is 1433, the official Internet Assigned Number Authority (IANA) socket number for SQL Server. After entering the port number, choose the Continue button.

6. Restart SQL Server.

CLIENT USING TCP/IP

You also must configure the client to use the proper Net_Library. You can use the Client Configuration Utility to set up the client.

STARTING SQL SERVER

The first thing you need to do after you finish the installation and connectivity configuration is to design the storage for the databases.

You can set up SQL Server to be started automatically by configuring the Startup option to be Automatic. You configure this option by opening the Control Panel, choosing the Server icon, and then choosing the Services menu option.

During installation, SQL Server sets up the SQL Server program group as shown in Figure 19.5.

Figure 19.5.
The SQL Server
program group.

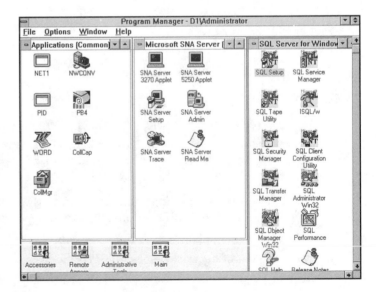

You need to click the SQL Administrator icon. The Connect Server dialog box then opens, as shown in Figure 19.6. In this dialog box, select the SQL Server name and user ID and password to connect to the SQL Server.

Figure 19.6.
The Connect Server
dialog box.

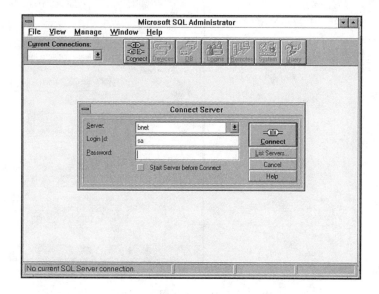

Once connected, you see the screen shown in Figure 19.7 without the Device Management dialog box. Click the Devices button, and the Device Management dialog box appears. This dialog box shows a list of devices that are available or you can create new ones.

Figure 19.7.
Device management.

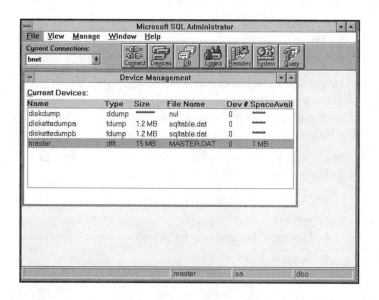

19

SQL SERVER

Click the DB button to access the Database Management window, as shown in Figure 19.8.

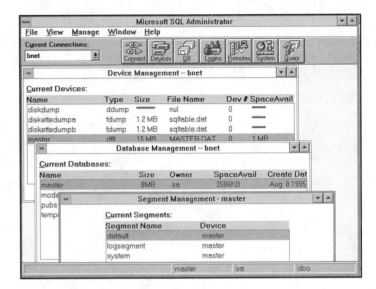

Figure 19.8.
Database management.

Double-click on the database name, and you get the Segment Management window. This shows the segments on which the database resides. You can add segments if you wish.

DEVICES AND DATABASES

SQL Server automatically creates the MASTER device and the MASTER, MODEL, TEMPDB, and PUBS databases. The administrator needs to create the devices and databases that will be used by the applications using SQL Server.

Devices are the operating system container files that act as the receptacle for the databases. Databases are logical structures that then allow the application to create and maintain tables and indexes inside them. Figure 19.9 shows the many ways in which you can configure databases to utilize disk drive storage efficiently.

Many rules and techniques are involved in device and database configuration. The following list is a summary of these techniques:

◆ You should create the devices on multiple disk drives to improve performance.

◆ Multiple devices can exist on the same disk drive.

◆ Devices have segments.

◆ Databases are made up of segments and therefore can span multiple storage devices. This effectively stripes the database for improved performance (see Chapter 2, "NT Design" for more information on striping).

◆ You can extend databases by adding additional segments on existing devices or on new devices that can be on existing or on new disk drives.

◆ Indexes and logs are elements inside a database; they live inside their own segments. As a result, indexes and logs can be on disk drives other than the main database. This is another way of improving performance.

Figure 19.9.
Storage structure.

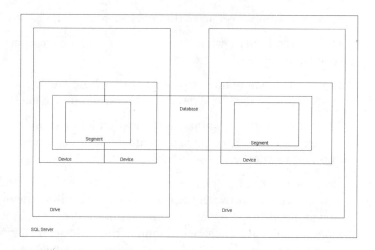

BACKUP AND RECOVERY

Administrators familiar with file-based database applications can relate to backing up files that contain important information because they can tell what data each file contains. In the case of SQL Server-type databases, the files are now tables, and they all reside inside container files called *devices*. You might then ask the question, "Do you back up these container files (which are plain-jane operating system files)?" The answer is no!

The SQL Server database backup is not simply a matter of backing up the media that contains the database but also *meta-data* (information about data). SQL Server provides several means of "dumping" databases in a form that can be used to re-create or load the database back in if it gets damaged or lost due to media failure.

The SQL Administrator applet provides a means of dumping databases by pointing at and clicking the database and selecting the dump device (which is just another operating system file and which is created by the administrator just like any other device). The device can be located on a disk volume or on a tape drive.

19

SQL SERVER

The ISQL command for this operation is

```
DUMP DATABASE database TO device_specification
```

The transaction logs can be dumped in a similar manner:

```
DUMP TRANSACTION database [TO device_specification] WITH TRUNCATE_ONLY ¦
➥WITH NO_LOG ¦ WITH NO_TRUNCATE]
```

This command removes the inactive part of the log after it is copied and then records the action in the active log.

WITH TRUNCATE_ONLY removes the inactive part of the log without making a backup.

WITH NO_LOG is used when the database runs out of space. It does not record the truncated segment in the log.

WITH NO_TRUNCATE makes it possible to back up the log even if the database is not accessible (the database device is damaged but the log device is accessible).

The topic related to database replication is too complicated to address here; just remember that it is possible to conduct online backup of both database information and logs to another "remote" SQL Server.

Recovering data is slightly more complicated because you have to be careful not to trample fresh data with stale copies from the dump device. Most of the time, the server mends itself whenever it is restarted. It does so by using automatic recovery from committed transactions found in the transaction log. You can force the writing of the log to the disk by using a technique called *checkpoint*. A system checkpoint forces pages of data that have been updated since they were last written to the disk.

When the automatic recovery does not work, you have to load a clean copy of your database from the dump device, as follows:

```
LOAD DATABASE database FROM device_specification
```

```
LOAD TRANSACTION database FROM device_specification
```

Unlike backup, recovery is not an online procedure. Usually, administrators load data into a test database and check it thoroughly before loading the real database, especially in case of partial loss of integrity.

Configuring Memory Usage

SQL Server for NT allows use of up to 2GB of virtual memory. Does this mean that if you do not intervene, it will take that memory away from the NOS? What is the optimum amount of memory that should be allocated to SQL Server? These and other questions are discussed in this section. In addition, allocation of memory can be different, depending on various hardware memory configurations.

NT Server provides each Win32 application a 4GB virtual address space, the lower 2GB of which are private per process and available for application use. The upper 2GB are reserved for system use. The 4GB address space is mapped to the available physical memory by the NT Virtual Memory Manager (VMM). The available physical memory can be up to 4GB, depending on the hardware platform.

SQL Server sees only virtual memory, not physical addresses. Virtual memory systems allow the over-committing of virtual memory, such that the virtual memory exceeds physical memory. If this situation is taken to an extreme, then the system will suffer performance degradation because of intensive memory paging. As a rule, SQL Server memory should have a 1:1 ratio of physical memory to virtual memory. Also, the NT Server system memory requirement must be considered; the additional memory for SQL Server should be about 12MB, with some variation depending on other application overhead.

Table 19.1 presents a rough figure of the memory configurations, assuming this computer is going to be a dedicated database server. The final determinant of memory optimization is the SQL Server cache hit ratio parameter as shown in the SQL Performance Monitor.

TABLE 19.1. MEMORY CONFIGURATIONS.

Server Memory	Memory Allocated to SQL Server
16MB	4MB
24MB	8MB
32MB	16MB
48MB	28MB
64MB	40MB
128MB	100MB

19

SQL SERVER

The minimum available memory for an x86 computer on which SQL Server for NT needs to run is 16MB. SQL Server for RISC requires more memory because of the lower density of RISC computer code. Adding more memory is usually a wise and inexpensive investment, and it is common for SQL Servers to be configured for 128MB or more memory, which they put to good use.

The easiest way to optimize memory is to use the SQL Server Performance Monitor and study the cache hit ratio while the system is under different loads. If the hit ratio is over 80 percent, adding memory will not help.

OTHER CONFIGURATION ISSUES

For effective optimization of SQL Server performance, it is necessary to identify the areas that will yield the largest performance increases over the widest variety of situations.

Multi-user concurrence and other issues aside, the greatest improvement in any database performance can be gained from improved logical database design, index design, and query design. If performance is a concern, concentrating on these areas first is wise because you can often achieve very large performance improvements with a relatively small time investment.

Memory configuration has already been discussed, so you know that having adequate memory and system resources definitely helps; however, performance gain from hardware resource optimization is incremental. SQL Server manages available hardware resources automatically, reducing the need for extensive system-level hand-tuning. The fastest computer can be bogged down with inefficient queries. Thus, even with the additional performance capacity SQL Server allows, optimizing the index, database, and query design is important.

EFFICIENT INDEX DESIGN

Unlike nonrelational databases, relational indexes are not part of the logical database design. Indexes can be deleted (dropped), added, and changed without having any impact on the database structure or application design. Experimenting with indexes is necessary to find the "sweet spot" of your database.

The SQL Server optimizer reliably chooses the most effective index in the majority of cases. The strategy is to provide a good selection of indexes to the optimizer and trust it to make the right decision. The following are index recommendations:

◆ Examine the WHERE clause of your SQL queries because it is the primary focus of the optimizer. Each column listed in the WHERE clause is a possible candidate for an index. If you have too many queries to examine, pick a representative set, or just the slow ones. If your development tool transparently generates SQL, picking a set will be more difficult. Many of these tools allow the logging of the generated SQL syntax to a file or screen for debugging purposes.

◆ Use single-column indexes. Single-column indexes are more effective than multi-column indexes. Single indexes have more rows per page and fewer index levels, thus boosting performance. Not many people know that the SQL Server optimizer maintains statistics only on the leftmost column of a multi-column index. If you do not pick the first column carefully, then that index will be ignored by the optimizer. The optimizer can check for hundreds or even thousands of index and join candidates. So provide many small indexes rather than few multi-column indexes. You should not try to design indexes to cover specific queries in the hope that an exact match will result in better performance. More often than not, over time, the query might change slightly, or due to infrequent usage the statistics will not be there, and the optimizer might ignore your carefully matched index. Restrict the number of indexes to those that are necessary to achieve adequate read performance because of the overhead involved in updating those indexes. This is true because even most update-oriented operations require far more reading than writing.

◆ Use clustered indexes; they can tremendously increase performance. In clustered indexes, the logical sequence matches the physical sequence of the index table. Even Update and Delete operations are often accelerated by clustered indexes because these operations require much reading. You can have only a single clustered index per table, so use this index wisely. Queries that return numerous rows or queries involving a range of values are good candidates for performance improvement by the use of a clustered index.

◆ Check for column uniqueness, which will help you decide what column is a candidate for a clustered index, non-clustered index, or no index. This process returns the number of unique values in the column. Compare this number to the total number of rows in the table. On a 20,000-row table, 10,000 unique values would make the column a good candidate for a non-clustered index. On the same table, 50 unique values would better suit a clustered index. Having 15 unique values means that the table should not be indexed at all. Here's a sample query to examine column uniqueness:

```
SELECT COUNT (DISTINCT CUSTKEY) FROM CUSTTABLE.
```

NORMALIZE LOGICAL DATABASE DESIGN

Proper normalization of the logical database design improves performance. Having a greater number of narrow tables shows that you have a normalized database. Having fewer but wider tables means that you have not normalized enough. On the other hand, a highly normalized database is usually associated with complex relational joins, which can hurt performance. But the SQL Server optimizer is very efficient at selecting rapid, efficient joins, as long as effective indexes are available. Normalization has the following benefits:

◆ It accelerates sorting and index creation because tables are narrower.

◆ It provides for more clustered indexes because more tables are available.

◆ Indexes tend to be narrower and more compact.

◆ Update performance is helped because there are fewer indexes per table.

◆ There are fewer NULLs and less redundant data, increasing database compactness.

◆ It reduces concurrency impact of DBCC diagnostics because the DBCC table locks will affect less data.

When you're using SQL Server, reasonable normalization most often helps performance rather than hurts it. A rule of thumb is to stop further normalization if your queries start to need over four-way joins.

Many times you are working with a database designed by others, and you do not have the freedom to normalize existing database designs. If you are designing the application, however, you can improve performance by splitting the databases into views and work through views. This way, you can hide the changes in the way you access the database.

EFFICIENT QUERY DESIGN

Some types of queries are inherently resource-intensive. This is related to fundamental database and index issues common to most databases, not just to SQL Server in particular. These queries are not inefficient; they are just resource-intensive, and the set-oriented nature of SQL may make them appear inefficient. Complex queries do more and therefore are costly when compared to more simple queries. SQL Server uses the most optimum access plan, but it is limited by the complexity and scope of the queries it has to satisfy.

The following are examples of complex resource-intensive queries:

◆ Large result sets, which mean more writing to disk

◆ IN, NOT IN, and OR queries, which result in more sequential access

◆ Non-unique WHERE clauses

◆ Use of "not equal" when using certain column functions, such as SUM

◆ Expressions or data conversions in WHERE clauses

◆ Local variables in WHERE clauses

◆ Complex views with GROUP BY or ORDER BY

The rule of thumb is to restrict the result set before applying the resource-intensive portion of the query. Large result sets are costly on most database systems. Do not return a large result set to the client for final data selection via browsing. Doing so also reduces network I/O and makes the application footprint smaller at the client. Restricting the result set is especially crucial when the clients are connected across slow remote communication links. It also improves concurrency-related performance as the application scales upward to more users.

HOW TO FIND BOTTLENECKS

To find bottlenecks, start by finding which queries are slow. Many times, an entire application may appear slow, when only a few of the SQL queries are slow. You need to know the SQL sent by the queries to SQL Server to be able to find the slow-moving queries. This is a simple, but effective approach for application development tools that use embedded SQL.

Note

If your development tool does not provide the SQL code, you can use the 4032 trace flag to capture the SQL statements sent to the server.

Once you suspect a slow query, you can take the following steps to find out what to do next:

1. Run the suspected query using ISQLW, and verify it is in fact slow. Also, run the query on the SQL Server computer itself, and redirect the output to a file. This process helps eliminate the network transport and screen I/O and application result buffering.

2. Use SET STATISTICS IO ON to examine the I/O consumed by the query. Check the count of logical page I/Os. Make a record of the logical I/O count to form a baseline number against which to measure improvement. It is often more effective to focus exclusively on the STATISTICS IO output and experiment with different query and index types than to use SET SHOWPLAN ON.

3. If the query is contained in a view or stored procedures, copy the query code into an ISQLW window and run it separately. This way, you can change the access plan as you experiment with different indexes. Taking this step also helps localize the problem to the query itself, versus how the optimizer handles views or stored procedures. If the problem is not in the query itself but appears only when the query is run as part of a view or stored procedure, running the query by itself will help determine this situation.

4. Check to see if there are triggers on the involved tables that can generate I/O as the trigger fires. It is best to remove any triggers involved in a slow query. Doing so helps determine if the problem is in the query itself or the trigger/view and, therefore, helps you find the reason for the slowness.

5. Check the indexes of the tables used by the slow query. As a rule of thumb, try indexing each column in your WHERE clause. Many times, problems are caused by not having a column in the WHERE clause indexed or by not having a useful index on such a column.

19

SQL SERVER

6. Run the query after making the index change and observe any change in I/O count.

7. After you have fixed the query, go back and check the whole application to see whether overall performance is better.

8. Check the program for I/O or CPU-bound behavior. For example, if a query is CPU bound, adding additional memory to SQL Server will not improve performance, because more memory only improves the cache hit ratio, which in this case may already be high. If, while running the query, the CPU% graph in SQL Performance Monitor is greater than 70 percent, this measurement indicates a CPU-bound state. If the CPU% graph is low, then the query is I/O bound.

ADMINISTRATION

With SQL Server, almost no day-to-day administration is necessary. Most organizations implementing SQL Server on the NT Server as their first client/server database will not need to hire a full-time database administrator (DBA). SQL Server can be automated to take care of itself. SQL Server for NT is integrated with the NT Performance Monitor.

STARTING SQL SERVER REMOTELY

The SQL Service Manager provides a way to start and stop SQL Server remotely. However, you cannot use the SQL Service Manager to start and stop SQL Server from a batch file or NT Command Prompt. The AT scheduler available in NT Server and the Remote Command Server from the NT version 3.5 Resource Kit both offer the ability to start and stop services from the NT Command Prompt, provided that you have privileges to start and stop services on the remote computer.

To use the AT scheduler, follow these steps:

1. Start the Schedule service on the remote computer.

2. Run the following NET TIME command to check the current time on the remote computer:

   ```
   NET TIME \\<Remote Computer>
   ```

3. Run the following AT command to schedule the desired program to run on the remote system about 1–2 minutes in the future:

   ```
   AT \\<Remote Computer> <Time> <Command>
   ```

Suppose that you want to stop SQL Server remotely on a computer named BNETServer. Start the Schedule service on BNETServer. Check the time on

BNETServer. For this example, say it is 2:00 p.m. Then run AT on the computer with which you want to control the computer BNETServer, as follows:

```
AT \\BNETServer 2:02:00pm NET STOP SQLSERVER
```

Note

This method does not work in a batch file because you need to know the current time of the remote computer.

TRUNCATING TRANSACTION LOGS

SQL Server for NT maintains a "% Full" counter of the SQLServer-Log object. You can use the value of this counter to decide when to dump or truncate the transaction log. Follow these steps:

1. Set up a text file called DU.SQL. This file will contain the SQL commands to dump or truncate the log. For instance,
    ```
    dump tran bnet with truncate_only
    go
    ```
2. Start the Performance Monitor, and add an alert that will run the script through ISQL when the log is more than 80 percent full.
3. Make sure that SQL Server is running.
4. Restart the Performance Monitor.
5. From the View menu, choose Alert.
6. Click on the + button to add an alert event.
7. Choose the object SQLServer-Log.
8. Choose the counter Log Space Used(%).
9. Choose the instance of the database you want to monitor—bnet in this example.
10. Click the Over button of the Alert if dialog box; then enter the percentage at which you want the log to be truncated in the box to the right of this button. Enter 80 to issue the truncate command when the log becomes more than 80 percent full.
11. Enter the ISQL command under Run Program on Alert. The command should launch your DU.SQL file. For example,
    ```
    isql -Sbnet -Usa -Ppassword -ic:\sql\du.sql
    ```
12. Click the Every Time button so that the log will be truncated every time the percentage full exceeds the specified threshold.

19

SQL SERVER

Note

So that you do not have to re-create this alert every time you start NT, you can save these settings using the File, Save Alert Settings dialog box.

Note

If you are using integrated security, you need to start the Performance Monitor under an administrator account or one that maps to the database's owner.

SQL SERVER REGISTRY ENTRIES

The SQL Server Monitor process uses a server-side Net-Library to communicate with clients and to search the following Registry key for network-specific parameters:

`HKEY_LOCAL_MACHINE\SOFTWARE\Microsoft\SQLServer\Server`

At startup, SQL Server sets a value for the `server_name` parameter in the SRV_CONFIG structure of Open Data Services. This value identifies in which Registry key SQL Server will look for values of the `ListenOn` and `connection_string` Registry entries. (By default, SQL Server looks in HKEY_LOCAL_MACHINE\SOFTWARE\ Microsoft\SQLServer\Server.)

Each `connection_string` Registry value is scanned and sent on to the associated Net-Library (such as named pipes) that is listed in the `ListenOn` field in the Server subkey. Each Net-Library acts upon the `connection_string` separately.

If no `connection_string` is associated with the Net-Library, SQL Server does one of the following:

◆ If the Registry entry is under the SQL#Server\Server subkey, no connection string is passed as the default.

◆ If the Registry entry is not under SQL#Server\Server, server_name is passed as the default. If the server_name subkey and the SQL#Server\ Server subtree do not exist, or the Registry cannot be found, SQL Server defaults to named pipes DLL (for the default Net-Library), and no parameter is passed. (You can turn off named pipes access by using the Registry Editor to explicitly delete the named pipes entry from the SQL#Server\Server subkey.)

Remote stored procedure calls and the SQL Administrator tool also use the DB-Library/Net-Library architecture under NT.

The following is a sample of what is added to the Registry for SQL Server on a Novell network:

```
HKEY_LOCAL_MACHINE\SOFTWARE\Microsoft\SQLServer\Server
ListenOn: REG_MULTI_SZ:    SSNMPNTW, \\.\pipe\sql\query
SSMSSPXN, BNET (computername)
```

Windows and OS/2 client workstations require the Novell NetWare 3.*x* or higher level of IPX. The SQL Client Configuration Utility is used to specify the default network that the Windows and OS/2 clients will use. If you choose Novell IPX/SPX, the required DBMSSPX3.DLL is automatically installed on the Windows client side, and DBMSSPXP.DLL is installed on the OS/2 client side. This adds the appropriate entries in the WIN.INI file or the OS/2.INI file, respectively.

SUMMARY

SQL Server offers a lot of power and flexibility, and at the same time it is easy to administer and manage. The administration of SQL Server is an ongoing process; the administrator has to make sure that

◆ Good backups are being made.

◆ Database integrity is not compromised.

◆ Databases do not outgrow the devices and choke the server.

◆ Transaction logs do not outgrow the devices and choke the server.

◆ When a breach occurs in the database, the transaction logs are readily accessible to conduct a rollback.

◆ Performance does not suffer because of lack of memory and processor resources.

Several books are available on the design, management, and administration of SQL Server; this chapter was intended just as an introduction.

19

SQL SERVER

- SNA Server Features

- Integration with NT
  Server

- Capacities

- System Requirements

- Installation

- SNA Server
  Administration

- SNA Server Clients

- Using Third-Party
  Emulators

- DOS Client Using
  IBM PC Support/400

CHAPTER 20

SNA Server

The SNA Server is an SNA gateway that connects LAN-based PCs with IBM host systems running Systems Network Architecture (SNA) protocols. The SNA Server has the following features:

◆ GUI tools for installation, administration, and troubleshooting

◆ Facilities for APIs, LU and PU protocols, and datalink protocols

◆ Centralized and remote administration, including administration via IBM NetView and RAS

◆ Support for centralized and branch configurations

◆ C2-level security

◆ Load balancing, hot backup, and other fault-tolerant features

◆ Support for key LAN protocols, including IPX/SPX and TCP/IP

◆ Symmetrical multiprocessing (SMP) enabled

◆ Portable between Intel x86 and RISC platforms

The SNA Server runs on the NT Server. It utilizes both the native NT communications protocol (such as TCP/IP or IPX) and IBM SNA protocols, acting as a high-speed gateway between the PC and IBM networks. The SNA Server's bidirectional communication provides terminal emulation, printer emulation, file transfer, and program-to-program communications. The SNA Server supports client functions on all the popular PC operating systems including NT, Windows 3.x, DOS, OS/2, UNIX, and Macintosh.

By supporting software such as 3270 or 5250 emulators, the SNA Server makes data and applications residing on IBM hosts available to PCs for use with desktop productivity software such as Microsoft Excel. For LAN-based PCs, the SNA Server acts as a server node to the IBM, allowing 3270 or 5250 screens to be displayed on the PC for seamless two-way communication. In addition, 3270 and 5250 printer emulation and file transfer are supported. Because the SNA Server runs on the NT Server, IBM NetView console operators can monitor and control activity on the server and also maintain secure access to corporate data. The SNA Server also provides remote access over a RAS connection. This enables remote system monitoring and management for the administrator, and seamless dial-up support for remote users to access the IBM host for normal sessions over phone-line connections (modem, ISDN, or X.25).

SNA SERVER FEATURES

The SNA Server has a full complement of features traditionally provided by hardware/software gateway products.

- ◆ Administrative Permissions. The administrative permissions that you can set in SNA Server Admin are read-only, read/write, full control, and no access.
- ◆ Full Audit Tracking. Full audit tracking is provided through integration with the NT Event Log.
- ◆ Hot Backup. The SNA Server implements hot backup through multiple connections within a single server, or through multiple servers within a domain. The SNA Server's LU pooling feature facilitates hot backup. An administrator groups LUs (from one or more servers) into a pool. If a data link on a server fails, the SNA Server can dynamically reroute lost sessions through other pooled LUs (using other data links). Similarly, if an entire server in a multiserver domain fails, the SNA Server can dynamically reroute sessions to pooled LUs on other servers.
- ◆ Protocol Independence. The SNA Server provides native support for named pipes, TCP/IP, IPX/SPX, Banyan VINES IP, AppleTalk, and RAS.
- ◆ SNANW. This component allows the SNA Server to communicate on a NetWare network.
- ◆ SNAAT. This component allows the SNA Server to communicate through AppleTalk.
- ◆ SNAIP. This component allows the SNA Server to communicate through TCP/IP.
- ◆ 3270 Applet. The SNA Server includes support for 3270 and 5250 emulators developed by independent software vendors. In addition, simple 3270 and 5250 applets are bundled with the SNA Server. These simple emulation tools facilitate evaluation and testing of the SNA Server and act as a test applications to problems when full-feature emulators do not operate properly. This program provides the following functions:

  Emulation of 3178 terminal models 2–5

  IND$FILE file transfer to/from TSO, VM/CMS, and CICS

  Single LU session

  Copy/paste via the Clipboard as well as the print screen feature
- ◆ 5250 Applet. This program provides the following functions:

  Emulation of 5250 terminal

  Single LU session

  Copy/paste via the Clipboard as well as the print screen feature

  TN3270 client support

20

SNA SERVER

◆ The APIs included with the SNA Server are as follows:

APPC: For developing 5250 emulators as well as applications that communicate peer-to-peer with other APPC applications using the LU 6.2 protocol. Management verbs are also supported.

CPI-C: For developing applications that communicate peer-to-peer with other applications using the LU 6.2 protocol.

CSV: For developing applications that include tracing of API calls, communication with NetView, and EBCDIC to ASCII conversion.

LUA: For developing applications (using LUA/RUI or LUA/SLI APIs) that need direct access to the LU 0, 1, 2, 3 data streams. Supports ISV 3270 emulators via the open 3270 EIS API.

EHLLAPI: For developing applications that interface with existing 3270 or 5250 applications. Note that EHLLAPI is offered by ISVs, but not by Microsoft. (EHLLAPI is not included in the 3270 and 5250 applets in the SNA Server.)

◆ Data Link Protocols. The SNA Server supports 802.2/LLC, SDLC, X.25/ QLLC, DFT, Twinax, and Channel attachment. For a complete list of compatible third-party data-link products from ISVs/IHVs, see the *Microsoft Companion Product Catalog*.

INTEGRATION WITH NT SERVER

The SNA Server works with NT Server to perform all administrative tasks on the SNA Server. The primary tools are the Control Panel, User Manager, Event Viewer, and Performance Monitor.

◆ The Control Panel on NT Program Manager contains many useful tools for the SNA Server.

◆ The Services applet controls the NVRunCmd service if you don't want a NetView operator to run commands on the SNA Server.

◆ The Network applet is used to install and configure protocol stacks used by the SNA Server.

◆ Error and event monitoring can be initiated in the Event Viewer feature in the SNA Server Admin utility. You can set the type (severity) of events to be recorded for the SNA Server.

◆ The Performance Monitor can be used to measure the performance of any SNA server accessible over the network. The parameters that can be monitored for SNA servers include throughput and transmission volume (in bytes, or in some instances, frames), and can be measured for connections, LUs, or adapters.

◆ The accounts established through the User Manager are also used by the SNA Server, so you need to create an account only once for use by the NT Server or SNA Server.

◆ Remote Access Service (RAS) is supported. RAS works with SNA Server in two ways. First, RAS can provide connectivity to SNA Server using asynchronous, X.25, or ISDN connections. This provides a remote connection to an SNA network or LAN by the use of a modem, X.25 card, or ISDN adapter as a network card. Second, RAS can run over SNA using LU 6.2 as a transport. This provides a way to connect to and manage an SNA server using the SNA network as the physical connection.

CAPACITIES

Depending on the NT Server platform provided for the SNA Server, the SNA Server has the following capacities:

◆ Up to 250 simultaneous connections (PUs) per server, in any combination of upstream (host), peer-to-peer, and downstream (DSPU) connections

◆ Up to 2,000 clients per server

◆ Up to 10,000 LU sessions per server

◆ Up to 50 SNA servers working together in an NT Server domain for load balancing and hot backup

SYSTEM REQUIREMENTS

The following system requirements are necessary to install and use SNA Server.

MINIMUM TOTAL RAM REQUIREMENT: SERVER
SNA Server on NT: 16MB

MINIMUM TOTAL RAM REQUIREMENT: CLIENT
NT Workstation: 14MB

ACTUAL RAM OCCUPANCY: DOS AND WINDOWS VERSION 3.*x* CLIENTS

◆ Base support for IBM PC Support functions	100K
◆ Base support for ISV 3270 emulator	50K
◆ Base support for APPC/LUA-RUI/CSV application	50K
◆ 3270 Applet	525K
◆ 5250 Applet	490K

◆ 3270 and 5250 Applet loaded at the same time   830K

◆ Base support for ISV 5250 emulator   185K

◆ Base support for ISV 3270 emulator   185K

◆ Base support for APPC/CPIC/LUA/CSV application   185K

The base support numbers shown in the preceding list do not include the application itself (such as the IBM PC Support components) or the SNA Server API DLLs loaded by the application.

HARD DISK REQUIREMENTS

◆ SNA Server only   8.0MB

◆ SNA Server including clients   18.0MB (for over-the-network client setup)

◆ SNA Server client running NT 7.5MB

◆ SNA Server client running Windows 3.*x*   2.0MB

◆ SNA Server client running DOS   1.0MB

◆ SNA Server client running OS/2   1.5MB

INSTALLATION

Follow these steps to install the SNA Server software:

1. From the NT File Manager, select the CD drive from which you are installing.

2. Double-click the file SETUP.BAT in the root directory.

3. When you see Welcome to Microsoft SNA Server Setup, click Continue.

4. When you see Software Licensing, type your name, company name, and product ID. Then click Continue.

5. When you see Installation Path, accept the default path or type in another. Then click Continue.

6. When you see Select Client/Server Protocols, select the client/server protocol(s) you are using. Then click Continue.

7. When you see Network Domain Name, type in the network domain name. Then click Continue.

8. When you see Change SNA Server Role, select Primary Configuration Server. Then click Continue.

9. When you see Review Settings, you can change your settings if you change your mind. Click Continue to copy the SNA Server files to the designated drive.

Do the following to install Link Service:

1. Highlight DLC 802.2 if you're using LAN connectivity. Then click Install.
2. The Link Service Configuration should show that the DLC 802.2 is installed and presents you with the opportunity to install another link service. Then click Continue.

See Figures 20.1 through 20.3.

Figure 20.1.
The Setup Options
dialog box.

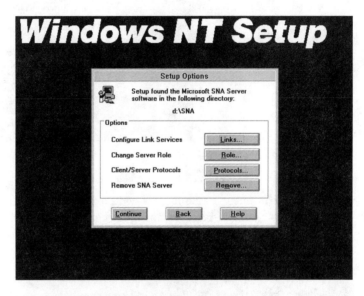

Figure 20.2.
The Link Service
Configuration
dialog box.

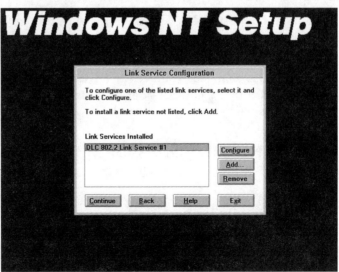

Figure 20.3.
The DLC 802.2 Link
Service Setup dialog
box.

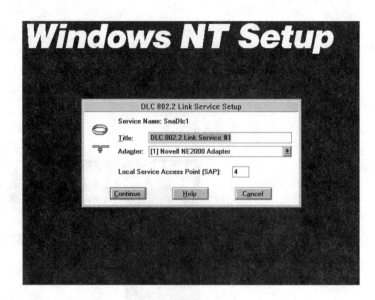

CHANGING THE NAME OF THE SNA SERVER

If the NT computer name is changed on a computer running SNA Server or SNA Workstation, the SNA Server configuration file continues to reflect the old computer name. As a result, the SNA Server fails to start. To update the SNA Server configuration file with the new server name, run the SNA Admin program as follows:

```
snaadmin c:\sna\system\config\com.cfg
```

You can change the SNA Server service name through the Server Properties dialog box. After you change the server name, save the configuration.

You may create other problems with AS/400 connections if the local control point name is also changed. You need to create a new APPC controller on the AS/400 associated with the new SNA Server control point name. Delete the old entry, and add a new one.

REMOVING THE SNA SERVER ADMINISTRATION PROGRAM

The SNA Server setup program automatically installs the SNA Server Administration program. The following steps are necessary to make the Administration program work.

1. Locate the SNA Server computer(s) running client installation over the network.

2. Locate the *<SNAROOT>*\CLIENTS\WINNT\SETUP.INF file.

3. Open SETUP.INF, locate the [DoAdminFiles] section (located on line 3450), and add the following two lines (new lines are bold):

```
[DoAdminFiles]
set Status = STATUS_SUCCESSFUL
set !InstallAdminFiles = $(!False)
return $(Status)
read-syms AdminFilesDlg
```

HOW TO START UP SNA SERVER

To start the SNA Server automatically when you start your system, use the Services application to configure the SNA Server service startup method as Automatic. Also, if you are using NetView alerts and the Run command, you should configure the NVAlert and NVRunCmd services to start automatically.

All other SNA Server services are automatically started by SNA Server as needed, even though they are configured for manual start (this includes any SNA Server link services and SnaNetMn). The SnaNetMn service displays an error message if the user attempts to start it through the Control Panel.

Following is a description of each SNA Server service and how each service is configured to start when SNA Server is installed:

◆ SnaBase: Automatic startup. You must start this service before any other SNA Server service can run.

◆ SnaServer: Manual startup. You can change this service to Automatic startup if desired. You also can start or stop it using the SNA Server Admin program.

◆ SNA Server link services (SnaDlc1, SnaSdlc1, and so on): Manual startup. The SNA Server automatically starts the link services as needed. These services should not be configured to start automatically using the Control Panel. Specifically, the SnaBase service starts these automatically. Also, the SnaServer service doesn't start unless all link services used by this server are running.

◆ NVAlert, NVRunCmd: Manual startup. You can change these services to Automatic startup if desired. SNA Server will not automatically start these services.

◆ SnaNetMn: Manual startup. SNA Server automatically starts this service if NetView connectivity is configured on an SNA Server connection. This service should not be configured to start automatically using Control Panel. It fails with the following error message if the administrator tries to start it manually:

```
SNA Server Error #0352
Unable to open the configuration file, rc=618
```

BACKING UP THE COM.CFG FILE

The first step to ensuring proper configuration recovery is to back up your SNA Server configuration file (COM.CFG). This file resides on your SNA Server primary configuration server and on any SNA Server backup configuration servers in your <*SNAROOT*>\SYSTEM\CONFIG directory, shared to network users as <*SERVER NAME*>\COMCFG\COM.CFG.

The COM.CFG file contains important configuration information about the SNA Server, including SNA Servers in the domain, SNA connections they own, 3270 and APPC LUs configured, LU pools, and SNA Server user/group information.

To back up the COM.CFG file, do the following:

1. From the File menu of SNA Admin, choose Backup.
2. Type the name of the configuration file. All backup COM.CFG files have an .SNA extension.
3. In the dialog box, specify the drive you want to back up. If you want to back up a network drive, select the Network checkbox, or press Alt+W, to establish a network connection.
4. When you are satisfied with your options, choose the OK button.

To restore your configuration, follow these steps:

1. From the File menu in SNA Admin, choose Restore.
2. Choose the path and filename you want to restore. This file replaces the COM.CFG in the <*SNAROOT*>\SYSTEM\CONFIG directory.

SNA SERVER ADMINISTRATION

The SNA Server Administration contains three windows, as shown in Figure 20.4. They are

◆ Servers and Connections
◆ LU Pools
◆ Users and Groups

Figure 20.4.
The SNA Server
Admin windows.

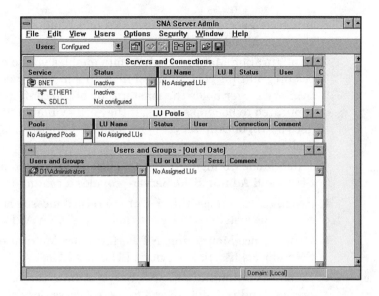

Drag-and-drop enables you to set up LU pools and assign users to them. Using icons, you can identify servers, connections, LU pools, and users, as well as the type of connection (SDLC, 802.2, and so on) and the type of LU pool (3270, LUA, downstream).

In an IBM mainframe environment, NetView communicates between SNA servers and host operators. The Admin program provides the following tools to manage SNA/LAN interaction:

◆ Link Services Management. You can install, configure, or remove link services using the SNA Server Setup. Admin displays the mapping between NT device driver names and SNA connections.

◆ Connection Management. Admin displays the status of SNA servers and connections (inactive, pending, active, stopping); it also allows you to create, delete, start, and stop them. A connection can be activated manually, at server startup, or on demand when a client accesses it. On-demand activation can be used for a dial-up SDLC connection that functions as a backup.

◆ LU Management. Admin enables you to create a range of LUs for a connection and group them into pools to provide user access. The name, status, and user activity for each LU are shown. Admin also enables you to reset LUs, view and modify LU properties, and move an LU from one pool to another.

◆ User Management. Admin displays users and groups as well as the sessions for users who have been given SNA access. Admin also enables you to assign LUs or LU pools to users, and to view or modify a user's properties (including permissions). You can filter the display to show active users only.

20

SNA SERVER

Integrated security is provided through Windows NT and managed with the User Manager.

◆ Configuration Management. Admin enables you to open, save, back up, and restore multiple configuration files. In a multiserver environment, the primary server holds the master copy of the configuration file; this copy is replicated to backup servers, if they are available. If the primary server goes down, backup servers provide the configuration information to clients and other servers.

◆ Batch-Mode Configuration. In addition to the graphical tools provided by Setup and Admin, SNA Server provides a command-line utility, snacfg.

◆ SNA Trace. You use this feature to record messages to and from SNA Server, as well as activity into and out of SNA APIs.

◆ Performance Monitoring. NT Performance Monitor enables you to monitor SNA objects like link services, PUs, and LUs.

◆ Remote Administration. SNA Server Admin can be used across routers and bridges, and remotely over a Remote Access Service (RAS) link. You can administer one domain at a time, or you can use the Select Domain command to connect to remote domains. In addition, an operator at a host console can use NVRunCmd to execute NT commands (through NetView) on an NT Server, with character-based output being displayed on the host console.

SNA SERVER CLIENTS

NT Server clients can use 3270 workstation emulation services. Running 3270 workstation emulation works a little differently for each type of client. The following sections discuss each type of SNA client.

WINDOWS-BASED CLIENTS

IBM Personal Communications/3270 WorkStation Program (IBM PC/3270) version 4.0 supports the SNA Server Windows client interface. To run this application on top of an SNA Server Windows client computer, follow these steps:

You must first install the SNA Server Windows client software on the WFW computer. You can select any SNA Server client/server connection method. On a PC running Windows 3.x, NT, connected through the LAN to an SNA server, do the following:

1. In File Manager, connect to your SNA Server CD.
2. In the CLIENTS subdirectory, select the subdirectory for your CPU type.
3. Double-click SETUP.EXE.

4. In the SNA Server Setup dialog box, click Continue.

5. In the Installation Path dialog box, accept the path or type in another; then click Continue.

6. In the SNA Server Location dialog box, select Remote Domain and Select Primary Server. Then type in the name of your SNA server. SNA Server Setup then copies files to your client computer.

7. In the Setup Complete dialog box, click Exit.

8. You will see the SNA Server icons.

Assign 3270 LUs to the user or group (or Everyone user) within the Users and Groups window of SNA Server Admin.

Configure PC/3270 to use this interface: Run the Personal Communications Start/Configure Sessions icon and then choose the Communication/Configure dialog box. Set the Adapter:LAN and Attachment:FMI Windows NT client. Next, choose the Configure button. Doing so automatically retrieves the 3270 LUs assigned to the user or group within the SNA Server configuration file at the SNA server. Select an LU from the list.

SPECIAL SETTINGS FOR WFW CLIENTS

The Microsoft IPX/SPX compatible transport (NWLink) is installed by default. When you configure the SNA Server client to use the "MS Network Client (named pipes)" interface, the NWLink transport is used automatically. This can pose a problem if the NT Server 3.5 Direct Hosting for WFW feature is turned on; this feature uses direct-hosted IPX/SPX connections rather than over NetBIOS.

You should add the following entry to the SYSTEM.INI on the WFW client computer:

```
[network]
DirectHost=NO
```

TCP/IP CLIENT

When you're connecting from an SNA Server client using the TCP/IP sockets interface to SNA Server, the following problems may occur if the NT TCP/IP Protocol is bound to more than one network card on the server, and different IP addresses are configured for each card.

When SNA Server is configured (using SNA Setup) to accept client sessions over TCP/IP sockets, SNA Server searches only for the first IP address that is configured on the server. The first IP address corresponds with the first adapter to which the TCP/IP Protocol is bound.

20

When an SNA client opens its "sponsor connection" to an SNA Server in the domain, SNA Server sends down the server name and IP address it finds. However, the SNA client may not be able to connect to the server over this first IP address because the IP address may be available only over the other server's network card.

To control which IP address is used by the SNA Server clients, configure the NT TCP/IP Protocol on SNA Server to bind to the desired adapter:

1. Open the Network icon in the Control Panel.
2. Choose the Bindings button.
3. Select the TCP/IP Protocol and choose OK.
4. Select the desired adapter and choose the up-arrow button on the right side of the Network Bindings dialog box. Move the adapter to make it the first in the list.
5. Choose OK.

CONFIGURING WINDOWS 3.*x* TCP/IP CLIENT

Run Setup and choose TCP/IP, or manually change the WIN.INI file. To change the WIN.INI file manually, follow these steps:

1. Set `LocalFlag=` (`REMOTE` ¦ `LOCAL`).
2. Use Remote if the domain or workgroup name of the SNA Server is different from the one used in the `WORKGROUP=` entry.
3. Use Local if the `WORKGROUP=` name is the same as the SNA Server. This `LocalFlag` entry is used by SETUP only to determine which option was selected.
4. Set `Remote =` (`domainname` ¦ `\\servername` ¦ `\\ipaddress`), where
   `domainname` is the NT domain name where the SNA Server resides.
   `\\servername` is the Windows NT computer name of an SNA Server in the domain.
   `\\ipaddress` is the NT IP address of SNA Server (for example, `\\121.1.1.4`)
5. Change `NosType=` (`TCPIP` ¦ `NOVELL` ¦ `LANMAN`) to `NosType=TCPIP`.
6. Change `NosSetup=` (`TCPIP` ¦ `NOVELL` ¦ `WFW`) to `NosSetup=TCPIP`.
7. Add `LogonUserName=` and `LogonDomainName=`. These entries specify the default username and logon domain for the workstation. These options are also used by the NetWare and Vines interfaces.

USING THIRD-PARTY EMULATORS

If you are using a Windows third-party emulator with SNA Server for NT, the following files are required:

SNA Server client files, located in the *<SNAROOT>* directory:

> WNAP.EXE—SNA Windows client (required)
>
> WPOPUP.EXE—Displays pop-ups if errors occur (required)
>
> SNAVER.EXE—Displays versions of the SNA Server client components
>
> WSHOWMEM.EXE—Displays internal memory tables and settings used by the SNA Server client software

SNA Server client DLLs required to run over NetWare:

> NWCLI.DLL—SNA client interface for NetWare
>
> NWNETAPI.DLL—NetWare API interface
>
> NWIPXSPX.DLL—NetWare IPX/SPX interface

Other SNA Server client DLLs:

> WDMOD.DLL—SNA client interface used by WNAP, SNA APIs, and third-party vendors using the Emulator Interface Specification (EIS) (required)
>
> WLOGTR.DLL—Required for logging and trace formatting (required)
>
> TOOLHELP.DLL—Used by WNAP to determine if an SNA Server client application has ended (required)
>
> WINTRC.DLL—Used only when message tracing is enabled
>
> CTL3D.DLL—Required by SNAVER; also used by 3270 and 5250 applets for 3D support
>
> YMGR.DLL—Yield manager, used only by earlier applications written to use the DCA/Microsoft Comm Server APPC interface

Used by 5250 emulation vendors:

> WINAPPC.DLL—APPC API support
>
> WINCSV.DLL—Common Service Verbs API support

Other SNA API interface DLLs:

> WINSLI.DLL—LUA Session Level Interface API support
>
> WINRUI.DLL—LUA Request Unit Interface API support
>
> WINCPIC.DLL—CPI-C API support
>
> WINMGT.DLL—APPC Management Verb API support

20

SNA SERVER

You must add the SNA client directory to the path in AUTOEXEC.BAT or put the files in a known path. You also need to add the following entries in the WIN.INI file of each workstation:

[Wnap]
WBinPath=(SNA Server client root directory, where *.EXEs are located)
Remote=(For NetWare, this must be set to the domain name where the SNA Server is running. For LAN Manager/Windows for Workgroups, this line is optional, though it must be set to the SNA Server machine name if the client is located in a different domain than the server, or is located remotely from the server.)
NosType=(Type of Network) [LANMAN ¦ NETWARE]
NosSetup=(Type of client) [LANMAN I WFW I NETWARE]
NetSetup=NO

DOS CLIENT USING IBM PC SUPPORT/400

When loaded, IBM PC Support/400 enables users to access their AS/400 through the SNA Server using an SNA Server DOS client.

At the NT Server SNA Server Admin, configure a connection to the AS/400. Add a Remote APPC LU to the connection by clicking Insert, and then select APPC (Remote). Then choose the following settings:

Add Remote LU Properties:

1. Enter LU Alias. Enter the Control Point Name of the AS/400 Network Name. Enter the AS/400 network name.
2. Enter the LU Name. This is the same as the LU Alias.
3. Enter the Uninterpreted LU Name. This is the same as LU Name (or you can leave it blank).
4. Answer Supports Parallel Sessions: Yes.
5. Answer Enables Automatic Partnering: Yes/No.
6. Choose OK.

To add a Local APPC LU to the server, follow these steps:

1. Highlight the Server (the computer name running SNA Server) and click Insert. In the New Logical Unit field, select APPC (Local).

Add Properties:

2. LU 6.2 Type: Independent
3. LU Alias: Username (or any unique LU name)

4. Network Name: Same as network name on node definition for this server (usually APPN)

5. LU Name: same as LU Alias

6. Partners (select): Select Add and then select the correct Partner LU (created in step 2 above) and partner with the "QPCSUPP" Mode (this is partnered by default). Then select Close on the Partner dialog box, and choose OK on the Properties dialog box.

Do the following on the SNA Server client workstation:

1. Install the SNA Server DOS client software (run the Setup program off the \\<SERVER>\CLIENTS\MSDOS directory)

2. Copy the SNA Server MS-DOS client ROUTER.EXE and INITRTR.EXE into your PCS directory.

3. In the CONFIG.PCS file, change the Network.LUName on the RTLN line to match the Network.LUName configured at the server. The network name should match the network name of the server, and the LUName should match the Local APPC LU name.

4. Start SNABASE and ROUTER.

After they have started, you should be able to use IBM PC Support/400.

SUMMARY

This chapter is intended as an introduction. It may help some administrators evaluate the SNA Server before they commit to using it. For administrators who are already conversant with SNA connectivity tools, this chapter is adequate as a starting point.

- Using NetBIOS to Advertise Available Services

- Using TCP/IP with NT

- NT's Native and Optional Routing Support

- Installing the TCP/IP Protocol

- Adding TCP/IP Support to an Installed NT Server

- Dynamic Host Control Protocol (DHCP)

CHAPTER 21

Microsoft TCP/IP Services

Note

In this book, the term "LAN" refers to an Ethernet, Token ring, or other type of local area network. The term "network" refers to the entire networked system of computers, LANs, WANs, protocols, NOS, and so on.

Internetwork   When multiple LANs are linked together with bridges or routers, the resulting network is called an internetwork.

Subnetwork   In an IP network, each logical LAN is designated as a subnetwork. A subnetwork is a single physical LAN or multiple LANs that are bridged together to seem like a single physical LAN. Each subnetwork constitutes a router destination for IP packets in an IP internetwork.

Non-Routable Protocol   Protocols that do not have logical addressing information in their packet headers and therefore cannot be passed over routers. NetBIOS and NetBEUI are two non-routable protocols used in Microsoft networks.

Packets   Network protocol data units that provide transport of data over a network and convey function codes between nodes. Packets are encapsulated into frames for delivery on a LAN.

Frames   LAN protocol data units that provide communication between nodes on a single LAN or between nodes in a bridged internetwork. Frames are specific to the type of LAN, that is, Ethernet or Token ring.

Note

The terms "packet" and "frame" represent two different layers of protocol. Packets are protocol units used by the NOS, and frames are LAN protocol units used between network adapters. Packets are encapsulated into frames for movement over a LAN.

Warning

Microsoft often uses the terms "frame" and "packet" interchangeably, and very often describes a packet as a frame. In many of their technical documents, they designate a NetBEUI packet as a NetBEUI Frame (NBF). In this book, these terms are used to distinguish the layer of protocol being discussed for greater clarity.

Server Message Block (SMB)   Microsoft's proprietary highest layer protocol and packet headers define a series of protocol codes used to pass information effectively between servers and client workstations.

UDP   User Datagram Protocol.

ARP   Address Resolution Protocol.

ICMP   Internet Control Message Protocol.

LMHOSTS   This file is commonly used on Microsoft networks to locate remote computers for network file, print, and remote procedure services and for domain services such as logons, browsing, replication, and so on.

WINS   The Windows Internet Name Service was designed to eliminate the need for broadcasts to resolve computer names to IP addresses and provide a dynamic database that maintains computer name to IP address mappings.

DHCP   Dynamic Host Configuration Protocol automatically assigns IP addresses.

RIP   Routing Information Protocol. A protocol used between routers to keep their routing tables updated.

SNMP   Simple Network Management Protocol. A protocol widely used in LAN/WAN monitoring devices.

FTP   File Transfer Protocol is used to transfer files from one computer to another.

NBNS   NetBIOS Naming Service.

HTML   HyperText Markup Language.

SMTP   Simple Mail Transfer Protocol.

NT provides native support for TCP/IP, but use of this stack with NT is not as slick as you might like it to be. You can configure an NT Server, NT Workstation, and Windows 95 computers with TCP/IP. Word For Windows (WFW) clients can obtain a free TCP/IP upgrade on Microsoft's CompuServe forum, from their FTP or Gopher Internet servers.

Configuring an NT network with TCP/IP provides some unique challenges, regardless of which protocol stack you use. This chapter helps you understand the many advantages, disadvantages, problems, and solutions in using a Microsoft TCP/IP network.

USING NetBIOS TO ADVERTISE AVAILABLE SERVICES

All computers configured to share files and/or printers on a Microsoft network rely on NetBIOS broadcasts to advertise their network presence. NetBIOS has been frowned on by network administrators and system analysts for many years because of its unreasonably "chatty" nature, its lack of routing support, and problems layering it with other protocols. Whenever NetBIOS is required, some system administrators clench their teeth and wish for relief.

Many NT purchasers are under the false impression that NT does not use NetBIOS; this simply is not true. Although Microsoft has apparently reduced references to the use of NetBIOS on the network, NetBIOS is still the foundation of current NT implementations, and Microsoft seemingly has no intention of eliminating this protocol.

NetBIOS BROADCAST STORMS

When a computer configured to share its files and/or printers comes up on the network, a volley of NetBIOS broadcasts are issued. Every time a node seeks to discover network resources, such as when File Manager is accessed, Windows sends out a NetBIOS query. Each query requires replies from every server advertising its services and Share names. At frequent intervals, broadcasts are issued to maintain awareness of the services. Many additional events touch off broadcasts. On larger networks, a simple episode such as entering File Manager can touch off a *broadcast storm*, a moment when virtually all available LAN bandwidth is saturated with NetBIOS traffic.

NetBIOS is also used to announce to all nodes the presence of the server, what services it has, the Share names (NetBIOS names) that are available, the group (or domain) to which the computer belongs, and many other statistics required to make the services available on the network. Each Share name that is configured adds to the number of NetBIOS packets required in a broadcast. Therefore, as your network grows in complexity, the number of NetBIOS broadcasts increases exponentially. In larger networks, the number of NetBIOS broadcasts that are periodically present amount to a broadcast storm.

ADMINISTRATION COMPLEXITY WHEN NetBIOS IS LAYERED WITH OTHER PROTOCOLS

Administrators would also like to eliminate other limitations to the NetBIOS protocol. Microsoft has done a commendable job on making this protocol as transparent as possible but has not eliminated the problems that result when layering it with other protocols.

The NT Server requires additional administrative work to map NetBIOS names to IP addresses within an NT Server network. Although Microsoft includes tools to provide NetBIOS broadcast support when using TCP/IP, you need to be aware of the pitfalls you may face in administering NetBIOS over a TCP/IP environment.

NetBIOS Is Not Routable

Another problem you may face is the fact that NetBIOS is not routable. To make shared resources available in an internetwork based on routers, therefore, administrators have to provide a method of forwarding NetBIOS broadcasts over the routers. Normally, routers are set to suppress NetBIOS broadcasts to eliminate NetBIOS broadcast storms. However, a router that suppresses NetBIOS broadcasts can also prevent you from accessing resources that are located on remote LAN segments.

Using TCP/IP with NT

When you're installing an NT Server, TCP/IP is the default protocol option. TCP/IP is the most widely used nonproprietary protocol in the world. It is used on the Internet and as the default protocol in Digital Equipment Corporation, Hewlett-Packard, Sun Microsystems, AT&T, and many other computer networks. Integrating NT into an existing TCP/IP network makes the most sense because all computers can communicate with a common protocol.

Benefits of Using TCP/IP

Microsoft's implementation of TCP/IP provides many benefits to network clients.

Note

TCP/IP is recommended in places where robust internetwork services are required. Employing the TCP/IP protocol stack is especially helpful when you're connecting to an existing TCP/IP network and you want Internet services.

NT Server 3.51 can be considered a native TCP/IP implementation, following IETF recommendations, such as RFC 1001 and RFC 1002. RFC 1001, Protocol Standards for a NetBIOS Service on a TCP/UDP Transport: Concepts and Methods, and RFC 1002, Protocol Standards for a NetBIOS Service on a TCP/UDP Transport define standards for using NetBIOS with TCP/IP.

IP TUNNELING

Microsoft, in NT Server 3.51, uses encapsulation (tunneling) to provide communication in a TCP/IP environment. Microsoft's TCP/IP solution for NT Server 3.51 encapsulates NetBIOS broadcasts into TCP/IP packets for delivery over IP routers. Microsoft has not yet stated that it will provide a truly native TCP/IP implementation of NT Server that eliminates the need for NetBIOS encapsulation.

WINS AND LMHOSTS LIMITATIONS

You use WINS and LMHOSTS configuration files to map NetBIOS names to IP addresses. Neither WINS nor LMHOSTS are used to locate resources, such as file servers and printers within the network. Browsing provides another database, separate from the WINS and DHCP databases, for tracking network resources.

Each domain has a master browser that is responsible for synchronizing resources between the domain's browse masters. The master browser and browse masters exchange NetBIOS names of domain resources, such as computers and printers. Clients query a browse master to search for a particular resource type, and the browse master returns a list of NetBIOS names of all matching resources. After receiving the NetBIOS name of the resource from the browse master, the client then either issues a broadcast or WINS query, or searches LMHOSTS files to locate the IP address of the resource. Each domain has a single browse master, with a backup browse master designated for about every 15 computers.

Each transport protocol (NetBEUI, NWLink, or NetBIOS encapsulated in TCP/IP) also has its own set of browsers. Backup browsers synchronize with the master browser every 15 minutes to exchange updates about the domain. After initialization, servers announce their resources to the master browser about every 12 minutes. Browse databases can be very slow to converge: in worst cases, it can take over 50 minutes before a backup browser realizes that a service is missing from the network.

In contrast, NetWare converges within five minutes of change. If a service disappears, every NetWare server will drop the missing service within five minutes. Every NT Server, NT Workstation, WFW and LAN Manager Server will send server announcements to the local network. When the master browser receives these server announcements, they are added to the browse list of the domain. As more services are added to the browse list, the browse database becomes large and hinders performance of browser queries.

The browse list for each domain also has finite size: The list of servers that the master browser maintains is limited to 64K of data. This size limits the number of computers that can be in a browse list in a single workgroup or domain to 2,000–3,000 computers. This limitation may impact the number of NT Workstations and

WFW clients in the network, forcing larger customers to use multiple domains to ensure that the 2,000–to–3,000-computer browse limit is not encountered.

BROWSING OVER TCP/IP

NT Server 3.51 networks that span TCP/IP subnets require a master browser and backup browsers for every IP segment. Each NT domain on each IP segment should have an NT Server acting as a browse master. The subnet master browsers contact the domain master browser every 15 minutes and exchange information about domain resources. WINS-enabled clients, such as NT Workstation, WFW, and Windows 95, may contact a WINS Server and locate domain master browsers. Non-WINS-enabled clients, such as DOS, Windows 3.1, and OS/2 clients, locate browse masters with NetBIOS broadcasts. NT Server segments that support non-WINS-enabled clients must have an NT Server, NT Workstation, or WFW computer located on the same subnet as the non-WINS-enabled clients. Otherwise, non-WINS-enabled clients cannot browse for resources.

NetBIOS Name Resolution over TCP/IP

Microsoft network computers advertise themselves and locate resources by NetBIOS names, not by IP addresses. When a NetBIOS broadcast is received, each node checks to see whether the same name already exists. Likewise, if a computer is to communicate with an NT server, it must find both the server's NetBIOS name and its IP address.

Because it is essential that every computer on the entire network must have a unique NetBIOS name, a corporate NetBIOS naming standard should be developed and enforced. Normally, NetBIOS over TCP/IP uses broadcasts to advertise the NetBIOS computer name and to locate other NetBIOS nodes. However, because NetBIOS broadcasts can saturate routers, LANs, or WANs, other mechanisms are often required for NetBIOS name advertisements and queries. RFCs 1001 and 1002 define possible NetBIOS name resolutions in a TCP/IP environment.

NT's Native and Optional Routing Support

Out of the box, NT Server 3.51 supports routing for IP only if Microsoft DHCP is used. It does not support common dynamic routing protocols such as RIP or OSPF, nor does it support IPX routing. NT Server 3.51 provides routing only for Remote Access Service clients but not for other types of clients such as local IPX, TCP/IP, or AppleTalk clients.

Note

Microsoft has been working on a Multi-Protocol Router add-on. Check on Microsoft's WINNT forum on CompuServe or their FTP or Gopher servers on the Internet for the latest update to this limitation.

INSTALLING THE TCP/IP PROTOCOL

You must be logged on as a member of the Administrators group for the local computer to install and configure TCP/IP.

To install TCP/IP on an NT computer, follow these steps:

1. Open the Control Panel and choose the Network icon. The Network Settings dialog box then appears. Click Add Software to display the Add Network Software dialog box.

2. Select TCP/IP Protocol And Related Components from the Network Software box, and then choose the Continue button.

3. In the NT TCP/IP Installation Options dialog box that appears, select the options for the TCP/IP components you want to install. After you have selected the options you want, choose the Continue button.

   TCP/IP Setup displays a message prompting for the full path to the NT distribution files on the CD.

4. In the TCP/IP Setup dialog box, enter the full path to the distribution files, and then choose the Continue button. You can select a CD-ROM drive or a shared network directory, or you can specify the Universal Naming Convention (UNC) pathname for a network resource, such as \\NTSETUP\BNET.

5. If you selected the options for installing the SNMP and FTP Server services, you are automatically requested to configure these services.

6. In the Network Settings dialog box, choose the OK button. If you selected the Enable Automatic DHCP Configuration option, and a DHCP server is available on your network, all configuration settings for TCP/IP are completed automatically.

   If you did not check the Enable Automatic DHCP Configuration option, continue with the configuration procedure. If you checked the DHCP Server Service or WINS Server Service options, you must complete the configuration steps for WINS.

7. Select TCP/IP Internetworking. When you choose this option, the TCP/IP protocol, NetBIOS over TCP/IP and Windows Sockets interfaces, and the TCP/IP diagnostic utilities are installed automatically.

8. Select Connectivity Utilities to install the connectivity utilities. Connectivity Utilities installs the TCP/IP utilities.

9. Select SNMP Service to allow this computer to be administered using remote management tools. SNMP Service installs the SNMP service, which enables you to monitor statistics for the TCP/IP services and WINS Servers using the Performance Monitor.

10. Select TCP/IP Network Printing Support if you want to print to UNIX print queues or TCP/IP printers that are connected directly to the network. TCP/IP Network Printing Support allows this computer to print directly over the network using TCP/IP. You must install this option if you want to use the Lpdsvr service so that UNIX computers can print to NT printers.

11. Select FTP Server Service if you want to use TCP/IP to share files with other computers. FTP Server Service allows files on this computer to be shared over the network with remote computers that support FTP and TCP/IP.

12. Select Simple TCP/IP Services to allow this computer to respond to requests from other systems that support these protocols. Simple TCP/IP Services provides the client software for the Character Generator, Daytime, Discard, Echo, and Quote of the Day services.

13. Select DHCP Server Service if this computer is to be a DHCP Server. If you select this option, you must manually configure the IP address, subnet mask, and default gateway for this computer. DHCP Server Service installs the server software to support automatic configuration and addressing for computers using TCP/IP on your internetwork. This option is available only for the NT Server.

14. Select WINS Server Service if this computer is to be installed as a primary or secondary WINS Server. Do not select this option if this computer will be a WINS proxy agent. WINS Server Service installs the server software to support WINS, a dynamic name resolution service for computers on a Windows internetwork. This option is available only for the NT Server.

15. Select Enable Automatic DHCP Configuration if a DHCP server is available on your internetwork to support dynamic host configuration. Enable Automatic DHCP Configuration turns on automatic configuration of TCP/IP parameters for this computer. This option is the preferred method for configuring TCP/IP on most NT computers. This option is not available if the DHCP Server Service or WINS Server Service option is selected. Figure 21.1 shows the last screen of this sequence.

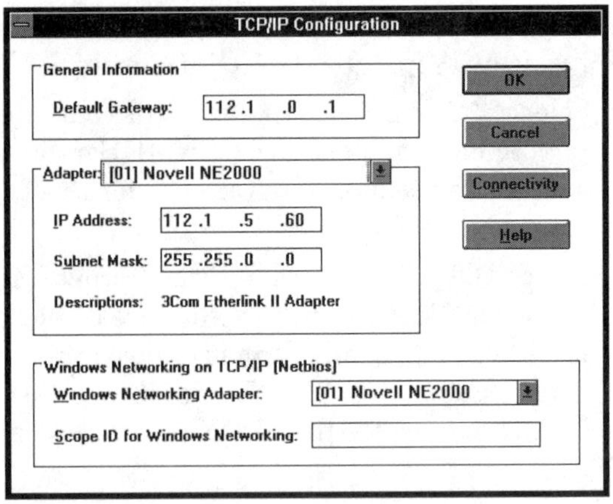

Figure 21.1.
TCP/IP Configuration.

After TCP/IP is installed, the *SYSTEMROOT*\SYSTEM32\DRIVERS\ETC directory contains several files, including default HOSTS, NETWORKS, PROTOCOLS, QUOTES, and SERVICES files, plus a sample LMHOSTS.SAM file that describes the format for this file.

ADDING TCP/IP SUPPORT TO AN INSTALLED NT SERVER

Theoretically, adding TCP/IP transport once a server is installed should be a simple matter. This option may work for any other protocol, but often you simply cannot add TCP/IP. If you have difficulty adding TCP/IP support to your server, simply reinstall the server from scratch. This process installs all the components and adds all the configuration details needed to install TCP/IP support effectively.

DYNAMIC HOST CONTROL PROTOCOL (DHCP)

DHCP allows centralized IP address assignment and administration by providing IP addressing information to clients, such as an IP address and the IP subnet mask. Unlike BOOTP, DHCP can lease IP addresses, providing an IP address to a client for a set period of time. DHCP also can provide other IP-related information to the client. Successful implementation of Microsoft's DHCP software usually requires updating IP routers with newer DHCP-aware software.

CONFIGURING DHCP SERVERS

One NT Server on each local LAN segment can be used as a DHCP server. NT 3.51's built-in internal router handles routing between the local segment and external networks.

The good news is that DHCP servers centralize the configuration process for using TCP/IP on a network, because you can handle all TCP/IP configuration for the network at the DHCP server.

The bad news is that IP host addresses are not necessarily assigned to the same client each time. When a specific client needs to have a specific IP address, the administrator can configure DHCP to assign a specific address to a specific node.

Note

Microsoft's Multi Protocol Router (now available) provides additional routing capabilities. This product is in an early release stage. You should check Microsoft's CompuServe forum, or its FTP or Gopher Internet server for the current release of this product.

You can find the Multi Protocol Router on Microsoft's CompuServe forum or its FTP or Gopher servers on the Internet at (ftp.microsoft.com or gopher.microsoft.com).

CREATING DHCP ADMINISTRATIVE SCOPES

The first step in configuring a DHCP Server that supplies IP addresses to DHCP Clients is to create a DHCP Scope, which consists of the following:

◆ A range of IP addresses that can be leased by DHCP Clients, often called an *IP address pool*. Each DHCP Server should have a unique pool of IP addresses that it can lease to DHCP Clients.

◆ A valid Subnet Mask for the pool of IP addresses.

◆ Any IP addresses in a range that need to be excluded so that they are not leased to DHCP Clients, such as the IP addresses of the DHCP Servers themselves.

◆ The duration of the IP address lease, which defaults to three days. The maximum lease duration can be set to either Unlimited or up to 999 days, 23 hours, and 59 minutes.

◆ A name (maximum of 128 characters) and comment for the DHCP Scope can also be supplied.

You create DHCP Scopes using the DHCP Manager utility, DHCPADMN.EXE, found in the Network Administration Program Manager group on a DHCP Server. Figure 21.2 shows the detailed property configuration information.

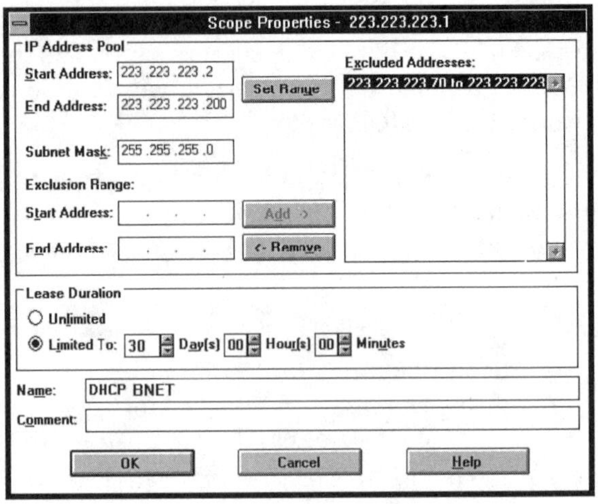

Figure 21.2.
DHCP Scope
Properties.

After you've created the administrative scope, you must activate it before the DHCP Server will lease any IP addresses from the DHCP's IP address pool. You can activate and deactivate a DHCP Scope from the DHCP Manager Scope menu. In DHCP Manager, active scopes are preceded by a yellow light bulb, and deactivated scopes are preceded by a gray light bulb.

After you've created a DHCP Scope, you can modify any of the scope's settings, such as the range of the IP address pool, from the Scope Properties menu.

RESERVING CLIENT IP ADDRESSES

When you use DHCP Manager, you can reserve a specific IP address for a client. This capability is useful in situations in which a user needs to install TCP/IP on a system that requires a specific IP address but is unfamiliar with configuring TCP/IP. The administrator can reserve the IP address required for the system using the Scope Add Reservations menu option in DHCP Manager and have the user simply enable automatic DHCP configuration. After you go through this step, when the system requests an IP address from the DHCP Server, the DHCP Server always returns the reserved IP address. Figure 21.3 shows this dialog box.

Figure 21.3.
Add Reserved Clients.

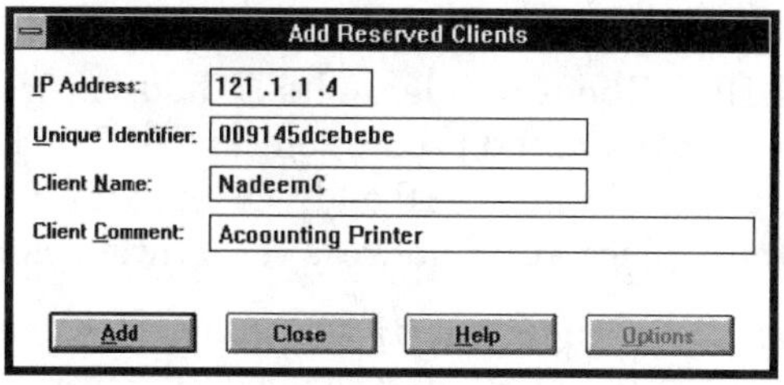

The two important entries in the Add Reserved Clients dialog box are

◆ Unique Identifier: This entry is the media access control (MAC) address (node address) for the DHCP Client. You can obtain this address by executing NET CONFIG RDR or IPCONFIG /ALL at a command prompt on the DHCP Client for which the IP address will be reserved. When you're reserving an IP address for a WFW system, this entry is the most important one that you must enter in the Add Reserved Clients dialog box because the DHCP Client sends its MAC address in its request to the DHCP Server for an IP address. If you enter this value incorrectly, it will not match the value sent by the DHCP Client, and the DHCP Server will assign the client any available IP address instead of the IP address reserved for the client.

◆ Client Name: This entry should be the computer name for the DHCP Client. However, it is used only for identification purposes in the DHCP Manager interface and thus does not have to be the same as the computer name. Different names will not affect the actual computer name. This entry is not available when adding reservations for DOS based DHCP Clients.

Note

An IP address reserved in DHCP Manager always takes precedence over any WINS static mappings if WINS is also being used.

ACTIVE DHCP CLIENT LEASES

You can use the Scope Active Leases menu in the DHCP Manager to see which DHCP Clients have leased an IP address from the DHCP Server. A dialog box appears when you choose this option displaying reserved IP addresses on the DHCP Server.

The Delete button in the dialog box removes the IP address lease for the selected DHCP Client. However, the DHCP Server does not notify the DHCP Client that its lease has been removed; therefore, no network activity results from removing a DHCP Client's IP address lease. The DHCP Client still can use TCP/IP with its leased IP address until it attempts to renew its lease, which will fail. The only way for a DHCP Client to release its IP address lease immediately is to use ipconfig / release at a command prompt on the DHCP Client. An administrator may want to delete a DHCP Client's IP address lease if it is a reserved IP address, because this is the only place an IP address reservation can be removed.

You can choose the Properties button to view the IP address, unique identifier, client name, client comment, and the lease expiration for the selected DHCP Client. The dialog box presented when this button is clicked is the same as the Add Reserved Clients dialog box; it includes on Options button, which is grayed out unless the selected DHCP Client has a reserved IP address. You can click the Options button to modify the DHCP Configuration options for the selected client only.

DHCP may seem to be an extra chore when you are setting up a TCP/IP network, but it is worth the effort. As your network grows, having a cleanly configured DHCP Server will help you in dealing with the day-to-day assignment of IP addresses.

WINDOWS INTERNET NAME SERVICES (WINS)

Windows Internet Name Service (WINS) maps NetBIOS names to IP addresses. WINS is simply a dynamic repository for NetBIOS names, mapping a 16-character NetBIOS name to an IP address. WINS is not used to locate resources, such as printers, servers, and so on. Instead, this job is handled by a separate database server known as the browse master. After a client has located a resource's NetBIOS name by browsing, it may use several mechanisms, including WINS, to convert the NetBIOS name to an IP address.

USING WINS TO REDUCE NETBIOS ADMINISTRATION

To ease administration of tracking NetBIOS names, NT Server provides WINS with NT Server 3.5. WINS is a NetBIOS Name Server (NBNS). It can register NetBIOS computer names and their respective IP addresses to the WINS database. It can respond to NetBIOS name queries by searching the WINS database, locating the NetBIOS name in question and responding with the respective IP address. WINS does not support NetBIOS name registration for DOS, Windows 3.1, or OS/2 clients.

INSTALLING A WINS SERVER

You install a WINS Server as part of the process of installing TCP/IP in NT Server. The following instructions assume you have already installed the NT Server operating system on the computer. You must be logged on as a member of the Administrators group to install a WINS Server.

1. Open the Control Panel and choose the Network option. The Network Settings dialog box then appears.

2. Choose the Add Software button to display the Add Network Software dialog box.

3. In the Network Software box, select TCP/IP Protocol And Related Components, and then choose the Continue button to display the Windows NT TCP/IP Installation Options dialog box.

4. Check the appropriate options to install, including at least one of the following options:

   WINS Server Service

   SNMP Service for configuring and monitoring WINS using SNMP or the Performance Monitor

5. Choose the OK button. NT Setup prompts you for the full path to the NT Server distribution files.

6. Type the full path to the NT Server distribution files, and then choose the Continue button.

7. Complete all the required procedures for manually configuring TCP/IP. The Network Settings dialog box appears again after you finish configuring TCP/IP.

8. Choose the Close button, and then reboot the computer. The TCP/IP and WINS Server software are now ready for use.

The Windows Internet Name Service is an NT service running on an NT computer. The support for WINS client software is automatically installed for the NT Server and for the NT Workstation when the basic operating system is installed.

To start, stop, pause, or continue the WINS service on any NT computer, follow these steps:

1. In the Control Panel, double-click the Services option, or from the Computer menu of Server Manager, choose Services. The Services dialog box appears.

2. Select the Windows Internet Name Service, and then choose the Start, Stop, Pause, or Continue button. Then choose the Close button.

3. You can start, stop, pause, or continue the WINS service at the command prompt using the commands `net start wins`, `net stop wins`, `net pause wins`, or `net continue wins`.

For each WINS Server, you must configure threshold intervals for triggering database replication, based on a specific time, a time period, or a certain number of new records. If you designate a specific time for replication, replication occurs one time only. If a time period is specified, replication is repeated at that interval.

CONFIGURING A WINS SERVER

To configure a WINS Server, follow these steps:

1. From the Server menu, choose the Configuration command. This command is available only if you are logged on as a member of the Administrators group for the WINS Server you want to configure.

2. To view all the options in this dialog box, choose the Advanced button.

3. For the configuration options in the WINS Server Configuration dialog box, specify time intervals as described in the following list.

   Renewal Interval: Specifies how often a client reregisters its name. The default is five hours.

   Extinction Interval: Specifies the interval between when an entry is marked as released and when it is marked as extinct. The default is dependent on the renewal interval and, if the WINS Server has replication partners, on the maximum replication time interval. The maximum allowable value is four days.

   Extinction Timeout: Specifies the interval between when an entry is marked extinct and when the entry is finally scavenged from the database. The default is dependent on the renewal interval and, if the WINS Server has replication partners, on the maximum replication time interval. The minimum allowable value is one day.

   Verify Interval: Specifies the interval after which the WINS Server must verify that old names it does not own are still active. The default is dependent on the extinction interval. The maximum allowable value is 24 days.

Figure 21.4 shows a WINS Server Configuration dialog box.

The replication interval for this WINS Server's pull partner is defined in the Preferences dialog box. The extinction interval, extinction timeout, and verify interval are derived from the renewal interval and the replication interval specified. The WINS Server adjusts the values specified by the administrator to keep the inconsistency between a WINS Server and its partners as small as possible.

Figure 21.4.
WINS Server
Configuration.

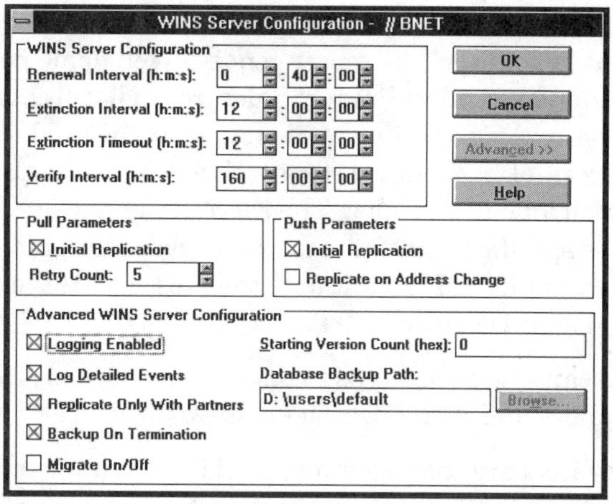

Take the following actions to manage the WINS Server.

1. If you want this WINS Server to pull replicas of new WINS database entries from its partners when the system is initialized or when a replication related parameter changes, select the Initial Replication in the Pull Parameters checkbox, and then type a value for Retry Count. The retry count is the number of times the server should attempt to connect (in case of failure) with a partner for pulling replicas. Retries are attempted at the replication interval specified in the Preferences dialog box. If all retries are unsuccessful, WINS waits for a period before starting replication again.

2. To inform partners of the database status when the system is initialized, select the Initial Replication checkbox in the Push Parameters group. To inform partners of the database status when an address changes in a mapping record, select the Replicate On Address Change checkbox.

3. Set any Advanced WINS Server Configuration options.

Using WINS is a better way to deal with name to IP address cross referencing. For some administrators, the complexity might be daunting in the beginning, but this service pays for itself in the long run.

WINDOWS NT RESOURCE KIT WEB SERVER

Bringing up a Web page on the World Wide Web is really popular today. You can get a jump on your competition if you establish your presence on the Internet to advertise your products, publicize your business, or sell information and information access.

The customer or user calling into the Web server might go through a sequence of steps as follows: The server sends a Web home page an HTML document that lets the customer select Product Sales from a list of choices. The server could then return a page with descriptions and pictures of the products. You show the prices, an e-mail address of a sales representative, and perhaps an option for the customer to download a full catalog. The server may have to use several protocols to carry out these specific tasks. If the customer chooses the sales representative e-mail address, for example, SMTP can carry the message. If the customer requests a copy of your catalog, it is sent via FTP.

You can also go so far as to have these responses and views built in real time using Gophers and WAIS search engines.

The links are managed by the HTTPS server, which maintains the HTML documents on the Web. Together with FTP and DNS, the NT EMWAC server package gives you almost everything to set up a WWW server. The only part missing is the SMTP server to handle e-mail. The Common Gateway Interface (CGI) 1.1 scripting standard is supported, but the target scripts must be NT-executable .EXE programs. This means that you need to do some programming. Instead, you could use Perl; the Web server manual shows examples of both methods. You can include WAIS searchable content, and you also can use the WAIS toolkit and the HTTPS server. Clickable images are also supported.

The Gopher Server for NT implements the Gopher protocol as described in RFC 1436. It runs as an NT service, just like the FTP server that comes with NT. The UNIX Gopher Server daemon is called *Gopherd*, and the NT Gopher Server service is called *Gophers* (which is pronounced Gopher-Ess). Gopher was named after the University of Minnesota mascot (where it was developed); it designates both the server and the client side.

How to Install and Configure the NT Resource Kit WEB Server

If you want to install and configure your MS WEB Server, follow these steps:

1. Log into your NT system as a user with administrative privileges.
2. The Gopher server is distributed in three versions: for the Intel, MIPS, and DEC Alpha architectures. Select the appropriate .ZIP file for your processor.
3. Unzip the file and look for the following files:

GOPHERS.EXE	The Gopher Server itself
GOPHERS.CPL	The Control Panel applet
GOPHERS.HLP	The Control Panel applet help file
READ.ME	Summary of new features and so on

4. Copy these files into the \WINNT35\SYSTEM32 directory, which is where many other services live. From the File Manager's Security menu, choose Permissions to ensure that the SYSTEM user has at least read permission for the files.

5. Start the Control Panel from the Program Manager to verify that the Gopher Server applet is represented as an icon.

6. Determine which version of Gophers you have. First, at the NT command prompt, type `gophers -version`; the version number is then displayed. You should also check the IP address of your computer using the command `gophers -ipaddress`; this command displays the name of your computer and its IP address as reported by the Windows Sockets API. If this information is incorrect, you need to reconfigure the TCP/IP software on your computer. The Gopher Server will not work if this address (or list of addresses if your computer has more than one network interface) is wrong.

7. Install Gophers into the table of NT Services and also register it with the Event Logger by running the program from the NT command line, specifying the `-install` flag. The program then registers itself and its location with the Service Manager and with the Event Logger, and it reports success or failure.

Note

You must execute the `gophers -ipaddress` command using the copy of GOPHERS.EXE, which you placed in the \WINNT35\SYSTEM32 directory.

8. To verify that the installation has succeeded, start the NT Control Panel and double-click the Services icon. The resulting dialog should list Gopher Server as one of the installed services.

If you plan to use the WAIS index searching capabilities of the Gopher Server, you should obtain and install the WAIS toolkit for Windows NT, available from EMWAC. Ensure that you place the WAISLOOK program in \WINNT35 \SYSTEM32.

The Gopher Service is known to the operating system as "GOPHERS." This means that the NT registry stores information about the service in a different place from earlier versions.

REMOVING THE GOPHER SERVER

If you want to remove the Gopher Server from your computer, or if you want to move the program to a new location, follow these steps:

1. If necessary, stop the Gopher Server by opening the Control Panel, choosing Services, and in the resulting Services dialog box, choosing the Stop button.

2. At the NT command line, run Gophers with the `-remove` option: `gophers -remove`. This command removes the Gopher Server from the Service Manager's list of services. It also deletes the Gopher Server's configuration information from the Registry.

3. If you are uninstalling the Gopher Server, simply delete the GOPHERS.EXE program, the GOPHERS.CPL Control Panel applet, and the GOPHERS.HLP help file.

4. If you want to move GOPHERS.EXE to a new location, you must move the file and then type `gophers -install`. This command informs the Service Manager and Event Logger of the new location of the program. You need to configure the Gopher Server and start it running again from the Control Panel.

CONFIGURING THE GOPHER SERVICE

You configure the Gopher Server using the Gopher Server applet in the Control Panel. The Gopher Server applet looks like Figure 21.5.

Figure 21.5.
Gopher Server.

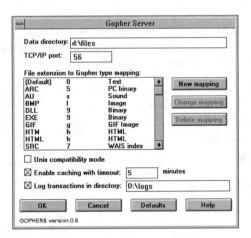

Note that the version number of the applet is displayed in the lower left-hand corner of the dialog box. The version number reported by the command `gophers -version` must be the same as the version number of the applet.

You can use this dialog to do the following:

♦ Set the root of the directory tree containing the files you want to make available using Gopher. Use the Data Directory field to make these changes. The default is D:\GOPHER. There are special considerations if the directory tree is located across a network on a server.

♦ Specify the TCP/IP port on which the Gopher Server listens for incoming connections. Use the TCP/IP Port field to make these changes. The value must be a positive integer representing a legal and otherwise unused port. The default is 70.

♦ Specify the Gopher type that corresponds to a given filename extension.

♦ Enable or disable whether caching is performed. Caching is disabled by default.

♦ Specify the timeout interval (in minutes) after which Gopher's cache files will be deemed to be out of date. Specify 0 to prevent cache files from being timed out. The default is 5 minutes.

♦ Enable and disable the logging of Gopher transactions. If this box is checked, the Gopher Server will record each Gopher request it receives in a log file. Logging is disabled by default.

♦ Specify the directory in which log files are stored. The default is the NT system directory (\WINNT35).

♦ Enable and disable a special UNIX Compatibility Mode. If this option is enabled, Gophers pays attention to files in the Data Directory with names starting with a dot. It treats such files (and also the .cap directory, if any) in the same way as the UNIX Gopherd program does. If you set the Data Directory to point to a FAT volume, you should not turn on this option because directory and filenames cannot begin with a dot on FAT volumes. The default is disabled.

♦ Restore the default values of all the configuration settings. Click the Defaults button to restore the values.

After you have finished making changes to the configuration, click the OK button. The configuration will take effect the next time you start the Gopher Server. If the Gopher Server is already running, a dialog box that reminds you to stop and restart it then appears.

The Gopher protocol represents the type of each file in a single byte. Several different types are defined in the protocol. The Gopher Server infers the type of a file from the filename extension, using a mapping table. The mapping table is configurable, using the list in the Control Panel applet and the buttons to its right, labeled New Mapping, Change Mapping, and Delete Mapping.

To change a mapping in the table, select the mapping in question from the list, and click the Change Mapping button. Figure 21.6 shows the resulting Change Mapping dialog box.

Figure 21.6.
Change Mapping
dialog box.

You can alter the extension you want to map using the Filename Extension field. From the list, you can select the Gopher type to which you want to map it (or you can enter the Gopher type character yourself if it's not in the list). Then choose OK to confirm your changes.

To create a new mapping, click on the New Mapping button in the Gopher Server dialog box. A dialog box, similar to the Change Mapping dialog box shown in Figure 21.6, then appears. You can use this box to specify the filename extension and to select the corresponding Gopher type. Note that you cannot create a new mapping for a filename extension already present in the mapping list—an extension can occur only once in the list.

To delete an existing mapping, select it from the list in the main Gopher Server dialog box, and click the Delete Mapping button.

If no entry for a particular extension exists in the mapping table, the Gopher Server will use the default extension mapping. This mapping is shown in the list with Default in the File Extension column. You can change the default extension mapping in the same way you change other mappings, but you cannot delete it.

If the directory tree that you want to make available to Gopher clients is located on a server instead of on the local NT computer, you will need to take special action. Normally, directories on the server are mapped to a drive letter on the local system. You might expect that simply using the mapped drive letter in the Gopher Server configuration dialog box would have the desired effect, and indeed it does, until you log off the local computer.

Drive mappings are established only when someone logs on to the NT computer. They are specific to a user, not to the computer. The Gopher Server is normally kept running, independently of whether someone is logged onto the computer or not.

Often, the Gopher Server is set to start up automatically when the operating system loads, when no one is logged in and, therefore, no drive mappings are in effect.

To overcome this problem, you can specify the Gopher Data Directory to the Gopher Configuration dialog box using a UNC form of directory name, for instance:

```
\\BNET\DATASERV
```

Here, BNET is the name of the server, and DATASERV is the Share name of the directory that is to be served using Gopher.

OPERATING THE GOPHER SERVICE

You use the Services dialog box in the NT Control Panel for managing Gophers operation. After you install Gophers, you can start it running by selecting it from the list of services in the Services dialog box and clicking the Start button. If all goes well, a message box containing a rotating timer will appear while the service starts up and will then disappear. The Gopher Server will then appear in the list of services with status Started and will be able to respond to Gopher clients.

You may want to arrange for the Gopher Server to start automatically when the system is started. You can do so by using the Startup button in the Services dialog box. You can also use this button to specify a different user ID under which Gophers can run.

Pausing the Gopher Server using the Pause button in the Services dialog box causes the following behavior:

◆ Any Gopher transactions currently underway are unaffected. They will run to completion.

◆ Any new Gopher connections are queued. When the service is resumed, they will be accepted and processed.

If more than five incoming connections are received while the service is paused, the extra connections will be rejected.

HTTP SERVER

The HTTP Server for NT implements the HTTP/1.0 protocol. It runs as an NT service, just like the FTP Server that comes with NT. The UNIX HTTP Server daemon is called httpd, and the NT HTTP Server service is called https. The HTTP Server service is configured using a Control Panel applet.

INSTALLING HTTP SERVER

To install the HTTP Server, follow these steps:

1. Log into your NT system as a user with administrative privileges.

2. The HTTP Server is distributed in three versions: for the Intel, MIPS, and DEC Alpha architectures. Select the appropriate ZIP file for your processor.

3. Unzip the file. You should have the following files:

HTTPS.EXE	The HTTP Server itself
HTTPS.CPL	The Control Panel applet
HTTPS.HLP	The Control Panel applet help file
CGISRIPT.ZIP	Sample CGI script programs
READ.ME	Summary of new features, and so on

4. Put HTTPS.EXE in the \WINNT35\SYSTEM32 directory, which is where many other services live. From the File Manager's Security menu, choose Permissions to verify that the SYSTEM user has read permission for the files.

5. Move HTTPS.CPL and HTTPS.HLP to the \WINNT35\SYSTEM32 directory. Start the Control Panel from the Program Manager to verify that the HTTP Server applet is represented as an icon.

6. Determine which version of HTTPS you have. At the NT Command prompt, type **https -version**; the version number is then displayed. You should also check the IP address of your computer by typing the command **https -ipaddress**; this command displays the name of your computer and its IP address as reported by the Windows Sockets API. If this information is incorrect, you need to reconfigure the TCP/IP software on your computer. The HTTP Server does not work if this address (or list of addresses if your computer has more than one network interface) is wrong.

7. Install HTTPS into the table of NT Services (and simultaneously register it with the Event Logger) by running the program from the NT command line, specifying the **-install** flag. The program registers itself with the Service Manager and with the Event Logger, and then reports success or failure.

8. To verify that the installation has succeeded, start the NT Control Panel and double-click the Services icon. The resulting dialog box should list HTTP Server as one of the installed services.

HTTPS CONFIGURATION

You configure the HTTP Server using the HTTP Server applet in the Control Panel. The HTTP Server applet looks like Figure 21.7.

Figure 21.7.
HTTP Server.

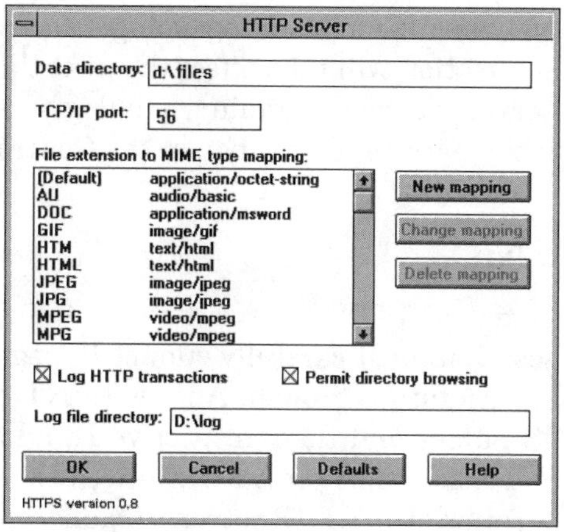

Note that the version number of the applet is displayed in the lower left-hand corner of the dialog box. The version number reported by the command `https -version` must be the same as the version number of the applet. If no version number appears in the lower left-hand corner, you are using version 0.2 of the applet.

You can use the HTTP Server dialog box to do the following:

◆ Set the root of the directory tree containing the files you want to make available on the World Wide Web. Use the Data Directory field to make these changes. The default is D:\HTTP.

◆ Specify the TCP/IP port on which the HTTP Server listens for incoming HTTP connections. Use the TCP/IP Port field to make this change. The value must be a positive integer representing a legal and otherwise unused port. The default is 80.

◆ Specify the MIME type that corresponds to a given filename extension.

◆ Enable and disable the logging of HTTP transactions. If this box is checked, the HTTP Server will record each HTTP request it receives in a log file. Logging is disabled by default.

◆ Specify the directory in which log files are stored. Use the Log File Directory field for this purpose. This capability is disabled unless the Log HTTP Transactions box is checked. The default is the NT System directory (\WINNT35).

◆ Permit the HTTP Data Directory tree to be browsed by HTTP clients. Browsing is disabled by default.

◆ Restore the default values of all the configuration settings. Click the Default button to restore the values.

After you have finished making changes to the configuration, click the OK button. The configuration will take effect the next time you start the HTTP Server. If the HTTP Server is already running, a dialog box that reminds you to stop and restart it (using the Services dialog box in the Control Panel) appears.

SUMMARY

Management of TCP/IP networks is not simple. You must assign and track IP addresses. You must carefully subnet IP segments to provide both segments and addresses for future growth. And, with NT Server, you must register and track NetBIOS names and their respective IP addresses throughout the network. Although NT Server 3.51 provides utilities to simplify some of this IP administration, administration of a TCP/IP network is generally considered more difficult than IPX. NT Server 3.51 provides Dynamic Host Configuration Protocol (DHCP) and Windows Internet Name Server (WINS) to alleviate IP administration and NetBIOS broadcast problems, respectively.

The NT Resource Kit includes the EMWAC programs to fill out Microsoft's TCP/IP and internetworking strategy.

The World Wide Web is the most popular of many Internet services you might peruse to make your presence known on the Internet. Its HyperText Transfer Protocol (HTTP) and HyperText Markup Language (HTML), working together, enable you to build electronic documents that can, in turn, enable you to use other powerful protocols such as Simple Mail Transfer Protocol (SMTP), File Transfer Protocol (FTP), Gopher, Wide Area Information Service (WAIS), and telnet.

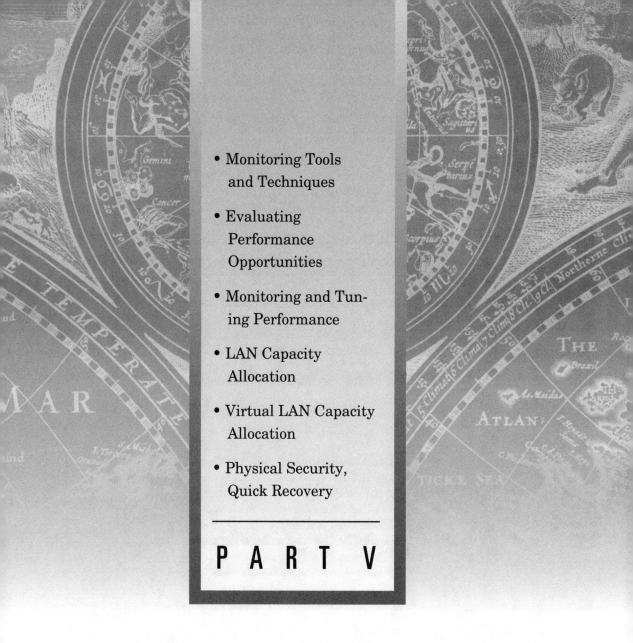

- Monitoring Tools and Techniques

- Evaluating Performance Opportunities

- Monitoring and Tuning Performance

- LAN Capacity Allocation

- Virtual LAN Capacity Allocation

- Physical Security, Quick Recovery

PART V

Optimizing Performance, Reducing Downtime

- Monitoring Local Area Networks

- Monitoring the NT Server Operating System

- Monitoring Server Usage

- Monitoring Disk Subsystems

CHAPTER 22

Monitoring Tools and Techniques

MAU   Multistation Access Unit (Token ring hub)

CAU   Control Access Unit (Intelligent Token ring hub)

LLC   Logical Link Control (IEEE 802.2 bridging protocol)

SNAP   Subnetwork Access Protocol (TCP/IP extensions to LLC)

A system administrator is responsible for monitoring the networks. You therefore need to monitor the following hardware subsystems of your network:

◆ Local area networks

◆ NT Server operating system

◆ Server usage

◆ Disk drive storage

This chapter discusses three goals to be achieved in monitoring each of these subsystems. You should monitor each subsystem for

1. Advance warning of impending failures

2. Potential problems as they develop

3. Opportunities for improving performance

This chapter discusses each of these subsystems. The focus of this chapter is to suggest tools and techniques you can use to monitor your network. Specifics of monitoring and troubleshooting these subsystems are discussed in greater depth in later chapters.

You also learn the goals of monitoring each subsystem. Particular attention is paid to the most common and most critical problems that you may encounter. This chapter discusses performance opportunities; however, because this topic is so important, Chapter 23, "Evaluating Performance Opportunities," explains this topic in greater depth.

MONITORING LOCAL AREA NETWORKS

Your Ethernet, Token ring, or other type of LAN is a complex subsystem. Although installation and configuration have been simplified, a LAN can develop problems that require immediate attention.

The performance and usability of your entire network rests upon the LAN. The LAN is a platform upon which servers, client workstations, printers, and other network resources all rely for effectiveness. If the LAN has problems, other components cannot work properly.

Each type of LAN works differently and has its own problems and symptoms. This section discusses Ethernet and Token ring LANs. The discussion of these two types of LANs includes Fast Ethernet and FDDI LANs, which are similar in scope with their predecessors.

The most common problems include

- Physical devices, including cabling, connectors, hubs, routers, and bridges
- Defective network adapter cards
- Improper configuration or defective drivers and protocol files

CABLING AND CONNECTORS

You should inspect your cabling periodically, especially cabling that is exposed and can be damaged. After any work is performed in a wiring closet or where cabling is present, you should inspect the cabling for any damage or movement that may have occurred.

Most LANs today run on unshielded twisted-pair cabling. Category 5 cabling can support bandwidths of up to 155 Mbps. Fast Ethernet has been effectively marketed for use with Category 3 through 5 unshielded twisted-pair cabling. This is a dangerous proposition because Ethernet relies on perfect cabling conditions for proper performance.

Always use EIA/TIA 568 cabling rules in cabling your LAN. This standard was developed to deal with all types of LANs. EIA/TIA 568 discusses selection and installation of Unshielded Twisted Pair (UTP), Shielded Twisted Pair (STP), and fiber optic cabling. Applications over 10 Mbps require category 5 UTP, STP, or fiber optic cabling.

EIA/TIA 568 limits "horizontal" cable segments to 90 meters from the outlet to the punchdown block, as shown in Figure 22.1. Horizontal cabling is defined as cabling systems from the wiring closet to the data outlet in the work area.

This cabling restriction does not include the patch cables from the data outlet to the network adapter card, or from the punchdown block to the wiring concentrator. The combined length of the patch cables should not exceed 10 meters, or 10 percent of the total combined length per cabling segment. All portions of a cabling segment should be of the same type of cable (category 5 versus 3).

Even though cabling and installation conforms to these specifications, external sources of interference can cause data errors, especially with UTP because it has little protection for external electromagnetic interference sources. Continuity and proper RJ-45 pin-out do not assure you that your cabling is good. You must evaluate other cabling factors to ensure the proper functioning of your LAN. Cabling must have the proper electronic characteristics including loss, attenuation, noise, and near-end crosstalk, as well as length and proper components.

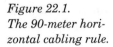

Figure 22.1.
The 90-meter hori-
zontal cabling rule.

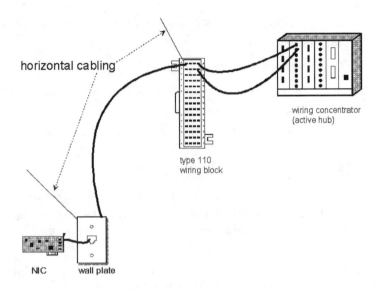

EIA/TIA 568 specifications provide minimum specifications for each of these parameters to meet category 3, 4, 5, and IBM type specifications. Chapter 30, "LAN Troubleshooting," discusses these specifications and how to certify your cabling to these specifications.

ETHERNET CABLING

Ethernet relies on perfect cabling conditions to operate properly. It uses the Carrier Sense Multiple Access with Collision Detection (CSMA/CD) access protocol to drive its operation. Though a Cyclic Redundancy Check (CRC) is present in the trailer of each frame, CSMA/CD does not make much provision for error control, reporting, or recovery. Therefore, monitoring is imperative if consistent productivity is to be assured.

When an Ethernet LAN has minor cabling problems, at the very least, usable bandwidth is limited. When cabling problems are minor, you may be able to log on, work, and function normally; however, problems surface when bandwidth utilization reaches higher levels. Because cabling problems statistically account for over half of all network disabilities (according to several recent surveys), if you cannot log on to an external server over the LAN, one of the first actions you should take is to inspect your cabling and connectors for damage.

Ethernet 10Base-T cabling must use category 3, 4, or 5 UTP. However, 100Base-TX requires strict compliance with category 5 specifications. It is also limited to no more than two repeaters in a series.

IEEE's 100Base-T4 standard provides for Fast Ethernet (100 Mbps) over category 3 (voice grade) cabling. However, you are required to have only one repeater in a series from any point to any point on your LAN.

You can link together 10Base-T, 100Base-TX, and 100Base-T4 LAN segments with bridges, switching hubs, or routers between them. In this configuration, each LAN segment is a separate physical subsystem. Bridges or routers form the boundaries between LANs.

Note

> Be sure to check your NT Server configuration for routing capabilities before you purchase or install a router. NT's routing support is quite limited. NT Server version 3.51 contains a router that routes only IP packets in the same server where Microsoft's DHCP is installed and working properly.
>
> NT Server version 3.51 does not support routing of IPX, NetBIOS, or NetBEUI protocols, or IP routing where host addresses have been assigned. Microsoft plans to release an upgrade or add-on that will support IPX and IP routing for assigned host addresses. Check with one of your Microsoft support vehicles for additional support.

Monitoring Ethernet

Because Ethernet is susceptible to cabling problems, virtually all major hub vendors provide monitoring devices and software for this purpose. Most monitoring software is vendor specific and manages intelligent hubs (a wiring concentrator with a CPU and a monitoring agent). The hub monitors the LAN's vital signs and reports any incidents perceived to be of concern to the monitoring software module.

Simple Network Management Protocol (SNMP) and Management Information Database (MIB)

Messages sent by an intelligent hub are usually transmitted through a special type of protocol data unit and error log. Although most vendors have standardized on the Simple Network Management Protocol (SNMP) as a strategy, SNMP is not always available to you unless you use TCP/IP protocols. Most SNMP-compatible software products collect SNMP messages and store them in a Management Information Database (MIB) for later retrieval and analysis.

You should check with your hub vendor for vendor-specific monitoring software. Many hubs can be upgraded with a monitoring agent, and many others are equipped with this capability although you may not have implemented the monitor.

OUT-OF-BAND MONITORING

Many monitors use out-of-band monitoring. A serial port is provided on the device to which you can attach a modem, or a null modem cable. You can then attach to a monitoring workstation and receive monitoring information over the serial link. This way, you can monitor the hub even when the LAN is non-functional.

NON-VENDOR-SPECIFIC MONITORING

You can use non-vendor-specific devices or software to monitor an Ethernet LAN. This capability is helpful when the LAN infrastructure consists of products from multiple vendors and when hubs are not equipped with monitoring agents.

Several excellent software packages are available to monitor Ethernet, including

> Microsoft's System Management Server
> Hewlett-Packard's OpenView
> Sun Microsystems' SunNet Manager
> Intel LANDesk Manager
> Novell's LANalyzer for Windows

HP's OpenView is available in UNIX and Windows versions, and uses SNMP to support its own and other vendors' products. OpenView for UNIX is far more robust than its Windows counterpart; however, this product is one of the finest Ethernet-monitoring packages that is not vendor specific.

Sun Microsystems' SunNet Manager is available in a UNIX version only. This product is among the very finest non-vendor-specific monitors, and it should be considered, despite this limitation. Because it uses SNMP, the SunNet Manager can accumulate error statistics from virtually any device that supports SNMP, provided you use TCP/IP transport.

Intel's LANDesk Manager has many other features, such as the capability to edit workstation configuration files and virus protection. LANDesk is universal but supports only its own error communication protocol. Therefore, products it monitors must be prepared for use with LANDesk Manager. In most cases, vendors have not been willing to spend the time to write drivers to support Intel's proprietary error notification system. If you purchase this product, make certain that your hubs, bridges, routers, and so on support this product.

PROTOCOL ANALYZERS

A protocol analyzer is far more than a monitor, but most protocol analyzers include monitoring functions. Several prominent protocol analyzers are available. They can monitor the Ethernet or Token ring LAN as well as capture LAN frames for later analysis.

The monitoring features are best typified by Novell's LANalyzer for NetWare. It is a software-only product that is geared more toward monitoring than it is toward full protocol analysis. LANalyzer runs on top of network adapters that have special promiscuous-mode drivers. A *promiscuous-mode* driver can capture all LAN frames instead of only the ones that are addressed to the MAC (node) address.

LANalyzer's opening screen shows the dashboard and the station monitor. This screen monitors LAN statistics and NetWare-specific server statistics. LANalyzer works with Ethernet and Token ring LANs only, and it provides minimal protocol encodes for IPX, NetBIOS, TCP/IP, and AppleTalk packet formats only.

The dashboard shows current levels of bandwidth utilization, packets per second, and errors per second. The station monitor has many columns showing traffic and error statistics, node addresses, and so on. You can double-click any column header to sort the list in descending or ascending order. Clicking the headers enables you to find the most active nodes, the ones with the highest error levels, and more.

You can select a trend analysis to show a time segment of utilization on several aspects of your traffic. LANalyzer's trend monitoring graphs utilization over an extended period.

Most protocol analyzers have these functions and more. The most expensive part of a protocol analyzer is the engineering that goes into protocol decodes. Network General decodes the largest list of protocols at all levels. This engineering takes a tremendous amount of labor and knowledge, which is important only to those people who need support for specific protocols.

Microsoft BackOffice System Management Server (SMS) includes a Network Monitor feature that includes many protocol analysis options. See Chapter 30, "LAN Troubleshooting," for more details on SMS.

Other protocol analyzers include

> Network General's Sniffer
> Hewlett-Packard's Network Analyzer
> Wandel & Goltermann's Domino
> Triticom's LANdecoder
> Network Communications Corporation's LANalyzer
> Dolphin Network's ESP Family

Protocol analysis of Ethernet and Token ring is discussed more fully in Chapter 30.

HARDWARE-BASED MONITORS

You can connect hardware-based monitors to your LAN cabling. An example of a hardware-based monitor is Network General's Watchdog. Network General makes the Sniffer protocol analyzer, but they sell the monitoring portion only for a much lower price. Watchdog includes a specially prepared network adapter and software. You must install the adapter only in specific types of computers where the bus and the card are well synchronized. Generally, you can purchase a PCMCIA network adapter for a notebook computer. PCMICA specifications are strict enough to provide a predictable interface for the special network adapter.

Watchdog monitors many error statistics and performance levels, gives a distribution of packet sizes, and much more. One of Watchdog's best features is an extensive report writer. You can print out reports on specific statistics to compare to previous levels; this way, you can tell if your network is growing in usage, whether traffic patterns have changed, and so on.

The products discussed here are just a few of the ones made to help you monitor your LAN. More products exist to provide tools for monitoring your Ethernet LANs. Consult with your network vendor for more suggestions.

WHAT TO LOOK FOR WHEN ANALYZING ETHERNET

Ethernet has little error control information that is available to detect problems. Generally, you may notice a few general errors that can indicate the source of problems. You should watch for the following statistics:

◆ Bad CRCs—If a frame has been damaged in any way, the CRC in the trailer will not compare with the CRC recalculation in the receiving node. A bad CRC may be the result of normal operations. Jabber control can generate bad CRCs in the normal course of operations. Generally, five errors per second or higher is an abnormal level.

Note

Bad cabling can be responsible for bad CRCs.

◆ Short frames—Each Ethernet frame must carry a minimum of 46 bytes in its data portion. Each IPX, IP, NetBIOS, NetBEUI, or other type of packet that the frame carries has at least a 46-byte header. The frame is padded with null data to the minimum (46 bytes) when no packet is included. However, there is no reason for a frame with no packet, so a small frame is an indication that frames are being sent unnecessarily or that the frame was interrupted during transmission.

Short frames are the result of normal jabber control, which prevents a node from dominating time on the wire. Jabber control, implemented in the transceiver, interrupts a transmission when it exceeds the maximum length for one frame.

A high level of short frames (more than a few per second) indicates a defective network adapter. Although this occurrence is less common than in the past, having short frames is still one of the most common errors to look for.

◆ Long frames—The Ethernet maximum frame length is about 1,500 bytes (depending on frame type) plus frame header and trailer data and the inter-frame gap. The presence of any frames that are too long indicates a defective network adapter, transceiver, or driver. There is not an acceptable level for this problem, because clearly even one long frame is a result of a defect.

◆ High Collision Level—As bandwidth utilization climbs, the likelihood of collisions increases. A utilization rate of 5 percent means that 5 percent of the time the wire is busy. This means that 5 percent of the time the *potential* for a collision is present. If the wire is busy, the network adapter card or workstation buffers will cache up backlogged frames and transmit them as soon as possible. Collisions occur when two cards start transmission simultaneously and find other bits on the wire during the first part of the transmission. The collision rate at low levels of utilization (under 30 percent) is negligible.

At higher levels of bandwidth utilization, collisions are a normal part of traffic. At 60 to 70 percent utilization, collisions are very high, almost to the point of restricting available bandwidth for data transmission.

A high level of collisions can be adequately measured only from a network device, not in a particular workstation. The device must set on the cable instead of on the other side of a transceiver.

High collision rates are normally the result of excessive levels of traffic and cannot be avoided unless you reduce the traffic levels. See "Bandwidth utilization" for better analysis of a LAN network with too much traffic.

◆ Bandwidth utilization—The percentage of time the cable is occupied with signaling is the bandwidth utilization. Because no more than one Ethernet frame can exist on the LAN at any given time, bandwidth is a measure of capacity, not speed.

When bandwidth utilization exceeds 30 percent, it is judged to be excessive. At this level, the likelihood of collisions increases, and too much capacity is eaten up with non-productive traffic. You should monitor excessive levels of bandwidth utilization, not for errors, but to assess the need to segment users into separate LANs.

◆ Frame type—Detecting the frame types in use and mapping them to nodes are important tasks if two nodes cannot communicate.

22

MONITORING TOOLS AND TECHNIQUES

You also can detect a few other statistics to asses the nature of traffic on your LAN. You can view frame size distributions to see what typical traffic should be like on your network. The distribution of protocols in use is of interest to managers who want to determine how much capacity is required for new users. Also, the presence of previously unknown node addresses indicates that a new network adapter, perhaps unauthorized, has been connected.

Many monitors attempt to diagnose problems by setting threshold levels for any of the preceding statistics. When a threshold is reached, the monitor can sound an alarm, execute an application that will notify the system administrator, and/or log error entries.

TOKEN RING

Token-passing ring access protocol is far more stable than Ethernet, can detect cabling problems, and can diagnose and report many error conditions. Over 50 types of MAC frames are used for this purpose, including the Beacon MAC frame type, which is most commonly found when problems occur.

Most later model Token ring network adapters can use either STP or UTP cabling. UTP requires a media filter, which is contained in the network adapter. Two ports are generally provided: a DB-9 for STP and an RJ-45 for category 5 UTP.

IBM's maximum cabling rules are complex and cumbersome. Today most vendors simply rely on EIA/TIA 568 standards. You can use IBM's STP charts for longer cabling runs. However, distances can vary according to the type of MAU/CAU used, the number of MAUs/CAUs, and how many nodes are to be installed. Most newer Token ring installations rely on category 5 UTP with the standard 90-meter (horizontal) cabling rule.

MONITORING TOKEN RING

Error-recovery procedures in token-passing access protocol become obvious. When performance degrades, all you have to do to determine the offending node or cabling segment is to stand at the MAU or CAU and listen to its switches or watch its indicator lights. A node that disconnects and reattaches is sure to subject the entire LAN to performance-robbing reconfigurations.

The presence of MAC frames (with the exception of the token) signals error detection or recovery in process. It is possible to detect these MAC frames and determine the nature of the problem, however. MAC frames have no addressing; they are simply passed around the ring (physically).

When error-detecting MAC frames are found, you must find the originating node. You accomplished this by "walking the ring," checking one node at a time until you find the originating node.

Less support is available for Token ring monitoring than is available for Ethernet. Far less Token ring is used than Ethernet, and many vendors share the business. IBM's Token Ring accounts for over 70 percent of all Token ring nodes and equipment. MAUs, CAUs, and Token ring network adapters are relatively expensive.

Several vendor-specific Token ring monitoring products are available. IBM's NetView is an excellent product for monitoring Token ring; however, it is usually used only in IBM Token Ring environments because it is designed to manage the entire network, including hosts.

Many protocol analyzers are available in both Ethernet and Token ring flavors. Check with your Token ring vendor, and with protocol analyzer vendors for a good Token ring monitoring/analysis tool.

BEACONING

Beaconing is the most common error-recovery procedure you can detect. When a node does not receive a free token for a set period of time, it sends a beacon MAC frame to its Nearest Active Downstream Neighbor (NADN). The NADN in turn beacons its NADN, and the beacon travels around the ring. If the beacon returns to its originator, all is well. If it does not, the beaconing node removes itself from the ring and later attempts to reinsert itself.

The presence of beaconing and reinsertion indicates a defective cable or network adapter. The node that removes itself and reinserts is the originating node. You can observe beaconing in process from the MAU or CAU (hub) by listening to the switches. When you hear a click, a node has disconnected or inserted into the ring. The switch that is clicking on and off regularly is the beaconing node and should be disconnected until the problem is fixed.

RING RE-INITIALIZATION

Ring re-initialization is another concern. This problem is the result of a serious ring failure. A re-initialization occurs whenever a serious error condition brings the ring down. Once this happens, Token ring's automatic error recovery feature re-initializes the ring as if it were coming up for the first time. When re-initialization occurs repeatedly, you must find and correct the source of this problem.

FRAME TYPES

Like Ethernet, Token ring also can be affected from dissimilar frame types. Token ring has two basic frame formats, and either one can have LLC or SNAP protocol data units.

In Token ring, all nodes on a ring must use the same frame type. Each frame passes through every network adapter on the LAN. When a node enters the ring with a different frame type, the entire ring can enter an error condition, causing total ring failure.

MONITORING THE NT SERVER OPERATING SYSTEM

NT provides a few tools for monitoring the operating system and software modules that run on NT. The Event Viewer and Dr. Watson for Windows NT are included in every NT installation. The Event Viewer automatically monitors and records system error messages that happen behind the scenes. You must configure Dr. Watson to log messages; it can monitor software application errors that are often missed by the Event Viewer. The NT Messages Database provides access to error messages, details, and explanations.

EVENT VIEWER

Whenever a server component cannot perform properly, an error message is logged in one of Event Viewer's logs. The error messages you read are in plain English—you don't have to run a debugger or know assembly language to understand what happened. You can find the Event Viewer in the Administrative Tools program group (see Figure 22.2).

Figure 22.2.
The Event Viewer.

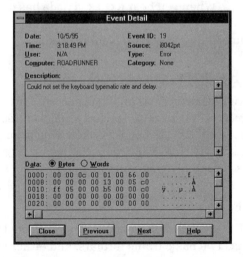

THE EVENT VIEWER'S THREE LOGS

The Event Viewer has three logs:

- System
- Security
- Application

These logs capture error messages generated by the operating system during boot and operation. The System and Application logs automatically capture messages during execution. The Security log captures messages only when Auditing is turned on.

When a driver fails to load, a security breach denies access, or an application fails, you should be able to look at the Event Viewer and figure out what has gone wrong.

MAINTAINING THE LOGS

As messages are recorded in your event logs, new messages overwrite older messages on a first-in-first-out basis. Check the Event Log Settings in Event Viewer for limitations on file sizes. You can limit the size of the log, limit the amount of time before events are removed, or allow the log to capture all entered until manually purged. You can delete the records from the logs by choosing Clear All Events from the Log menu in the Event Viewer.

Note

You can turn off event logging in Control Panel's, Services utility. However, if you do, you will lose the ability to find background error messages in case of a system failure. Turning off event logging is not recommended.

To control the types of security events to be audited, choose Audit from the Policies menu in User Manager. To control the auditing of file and directory access, choose Auditing from the Security menu in File Manager.

DR. WATSON FOR WINDOWS NT

Another tool that is available with NT is the Dr. Watson for Windows NT utility. This application error debugger can monitor software application messages. These messages relate more directly with software applications you buy and install on your NT computer. You should turn on and monitor software modules before calling for technical support.

Dr. Watson's error log is contained in the file DRWTSN32.LOG in the *<winroot>*\System32 directory. This file can be uploaded to support personnel for analysis.

You can turn on the binary crash dump option in Dr. Watson. This way, you or software support personnel can load the contents of memory at the time the crash occurred into the Windows NT debugger for analysis.

SETTING UP THE DR. WATSON UTILITY

To install Dr. Watson as an icon on your desktop, simply choose New from the File menu, and find the DRWTSN32.EXE in the *<winroot>*\system32 directory. You can also execute Dr. Watson from File Manager, Program Manager (File, Run), or from the command prompt.

After you have installed Dr. Watson, you can view its Application Error log, as shown in Figure 22.3.

Figure 22.3.
The Dr. Watson utility.

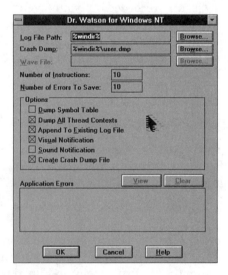

When applications generate errors, you see a dialog box on your screen. However, Dr. Watson intercepts exception handlers that the software generates to produce the error message you see on your screen.

If no exception handler is found, the system checks the Registry for an application debugger that may have been provided by the software developer. You will find the Debugger and Auto values in \\HKEY_LOCAL_MACHINE\ Software\Microsoft\Windows NT\CurrentVersion\AeDebug. The two values provide the following information:

Debugger: The name of the debugger module provided by the developer that can be used to analyze software-specific errors.

Auto: A value set to zero or one. A zero indicates that a message box will appear when an error occurs, and you will be able to start the debugger named in the Debugger value. A value of one indicates that the debugger will automatically start the debugger named in the Debugger value.

The default from a normal NT installation sets the Debugger value to DRWTSN32 and the Auto value to one. This way, Dr. Watson can track and debug the error, and log the error information.

Note

If you have installed a different debugger and want to revert to Dr. Watson, enter `DRWTSN32.EXE -I` at a command prompt. The `-I` switch causes the Registry to be updated.

Setting Up the Microsoft Windows NT Messages Database

The NT CD-ROM has a full error messages database and search engine that you can install. These options are not installed on your hard drive by default. These modules take up less than 5MB of disk space and make error chasing much easier. The NT Messages search application is shown in Figure 22.4.

Figure 22.4.
The Microsoft Win-
dows NT Messages
search application.

To install the NT Messages database, run the Setup program located in the \SUPPORT\WINNTMSG directory on your installation CD-ROM. This program creates a Microsoft Windows NT Messages common program group with four icons:

◆ Windows NT Messages
◆ Compact Database
◆ Read Me
◆ Change Workgroup

The Windows NT Messages applet provides a method of viewing error messages and searching the error message database from entries displayed on the screen.

You can compress your log entries by selecting the Compact Database applet.

You can read additional instructions that may not be included elsewhere.

Change Workgroup enables you to select and monitor an error log on another server (provided you have appropriate access permissions).

For more information about troubleshooting and resolving problems, see Chapter 27, "Physical Security, Quick Recovery."

MONITORING SERVER USAGE

Monitoring an NT Server is an important task. Microsoft provides many tools in an NT Server to allow for monitoring of virtually every aspect of your system. Tools that are provided enable you to watch the usage of almost every process, task, and resource in your server.

For example, the Performance Monitor utility enables you to observe RAM usage in the form of a trend graph (see Figure 22.5). This tool enables you at a glance to determine whether you have enough RAM in your server. You can find the Performance Monitor in the Administrative Tools program group.

Figure 22.5.
Performance Monitor.

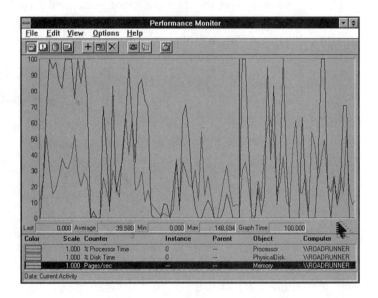

You can also monitor software applications running on your server, such as the SQL Server. Monitoring these applications enables you to get a peek into the execution of modules and the resources used as a result of program execution, database searches, merging, indexing, and other software application-related activities.

The NT Server is packed with a plethora of resources, each of which requires RAM and processor time. Each process requires resources, and you can have a ringside seat observing resource usage.

Because monitoring usage is so important, this book devotes an entire chapter to this topic alone. See Chapter 23, "Evaluating Performance Opportunities," for more detail on monitoring your server.

MONITORING DISK SUBSYSTEMS

Disk drives and disk subsystems require constant monitoring. Your disk storage subsystem is the heart of your network. The server operating system and all data files reside on one or more disk drives. Though drive failure is not the most frequent problem you will face, it can be the most serious.

In many systems, fault tolerance has a serious downside. The biggest problem may be that when a drive goes down you may not even be aware of it. When a drive is down in a mirrored or stripe set, and you expect your disk subsystem to recover from further disabilities, you will be sadly disappointed. You should check the fitness of your disk drives on a frequent basis.

VIEWING DISK PARTITIONS

You can use the Disk Administrator to view the partitions on your server's disk drives. The Disk Administrator cannot show you much about your drives' operation; it shows you only the partitions, type of partitions, striping information, and enables you to perform a few tasks, such as renaming a volume.

You can find the Disk Administrator in the Administrative Tools program group; it is shown in Figure 22.6.

Figure 22.6.
Disk Administrator.

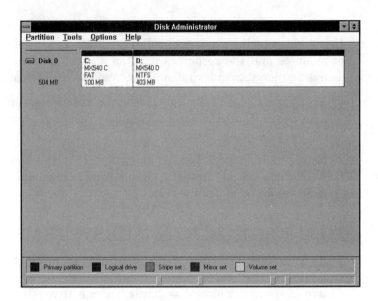

CHECKING THE FILE SYSTEM

NT's CHKDSK is designed to scan file system integrity for lost clusters, cross-linked files, and so on. NT's CHKDSK can scan NTFS, HPFS, and FAT partitions. If errors are found, CHKDSK attempts to repair them. However, when CHKDSK is run without any switches, it is in a read-only mode, so repairs are not saved to disk.

Note

When file system damage is detected during boot, NT automatically runs CHKDSK as part of its boot procedure.

CHKDSK reports the following:

> Type of file system
> Total disk space
> Disk space in use
> Disk space available
> Allocation unit information

CHKDSK has three option switches:

> /FFixes errors found in the file system
> /vProvides verbose listing of files during usage
> /RLocates bad sectors and recovers readable information

When you run CHKDSK, first run it without switches. If lost clusters exist, then run CHKDSK using the /F switch. You can run CHKDSK from a command prompt within Windows NT. If the volume being checked is a Share that is in use by a client, CHKDSK will ask if you want to allow CHKDSK to run the next time NT is brought up.

Under certain conditions, you cannot run CHKDSK. For example, when you run CHKDSK on a volume that contains an active paging file, it cannot complete its scan. Under these conditions, elect to run CHKDSK the next time the system is booted.

DISK UTILITIES TO CHECK THE PHYSICAL DISK SUBSYSTEM

NT does not provide utilities to check the physical stability of your disk subsystem. You should use utilities provided with your disk adapter for this purpose.

SCSI disk adapter developers provide either a program on disk with their adapters or a BIOS chip on the SCSI adapter to perform setup, formatting, surface analysis, and diagnostics.

If your file system develops file-corruption problems on a frequent basis, your disk adapter may be a contributing factor. Though poorly written software applications can cause file corruption problems, more commonly these problems result from disk media defects. You should scan the surface of your disk periodically to check on the presence of media defects that may have developed.

When you're checking a disk for media defects, always run a non-destructive test on data areas and a destructive test on non-data areas. If a drive is failing, replace it immediately. Considering the cost of disk drives today, attempting to repair a failing drive is not an economically sound practice. At the first sign of trouble, remove the failing drive, and replace it with a new, good drive. This is not the place to cut corners.

To prevent media defects, keep your servers in a secure place, free from vibration, electromechanical interference, and other forms of physical abuse.

SUMMARY

This chapter briefly discussed some of the tools available to you in monitoring LANs, your server, the server operating system, and its disk subsystems. For more information on troubleshooting and resolving problems, several chapters in Part VI of this book contain more detail on each aspect of troubleshooting.

- Processor, Threads, and the Queue

- Prioritizing Foreground Application Versus Server Performance

- Interaction of SERVER Service with the Cache

- Memory Optimization

- Hard Disk Adapters

- Cache Memory

- Server Network Cards

- Truncate Event Logs

- Disable BIOS Shadowing

CHAPTER 23

Evaluating Performance Opportunities

NT Server can be used for such a wide variety of functions that the default settings provided by the designers can be unsuitable for your specific situation. On the other hand, NT is self tuning and has many adaptive features. In addition, NT's designers have made NT Server very configurable and it can be tuned to meet the requirements of specific situations. The areas covered in this section are not the only places you can apply adjustments, but these are the areas where the improvement yields the most performance in proportion to the administrator's effort.

Another way to improve performance is to change the hardware platform's design. You can make certain changes to the hardware that have more impact on performance than other approaches. The most important areas to change are the processor, memory, the storage channel, and the network.

PROCESSOR, THREADS, AND THE QUEUE

The processor serves the queue: that means that the nature of the load on the processor depends on what is pending in the queue. The schedule of processes in the queue is established by preemptive multitasking and the relative duration and priority of the processes. This means that the highest priority thread that is ready to run executes program instructions. If another thread is waiting, what happens depends on its priority. If it is a lower priority than the executing thread, it will mostly wait, only occasionally getting processor time to prevent total starvation. If it has the same priority as the executing thread, the two will share the processor. The system will periodically switch from one thread to the other in order to let them both have processor access.

Priorities are assigned at two levels. The process is assigned a priority class based on how the user starts and interacts with it. Then, within the process's priority class, its threads are assigned priorities that can change depending on requests by the thread itself, or because of interactions with peripherals or with the user. When the thread uses the processor, its priority is lowered; when it accesses peripherals, it is raised; and when it accesses such peripherals as the keyboard, it is upgraded even more. Threads get this priority upgrade as long as peripheral access goes through the NT Executive.

If a computer has multiple processors, a ready thread can run on any of them. The system attempts to run a thread on the same processor it last ran on. This method of rescheduling is called *soft affinity*. This helps reuse data left in the processor's memory caches from the previous execution of the thread. A thread could be restricted to run on only certain processors, but that is uncommon.

PRIORITIZING FOREGROUND APPLICATION VERSUS SERVER PERFORMANCE

Most applications started by users during system operation run in the Normal Priority class. When the user who is interacting with an application uses the keyboard or the mouse, that application gets focus in the foreground. The foreground processes get an upgraded base priority of nine instead of the level eight assigned to other Normal Priority class processes. When an application gives up the foreground, it gets background priority of seven.

The significance of this is that when the foreground application uses the processor heavily, it can lock out all lower priority processes from execution. Because responding quickly to the user is usually the system's goal, this is the chosen default for NT operation. For NT Server computers, you should use the "Foreground Equals Background" setting under Tasking in the System applet of the Control Panel. Experimenting with this setting becomes significant when NT Server is used as an application server.

Processes and threads run at priorities assigned during application installation. The SERVER service competes with the active foreground process. The interaction between the two is not a simple one. It is important to understand the relationship between the SERVER service priority and the foreground process priority.

During NT Server setup, the SERVER service priority is set equal to the foreground process priority. On the other hand, NT Workstation sets the foreground at a higher priority than the SERVER service. You can change the Tasking option in the System applet of the Control Panel to adjust the SERVER service priority. You can also change the interaction between the foreground and SERVER priority by changing Registry parameters.

You can change the priority of all SERVER service threads in relation to the base priority of the foreground process. Higher priority can give better server performance at the cost of foreground application responsiveness. Lower SERVER priority gives preference to other processes on the system.

1. Start the Registry Editor (REGEDT32.EXE) and go to the subkey, HKEY_LOCAL_MACHINE\SYSTEM\CurrentControlSet\Services\LanmanServer\Parameters.

2. From the Edit menu, choose Add Value.

3. Enter the following values:
```
Value Name: ThreadPriority
Data Type:  REG_DWORD
Decimal: <0 Process runs at background priority
      1 SERVER threads priority equal to foreground
      2 SERVER threads priority higher than foreground
      15 SERVER threads at real-time priority
```

4. Quit Registry Editor and restart NT.

Note

A value of 15 should never be used in practice. If the server becomes busy, other important system processes could become resource starved.

Warning

When the SERVER ThreadPriority is 1, changing the Tasking option to Foreground and Background Applications Equally Responsive sets the SERVER service priority equal to foreground and background priorities. This can cause the SERVER service's performance to degrade because it must now share time equally with other background processes.

The settings you use depend on your specific situation; if there are no server-based applications (such as SQL Server or Exchange Server) you can give the SERVER a setting of 2.

INTERACTION OF SERVER SERVICE WITH THE CACHE

Sometimes the interaction between the SERVER service and the cache can cause system degradation. This problem can be addressed by tuning the server to balance memory use. To do this, perform the following steps:

1. In the Control Panel window, choose the Network icon.

2. From the Installed Network Software box, select Server, and then choose the Configure button.

3. If either of the options Maximize Throughput for File Sharing or Maximize Throughput for Network Applications is currently selected, you may get better performance during large file copy operations by selecting the Balance option. If Balance or Minimize Memory Used is already selected, this method does not help the problem you are having.

4. If you elected to make a change in step 3 above, restart your computer so the change can take effect.

There are two options designed to maximize network throughput; each permits the system cache to use more available memory than it would otherwise. In this situation, the available memory can drop to levels resulting in heavy swapping activity on the hard disks in order to accommodate requests from user or system applications that may subsequently need to be swapped into memory.

The cache manager periodically gives up memory that it has allocated so that the system will never run completely out of memory due to caching alone. This can happen whenever a file copy operation is complete or when a threshold value is reached. This means that the problem described previously does not occur if a series of smaller files are copied. The threshold value for the Balance option is nominally higher than the threshold values for the options designed to maximize throughput that the problem does not occur there either.

This problem is also more noticeable on computers with lower total physical memory. When more total physical memory is available, the minimum available memory threshold is also higher, which can alleviate this problem.

MEMORY OPTIMIZATION

On ISA bus computers, memory above 16MB is accessed via the NT Virtual Direct Memory Access method. This access method compensates for the limitations inherent in the 24-bit ISA memory address limitation (16MB) using DMA double buffering. Double buffering provides much better performance than normal ISA I/O access but is a limited approach when compared to 32-bit bus mastering architectures such as EISA, MCA, or PCI. Generally speaking, NT takes full advantage of RAM in computers with ISA, EISA, PCI, and MCA, up to a maximum of 4GB.

A few ISA-based computers have unusually poor hardware secondary cache schemes. On these machines, increasing memory beyond 16MB actually degrades performance. It is best to disable secondary cache on these computers.

PAGEFILE AND VIRTUAL MEMORY

NT uses a paging file for virtual memory called PAGEFILE.SYS. This file is created during NT Setup and is located in the root directory by default. NT requires a paging file, but it does not have to be in the root directory of the system logical drive.

The paging file is not necessarily a single file; it can be a group of files stored in various locations across hard disks and partitions. The files are collectively referred to as "the paging file." When thinking about the size of the paging file, the sum of all the files that make up the paging file is the only value you need to keep in mind. The following rules apply when optimizing the paging file:

1. The paging file's size is calculated as system RAM plus 12MB. There is a minimum of 22MB required for the Executive. If system RAM plus 12MB is less than 22MB, you should increase the size until the system RAM plus paging file is at least 22MB. Also, if you have enough surplus RAM to support the operating system and application memory requirements, the need for a large paging file is lessened. If you have 64MB of RAM, you can

reduce the paging file to a very small size. You should keep a small initial paging file but your maximum paging file size should be large in case any application on the server requires a large amount of memory for a short period of time.

Note

> The Executive needs only 22MB. For reasonable application performance, a 40MB total is recommended. These sizes are recommended because NT requires backing storage for everything it keeps in RAM. If NT requires more space in RAM, it must be able to swap out code and data to either the paging file or the original executable file. If NT cannot do this, out of memory errors are generated.

2. If you have multiple hard disks, splitting up the paging file to speed up the access time is highly recommended. If you have two hard disks, and you split the paging file, both hard disks can be accessing the paging files simultaneously, almost doubling the throughput. However, if you have two hard disks, and one is faster than the other, it may be more effective to store the paging file on the faster hard disk.

Note

> There is no point in splitting up the paging file between multiple partitions because it does not increase the hard disk's ability to access the paging file. This may help if the logical drives are not large enough for the entire paging file.

WORKING SETS

A *working set* is defined as the footprint in memory of a process and its threads. Other related topics covered here are *nonpaged pool*, and locking pages into physical memory via VirtualLock().

A process's working set is the set of pages that it has currently in memory. The values for the maximum working set and the minimum working set are hard-coded in NT and are not changeable.

The system tries to keep about 4MB free to reduce the paging that occurs when loading a new process, allocating memory, and so forth. Any free RAM beyond what the system requires is available for the system to use to increase the working set size if the process is doing a lot of paging.

Process pages that are paged out of the process space are moved into the standby list where they remain until sufficient free RAM is available or until system memory is low and they need to be reused. If these pages are accessed by your process while they are still on the standby list and more RAM has become available, they are soft-faulted back into the working set. This does not require any disk access, so it is very quick.

Therefore, even though you have an upper limit to the size of your working set, you can still have quite a few process pages in memory that can be pulled back into your working set very quickly.

One way to help an application receive a larger working set is to use the Network application in the Control Panel to set the server configuration to Maximize Throughput for Network Applications.

PAGED AND NONPAGED MEMORY POOLS

Paged and NonPaged memory pools are maintained by NT. The NonPaged pool is used by processes that cannot be deprived of memory. Each NIC gets a NonPaged amount of memory. This memory is never released. On the other hand, Paged memory can be written to the pagefile when higher priority process demands memory.

NT is a 32-bit operating system that can run both 16-bit and 32-bit applications. System calls of 16-bit applications are translated to 32 bits. As a result, a program can use 4GB of memory. The upper half of this is devoted to system code and data and is only visible to the process when it is in privileged mode. The lower half is available to the user program when it is in user mode, and to those user-mode system services called by the program.

The memory is allocated in pages. Page size varies with the computer's processor type. Page size is 4096 bytes (4K) for 386, 486, and Pentium processors, the same for MIPS processors, and 8192 (8K) for DEC Alpha processors.

When a page of code or data is required from a peripheral, the NT memory manager finds a free page frame in which to place the required page. The system transfers the required page, and processing can continue. If no page frame is free, the memory manager must select one to reuse. The memory manager tries to find a page frame whose contents have not been used for some time. When the memory manager finds a suitable page frame, it discards the page in it if that page has not been modified since it was placed into RAM. Otherwise, the changed page must be written back to its original location on the disk before the new page can replace it. The memory manager uses many algorithms to minimize and anticipate page traffic and thus reduce the possibility that paging traffic will saturate the disks.

Usually, programs execute by fetching one instruction after another from a program code page until they call or return to a routine in some other code page, or make a jump to code in another page. Or, they can simply come to the end of the current page and need the next one. Such a transfer of instruction control to a new page causes a page fault if the needed page is not currently in the working set of the process. The working set of the process is the set of pages currently visible to the process in RAM.

A page fault can be resolved quickly if the memory manager finds the page elsewhere in RAM. It might be in the working set of some other process or processes, or it might have been removed from this process's working set by the memory manager in an aggressive trimming attempt. The memory manager places such pages on a list of page frames called the standby list, and they can be reinserted into a process's working set very quickly. But if the page is not elsewhere in RAM, the memory manager must find a free page frame, or make one free as described above, and then fetch the required page from the peripheral. One characteristic of code pages is that you do not need to modify code while in RAM, so code pages can be discarded without being written back to disk.

Data pages are accessed in a more random manner than code pages. Each instruction in a program can reference data allocated anywhere in the address space of a process. The idea is the same. If an attempt is made to access a data page not in the process's working set, a page fault occurs. From that point on, the process is just as described for code pages. The only difference between data pages and code pages is that data pages are frequently changed by the processes that access them, so the memory manager must take care to write them on the peripheral before replacing them with another page.

To see how much memory NT thinks the system has, switch to Program Manager and choose About Program Manager from the Help menu. For testing purposes, you can reduce the amount of memory that NT thinks the computer has by modifying the BOOT.INI file. This file has protected attributes. If you want to modify BOOT.INI, make a copy of it first, and then use ATTRIB to turn off the Read Only, Hidden, and System attributes for BOOT.INI.

Warning

By turning off the protected attributes, you can now overwrite BOOT.INI. Some mistakes written to BOOT.INI can prevent NT from starting.

To observe paging in action, it is useful to make the system think it has less memory. This forces the memory manager into more activity that we can easily observe. Find the line indicating the NT operating system with which you want to boot. Add a /MAXMEM=n parameter to the end of the NT version line. The *n* is the number of megabytes you want to test. It is important that you do not make this less than eight. Following is an example of a BOOT.INI file set up with four versions of NT, each configured to use different amounts of memory.

```
[boot loader]
timeout=30
default=multi(0)disk(0)rdisk(0)partition(1)\winnt
[operating systems]
multi(0)disk(0)rdisk(0)partition(1)\winnt="Windows NT Version 3.5"
multi(0)disk(0)rdisk(0)partition(1)\winnt="Windows NT 3.5, 12Mb" /MAXMEM=12
multi(0)disk(0)rdisk(0)partition(1)\winnt="Windows NT 3.5, 10Mb" /MAXMEM=10
multi(0)disk(0)rdisk(0)partition(1)\winnt="Windows NT 3.5, 8Mb" /MAXMEM=8
c:\="MS-DOS"
```

NT calculates NonPagedPoolSize and PagedPoolSize based on the amount of physical memory present in the computer at boot time. These values can be changed by using the Registry Editor.

```
MinimumNonPagedPoolSize = 256K
MinAdditionNonPagedPoolPerMb = 32K
DefaultMaximumNonPagedPool = 1 MB
MaxAdditionNonPagedPoolPerMb = 400K
PTE_PER_PAGE = 1024
PAGE_SIZE=4096
```

The page pooled memory management parameters are located in:

```
HKEY_LOCAL_MACHINE\SYSTEM\CurrentControlSet\Control\Session Manager\Memory Manage-
ment
```

THE LARGESYSTEMCACHE SUBKEY

If the paging file is being accessed excessively and unnecessarily, you can check that by using the Performance Monitor. You can also observe that the disk is constantly busy.

This behavior could be because LargeSystemCache is set to 1. Check the following subkey using the Registry Editor:

```
HKEY_LOCAL_MACHINE\SYSTEM\CurrentControlSet\Control\Session Manager\Memory Manage-
ment
```

For a non-zero value, LargeSystemCache specifies that the system favors the system-cache working set rather than the processes working set. Change the value of LargeSystemCache to 0.

THE NOT_ENOUGH_QUOTA SUBKEY

Each NT object created requires a block of nonpaged pool. In fact, it is the availability of nonpaged pool that determines how many processes, threads, and other such objects can be created. The error that you receive if you have too many object handles open is

```
1816 (ERROR_NOT_ENOUGH_QUOTA)
```

This error happens if some objects are too large, sharing an object caused excessive quota charges, or the quota limits option was set too low.

Quota is only charged once per object rather than once per handle. The quota mechanism dynamically raises and lowers the quota limits as you bump into the limits. Before raising a limit, it coordinates this with the memory manager to make sure you can safely have the limit raised without using up all of the system resources.

VirtualLock()

Programmers and software developers can control NT Server paging activity by using the WIN32 API.

To lock a particular page into memory so that it cannot be swapped out to disk, you should use `VirtualLock()`. The documentation for `VirtualLock()` states that "Locking pages into memory may degrade the performance of the system by reducing the available RAM and forcing the system to swap out other critical pages to the paging file." There is a limit on the number of pages that can be locked: 30 pages. "The limit is intentionally small to avoid severe performance degradation."

NT allows processes to increase their working set size by using `SetProcessWorkingSetSize()`. Because each process has the default minimum working set size reserved, no matter how small the process actually is, this API is also useful to trim the minimum working set size if you want to run many processes at once.

HARD DISK ADAPTERS

If you can provide plenty of memory, there are a number of ways you can improve disk throughput. Find out about the disk controller from the manufacturer if it does 8-bit, 16-bit, or 32-bit transfers. The more bits in the transfer operation, the faster the controller moves data.

A server should have a 32-bit EISA, MCA, or PCI bus, and you should use 32-bit bus mastering disk adapters. The computer's I/O bus architecture has tremendous effect on the performance during heavy I/O operations. EISA, MCA, and PCI buses have much greater bandwidth than ISA buses and can accommodate many times as much data in a burst. Many computers also have a turbo switch that affects bus speed. Make sure it is set to on if you have such a switch. ISA buses cannot see above 16MB of RAM. To place data above 16MB of RAM, the driver must arrange a copy of the data from the area below 16MB. This can slow down the computer.

Bus mastering also has a tremendous effect on lowering CPU utilization. Non-bus mastering devices rely on the CPU to drive I/O, but bus mastering devices have their own processors that significantly improve performance while reducing system resource usage. Although 16-bit DMA and bus mastering implementations provide good performance improvements, EISA, MCA, and PCI bus mastering are significantly more effective.

A more detailed discussion of bus mastering 32-bit bus design is found in Chapter 3, "Building the Server."

CACHE MEMORY

NT uses a single cache for all file systems. Before going to fetch the data from disk or network card, the file system first asks the NT I/O Manager if the data is in the cache. If it is, the cache manager returns the data directly from the cache. That means every time the cache manager is asked for such data, it is there.

Some disk controllers feature built-in caches. The benefit of this depends a lot on the access patterns of your system. If you are going to purchase the RAM anyway, you might want to consider putting it in the computer's main memory instead of on the disk controller card; that way the operating system can control it and make best use of it under changing conditions. Because NT adapts the disk cache size to the amount of memory available, when memory is needed for something besides disk caching, it is available but at the expense of the disk cache.

If the disk adapter has been checked out, the problem may be the configuration of the disk subsystem as a whole. If you have all the load concentrated on one disk and one controller, consider getting a second disk and even a second controller.

There is no limitation on the number of disk adapters except for the limited number of slots on the motherboard. Chapter 31, "File System and Disk Subsystem Problems," covers multiple disk geometry in more detail.

PHYSICAL DISK DRIVE CONFIGURATIONS

NT's preference for SCSI drives has been discussed in previous chapters. SCSI has become the defacto hard disk interface for high-end computers, especially servers. The technology is mature, proven, and new improvements have defined capacities and throughput unparalleled in personal computer disk storage.

SCSI is preferred for several reasons.

◆ SCSI has much higher capacities than other non-proprietary disk interfaces, such as IDE. SCSI adapters are available in 32-bit bus mastering varieties for all types of computer busses.

◆ SCSI is compatible with NT's sector sparing (hot fix).

◆ You can use common SCSI hardware and drives to implement NT's striping, mirroring, and RAID 5 configuration features for better performance and fault tolerance.

◆ You can attach several different types of devices to a SCSI adapter, including

> disk drives
> CD-ROM drives
> tape drives
> optical drives
> scanners

◆ NT drivers are available for most SCSI adapters. If you have an NT driver for an adapter, chances are any devices you connect to the adapter will work with NT.

Newer model SCSI drives rotate at 7200 RPMs or higher (drives typically rotated at 3600 RPMs until recently). As you can imagine, this speed significantly reduces access rate and latency times. There are a few additional SCSI benefits.

◆ SCSI peripheral devices of the same type have similar characteristics so you can often replace failed devices with new ones that do not have to be from the same vendor. In most cases, a different brand and model replacement SCSI adapter can be used with a disk drive laden with data without losing the data. Many older types of disk adapters required the drive to be low-level formatted before use to suit the adapter, which meant losing all data.

◆ SCSI devices are intelligent and independent as a controller is built onto each SCSI device. Like bus mastering, this relieves the CPU from having to do low level work, and provides multitasking abilities.

◆ Later SCSI adapters allow you to connect different device types using the same cable. In a non-SCSI environment, such as IDE, sound cards, or proprietary controllers, each device requires its own dedicated adapter.

◆ SCSI is faster than other disk interface standards with maximum burst transfer rates ranging from 5 to 40 million bytes per second. See Table 23.1 for a chart with more specific specifications.

◆ SCSI I/O is independent of the system bus, and adapters are available for every type of PC bus. This allows peripheral devices to be moved from one system to another, which preserves a company's hardware investment. It also enables quick recovery. If a server fails and the data is intact, the drives can be moved to another system without having to restore data, even if the system has a different bus type.

◆ Multithreaded operating systems, such as NT, can use split seeks to take full advantage of the multitasking capabilities of the SCSI bus (often called the "SCSI detach feature"). When an NT thread requests to read a logical block on SCSI disk 1, and at the same time, a second thread requests to write some data to SCSI disk 2, the following may occur:

> The SCSI host adapter processes the first request made by NT executive by arbitrating the SCSI bus and making a connection to disk 1.

> After the connection is made, disk 1 disconnects and gives up the bus (bus free) so that other requests can be made by the host.

> The first thread stops executing and waits while the slow I/O device completes a data transfer.

> As the seek is carried out on disk 1, the second thread request is processed in the same manner as the first, because NT can issue a "context switch" to allow for a thread of execution while another is still being completed.

> Because the bus is free at this time, the host (initiator) is able to make a connection with disk 2. Disk 2 then disconnects and performs a write of some data to a logical location on the disk. At the same time, disk 1 may still be seeking the block to read. The two devices are therefore performing task (read, write) simultaneously.

Table 23.1 describes the configuration attributes of the SCSI interface configurations.

TABLE 23.1. SCSI PERFORMANCE CHARACTERISTICS

ANSI Spec	Bus Width	Common Name	# devices	Transfer Rate (Mbytes/sec)
SCSI-1*	8-bit	Async SCSI	8	5
SCSI-2*	8-bit	Fast SCSI	8	10
SCSI-2**	16-bit	Fast-Wide SCSI	8	20
SCSI-3*	32-bit	Fast SCSI	8	10
SCSI-3**	16-bit	Fast-Wide SCSI	16	20
SCSI-3**	32-bit	Fast-Wide SCSI	32	40

* = with 1 cable
** = with 2 cables

23

EVALUATING PERFORMANCE OPPORTUNITIES

ANSI Spec: The formal American National Standards Institute specification for the device.

Bus width: The SCSI bus width used between the SCSI adapter and its devices.

Common Name: The design name most often used in marketing and sales literature.

Transfer Rate (MBytes/sec): The maximum bandwidth supported in a momentary burst.

devices: The maximum number of devices supported for a single adapter.

Asynchronous: A handshaking protocol that requires a handshake for every byte transferred (synchronous transfers a series of bytes before handshaking occurs, which speeds data transfer rate).

Fast SCSI is an option that doubles the synchronous data transfer rate. The rate is achieved by removing excess margins from various times and delays. To use the fast SCSI option, high quality cables are required. This option is compatible with normal synchronous SCSI and has:

◆ Up to 10 (megabytes) MBytes/sec over an 8-bit bus.

◆ Synchronous data transfer negotiation required.

◆ Single-ended implementation recommendations: maximum cable length of 3 meters and active terminators.

Wide SCSI is an option that adds a second SCSI cable of 68 conductors. This cable provides a data path for 16- or 32-bit data. This path has separate handshake signals and is for data transfer only. The transfer rate is two or four times the present transfer rate of SCSI-1. With the second cable, SCSI-2 remains compatible with the 8-bit SCSI.

SCSI TAGGED COMMAND QUEUING

SCSI tagged command queuing (not available in SCSI-1) allows a SCSI host adapter to queue up multiple SCSI commands to a device before receiving a response for any of the commands. By default this feature is disabled by NT. The SCSI host adapter must wait for a command response before sending another command. In most systems, enabling SCSI-tagged command queuing results in improved system performance.

To enable SCSI-tagged command queuing for a PCI SCSI host adapter, perform the following steps:

1. Log on to Windows NT as an administrator.

2. Start Registry Editor.

3. From the HKEY_LOCAL_MACHINE subtree, go to the \SYSTEM \CurrentControlSet\Services\sparrow key.

4. From the Edit menu, select Add Key.

5. In the Key Name text box, enter `Device`, and then choose OK.

6. Select the Device subkey.

7. From the Edit menu, choose Add Value.

8. Enter the following:

```
Value Name: DriverParameter
Data Type:  REG_SZ
String:     UseTags=1
```

9. Exit Registry Editor and restart NT.

SERVER NETWORK CARDS

One of the most significant bottlenecks in many networks today is the server network cards. Especially when you're using 100Mbps LAN technology, such as Fast Ethernet or FDDI, you should use 32-bit EISA, MCA, or PCI bus mastering network cards in the server.

NT is a 32-bit operating system that is significantly crippled by handling 16-bit I/O operations. The overhead placed on the system CPU to service the I/O operations drives CPU utilization very high. System performance is often limited by CPU saturation; the server becomes I/O bound because the CPU has approached 100% utilization.

Bus mastering reduces CPU utilization by offloading I/O operations to the network card's on-board processor. Bus mastering can be most effective when the bus is designed for sharing among multiple masters. ISA was not designed this way, so bus mastering cannot be optimized in an ISA bus, regardless of how many design improvements developers make.

A more detailed discussion of bus mastering 32-bit bus design is in Chapter 3, "Building the Server."

TRUNCATE EVENT LOGS

The Event Viewer logs all events and error messages. These logs can become very large. In addition, as time goes on, the Event Viewer starts to take more and more memory. It sometimes does not release memory properly when it performs certain operations on the event log. This problem occurs even when you instruct Event Viewer to keep to a maximum event log size. You should check the size of the event logs and delete them periodically.

Disable BIOS Shadowing

Most computers provide the ROM BIOS shadowing option. This feature provides an advantage when running DOS; it is not an advantage when running NT.

ROM BIOS shadowing means copying the BIOS from ROM into RAM and using either hardware or 386 enhanced mode to remap the RAM into the normal address space of the BIOS. Because reading RAM is much faster than reading ROM, BIOS-intensive operations are substantially faster.

NT does not use the BIOS; therefore, no performance is gained by shadowing. If ROM BIOS shadowing is not used, more RAM is available to NT, so there is an advantage to disabling the ROM BIOS shadowing option.

This applies to other BIOS shadowing schemes as well. Typically the CMOS settings allow the system to shadow any BIOS.

Upgrading to RISC- and Multiprocessor-Based Computers

One of the obvious things you can do to increase performance is to upgrade your server computer to a multiprocessor or SMP system. NT Server allows the use of up to eight processors that can work in unison in a symmetric multiprocessing process. Some of the reduced instruction set computers (RISC) provide higher performance. These include DEC ALPHA AXP, MIPS R4000, and IBM PowerPC.

Upgrading to a Multiprocessor Computer

For each processor you add, theoretically you get 100% of a processor's worth of work done. Things are not always so in practice. There are many reasons why adding processors may not yield the response time improvements. For example, if the bottleneck is not in the processors at all, adding more does not help. If the disk subsystem is overloaded, adding a processor does not increase the work done.

More subtle problems can cause less than 100% improvement. These all revolve around the contention for shared resources. The processes share more than just the code they execute. Because code is only read and not written, each processor can have a copy of the code in its primary and secondary memory caches; as they execute they do not even have to share access to the RAM that holds the code. Programs frequently operate independently like this, but in actual practice they tend to use shared system resources and thus mutually develop bottlenecks as they contend for those resources.

NT Resource Kit Upgrade Utility

To upgrade a single-processor system to a multiprocessor system, use UPTOMP.EXE. UPTOMP.EXE is included in the Resource Kit for Windows NT version 3.5. This tool is located under Performance and System Monitoring Tools in Resource Kit Tools Help.

Summary

The rich set of features available in the NT system allows administrators the flexibility to fine-tune the system to suit their specific needs. The areas of functionality covered in this chapter are a good place to start. In due time, third- party tools will emerge allowing even more improvements. There is, of course, the next version of NT on the horizon. Once the dust has settled in the major upgrade rush for Windows 95, NT will again gain the attention of the designers and also the large number of third-party developers.

- Overview

- Performance Monitor
  Internals

- Performance Monitor
  Operations

- How to Deal with
  Bottlenecks

- Monitoring an
  Application

- Monitoring the
  Network

- Performance Tuning

- Miscellaneous Tuning

CHAPTER 24

Monitoring and Tuning
Performance

Bottleneck   A system component that restricts overall system performance.

Task   A task is any kind of an operation. It could be updating a word-processing document or sending an e-mail message.

Working set   A working set is the memory (RAM) that a process allocates while it is running.

OVERVIEW

This chapter is about NT Server performance. It considers problems in reaching maximum server performance and then explores Server tools designed to help the network administrator monitor and track various server behaviors. This chapter shows how these tools can generate logs and statistics that, as the administrator, you can use to identify and eliminate the causes of the problems. It also includes information about the Server Alerter service that can notify administrators about important errors and events.

To illustrate a typical performance problem let's look at a typical computer system. The processor and the cache/RAM are busy during the execution of instructions. We consider the processor and memory as a unit when we think of the processor. When memory is suspected of being a bottleneck, we are concerned about its size, not its speed. On single processor systems we just lump memory speed into processor speed. When memory is too small, there is not enough room in memory for all the needed pages of program code and data. The system starts to spend a lot of time moving pages between disk and RAM. What you notice is the resulting high disk utilization.

By the definition of bottleneck, you will suspect the disk. What you really need is more memory. Although the disk is, strictly speaking, the bottleneck in the system, the reason it is the bottleneck is lack of memory. There is a counter (Memory: Pages/sec) that clearly shows this to be the case.

Lack of memory is by far the most common cause of serious performance problems in computer systems.

What are the most common causes of performance problems?

- ◆ Resources that are not utilized efficiently
- ◆ Resources that are not utilized fairly
- ◆ Resources that are too slow
- ◆ Resources that are too small

◆ Virtual Memory systems. All classes of virtual memory operating systems have certain generic performance problems in common. These include

Memory problems

Hardware problems

Software problems

NT Server Performance Monitor provides essential information for problem detection and performance optimization. NT Server provides the mechanism for collecting raw data for analysis. By maintaining a record of the network during normal operation, the administrator can build an understanding of reasonable performance values. This provides a baseline against which the current system performance can be compared when some components need to be upgraded or replaced. Without this baseline, problem detection can be difficult. A major design goal of NT Server is to eliminate the many obscure performance parameters that characterized earlier network operating systems. Adaptive algorithms have been incorporated into NT Server so the correct values are determined by the system as it runs. The 32-bit address space removes many limitations on memory and the corresponding need for users to partition it manually with tuning parameters. NT Server can adequately tune itself for generic problems by dynamically adjusting itself; it redistributes its resources as needed without notifying the administrator.

NT Server is designed from the ground up to be self tuning. The system monitors several counters and adjusts related parameters to provide better performance. In addition to the automatically adapted parameters, there are other parameters that can be adjusted by the administrator. These parameters may need adjustment mainly because NT Server cannot determine what kind of load will be put on the server. Default values for all parameters are assigned to address a broad range of normal system use, and they rarely need to be altered. In other situations changes might be advisable. The few tuning parameters that you can adjust are discussed in this section.

Optimizing NT does not mean that you have to manually adjust many conflicting parameters. Optimizing NT is the process of determining what hardware resource is most in demand, and then adjusting the operating system to relieve the congestion caused by the overloading of that hardware resource. The critical tool in finding the overloaded resource is Performance Monitor.

A discussion of NT parameters requires a short review of how programs execute on the NT platform. Programs contain instructions or code that is loaded from the disk drive. The processor executes the code, fetches and stores data as needed and navigates the logic dictated by the code. A typical Intel 486 or Pentium processor executes between two and three million instructions per second. RISC-based processors need to execute fewer instructions but require more program code, thus requiring more memory for execution. NT brings the program code into RAM in sections called pages. This way pages are brought into memory according to the demands of the program logic. The randomness introduced by program behavior can cause excessive memory paging.

The program asks NT to read data from a file or write data to a file on a local or network disk. This causes the data to pass from RAM to the network card, which takes care of transferring data to or from the disk at the server. When the data is received by the network card it interrupts the processor and the processor copies that data from the network card buffer to the program's active data page.

When the program is executed, the results may have to go to the graphic adapter to be displayed on the monitor. The conversion to bits of the data stored in memory and the transferrence of these bits to the memory in the graphic adapter are also the processor's job. The program can also ask NT to notify it when the user presses a key or moves the mouse.

All this data travels on the I/O and memory bus. The bus is really a set of electronic paths along which electrons travel at high speed. PCI and EISA bus designs partition the system hardware into two separate buses, so slower I/O traffic does not interfere with the high-speed processor memory traffic. These buses are fast enough that they seldom cause a computer system bottleneck. There are exceptions, however, and those cases are covered later on in this section.

There are two kinds of memory caches. The built-in cache in the 486/Pentium processor holds recently used code and data. This makes use of program behavior in that they use many of the memory bytes that they have used in the recent past. By keeping these bytes near the processor in high-speed memory, access to them is very fast. It takes one processor cycle to get data from the processor cache.

The external, or level 2, cache is larger but slower than the processor cache. Generally, very fast SRAM is used for this purpose. This kind of cache can usually be accessed in two or more processor cycles. Compare that to the main memory access which takes around 10 processor cycles. Obviously, the caches provide a huge performance gain when the data is present there. The presence of the cache hierarchy in the 486 and Pentium is the main reason for their large performance improvements over the 386.

The advent of multi-processor systems allows multiple programs or independent logical program execution paths, called threads, to execute concurrently. Cache design is even more important to reduce memory traffic and the potential for memory to be a bottleneck in multi-processor systems. The common memory is the usual limitation to the degree of concurrence that can be achieved.

NT Server self-monitoring capabilities are

- To improve performance based on the existing configuration
- To provide for capacity planning and forecasting
- To maintain adequate hardware resources

Performance Monitor Internals

This section deals with the concepts used in the Performance Monitor program included with NT Server. In simple terms, we are interested in measuring the throughput, duty cycle, or the delays involved with different system components. In addition, as a result of the monitoring action itself, we want to minimize the impact on the component under test.

Performance Monitor uses counters that run within units of time to measure what transpires within those units of time. Before we proceed with the details of these counters we discuss some general concepts related to system performance.

Transaction

A *transaction* is a unit of work on the system. This could be a user interaction with an application, a reading of a file from a network server, or an e-mail message sent across the LAN. The most important thing is the total time the transaction uses on each unit of hardware on the computer. Call this the *demand* for the device, and measure it in seconds.

The system device with the smallest maximum throughput for this transaction determines the maximum throughput the system can provide. This device is where the bottleneck occurs. Notice that making any other device faster can never yield more throughput; it can only make the faster device have lower utilization. This is why it is so important to discover a system's bottleneck before adding more hardware capability.

A sample calculation can be used to illustrate the bottleneck phenomenon. If a transaction takes .25 seconds of processor time and .5 seconds of disk time, the processor can handle four transactions per second, while the disk can handle two transactions per second. So the overall system can handle only two transactions per second, at which point the disk will be saturated (utilization = 1). The utilization of the processor at that point is .25/.5 = .5, or 50%.

NT Performance Monitor counts and displays basic elements such as the utilization, visits, and service time for each device. Sometimes it displays only some of these values and computes the others.

COUNTERS

NT monitors hardware devices according to the count of visits to the device. The physical disk device has, for example, a count of disk transfers made expressed as Transfers/sec. Often these visits are broken down into categories for a more precise indication of the cause of the activity. For example, counters for Disk Reads/sec and Disk Writes/sec give you a better understanding of the cause of disk overloading. Counters are expressed as rates per second, and timers as the fraction of time that a device is used as a percentage.

When memory is inadequate, there is not enough room in memory for all the needed pages of program code and data. The system starts to spend a lot of time moving pages between disk and RAM. What you observe is high disk utilization. Your first impression might be to upgrade your disk to a faster one. What you really need is more memory. Although the disk seems to be where the bottleneck occurs, the real reason it is the bottleneck is lack of memory. There is an NT counter (Memory: Pages/sec) that clearly shows this to be the case, and there are a number of other counters to help you confirm this behavior. Lack of memory is by far the most common cause of serious performance problems in computer systems, especially in virtual memory systems.

SAMPLE COUNTERS

The following list of objects shows what counters you can use, and provides some potential factors to look for when using Performance Monitor.

Object	Type of Counter	What to Look For
Processor	%Processor Tune	If this value is consistently high, and disk and network counter values are low, suspect the processor.
Physical Disk	%Disk Time	If this value is consistently high, and Disk Queue is greater than 2, suspect the disk.
Memory	Pages/sec	If counter value is consistently greater than 5, suspect memory.
Server	Bytes Total/sec	If the sum of Total Bytes/sec for all servers is roughly equal to the maximum transfer rates of your network, you may need to segment the network.

Using Performance Monitor to monitor disk activity increases disk access time by 1.5 percent on the average. Because of this, disk activity monitoring is not turned on by default. Disk monitoring can be turned on in server machines using a 486 or higher. To activate disk monitoring, you need to do the following:

◆ Activate disk activity monitoring by entering `diskperf -y [\\Computer name]`

◆ To deactivate disk activity monitoring, enter `diskperf -n [\\Computer name]`

The optional computer name parameter allows disk activity monitoring to be turned on by a central system administrator.

PERFORMANCE MONITOR OPERATIONS

Performance Monitor is a tool for tracking computer performance. Figure 24.1 shows the first screen.

Figure 24.1.
Performance Monitor.

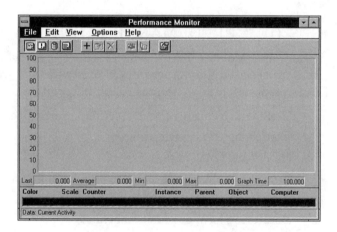

Performance Monitor is based on a series of *counters* that track such things as

◆ The number of processes waiting for disk time
◆ The number of network packets transmitted per second
◆ The percentage of processor utilization

Collected over time, *counter statistics* show performance trends. These can help an administrator tune the network. They can also provide data that is useful for troubleshooting and network expansion.

SECURITY

Performance Monitoring can potentially render a system unusable if testing is too rigorous. Usually, testing should be carried out when the system is not in use (unless

24

MONITORING AND TUNING PERFORMANCE

symptoms only appear when the system is under normal load). Administrators need to control the access to the monitoring functions. In addition, administrators do not want other users to interfere with an ongoing test. NT Server provides security features as part of the Performance Monitor program. There are two Performance Monitor security functions that are available only to members of the Administrators group.

◆ The ability to run Performance Monitor with realtime processing priority.

◆ The ability to activate disk counters.

Realtime processing is important if you intend to run Performance Monitor as a background application. Performance Monitor was designed to identify the majority of performance problems (bottlenecks).

Performance Monitor's entire operation is based on the premise that objects use counters, and counters use instances.

USES OF PERFORMANCE MONITOR

Performance Monitor covers a wide range of system behavior. Some of the measurements can be used daily, others may be used when you are trying to isolate problems. Performance Monitor generates useful information by doing the following:

◆ Monitoring realtime and historical performance

◆ Identifying trends over time

◆ Identifying bottlenecks

◆ Monitoring effects of system configuration changes

◆ Determining system capacity

◆ Monitoring local or remote machines

◆ Notifying administrators of significant monitored events that exceed threshold values

◆ Determining the frequency with which Performance Monitor updates information in logs, graphs, and reports. (Each of the values is an average of the last two data reads separated by the length of the time interval. Time-interval settings can also affect the amount of memory and processor time used by Performance Monitor.)

◆ Exporting Performance Monitor counter data to other products, such as spreadsheets and databases, for further data reduction and analysis.

Objects That Can Be Viewed

If you've played around with Performance Monitor at all, you've noticed it has a lot of counters. To cope with this flood of data, the counters are organized into a logical hierarchy. This hierarchy is defined by the structure of the (measurable) hardware equipment and (measurable) software elements.

At the top of the hierarchy is the domain. Each domain contains computers. For our purposes, each computer has distinct elements called *objects*. There are objects for physical components such as processors, physical disks, and memory. There are other objects, such as process and paging file. Each object has a set of *counters* defined for it. An object's counters record the activity level of the object. We use the following typographical convention to name a counter of a particular object: *object: counter*.

Some objects have multiple *instances*. For example, a computer can have multiple physical disk drives. Each of these disk drives is an instance of the Physical Disk object. Each of these disk drives has a name; in the case of Physical Disks it is its physical unit number. All the instances of a particular object have the same counters defined for them. The % Disk Time counter is the main indicator of how busy a disk is. Each physical disk drive has a counter that measures % Disk Time. We use the following typographical convention to denote a particular counter of an object with instances: `object: counter[instance name]`.

This structure is used in the dialog box where you select counters for measurement. This dialog box is shown in the following section.

Performance Monitor tracks many Server objects, including:

◆ Cache
◆ Logical disk
◆ Memory
◆ Physical disk
◆ Process
◆ Processor
◆ System
◆ Thread
◆ Network-related objects (server/workstation)
◆ Printers

24

Monitoring and Tuning Performance

Each of these objects has subcategories called *counters* that can also be monitored. In fact, Performance Monitor actually reports on the counters instead of the objects. The following counters can apply to all objects.

◆ Objects/counters: Counters usually include a reference to their object and are written as OBJECT: COUNTER. For example, PROCESSOR: %PROCESSOR TIME% tracks the percent of utilization for a given processor.

◆ Multiple instances: An object type can have several instances. For example, the Processor object type will have multiple instances if a system has multiple processors. If an object type has multiple instances, each instance may use the same set of counters. The process object, for example, has many instances—one for each active process. In a case where four processes are active at once, Performance Monitor generates four instances. An NT process is created when a program runs. A process may be one of the following:

An application (EXCEL)

A service (Event Log)

A subsystem (print spooler)

◆ Addresses and Threads: In addition to an executable program, every process consists of a set of virtual memory addresses and at least one thread. Threads make it possible for different parts of a process to execute on different processors simultaneously. Each thread running on a system shows up as an instance for the thread object type and is identified by association with its parent process. For example, if Print Manager has two active threads, Performance Monitor identifies them as thread object instances Printman = 0 and Printman = 1.

◆ The Counters: Every object contains counters that generate data about aspects of the object's performance. There are more than 300 counters available in NT Server.

CHARTING

Figure 24.2 and Figure 24.3 show the pick list for adding counters to the chart using the Add button in Performance Monitor. Figure 24.4 shows the chart as it moves across in time on the horizontal axis. The time scale can be adjusted from the Chart Options dialog box.

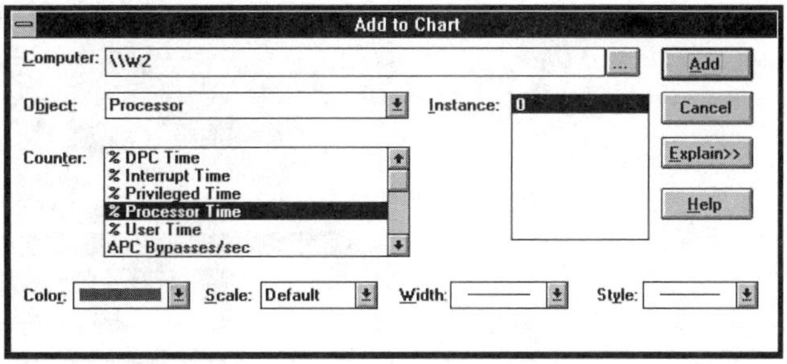

Figure 24.2.
Processor chart counter
selection.

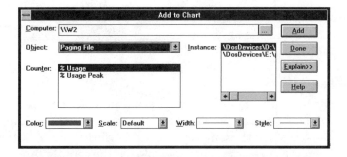

Figure 24.3.
Paging file chart
counter selection.

Figure 24.4.
Chart view in Perfor-
mance Monitor.

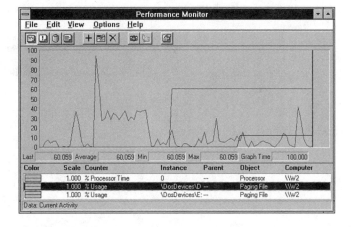

LOGS

You can create a log of counter values. Logging saves counter values to disk for further analysis. Using Performance Monitor, you can replay log files to create charts, alerts, or reports from the logged data. Figure 24.5 shows some data being selected for logging.

Viewing data from a log file is very similar to viewing current activity. You can create charts, alerts, reports, and even new log files. But because the data already exists, you don't have to wait for it to materialize.

24

MONITORING AND TUNING PERFORMANCE

Figure 24.5.
Log selection in the
Performance Monitor.

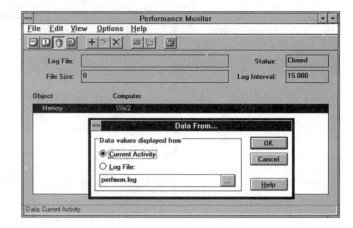

REPORTS

Reports allow monitoring of realtime performance of the selected counters. The reports present the values of the counters in a column format. You can create a report of all the counters in the Performance Monitor, and you can report on a counter. A report shows the value of the counter, and you can create a report of all the counters in Performance Monitor. Figure 24.6 shows a report.

Figure 24.6.
Report view in the
Performance Monitor.

ALERT

Realtime alerts allow you to continue working while Performance Monitor tracks events. Performance Monitor notifies you when a counter exceeds a threshold value that you can set indicating the counter has reached a level that deserves attention. Notification can occur the first time a counter reaches the threshold value, or each time it exceeds that value.

You can set an alert on a counter. This causes the display of an event when the counter reaches a threshold value that you have set. You can monitor many alerts at one time.

A maximum of 1000 events are recorded in the alert view. After that, the oldest one is deleted when a new alert occurs. Figure 24.7 shows how to set the alerts on counters.

Figure 24.7.
Alert selection in the
Performance Monitor.

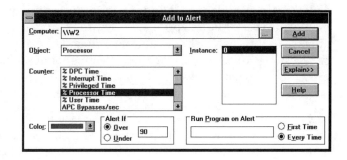

GRAPHING LOGGED DATA

You select objects, counters, and instances for charts of logged data just as you do when charting current activity; however, displaying time on the chart is different.

For best results, first consider charting in the graph mode. You should log on for a sufficient time to accumulate more than 100 values. Performance Monitor attempts to graph 100 points in order to fill the chart window with a smooth line. If there are fewer than 100 data snapshots in the log file, you see every point graphed, and the graph does not reach the right-hand edge of the window. In the Chart Options dialog box, you see that the Update Time group is unavailable because it is not relevant when playing back a log.

Log files are self-contained; you can view them at any NT machine. If you were to use Performance Monitor, you could check the Explain button to learn more about the statistics. However, there is no Explain help file when using the log file. To see counter explanations you must use Performance Monitor when viewing Current Activity.

HOW TO DEAL WITH BOTTLENECKS

To eliminate bottlenecks, you must first discover where the bottlenecks are, then work to improve performance of that particular subsystem. Several subsystems reveal the sources of the most common bottlenecks and are therefore discussed in this section.

Processor Bottlenecks

For best performance, NT requires the fastest processor speed you can afford. You should have a Pentium, Pentium Pro, or RISC processor. Although NT runs fine on a fast 486, heavy server loads and server-based applications require more fire power.

Attempting to overcome an underpowered processor by upgrading to a 486DX2 or 486DX4 (internal clock doubling or tripling) processor does not provide the improvement you expect. File and print services are I/O-paced integer functions that are not affected by internal clock doubling or tripling. The external I/O of a 486DX, Pentium, or Pentium Pro processor is the most effective at improving performance. Even RISC processors are not necessarily faster at processing I/O. A RISC processor's benefit is specific to server-based application processing and graphics or math calcuations.

Another thing you can do is increase the size of your external (level 2) cache by adding more SRAM to your motherboard. Many computers accept a range of external cache sizes from 0KB to 512 KB or more. Most computers sold for use as a server already have between 256KB and 512KB of external cache. Check your computer (or motherboard) documentation to see if you are able to upgrade your external cache.

Adding memory without upgrading the secondary cache size sometimes even degrades processor performance. This is because the secondary cache now has to map the larger memory space, usually resulting in lowered hit rates in the cache. This slows down processor-bound programs because they are scattered more widely in memory after memory has been added. If you suspect such a slowdown, create a processor-bound test with Response Probe that touches a lot of memory, but fits in the original memory size without sustained paging. Run this test before and after adding the memory, and you may well see that the test is slower with more memory. Disable the secondary cache using the BIOS setup utility, and repeat the experiment with both memory sizes. They should now perform the same. If they do, you have isolated the problem to the secondary cache design.

Finally, you might benefit from adding additional processors to use NT's Symmetrical Multiprocessing (SMP) capability. Only minor degrees of improvement are realized except in specific circumstances. SMP helps only when you have a bottleneck involving more than one thread capable of asynchronous execution. To the extent that threads can execute in parallel, adding processors provides relief. The expected benefits of adding SMP support is recommended to help server-based applications perform better. The degree of expected improvement is entirely dependent on the application.

You should only use 32-bit bus mastering disk and network adapters in a server. These devices consume the least amount of CPU time, because most I/O tasks are handled by the adapter's on-board processor. EISA, MCA, and PCI bus designs use on-board bus controllers instead of CPU time to acquire the bus and transfer data to RAM without CPU intervention. Older style 16-bit ISA cards are acceptable only where the smallest systems are concerned. ISA 8-bit adapters are not acceptable for servers, because they consume excessive CPU time and restrict flow to and from the LAN.

ISA alternate DMA configurations are effective at reducing the effect a 16-bit card has on your processor. However, if your disk or network adapters can be configured using alternate DMA channels, you may still suffer from high levels of CPU utilization. See Chapter 25, "LAN Capacity Allocation" for a more detailed discussion on selecting server network cards.

DISK BOTTLENECKS

Disk performance affects memory performance because backlogged disk requests are held in RAM. If you discover a disk bottleneck, the first thing you need to determine is whether more memory is required. To restate a critical truth, if you are short on memory, you will see symptomatic lost performance reflected as a disk bottleneck.

If memory is not the problem, there are a number of possible avenues to pursue to improve disk throughput. First, consider your disk adapter card. Research the product documentation to see if it does 8-bit, 16-bit, or 32-bit data transfers in each cycle. The more bits in the transfer operation, the faster the controller moves data.

Your I/O bus architecture comes into play here. EISA, MCA, and PCI buses transfer data at much higher throughput than ISA buses. Some ISA computers also have a physical or software turbo switch that affects bus speed. Make sure it is set to on if you have such a switch, but if you do set it to on, watch out for malfunctioning cards that cannot use turbo speeds. ISA buses cannot see above 16MB of RAM. To support ISA computers with more than 16MB of RAM, NT drivers remap data from the area below 16MB to the memory segment above 16MB. This can slow processing significantly.

If you have an ISA 16-bit adapter that can use an alternate direct memory access (DMA) channel, this option should be turned on. DMA can noticeably improve transfer speeds and reduce processor utilization. Better yet, use a 32-bit (EISA, MCA, or PCI) bus mastering adapter.

Some disk adapters have on-board caches. The benefit of this depends a lot on your system's access patterns. If you are going to purchase the RAM anyway, you might want to consider putting it in the computer's main memory instead of on the adapter card. Because NT features adaptive disk cache size, when memory is needed for something besides disk caching, it is available. It is also available to disk drives on other adapters, as well as to network file systems. Some computers have a limited amount of main memory they can use, in which case adding memory to a disk adapter may be appropriate.

If you have done the best you can with your disk adapter, you can consider a different disk subsystem configuration. If you have all your activity focused on one disk and one adapter, consider getting a second disk and even a second adapter and spread the load across them. Prices for disk drives are constantly coming down and adding more spindles is the easiest way of adding performance to your system. You can hook up several drives to a single controller and still derive the benefit of multiple spindles. When attaching several disk drives to the same SCSI cable be careful in selecting the cables and connectors. SCSI bus specification requires stringent electrical characteristics for each device attached to the SCSI bus.

MEMORY BOTTLENECKS

When your NT computer has insufficient memory, it appears as though the disk has a problem until you check the queue length. In most cases you will find that excessive queue length results from lack of memory. In fact, the disk I/O requests are delayed while they wait in queue.

In most memory bottleneck situations, you just do not have enough memory. Once Performance Monitor has told you so, you just go and buy some more memory.

Other memory problems are more insidious. With memory leakage for instance, it's as if your computer were bleeding to death. A memory leak occurs when a memory pool allocates some of its memory to a process and the process does not return the memory. When this happens repeatedly, the memory pool is depleted.

So how do you identify a memory leak? You find a counter that shows pool memory is being allocated, and the available amount of pool memory is continuously being depleted, then you identify the process that is being allocated memory, but not returning it.

The Memory, Objects, and Processes objects should always be selected when you are looking for a pool leak. All counters under each object should be selected. Other object counters can also be selected to help you identify a specific problem. You then simply view all charted objects until one or more objects show a trend that could be a pool leak and then investigate the problem.

When you chart memory resources, it should be clear that one or more memory pools are allocating memory and the available memory in one or more memory pools is being continuously depleted. When charted, a memory pool may display a continuously climbing stair-step effect while the process leaking memory is running. However, during times of inactivity, it is common to see the charted line remain flat. The charted line will continue the stair pattern the next time the process leaking memory is run.

When you chart threads, it should be evident that the thread count grows in a manner similar to the tagged pool memory allocs and bytes discussed in the previous paragraph. Depending on the amount of threads that are created, the Threads object may jump to a high value immediately.

Charting Processes should help determine which process is causing the leak. Object counters such as Pool Nonpaged Bytes, Pool Paged Bytes, and Thread Count should all be charted. The process leaking memory should show up in a chart as the cause of the stair-step pattern.

Usually it is hard to find the specific process that is leaking memory. A trend can often be identified that shows a memory leak, but an exact process may not be identifiable as the cause of the memory leak. If the process leaking memory is a service, you can identify the process using Control Panel (Services) and Performance Monitor.

1. If the process has been running long enough to show signs of the memory leak, use Performance Monitor to chart the object counter Objects: Threads. The number of threads running depend on many factors, but the number grows larger as the process leaking memory continues to run.

2. Run Control Panel and choose Services.

3. Tile the windows so you can see both Control Panel and Performance Monitor.

4. Using Control Panel, start and stop the services one at a time. If the process that is leaking memory has been running long enough, there will be a drastic reduction in threads when that process is stopped. The process leaking memory does not have to be a service to use this method. If the process leaking memory is a regular program, closing the program will also cause the thread count to drop.

CACHE BOTTLENECKS

On DOS systems, the primary tuning parameter in the system is the size of the disk cache. Recent versions of DOS and Windows have reduced the need for you to tweak this parameter because they adapt to the memory size of the machine. Still, few users of those systems can resist the temptation to play with the tuning parameters of the cache.

The NT Server cache adapts itself automatically to memory size and loading on the computer and has few tuning controls. This section covers the workings of the file system cache on NT and shows how you can determine if it is the primary focus of system activity.

The file system cache is a buffer that holds data coming from or destined for disks, LANs, and other peripherals. NT uses a single file system cache for all cacheable peripheral devices. For simplicity you can refer primarily to the disk as the source of data, but keep in mind this is a simplification, and any time the word "disk" is used in this section you may substitute LAN or the high speed peripheral of your choice.

Unless an application specifies the FILE_FLAG_NO_BUFFERING parameter in its call when opening a file, the file system cache is used when the disk is accessed. On reads from the device, the data is first placed into the cache. On writes, the data goes into the cache before going to the disk.

Unbuffered I/O requests have a unique restriction; the I/O must be done in a multiple of the disk device's sector size. Because buffering usually helps performance, it is rather unusual for a file to be opened without buffering enabled. The applications that do this are typically server applications like SQL Server that manage their own buffers. For the purposes of this section, you can consider all file activity to be buffered by the file system cache.

When NT first opens a file, the cache maps the file into its address space, and can then read the file as if it were an array of records in memory. When an application requests file data, the file system first looks in the cache to see if the data is there, and the cache tries to copy the record to the application's buffer. If the page is not in the working set of the cache, a page fault occurs. Cache references to absent file pages are resolved by the memory manager.

If the page is in memory, it is mapped (not copied) into the cache's working set. This means a page table entry is validated to point to the correct page frame in memory. If the page is not in memory, the memory manager gets the page from the correct file on the peripheral. This is how the cache manager uses the memory manager to do its input. The cache is treated much like the working set of a process. It grows and shrinks as demand dictates.

On NT Server, you can tune cache versus process working set behavior by using the Network option of Control Panel. After choosing the Network icon, in the Installed Network Software list box select Server and choose the Configure button. In the Server dialog box, select Maximize Throughput for File Sharing, to give more priority to the cache. To select process working sets, select Maximize Throughput for Network Applications.

LAN BOTTLENECKS

A LAN further complicates the picture. To begin with, you may have several client computers and perhaps even several different servers. In addition to these factors, you have the LAN, and possibly multiple network protocols that complicate your analysis. Inside this complex system of equipment and logic there might be hidden a bottleneck.

One good thing about searching for network bottlenecks is that everything we have covered in the previous sections still applies. A server that has a disk bottleneck because memory is too tight is still a computer that has a disk bottleneck because memory is too tight. The fact that it is a server just makes it more annoying because more people are affected. So what you have learned thus far is not wasted, we just have to add a bit more knowledge. We need to look at the counters reflecting network traffic and gain some understanding of their capacities under various configurations.

WAN analysis and LAN analysis is much the same, except bandwidth is far more restricted on WANs. Your choice of network protocol and configuration parameters is quite important when WANs are factored into your network configuration.

NT ships with a number of network protocol options including IPX/SPX (Novell NetWare compatible protocol). Performance Monitor has counters on each of these protocols. If you have installed a third-party protocol, it may or may not include extended object counters added for Performance Monitor support. If so, you will undoubtedly find that the guidelines discussed here even apply to your situation.

Another factor to watch out for is NetBIOS broadcast storms. Regardless of which transport protocol you have chosen, NT uses NetBIOS to publish share availability on the network. If you have a very large network with many computers sharing devices, use a protocol analyzer to determine the source of your traffic jams. Chapter 30, "LAN Troubleshooting," discusses analyzing protocols and what to look for.

MONITORING AN APPLICATION

The four counters below are especially helpful resources. They present a reasonable overview of total system use by any given application, and they can tell the administrator how various applications use memory, the processor, and I/O time.

- ◆ %Processor Time: The percentage of elapsed time that a processor is busy executing a thread for a particular process.

- ◆ Working Set: The current number of memory bytes used by or allocated to a process. This value may be larger than the minimum number of bytes actually needed by the process.

◆ Read Operations/sec: The rate (number per second) of read operations on peripheral devices, such as hard disks or printers, issued by threads in a process.

◆ Write Operations/sec: The rate (number per second) of write operations on peripheral devices issued by threads in a process.

Capacity planning requires regular measurements on a daily basis. Begin by logging in at 5-minute intervals all day, and then re-log the files with the intervals increased to 15 minutes. Focus on the most active two hours of the day, and create an ongoing archive of log files containing this information.

The following list offers a good starting point for analyzing your system's performance. To locate the most common bottlenecks, evaluate the following objects and counters.

Object type	Counter
Process	%Processor Time, Interrupts/sec
System	Read/write operations/sec
Memory	Pages/sec, Cache Pages/sec, Available Pages
Server	Total Bytes/sec Physical Disk
%Disk time	Average Disk sec/Transfer
Logical Disk	%Free Space

The above objects and counters provide the tools for investigating the following:

◆ Why an application is performing poorly.

◆ Intermittent performance problems.

◆ Where increased capacity such as memory or hard-disk storage would be useful.

◆ You can chart each counter with a different color line. Each time you add a counter, its values are graphed over time. Many counters can be charted at the same time.

◆ Charting these counters allows you to record performance trends so that they can be viewed at a later time. Viewing performance trends over time can help with capacity planning.

◆ You can save your monitor statistics to log files for further analysis. Once the statistics are logged, you can feed the log file back into the Performance Monitor to create charts, reports, or alerts from the logged data as if you are monitoring the data in realtime.

◆ Many people recognize problems better in a chart than from viewing raw data, but charts only present a two-dimensional picture of system activity.

Logs, on the other hand, can reveal the true nature of a system's behavior under different conditions by providing data for long-term trend analysis. Use your log files to search for inconsistencies and aberrant values. You can correlate aberrant values with operations that are occurring to reveal the source and causes of bottlenecks and poor performance.

THE PROCESSOR AS A BOTTLENECK

The processor does not become a bottleneck until the total processor sustains 80 percent utilization or more. When processor use approaches 100 percent, it may indicate that the processor is not adequate to support demand. In addition to the processor capacity, you need to make sure that the server is only using good 32-bit bus mastering network and disk adapters. What may look like a processor bottleneck is sometimes due to peripherals.

If you have eliminated other components as the cause of the bottleneck and the processor consistently shows high utilization, upgrading your processor may be in order. A more powerful processor or a multiprocessor system may solve the problem. However, acceptable processor usage may depend on computer activity. Use the Performance Monitor to chart the counter called Process: %Processor Time for all processes. If more than a couple of processes are contending for the majority of the processor time, then a faster processor or an additional processor in an SMP (symmetric multiprocessor) machine should be considered.

Tip

Be sure to schedule during off hours those tasks that are not time sensitive. There is no reason to affect peak productivity hours with tasks that can be run during off hours. NT's AT.EXE utility can be used to kick off unattended processes at any time of the day.

PROCESSOR QUEUE LENGTH

The number of threads indicated by the processor queue length is a significant indicator because each thread requires a certain number of processor cycles. If demand exceeds supply, long processor queues develop and system response suffers. Therefore, a sustained processor queue length of >2 generally indicates the processor is a bottleneck. This counter will always be 0 unless you monitor a thread counter as well.

PROCESSOR TIME

The counter called %Processor Time indicates how busy a processor is. It shows the percentage of elapsed time that a processor is busy executing non-idle threads.

SERVICE REQUESTS

The Interrupts/sec counter, which measures the rate of service requests from I/O devices, is also an important processor counter. A dramatic increase in this counter value without a corresponding increase in system activity indicates a hardware problem.

AVERAGE QUEUE TIME

Disk queue length can be thought of as the number of disk access requests waiting in the queue to be processed. It is a temporary value that grows and shrinks rapidly. You may want to watch this figure over a period of time to determine a baseline and average. The Avg. Disk sec/Transfer counter is the average amount of time for a disk transfer (either reads or writes). Reads and writes are monitored separately as well, if you are interested in closer examination of disk utilization. Use the following formula to find the average disk queue time:

Avg.Queue Time = Disk Queue Length × Avg. Disk sec/Transfer

Multiplying Disk Queue Length by Avg. Disk sec/transfer gives an estimate of the amount of time each disk I/O will actually take on that logical drive (average disk queue time, not in the Performance Monitor). This information is a relative performance measurement and should be compared with other hard disk drives in your system. Compute the figures for all logical disks in your system. To increase system performance, you may want to distribute paging files to the logical drives with the lowest total disk I/O time. Up to 16 volumes can have paging files. The number of disk commands waiting in the queue is usually the factor that slows disk performance by increasing the average disk queue time.

MONITORING THE NETWORK

The network can account for a large number of performance problems. It is usually difficult to figure out if the problems are related to the network hardware or the cable plant or something is happening to the network traffic. Performance Monitor provides counters for measuring the network traffic as it passes through the server. The network traffic is handled by the redirector and server software running at the server.

NT redirector software (RDR.SYS) transmits requests while server software (SRV.SYS) receives and interprets incoming messages. Each computer also uses at least one type of protocol software to handle packet formatting and routing. NT supports several protocols, including NetBEUI and TCP/IP. The server, the redirector, NetBEUI, and TCP/IP each generate a set of statistics that appear as Performance Monitor counters. Abnormal network counter values often indicate problems with a server's memory, processor, or disk(s). Therefore, the best approach to monitoring a server is to watch network counters in conjunction with other counters such as %Processor Time, %Disk Time, and Pages/sec.

For example, if a server shows a sharp increase in Pages/sec accompanied by a drop in Total Bytes/sec, it may indicate that the computer is running short of physical memory for network operations. Tracking the counter values in the following chart over an extended period is a good way to understand network operations.

NETWORK COUNTERS

The following table shows the different counters you may have to monitor to get an idea of the behavior of the network. The complete picture emerges when you study all the information together.

Object type	Counter	Description
Server	Pool Nonpaged	Monitors the number of times allocations from the nonpaged pool have been denied, which indicates the computer's physical memory is too limited.
Server	Pool Nonpaged Peak	Maximum number of bytes of nonpaged pool that the server used at a given time. This maximum indicates the amount of memory (RAM) required in the server.
Server	Total Bytes/sec	The number of bytes sent and received each second. This value gives an indication of how busy the network is.

24

NetBEUI Bytes	Frame Received/sec	Bytes and frames sent. The ratio of Frame Bytes to Frames Received.
Frames Rejected	Frames Rejected	Frames received that were incorrect and had to be resent.
NetBEUI	Times Exhausted	This is a sum counter that indicates the number of times since system startup that all the resources (buffers) were in use. Values for instances 0 through 4 link addresses.

Note

In the above table, the term *frame* is used inconsistently from the rest of this book. Though the term frame usually refers to a LAN protocol data unit, some Microsoft documentation refers to NetBEUI packets as frames.

As an illustration, you can use Performance Monitor to track TCP/IP performance by following the steps below:

1. In the Administrative Tools group in Program Manager, double-click Performance Monitor.

2. From the Edit menu, choose Add To Chart.

3. In the Computer list in the Add To Chart dialog box, select the computer you want to monitor.

4. In the Object list, select the TCP/IP-related process you want to monitor: FTP Server, ICMP, IP, Network Interface, TCP, UDP, or WINS Server.

5. In the Counter list, select the counters you want to monitor for each process, and then choose the Add button.

6. When you have selected all the counters you want for a particular chart, choose the Done button.

PERFORMANCE TUNING

Up to now, the discussion has centered on measurements and analysis. This section discusses methods of interpreting the data gathered by Performance Monitor. Once you have a clear idea of where the problems are located, you can start making improvements. The normal response to performance problems is to add more resources. This can be an expensive solution. If it is not carefully planned, it may not fix the problem.

SERVER TUNING

The following are some improvements you can make to the server:

◆ Create multiple paging files. If you have more than one physical disk, create a paging file for each physical disk.

◆ Schedule memory-intensive applications. This means running memory-intensive applications when the system is not busy, or run them on the highest performance computers.

◆ Balance the server load. You can distribute applications among servers until each computer displays a reasonably equivalent load.

◆ Unbind idle network adapters.

◆ Plan workgroup placement. You can configure the network so that servers are on the same network segment as the people who access them.

Another method of improving performance without redesigning the entire system is to set the priorities at the server. Changing the priority can have a dramatic effect on the behavior of the system. NT Server defaults to the wrong priority. It defaults to Best foreground application response time. An administrator can turn to NT Server Tasking options if certain applications cause other applications to appear to severely slow down or stop. Use the Control Panel System option. On the System option, choose the Tasking button. The Tasking dialog box appears, presenting three Tasking options for manipulating an application's normal thread priority.

The following list shows the available options:

◆ Best foreground application response time   This means that the foreground session has the highest priority. This gives the foreground process a priority boost (up two thread levels to priority 9).

◆ Foreground application more responsive   This means that the foreground application has higher priority than the background. This gives the foreground a smaller priority boost (up one thread level to priority 8).

◆ Foreground and Background Equally Responsive   This is the preferred setting for NT Server, because it balances the foreground and background. In effect, it gives priority to the background because there should be no foreground activity at the server (if it is not being used as an application server). Both forground and background are at priority 7. This may also help performance of the Server service because several of its threads within the process run at a base priority of 8 and would be superseded by the active window when it receives a priority boost to 9.

◆ You can apply a finer adjustment using thread priorities. The normal execution of threads within a process occurs at priority 7. The thread executing the foreground process gets a slight priority boost so that the active process will be more responsive to the users' needs. This priority boost can be regulated by selecting from the Tasking options.

IMPROVING DISK PERFORMANCE

There are a couple of simple ways to improve disk performance in your system, perhaps without even changing hardware. Striping a logical volume over multiple physical disk drives (RAID 1) improves performance in a SCSI disk subsystem. SCSI devices are intelligent and can operate independently of one another. A volume striped over two disk drives can double I/O throughput because double the amount of data can be read or written simultaneously. Striping is done in 64KB sections.

Consider striping a logical volume when you have multiple disk drives. Compare the average disk queue time (Avg.Disk sec/Transfer multiplied by Disk Queue Length) for the disk drives to the average disk queuing time of the existing disk divided by the number of drives to be striped. This assumes a totally random access pattern on the logical volume. If the majority of the disk access is localized to a single file or area of the disk, this solution may not increase performance.

Another factor to consider is relocating data files onto different volumes. You can balance user file access I/O over multiple disk drives. An administrator should locate applications and data in a way that makes the best use of existing resources.

NT SERVER MEMORY

The NT Server memory uses a 32-bit, flat, linear addressing scheme that can address up to 4GB of memory. When an application attempts to access memory, it simply specifies a 32-bit memory address. This overcomes the problems associated with accessing memory based on the 64KB segment model. The linear addressing scheme makes NT portable because it is compatible with the memory addressing in processors such as the MIPS R4000 and the DEC Alpha. This still does not solve the problem of not having enough memory under some circumstances.

PAGING AND VIRTUAL MEMORY

When application space is limited, NT Server creates virtual memory through a process called *paging*. NT Server is designed to meet immediate memory demand by loading a program into RAM while swapping out inactive code into virtual memory. This process is called demand paging.

Paging physically transfers unused data from RAM to the paging file (PAGEFILE.SYS) on the system partition of the hard disk. It then retrieves the data from the physical disk file when an application needs it. The virtual memory available on a computer is equal to its available physical RAM plus the paging file.

During Setup, NT Server automatically calculates the size of the paging file for best performance based on the amount of RAM and disk space available.

PAGING FILE SIZING AND PLACEMENT

The recommended size of the paging file is equal to the total RAM plus 12MB. During Setup, if the amount of free space available on the hard disk when the paging file is created is less than the total RAM, the default size of the paging file will be equal to the amount of free space available. If the +PAGEFILE.SYS is configured with less than 22MB, the System Control Panel application automatically runs during boot and prompts you to reconfigure the paging file. In theory, a system with 32MB of RAM does not need a paging file; however, the minimum required paging file size is 2MB.

You cannot delete PAGEFILE.SYS in NT. If you are running another operating system and you delete PAGEFILE.SYS, NT creates a new paging file automatically the next time NT is started.

The paging file can grow if it is needed, but expanding a paging file adds time to the paging process. Therefore, it is best that the paging file not be required to grow during normal operations. PAGEFILE.SYS shrinks dynamically if there are free pages at the end of the file. Growing the paging file requires additional disk access to allocate the needed sectors, update any allocation, and free sector tables used by the file system. The Memory: Commit Limit is the Performance Monitor counter that indicates the number of bytes that can be committed to the paging file without extending the paging file (this counter is found under the Memory category). Thus, the lower the counter, the greater the possibility that the paging file will grow. To allow time to react to the pending problem, it is best not to let the commit limit dip below 10 to 20 percent of the existing size of the paging file. This provides a buffer to cushion any instant needs for the paging file.

Note

> If PAGEFILE.SYS is located on an NTFS partition, the displayed size is not updated as the page file grows or shrinks. This information is only updated on NTFS partitions when the file is closed or when an attempt is made to delete it.

Paging file behavior can be a valuable indicator of system problems. If a significant amount of paging occurs, it can be an indication of system problems.

Pages/sec times the Logical Disk: Avg. Disk sec/Transfer (where the Logical Disk object represents the location of PAGEFILE.SYS) gives you an indication of system problems.

The product of these counters is the percentage of the disk access time used by paging. If this number is regularly greater than 10 percent (0.1), the system needs more memory. If excessive paging has been detected, the next step is to determine the additional memory needs. This is done by monitoring the Process: Working Set (found in the Process category) for each active process in the system. Terminate processes starting with the largest working set present and proceed toward the smallest. Check the statistics until the paging drops below the excessive mark. Add up the size of the working sets of the processes killed. This provides a rough estimate of the additional memory required. The strategy used here is to check the working set size, then kill a process, check the working set size again, kill another process, check the working set size, and so on.

TUNING LAN HARDWARE

Most LAN hardware is built to operate under optimal conditions. Most Ethernet and Token ring hardware built today works at maximum efficiency without any configuration intervention. However, there are a few factors you should consider when evaluating your network's performance.

- ◆ Choose a good network card
- ◆ Use the 32-bit bus mastering network cards
- ◆ Choose only NDIS 3.*x* -certified network cards and drivers

Although little can be done to tune the network card directly, choosing the correct adapter for your NT Server may potentially double performance. More importantly, server network cards can have dramatic effects on your server and may become a bottleneck for all LAN users. Choose network cards carefully, taking all factors into consideration. Evaluate performance, technical support, warranty, vendor stability, and price in that order. You will find that the top network cards do not cost significantly less than lower quality cards. This is especially true when you spread the cost of the card over all the users who access it from their client computers.

All but the smallest network demands require 32-bit bus mastering network adapters. Choose one that uses the full width of the I/O bus in your system. ISA 16-bit or 8-bit cards eat up processor time and degrade total system performance. Though 16-bit cards can provide the same level of throughput as a 32-bit card in a 10 Mbps Ethernet environment, higher bandwidths require the higher capacities of EISA, MCA, or PCI. Additionally, an ISA card consumes many more CPU cycles to drive its I/O. Most later model 32-bit bus mastering devices keep processor utilization very low while delivering high levels of I/O.

Note

You will find that PCI network cards provide the best cost to performance ratio. PCI bus mastering is simpler and less costly to develop than EISA or MCA. Most of the technical mechanics are built into the computer chipset and not the card; therefore, PCI cards are generally less expensive and easier to build. The quality of the bus mastering implementation is better for the same reason.

Avoid VESA VL-bus network cards! While this technology is great for video, it has never garnered much support for network adapters. NDIS 3.x–certified drivers are rare, deeply imbedded driver defects are quite common, and future support is questionable.

Additionally, choose the network adapter and driver as a team. You should choose an adapter that is NDIS 3.x–certified. A defective driver can cause significant global performance problems. You can find tested adapters on the NT Hardware Compatibility list.

TUNING THE WORKSTATION SERVICE

Though the default NT redirector (client software) is fairly self-tuning, an administrator should be aware of several indicators in Performance Monitor.

CURRENT COMMANDS

Current Commands is a counter that shows the number of commands from client redirectors currently queued up. If this number is greater than one per client, the redirector may be where a bottleneck occurs in the system. This can occur for three reasons.

1. The server with which the redirector is communicating is slower than the redirector.

2. The redirector is busier than the client network adapter can keep up with.

3. LAN capacity may be insufficient to support current demand levels.

If LAN capacity problems are identified, it may be necessary to segment the LAN in an attempt to partition network traffic. Or you can try to make the following changes to see if tuning the Registry parameters can help:

◆ The Current Commands maximum is set by a parameter in the Registry in the `LanmanWorkstation` parameter key.

◆ `MaximumNumberOfCommands` determines the maximum number of commands the redirector will accept before rejecting requests. The default is 50 and can be set as high as 255. If Current Commands grows on a steady basis to within 10% to 20% of `MaximumNumberOfCommands`, the administrator should consider increasing the value in the Registry.

NETWORK ERRORS/SEC

Network Errors/sec is a Performance Monitor value that counts the number of serious network errors detected by the redirector. This is an indication that further research is needed. Start by looking at the Event Log on the machine that identified the error.

REMOTE SERVER PROBLEMS

Reads Denied/sec and Writes Denied/sec are two Performance Monitor values that indicate if the remote servers are having problems with memory allocation. Check the servers to or from which the workstation will be doing large file transfers. If it is not possible to increase memory used by RAW 1/0 at the server level, the workstation can be instructed not to use RAW 1/0. This is done by setting the Registry entries `UseRawReads` and/or `UseRawWrites` to False.

TUNING THE SERVER SERVICE

You can optimize the following parameters:

◆ Minimize Memory Used

◆ Balance

◆ Maximize throughput for File Sharing

◆ Maximize throughput for Network Applications.

◆ Make Browser Broadcasts to LAN Manager 2.*x* Clients

First, there is less need to tune the user interface components, such as the keyboard, mouse, and video. Under most circumstances, the server computer should not be used as a workstation. Second, it is very likely the server component performance will outweigh individual client redirector demands.

If server memory becomes a constraint, you may want to adjust the client redirector parameters down so that more memory is available for the server processes.

If the server is running client-server applications such as a SQL Server, SNA Server, or an RPC (remote procedure calls) server, fewer applications will be accessing the disk. Distributing files across multiple disks may prove to be more fruitful.

The `MaximizeThroughputForFileSharing` parameter initially allocates memory for an unlimited number of connections (71,000 connections). This number is quite excessive, and should be reduced according to your requirements. As a rule of thumb, you can set this parameter to the number of users times twenty for a comfortable level.

MISCELLANEOUS TUNING

You can find performance in many unsuspected places. As you become familiar with NT Server and the network as a whole, you may find many areas where improvements can be made. The following are some examples of such unlikely places.

CHANGING DEFAULT SPOOL DIRECTORY

To change the default printer spool directory for all printers to spread the load over more than one physical disk by following these steps:

1. Start Registry Editor.
2. From the HKEY_LOCAL_MACHINE subtree, go to the subkey \SYSTEM\CurrentControlSet\Control\Print\Printers.
3. Select the Printers key.
4. From the Edit menu choose Add Value.
5. Add a value using the following information:
   ```
   Value Name: DefaultSpoolDirectory
   Data Type:  REG_SZ
   String:     <full path to printer spool directory>
   ```
6. Exit Registry Editor and restart NT.

To change the printer spool directory for specific printers, follow these steps:

1. Start Registry Editor.

2. From the HKEY_LOCAL_MACHINE subtree, go to the subkey
   \SYSTEM\CurrentControlSet\Control\Print\Printers\<specific
   printer>\SpoolDirectory.

3. Select the Printers key.

4. From the Edit menu choose Add Value.

5. Add a value using the following information:

```
Value Name: SpoolDirectory
Data Type:  REG_SZ
String:     <full path to printer spool directory>
```

6. Exit Registry Editor and restart NT.

Note

Neither DefaultSpoolDirectory nor SpoolDirectory are set by default.
The global default location for all printers' spool files is
%SYSTEMROOT%\SYSTEM32\SPOOL\PRINTERS.
DefaultSpoolDirectory defines a new global default location for all
printers to put their spool files. SpoolDirectory defines a new printer-
specific location for spool files that overrides the global default on a
per-printer basis.

SHUT DOWN PRINT JOB LOGGING

By default, NT Server logs in the System Log every print job processed by the server.
This section explains how to disable that logging. Administrators who want to
disable the logging of every print job can follow these steps:

1. Run REGEDT32.EXE.

2. Find
   \HKEY_LOCAL_MACHINE\SYSTEM\CurrentControlSet\Control\Print\Providers.

3. From the Edit menu, choose Add Value.

4. In the Value Name field of the Add Value dialog box, type `EventLog`.

5. In the Data Type box, select REG_DWORD.

6. In the Dword Editor dialog box, type a `0` (zero) in the Data box.

7. Choose the OK button.

8. Quit REGEDT32.EXE.

9. Restart the computer.

SETTING RAW READ/WRITES

Normal CORE mode read and write operations occur in approximately 8KB units. For each 8KB the redirector must submit a new SMB (server message block); this is adequate for most file operations. Many applications want to override CORE mode to send larger data blocks with each SMB. As an optimization, Microsoft networks can use RAW mode to send data in 64KB units, requiring one SMB for every 64KB. The transport subdivides this buffer as needed. One stipulation of RAW mode is that the Virtual Circuit must be tied up while the operation is in progress because the data frames contain no SMB information to correlate it. No other SMB can be allowed during this time.

NT introduced a new SMB called `NTNotifyDirectoryChange`. This causes the server to notify the client if directory information changes. For example, if another client adds a file to a directory, NT File Manager uses `NTNotifyDirectoryChange`.

This SMB is classified as a long-term request. The SMB is received by the server but is not returned until a change occurs (or until the SMB is canceled by the client). Because the client does not know when the server completes the SMB, it cannot tie up the virtual circuit. Therefore, the client does not use RAW mode when an `NTNotifyDirectoryChange` is pending.

When necessary, File Manager cancels the request to take advantage of RAW mode. However, other processes such as NTVDM or SETUP are not aware that RAW mode has been disabled.

The file I/O optimizations in NT File Manager can cause other processes' calls to Raw Write and Raw Read to fail. To correct this problem, follow these steps:

1. Always use File Manager to copy or write files. File Manager cancels the `NTNotifyDirectoryChange` SMB before submitting the RAW read/write operation.

2. Modify the NT Registry as follows:

   Run Registry Editor (REGEDT32.EXE).

   From the \HKEY_CURRENT_USER subtree, go to the \Software \Microsoft\FileManager\Settings key.

   From the Edit menu, choose Add Value.

3. Enter the following:

```
Value Name: ChangeNotifyTime
Data Type:  REG_SZ
String:     0 (disable; 1 for enable)
```

24

MONITORING AND TUNING PERFORMANCE

SUMMARY

Performance monitoring and tuning are difficult and time-consuming activities. You should make sure to run some benchmark counters on a newly installed system and save the logs for replay later. Also, do not try to start tuning immediately after the system is installed; let the users settle into their usage patterns so that you do not have to constantly tweak the system in response to changing user habits. Make sure that you tune one factor at a time and make measurements. Keep a log and the .PMC and .PML files for later use to re-create the same situations to confirm your results.

- What Is Bandwidth?

- Monitoring
  Bandwidth

- Bandwidth Solutions

- Higher Capacity
  LANs

- Internetworking
  Solutions—
  Segmenting LANs

- Switching Hubs
  and Virtual LANs
  (VLANs)

- Monitoring LAN
  Bandwidth

CHAPTER 25

LAN Capacity Allocation

LAN capacity may not be sufficient when a number of users share a single LAN. EtherNet and Token ring have limited capacity in relation to the many demands made on today's LANs. Even higher capacity LANs (Fast Ethernet, FDDI, 100VG, ATM) have a limit as to how many users can be supported on one LAN.

Note

> In this book, the term *LAN* refers to an EtherNet, Token ring, or other type of local area network. The term *network* refers to the entire networked system of computers: LANs, WANs, protocols, network operating systems (NOS), and so on.

Servers are far more powerful than they were last year, and next year's servers will be more powerful yet. In the past, one server and one LAN have been allocated to a number of users, generally on a workgroup basis. That is, one server and one LAN would be installed for an accounting department, an accounts receivable department, or an invoicing department according to the expected traffic demands. The composite system has been the focal point of providing capacity.

Consolidating servers is a trend in larger organizations today. As more users are added to a network, management invariably adds more servers to service workgroup needs. Because server power is growing rapidly, the trend is to put more users on each server or to consolidate existing servers. In this chapter, this scenario is called the *one-server-to-one-LAN* model.

The one-server-to-one-LAN model has always worked in the past, but in today's networks, the bottleneck in network capacity is not the server. In most situations, the individual LAN will at times pace the level of traffic due to its limited capacity.

NT Server can accommodate up to 16 network adapters in a single server. The old one-server-to-one-LAN model can now be discarded. By using a 32-bit bus mastering server design, you can accommodate several network interface cards in one server without bus or processor bottleneck.

The solution this chapter explores is a new one-server-to-several-LANs approach as well as other approaches. Even if some of the LANs are 100 Mbps or better, this new model provides built-in capacity to an already existing system.

The trend towards server consolidations can be tempered with well-researched LAN capacity allocation. A system analyst should evaluate traffic levels and suggest capacity allocation methods that work for the organization.

The ratio of users to a LAN is now the critical issue. More accurately, the system analyst needs to determine at what level users need to be divided into separate LANs instead of separate networks.

WHAT IS BANDWIDTH?

The speed of your LAN is called *bandwidth*. The first issue to be addressed in this chapter is the issue of what 10 or 100 Mbps really means to you in quantitative performance. The answer is quite complex, but the bottom line is that bandwidth is a matter of *capacity*, not of speed.

CAPACITY, NOT SPEED

A 100 Mbps LAN has 10 times more capacity (not speed) than a 10 Mbps LAN. The classic simile of a pipe is often used by electronic engineers to explain the bandwidth issue. A 100-gallon-per-minute pipe has 10 times more capacity than a 10-gallon-per-minute pipe. Ultimately, water may or may not flow faster through the bigger pipe, depending upon whether capacity is smaller than water flow demand.

Speed is an electrical issue relative to the type and quality of cabling. An electron, and therefore a bit, travels down a wire at a given, constant rate. This rate is called the *nominal velocity of propagation* (NVP). A category 3 UTP cable's NVP is about 62 percent of the speed of light. Bits travel down the wire at this speed regardless of whether they are signaled at the rate of 10 or 100 MHz.

100 Mbps means that the bits are signaled at the rate of 100 MHz and therefore 100 million bits per second because simple baseband Manchester digital signaling is used in Fast Ethernet. The first bit in a frame will reach its destination regardless of whether it is signaled at 10 or 100 MHz. Frames are therefore propagated at the same speed.

HIGHER BANDWIDTH AND TRANSMISSION TIME

Bandwidth measures how much time is occupied during transmission of a frame on the wire and therefore how much time is available for other frames to be transmitted. No more than one frame ever exists on a 10 Mbps Ethernet LAN at any given time. Therefore, the issue is that 100 Mbps Ethernet addresses is the amount of *time* a frame occupies the wire.

Because a frame signaled at the rate of 100 Mbps takes one-tenth the amount of time to put on the wire, 10 times more free time is available for other users' demands. The frame actually arrives at the same rate of speed, but the available time on the wire is increased. In Figure 25.1, a 10 Mbps frame is represented in terms of space. When the same frame is signaled at 100 Mbps, ten times as much free time is available between frames.

This time model is more accurate than a speed model. Network/transport protocols (that is, NetBIOS, NetBEUI, IPX/NCP, TCP/IP, and so on) pace the flow of packets (encapsulated into frames on a one-to-one ratio) through a connection-oriented flow—an acknowledgment must be returned before the next packet is sent.

Figure 25.1.
Frames transmitted at
10 versus 100 MHz.

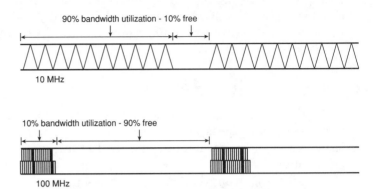

BANDWIDTH CONCLUSION

A user may not experience significantly greater performance after switching to a 100 Mbps LAN. Instead, the LAN has more capacity available to service user demands than in a lower bandwidth LAN. A 100 Mbps LAN has approximately 10 times more capacity than a 10 Mbps LAN.

On many occasions, system analysts dealing with WANs have experienced this same phenomenon. When upgrading from a 64-Kbps data line to a T-1 (1.544 Mbps), better performance is often not realized. Unless demand exceeds the limit of 56 Kbps (64 Kbps minus the 8-Kbps Robbed Bit Signal overhead), the T-1 line does not provide greater performance. The T-1 line provides greater capacity, not speed.

Before upgrading your LAN to 100 Mbps, you must analyze the current level of bandwidth utilization to make a good decision on upgrading.

THEORETICAL VERSUS USABLE BANDWIDTH

Bandwidth is measured in the percentage currently in use versus theoretical capacity. Keep in mind that Ethernet cannot push the theoretical limits of bandwidth due to collisions and the contention-oriented nature of CSMA/CD access protocol. You are lucky to squeeze 80 percent bandwidth utilization out of EtherNet, whereas token-passing ring and other types of deterministic access protocols can consistently deliver 90-95 percent bandwidth utilization. While the theoretical bandwidth of 10 Mbps Ethernet is 10 Mbps, the usable bandwidth translates to 8 Mbps or so, while the usable bandwidth of 16 Mbps Token ring approaches 1.9 Mbps.

Token ring, FDDI, 100VG-AnyLAN, and ATM overcome the limitation that EtherNet/Fast EtherNet faces. An FDDI LAN can accommodate 90-95 Mbps, whereas a Fast

EtherNet LAN may only produce 7-8 Mbps (under ideal conditions) due to many technical factors. Your usable bandwidth may be less in EtherNet depending upon the length and quality of your cabling.

Note

Always consider the usable instead of theoretical bandwidth when planning capacity allocation.

CATEGORIZING BANDWIDTH NEEDS

Bandwidth allocation should be proportioned according to user demands. Most users do word processing and send electronic mail over LANs. Other users save and retrieve large graphics files on file servers over the LAN. The two types of applications demonstrate the diversity of bandwidth demand.

The four most popular applications used on a LAN today are:

♦ Word processing
♦ Spreadsheets
♦ Electronic mail
♦ Shared databases

The first three of these applications consume very little bandwidth, and many database applications only rarely consume large amounts of bandwidth. User demands are of short duration, and are widely spaced over long time periods. A word-processing or spreadsheet user may pull up a document, work on it for an extended period of time, then save the document. The LAN activity would show a very short burst of traffic, followed by an extended period of dormancy, then another short burst of traffic.

Even a 2.5 Mbps ARCnet LAN can accommodate many users under such conditions. A single 10 Mbps EtherNet LAN can accommodate 100 or more such users, provided that their activities are as sporadic as indicated.

When a database activity is factored in, bandwidth can be quickly consumed. Many database applications are heavily used, and/or utilize update activity that is very I/O-intensive. All it takes is one user doing a database merge, massive update, or file reorganization to fill the LAN to capacity. Printing also provides a steady massive stream of data flow, especially when a Hewlett-Packard laser printer with a built-in network adapter and a modular I/O channel is used. A solitary network printer can saturate a LAN's bandwidth easily.

Now that inexpensive 100 Mbps technology has arrived, more bandwidth-hungry applications are becoming popular. Scanning documents for later retrieval is a popular new activity that can really stress out 10 Mbps EtherNet's limit.

The practice of document imaging, storage, and retrieval has become very popular now that disk drives, optical drives, CD-ROMs, 100 Mbps LANs, and powerful computers are available at low prices. LANs will be buried with such demands in the years to come.

A system analyst must take into consideration the profile of work to be done on the LAN and evaluate future demand based on current and future usage.

MONITORING BANDWIDTH

You can monitor bandwidth utilization with a LAN monitor or a protocol analyzer. When the Network Monitoring Agent is installed from the NT control panel Network applet, a new item appears in the Performance Monitor drop-down box. The Network Segment option enables you to view traffic levels on directly connected LAN segments. Additionally, System Management Server provides a complete network frame capture utility that identifies current network utilization and error levels for each LAN segment.

A useful analysis must include watching bandwidth utilization over an extended period of time. A given moment does not tell you how often or how long traffic has been inhibited by high levels of utilization. A trend analysis is therefore preferred to simple monitoring.

Figure 25.2 shows LANalyzer for Windows' bandwidth utilization trend analysis over an extended period. The factors you should consider are:

◆ Bandwidth peaks
◆ Duration of the spikes

In Figure 25.2, you can see that bandwidth has peaked to a plateau maximum level a few times. The peaks represent the maximum level of available bandwidth. The plateaus represent how long bandwidth has remained restricted.

How high spikes go is a valid measure; however, how long bandwidth remains at peak level is more important. The plateaus are of the most significance in this illustration. They tell us how much delay users experienced. During one of the spikes, user traffic is delayed, sometimes resulting in pauses in software application processing.

Given the randomness of user traffic demands, user traffic will overlap periodically. The nature of network traffic patterns is to be "bursty" with no regularity. Therefore, overlap is inevitable at times.

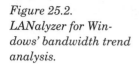

Figure 25.2.
LANalyzer for Win-
dows' bandwidth trend
analysis.

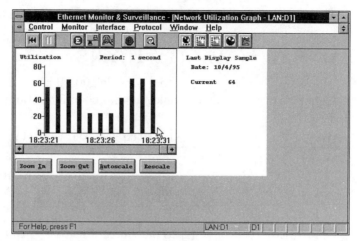

High bandwidth utilization spikes can appear frequently, but unless the duration exceeds a few seconds, users will scarcely notice any degradation.

To adequately analyze network bandwidth, you must compare traffic patterns with what level of traffic is acceptable. The level you will accept depends upon experience.

Baselining

You cannot plan capacity to fill all demand at all times. Your network traffic should be baselined to reveal normal traffic patterns. You can then compare current traffic patterns to your baseline of normal traffic patterns.

Baselining consists of saving trend analysis graphs such as the one shown previously in Figure 25.2. You can compare future trend analysis graphs to develop a feel for whether a trend of increasing traffic has developed or if the current level is an extraordinary event.

Bandwidth Solutions

Once you have determined that current capacity is insufficient to satisfy the normal traffic patterns, you have several options. You can do any of the following:

- ◆ Upgrade to a higher capacity LAN
- ◆ Allocate users among a few LANs
- ◆ Use bridges or routers to segment a large LAN into a few smaller ones
- ◆ Use a switching hub to segment LANs and users automatically
- ◆ Use a combination of these approaches

These approaches are discussed in greater detail in the following sections.

HIGHER CAPACITY LANS

There are a few LAN types that provide 100 Mbps or more bandwidth. Table 25.1 explores current LAN technologies that should be stable for the next few years.

TABLE 25.1. HIGHER BANDWIDTH LAN CAPACITY COMPARISON.

Type of LAN	Standard	Theoretical Bandwidth (Mbps)	Usable Bandwidth (%)
Fast EtherNet	IEEE 802.3u 10Base-TX	100	70
Fast EtherNet	IEEE 802.3u 100Base-T4	100	70
FDDI	ANSI ASCX3T9.5	100	93
100VG-AnyLAN	IEEE 802.12	100	90
TCNS (Thomas-Conrad)	no standard	100	65
ATM	ATM Forum	25-155	90

Note

Usable bandwidth statistics in this chart are conservative estimates of maximum usable levels based on experience. Various combinations of network card, server, and cabling installation can vary by as much as 15 percent.

COMPARISON OF LAN AVAILABLE BANDWIDTH AND BUS CAPACITY IN A SERVER

When adding more than one network card to your server, you should take care to provide the proper bus design to accommodate your configuration. You do not need a mainframe to handle the traffic a few network cards and a couple of SCSI disk adapters can handle.

In comparing available bandwidth levels among the most popular types of LANs, you will find Figure 25.3 helpful. In this graph, popular LANs are compared against bus bandwidths to help you select the appropriate technology for your server.

*Figure 25.3.
Comparisons of
popular LANs and bus
bandwidths.*

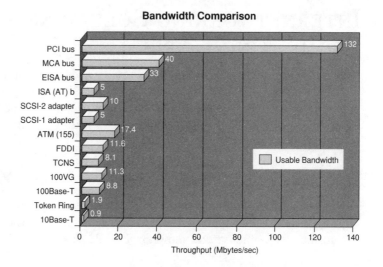

Bandwidth Comparison

PCI bus 132
MCA bus 40
EISA bus 33
ISA (AT) b 5
SCSI-2 adapter 10
SCSI-1 adapter 5
ATM (155) 17.4
FDDI 11.6
TCNS 8.1
100VG 11.3
100Base-T 8.8
Token Ring 1.9
10Base-T 0.9

Usable Bandwidth

Throughput (Mbytes/sec)

Note

Throughput (I/O) statistics are expressed in *bytes* per second, and
LAN standards are expressed in *bits* per second. Figure 25.3 shows all
statistics in Mbytes/sec, whereas theoretical LAN capacities are
normally expressed in Mbps.

Figure 25.3 shows that one EISA or Microchannel (MCA) bus can accommodate a
combination of several network cards and SCSI adapters. However, when 100 Mbps
network cards are added, even EISA, MCA, and Microchannel busses prove
insufficient. For this reason, Peripheral Component Interface (PCI) has been
developed.

Tip

When combining more than one network card and one disk adapter in
a busy server, you should use only 32-bit bus mastering cards. Bus
mastering offloads I/O processing to the onboard processors. This
alleviates processing bottlenecks caused by non-bus mastering devices
which drive CPU utilization to 100 percent.

INTERNETWORKING SOLUTIONS— SEGMENTING LANs

Each user's frames are propagated to every node on a single LAN. When these users share the same LAN, their capacity is limited. Separating users by connecting them to separate LANs is one way of allocating capacity. When LANs are joined together, an internetwork is formed. Bridges and routers form the boundaries between separate LANs.

INTERNETWORK DESIGN

It becomes apparent that more than one server is required for an internetwork to provide increased capacity. If only one server is used, the internetwork configuration may be inefficient, as shown in Figure 25.4.

Figure 25.4.
One server and an
internetwork.

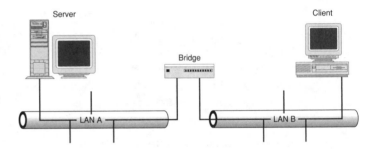

Figure 25.4 illustrates a configuration that may be necessary due to physical constraints. For example, the total length of the internetwork may exceed limitation of a single LAN. This configuration is inefficient, however, because all network packets from remote LAN users must travel over a bridge or router. Excessive latency may be introduced when the bridges/routers become congested.

BACKBONE LANs

The most common configuration used to internetwork uses a single high-capacity LAN to join several lower bandwidth LANs together, as shown in Figure 25.5. In this illustration, a router stands between each departmental LAN and the backbone LAN. One or several servers are placed on the backbone LAN to provide immediate access with the fewest number of hops over routers/bridges.

Because the backbone LAN has high capacity, and local LANs have less capacity, the local LANs become a factor limiting the throughput to the backbone LAN. In this scenario, the backbone rarely becomes congested. This configuration provides many benefits, including flexibility to add servers and other services on the backbone.

Figure 25.5.
A backbone LAN.

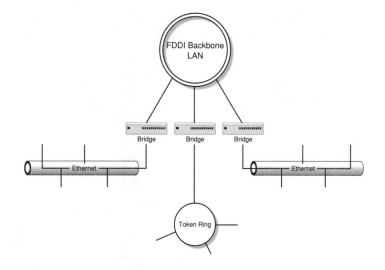

BRIDGES, ROUTERS, AND BROUTERS

Although many people use the terms *bridge* and *router* interchangeably, these two types of devices are quite different. Each works at a different layer of protocol and has differing features and benefits.

BRIDGES

A simple bridge filters and forwards LAN frames by examining the node (MAC) addresses in the LAN frame header. The bridge keeps track of which nodes are located on each port. These bridges are called *MAC layer bridges* because they process addresses in the IEEE Media Access Control (MAC) frame header. Figure 25.6 shows the functionality of a MAC layer bridge.

Figure 25.6.
A MAC layer bridge.

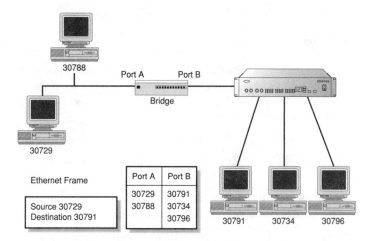

MAC layer bridges are limited in their abilities. When more complex internetworks are formed, frames can go into infinite loops as shown in Figure 25.7.

Figure 25.7.
A loop in a complex
internetwork.

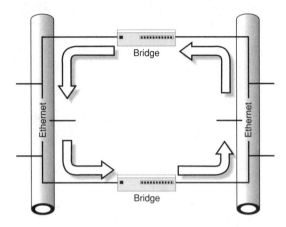

To handle more complex bridges, some bridges add another layer of protocol to the frame header. Using Logical Link Control (LLC) or SubNetwork Access Protocol (SNAP), intermediate addresses are added to specify the route to be taken.

ROUTERS

Routers process the packet protocol contained inside of a LAN frame. This distinguishes a router for two important reasons:

◆ The router processes the network layer protocol header information and its logical addressing.

◆ The router can process only network protocols that are routable. This includes IPX, IP, and AppleTalk protocols. A router cannot route NetBIOS, NetBEUI, and SNA protocols.

Note

The terms *packet* and *frame* represent two different layers of protocol. Packets are protocol units generated and used by the NOS. Frames are protocol units used between network cards. Packets are encapsulated into frames for movement over a LAN.

Although these terms are often used interchangeably, they are used more precisely in this book.

The routing process is shown in Figure 25.8. The LAN frame is discarded when the router receives the frame. The router processes the packet, not the frame addressing. If the packet needs to be forwarded, the router sends the packet to the destination network adapter driver for encapsulation in a new frame. In Figure 25.8, the first frame has fulfilled its purpose when it delivers the packet to the router's #1 network adapter. When the packet is forwarded to LAN B, a new frame is assembled, in which the source is the router's #2 network adapter.

Figure 25.8.
A router filtering and
forwarding packets.

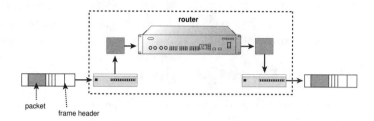

packet

frame header

Brouters

Routers that contain bridging functions are called *brouters, bridging routers,* or *routing bridges.* This type of device always routes first if the network protocol is routable, and it bridges only when a non-routable protocol is detected.

To Route or to Bridge; That Is the Question

The real question is whether you should choose a bridge or a router as the primary strategy for your internetwork. The following discussion should help you decide.

Generally, bridges are simple and inexpensive devices that are easy to install and configure. MAC layer bridges linking two LANs together require virtually no configuration at all. If your network uses only non-routable protocols (NetBIOS, NetBEUI, and SNA protocols), bridges are the logical choice.

Routers are generally more complex and therefore more difficult to manage. The logical addressing for IP and IPX networks and hosts must be assigned by the administrator. Installing and configuring these devices requires either knowledge of the existing internetwork addressing, or familiarity with administration of addresses.

Routers are programmable: They can filter packets based on any field in the packet header or in the data portion of the packet. Because bridges do not process the packet header, this information is not available.

Routers can change path decisions based on changing network conditions. Any time a new path becomes available, the router can change the path the packets will take. For the most part, this is not possible with bridges—once they are installed, their path instructions generally remain fixed.

Routers can use a variety of protocols to communicate between them. Many routers use Router Information Protocol (RIP), some use Open Shortest Path First (OSPF), and others use proprietary link-state protocols to define different bases for making routing decisions. When multiple paths exist, you may want to consider the best path decision based upon hops, time, or cost of the media.

As you can imagine, routers generally cost more than bridges. The most important consideration, however, is the routable protocol knowledge the system integrator and the administrator must possess to install and manage the internetwork.

MIXING BRIDGES AND ROUTERS

Each time an IP or IPX packet is routed, an increment is added to the hop count field in the packet header (IPX=transport control, IP=time to live). RIP-based routers often make poor routing decisions when bridges and routers are present in redundant paths. The bridges are not taken into consideration in the hop count, so the bridged path looks as if it has fewer hops. Therefore, mixing bridges and routers is not recommended where redundant paths exist.

SWITCHING HUBS AND VIRTUAL LANS (VLANS)

Switching hubs have become quite popular lately in an EtherNet environment. Although there are at least three different designs for these devices, the basic concept is to put a switch between ports that can automatically switch from a repeater to a bridge. When a path through a switching hub is used more often, a repeater makes the connection. Less frequently used paths are bridged.

A switching hub automatically segments traffic between clients and servers. For this reason, the term *Virtual LAN,* or *VLAN,* has been coined to describe the internetwork configuration, because the switch automatically segments the LAN into separately bridged LANs. The term indicates that separate LANs are administered by the hub to create virtual (not fixed) bridge links.

When a large network with multiple servers is controlled by a switching hub, the LAN is automatically segmented into separate LANs as shown in Figure 25.9. This configuration improves performance without any additional administrative intervention.

Physically dividing the users into two separate LANs with a bridge would accomplish the same effect as the illustration in Figure 25.9. However, a switching hub provides two advantages: first, less network design, planning, and administration is involved; second, the bridge can dynamically change its configuration when users change their port positions. Every time the user accesses a different server, the bridge reconfigures the ports accordingly.

Figure 25.9.
Two servers and a
switching hub segment-
ing traffic.

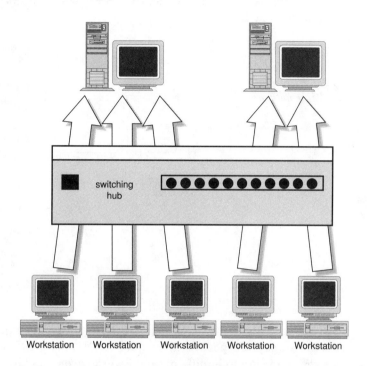

Workstation   Workstation   Workstation   Workstation   Workstation

When the network is configured with only one server, as shown in Figure 25.9, the bridging effect is of no value. However, most switching hubs cache frames and switch each cabling segment as a separate LAN. This gives each workstation a dedicated segment, which it does not have to share with other nodes. The total LAN capacity is thereby increased.

When a combination 10/100 Mbps switching hub is used, the network functions just like a backbone LAN configuration (discussed earlier in this chapter). The clients have dedicated 10 Mbps segments, while the server has a 100 Mbps segment. This is the concept behind 100VG-AnyLAN—this network is designed to support 10 Mbps EtherNet, 16 Mbps Token ring, and 100 Mbps 100VG nodes.

NT MULTIPLE NETWORK ADAPTERS

As discussed previously, you can put up to 16 network cards in a server. This is a convenient way to eliminate LAN bottlenecks. If many active users are connected to a server with one network card and one LAN, the LAN may have high levels of utilization.

ADDING LAN CAPACITY

To improve LAN capacity, break up large LANs into smaller LANs, using two or three network cards in the server as shown in Figure 25.10. This technique increases capacity.

Figure 25.10.
Adding more LAN
capacity by using
multiple network
cards in a server.

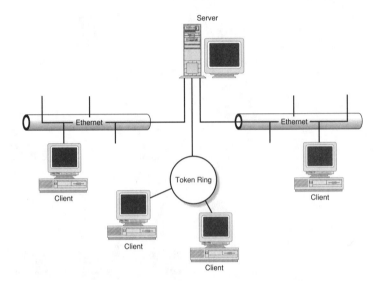

Using two cards doubles LAN capacity by doubling the number of LANs. Using three network adapters potentially triples LAN capacity. Your only limitation is the server's capacity to handle more network cards and traffic.

Most servers today are powerful enough to handle the increased levels of traffic. However, if you use a 16-bit ISA (standard AT) bus, your bus will become congested, resulting in decreased capacity. The bus becomes congested mainly because the CPU is too busy at times (at 100% utilization) processing I/O.

Bus mastering was developed to eliminate bus congestion due to processor-bound I/O and limited bus capacity. You should always use 32-bit bus mastering network cards and disk adapters to eliminate bus congestion and processor-bound I/O cycles. A bus mastering card has its own processor and offloads I/O processing to the card's own processor.

EISA, Microchannel (MCA), and PCI busses have greater capacity and the ability to arbitrate bus mastering much better than ISA busses can. Though 16-bit bus mastering is possible, its effects are limited, and limited bus capacity is still a concern. Industry-standard bus capacities are shown in Table 25.2.

TABLE 25 2. BUS CAPACITIES AND STATISTICS.

Bus	Data Path	Throughput
ISA	16-bit	5 Mbytes/sec
EISA	32	33
MCA	32	40
PCI	32	132

Tip

You will find that PCI network cards provide the best cost-to-performance ratio. PCI bus mastering is simpler and less costly to develop than EISA or MCA. Most of the technical mechanics are built into the computer chipset and not the card, so PCI cards are generally less expensive and easier to build. The quality of the bus mastering implementation is better for the same reason.

Avoid VESA VL-bus network cards like the plague! This technology is great for video, but it has never garnered much support for network adapters or SCSI disk adapters. NDIS 3.x certified drivers are rare, deeply embedded driver defects are quite common, and future support is questionable.

Refer to Figure 25.3 earlier in this chapter for comparison of bus capacities versus LAN and SCSI adapters. An EISA, MCA, or PCI bus can easily handle several network cards and SCSI host adapters. An ISA bus is poorly equipped to handle more than a single network card and one SCSI host adapter, even if cards are configured with alternate DMA channels.

MONITORING LAN BANDWIDTH

You can monitor your LANs with several devices. Almost any intelligent hub, monitor, or protocol analyzer includes this statistic. The way the data is presented and analyzed differs significantly, however. Many intelligent hubs simply poll every second or so and send raw data, which can then be imported into a spreadsheet for graphing. Other devices provide graphical trend charts that are quick, easy, and self-explanatory.

The following examples show how a Windows GUI interface is used to provide graphic tools.

MICROSOFT BACKOFFICE SYSTEM MANAGEMENT SERVER (SMS)

Microsoft BackOffice Suite's System Management Server contains a Network Monitor feature that provides this functionality.

W & G'S DOMINO

Wandel & Goltermann have made sensitive electronic test equipment for many years. The Domino network analyzer is the product of many generations of testing equipment.

Domino has a unique configuration in that the analyzer is a separate small box that relays information to your computer through its parallel port. This allows the Domino to capture all traffic without missing any frames. Missing frames when traffic is at its peak is a concern with most protocol analyzers because inexpensive network cards, computers, and busses are not fast enough to capture high levels of traffic. Domino also has built-in software-configurable RJ-45, BNC, AUI, and DB-9 ports. The RJ-45 port can be configured for either 10Base-T or UTP Token ring LANs. The DB-9 is for STP Token ring. The software used to configure the ports is shown in Figure 25.11.

Figure 25.11.
W & G's Domino port configuration graphical utility.

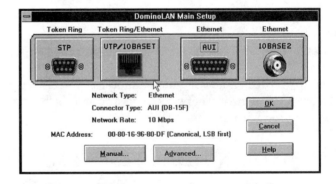

Domino's Windows-based collection of software modules enables the user to learn to use its many robust features easily. It also enables you to switch between various functions quickly with little effort. A Windows interface for a complex product like this is virtually mandatory.

Domino's Network Utilization Graph is shown in Figure 25.12. The trend analysis allows you to analyze bandwidth levels over an extended period of time.

Figure 25.12.
Domino's Network
Utilization Graph.

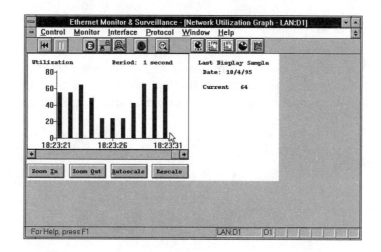

25

LANALYZER FOR WINDOWS

LANalyzer for Windows has a simple Windows-based interface, but it lacks many of the more sophisticated features of other protocol analyzers. It is a software-only product that works with network cards that implement a "promiscuous mode."

LANalyzer's Windows interface is one of the simplest to understand and use from the outset, partly because the interface lacks the many features that other protocol analyzers have. LANalyzer's network utilization trend chart is shown in Figure 25.13.

Figure 25.13.
LANalyzer's network
utilization trend chart.

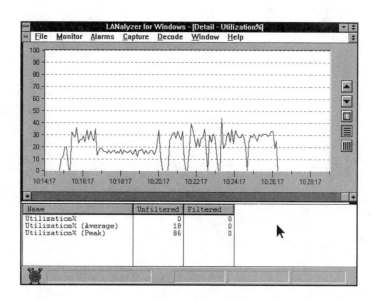

SUMMARY

Many tools are available for LAN analysis and monitoring. The integrator, system analyst, or system administrator can use every tool at his/her disposal to design a network or internetwork that optimizes resources as discussed in this chapter. In many cases, better network design is simply a matter of configuration.

- Virtual LANs: The Automatic Solution

- Switching Hub Benefits and Limitations

- Planning

- Joining Different Bandwidth Nodes

CHAPTER 26

Virtual LAN Capacity Allocation

When a single LAN and a single server can no longer handle the traffic on your network, you should seek an upgrade path. Most servers can handle far more traffic than a single LAN can generate, so the most likely bottleneck you will find is in the LAN. One LAN rarely serves the needs of more than a handful of busy clients.

One solution to this problem is a switching hub, which provides dedicated connections between pairs of nodes at any given moment. This type of device provides a few benefits. Switching hubs can do the following:

◆ Improve bandwidth

◆ Reduce collisions in an Ethernet environment

◆ Reduce latency

◆ Dynamically reconfigure connections

At times, switching hubs are not as automatic as advertisements make them seem. Based on how your network is designed, there are many limitations and considerations in selecting a hub and implementing it. You might spend thousands of dollars on a switching hub and not receive any benefit.

This chapter discusses your options of how to select and implement switching hubs to manage network capacity. The previous chapter discusses LAN capacity allocation in more general terms, while this chapter specifically discusses considerations when using switching hubs as a capacity allocation method.

Virtual LANs: The Automatic Solution

The terms *switch* and *VLANs* are often used in industry articles without defining what these terms mean. Even the most technical people are often a little off-balance when reading articles in magazines because these terms are not standardized and can be used differently by different writers.

A *switch* most often refers to a type of bridge that automatically switches between bridging and repeater functions for each port. Switches are used to bridge between different types of LANs. For example, 100VG-AnyLAN is designed with a hub that can switch between 10-Mbps Ethernet, 100VG, and 16-Mbps Token ring. When bridging between similar and dissimilar LAN types, movement from same-to-same LANs uses a repeater, whereas the switch changes to a bridge to handle traffic between dissimilar LAN nodes. A switch is a device that separates (bridges) the two LANs.

A switching hub normally switches several LAN cabling segments together. The switches can link two cabling segments together into a single LAN or bridge two cabling segments together as two separate LANs. In the latter case, each cabling segment is a separate LAN and does not share bandwidth between two users.

Instead, each user has a full allocation of bandwidth all to itself. The frames from each node are often buffered at the hub and forwarded to the other segment without having to share bandwidth with other nodes.

Two or more virtual LANs are created whenever a switching hub segments traffic between ports. The term *virtual* refers to the fact that most switching hubs automatically reconfigure separate paths on-the-fly instead of requiring physical separation by the LAN administrator (see Figure 26.1, box B).

A switching hub will at least reduce or eliminate collisions in an Ethernet environment. This in itself allows a greater percentage of the theoretical bandwidth to be available for productive traffic. However, that is not the only benefit of a switching hub. In some network configurations, the hub actually allows two or more pairs of nodes to communicate simultaneously. Figure 26.1 shows how a single switching hub divides a single LAN into two separate virtual LANs (network A). Usually, it would take two separate hubs to accomplish the same results (network B).

Figure 26.1.
A switching hub with
two servers (A) allows
twice as much traffic
through one device.

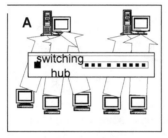
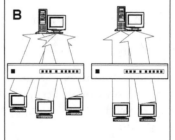

When a switching hub separates traffic in this manner, two "virtual LANs" are automatically configured, as shown in box A of Figure 26.1.

SWITCHING HUB BENEFITS AND LIMITATIONS

If network traffic and layout are appropriate, a switching hub can provide many benefits, including:

- ◆ Reduced collisions
- ◆ Increased usable bandwidth
- ◆ Less administration

In short, a switching hub can, in many cases, automatically optimize network configuration. Additionally, some switching hubs can automatically reconfigure as traffic patterns change, optimizing the network at all times.

A perfect candidate for virtual LAN segmentation is the large, unsegmented LAN where perhaps 100 users all share the same LAN. Many large networks are put together this way when a mainframe or minicomputer connects many terminals, or when workstations run simple word-processing, spreadsheet, and electronic mail applications. Many users can share a single LAN with little overlap of demand.

When users actively use shared databases, use graphics applications, and send large print jobs over the network, available LAN traffic proves overwhelming at times. In this situation, more capacity is needed. Instead of upgrading all users to a larger capacity type of LAN (such as Fast Ethernet), the administrator should use all capacity allocation methods at his/her disposal.

Some network traffic patterns and network layouts are not suitable for the virtual segmentation that a switching hub affords. For example, if all users access a single server, there is less you can do to segment the traffic. The bottleneck is in the path to the server, and the LAN is only one part of the path.

PLANNING

There are a few different designs that competing switching hubs are based upon. Some hubs may assist in reconfiguring your network to perform properly—in other cases, switching hubs may add no value to your network at all.

Proper planning is required to implement a capacity allocation solution that will definitely produce results. Many system analysts simply specify the highest level of product in every category, hoping that the combined effect will provide the required results.

SELECTING THE BEST HUB FOR YOUR NETWORK

The first step in capacity allocation is to analyze the existing network traffic patterns. This topic is discussed in Chapter 25 under the topic of baselining. You must be familiar with traffic patterns, user-to-server pairings, and changing demands.

If the network is an existing network, this analysis is simple, and most system administrators should be able to draw a diagram that summarizes these factors. Part B of this first step is to verify that the overall network traffic corresponds with the administrator's understanding. Most larger networks are so complex that it is very easy to mistake traffic patterns. A protocol analyzer is a perfect tool for monitoring and baselining network traffic patterns.

In a proposed network, it is not so simple. In many cases, the system analyst must interview users and managers and attempt to project what traffic patterns will emerge. Although this is more difficult, it is easier to put a design together that will handle potential traffic demands based on a few alternate scenarios.

SWITCH DESIGN

There are three basic switch designs. One type of switch relies on software and CPU power to switch frames; the other two rely on hardware components to handle frame traffic.

BUS SWITCHING

The first and simplest switch design is the bus switch. In this design, all ports are on a single parallel bus, as shown in Figure 26.2. The bus is a hardware-driven system that relies entirely on the performance of hardware components.

Figure 26.2.
Bus switching design.

Workstation

A *bus switch* works similarly to a basic Ethernet LAN. In this type of switch, each port is a node on a bus. Incoming frames travel down the bus, and take the path to the port where the destination node is connected. The path to be taken depends upon the MAC layer node address in the frame header. Using time division multiplexing, the bus controller allocates a time segment large enough to accommodate one full-sized frame for each frame to make its trip down the bus—only one frame exists on the bus at any given time.

Most switches of this nature are configured by the LAN administrator. Once a connection has been established between two ports, a direct connection exists, and a bridged connection exists between the sending port and all other ports. The virtual connections are static and usually require manual reconfiguration to establish different repeater/bridge port assignments.

Buffers handle the incoming frames, so the switch fabric changes the direct and bridged connections each time a frame comes up for a trip on the bus. The buffers also permit input and output to be mismatched; for example, some ports can run at 10 Mbps and some at 100 Mbps. The basic design also allows more than one node to be connected to each port.

This design has certain advantages and disadvantages. This type of switch is simple and efficient; it can handle a large number of frames without serious latency. It is flexible—it handles broadcasts and multicasts with few complications. It is expand-able—you can attach a multinode segment to one port. It is manageable—only one frame is on the bus at any time, so a monitoring agent can monitor all traffic. Because this type of switch is hardware-driven, its performance does not suffer when higher levels of traffic are present.

Setup and configuration are not automatic, however. Changes to the configuration between repeater/bridged ports typically must be handled by an administrator, and the configuration remains static until manually changed. It is also a more expensive design than the other two basic switch designs because each switch is both a repeater and a bridge.

MATRIX SWITCHING

Matrix switching is also a hardware-based design, but it relies on a more complex set of port connections configured into a mesh, as shown in Figure 26.3.

Figure 26.3.
A matrix switch.

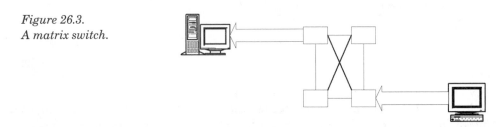

In this design, physical circuits are set up between the matrix of connections between switches. Each port has a switch to each other port. When a frame enters the hub, the MAC layer node address in the header defines the path between the source and the destination. At that time, a connection is created between the source and destination port. Once the transmission is completed, the connection is termi-nated. The fabric of the switch configures the physical connection between the two with a repeater. The mesh design dynamically reconfigures every time a frame enters a port. No bridging is necessary, as connections are dedicated between each source and each destination on an individual case basis.

This is a basic hardware design that is quite expensive. In this type of device, each port must have a dedicated path and switch to every other port. A 4-port hub would have 16 switches (4 ports×4 ports), and an 8-port hub would have 64 switches (8 ports×8 ports), and so on. As you can tell, this type of device can be quite expensive.

A matrix switch can generally provide higher performance than a bus switch. If a connection is unused, no buffering is necessary. If two or more sets of communica-tions take different paths, no buffering is necessary, and both can operate at the same time. However, when two or more nodes need to communicate with the same port, buffering is still necessary.

Matrix switches have different advantages and disadvantages. A powerful advantage is the switch's ability to dynamically change its configuration without administrator intervention. As node-to-node connections change, each switch can reconfigure independently. This design is theoretically faster because buffering is not necessary all the time. Also, when two different paths are used at the same time, bandwidth is theoretically doubled (three paths tripled, four quadrupled, and so on). This factor is fine in a peer-to-peer environment but is not available in a single-server, client-server network.

The downside of this design is that it is not very manageable. Because parallel connections can exist at the same time, no single agent can monitor all the connections. In this design, each port has its own buffers, so input and output rates must be approximately equal, or a large amount of RAM will be required for higher bandwidth port. Another drawback is the lack of provision for broadcasts and multicasts. When a single frame needs to be sent to multiple nodes, this design is poorly equipped to provide the mechanism.

SOFT SWITCHES

Software-based switches are based on router design, and all work basically the same way. Because the design is simple and software-based, developers can build in many features. In this type of switch, frames are buffered, examined, and forwarded on a one-by-one basis to each port, as shown in Figure 26.4. A processor examines and moves the frames from one port to another, reading the MAC destination node address and configuring a single switch to the destination port. Each frame is switched independently and therefore reconfigures paths on-the-fly.

Figure 26.4.
Software-based switch.

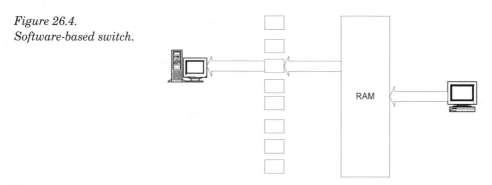

This type of design is theoretically slower than a hardware switch; however, fast RISC processors, high speed busses, and static RAM are often used to make up for the latency factors. This may drive up the price of the hub, but the hub software can be upgraded, which is not possible for hardware switches.

This design has advantages and disadvantages. The advantages are obvious: it is completely flexible in path assignments, manageable, upgradable, and configurable. No wonder this is the design selected by most major vendors. Different bandwidth ports can be set up (that is, 10 versus 100 Mbps), and each port can contain more than one node.

The disadvantages are mainly higher cost due to processor, RAM, and software development labor. Slower speed is also a factor. Not only is latency introduced every time a frame is processed, but only one port connection is active at any given moment, unlike matrix switches where two or more connections can be active at the same time.

JOINING DIFFERENT BANDWIDTH NODES

Now that Fast Ethernet and 100VG-AnyLAN have provided less expensive 100-Mbps networking, the demand for 10- to 100-Mbps switching is high. The natural upgrade path would be to upgrade servers and power users to 100 Mbps and retain 10-Mbps nodes where possible. A switching hub is the solution to this dilemma. A few ports can be at 100 Mbps, while most ports are at 10 Mbps. Buffering can handle different input and output rates.

In practical usage, it has been discovered that servers connected at 100 Mbps cause the buffers to overflow when the client is connected at 10 Mbps. A 10-Mbps workstation can only receive the frames at one-tenth the rate that the server can feed them. When a long dialog between a client and server occurs, the buffers often overflow when the server responds to the client. The buffer overflow blocks other nodes from accessing the hub, causing a major bottleneck. The problem is inherent to all switch designs.

MULTIPLE SERVER NETWORK CARDS TO A SINGLE SWITCH

One basic solution to bandwidth limitations is the practice of putting two or more network adapter cards in a server, all of which are connected to a single switching hub, as shown in Figure 26.5.

In the scenario shown in Figure 26.5, several clients are load-balanced over the two network adapters. Two cards potentially double the throughput to the server. Because server busses and processors can handle far more traffic than one 10-Mbps Ethernet card can generate, this design works well.

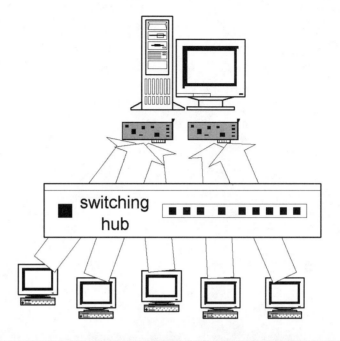

Figure 26.5.
Doubling the band-
width to a server.

Tip

When multiple network cards are used in a server, 32-bit bus mastering network cards and disk adapters should be used to reduce the
CPU load.

SUMMARY

Switching hubs are not the fix-all some advertisements make them out to be.
However, a switching hub can solve traffic jams in a too-busy network. The system
analyst should evaluate the network and the potential effect a switching hub can
have on it. Not all network configurations will benefit, and not all switching hubs
work the same way.

- Backup and Restore

- Rapid Recovery Procedures

- Disk Subsystem Fault Tolerance

- Uninterruptible Power Supplies (UPSs)

CHAPTER 27

Physical Security, Quick Recovery

The physical security of your network is most important. A system administrator needs to strive for 100 percent uptime. In case of the inevitable, the system administrator needs to plan for an expedient and graceful recovery, reducing the amount of lost productivity. That means reducing the amount of time required to get the system operative and reducing lost data from restoring backups. This chapter discusses these topics in a general sense. The advice given here pertains to any network and any NOS.

BACKUP AND RESTORE

There are several backup issues to consider:

◆ Backup devices and software

◆ Backing up open files

◆ Backing up and restoring the Registry

◆ Restoring the NT operating system

These topics are discussed in more detail in this section.

BACKUP DEVICES AND SOFTWARE

A backup device and accompanying software packages are not designed to back up all operating systems. Each individual operating system has some unique properties that may cause flaws in your backup. There are two issues to consider about backup devices.

First, is the device compatible with NT? If you decide to install your backup device on an NT computer, it had better be compatible, or it simply will not work. Second, does the backup software support backing up NT system files, such as the Registry and the Security Account Manager database? There is good news and bad news on this point. If your software does not fully support NT file system security features, the good news is that you may be able to use the NT Backup utility. The bad news is that any file compression or other added features that the native software supported may not be supported with the NT Backup utility.

Check the Hardware Compatibility List for details on supported devices and backup software packages. Check with your vendor and make sure they know that you intend to use the device with NT. Your vendor should provide a money-back guarantee in case operation is not to your satisfaction. You should back up and restore a system to another computer to make sure that restoring the system is effective.

Backup software should be expressly designed for backing up NT Server. MS-DOS is the simplest of operating systems, so if you use simple backup software for backing up a DOS system, you may run into some heartbreaking news when you restore your data after a system failure.

Backing Up Open Files

Your backup software should support the option to back up files that are open. Files may be left open for one of many reasons. Though some files are opened and locked by the operating system, a file that is left open and locked by an application can cause serious problems. If your backup software does not back up open files, you may find that your backups have some serious holes—files that were open and therefore not backed up.

The NT Backup utility supports backup of local files that are exclusively locked by the operating system, such as event logs and Registry files. However, it does not back up files that are open and in use.

The Skip Open Files Wait Time dialog box enables you to specify an internal timer to be started. By default, NT Backup waits 30 seconds for the file to become available. If the file does not become available during the 30-second waiting period, NT Backup skips the file, notes an exception in the backup log file (if the log is enabled) or marks it as skipped, and continues to the next file.

You can modify the following Registry entries to adjust the skipped files options, as follows:

```
HKEY_CURRENT_USER\SOFTWARE\MICROSOFT\NTBACKUP\User Interface
Name:          Skip open files
Type:          REG_SZ
Default:       0
Definition:
0 = do not skip, wait
1 = skip files that are opened unreadable
2 = wait on open files for "Wait time"
Name:          Wait time
Type:          REG_SZ
Data:          30
Definition:
Maximum time (seconds) to wait for open files. Default is 30 seconds.
Maximum value is 65535
```

Files NT Backup Skips by Default

NT Backup skips the following files by default:

- Files you do not have permission to read. Only those with backup rights can copy files they do not own in NT Backup.
- Files that are temporary in nature—such as PAGEFILE.SYS, WIN386.SWP, 386SPART.PAR, BACKUP.LOG, and RESTORE.LOG.

These are neither backed up nor restored by NT Backup. The list of skipped files is hard-coded into NT Backup and cannot be changed.

◆ Registry files on remote computers. NT backs up only local registry files.

BACKUP AND RESTORING THE REGISTRY

Backing up and restoring Registry information is an exercise every administrator should go through at least once. Some day you may have to restore under adverse conditions when a piece of hardware fails and you have to put the system back together again.

How this restoration is done depends on what hardware is available and what file system is in use. You can, of course, only restore what you have backed up.

Warning

Make frequent and consistent backup sets of all important files, including system files. Many administrators forget to make backups of system information, thinking that nothing of significance has changed. NT is a dynamic system, and changes are occurring behind the scenes.

A regular backup routine should include using the Configuration Save command in Disk Administrator to maintain an up-to-date Emergency Repair disk for restoring the NT system.

BACKING UP REGISTRY HIVES

The Registry is a data set that is very important to the stability of your NT operating system. There are four predefined keys and hundreds of subkeys in your Registry files. Hives are backup files that contain backup information for all the subkeys and values within a subtree in a Registry key. The Registry is discussed in much greater detail in Chapter 14, "Managing the Network Registry."

You can back up Registry keys, subkeys, and hives in four different ways:

◆ Use a tape drive and the NT Backup program, and select the Backup Local Registry option in the Backup Information dialog box to automatically include a copy of the local Registry files in the backup set. This is the preferred method for creating backups if you have a tape drive.

◆ If you do not have a tape drive, run the REGBACK.EXE or REPAIR.EXE program, or use another tool that uses the same techniques to back up Registry files.

◆ Start the computer using a different operating system. Then copy all files in the <winroot>\SYSTEM32\CONFIG directory to a safe backup location. For example, use another instance of NT if the Registry is stored on an NTFS partition, or use DOS if the Registry is stored on a FAT partition.

◆ Use the Save Key command in Registry Editor, which essentially performs the RegBack procedure manually.

To do this, you should save hives for each essential subtree. For each direct subkey of HKEY_LOCAL_MACHINE and HKEY_USERS, you must choose the Save Key command from the Registry menu, specifying filenames that match the key names. For example, save the SYSTEM key to \BACKDIR\SYSTEM. On the FAT file system, the filename should not have an extension.

Do not use Save Key with the Hardware hive, which is volatile. You will not get any data, because Save Key cannot save volatile keys to disk.

RESTORING REGISTRY HIVES

If you have a good set of backup files, which you update regularly, you can restore Registry hives that are damaged or missing.

You cannot, however, use Registry Editor to fully restore hives, because active parts of the Registry require use of the ReplaceKey operation for restoration, which Registry Editor cannot perform.

To restore a damaged system, you must first restore the basic operating system installation. You might do this by using the Emergency Repair disk to restore your system to what it looked like just after installation, or simply run NT Setup again. Such a restoration results in a system that starts the computer but lacks changes made since you first set it up. Most of those changes are recovered by copying files from backups by using the NT Backup program for tape backups or by copying from disk backups.

However, you cannot merely copy the backups of Registry hive files, because those files are protected while NT is running. So, after the system and all of the additional files such as device drivers are restored, you must restore the Registry. You might do this in one of the following ways, depending on which backup mechanism you used:

◆ For tape backups, you can use the NT Restore program to restore the Registry. Then restart the computer.

◆ Start the computer using an alternate instance of the operating system or using DOS if the system files are on a FAT partition. Copy the files back to the <winroot>\SYSTEM32\CONFIG directory. Then restart the computer using the regular operating system.

◆ Use the REPAIR.EXE program from the Resource Guide disk (if you purchased the NT Resource Kit).

◆ Use the REGREST.EXE program from the Resource Guide disk. The RegRest program performs a ReplaceKey operation, which swaps backup files for the default files that the Emergency Repair or NT Setup programs installed and saves the default files under other filenames. Restart the computer after running the RegRest program to see the restored Registry.

RESTORING NT SYSTEM VOLUME

If you lose your NT system volume, you can restore NT system and preserve your data if you have a backup copy of the NT system volume.

Note

You must override the default settings of the NT Backup program (NTBACKUP) for the Registry settings to be backed up.

TO RESTORE NT SYSTEM

1. From NT Backup, restore the following directory and all the Registry files:

   `<winroot>\system32\config`

2. Reboot your computer.

3. Restore the entire backup set except for the Registry files.

4. Reboot your computer again.

The volume should be back to its original state.

Note

If you use Arcada backup software tape by Arcada, you can use NTBACKUP.EXE using this backup tape. Choose <winroot>\ SYSTEM32\CONFIG and all Registry files. Your program groups and accounts should be restored. The Arcada backup doesn't allow you to explicitly specify the Registry files for backup or restore.

TO RESTORE NT SYSTEM ON A DIFFERENT DISK

If the primary physical disk and adapter was changed because of failure or because of an upgrade, the restore procedure is slightly different. Also, you have to maintain user accounts and desktop settings after you have reinstalled NT.

This situation may occur when you need larger disk capacity or a more versatile disk controller. One example of such a situation is when NT is installed on an IDE drive and you want to upgrade to a large SCSI drive without losing user accounts or desktop settings.

To change the primary physical disk and controller while maintaining user account and desktop settings, perform the following steps:

1. Create a startup DOS disk and copy FDISK.EXE, FORMAT.COM, and SYS.COM to it.
2. Configure both drives.
3. Place a primary FAT partition on the new drive and format it.
4. Use XCOPY to copy NT files and directories from the old drive to the new drive.
5. Create a directory called CONFIG off the root directory of the new drive and copy %WINNT_ROOT%\SYSTEM32\CONFIG*.* to it.
6. Remove the %WINNT_ROOT%\SYSTEM32 subdirectory and all of its subdirectories on the new drive.
7. Shut down the computer and physically remove or disconnect the old disk.
8. Restart the computer, run CMOS, and remove the old disk reference.
9. Insert the startup disk and use the SYS command to restore the system on the new disk (A:\SYS C:).
10. Remove the startup disk and verify the new disk starts.
11. Reinstall NT over the old installation.
12. After you reinstall NT, start DOS, and change to the CONFIG directory you created in step 5.
13. Delete *.EVT and SYSTEM.* files.
14. Copy the remaining files to the <winroot>\SYSTEM32\CONFIG directory.

When you restart NT, user accounts and desktop settings should be maintained.

RAPID RECOVERY PROCEDURES

There are times when a complete reinstallation will save time and headaches. Reinstalling NT is not the terrible nightmare that the original installation might have been. However, you should be prepared to install NT taking to heart all the lessons you learned when you first installed NT. That means that you should have all drivers and configuration parameters at your fingertips. Any special procedures that were required should also be noted and available for reference.

An upgrade is a different situation. You should be more prepared for a reinstallation under emergency circumstances than you would for an upgrade. A reinstallation and an upgrade require the same level of preparedness.

REINSTALLING NT

Reinstalling NT over an existing system may become necessary if you have suffered heavy file corruption or a similar problem. Here the reinstall may be required if you want to move all of your data disks from one server to another. The same procedure applies if you want to install NT to another directory or disk on a computer that already has NT installed so that you can save the share names that exist on the original NT installation, including any permissions assigned to those shares.

To save only the existing share names and their permissions on NT, follow these steps:

1. On the existing NT installation containing the share names and permissions that you want to save, run the Registry Editor (REGEDT32.EXE).

2. From the HKEY_LOCAL_MACHINE subtree, go to the following key:

   SYSTEM\CurrentControlSet\Services\LanmanServer\Shares

3. Choose Save Key from the Registry menu.

4. Type a new filename (a file extension is not necessary) and save the file to a floppy disk.

5. Reinstall NT.

6. Run Registry Editor.

7. From the HKEY_LOCAL_MACHINE subtree, go to the following key:

   SYSTEM\CurrentControlSet\Services\LanmanServer\Shares

8. From the Registry menu, choose Restore.

9. Type the path and filename of the file that you saved in step 4.

Warning

This step overrides whatever shares already exist on the NT computer with the share names and permissions that exist in the file you are restoring. You are warned about this before restoring the key.

Note

If, after completing the nine-step procedure, you decide that you should not have restored the Shares key, restart the computer and press the spacebar to use the Last Known Good Configuration.

After restoring the Shares key, the shares can be used by network clients. Although running NET SHARES on the server displays the shares, File Manager does not. To make File Manager aware of the newly restored shares, create a new share on the server. File Manager will then display all of the other shares after you reboot the server or stop and restart the Server service.

If you choose Stop Sharing in File Manager, the restored shares will still show up, but they are grayed out.

Only permissions for domain users are restored. If a local user was created in the previous NT installation, that local user's unique security identifier (SID) is lost.

NTFS permissions on directories and files are not affected when you save and restore the Shares key.

Emergency Repair Process

As part of the repair process, Setup will perform each of the optional tasks shown in the following list with an "X" in its checkbox.

[X] Inspect registry files.
[X] Inspect startup environment.
[X] Verify NT system files.
[X] Inspect boot sector.

Explanation of Repair Options

- Inspect Configuration Registry Files: Choosing this option takes you to a second screen. This option attempts to load each file in the Registry that is selected from that screen to determine whether or not it may have become corrupt. If Setup determines that part of the Registry has become corrupted, it recommends that the file be restored. You can accept or ignore the recommendation.

- Inspect Startup environment: This option checks the boot files such as NTLDR, NTDETECT.COM, and so on.

- Verify NT System Files: This selection uses a checksum to verify that each file in the installation is good and matches the files that were originally installed. If files are missing or corrupt, they can be restored from the installation disks or CD.

- Inspect Boot Sector: This option repairs the boot sector on disk C and reinstalls the Boot Loader functionality.

EMERGENCY REPAIR ON RISC COMPUTERS

On an x86-based system, the repair utility is run by booting from a startup disk that was created during the installation of NT. On a RISC-based computer, no startup disk is created—the RISC-based computers do not boot from a floppy disk.

Use the following procedure to use the emergency repair disk on a RISC-based computer:

1. Insert the NT CD into the CD-ROM drive.
2. Start your computer.
3. From the list of choices on the firmware menu, select Run A Program.
4. When you are prompted for the program to run, type `D:\MIPS\SETUPLDR.EXE` and then press Enter (assuming D: is your CD-ROM drive).
5. When the setup screen appears, type `R` to run the repair utility.
6. Insert the repair disk into drive A: as prompted and continue to follow the instructions on the screen.

Warning

You must not convert the boot partition to NTFS on a RISC-based computer. This is because the firmware on RISC-based computers loads the first system files in the NT boot process, and the firmware understands only the FAT file system. Create a small boot partition (1 MB or larger) to hold the HAL.DLL and OSLOADER.EXE files. The rest of the disk can be used as an NTFS partition.

ADJUSTING THE BOOT.INI FILE AFTER REINSTALL

You may need to edit the BOOT.INI parameters after reinstalling. There are different considerations depending upon whether your system is an Intel or RISC and whether a FAT or NTFS file system is used.

ADDING OR REMOVING PARTITIONS ON A RISC COMPUTER

When you use Disk Administrator to create new partitions on a disk drive that has the NT system files on it, under certain circumstances, the Advanced RISC Computing (ARC) path to the NT files changes. When this happens, a dialog box appears when you exit Disk Administrator, warning that the BOOT.INI needs to be changed to reflect the new path. You need to edit the BOOT.INI file before choosing the OK button in the dialog box because the next option restarts the system. This situation occurs only with a system that has a drive configuration C:, D:, FREE SPACE where NT is located on drive D:, and it is a logical drive in an extended partition. Also, it is assumed that the free space is not part of the extended partition. In this situation, any new partition created in this space (which would have to be created as a primary partition, because an extended partition already exists) causes the ARC path to the extended partition to change, because the ARC specifications count primary drives before those in extended partitions. When the warning dialog box appears, do not choose the OK button in the dialog box. Use Task Switch (by pressing either Alt+Tab or Ctrl+Esc) to switch to a text editor. Edit the BOOT.INI file to reflect the new path to the NT files. This involves editing a line similar to the following:

```
scsi(0)disk(0)rdisk(0)partition(1)\winnt
```

Change partition(x) to partition(x+1) to correctly modify the ARC path to the NT files.

If you have already restarted the computer without editing the BOOT.INI file, the startup will fail due to the system being unable to find the NT system files. To correct this problem, use one of the following two procedures. If your C: drive is FAT, perform the following step:

1. Restart the computer into DOS from either the multiboot screen, or with a startup disk.
2. At the prompt, type: **ATTRIB -R -S -H BOOT.INI**
3. At the prompt, type: **EDIT BOOT.INI**
4. Change partition(x) to partition(x+1).
5. Save the file and quit out of the editor.
6. Restart the computer.

If your C: drive is not FAT, use the following procedure:

1. Go to another computer running NT and format a floppy disk. It will now have the NT boot sector on it.
2. Copy the following files onto the disk: NTLDR, NTDETECT.COM, and BOOT.INI.
3. Edit the BOOT.INI file (on the floppy disk) and change the ARC path so that it is correct for the computer that is unable to start NT.
4. Use the startup disk to restart the computer that was unable to start NT.
5. Follow steps 2 through 6 of the first procedure to edit the BOOT.INI file on the hard disk drive.

ADDING OR REMOVING ADAPTERS

NT may not boot after you remove an adapter even if it is not the primary adapter. This is because NT stores references to adapters statically. When you remove an adapter, the adapter number may change at the hardware level. For example, if you had two SCSI hard disk adapters, numbered 0 and 1, removing the first makes the second become number 0. When NT tries to access the information on the second adapter, it looks for adapter number 1, which no longer exists.

If this problem occurs, you need to modify an entry in the BOOT.INI file to accurately reflect the adapter number. For example, the following entry may be in the BOOT.INI file:

```
scsi(1)disk(0)rdisk(0)partition(1)\winnt ="NT 3.5"/SCSIORDINAL:0
```

In this example, you would need to change the value in SCSI(1) to SCSI(0).

Note

On non-x86-based computers, you need to modify system boot parameters.

In general, you should disable an adapter and test to see if NT boots before physically removing it. In this manner, if NT fails to boot, you can power down and restart NT to revert to the last known good control set.

REMOVING NT FROM THE BOOT PARTITION

The procedures described in this section enable you to remove the NT boot sector from your system.

REMOVING NT FROM THE BOOT SEQUENCE

There are two ways to remove the NT boot sector from your computer:

◆ If you want to return to your original DOS configuration, boot DOS and type **sys c:**. This command replaces the NT boot sector with the DOS boot sector and enables your computer to boot straight into DOS. The following files are left in the root directory and can be deleted after you perform the SYS operation: PAGEFILE.SYS, BOOT.INI, NTLDR, NTDETECT.COM, and NTBOOTDD.SYS.

◆ If you want to leave NTLDR on the disk, you can boot DOS without prompting by changing the startup operating system and time-out value. To do so, choose the System icon in the Control Panel, select DOS in the Startup box, and type **0** in the Show List For box.

Note

If the primary partition was converted to NTFS, the only way to return to starting DOS is to reformat the drive and reinstall DOS.

Removing a Primary NTFS Partition

If you have attempted to modify the primary, bootable, NTFS partitions and have not succeeded, it may have been for the following reasons:

♦ DOS versions 5.0 and 6.0 do not recognize an NTFS partition. The DOS FDISK program reports an NTFS partition as a high-performance file system (HPFS) partition.

♦ You cannot modify or delete an NTFS primary partition within itself.

To delete or modify a primary NTFS partition, perform any one of the following four procedures:

♦ Boot DOS version 6.0 from a floppy disk and press Enter to continue installing DOS 6. When prompted to do so, choose Remove files.

♦ Initiate NT installation from floppy disks or CD. When prompted to do so, choose P to remove the partition.

♦ Boot OS/2 version 1.x from a floppy disk and run its FDISK program. To remove the partition, specify the /D option.

Virus Prevention, Detection, and Removal

When you start your computer with a floppy disk that is infected with a virus, NT is not capable of detecting it, which is true with many operating systems. Some viruses, such as the FORMS virus, may infect the boot sector of your hard disk drive. This section discusses some methods of protecting the boot sector of the hard disk drive from viruses.

There is a misconception that if the partition of the hard disk drive is NTFS, the information in the partition is secure. NTFS, FAT, and NS HPFS file systems are *not* recognized until NT starts the service for the file system. The boot sector is separate from the file system in that boot instructions are recognized by the system BIOS upon starting the computer.

In order to provide C2-level government security, the environment surrounding the system must meet the same level of security that NT provides. The C2 standard requires physical security, such as locking the computer.

In order to protect your system from any type of virus infection in NT and possibly recover the boot sector of the hard drive, you can do the following:

◆ Remove any floppy disk in drive A: after shutting down NT.

◆ Configure the system BIOS to disable floppy disk booting (no floppy seek) or change the order of the boot process to hard drive first.

◆ Configure the system BIOS to enable system password protection.

◆ To possibly fix the boot sector, boot with an MS-DOS system disk and run the following command: FDISK /MBR.

◆ Run the Repair utility to verify and recover NT boot files.

FDISK/MBR works only on hard disk drives that are within the limitations of DOS. If you are accessing devices that are beyond the 1024-cylinder limit, you will not be able to perform the FDISK/MBR command, and error code 1762 will appear.

If a virus has infected the MBR, you will not be able to run the Emergency Repair Disk until the virus is cleaned. Most virus programs have the same limitation as DOS, so you will not be able to run a scan against the hard disk drive; however, DOS 6.22 MSAV.EXE will clean the Master boot record and RAM of the computer.

RECOVERING FROM SECURITY ACCESS MANAGER (SAM) CORRUPTION

Just about the worst disaster that can confront an administrator is corruption of the SAM database. Chapter 14, "Managing the Network Registry," deals with the details of backing up and restoring SAM, but in that chapter, it is assumed that you do not have media corruption.

WHAT TO DO WHEN THE VOLUME CONTAINING SAM IS DAMAGED

If you experience a hard disk or data corruption problem and lose your NT system volume, you can restore NT Server and preserve your data if you made backup copies of the NT Server system volume.

Note

You must override the default settings of the NT Backup program (NTBACKUP) for the Registry settings to be backed up.

To restore NT, use the following procedure:

1. From NT Backup, restore the following directory and all the Registry files: <winroot>\SYSTEM32\CONFIG.

2. Reboot your computer.

3. Restore the entire backup set except for the Registry files.

4. Reboot your computer again.

The volume should be back to its original state.

Note

If you use Arcada tape backup software, you can use NTBACKUP.EXE with your tapes. Choose <winroot>\SYSTEM32\CONFIG and all Registry files. Your program groups and accounts should be restored. The Arcada backup does not allow you to explicitly specify the Registry files for backup or restore.

IF YOU CANNOT ACCESS THE NETWORK

There are three situations in which you will receive an Access Denied message across untrusted domains when accessing a resource that has permissions for Everyone.

1. When a user from an untrusted domain attempts to access the server and he has the same user name for both domains but different passwords in each, he is prompted for a password. If the password is not correct for the domain in which the server resides the user usually receives an Access Denied message (depending on the operation). You can work around this problem by entering the correct <domain>/<username> in the Connect As dialog box in File Manager and then providing the correct password. A simple way to avoid this problem is to make sure that the passwords match in both domains, or to set up a two-way trust relationship between the two domains.

2. The Guest Account on the domain is disabled. This is the default for NT Server. If a user from an untrusted domain is trying to access the server remotely, he receives an Access Denied message because there is no valid user name that he can use to make the connection. To deal with this, enable the Guest account on the NT Server.

3. If your account or all of the groups you belong to do not have the right to "access this computer from network," you will receive this error message. To deal with this, use User Manager to add the "access this computer from network" right to your account.

AUTOMATICALLY DISCONNECTING USERS

If you want to restrict the number of users on an NT Server because of licensing or loading restrictions, you can do so by automatically disconnecting inactive users. This technique can also be used to disconnect users so that the backup program does not encounter files left open by careless users who forget to log out at the end of the day.

Essentially, the limit is the number of simultaneous user sessions the server allows. However, this limit does not affect the number of simultaneous null sessions that are used by many services and some of the administrative tools. In addition, the limit does not apply to anything that does not use the server and runs directly over the transport, such as Windows Sockets.

Any session that does not have any activity on it will be automatically disconnected after the AutoDisconnect time has expired; the default for this is 15 minutes. Once the session is disconnected, that session will be made available so that another user can connect to the NT Server. Therefore, lowering the AutoDisconnect time can help to reduce the number of users on the system.

You can configure the AutoDisconnect time by running the following command from a command prompt and specifying the *<time_before_autodisconnect>* in minutes:

```
NET CONFIG SERVER /AUTODISCONNECT:<time_before_autodisconnect>
```

DISK SPACE ALERT

By default, Event Viewer may report Event ID 2013 if a partition has 10 percent or less disk space available. Event ID 2013 says the following: The disk is at or near capacity. You may need to delete some files.

You can change the DiskSpaceThreshold value to alter the percentage of free disk space available before an alert is logged. The registry parameter is defined as follows:

```
Value: DiskSpaceThreshold    REG_DWORD
Range: 0 to 99 percent
Default: 10 percent
```

Description: Specifies the percentage of free disk space remaining before an alert is sent.

To modify the DiskSpaceThreshold value, perform the following steps.

1. Start REGEDT32.EXE.

2. Select the following path:
   HKEY_LOCAL_MACHINE\SYSTEM\CurrentControlSet\Services\
   LanmanServer\Parameters

3. From the Edit menu, choose Add Value.

4. Enter `DiskSpaceThreshold` in the Value Name field.

5. Change the Data Type to REG_DWORD.

6. Enter the desired percentage value in the Data field.

7. Shut down and restart NT.

FAULT TOLERANCE

FtDisk, the NT fault-tolerant driver, provides the mechanisms for redundant data storage, volume management, and dynamic data recovery. Dynamic data recovery is only available on SCSI drives. FtDisk works between the physical disk drivers and the file system drivers, and works with all the supported file systems (FAT, HPFS, and NTFS). NT file system (NTFS) is the only file system with built-in data recovery mechanisms.

When you have FtDisk installed on a SCSI NTFS drive with spare sectors, the following fault-tolerant features are available. The following features are for a fault-tolerant volume:

◆ FtDisk can recover data.

◆ FtDisk uses sector sparing.

◆ File system is unaware of the error.

The following features are for a non-fault-tolerant volume:

◆ FtDisk cannot recover data.

◆ FtDisk sends bad sector error message to file system.

◆ NTFS performs cluster remapping and data is lost.

Fault-tolerant volumes include mirror sets (RAID 1) and stripe sets with parity (RAID 5).

27

Note

If FtDisk finds a bad sector on a fault-tolerant volume, and the physical disk supports spare sectors and has spare sectors available, FtDisk replaces the sector. This is true for all three supported file systems (FAT, HPFS, and NTFS); the file system remains unaware of this mechanism.

NTFS INTERNAL TABLES

NTFS includes several system files, all of which are hidden from view on the NTFS volume. A system file is one used by the file system to store its metadata and to implement the file system. System files are placed on the volume by the Format utility.

The NTFS system files are listed in Table 27.1.

TABLE 27.1. NTFS SYSTEM FILES.

System file	Filename	Description
Master File Table	$Mft	A list of all contents of the NTFS volume
Master File Table2	$MftMirr	A mirror of the important parts of the MFT, used to guarantee access to the MFT in the case of a single-sector failure
Log File	$LogFile	A list of transaction steps, used by the Log File System for recoverability
Volume	$Volume	The name, version, and other information about the volume
Attribute Definitions	$AttrDef	A table of attribute names, numbers, and descriptions
Root Filename Index	$.	Root directory
Cluster Bitmap	$Bitmap	A representation of the volume showing which allocation units are in use
Boot File	$Boot	Includes the bootstrap for the volume, if this is a bootable volume
Bad Cluster File	$BadClus	A location where all the bad clusters in the volume are located

DISK SUBSYSTEM FAULT TOLERANCE

NTFS is a recoverable file system. It combines the speed of a lazy-write file system with virtually instant recovery.

NTFS guarantees the consistency of the volume by using standard transaction logging and recovery techniques. It includes a lazy writing technique plus a system of volume recovery that takes typically only a second or two after the computer is rebooted. The transaction logging, which allows NTFS to recover quickly, requires a very small amount of overhead compared with careful-write file systems.

When used on a partition on a single device, NTFS can recover from a system crash, yet it may lose data as the result of an I/O error. In conjunction with the mirroring or parity striping support implemented by the fault-tolerance driver, NTFS can survive any single point of failure. The NTFS partition still remains accessible, though potentially not bootable. That is, even if the boot sector is lost and the bootstrap cannot transfer control to the NTFS copy of the boot sector, you can still boot the computer from another partition or another physical drive, and you can still access the NTFS partition.

Sector Sparing (Hot Fix)

NTFS also supports hot-fixing, so that if an error occurs because of a bad sector, the file system moves the information to a different sector and marks the original sector as bad. This is transparent to any applications performing disk I/O. Hot-fixing eliminates error messages such as the "Abort, Retry, or Fail?" error message that occurs when a file system such as FAT encounters a bad sector.

However, when NTFS is used on a fault-tolerant device and an error is detected on one copy of a cluster, data can be recovered. The bad cluster is migrated to the Bad Cluster File, and it is replaced by another cluster. Then a copy of the original data is written to the new cluster.

Note

NTFS supports cluster sizes of 512, 1024, 2048, and 4096. Although the FORMAT command automatically selects an appropriate cluster size based on its examination of your disk, you can use the /a option to specify a particular cluster size. Type FORMAT /? at the command line for more syntax information.

Remirroring a Fault-Tolerant File System

If the partition containing the NT Advanced Server system files is mirrored and then lost, you can use a fault-tolerant boot floppy disk to restart NT Server and access the mirror of the lost drive.

A fault-tolerant boot floppy contains the files necessary to boot NT from a mirrored partition. You can create a fault-tolerant floppy at installation time or by running RDISK from the File, Run menu.

Once NT is successfully booted from the fault-tolerant boot floppy, the files and directories on the mirror drive are available for normal disk operations. Even if the disk containing the primary partition is lost, no differences are apparent to you (unless you study the status information displayed in Disk Administrator). Fault tolerance no longer exists, however. If the remaining partition is lost, all its data is lost also. So it is safer to break the current mirror set, configure a new boot and system partition, and create a new mirror.

ALTERNATE METHOD OF CREATING A FAULT-TOLERANT FLOPPY

If the primary partition of a mirror set is lost, you cannot start NT Server, and no other NT system is available from which to create a fault-tolerant boot floppy, follow these steps:

1. Boot to DOS, either at another system or with a floppy on the current system.

2. Copy the NT Advanced Server Setup Disk 1 for floppy disk installation to a blank floppy disk with the DISKCOPY utility (or another utility that will copy a mirror image of the original disk, including the boot sector).

3. Delete all files on the copied disk except NTDETECT.COM and NTLDR.

4. Expand NTLDR as SETUPLDR using the command EXPAND NTLDR SETUPLDR.

5. If the mirrored drive is a SCSI disk requiring a SCSI driver to work with NT, copy and expand the appropriate SCSI driver from the NT Server Setup Disk 1, then rename it to NTBOOTDD.SYS.

6. Using a text editor such as EDIT.COM, create a BOOT.INI file with an ARC path that points to the NT directory on the mirror partition. The disk is now ready for use as a fault-tolerant boot floppy.

When NT is installed on an NT file system (NTFS) formatted boot drive, recovering from a boot failure can be difficult because you cannot access the NTFS partition unless NT is running.

Here are a few boot-failure scenarios, and how to recover from them, or at least gain access to the partition. These are general guidelines on methods of gaining access to an NTFS boot partition.

CREATING AN NTFS BOOT FLOPPY

This section shows how to create a boot disk to access a drive with a faulty boot sequence and an NTFS file system. This can be useful when an incorrect hardware driver replaced a working one and there is no Emergency Repair Disk to repair the boot files.

To create a boot disk for an NTFS partition:

1. Make a disk copy of the first Setup Disk.

2. Delete all files on the new disk.

3. Copy NTDETECT.COM and NTLDR to the new disk.

4. Rename NTLDR to SETUPLDR.BIN.

5. Create a BOOT.INI file with the following lines (this example is for a single partition SCSI drive with NT installed under \WINNT):

```
[boot loader]
timeout=30
Default= scsi(0)disk(0)rdisk(0)partition(1)\winnt
[operating systems]
scsi(0)disk(0)rdisk(0)partition(1)\winnt="Windows NT"
```

The following files are usually set with their attributes as System, Hidden, Read-Only: BOOT.INI, NTLDR, and NTDETECT.COM.

If you run out of space on the disk, remove driver files that you will not need.

Boot from the floppy disk and log on to NT.

You might get these messages if problems persist:

♦ The following message appears when the path to the system files is incorrect or includes the drive letter: Windows NT could not start because of the following ARC firmware boot configuration problem: Did not properly generate ARC name for HAL and system paths.

♦ The following message appears when the incorrect SCSI driver has been selected for the system or the NTBOOTDD.SYS does not exist: Windows NT could not start because of a computer disk hardware configuration problem. Could not read from selected boot disk. Check boot path and disk hardware.

Non-Setup-Related Boot Failures

If you have been running NT successfully, and it fails to boot, you can use the following simple procedure to try to recover from the problem:

1. Verify that the problem has not been caused by changes or failures in the hardware. Loose cables, bad cables, new cards, new drives, and even new settings on existing controllers can all cause boot problems.

2. If NT failed to boot after you installed a new device driver, try pressing the spacebar at the OSLOADER screen and selecting the Last Known Good option. If the boot process failed before you logged on to the system, this should correct the problem.

3. Try creating an NTFS boot disk as described in the previous section.

4. Boot from the NT Setup disk (or run SETUPLDR on a RISC-based computer) and run the emergency repair process. An emergency repair disk may not be required but can help if the repair directory on the hard drive is damaged. This will solve most boot problems that involve bad system files or a corrupted registry.

SETUP-RELATED BOOT FAILURES

If you were installing NT and NT failed to boot, and Setup was interrupted, the recovery steps listed previously will generally not work (unless you aborted Setup at a very early stage). Assuming that the failure was not some easily correctable problem (bad installation media, incompatible or malfunctioning hardware), there are two methods you can use to gain access to your drive and data:

1. If you have enough free disk space, try installing NT again into a different directory. This sometimes works when an upgrade failed and in any situation where you have to get access to the data but have been unable to get your current installation of NT to boot. This also enables you to fix boot problems that involve bad drivers or other configuration problems that the methods described in the preceding section did not help with. In many cases, you can simply boot the alternate NT installation and delete the bad driver in question.

2. If all other attempts to gain access to an NTFS partition have failed, including installing NT to a new directory, try removing the hard disk drive and installing it in a computer that is running NT. The computer you move the drive to must be running a version of NT that is equal to or greater than the one that failed. This allows for changes in the file system drivers. Alternatively, you can install a new boot drive in the computer that is failing to boot NT, and then install NT on that drive. In either case, when you are moving SCSI drives from one computer to another, make sure that both computers use SCSI controllers made by the same manufacturer and that both are configured the same way. Different controllers can use different translation schemes and different settings.

In any situation, it may be best to simply reinstall and restore from a recent backup. Most of the these instructions are for situations where you do not have a recent backup and must either get your current copy of NT working or gain access to important data. None of these methods should be a considered a replacement for frequent backups or other methods of ensuring data recoverability (such as stripe sets, mirror drives, and so on).

UNINTERRUPTIBLE POWER SUPPLIES (UPSs)

A UPS is a power supply that uses a storage battery to keep the server running during a power failure. Most UPSs also provide power conditioning: they filter spikes, surges, sags, and noise. The length of time the server can run on the UPS depends on the specifications for that particular UPS and the load it must support.

Many UPS devices offer the ability to interface to the server. During a power failure, the UPS sends a signal that causes the UPS service to initiate a graceful shutdown of the server so that all active sessions and files are closed properly before the battery becomes exhausted. The UPS service, when used in combination with the Alerter and Messenger services, can also be configured to notify the administrator when a power failure has occurred.

The UPS service should be used in conjunction with the Alerter, Messenger, and Event Log services. This is to ensure that events related to the UPS service, such as a power failure or a UPS connection failure, are recorded in the system log of the Event Viewer and that designated users are notified of these events over the network.

The Server option in the Control Panel is used to designate which users and/or computers should receive UPS alerts and warning messages.

UPS SERVICE PARAMETERS

The following options in the UPS Control Panel application are used to configure the UPS service:

- ◆ Activate UPS service and select serial port COM1: through COM4:
- ◆ UPS Configuration

To support contact-closure type UPS devices, the UPS service always does the following:

- ◆ TXD (Transmit Data) is set permanently low.
- ◆ RTS (Request to Send) is set permanently high.
- ◆ Execute command file

Use this option to specify a file that should be executed prior to system shutdown. The command file can contain commands for closing connections, for example.

This command must be executed within 30 seconds to guarantee safe shutdown of the server. The file must be located in \WINNT\SYSTEM32 with one of the following extensions: .BAT, .CMD, .EXE, or .COM.

◆ Expected Battery Life is used to specify the time in minutes that the system can run on battery power.

◆ Battery Recharge Time is used to specify the time in minutes that the battery must be recharged.

These options apply only if the UPS cannot provide a low battery signal.

◆ Time Between Power is used to specify the time in seconds between Failure and Initial Warning Message—when a power failure occurs and when the first message is sent to users.

◆ Delay Between Warning Messages is used to specify the interval, in seconds, between the messages that are sent to notify users of a power failure.

CABLE PIN ASSIGNMENTS

Making a cable for your UPS is easy if you have the pin assignments. The following information applies to APC Back-UPS models 250, 400, 450, 600, 900, and 1250. Make sure the following pins are connected: DB9 9-Pin Male Connector to PC serial port UPS connector.

Pin #5	Ground	Pin #4
Pin #8	Power Failure	Pin #2
Pin #4	UPS Shutdown	Pin #1
Pin #1	Low Battery	Pin #5—[10k ohm]—Pin #8

Note: unlisted pins need not be connected.

SUMMARY

Time is of the essence when a system fails. Each hour of downtime more than likely costs your company thousands of dollars in lost productivity. This chapter discusses some very important topics that a system administrator must be aware of in case of a system failure. A recovery plan should be in effect, and fire drills should be conducted periodically to ensure that the procedures you have developed work flawlessly.

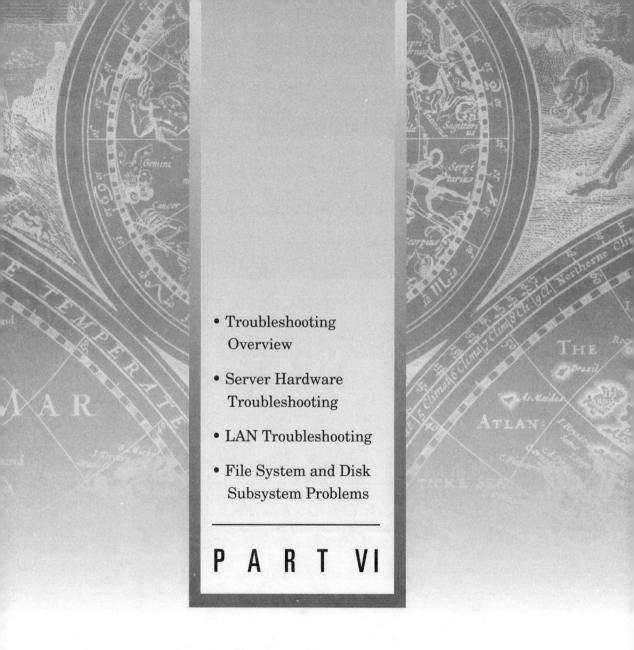

- Troubleshooting
  Overview

- Server Hardware
  Troubleshooting

- LAN Troubleshooting

- File System and Disk
  Subsystem Problems

PART VI

Troubleshooting

- NT Server Hangs During Boot

- Logon Script Problems

- Dropped Connections

- JetDirect Printer Debugging

- BrowseMaster Conflicts

- Adjusting NWLink Packet Size

- Dr. Watson

- Removing COM Ports

- Removing Printers

CHAPTER 28

Troubleshooting Overview

NT Server has an endearing quality of being simple to install and get running, and it hides its sophisticated side from a novice installer. On the other hand, it is trying to be everything to everyone, so it may not be tuned for the hardware configuration and task you are using it for.

The catch is that as soon as you tinker with the default configuration, things start getting out of hand. So here are some simple rules to live by, or you will forever be reinstalling.

◆ Keep a backup of the boot on a disk, in addition to the Emergency Repair Disk.

◆ Keep a backup of the entire WINNT directory, preferably on a FAT drive.

◆ Run Performance Monitor and save a log of typical system behavior.

◆ Every time you make changes, freshen up your Emergency Repair Disk and both of your backups.

◆ Change only one thing at a time and keep good notes of the combination of things you have tried.

◆ If you are working on a new network, recruit one of the workstations to be a backup NT Server. You may have to upgrade the RAM to 16 M to install NT Server, but after the installation, you can reduce it back to 8 M. NT Server runs fine with 8 M. This could be your reference computer; it can be used as the repository of your backups.

◆ Reinstalling NT Server is not destructive. If you are careful, you can reinstall NT Server many times without hurting your data. Of course, throughout the book, we recommend having a separate system drive for NT Server; this can make it less frightening to attempt a reinstall.

This chapter is going to be haphazard because there is no organized way of discussing troubleshooting. The topics discussed are common problems encountered on NT networks.

NT SERVER HANGS DURING BOOT

After you install NT Server version 3.5, your system may stop responding (hang) when you select the Shutdown and Restart option. This behavior does not occur if you select Shutdown. However, when you select Restart in the Shutdown Computer dialog box, the same problem occurs.

This problem occurs when the NT Server version 3.5 Setup program calls the computer BIOS to obtain computer configuration information. On several computers, the BIOS returns invalid information for the number of processors installed on the computer. For example, a multiprocessor Hardware Abstraction Layer (HAL) is installed instead of required uniprocessor HAL.

A possible workaround for this problem is to reinstall NT Server version 3.5 and run Custom Setup. Configure the Computer type for Standard PC instead of the one selected by default. This forces the Setup program to install the uniprocessor HAL. Reinstalling NT Server version 3.5 to the same location of the previously installed one will update the HAL without losing any user accounts and important Registry information.

Note

If you choose to upgrade to NT Server version 3.5 instead of performing a complete installation of NT Server version 3.5, you will not be offered the option of changing the HAL.

LOGON SCRIPT PROBLEMS

Here is a checklist of potential problems with local logon scripts. A logon script is similar to a batch file because it performs a series of commands when a user logs in to his or her account. If problems arise with a logon script, use the following list to troubleshoot the problem:

◆ Make sure the logon script is in the directory \WINNT\SYSTEM32\ REPL\IMPORT\SCRIPTS. The only valid path option is a subdirectory of the default logon script directory. A path to any other directory or using the environment variable %HOMEPATH% will cause the logon script to fail.

◆ If the file system on the partition containing the logon script directory is NTFS, make sure the user has read rights to the logon script directory. If no rights have been explicitly assigned, the logon script may fail without providing an error message.

◆ Make sure that the logon script has a filename extension of either .CMD or .BAT. A script with any other extension will fail. The .EXE extension is also supported, but only for genuine executable programs. Attempting to use the .EXE extension for a script file will result in the following error message: NTVDM CPU has encountered an illegal instruction. To remove the error, terminate the application or the virtual DOS machine (VDM).

◆ If the logon script is to be set up for a WFW computer, the WFW computer must have the NT Server domain specified in the LAN Manager domain portion of Control Panel networks, rather than just assigned to that workgroup.

◆ It will take a period of time for a recently created logon script to be replicated from the Primary Domain Controller to all the member servers. Thus, if a workstation is validated by a server other than the PDC, recently created logon script changes may not be in effect.

28

TROUBLESHOOTING OVERVIEW

Many problems are caused by lack of access to resources on the network. They do not manifest themselves as such and can seem to be something else. Also, NT Domain architecture is more complicated than WFW architecture and the single-server design of NetWare 3.*x*. An example here illustrates some of the subtle ways that these access problems can manifest themselves.

Suppose RickS logs on to an NT domain with the password Smart. He wants to view the shared resources on a server named \\BNET, but his password there is Dumbo. Because of this situation, Rick sees the following message displayed on the screen: `Error 5: Access has been denied.`

RickS asks the administrator of \\BNET to change his password, but the administrator leaves the User Must Change Password At Next Logon checkbox checked. When RickS tries to view the server's shared resources this time, he sees the following message displayed on the screen: `Error 2242: The password of this user has expired.`

When the administrator of \\BNET clears the User Must Change Password At Next Logon checkbox, RickS is finally able to see the server's shared resources.

Suppose RickS is logged on to an NT domain with the password Smart but wants to connect to a shared directory on \\BNET where his password is Dumbo. Even though \\BNET has a Guest account because there is an account for RickS, he is not allowed to gain access through the Guest account. Instead, NT prompts RickS for the valid password on \\BNET.

On the other hand, NadeemC wants to access the same shared directory and has no account on \\BNET. He is allowed access to this resource through the Guest account for \\BNET and is assigned the permissions associated with that account.

This illustrates the way NT authentication works. See Chapter 11, "Setting Up the User Environment," for details.

DROPPED CONNECTIONS

Intermittent problems are very difficult to deal with. Perhaps a connection works but drops off after a while. Sometimes you can connect, but other times you cannot. The preponderance of clients on NT Server networks are WFW clients. The following discussion addresses time-related problems.

A session between a WFW client and an NT Server over IPX with NetBIOS protocol may be dropped. Several problems may occur with WFW clients when this happens, including experiencing a general protection (GP) fault, or receiving an SMB error 1,6 indicating an Invalid File Handle during file I/O after the session has been idle for three or four minutes.

This problem usually occurs when WFW clients are running applications on the NT Server and have several files open on the server. Net Sessions on the NT Server displays the active sessions on the server; if the session remains idle for a few minutes, the session is dropped and when you attempt any operation related to the open files, you may experience a GP fault. The network sessions get dropped because the WFW client does not respond to the keep-alive packets from the server if they are sent at 30-second intervals, which is the default of NWNBLINK.

To fix this problem, change the KeepAliveTimeout value in the NT Server Registry from 60 (this value represents half-seconds) to 30. The Registry entry for KeepAliveTimeout is in the following location: LocalMachine\System\ CurrentControlSet\Services\NWNBLINK\Parameters.

When you change the KeepAliveTimeout value to 30, the keep-alive packets are sent every 15 seconds. This helps maintain the session and eliminates GP faults.

In NT Server, when a TCP/IP connection idles for a certain period, TCP/IP will generate keep-alive traffic. When TCP/IP determines that no activity has occurred on the connection within the specified time (default 120 seconds), it generates keep-alive traffic to probe the connection. After trying the configured number of times to deliver the keep-alive traffic without success, it marks the connection as down, and the client connection is dropped as a result.

To fix this problem, you can add the Registry entry, or modify it if you already have one, in the following path: HKEY_LOCAL_MACHINE\SYSTEM\ CurrentControlSet\Services\Tcpip\ParametersTcpKeepCnt. Set it to the number (in seconds) you prefer. To keep the connection alive forever, you should set the value to 0. For example, TcpKeepCnt:REG_DWORD:0.

The disconnection problem may not occur with your particular application if the application can automatically reconnect after the connection is dropped. This problem does not occur in SQL Server for NT Server version 4.21 because the Setup program has been enhanced to automatically set the TCP/IP parameters in the Registry. If you have installed SQL Server 4.21, you do not need to manually modify the Registry.

JETDIRECT PRINTER DEBUGGING

NT Server may lose connections with Hewlett-Packard (HP) JetDirect printers. This can result in a continuous Online or Status Unknown for the printer in Print Manager. The print queue then stops responding (hangs) and does not restart until the server is restarted.

28

To correct this problem, do the following:

◆ Make sure that the latest version of HPMON.DLL is loaded. Run Print Manager. Select any print queue using an HP JetDirect. From the Printer menu, choose Properties, and then choose Settings. Choose the About button to display the version information. It should be version A.00.14. This is the version shipping with NT Server version 3.5.

◆ Increase the DLC Timers settings located in Print Manager to be similar to the version information in the preceding paragraph. To adjust the DLC Timers, select a printer using a JetDirect, and then choose Properties from the Printer menu. Choose the Settings button, and then choose Options (do this from the server because HPMON.DLL cannot run remotely). The range for each of the three settings of the DLC Timers is 1 to 10. Try doubling each setting first, and then adjust them more if you need to. This affects HPMON as a whole for the server, so you only need to make this adjustment on one printer.

Note

The new settings will not take effect until you restart the server.

◆ HPMON by default uses windowing to communicate with the JetDirect card. This means that HPMON will send, for example, five packets to the JetDirect and expect only one acknowledgment for all five. Sometimes if the printer is slow to accept incoming data, the buffers on the JetDirect will become full, and the JetDirect cannot accept all of the packets at once. The JetDirect will not send the acknowledgment, and HPMON must attempt to synchronize between the two. Under stress, this causes problems because traffic increases between HPMON and the JetDirect with retransmissions. The connection may fail during this time. In cases like this, it is best to turn the windowing off. If you do so, HPMON will send one packet and wait for an acknowledgment before sending the second packet. This provides for much better error handling. Although this change does affect the network speed to the printer, the speed is only moderately affected and is still much faster than printers can render the print. Such cases of flow control can actually be faster than with the retransmissions of failed windows of data.

To disable windowing, you can modify the Registry. However, if you extract the new HPMON available on MSDL and the Internet with the -D parameter, and then run the automated Install program for HPMON, you do not have to modify the Registry.

1. Start REGEDT32.EXE and locate the following Registry subkey: HKEY_LOCAL_MACHINE\SYSTEM\CurrentControlSet\Control\ Print\Monitors\Hewlett-Packard Network Port\Options.

2. From the Edit menu, choose Add Value. Enter `MaximumXmitsWindow` in the Value Name field. Select REG_DWORD for the Data Type. Enter 1 in the Data field and choose OK.

3. From the Edit menu, choose Add Value. Enter `MinimumXmitsWindow` in the Value Name field. Select REG_DWORD for the Data Type. Enter 1 in the Data field, and choose OK.

4. Exit REGEDT32.

BROWSEMASTER CONFLICTS

BrowseMaster contentions can occur between WFW workstations and NT Server when a workgroup or domain contains at least one computer of each type. You may have difficulty seeing servers in an NT Server network from a WFW workstation if the workstation is a backup BrowseMaster and not registered in the NT Server network. To work around this problem, do one of the following:

◆ Make sure there is a guest account enabled in the NT Server domain.

◆ Add the following line to the [network] section of the SYSTEM.INI files in all WFW computers on the network: MaintainServerList=no.

This workaround stops all WFW workstations from trying to be BrowseMasters. If you use this workaround, you need to ensure that at least one NT Server computer (workstation or server) in the workgroup or domain is running at all times. Until an NT Server computer is running or a user changes the value of the MaintainServerList variable to "auto" and reboots, no browsing can occur (you receive error 6118).

You can also log on to the domain or workgroup with a valid account (even a guest account works). Guest accounts should remain enabled on domain controllers. Instead of removing guest accounts to restrict access to certain services, simply remove any of the undesired or all of the guest account rights in User Manager.

There should not be user name duplicates on different domains. If a user name is duplicated across different domains, there will be inconsistent results when a logon is attempted from a WFW workstation on that NT Server network.

ADJUSTING NWLINK PACKET SIZE

This situation can happen on mixed networks. When you cross Novell routers (file servers or multiprotocol routers) using NWLink, you may receive some erratic behavior unless a Registry entry is made for maximum packet size.

The symptoms for this problem vary. In some cases, the response to a drive connection in File Manager takes minutes to complete. In other cases, File Manager stops responding (hangs). Sometimes, error messages are returned indicating a

28

TROUBLESHOOTING OVERVIEW

network problem. Even if a connection takes place, erroneous results may be returned. This problem has been reported in both Token ring and Ethernet environments.

For example, share the WINNT\SYSTEM32 directory, which contains greater than 500 on one NT Server computer. When you attempt to connect to this share (as Administrator) from a different NT Server, you will receive a "No Files Found" error message. In this example, the only computers on this internetwork are the two NT Servers and a NetWare 3.11 file server acting as a router. The following NLMs are loaded on the NetWare server: ISADISK, TOKEN, NMAGENT, and MONITOR.

Making the same connection when both NT Server computers are connected to the same Token ring produces the correct result. Directories containing only a few files may not exhibit these behaviors.

Ethernet problems can occur in complex WAN environments. Lowering the packet size can resolve the issue without any other changes being required. The symptom in this case is the inability to remotely administer one NT Server from another one separated by a wide area link.

The workaround to this problem is to add an entry to the Registries of the NT Server computers as follows:

1. At a command prompt, type `REGEDT32`.
2. Single-click on HKEY_LOCAL_MACHINE window.
3. Double-click the following in the order listed: SYSTEM, CurrentControlSet, Services.
4. Scroll to NWLINKIPX.
5. Double-click the following in the order listed: NWLINKIPX, NetConfig, Driver01.
6. Check to see if there is a MaxPktSize entry in the box on the right.
7. If MaxPktSize does not exist, select choose Add Value from the Edit menu. In the Value Name field, type `MaxPktSize`. Change the Data Type field to REG_DWORD. Choose OK.
8. Change the Radix field to Decimal. For Token ring, enter 1500 in the Data field. For Ethernet, enter 1000 in the Data field (higher values may be possible). Choose OK.
9. Quit the Registry Editor, quit all open applications, and shut down and restart the computer.

DR. WATSON

NT includes Dr. Watson, DRWTSN32.EXE, which serves the function of NT Post Mortem Debugger. This utility is similar to the Windows 3.1 Dr. Watson program.

Dr. Watson automatically catches any Win32 application errors and logs them. The following data is saved in the log:

1. Exception information, such as exception number and name.
2. System information, such as computer name, user name, OS version, and so on.
3. Task list.
4. A state dump for each thread, including a register dump, disassembly, stack walk, and symbol table.

By default, the Dr. Watson log file, DRWTSN32.LOG, is located in the \<winntroot>\SYSTEM32 directory.

NT application log (which can be viewed through Event Viewer) also contains a record of the application error.

ENABLING AND DISABLING DR. WATSON

Dr. Watson is enabled when NT is installed. To disable Dr. Watson, the following Registry value must be changed from a 1 to a 0 (zero):

```
\HKEY_LOCAL_MACHINE\SOFTWARE\Microsoft\Windows NT\CurrentVersion\AeDebug:Auto
```

To re-enable Dr. Watson, change the Auto value from 0 (zero) to 1. Doing so launches whatever debugger, or application, is under ...\AeDebug:Debugger. For Dr. Watson, the ...\AeDebug:Debugger value should contain:

```
drwtsn32 -p %ld -e %ld -g
```

Note

> When Dr. Watson is enabled, it does not appear as an icon on the desktop, or in the Task List. It only shows up when a Win32 application causes an application error.

CONFIGURING DR. WATSON

Start DRWTSN32.EXE from the command line or a Program Manager icon. Figure 28.1 shows the configuration options for Dr. Watson.

28

TROUBLESHOOTING OVERVIEW

Figure 28.1.
Dr. Watson.

All of the Dr. Watson configuration information is stored in the Registry under:

`\HKEY_LOCAL_MACHINE\SOFTWARE\Microsoft\DrWatson`

Dr. Watson prints reports, such as the System Information report shown in Listing 28.1.

LISTING 28.1. SAMPLE OUTPUT.

```
*----> System Information <----*
        Computer Name: BNET
        User Name: Administrator
        Number of Processors: 1
        Processor Type: Intel 386
        Windows Version: 3.50
        Current Build: 782
        Current Type: Uniprocessor Free
        Registered Organization: BusinessNet
        Registered Owner: Nadeem Chagtai
*----> Task List <----*
*----> Module List <----*
(019e0000 - 01a0f000) exe\perfmon.DBG
(77f70000 - 77fb6000) dll\ntdll.DBG
(71000000 - 71012000) dll\shell32.DBG
(77f00000 - 77f63000) dll\kernel32.DBG
(60a00000 - 60a38000) dll\user32.DBG
(64000000 - 64033000) dll\gdi32.DBG
(62600000 - 6261f000) drv\winspool.DBG
(67b00000 - 67b37000) dll\rpcrt4.DBG
(77df0000 - 77e23000) dll\advapi32.DBG
(77d70000 - 77d9c000) dll\crtdll.DBG
```

```
(77dc0000 - 77de7000) dll\comdlg32.DBG
(77d50000 - 77d63000) dll\comctl32.DBG
(77e30000 - 77e38000) dll\rpcltc1.DBG
(77c20000 - 77c30000) dll\mpr.DBG
(77b50000 - 77b65000) dll\mprui.DBG
(77d10000 - 77d25000) dll\netui0.DBG
(77bc0000 - 77c0f000) dll\netui2.DBG
(77cd0000 - 77d0f000) dll\netui1.DBG
(61800000 - 61843000) dll\netapi32.DBG
(77cc0000 - 77cca000) dll\NetRap.DBG
(77c10000 - 77c20000) dll\samlib.DBG
(77c90000 - 77cb2000) dll\netmsg.DBG
(77c30000 - 77c3c000) dll\ntlanman.DBG
(77710000 - 77718000) dll\ftpctrs.DBG
(776f0000 - 776fa000) dll\ftpsvapi.DBG
(76e10000 - 76e21000) dll\perfctrs.DBG
(765e0000 - 765fd000) dll\wsock32.DBG
(00400000 - 0040f000) D:\SQL\DLL\SQLCTRS.dll
(00380000 - 003bb000) D:\WINNT35\system32\ntwdblib.dll
(003e0000 - 003eb000) D:\WINNT35\system32\DBNMPNTW.dll
State Dump for Thread Id 0x73
eax=0016a16c ebx=0016a5d8 ecx=0012ffe0 edx=00140538 esi=00000000 edi=0016a16c
eip=77f8e061 esp=0012f01c ebp=0012f170 iopl=0         nv up ei pl nz na pe nc
cs=001b  ss=0023  ds=0023  es=0023  fs=003b  gs=0000          efl=00000202
function: <nosymbols>
77f8e04d 6685f6            test    si,si
77f8e050 75ed              jnz     77f8e03f
77f8e052 5f                pop     edi
77f8e053 5e                pop     esi
77f8e054 c3                ret
77f8e055 8b442404          mov     eax,[esp+0x4] ss:0083dc57=????????
77f8e059 56                push    esi
77f8e05a 8b74240c          mov     esi,[esp+0xc] ss:0083dc57=????????
77f8e05e 57                push    edi
77f8e05f 8bf8              mov     edi,eax
FAULT ->77f8e061 668b0e            mov     cx,[esi] ds:00000000=????
77f8e064 8bd7              mov     edx,edi
77f8e066 66890a            mov     [edx],cx ds:00140538=70c0
77f8e069 83c702            add     edi,0x2
77f8e06c 83c602            add     esi,0x2
77f8e06f 6685c9            test    cx,cx
77f8e072 75ed              jnz     77f8e061
77f8e074 5f                pop     edi
77f8e075 5e                pop     esi
77f8e076 c3                ret
77f8e077 668b442408        mov     ax,[esp+0x8] ss:0083dc58=????
77f8e07c 8b542404          mov     edx,[esp+0x4] ss:0083dc57=????????
```

As you can see, the information provided by Dr. Watson is not suitable for consumption by mere mortals. In reality, this information is seldom used except to send back to the offending vendor's technical support department. It can also be of use to software developers or computer nerds.

REMOVING COM PORTS

Some problems administrators experience with NT Server are related to undoing some of the automatically configured parameters. Many times you are having a conflict, and you know it is a COM port. You do not use the port, but you cannot remove the definition of the port in the NT Server Registry. NT Server and NT Workstation can support up to 256 COM ports on each computer. Use the Ports application in the NT Server Control Panel to add ports.

If you attempt to delete a COM port from Control Panel's Ports utility you may be successful, or you may receive a dialog box indicating that you must be logged on as Administrator for the computer to execute the command (even though you are logged on as Administrator). To remove a COM port that cannot be removed from Control Panel's Ports utility, you must use the Registry Editor utility. Perform the following five steps to remove a COM port from an NT Server or NT Workstation:

1. Start the Registry Editor (REGEDT32.EXE).
2. Find the following key:
   \HKEY_LOCAL_MACHINE\System\CurrentControlSet\Services\ Serial\Parameters.
3. The Parameters key has several subkeys such as Serial10000, Serial10001, and so on. Each of these subkeys corresponds to a COM port. To determine the COM port to which each applies, check the corresponding DosDevices value.
4. After you determine the COM port to remove, choose the appropriate Serial<*xxxxx*> subkey, and choose Delete from the Edit menu.
5. Close the Registry Editor, and then shut down and restart your system.

REMOVING PRINTERS

Print Manager enables you to create a new printer destination, but it does not allow you to remove an old one. To remove an old one, you must remove an entry from the Registry. Printer destinations can be any of the following types: Local Port, Hewlett-Packard Network Port, or AppleTalk Printing Devices.

REMOVING A HEWLETT-PACKARD NETWORK PRINTER DESTINATION

In Registry Editor, delete the Hewlett-Packard network printer from the following key: HKEY_LOCAL_MACHINE\System\CurrentControlSet\Control\Print\ Monitors\Hewlett-Packard Network Port\Portnames.

Removing an AppleTalk Printer Destination

In Registry Editor, delete the AppleTalk printer from the following key: HKEY_LOCAL_MACHINE\System\CurrentControlSet\Control\Print\Monitors\ AppleTalk Printing Devices\Ports.

Removing Control Panel Components

One of the clever tricks administrators use to restrict other users from changing things is to remove some of the critical icons in Control Panel. Granted, you can restrict users or even members of the admin group by selectively granting permissions, but sometimes you have to go even further. You can prevent individual Control Panel components from loading under NT Server by modifying the Registry.

In NT Server, a cache mechanism is implemented to speed the loading of Control Panel components. When you run Control Panel for the first time, a cache is created that includes information regarding each component in the Control Panel. Therefore, Registry entries specifying certain components not to load are not read in NT Server version 3.5.

To do this, add the /CACHE switch to the Control Panel Command Line in the Program Manager Program Item Properties dialog box after you modify the Registry, for example: CONTROL.EXE /cache.

You can use the following procedure to prevent Control Panel components from loading.

1. Run Registry Editor (REGEDT32.EXE).
2. From the HKEY_CURRENT_USER subtree, go to the following key:
   \Control Panel
3. From the Edit menu, choose Add Key.
4. Type **Don't Load** in the Key Name text box and choose OK.
5. Select Don't Load.
6. From the Edit menu, choose Add Value.
7. Type the following in the appropriate text boxes:

```
Value Name:  <Control Panel component>
Data Type:   REG_SZ
String:      0 or 1 (Either string value will prevent the Control component
from loading)
```

The default Control Panel component names are:

```
Color        International      Desktop
Fonts        System            Keyboard
Ports        Date/Time         Printers
```

```
Mouse        Network          Devices
Drivers      Sound            Cursors
Server       Services         UPS
Display (NT Server version 3.5 only)
MIDI Mapper (NT Server version 3.1 only)
```

8. Quit Registry Editor and restart Control Panel.

Note

If you need to modify the Registry again to prevent additional Control Panel components from loading, do not repeat steps 3 and 4.

DISABLING PRINTER MESSAGES

Some applications can be stopped from processing if they are interrupted by a pop-up printer message. For example, Great Plains Dynamics accounting requires that it not be interrupted during a posting operation. Under NT Server, it is possible to disable the Printing Notification network dialog boxes sent by the Spooler on a Print Server when a print job has been completed, an error has occurred, or a job has been deleted. This setting applies globally to all the printers on a particular print server. It is not possible to set this option on a per-printer basis.

To disable Printing Notification network dialog boxes, use Registry Editor as follows:

1. Start Registry Editor.
2. From the HKEY_LOCAL_MACHINE subtree, go to the following subkey: \SYSTEM\CurrentControlSet\Control\Print\Providers.
3. From the Edit menu, choose Add Value.
4. In the Value Name field of the Add Value dialog box, type the following: `NetPopup`.
5. Select REG_DWORD for the Data Type.
6. Choose OK.
7. In the Dword Editor dialog box, type **0** (zero) in the Data field.
8. Choose OK.
9. Exit Registry Editor.
10. Stop and restart the Spooler service from the Services portion of Control Panel so the new setting will take effect.

Note

> If the print notification is turned off for direct-connected printers (parallel and serial), error conditions will result in an error dialog box appearing on the server. While this error is displayed, printing will not resume to the printer even if the cause of the error is cleared from the printer. You will need to log on to the server and choose Retry or Cancel in the error dialog box. This problem does not affect network-connected printers.

ENABLING/DISABLING SHUTDOWN BUTTON

The shutdown button on NT Workstation is available in the Welcome screen after pressing Ctrl+Alt+Del to log on. However, in NT Server version 3.5, the Shutdown button is not available by default. The ability to display the Shutdown button is configurable for both Workstation and Server versions of the operating system through the Registry. Follow these steps to configure this option for NT Workstation and NT Server:

1. Start REGEDT32.
2. Open HKEY_LOCAL_MACHINE\SOFTWARE\Microsoft\WindowsNT \CurrentVersion\Winlogon.
3. Double-click the ShutdownWithoutLogon parameter.
4. Change the value of the string to 1 to make the Shutdown button available.

CHANGING THE DOMAIN FOR A COMPUTER

One of the most perplexing problems an administrator can encounter is to be caught in a name conflict or not be able to access the PDC because the workstation in question has been moved and has to be added back into another domain. If you have an NT workstation in an NT Server domain and you want to change the computer's computer name, the computer must leave the domain and rejoin the domain in order for the change to take effect.

1. Have the NT Server domain administrator create an account for the new computer name.
2. In the Network Settings dialog box, choose the Change button next to the computer name.

3. In the Computer Name dialog box, type a unique name (the new name) for the computer, and choose OK. This procedure results in your NT workstation being unable to log on in the NT Server domain with any user account. (It makes no difference if the NT Server domain administrator creates the computer name before or after the computer name change.) If you find that you are unable to log on in an NT Server domain after a name change, you should log on to your local database as an admin user. Next, leave the NT Server domain either by joining another NT Server domain or by selecting any workgroup. After you reboot the system, your computer can rejoin the original domain with the new computer name; you will be correctly prompted with the "WELCOME TO THE *<original domain>* DOMAIN" message.

Note

You cannot add the new computer name for the NT Workstation in the domain by re-entering the current domain name and providing an admin account for the domain. The computer must leave and rejoin the domain.

4. Create a new computer account for the NT workstation in the new domain.

5. Choose the Network icon in Control Panel, choose the Change button next to the current domain name, and enter any workgroup name or the name of another NT Server domain.

Note

If you choose another NT Server domain, you will need an administrator of that domain to create a computer account for you in Server Manager, or you will need to provide an admin account and password so that you can add the computer account to the NT Server domain.

6. Choose the Network icon in Control Panel and change the computer name of the NT workstation to the new name.

Note

Once a computer name is changed, the Change button for the domain named is dimmed, which indicates that you cannot change the computer name and the domain name at the same time unless you change the domain name first, as indicated by the order of steps 1-6.

7. When prompted, reboot the system in order for the domain name and computer name changes to take effect.

8. Log on to the local computer with Admin privileges.

9. Choose the Network icon in Control Panel, choose the Change button next to the domain name, and enter the original domain name. In the first step, you created a new computer account, and as a result, you will not need to provide a valid administrator and password for the original domain. You will receive the "WELCOME TO THE *<original domain>* DOMAIN" message.

10. When prompted, reboot the system so that the domain name change can take effect. You should now be able to log on to the NT Server domain with any valid account.

SUMMARY

This chapter should give you an idea how to go about troubleshooting some typical problems encountered in administering NT Server networks. It is by no means a complete treatment. All through this book are many practical examples of problems and the keys to solving them.

28

TROUBLESHOOTING OVERVIEW

- How to Identify a
  Server Hardware
  Problem

- Isolating the Offend-
  ing Component

CHAPTER 29

Server Hardware
Troubleshooting

In a client-server network, your server is the heart of the network. Even slight hardware problems can cause serious complications, including file corruption, damage to the Registry, or simply downtime from total or partial equipment failure. The problem itself is not as much a concern as the complications and the related costs of downtime.

Of course, you should have the best server hardware your budget can afford. A reliable computer manufacturer offering dependable technical support and quick availability of replacement parts is important. NT compatibility is very crucial, and knowledgeable technical support is often required to resolve problems built into the system board components of your server.

Tip

> One of the most common problems that disables an NT server is RAM failure. Purchasing a server with ECC memory will reduce or eliminate parity errors that crash your server.

Refer to Chapter 3, "Building the Server," for tips on how to put together a dependable server.

HOW TO IDENTIFY A SERVER HARDWARE PROBLEM

A server hardware problem is often difficult to distinguish from an operating system crash. NT may crash if the Registry is corrupted, file corruption occurs, a hardware fault is present, or any number of other reasons. For example, if a driver file becomes corrupted, the device may not load properly, and may even prevent your server from coming up at all.

NT is pretty stable when it comes to preventing server downtime due to driver or device problems. If a device does not work, NT's preemptive processing kernel will simply fail to load the device driver, and bring up the operating system, hardware permitting. If the device failure prevents one of the computer's major components from working, of course NT cannot recover for you.

Driver software functions between the hardware abstraction layer and the device itself. Defective or corrupted drivers can therefore have a more serious effect on the server than just about any other software loaded on your system. Always check drivers carefully before assuming a hardware failure.

Hardware problems identify themselves through various methods. The Event Viewer monitors hardware events and can be checked if the server operating system can come up. However, if the operating system cannot be initialized, the Event View cannot be used.

Hardware Incompatibilities and Configuration Problems

Because of NT's hardware abstraction design, NT relies on your system BIOS and chipset to control hardware functionality. If some minor incompatibility problems or bugs exist in the BIOS or chipset, NT may run trouble-free for a while, only to crash on later occasions. This kind of problem is quite perplexing.

Tip

> To protect yourself from many hours of lost productivity, make sure your base computer is a good brand and is listed on Microsoft's hardware compatibility listing. It is very helpful to purchase a server that is factory preconfigured and guaranteed to be 100 percent NT-compatible.
>
> You may even have a server that ran fine under NetWare or DOS but has continual problems running under NT. This is because NetWare and DOS are designed strictly for the Intel x86 platforms. DOS is not so sensitive to hardware incompatibilities in the "real mode," and NetWare bypasses the system BIOS to take nonpreemptive control of the system hardware. NT's orderly protection and hardware abstraction sometimes become a trade-off for hardware compatibility.

The NT Compatibility list is provided and updated frequently to include computers, system boards, main subsystems, and other components that are known to be fully compatible with NT. You can obtain the NT Compatibility list from Microsoft's CompuServe NT forum, the Microsoft FTP server on the Internet, or other Microsoft sources.

NT is very sensitive to the following conditions:

◆ Incompatible BIOS, chipsets, and glue logic

◆ RAM chips that do not match one another (that is, different brands or mixing different speed chips)

◆ RAM chips without parity (cannot send message concerning parity error)

◆ Processor external cache problems (static RAM chips that do not work properly or are configured improperly)

◆ PCI devices with assigned interrupts

Tip

> Always assign interrupts manually—see your advanced BIOS Setup configuration screens.

These are some of the most difficult problems to find. Most often, these problems occur intermittently depending on which modules are in use at any given time.

Look for STOP messages during the boot procedure with error text that indicates the source of the problem. STOP messages are discussed in greater detail in a later part of this chapter.

SERVER HARDWARE FAILURE SIGNS

Main system board failures are relatively uncommon. More frequently, your computer will fail due to disk drive, RAM, power supply, or the interface card failure. Each of these problems can cause your computer to halt and prevent your computer from booting.

Tip

> When you experience a hardware failure, check all interface boards and memory modules for proper seating. Wiggle the boards, SIMMs, or chips in their slots/sockets, or pull and reseat them.
>
> Oxidation may cause interface cards to lose contact. You should clean all board contacts and reseat them, making sure that the board is pushed down into its slot into proper position.

Different brands of computers display different symptoms when a failure occurs.

POWER ON SELF TEST (POST)

Each system board is designed with diagnostic sound signals that indicate the nature of the problem. This is part of the Power On Self Test (POST) procedure each computer goes through during a cold boot. If the POST finds errors when polling for known hardware devices, the computer will beep, providing information about which subsystem has failed. For example, a repeating series of three beeps during boot on many system boards indicates a RAM problem. Each computer's codes differ. Read your system manual or contact the system developer's technical support department to determine what the beep sequence means.

SETUP ERRORS

Other Setup errors can occur if a hardware device or RAM fails the POST. Observe the Setup error, and run Setup to see if the error is from a configuration error. If the Setup error persists even though all hardware devices are properly set up, check to see if the hardware device is operative.

If system RAM fails, the amount of RAM seen by Setup is truncated at the memory address of the failed RAM chip. Setup will truncate the usable memory when you run Setup, but all your memory will not be available. In this case, run RAM tests as indicated later in this section, and replace the defective RAM chip, bank of RAM chips, or SIMM.

Tip

If your computer displays a Setup error during boot, check your system board battery. When the battery fails, Setup loses the system configuration information needed to bring the system up and access devices.

INTERMITTENT FAILURES

Quite often, hardware devices fail intermittently, sometimes working for extended periods, sometimes not working at all. Generally, a problem that is intermittent is seated in electronic devices.

A device that fails intermittently will not get better. If you can identify a failing device, you should replace it. You may find that the intermittent nature of the problem causes more problems such as file damage or corruption. If you cannot count on the system to work reliably, it is of little use.

A server that has an intermittent problem should be observed under stress testing (described in the following section) or under extended heavy production circumstances. Failure is more likely to occur at these times, and stress tests will help you identify the failure.

DISK INTERFACE CARD PROBLEMS

Should your disk interface card or cable fail, your primary disk drive will not boot. You will receive one of many different screen messages that indicates that your disk drive will not boot, no bootable device is found, or that a hard disk drive failure was detected.

To verify that this is your problem, boot from a bootable DOS disk placed in drive A:.

> *Note*
>
> If you are unable to boot from drive A:, check your computer Setup program to see if booting from drive A: has been disabled.

First, check your drive cables for damage and see that the ends are properly seated. If you have a SCSI adapter, it should have a diagnostic program that can test the SCSI subsystem including storage devices attached to it.

TESTING A SERVER'S DURABILITY

Any time you feel uncomfortable about a server's durability, you should schedule a time soon when you can stress test it. A stress test consists of running the computer under unusually high loads that can cause flaws to appear.

You can run a multiuser network testing utility, such as the ServerBench from Ziff-Davis (publishers of *PC Magazine* and *PC Week*). You can request a complimentary copy of this testing product from Ziff-Davis:

Fax to: (919) 380-2879

Mail to: Ziff-Davis Benchmark Operation
               One Copley Parkway, Suite 510
               Morrisville, NC 27560

In addition, you can run a looping batch file on the server itself. In short, put as much load on the server as possible for an extended period of time.

Heat also causes flaws in chips to surface. If possible, put the server in an enclosed space and warm up the space up to 90 degrees (Fahrenheit) or higher. As the chips warm up with heavy usage, the additional warmth of the room may cause intermittent problems to surface.

If any problems are going to appear, they should appear under these circumstances. If the server survives a 12-hour heat test that stresses the server to its limits, you can feel more comfortable about keeping it in service.

MOVING DATA STORAGE TO ANOTHER SERVER

When a server's reliability is questionable, you might consider temporarily moving disk storage devices or files to another computer that can function as a replacement server. If the drives are okay, there is no reason to suffer through server failures.

They can be transferred without even restoring a backup. A standby server can provide temporary service while the primary server is taken out of service for a comprehensive physical examination, repair, and/or replacement as illustrated in Figure 29.1.

Figure 29.1.
Transferring the
secondary disk sub-
system to a standby
server.

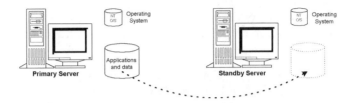

Moving the operating system drive to another computer is possible, but this is not a desirable procedure. The operating system configuration for the hardware devices and computer is specific to the server and may require extensive modification.

Tip

Install two separate disk subsystems in your server: one for the operating system, a second for applications and data. Removal of the secondary disk subsystem and installation into a standby server is then possible with fewer complications.

A standby server can also have a disk subsystem with the NT Server operating system. The secondary disk subsystem can be transferred from the primary to the standby server without having to reconfigure the operating system.

It is a good idea to separate the operating system from user data and applications. You are well advised to install a separate NT Server operating system on the standby computer. The data and applications can reside on a separate SCSI subsystem. This way, you can just copy the data to the standby server without altering the operating system and its configuration.

For this reason as well as others, it is best to install servers with at least two separate disk drive subsystems: one for the operating system, the other for user applications and data. This way, the secondary drive(s) with user applications and data can be moved at will without disturbing the operating system installed on the bootable primary drive subsystem.

HOT ONLINE BACKUP SERVER

Another suggestion is to keep a secondary server online that can stand in as a server should the primary server fail. This computer can be a personal computer, perhaps the system administrator's computer or a computer purchased for this purpose.

If the backup server is dedicated to this purpose, it can be online standing by for action. You can copy files to it frequently, and switch over to the standby server whenever necessary.

FREQUENT SERVER REPLACEMENT

A server should be replaced every couple of years. The first two years of a computer's life are normally pretty trouble-free. The old server can be rotated to a user workstation, while the new server provides more and better performance and a renewed life span.

This concept is employed by car rental companies to continually provide new automobiles that are dependable and have low maintenance. The same practice is even more desirable for a server, because the old one does not have to be sold or discarded—it can be used as a user workstation.

ISOLATING THE OFFENDING COMPONENT

Using diagnostic software to isolate the bad component is pretty simple in today's PCs. Most better brands of computers are shipped with a diagnostic utility that can generally isolate the problem if the computer is bootable and can run the diagnostics program.

Other diagnostics programs are available for testing PCs. You can purchase a hardware testing utility from most computer software stores. A few top utilities that you might consider are

>CheckIt
>QA Plus
>System Sleuth

Another method is far less sophisticated but works almost every time. The simplest method of locating the component that has failed is to swap the suspected component for a new one, or put the suspect component in another computer.

If the component has failed in one computer, chances are pretty good that it will also fail in another computer. If a known good component is swapped for a failed one, you have isolated your problem.

REVIEWING THE EVENT LOG

Whenever a system problem is detected during NT boot, the Event Log processor notes the problem and places an entry in the system event log. This log can be viewed by clicking on the Event Viewer in your Administrative Tools program group.

Enter Event Viewer, select Log, System, then you can view the list of exceptions that have occurred, as shown in Figure 29.2. The list of messages is divided into three types: Information, Error, and Warning. Each entry starts with an icon indicating its type. Double-click on an entry to view its detail as shown in Figure 29.3.

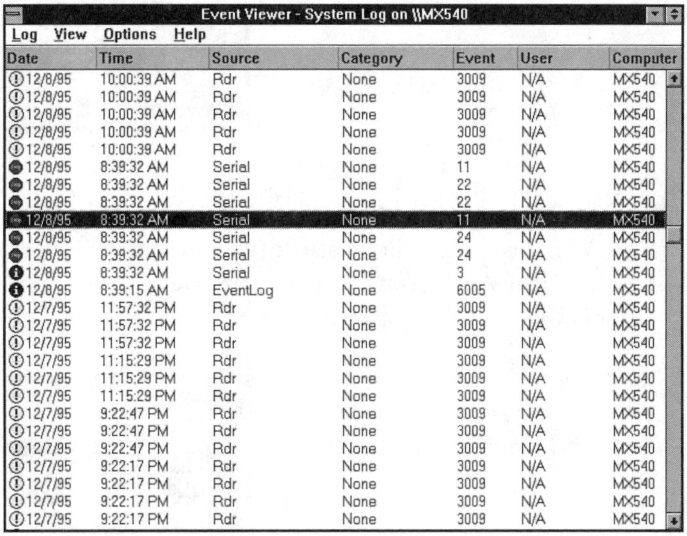

Date	Time	Source	Category	Event	User	Computer
12/8/95	10:00:39 AM	Rdr	None	3009	N/A	MX540
12/8/95	10:00:39 AM	Rdr	None	3009	N/A	MX540
12/8/95	10:00:39 AM	Rdr	None	3009	N/A	MX540
12/8/95	10:00:39 AM	Rdr	None	3009	N/A	MX540
12/8/95	10:00:39 AM	Rdr	None	3009	N/A	MX540
12/8/95	8:39:32 AM	Serial	None	11	N/A	MX540
12/8/95	8:39:32 AM	Serial	None	22	N/A	MX540
12/8/95	8:39:32 AM	Serial	None	22	N/A	MX540
12/8/95	8:39:32 AM	Serial	None	11	N/A	MX540
12/8/95	8:39:32 AM	Serial	None	24	N/A	MX540
12/8/95	8:39:32 AM	Serial	None	24	N/A	MX540
12/8/95	8:39:32 AM	Serial	None	3	N/A	MX540
12/8/95	8:39:15 AM	EventLog	None	6005	N/A	MX540
12/7/95	11:57:32 PM	Rdr	None	3009	N/A	MX540
12/7/95	11:57:32 PM	Rdr	None	3009	N/A	MX540
12/7/95	11:57:32 PM	Rdr	None	3009	N/A	MX540
12/7/95	11:15:29 PM	Rdr	None	3009	N/A	MX540
12/7/95	11:15:29 PM	Rdr	None	3009	N/A	MX540
12/7/95	11:15:29 PM	Rdr	None	3009	N/A	MX540
12/7/95	9:22:47 PM	Rdr	None	3009	N/A	MX540
12/7/95	9:22:47 PM	Rdr	None	3009	N/A	MX540
12/7/95	9:22:47 PM	Rdr	None	3009	N/A	MX540
12/7/95	9:22:17 PM	Rdr	None	3009	N/A	MX540
12/7/95	9:22:17 PM	Rdr	None	3009	N/A	MX540
12/7/95	9:22:17 PM	Rdr	None	3009	N/A	MX540
12/7/95	9:22:17 PM	Rdr	None	3009	N/A	MX540

Figure 29.2. Event Viewer's system log.

The specific error message shown in Figure 29.3 indicates that the tape device driver for a QIC tape device did not load.

You can filter events in this log to locate specific entries that you are interested in. From Event Viewer's main menu bar, select View, Filter Events.

In Event Viewer, select View, Filter Events, Source to see each process on your NT operating system. Click on the arrow to the right of the Source box, and you can find any process occurring on the server. Selecting a Source process will restrict the events listed to ones pertaining to the selected Category.

Figure 29.3.
Event detail.

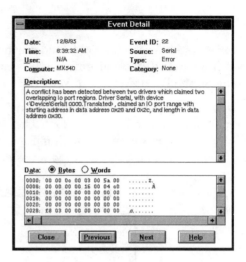

RUNNING THE DIAGNOSTICS UTILITY

The Windows NT Diagnostic utility is the NT version of the older Microsoft Diagnostics (MSD). You can select and view several hardware configuration options from NT Diagnostic utility's main menu as shown in Figure 29.4.

Figure 29.4.
Windows NT Diagnos-
tics utility main menu.

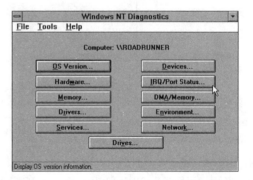

This utility shows the configuration of each hardware device in detail. It is helpful in finding device conflicts. The screen shown in Figure 29.5 shows a serial port configuration. This type of information can show you which interrupt, memory addresses, DMA channels, and port addresses each device is using. If you have two devices configured for one of the same configuration parameters, you can find the mistake here.

Figure 29.5.
IRQ / Port Status in NT
diagnostics.

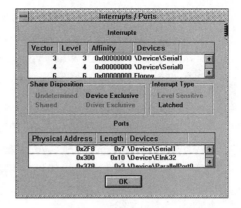

Control Panel's Device Applet

You can select the Device applet to see what devices are operative at the moment. This program shows the current state of each device driver when the device driver is loaded.

This information tells you if a device drive is loaded and functioning. This information is helpful to determine why a device may not be functioning, or to see which device is not functioning. When a device driver loads, it tests the hardware device to see if it is responding. If the device fails to respond, the device driver does not load and will therefore show that the device driver is not running in this utility.

Dealing with Intermittent Problems

Intermittent problems are most difficult to find, because everything may be working correctly at the moment that you attempt to isolate a problem. The only sure way to locate the problem is to observe the failure and be able to re-create it at will.

To force an intermittent problem to surface is often not difficult. Generally, intermittent problems are related to electronic components. A surefire way to bring intermittent problems out is to run the component that intermittently fails at full capacity for extended periods. For example, if a disk drive produces a write error periodically, run a repeating I/O test over and over until the failure occurs.

Heat also brings out intermittently flawed electronic components. Usually an electronic component operates at a higher temperature when under extreme load for extended periods. By running a full load test, especially in a warm room (80 degrees Fahrenheit or higher), you can force some of these errors to surface.

TESTING RAM

RAM problems are most often intermittent. A failing RAM chip heats up when under extreme load—and that is usually when your parity error occurs. QA Plus, CheckIt, and System Sleuth all have RAM testing utilities that can cause intermittent RAM errors to surface. Select the most comprehensive RAM testing method that your utility supports and run it continuously overnight. You can generally come in and find the offending memory address in the morning.

Most of these utilities have a memory layout screen that will help you identify which chip has failed from the parity error that is generated.

TESTING DISK DRIVES

Your disk vendor or SCSI adapter vendor provides a disk formatting and testing utility that can help identify disk problems. Several computer hardware testing utilities have a disk drive testing utility that can help diagnose bad disk media with a non-destructive surface scan.

Note

Generally, the testing program for disk drives is supplied with a SCSI adapter. Testing programs are generally not made available by IDE drive manufacturers.

WHEN THE SERVER CANNOT BOOT

When the NT operating system cannot come up, you will not be able to run NT, so you will not be able to view the Event Viewer or any of the error files. In short, your options to troubleshoot are restricted to normal hardware troubleshooting procedures under MS-DOS.

In order to protect yourself against this eventuality, you can enable the WINDBG debugger with the recover option enabled. This option causes the debugger to save a memory dump to the boot partition upon failure so you can view the contents in memory. A memory dump is useful if you can get a highly trained support specialist (a programmer) to accept your dump and debug it.

You cannot perform this procedure if the server cannot boot. If you want this option to be available, you must configure WINDBG (as discussed later in this chapter) while your server is still operative.

Note

> If your primary partition is an NTFS partition, you will not be able to view it under DOS. You might therefore consider having a FAT primary partition (drive C:) and an NTFS secondary partition (drive D:). This will allow the debugger to write the memory dump to the FAT DOS partition so you can view it.

A memory dump saves the raw contents of memory to disk. This requires as much disk space as RAM—for example, if you have 48MB of RAM in your server, the dump file will contain 48MB of data.

To configure WINDBG to save during a failed boot:

1. Select System options in Control Panel.

2. Click on the Recover button.

3. Select the options shown in Figure 29.6.

Figure 29.6.
The Recovery option in
the Control Panel
System applet.

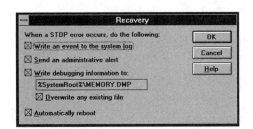

STOP Messages During Boot

When some serious hardware problems occur, NT may stop during boot, and display a STOP error message. These messages represent Microsoft's attempt to display the breakpoint in kernel execution. The breakpoint theoretically should point you to the source of the reason for the STOP. However, these messages are often only usable to Microsoft factory technicians. Generally, the only real benefit occurs when a specific STOP error is common and can be associated with a more specific problem.

Quite often, STOP messages refer to a dependency module that does not work because another service did not work, which in turn may not work because a hardware device did not work. The messages refer to a thread, or resource label, and at times may not at all describe the offending component.

The STOP messages come from the NT Executive. You can find out more about these messages in Chapter 2 of the NT Messages manual. You can find this material in NT Server's Books Online (see the MAIN program group). Check the table of contents for the Messages manual, and see Chapter 2, "Windows NT Executive Messages."

Very often the STOP is caused by a hardware device malfunction, or a deeply embedded hardware compatibility problem, perhaps in the BIOS or chipset. STOP messages from the operating system are often misleading, providing textual references that may even confuse you.

If an NT server has been running reliably, never had the same problem before, and is performing the same types of jobs it was doing before, look for a hardware device failure.

If your NT server was recently installed, or its system or interface card hardware was upgraded or reconfigured, you may have encountered a system incompatibility that has gone undetected up to this point.

USING THE WINDOWS NT DEBUGGER

The Windows debugger is helpful for Microsoft factory support engineers to determine where the source of a problem lies. Few service technicians or system administrators will find the debug messages and addresses helpful in finding a problem.

Note

If you believe the NT debugger can be useful to you, read on. Most technicians are advised to forget about this tool, as it is kernel-code specific and not of use to most.

The NT debugger, WINDBG.EXE, is not installed in NT's Setup program. You must install it manually by copying the files from the \SUPPORT\DEBUG*<platform>* directory (*<platform>* represents i386, ALPHA, MIPS, or PPC directory, depending upon your type of computer).

Debugging must be done from a separate NT computer, connected to the crashed server by a serial connection to one of the server's COM ports. This can be done locally using a null modem cable (a modem cable where pins 2 and 3 are crossed), or with local and remote modems connecting the path.

Once the debugger is installed, the serial connection is established, and the debugger is run, you can find STOP messages and peruse the debugger for breakpoints, dependency links, and so on. You will find help by typing **HELP** at a debug prompt.

Note

Do not expect WINDBG errors and parameters to be helpful unless you have kernel source code at your side. This information is helpful to Microsoft in-house programmers, but may be indecipherable and even misleading to the average technician.

The services you see listed are most often dependencies, driven by other modules and devices. The addresses refer to assembled code execution statements in memory. The line cited in the STOP message may refer to any line of code being executed and may not necessarily point you to the problem, even if you could disassemble the code.

You can find material relating to installing and using WINDBG in NT Server's Books Online (see the MAIN program group). Check the table of contents for the Messages manual, then see Chapter 2, "Windows NT Executive Messages."

WORKING AROUND A FAILED COMPONENT

Although you may have a device that has failed, you may be able to run without it and avoid downtime until you get it fixed. When a device is removed, the operating system notes this condition during boot, runs anyway (if possible), then writes the altered configuration information to the Registry if necessary.

If a failed device prevents NT from booting, physically remove the device, use the Emergency Repair Disk if necessary to remove the device driver from the configuration, then attempt to bring your server up again.

REPLACING SUSPECTED COMPONENTS

The basic common-sense approach to troubleshooting involves simply replacing suspected hardware devices until the problem disappears. Although this sounds crude and perhaps expensive, consider that it is often the fastest and most direct method of resolving a problem.

Replacing suspect components is also often the least costly in terms of time. Simply swapping out a component can take minutes and can resolve a problem immediately. The cost of an hour of downtime in a Fortune 1000 company can range between $32,000 to $72,000 according to recent industry surveys. The cost of several hours of technician time can also be costly and may still involve downtime.

If you can narrow down the problem to one or a few suspected components, you can install a component known to be good. If the problem is not solved, you have spent a little money to purchase a spare component, which can possibly be used in another computer, or as a spare should the server component fail. If the component is very expensive, this approach may not be practical. This is not such a big risk to take where system RAM, SCSI, or other storage device controllers, network interface cards, and other devices are concerned. Even main system boards are far less expensive than the alternative quite often.

SUMMARY

Troubleshooting a failed server is no different from troubleshooting any other computer. There are, however, a few tools and a few additional considerations when running NT.

A debugger is available; this is a good tool if you know how to debug code. Even under these conditions, debugging may not prove fruitful unless you have NT code available to read procedures and dependency modules that may be cited in the error messages.

The Event Viewer and NT Diagnostics utilities are helpful to find hints as to what has gone wrong. Regular old hardware troubleshooting skills and good knowledge of computer hardware go a long way in securing the health of your system.

- The Protocol Analysis Approach to Trouble-shooting

- Troubleshooting the Physical Layer

- The LAN Layer

- Analyzing NetBIOS

- Analyzing Transport Protocols

- Analyzing SMB

CHAPTER 30

LAN Troubleshooting

Local Area Network   The cabling, network adapter cards, connectors, and intermediate connection devices (such as hubs and MAUs) used to connect computers together.

Note

In this book, the term *LAN* refers to an Ethernet, Token ring, or other type of local area network. The term *network* refers to the entire networked system of computers, LANs, WANs, protocols, NOS, and so on.

frames   The unit of data and protocol header/trailer information that is propagated on a LAN.

packets   The unit of data and protocol header information that transports data over a LAN. Packets carry header information for TCP/IP, NetBIOS, NetBEUI, IPX/SPX/NCP, and other network and transport protocols.

Note

The terms *packet* and *frame* represent two different layers of protocol. Packets are protocol units generated used by the NOS, whereas frames are protocol units used between network cards. Packets are encapsulated into frames for movement over a LAN.

Although these terms are often used interchangeably, this book uses them more precisely.

IEEE   Institute of Electrical and Electronic Engineers. IEEE has standardized LAN characteristics and cabling specifications to enable competing vendors' products to work together.

EIA   Electronic Industry Association.

TIA   Telecommunications Industry Association.

FDDI   Fiber Distributed Data Interface. A type of LAN based in token-passing, ring access protocol using optical fiber cabling. FDDI is more stable and secure than other types of LANs and supports 100 Mbps bandwidth.

CDDI   Copper Distributed Data Interface. The solid wire equivalent of FDDI. FDDI can run on Category 5 UTP. There is no standard for this variation, but for all intents and purposes, it's simply FDDI running on copper wire.

STP Shielded twisted pair. Note that STP is 150 ohm wire and must not be substituted for UTP, which is 100 ohm wire.

UTP Unshielded twisted pair. Category 3, 4 (voice grade), or 5 (data grade) cable is acceptable for 10Base-T; however, Category 5 is required for Token ring, CDDI, ATM, and Fast Ethernet.

EMI Electromagnetic interference. Electrical current generates a magnetic field at a 90 degree angle from the direction of the flow. This field induces electrical propagation in wire nearby, causing interference.

Networks are often mysterious and difficult to troubleshoot. In most cases, technicians are not certain of where a problem lies; they simply try different fixes until they finally hit on the problem that was preventing communications. This is why troubleshooting a network is often considered "black magic" and why effective troubleshooters are often regarded as "gurus." If the mechanics are understood, this is a learned science, not magic.

This trial-and-error method of troubleshooting is often effective for two reasons. First, a few common problems are most often responsible; second, an experienced system administrator becomes familiar with the symptoms of the most common problems. However, a more comprehensive approach is required for uncommon problems, intermittent occurrences, and performance evaluation. System administrators also need to stay a step ahead of disasters, resolving problems when they are minor—before they disable the network. This chapter discusses troubleshooting procedures in your network.

THE PROTOCOL ANALYSIS APPROACH TO TROUBLESHOOTING

Several problems can cause communications to fail, and only part of them relate directly to the LAN itself. A protocol analyzer is a passive listening device that captures LAN frames and buffers them for examination. It also accumulates performance and error statistics. The analyzer can determine which layer is responsible for problems and enable you to locate exactly what the problem is from protocol header information contained in the frame or packet headers.

The protocol analysis approach taken by large system troubleshooters generally involves dissecting the network into layers. Network design is often categorized in layers equivalent to the layers of the Open Systems Interconnection (OSI) model from the International Standards Organization; however, Microsoft uses many terms differently from OSI, so it is confusing to map protocols to OSI layers as most protocol analyzers do.

30

LAN TROUBLESHOOTING

Note

Microsoft uses some terms differently from other network industry vendors. If you refrain from applying existing protocol knowledge to Microsoft documentation, you will save yourself a lot of confusion.

This chapter discusses protocol terminology that is more consistent with Microsoft documentation.

The only certain solution to locating communications problems is using a protocol analyzer or similar device to pinpoint the source and nature of the problem. Protocols generally do not generate screen error messages that tell us what is wrong. Exchanges of data between clients and servers are carried by packets and frames from the sender to the receiver. By observing the packet and frame header information, most specifically error codes, you can ascertain exactly why a problem occurs. Of course, this is only possible by using a protocol analyzer of some software that reveals protocol information on your network. A protocol analyzer is a sophisticated tool that captures LAN frames and encodes the frame and packet header information so you can find the specifics of the problem.

Protocol interaction is extremely complex because protocols are layered one upon another. However, you can pinpoint problems by looking for a few specific protocol errors and dialog exchanges that are not consistent with normal communications. Problems can relate to several aspects of your network.

The first layer to examine is the physical layer. Problems at this layer show up in error statistics. Error information is specific to the type of LAN (Ethernet, Token ring, and so on) so there are no simple instructions on how to find physical layer problems; they are often difficult to spot. Ethernet errors are far more general than Token ring errors, and physical layer problems are often intermittent. You might have good continuity and the proper pinout in your cabling, but other electrical characteristics can introduce high data error rates. A protocol analyzer only helps identify the source of the problem. From there, the most comprehensive and certain way to find problems at this layer is to use a cable tester or certification device.

WHICH PROTOCOL ANALYZER TO USE

The market today features many brands and models of protocol analyzers. Of course, some have more features than others, and some cost far more than others. Several good analyzers are available, and prices have fallen in recent years. You can spend between $1,500 to $50,000 for a protocol analyzer.

The most important factor to look for in a protocol analyzer is the supported protocol decodes. Protocol headers have many codes that must be translated into plain English (or another language). Always check to see that all protocols in use in your network are supported by the analyzer before you purchase it. Many analyzers lack good support for Microsoft protocols because there has been little demand for some of these protocol decodes in the past. Network General's Sniffer supports more protocol decodes than any other analyzer on the market.

Another important factor to look for is an easy-to-understand user interface. Of course, a Windows interface is a valuable feature; unfortunately, many analyzers still use a DOS interface. A few run on UNIX and use a window type of interface that is very good. One of the easiest Windows-based interfaces to use is Wandel & Goltermann's Domino analyzer. Another good interface is Novell's LANalyzer for Windows; however, it has limited support for Microsoft protocols. The Network Monitor in Microsoft's System Management Server (SMS) is a natural addition to your NT Server based network.

Also important is the capability to capture all LAN frames regardless of how active your LAN is. Some analyzers are software only, and others include their own network cards and are often bundled with a computer. Traditionally, better protocol analyzers have been hardware-software combinations to ensure that all frames are captured. The current recommendation is that you use a Pentium computer for your analyzer. Software-only analyzers require a network card that can operate in the *promiscuous mode.* The promiscuous mode enables the network card to capture all frames present on the LAN. It is also important to use a high-performance network card. PCMCIA or PCI network cards are preferred because the bus interface has very high capacity.

Some analyzers employ another method of capturing frames. A separate piece of hardware captures frames, buffers, and sends them to the computer for examination. Wandel & Goltermann's Domino is built this way and has the capability to handle 100 Mbps traffic and feed it to a computer without losing frames. This type of configuration is more expensive but is absolutely required to ensure that all frames are captured at higher speeds.

TROUBLESHOOTING BY LAYER

When you look inside the network, you see layer upon layer of complexity. The old 80-20 rule applies here; approximately 80 percent of the symptoms are caused by 20 percent of the potential problems. Having just a little knowledge of each layer is important. The layers involved are the following:

Physical layer   Cabling, connectors, and LAN devices such as hubs comprise the physical aspects of your LAN. You cannot analyze this layer, but problems related to this layer show up in LAN layer error codes. Physical layer problems statistically account for over half of all network disabilities.

30

LAN TROUBLESHOOTING

LAN layer   Ethernet, Token ring, or other types of network cards exchange data between nodes that are connected to the same LAN or over a bridge. Problems specific to network-card firmware and drivers show up at this layer and can be identified with a great degree of certainty. This layer is analyzed by capturing and viewing frame header information.

Transport layer   IPX/SPX, TCP/IP, or NetBEUI protocols are responsible for logical communications data between network nodes. Each transport protocol works differently and has different problems. This layer is analyzed by viewing the transport protocol header information specific to the transport protocol in use. All protocol headers show very little information about transporting data; however, IPX and IP routing problems and inefficiencies show up here.

Note

Technically speaking, IPX and IP are network protocols (as defined by the OSI model); however, Microsoft uses these protocols to transport NetBIOS and SMB packets, which often contain data. Microsoft refers to these protocols as transport protocols, so this book refers to them as such to be consistent with Microsoft documentation and configuration screen information.

Virtual circuit management layer   The NetBIOS protocol handles most exchanges of share names, workgroup/domain names, and virtual circuits (logical communication) establishment between nodes. It also handles the exchange of information concerning access privileges. Each NetBIOS packet is encapsulated in an IPX, IP, or NetBEUI packet for transport, but it's there even though you might think it isn't. Every time your operating system needs to look for other nodes, it issues a NetBIOS broadcast requesting names. Each computer configured to share devices responds by issuing a NetBIOS broadcast for each share name that contains various configuration details such as group names, domain name, and access permissions.

NetBIOS is the foundation of Microsoft connectivity. It is a quite persistent and inefficient protocol that rarely fails completely. When problems appear, it can cause serious performance degradation. You can often find the reasons for performance and server access failures by tracing NetBIOS exchanges. Very often, NetBIOS inefficiency is related to cabling or other intermittent problems on your network.

Highest layer   SMB protocol is Microsoft's top layer protocol that relays operating system requests from node to node. It is mainly responsible for handling file access and print jobs. SMB carries the access tokens and mechanics that provide permission to access network shares and services. SMB calls upon processes in the server to provide network services. SMB serves a couple other miscellaneous functions, but when file access is not accomplished, you can usually find the reasons by tracing dialogs in the SMB request and reply sequences between nodes.

You can observe various problems specific to each layer and find typical problems by analyzing these layers. Later in this chapter is a more detailed discussion of each layer.

TROUBLESHOOTING THE PHYSICAL LAYER

Physical cabling and connector problems account for well over half of all network disabilities. The following information is important for troubleshooting, but you should also review it before cabling a network.

Problems at this layer are only evidenced by a protocol analyzer. A protocol analyzer can often pinpoint the location of a physical problem through filtering frames that are involved in the problem. After good communications are filtered out, the remaining frames often locate one or more nodes that are related to the problem.

The most common problems to look for include the following:

◆ Cable connectors—Frayed connections or damaged connectors can introduce electrical problems that cause intermittent problems with connectivity or introduce high error rates.

◆ Cabling—Wrong wire, segments that are too long, kinks, and broken or shorted cable can cause problems.

◆ Malfunctioning LAN devices—Like any other electronic device, hubs, repeaters, MAUs, and wiring concentrators can malfunction. When they do, they intermittently or completely disrupt network traffic or introduce high error rates.

Protocol analysis cannot really examine the physical layer because it doesn't have protocol information directly relating to it. Ethernet, Fast Ethernet, and 100VG are notoriously simple but general in error detection. Token ring and FDDI are far more specific; for example, Token ring can generate 52 types of error detection and recovery frames, such as a beacon frame or frames identifying a ring failure. Many of these errors are very specific and point to problems with cabling or the physical layer. For all types of LANs, once the protocol analyst determines that the problem is probably physical, he must examine the cabling and LAN devices.

CABLE CONFIGURATION, TESTING, AND CERTIFICATION

Cabling problems cost organizations thousands of dollars per year in lost productivity, idle resources, and lost revenues. This section reviews troubleshooting and certification of cabling systems typically used in LAN installations. Most LAN systems run on twisted pair or coax, although a small but growing percentage runs on fiber optic cabling. This section explains the causes and treatment of most common cabling problems along with what is required to certify your cabling and reviews some installation tips to help you prevent costly network down time.

Many system administrators are responsible for software operations only, leaving cabling to the data communications crew. It is important for all network technicians to know a little about cabling even if someone else is responsible for it.

Often effective are simple troubleshooting devices, such as a continuity tester or ohm meter; however, they do not tell the whole story. You can have continuity, but the characteristics of the cabling might not be suitable for your type of LAN. That's why cable testers are used to locate cable faults. If you want to ensure that cabling will support the type of LAN you are using, a more sophisticated tester can certify the cable for suitability with various types of LANs.

Protocol analysis can narrow the scope of the troubleshooting, and from that point on, you should use cable testers to determine exactly where the problem is.

COAXIAL CABLE PROBLEMS

Many computer technicians believe that if they have followed their cabling guidelines and they have continuity, their cabling is good. This is not the case at all. Access protocols, especially CSMA/CD, rely heavily on the appropriate cabling characteristics for proper operation. Several factors must be correct in order so that your cabling will provide good performance.

ATTENUATION

Any electromagnetic signal loses strength as it moves away from its source, and LAN signals over coax are no exception! This signal loss with distance is called *attenuation*. One of the most common problems in coaxial networks is the slow and steady growth of the cabling segment until it exceeds the length limitation. For 10Base2 Ethernet systems, this is 200 meters (10Base2 means 10 Mbps, baseband, for 200 meters, which was later changed to 185 meters). If the length is too great, the signal might have too much attenuation, and you will experience degraded performance. How do you measure length? You use Time Domain Reflectometry (TDR), which is a technical way of saying "cable radar." TDR is conceptualized in Figure 30.1.

Figure 30.1.
Time Domain Reflecto-
metry (TDR).

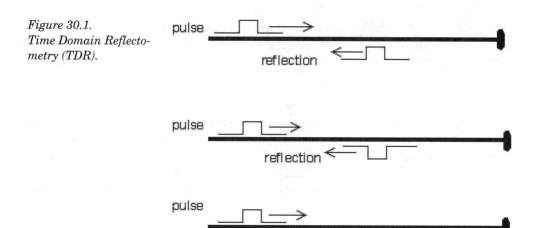

TDRs are built into almost all cable testers today, and they are an invaluable tool for measuring cable length, finding cable mismatches, and finding shorts, opens, and breaks. The method is simple. A pulse is sent from the tester down the cable. When the pulse encounters a change in cable impedance (usually an open or short), it is reflected back to the tester. The tester measures the elapsed time and, knowing how fast electrons travel in the cable, calculates and displays the distance to the fault.

COAXIAL CABLE

Although it's rapidly being eclipsed by its twisted pair rival, coaxial cabling still enjoys a large installed base and is often a good choice for small networks. Coaxial cable is familiar to most of us in its cable TV application, but keep in mind that TV coaxial cable is not the correct cable for an Ethernet LAN.

Physically, coaxial cable is simple. There are several concentric layers of material surrounding a common axis, the co-axis or *coax*. Typically, there is a central solid copper core conductor surrounded by a non-conducting material, which is in turn surrounded with a foil or braided shield and finally covered by an abrasion-resistant jacket. You can use stranded core for better flexibility. Teflon-coated (plenum) cable is also used for applications where the cable is pulled through air ducting.

Coaxial cable was the preferred Ethernet cabling choice for many years because the radial grounded shield protects the inner core where the signal is present. However, coaxial cable is more difficult to install and brings many problems that relate to the LAN topology (how the cable is laid out).

Coaxial cabling often presents a problem because it generally includes several computers on the same cable. The linear-bus topology (daisy chain) design for coaxial-based Ethernet is unstable; if any part of the cable is broken, all nodes on that cabling segment are down. This makes troubleshooting more difficult because communications are totally disabled.

CABLE MISMATCHES

One common problem is connecting different types of coaxial cable together. Just because there are connectors made to join different types of coaxial cable does not mean that you should put together a LAN with them. It is possible to connect a 50 ohm Ethernet cable to a 93 ohm ARCnet cable and achieve continuity, but you will have a major mismatch in impedance. You can easily find impedance mismatches using a TDR.

Note

Check your cable carefully before installation. Thin Ethernet is RG58U (50 ohm). You must not substitute TV coaxial (RG59U) or ARCnet (RG62U). Although you might be able to log in, this causes extensive LAN errors and limits capacity severely. These errors are accentuated when more traffic is present.

PHYSICAL PROBLEMS

Stretching a cable, tugging on a cable, keeping an intermittent connection, or leaving the cable in a hostile environment often leads to cable breaks, opens, and shorts. Be especially careful to route cables near workstations in such a way as to minimize the risk of accidental cable damage. You can easily find these types of faults with a TDR.

TERMINATORS

Terminators for coaxial cables are nothing more than resistors soldered into a small can. They can break when dropped. It's a good idea to have spares on hand. Be sure they are the right type (50 ohms for Ethernet).

Note

You should check and verify terminator resistance for 50 ohms, especially if you cannot communicate over your cabling. ARCnet and TV terminators look identical and are often not marked.

TWISTED PAIR CABLE, EIA/TIA 568 CABLING SPECIFICATIONS

By far the most popular type of LAN cabling is *unshielded twisted pair* (UTP). It is easy to work with, flexible, low in cost, small diameter, lightweight, and simple to connect and terminate, and its application is universal. UTP supports wide-ranging applications including voice, ISDN, Ethernet, Token ring, Fast Ethernet, and most other types of LANs.

UTP commonly consists of four pairs of 24 AWG solid or stranded copper wire surrounded by a thin insulating jacket. IEEE specifications indicate cabling characteristics that are suitable for various types of LANs. However, Electronics Industry Association (EIA) and Telecommunications Industry Association (TIA) engineers have defined cable rating and labeling requirements that make the job of selecting cabling much simpler.

The most important standards reference for those interested in LAN cabling is the EIA/TIA 568 standard. Because UTP is so common these days for LANs, EIA and TIA combined cabling specifications to define a standard set of UTP cabling rules that is suitable for networking virtually any type of LAN with up to 100 Mbps bandwidth. The following types of LANs can use EIA/TIA 568 rules:

- ◆ Ethernet
- ◆ Fast Ethernet
- ◆ Token ring
- ◆ FDDI on UTP (sometimes called CDDI or TP-DDI)
- ◆ 100VG-AnyLAN (802.12)
- ◆ ARCnet
- ◆ ATM

The EIA/TIA 568 cable specification is not only standardized for many types of LANs, but it is also very simple and precise. A system designer can specify simply EIA/TIA 568A or EIA/TIA 568B, and all related specifications are known to the cabling vendors and contractors. Table 30.1 indicates the EIA/TIA category rating system for cabling.

30

LAN TROUBLESHOOTING

TABLE 30.1. THE EIA/TIA CATEGORY SYSTEM.

Category	Description	Typical Application	Classification
Category 1	Intended for basic communications and power limited circuit cable. There are no performance criteria for this category. Functional equivalent of UL Level 1.	Not rated for any application.	Non-data grade
Category 2	Low performance UTP. Typical applications include voice and low speed data. Not specified in EIA/TIA 568A for data use. Functional equivalent of UL Level 2 or IBM Type 3.	IBM Type 3 Voice/PBX Alarm wiring	Voice grade
Category 3	Applies to UTP cables and associated connecting hardware with transmission characteristics up to 16 MHz. Functional equivalent of UL Level 3.	10Base-T 4 Mbps Token ring ARCnet 100Base-VG 100Base-T4	Voice grade
Category 4	Applies to UTP cables and associated connecting hardware with transmission characteristics up to 20 MHz. Functional equivalent of UL Level 4.	16 Mbps Token ring Low loss 10Base-T	Data grade

Category	Description	Typical Application	Classification
Category 5	Applies to UTP, ScTP or STP cables and associated connecting hardware with transmission characteristics up to 100 MHz. Functional equivalent of UL Level 5.	ATM over copper TP-PMD CDDI 100Base-T	Data grade

Signal Degradation

Any time you have electricity carrying data down a wire, there will be some signal degradation. There are four factors that must fall within allowable ranges in order to eliminate problems. Cabling is rated to the categories discussed in Table 30.1 according to how much of each of these factors can be present over a specified cable length. The factors that are considered include the following:

◆ Length

◆ Noise

◆ Near End Crosstalk (NeXT)

◆ Attenuation

Each of these factors is discussed in the following sections.

Length

Each type of LAN has cabling rules for each type of cable to be used. For example, 10Base-T Ethernet allows 100 meters per cabling segment from the wiring concentrator to the network card.

When your cabling is longer than specifications allow, you may sporadically experience connection problems. Problems can affect the entire LAN. It is necessary to test all cable runs to be sure they do not exceed specifications.

Noise

Any interference introduced from an external source is called noise. Any time you have a flow of electricity, a magnetic field is generated in a 90 degree angle from the flow. This electromagnetic interference (EMI) causes data errors on nearby LAN cabling, especially UTP, which is highly susceptible to EMI because the inner wires are not shielded.

30

LAN Troubleshooting

Although it is not possible to eliminate noise from a UTP cable plant, the amount of noise allowed to achieve category 3, 4, or 5 rating varies according to the combination of signaling rate (such as 10 MHz versus 100 MHz) and distance. When you use a cable tester, your tester first calculates the length of the cable and then tests the noise at a specified signaling rate. The cable either falls into range for certification at a category level or fails the test entirely, which means the cabling is not suitable for a LAN at the given length.

UTP can handle a relatively high level of noise because the twists in the cable and the electronic circuitry in the network adapter cards and LAN devices. Almost every LAN that uses UTP has one (or more) transmit pair of wires and a receive pair. On each pair, one wire carries a positive signal and the other wire in the pair carries a negative signal as shown in Figure 30.2.

Figure 30.2.
A UTP wire pair.

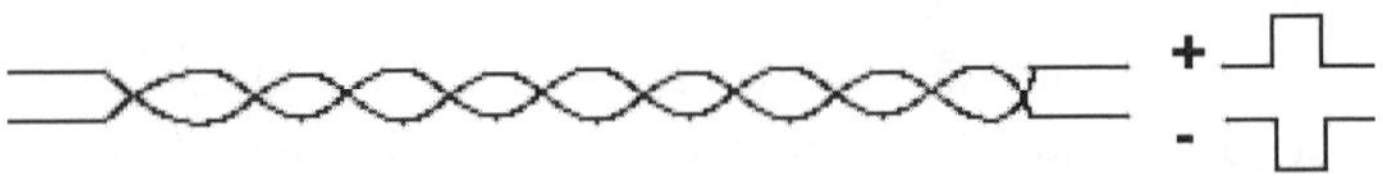

In this situation, any signal placed on one wire should have an exact reciprocal on the other wire in the pair. The twists cause "resonance," where the positive signal generates EMI that induces more signal strength on the negative signal and visa versa. Whenever a signal is detected that does not exist on the other wire in the pair, it is known to be noise and therefore is canceled out.

NEAR END CROSSTALK (NEXT)

Any flow of electricity generates an electromagnetic field around the wire that can interfere with signals on adjacent wires. In UTP, two wires are twisted together to form a pair because this enables opposing fields in the wire pair to cancel and strengthen each other. The tighter the twist, the more effective the cancellation, and the higher the data rate supported by the cable.

Note

Maintaining a tight, consistent wire twist from end to end is the single most important factor in good UTP cable quality and a good cabling installation.

Loosely twisted pairs, substandard connectors, and casual termination will cause excessive NeXT. If you have ever experienced a telephone conversation where you could hear another conversation faintly in the background, you have experienced an example of NeXT, and it is deadly to LAN traffic. In LAN applications, NeXT occurs when the transmitting pair radiates energy that is coupled into the adjacent receiving pair and is erroneously interpreted as the intended receive signal. The NeXT between two adjacent pairs is shown in Figure 30.3.

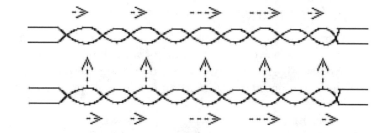

Figure 30.3.
Near End Crosstalk
(NeXT).

NeXT is measured as the difference between the strength of the transmitted signal one pair and the strength of the transmitted signal on the adjacent pair. A large number (such as 50 dB) is preferred over a small number (such as 20 dB).

Note

When a tester indicates "High NeXT", you need to find out if it means a high number (which is good) or a high amount of crosstalk (which is bad). The normal convention is to refer to the amount of crosstalk, so "low crosstalk" means a good cable.

Note that most UTP have four wire pairs, and because NeXT occurs between all pair combinations, there are six different NeXT measurements required per cable. If you only measure the NeXT on the 1-2/3-6 pairs (used with Ethernet), that won't tell you anything about how the cabling will perform for Token ring applications (which use wires 3-6/4-5) or Fast Ethernet 100Base-X (which use 1-2/7-8). The *worst* measurement of the six is the one used to rate the cable. If this sounds complicated, don't worry. Most test tools automate the whole process, making all the measurements, comparing the results to appropriate pass/fail standards, and then giving you a pass or fail result.

Table 30.2 indicates some of the causes and recommended actions when trouble-shooting NeXT problems.

TABLE 30.2. NeXT PROBLEMS AND SOLUTIONS.

Possible Cause of NeXT	Recommendation
Pairs untwisted	Examine cable for loose or untwisted cabling, particularly at connection points.
Use of silversatin (untwisted) patch cables	Discard and replace with data grade patch cables.
Split pairs	Ensure logical pairs are twisted together (see the section titled "Split Pairs").
Multiple applications in common sheath	Never run voice and data applications in the same sheath.

LOSS/ATTENUATION

Attenuation is a measurement of the loss of power or signal distortion. Every 6 dB doubles the power. –10dB is four times the power of –22 dB because it is 12 dB stronger. Figure 30.4 illustrates a digital signal that has attenuated over a distance. A certain amount of attenuation is allowable for each category rating.

Figure 30.4.
Signal loss/
attenuation.

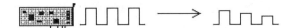

Table 30.3 provides some suggestions for troubleshooting attenuation problems.

TABLE 30.3. TROUBLESHOOTING ATTENUATION PROBLEMS.

Possible Cause of Excess Attenuation	Recommendation
Excessive length	Check with TDR; add repeater or change to a higher grade of cable if necessary.
Inadequate grade of cable	Replace cable with higher grade (Category 5 recommended).
Non-twisted patch cable	Replace with twisted pair cable.
Poor punch block connections	Check and reconnect if necessary.
Poor jack connections	Verify conductors are seated properly and check for tight wire twists right up to point of termination.
High temperature environment	Attenuation increases with temperature. If cable is subject to extreme heat (>40 C) this can severely impact performance. Remove or shield from heat source.

CROSSED PAIRS

Crossed pairs are a typical installation problem that is easily detected with a cable tester that includes a wire map function. (See Figure 30.5.) In this example, pins 1 and 2 have been crossed, which results in the inability to communicate.

Figure 30.5.
Crossed pairs (1-2
crossed, 3-4 okay).

SPLIT PAIRS

Although crossed pairs are relatively easy to find, split pairs are a bit trickier. Split pairs occur when physical continuity is maintained but wires from logical pairs are split up. (See Figure 30.6.) This error is much tougher to isolate because there is still a pin-to-pin correspondence. A wire map test would show no problem. However, with split pairs, all the benefits of twisting are lost, and Category 5 cables degrade to Category 2 performance very quickly. Split-paired cabling might support 10Base-T for short distances, but the additional NeXT that is induced will severely limit high speed communications.

Figure 30.6.
Split pairs (1-2/3-6
split).

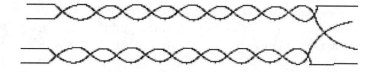

Split pairs are best found by measuring Near End Crosstalk. If you are using data grade components and get a NeXT result of less than 22 dB, suspect split pairs.

CONNECTOR PROBLEMS

All 8-pin modular jacks are not the same. Careful inspection will reveal there are two main types: those designed to work with solid-core UTP and those designed to work with stranded UTP. (See Figure 30.7.) In the solid-core design, the blade in the pin connection is split into two tines, which can firmly grasp the solid wire. In the stranded wire design, the blade is designed to pierce the strand. If you use the wrong type of connector, you will probably get an intermittent connection.

Figure 30.7.
Solid core versus
stranded modular
8-jacks.

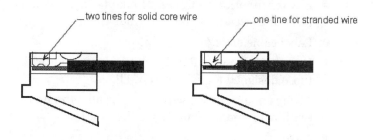

Modular 8-pin jacks are also designed for flat (silver satin) and twisted pair wire. The jack for silver satin has a smaller, flatter opening for the cabling. You will not be able to easily get the outer jacket of a twisted pair cable into this type of jack, and therefore, you will need to strip back more of the outer jacket than allowed. Also, your crimp will not hold properly, resulting in an intermittent connection.

Note

You should always use Category 5 rated connectors and wire blocks, even if you use Category 3 cabling. Category 5 connectors are generally easier to put on and in most cases provide a positive connection.

TERMINATION PRACTICES

Physical continuity does not guarantee high-speed performance. Using old style telephone wire installation techniques with data-grade cabling and components gives you voice-grade performance. For example, in voice applications, it's okay to strip off three inches of insulation, pull the wires apart for easy access, and then connect them to the punch block or wall plate. Such techniques will clobber an intended Category 5 installation and might not even certify at Category 3.

Note

EIA/TIA 568A requires all terminations to have no more than 13 mm (0.5 inches) of untwisted wire at *any* location on the LAN.

UTP INSTALLATION TIPS

You will save yourself future LAN down time if you use the following UTP installation guidelines:

◆ Buy the best UTP you can afford.

◆ Buy termination equipment (modular 8 jacks, punch blocks, and so on) that meet or exceed the quality of your cable.

◆ Label cable ends.

◆ Do not mix up modular 8 jacks designed to work with stranded UTP with those designed for solid-core UTP.

◆ Always maintain the wire twist for all pairs up to the points of termination (within 13 mm for Category 5 installations).

◆ Never share voice and data applications in the same cable.

- Always terminate voice and data cables into different punch blocks or racks.
- Strive to minimize the number of connections between the network card and LAN devices.
- Use a minimum bend radius of ten times the cable diameter.
- Tie and dress cables neatly.
- Never use bridged taps (multiple appearances of the same cable pair at several distribution points).
- Allow at least one square foot of closet floor space for every 250 square feet of usable floor space.
- Allow for sufficient cooling and air flow in the wire closet.
- Put a lock on the wire closet and use it.
- On multi-floor installations, locate the wiring closet where there is common vertical access, preferably in a location less than 100 meters (328 feet) from the furthest user connection. The location is often near the center of the floor, which helps ensure cable distances don't exceed the maximum. AT&T research has shown that 99 percent of the time user stations are located 93 meters or less from a wiring closet.
- Install sufficient power outlets for future unanticipated equipment.
- Be sure you have permission to work in the wiring closet. In some buildings, the owners of the closet are not the tenants.
- Do not use old type 66 blocks (voice grade, which exhibits high frequency attenuation and poor NeXT). Instead, use type 110 (Category 5—data grade) blocks.
- Do not use screw type terminations. Use clip or barrel IDC (insulation displacement contact) connections such as those used in type 110 blocks.
- Pay very careful attention to termination practices. Maintain a tight wire twist up to the point of termination at punch blocks, wire plates, and connectors.
- Check building and fire codes and follow them.
- Avoid routing cables near EMI noise sources, such as florescent light fixtures, motors, and AC power lines. Never pull LAN cabling through the same holes or conduit with other electrical cable.
- Use the same cable throughout. Avoid mixing up cabling from different manufacturers in the same installation.
- Keep patch cables as short as possible, and choose Category 5 patch cable if possible.

◆ Do not use silversatin (untwisted flat ribbon) patch cables, especially from the wall plate to the network adapter card.

◆ Insist the installation be tested with equipment that meets or exceeds the requirements for the installation, and get a certification report for each cable. A toner or DMM is insufficient. Such tools tell you nothing about the cable's capability to reliably transfer high speed data.

FIBER OPTIC CABLE

Fiber optic cabling has a far lower incidence of trouble than copper cabling, principally because it is usually found only on the backbone or in well protected areas. Fiber optic troubleshooting is done with either a power meter, which measures attenuation, or an Optical TDR, which measures distance and finds faults. Aside from catastrophic failures (such as those caused by your friendly neighborhood backhoe), most fiber optic problems are due to poor quality splices and connections, which you can find using a power meter.

Note

Fiber optic cabling is no longer significantly more expensive than Category 5 UTP. Optical fiber termination has become more afford-able with new tools that have been developed. Check with your cabling vendor before deciding that optical fiber is too expensive.

What is expensive about fiber optics is the electronics on board network interface cards, wiring concentrators, and repeater links.

CABLE TROUBLESHOOTING TOOLS

Cable troubleshooting tools fall into three broad classes with increasing price and capability:

◆ Continuity testers

◆ Troubleshooting tools

◆ Certification devices

Each of these types of devices are discussed in the following section.

CONTINUITY TESTERS

The simplest cable troubleshooting tools are toners and continuity checkers. These are generally less than $100 and verify end-to-end connectivity and continuity, and in some cases, they can check for crossed pairs. A simple cable continuity tester has two RJ-45s and four lights, one for each pair.

A continuity tester is the primary tool an installer uses to make sure he has put the ends on correctly. It will tell you that your cable is pinned out correctly and there is good continuity. The cable should be okay, providing you have used the right cable, it does not exceed length specifications, and there are no bad connection points or EMI sources.

There are many manufacturers of continuity testers including Paladin, Progressive Electronics, and the Siemon Company. They are available from the catalog supply companies. Probably the most popular tool in this class is the ubiquitous toner from Progressive Electronics. These are useful tools for simple troubleshooting but are inadequate to diagnose many hidden problems on LANs.

TROUBLESHOOTING TOOLS

Cable testers for troubleshooting are virtually a requirement wherever new cabling is added periodically or cabling is subject to abuse. This class of tool includes the functionality of the previous group but adds TDR, attenuation and NeXT measurement, and the intelligence to interpret most results. Prices range from around $500 to $2,500, but compared to cost of LAN down time, they are a bargain.

Cable testers test the characteristics of the signal for a given LAN application and simply pass or fail the cable. Older models provide only raw data that you must interpret. Newer models always calculate data to a pass/fail decision.

In many cases, the number being measured has to be compared to the length of the cable being tested at the signaling rate to be used (for example, 47 meters of cable at 100 MHz). The testing parameters are stated per 1,000 feet, so you can quickly become involved in an extensive mathematical project if not for the cable tester.

Most newer cable testers are generally easy to use, lightweight, and portable. Most cable testers today feature one-button testing for most common LANs, digital information readout, and rechargeable batteries. Common manufacturers include Microtest, Fluke, and Wavetek. These products are generally available from electronics retailers, cabling resellers, and large networking product distributors. The Microtest MT350 is a good choice in this class of tools.

Note

Given that cable faults account for over 50 percent of all LAN failures, a cable troubleshooting or certification tool is an essential first line of defense for any LAN greater than 25 nodes. Continuity testers tell you nothing about the cable's capability to successfully transmit *high speed* data. Many users are surprised to find cable scanners often pay for themselves within their first 30 days.

CERTIFICATION TOOLS

Cable certification is required when you need to be sure that the cable you intend to use will work for the intended application. Cable certification tools rate the cable segment's usefulness for the intended purpose, and (for twisted pair) assigns a category classification for the entire length of the segment, including connections. Proper cable certification ensures that the cable will support the type of LAN and signaling rate for which it was tested.

Cable can be certified in either a category classification (such as Category 5) or whether the installation is suitable for a specific LAN application (such as 100Base-T). When you perform cable certification, a test tool runs a prescribed series of tests, stores the results, compares each result to its particular pass/fail parameter for that measurement, and then provides an overall pass/fail and Category rating. Many devices can attach to a PC, upload test results, and provide extensive reports including specific raw and interpreted data. Others hook up to a printer and print out test results. Many have extensive programmable features and support all types of cable used in LAN installations.

Cable certification tools are actually the best cable troubleshooting tools because they take all the effort and analysis out of the test. They can ensure that your cabling will work for your intended purpose (such as Fast Ethernet). You run one test, and then the tester either indicates that the cable is okay for the application or explains exactly why it failed. Such tools eliminate the guesswork of which test to run or how to interpret the results.

Certification tools include the functionality of the previous group of simpler cable testers but add the additional measurements and extended range needed to completely certify LANs or cables. Prices have fallen significantly in recent years, and very good cable testers now range from $500 to $5,000 in price. They are available from the same sorts of suppliers as the previous group. The most popular cable testers are sold by Microtest, Fluke, StarTeck, Hewlett-Packard, and many others.

The PentaScanner from Microtest is capable of full Category 1-5 certification at 100 MHz. It also offers LAN monitoring and includes all the troubleshooting tests needed for Ethernet, Token ring, Fast Ethernet, 100VG, ARCnet, CDDI, and many other types of LANs. The PentaScanner is also available in optical fiber varieties. Optical fiber scanners are more expensive.

Tip

When you are having cabling installed, you should have your cabling certified by an independent third party with a high quality cable certification tool. The cable should be certified at the intended signaling rate (for example, 100 MHz). Cable can rate Category 5 at 10 MHz but rate only Category 4 or 3 at 100 MHz.

At the outset of your contract, you can usually retain part of your final payment until the cable has been certified to your specifications. For example, if you have a contractor install Category 5 cable and connectors, ask a separate cabling technician to test each cable. Once each cable certifies Category 5 end-to-end, release the final payment. This common practice is called "retention billing" in the building industry. Under Uniform Commercial Code legal practices, you are entitled to fitness of intended purpose. Cable certification is the quantitative measure of such fitness.

THE LAN LAYER

The LAN layer is represented by the Ethernet, Token ring, or other type of LAN frame. Information at this level is pretty elementary and only pertains to the operation of the LAN and delivery to a specific MAC address (node address). Information gleaned from this layer can reveal the following:

- ◆ Malfunctioning or improperly configured network cards
- ◆ Driver software or driver configuration
- ◆ Frame type not matching between server and clients

The LAN layer has a sublayer that is used by complex bridges, such as Token ring source-route bridges, Logical Link Control (LLC), and SubNetwork Access Protocol (SNAP) bridges. It is generally identified as the 802.2 (LLC) layer by most protocol analyzers.

Because Ethernet and Token ring account for the vast majority of installed LANs, I devote separate sections to each one. Analysis of Ethernet, Fast Ethernet, and 100VG are pretty similar. Analysis of Token ring and FDDI are very similar. You must have a protocol analyzer capable of analyzing your specific type of LAN.

ETHERNET PROTOCOL ANALYSIS

Ultimately, the only way to definitely know where the problem is in a LAN is to use a protocol analyzer. This type of device captures the frames circulating on a LAN for analysis. It also reports error statistics and identifies the nodes involved in the errors.

Because the access protocol and the frame formats in Ethernet are so simple, there is little error control, recovery, or reporting built in to Ethernet. Most of this job must be handled by monitoring devices or protocol analysis. Using a protocol analyzer can pinpoint exactly where a problem occurs; however, interpretation of error statistics is most important because the errors are so general in nature.

The factors you should look for in analyzing an Ethernet LAN are:

◆ Consistent frame format between clients and servers

◆ Frames that are too short

◆ Frames that are too long

Error levels that you should monitor include:

◆ Collisions

◆ Bandwidth utilization (percentage of available bandwidth in use)

◆ Cyclic Redundancy Check (CRC) error rate per second

◆ Short frame error rate per second

You must interpret these incidents, levels, and error rates in context of what is occurring at the time and what level is acceptable. Each type of protocol analyzer reports these levels; however, few of them identify, first, whether the level indicates a problem is present and, second, why the problem is occurring.

Each of these errors and levels are discussed in the following sections.

ETHERNET FRAME FORMATS

There are four different formats for Ethernet frames. The frame format is configured when the network adapter driver is installed. If two computers attempt to communicate, they must use the same frame format or the attempt will fail.

When you're installing Windows for Workgroups (WFW), Windows 95, or NT network adapter drivers, Setup asks for the frame type. If a frame type is not already in use, Setup suggests using the Ethernet 802.2 frame type. You also have the option to install all frame types. Although this certainly resolves the problem of incompatible frame format, it is not the most preferred method of handling the problem because it makes your protocol bindings needlessly complex.

The four frame types shown in Figure 30.8 are described as follows:

◆ Ethernet II—This frame format is the original Ethernet II specification format defined by Digital, Intel, and Xerox. IEEE's 802.3 workgroup redefined the frame format. It is very similar to the other frame formats but differs in two ways: it has no LLC or SNAP header, and the two-byte field used to define the length of the encapsulated data packet in other formats is used to define the type of data packet.

◆ Ethernet 802.3—This frame format is identical to the 802.2 frame except it does not include the LLC protocol header information. This frame format was never officially sanctioned by the 802.3 workgroup and is therefore used less often.

◆ Ethernet 802.2—This frame format is the same as the 802.3 frame but includes a Logical Link Control (LLC) protocol data unit header, which is used in certain types of bridges. This is the IEEE 802.3 officially approved frame format. Even if the LLC header information is not used, this frame format will work just fine, as long as other nodes also use it.

◆ Ethernet SNAP—This frame format includes a SubNetwork Access Protocol data unit header in place of the LLC header. The Internet Engineering Task Force (IETF) defined SNAP for use in bridges to be used with TCP/IP and connected to the Internet. SNAP defines extensions to LLC and is very similar. This is the most commonly used frame format for TCP/IP vendors. It is also the frame format required in Apple Phase II EtherTalk networks.

As you can see, you should simply use the same frame format throughout your network. Microsoft and NetWare nodes can use any frame format; however, you might find that other systems require a specific frame format. In that case, configure your Microsoft and NetWare nodes to the same frame format, or install support for multiple frame formats in your Microsoft and NetWare nodes.

You can use a protocol analyzer to find out exactly which frame formats are in use on your network. Every Ethernet protocol analyzer reports the frame format for each frame. Figure 30.9 shows the Wandel & Goltermann Domino analyzer reporting frame formats. Each protocol analyzer works differently, but you will find that each enables you to configure a view that depicts the frame formats.

The media access protocol used by Ethernet (CSMA/CD) is very dependent on good cabling for error control. Collision detection depends on the length of cable, characteristics of the cabling and connections, configuration of cable segments, and many other factors to control access to the bus. Even minor cabling or connector damage can cause reflections, which transceivers might perceive as (false) collisions, causing further problems. Many Ethernet vendors produce "smart" LAN devices that can detect these conditions and report them to the management software modules for your information. These are sometimes called *managed* devices.

30

LAN TROUBLESHOOTING

Figure 30.8.
Ethernet frame
formats.

Ethernet II

(Used in AppleTalk Phase I and TCP/IP vendors)

preamble	destination address	source address	type	data	pad	crc
8 bytes	6	6	2	46 - 1518		4

802.3

(used in early NetWare environments)

preamble	destination address	source address	length	data	pad	crc
7 + 1 bytes	6	6	2	46 - 1518		4

802.2

(802.3 standard, used in later NetWare and TCP/IP environments)

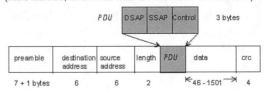

| | PDU | DSAP | SSAP | Control | | 3 bytes |

preamble	destination address	source address	length	PDU	data	crc
7 + 1 bytes	6	6	2		46 - 1501	4

SNAP

(used in AppleTalk Phase II and Internet Community)

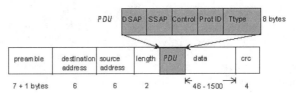

| | PDU | DSAP | SSAP | Control | Prot ID | Ttype | 8 bytes |

preamble	destination address	source address	length	PDU	data	crc
7 + 1 bytes	6	6	2		46 - 1500	4

You can monitor several conditions to determine what types of errors might be reducing performance or interrupting communications on your Ethernet LAN. Each one is discussed in the following sections.

COLLISIONS AND BANDWIDTH UTILIZATION

On a busy Ethernet LAN, it is common to experience collisions when two or more network cards attempt to transmit at the same time. Collisions cannot be avoided on Ethernet LANs because CSMA/CD is a demand-based contention access protocol. Although collisions are considered normal for Ethernet LANs, excessive collisions reduce the overall throughput of the network. So how much is too much?

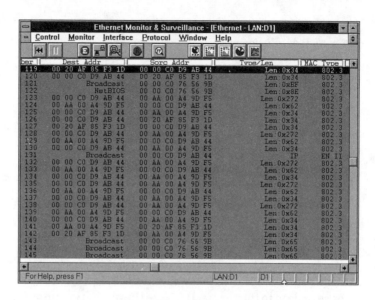

Figure 30.9.
Wandel &
Goltermann's Domino
showing frame formats.

The number of collisions is directly related to bandwidth utilization, as shown in Figure 30.10. Bandwidth utilization is expressed as a percentage of theoretical capacity (10 Mbps for Ethernet). With less than 25-percent bandwidth utilization, the probability of a collision is low. As bandwidth utilization increases, or as long cable plants are used, the likelihood of generating collisions increases exponentially. Depending on cabling conditions, collisions can make the network unusable at somewhere between 60 to 90 percent of theoretical bandwidth utilization. Even the best and shortest cable plant cannot handle levels higher than about 90 percent of theoretical bandwidth utilization.

Note

Because not every cable plant is capable of reaching the theoretical high bandwidth utilization of 90 percent, you should not expect your LAN to perform as well as some benchmark tests you might have seen in magazines, which are run under ideal conditions. Normal conditions generally limit Ethernet LANs to between 60 and 75 percent utilization.

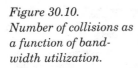

Figure 30.10.
Number of collisions as
a function of band-
width utilization.

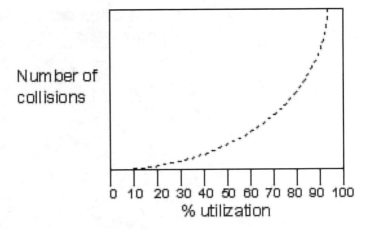

It is important to realize that LAN utilization is not a constant factor. It is by nature very "bursty" because users might decide at any time to retrieve information from or save data to the server. Because this activity is unpredictable, it is difficult for you to determine if excessive traffic is causing a problem. To compensate for this possibility, a figure of 25 to 30-percent bandwidth utilization is considered an acceptable level. At about 70 to 80 percent bandwidth utilization, your LAN generally becomes fully saturated.

Usually you can tell when the LAN is extremely busy based on the response time observed at a workstation; however, this does not identify the source of excessive network load. Also, under normal conditions, global collisions on a LAN cannot be detected at any single network card. Each network card's firmware is designed to only listen to frames addressed specifically to it or to those that are addressed as a broadcast. Some wiring concentrators have collision-indicator LEDs, whereas some simply have no indication of collision counts.

Note

A wiring concentrator is an excellent listening device for collisions because network interface cards can only detect collisions in which they are involved. A wiring concentrator can detect collisions anywhere on a physical LAN to which it is attached. Many wiring concentrators have collision LEDs or an SNMP agent that reports collision levels.

Many "intelligent" wiring concentrators contain a monitoring agent that listens for various potential error conditions. It then reports them to a software-management module running at a console located somewhere on the LAN. Many use an out-of-bandwidth serial port on the wiring concentrator to enable communications even if the LAN goes down. These devices generally use Simple Network Management Protocol (SNMP) to report problems to vendor-specific software modules.

Warning

> To determine if a condition is unusual, it is necessary to understand what the "normal" condition is. All LANs are unique in their configurations. What is normal for one network might not be considered normal for another.

You need to *baseline* the normal activity for your network. Baseline information relates to bandwidth utilization and should contain data to help you answer the following questions:

◆ What is the bandwidth utilization as a function of time over a normal working day and throughout the week?

◆ What types of protocols are using the bandwidth?

◆ Which users are taking up most of the bandwidth?

One of the standard baselining recommendations is to monitor your LAN over a long period of time to gather statistically significant information. For best results, perform this over a period of at least one month, so you can gather information on processes that happen only once a week or once a month. This information also can help you in planning for network growth.

Bandwidth utilization is, therefore, a good indicator of collision likelihood. When you're monitoring an Ethernet LAN, you should be concerned with a bandwidth utilization level of 30 percent or higher. As bandwidth utilization increases, the likelihood of collisions increases exponentially. Frequent high utilization levels indicate that too much demand is placed on the LAN, which can lead to excessive collisions and throughput degradation. When high levels of bandwidth utilization are frequently encountered, it is recommended that you *segement* your LAN. You can do this by breaking it into separate physical LANs connected to multiple network cards in the server or by using bridges or routers.

Tip

> When doing baselining or examining bandwidth utilization, you should take into account how your particular business operates. For example, if yours is an accounting firm, high utilization can be expected during month ends and tax-return time. You should have a number of different baselines for different periods of your business year.

30

LAN TROUBLESHOOTING

LOCAL AND REMOTE COLLISIONS

When looking at the statistics from Ethernet LAN monitors, you will see counters for local collisions and remote collisions. Local collisions are collisions that occur on the local cabling segment, whereas remote collisions are separated by a repeater (including a wiring concentrator).

Collisions are detected by the collision-detection circuitry in the network interface card's transceiver (or external transceiver). As a result of a collision, collision fragments appear on the cable. A collision fragment is less than 64 bytes in length and has an invalid CRC.

Note

There is some confusion in the industry about referring to a frame or a packet. In this book, the frame is the LAN protocol unit (Ethernet, Token ring, and so on) that contains a packet. The packet is the transport protocol unit packet (NetBIOS, NetBEUI, IPX, or IP) that is encapsulated in the frame.

A frame includes the LAN header, the packet, and the trailer but excludes the preamble.

Remote collisions occur on the other side of a repeater (or other cabling segments connected to the wiring concentrator). A remote collision is assumed when a collision fragment is detected without triggering the collision-detection circuitry. Repeaters only repeat bits and therefore pass on collision fragments to all connected cabling segments, whereas bridges and routers do not. Table 30.4 compares local and remote collisions.

TABLE 30.4. COMPARISON OF LOCAL AND REMOTE COLLISIONS.

Collision Type	Frame Size	Bad CRC?	CD Pair Triggered?
Local	Less than 64 bytes	Yes	Yes
Remote	Less than 64 bytes	Yes	No

Ethernet network cards recover from detected collisions by resending the frames that were involved in collisions. What is an acceptable collision level? Depending on the type of work done, the network can reach various collision levels before noticeable performance degradation occurs. The network has reached an unacceptable threshold level whenever you get user complaints. The general rule of thumb for an acceptable level is that your collision count should be no more than 5 percent of the total transmitted packets.

When you are troubleshooting excessive collision problems, it is important also to look at the bandwidth utilization. This information helps you to determine whether the excessive collisions are due to an overloaded LAN or a faulty component. If bandwidth utilization and collision counts are both high, then it is likely the collisions are a result of higher traffic volume on the LAN. One possible solution is to segment traffic using bridges or routers.

If collision counts are high while bandwidth utilization remains normal, then it is possible that your cable segment length exceeds the maximum allowed by specifications, there are faults in your cabling, or there are violations of repeaters in series rule. You should have no more than four repeaters in series for 10Base-T, no more than two repeaters in series for 100Base-T, and no more than one repeater in series for 100Base-T4.

Under these conditions, devices at the far end of the cable might consider the cable to be free when in fact a frame is on the wire. Because the frame on the wire might not have propagated throughout the cabling system, devices at the far end could continue to transmit, thus causing a collision. If the cabling length is past specifications or too many repeaters are used, the collision might even go undetected. This results in the loss of frames, requiring a higher-level network protocol (normally SMB) to detect the loss of data and resend it.

Tip

If you observe a high number of remote collisions, it is an indication that the cabling segment on the other side of the repeater is experiencing high local collisions. To reduce the amount of remote collisions reaching your local cabling segment, isolate your cabling segment from the remote and then troubleshoot for the cause of high collision counts on that remote cabling segment.

Note

A LAN with multiple cabling segments connected by repeaters should have about the same amount of traffic on all cabling segments because all traffic is "repeated" and not filtered. If one cabling segment is showing more collisions than others, it might be the result of faulty hardware on that particular cabling segment.

SIGNAL QUALITY ERROR (SQE)

Sometimes false collisions are caused by the presence of a Signal Quality Error (SQE—also known as "heartbeat") signal when it is not required. Ethernet Version

2.0 transceivers send a SQE signal through the collision-detection pair back to the network card right after each frame is sent to verify that the collision-detection circuitry is working. Ethernet Version 1.0 transceivers do not do this. Most network cards in use today do not support this feature. As a result, using SQE with such a network card causes the network card to think there is a collision when there isn't one.

A repeater is not designed to recognize SQE; therefore, whenever you use a repeater (or wiring concentrator), SQE must be disabled. This is usually done through a dip switch or a jumper. If SQE is not disabled, the repeater interprets this signal as a collision, and according to the specifications, it generates a jam (62 bits on the wire to guarantee devices on that segment recognize a collision). Jamming is used for *jabber control*, which prevents a busy node from dominating the LAN. With SQE enabled, the jam sequence is sent after each frame transmitted on the LAN, and a significant amount of bandwidth is consumed needlessly, potentially affecting all others' performance.

Warning

When using external transceivers, disable SQE.

LATE COLLISIONS, CRC, AND ALIGNMENT ERRORS

When a frame of a size between 64 and 1518 bytes with an invalid CRC is detected, the condition is known as a *late collision*. This collision also fires the collision-detection circuitry in the network card if it happens on the local segment and cannot be distinguished from a normal collision. If a bad CRC is detected without the network card's collision-detection circuitry firing, then the condition is called a CRC error, and it is assumed to have occurred on a remote segment.

Usually a frame ends on an 8-bit (or byte) boundary. For example, one does not usually get a frame that is 75 bytes and 2 bits long. If a frame does not end on an 8-bit boundary, an alignment error has occurred. By convention, both CRC errors and alignments are grouped together as CRC/alignment errors during reporting.

Unlike local and remote collisions, which are normal for Ethernet LANs, bad CRCs, alignment errors, and late collisions are not healthy symptoms. They are usually caused by hardware problems, such as faulty cabling or network cards. Some of the most common causes include the following:

◆ A cable segment that is too long.

◆ Improper termination.

- Spacing between taps that is less than the recommended minimum (a common error in 10Base2 and 10Base5 environment).
- Noisy cable due to induced electromagnetic interference from nearby sources, such as florescent lights and the motors in ceiling fans.
- Improper grounding of the cabling segment, resulting in ground-loop.
- Network card failure to detect a collision or frame on the wire. Such a node is sometimes known as a *deaf node*.

Tip

When running cables, do not push the maximum allowable distance. A rule of thumb is to use about 80 percent of recommended maximum distance. This allows for signal loss because of noise on the wire.

Warning

For long coaxial cable runs, make sure only one end of the cable is grounded. Grounding both ends, especially to different grounds, might cause ground loops (and data corruption as a result).

FRAGMENTED FRAMES

Frame fragments are less than 64 bytes in size with an invalid CRC. They usually result from local or remote collisions. There are always some fragment frames on your LAN because collision is unavoidable in Ethernet; however, the number of fragmented frames should be less than 10 percent of your overall frames. Otherwise, your LAN is approaching saturation and should be segmented into separate LANs.

ILLEGAL LENGTH FRAMES AND JABBERS

A legal Ethernet frame must be between 64 bytes and 1518 bytes in length. If a frame is less than 64 bytes in length and contains a valid CRC, it is known as a short frame or a *runt*. A frame that is longer than 1518 bytes and has a valid CRC is known as a *long frame*. These illegal frames are usually caused by faulty drivers. Updating to the latest version of the driver should cure these problems.

A *jabber* is a frame that is over 1518 bytes in length with an invalid CRC. This is usually caused by a faulty transceiver. By design, a transceiver can only transmit for 150 milliseconds, long enough to transmit 1518 bytes. If the transceiver does not stop after transmitting 1518 bytes, a jabber condition has occurred.

Tip

> If you suspect a jabbering node, check the transmit light on the
> network card or transceiver to see if it's lit continuously.

Opposite of a deaf node is a *chatty node*. This is when a transceiver or network card goes on and on generating any one of several types of signals that then get interpreted as collisions. This could bring the whole LAN to a grinding halt because no other device can transmit.

This section defined various Ethernet frame errors, as summarized in Table 30.5. Understanding how they occur helps you to better monitor your LAN and set alarm thresholds to manage these errors before they degrade your network communications.

TABLE 30.5. VARIOUS ETHERNET ERROR TYPES AND THEIR CONDITIONS.

Error Type	Error Condition
Local collision	Less than 64 bytes
	Bad CRC
	Collision-Detection (CD) pair triggered
Remote collision	Less then 64 bytes
	Bad CRC
	CD pair *not* triggered
Late collision	Between 64 and 1518 bytes
	Bad CRC
	CD pair *may* be triggered
CRC error	Between 64 and 1518 bytes
	Bad CRC
	CD pair not triggered
Alignment error	Between 64 and 1518 bytes
	Bad CRC
	Does not end on 8-bit boundary
Short frame (runt)	Less than 64 bytes
	Good CRC
Long frame	More than 1518 bytes
	Good CRC
Jabber	More than 1518 bytes
	Bad CRC

Token Ring Analysis

Token-passing ring access protocol has many built-in self-management features. These are effected through MAC frames (a token is one type of MAC frame; there are 52 different MAC frame types). Some types of MAC frames provide recovery from ring troubles such as the loss of Active Monitor, the loss or corruption of frames or tokens, and intermittent hardware faults. They also provide constant updating of upstream neighbor's addresses, which is essential in the isolation of a fault domain during troubleshooting processes.

To facilitate self-management, Token ring architecture specifies five *functional stations*.

- Active Monitor
- Standby Monitor
- Ring Parameter Server
- Ring Error Monitor
- Configuration Report Server (also known as Network Manager)

Functional stations are special "software" devices that take on specific station functions. Active and Standby Monitor functions are built into each network card as part of the chip set functions. The remaining three are all enabled through special software (such as the IBM LAN Manager software). These three stations do not have to exist on a ring in order for the ring to function. The following is a brief description of their functions:

- **Active Monitor** provides master clocking for the ring and ensures the presence of a token. Usually, it is the first active device on the ring.

- **Standby Monitor** is any device that is not an Active Monitor. They ensure that there is an Active Monitor on the ring.

- **Ring Parameter Server** provides parameter settings for devices at the time of insertion into the ring.

- **Ring Error Monitor** is a central "console" for collecting errors from other ring devices.

- **Configuration Report Server (Network Manager)** keeps track of the current ring configuration and controls individual network card parameters, such as various timers.

There are two types of errors in the token ring protocol: soft errors and hard errors. *Soft errors* are intermittent errors from which the ring can generally recover without disrupting ring functionality. Some *hard errors* might be resolved by the use of Media Control MAC frames, whereas some might require manual intervention.

30

LAN Troubleshooting

In this section, I examine some of the most important Media Control MAC frames in Token ring. I also look at the most common causes of soft errors. You see how they can help you diagnose the health of your rings and find a cure for problems.

RING POLL

Every seven seconds, the Active Monitor initiates a ring poll process to perform the following tasks:

1. Inform all Standby Monitors that an Active Monitor is present.
2. Inform all ring devices that the ring is functioning properly.
3. Enable ring devices to update the address of their Nearest Active Upstream Neighbor (NAUN).

This process happens regardless of whether there is any traffic on the ring (except when the ring is beaconing). In IBM terminology, this is known as the Neighbor Notification process.

Warning

If you cannot detect the ring poll process occurring every seven seconds, you have a serious token-passing ring protocol problem. If this is happening on your ring, locate the Active Monitor because it is likely that it has a faulty network card or that its Active Monitor Timer has been changed. If you do not correct this, you might notice many MAC frames of the Active Monitor Present and Neighbor Notification Incomplete type and possibly a nonfunctioning ring. This condition is rare.

Tip

You can determine the physical order (as connected into the MSAU) of the Token ring devices based on the ring poll frames. This is useful information to have when troubleshooting (see the section titled *Beaconing*) and for documentation purposes.

RING RECONFIGURATION

Each Token ring device keeps track of the hardware MAC address of its nearest active upstream neighbor (NAUN). This is usually learned from the ring poll MAC frames; however, when a new device is inserted into or removed from the ring, a Ring Change frame is sent by its immediate downstream neighbor to the ring error monitor. Usually, the number of such frames are small. They occur in the morning when users turn on their workstations, over lunch period when people power off/on their machines, and at the end of the working day when workstations are powered off.

Tip

> If you notice a large number of ring change MAC frames outside of the normal hours, it is likely that you have one or more Token ring devices constantly inserting and deinserting from the ring. Check for possible faulty wiring, hardware, or LAN drivers. Use a protocol analyzer, such as the ones described in this chapter to isolate the faulty device.

RING PURGES

When the Active Monitor detects a lost token or frame, it must determine if the ring is functioning properly before releasing a new token. The way the Active Monitor checks the general health of the LAN is by transmitting purge frames. They are transmitted in 4-millisecond intervals for up to one second. As soon as the Active Monitor receives back just one uncorrupted purge frame, it assumes the ring is healthy and releases a free token. This is the first step taken by the token-passing ring access protocol in trying to recover from a hard error.

Tip

> There will always be a small amount of purge frames on your ring. They are usually caused by stations entering and leaving the ring. If you detect a constant stream of purge frames on your ring, you are having an intermittent physical problem with cables, connections, MSAUs, or network cards. You will also notice that the performance of your LAN grinds to a halt.

If the Active Monitor does not receive an uncorrupted purge frame within one second, the ring goes into ring recovery.

RING RECOVERY (LOSS OF ACTIVE MONITOR)

In most Token ring protocol monitors, there is a ring recovery counter. This counter is incremented every time a monitor contention process occurs to elect a new Active Monitor. In IBM terminology, this is also known as the Claim Token process, and it happens under the following conditions:

◆ The Active Monitor does not detect an error-free purge frame within one second after it started transmitting purge frames.

30

LAN Troubleshooting

◆ The Active Monitor does not detect the completion of the ring poll process within a given time.

◆ A Standby Monitor detects the lack of a ring poll process within a given length of time (about 12 seconds).

As with ring purges, it is normal to have a few ring recoveries, but as with purge frames, they should be few and far between. This is the second stage in the Token ring physical error recovery scheme.

Warning

If you detect a constant level of purge frames, your ring is ill and you are suffering a performance hit. If the ring recovery counter is steadily increasing, your LAN is in serious trouble and you should take immediate action.

When the ring cannot complete a monitor contention process within one second, it goes into the third and final stage of hard-error recovery, a process called *beaconing*. If the error is resolved by monitor contention, a ring purge follows and the ring is back to normal operation status.

Beaconing

Beaconing is the last desperate attempt by the token-passing ring access protocol to recover from a hard error. When the ring is beaconing, the ring is nonfunctional; no new device can insert into the ring, and no user data will be transmitted by the stations. All LAN access is halted.

If the hard error is due to a faulty Token ring adapter or cable lobe, the beaconing process can usually recover the ring. Most problems that cause beaconing require manual intervention to resolve. Fortunately, the beacon MAC frame contains information indicating the cause of the error, as well as an indication of a fault domain. A *fault domain* is the area between the station reporting the beaconing and its active upstream neighbor.

Tip

Having a list of MAC addresses of Token ring network cards and their location on your ring greatly helps you in locating the physical device that is causing the beaconing. You can generate this list by examining ring poll frames.

Warning

One of the most common causes of beaconing is a loose cable at the network card end of the connection.

Probably the most common cause of beaconing on a ring is mixing Token ring network cards that are set for different speeds. You cannot have even one network card set at 4 Mbps on a 16 Mbps ring or vice versa. Most Token ring network cards are shipped with 4 Mbps as the default speed setting. Check this before installation.

If you run the IBM PS/2 Reference Disk to autoconfigure your cards, the Token ring card will be set to 4 Mbps.

Once the cause of the beaconing is resolved, the ring performs a monitor contention, followed by a ring purge, and then the ring is back to normal.

SOFT ERRORS

Soft errors are intermittent errors from which the ring can recover easily and automatically. Sometimes it is difficult to classify what is a hard error and what is a soft error. Some experts consider beaconing a hard error and everything else a soft error. Token ring protocol defines the following four types of errors:

◆ Type 1: Errors that require no recovery procedure by the ring.

◆ Type 2: Errors that are corrected by a ring purge process.

◆ Type 3: Errors that are resolved by a monitor contention.

◆ Type 4: Errors that require beaconing.

Each of these errors are generated by specific conditions.

TYPE 1 ERRORS

Typical Type 1 errors are Receiving Congestion and Frame Copied errors. Congestion errors are discussed in greater detail in the next section of this chapter. Recall from Chapter 2 the discussion of how Token ring works; when a data frame reaches the destination node, the receiving node changes two bits in the trailer (the Addresses Recognized Indicator, ARI, and the Frame Copied Indicator, FCI). A Frame Copied error occurs when a station detects a frame addressed to its specified address and either or both of the ARI and FCI bits are *already* set. This is normally caused by line noise that corrupts the frame.

TYPE 2 ERRORS

The most common Type 2 soft error is the Burst 5 error. It constitutes over 90 percent of all observed soft error counts.

30

LAN TROUBLESHOOTING

Note

A Burst 5 error is when a station detects five half-bits of the differential Manchester signal without a phase change. In other words, in five half-bit times, no data was detected. (A *bit time* is how long it takes to transmit a bit on the ring.)

Whenever a station is inserted into or removed from the ring, the integrity of the ring is temporarily broken. This causes a Burst 5 error (more commonly referred to as a Burst error). There are always a small amount of Burst errors on your ring. This is because of users turning on and off their workstations. However, the errors should usually occur only in the early morning, around noon, and in the late afternoon. If you observe a large number of Burst errors during other hours of the day, you should investigate the cause. This is because Burst errors cause ring purges, and ring purges use up a ring's bandwidth. If there is a constant level of Burst errors, there will be a constant level of ring purges, and this causes performance degradation.

Tip

Burst errors are isolating errors. When a device reports a Burst error, it includes the address of its upstream neighbor. From the address of the station reporting the Burst error and its upstream neighbor's address, you have a fault domain to troubleshoot.

A constant level of Burst error is usually due to faulty cabling or connectors.

Warning

If you observe Burst errors from *all* devices on your ring, it is very likely that your cabling system is out of specification (for example, using Type 3 cables instead of Type 1 for 16 Mbps operation).

You will also observe Lost Token and Lost Frame errors (both are Type 2 soft errors) when you detect Burst errors.

TYPE 3 ERRORS

Lost Monitor is a Type 3 error. This is reported by a Standby Monitor when it detects that the Active Monitor has left the ring. A monitor contention process is initiated to elect a new Active Monitor.

TYPE 4 ERRORS

Type 4 errors are any errors that cannot be resolved by a monitor contention and therefore lead to beaconing. It is generally agreed that a Type 4 soft error is the same as a hard error.

CONGESTION

Congestion error is one of the more common Type 1 errors. It occurs when a station detects a frame that is addressed to its specific location but has insufficient buffer or time to copy it. In most cases, it is due to a slow network card in the station.

Tip

> The network card in the file server and any bridge or router should be the fastest on the ring. Otherwise, they would be the cause of Congestion errors.

In some cases, congestion can be caused by a memory conflict in the workstation. For example, when a RAM buffer or ROM address used by the Token ring network card overlaps with an expanded or extended memory address in use, the network card's buffer space can be reduced, which in turn leads to insufficient buffer for copying frames.

TOKEN ROTATION TIME

Token rotation time is one of three basic vital sign statistics to be monitored periodically on every Token ring. The three vital signs are

◆ Token rotation time

◆ The number of purge frames

◆ The number of ring recoveries

Token rotation time is a measure (in microseconds) of how often a Token ring device detects a free token. For example, a token rotation time of 30 microseconds means that, on average, a station can capture a free token every 30 microseconds.

Tip

> There is no typical token rotation time. Every ring is different. From experience, it is observed that for a 16-Mbps ring with 386-type workstations, you can expect a token rotation time of 1 microsecond per active device on the ring. That is, if there are 20 active devices on at the time, you can expect a token rotation time of about 20 microseconds.

As the bandwidth utilization increases, token rotation time also increases. This is very similar to the principle that the amount of collision in Ethernet is a function of utilization. You will observe that token rotation time increases when ring purge, monitor contention, and (especially) beaconing processes are happening. This is because no free token is available when these processes are going on.

Tip

You should baseline your token rotation time when you think your ring is performing well. Keep an eye on this timing information to determine if your LAN usage is increasing or if you are having a ring problem.

The other two vital signs—ring purges and ring recoveries—were discussed in detail earlier in this chapter.

Warning

As the three vital-sign counters increase, it is an indication that your ring is having problems. Resolve them before your ring beacons.

ANALYZING NETBIOS

NetBIOS is used in all Microsoft networks as a virtual circuit management layer protocol. A virtual circuit management protocol establishes a virtual circuit where a receiver is listening for the sender's message. Just as a telephone conversation must be preceded by a dial tone, dialing, and then a physical circuit establishment, a virtual circuit using NetBIOS precedes all data exchanges between clients and servers. NetBIOS performs this function in all Microsoft configurations regardless of which transport protocol is used. Once the connection has been established and share information is checked, data can flow between nodes.

The following problems occur due to errors at this protocol level:

◆ Failed logon requests

◆ Failure to access a share

◆ Excessive delays when accessing a network resource

◆ Message transfer failure

◆ General poor performance

Using a protocol analyzer, you can check for NetBIOS broadcasts when a client accessed a share, such as when the client enters File Manager. Whenever a share is accessed, the client sends out a NetBIOS request to which computers set up to share their file systems respond with distribution share information.

NetBIOS packets are encapsulated into LAN frames for transport over the LAN. NetBIOS packets are never used to transport data in later Microsoft networks; the packet header contains codes that communicate NetBIOS information between clients and servers.

ANALYZING TRANSPORT PROTOCOLS

The transport protocol carries higher layer protocol information (and sometimes data) from the sender to the receiver. The transport protocol packet header is appended to the higher layer protocol packet and encapsulated into the LAN frame for delivery on the LAN as shown in Figure 30.11. Before the transport protocol packet can be sent, a virtual connection must be established by NetBIOS.

Figure 30.11.
Transport protocol
encapsulated into LAN
frame for delivery.

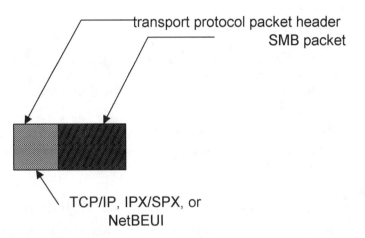

transport protocol packet header
SMB packet

TCP/IP, IPX/SPX, or
NetBEUI

In a Microsoft network, the transport layer can be implemented with IPX/SPX, TCP/IP, or NetBEUI protocols. In a Microsoft network, evaluating these packet headers is normally fruitless, and when it's performing properly, examining the layer elicits nothing but yawns. The connection mechanics generally used with these protocols is replaced by NetBIOS. Many of the errors you would watch for are therefore not applicable in a Microsoft network. What is left is a simple transport of NetBIOS or SMB packets from source to destination.

This layer is sandwiched between the LAN frame and the NetBIOS or SMB packet headers. The Network utility handles the task of installing and configuring these protocols and their bindings. Problems that relate to the transport protocol layer are therefore rarely encountered.

If you have configured servers and clients to communicate with the same protocols, you probably won't find too many problems at the transport layer. You usually view this layer to ensure that all nodes communicate with the same protocol. TCP/IP is more complex, so when there are transport problems, there are more problems to troubleshoot than there is for IPX or NetBEUI.

The following problems are often discovered through protocol analysis of transport protocols:

◆ Protocols not matching between server and clients

◆ Incorrect protocol configuration (common with TCP/IP)

◆ Routing information that might identify routing inefficiencies

Although the protocols discussed in this section encompass both the OSI Network and Transport layers, Microsoft refers to them as transport protocols or sometimes just transports.

NETBEUI

NetBEUI is the simplest of all transport mechanisms used in a Microsoft network. It is very short and specific; because virtual circuits are established by NetBIOS, all NetBEUI has to do is move a NetBIOS or SMB packet from its source to its destination.

To many analyzers, NetBEUI is simply a later version of NetBIOS. There is little to monitor on this protocol, and most documentation about its functions is contained in documents on NetBIOS.

ANALYZING IPX/SPX IN A MICROSOFT NETWORK

Novell protocols are well supported because they are the most widely used protocols. Novell uses IPX (Internetwork Packet Exchange) to communicate with routers, but it relies on NetWare Core Protocol (NCP) to do most of the transporting functions. Usually, IPX is used only for routing information.

In a Microsoft network, IPX is used to transport a NetBIOS or SMB packet to its destination. Novell's NCP is not used for any Microsoft functions. Using this protocol enables you to use external routers to move data over internetworks. It is also used in the same way as NetBEUI, simply to transport. Most of the IPX information either is not used or is also contained in the frame header. The IPX packet header enables transport over routers that can process IPX.

You use SPX (Sequenced Packet Exchange) when delivery of data must be verified. SPX communications add an acknowledgment and checksum, which incurs additional network bandwidth and computer checksum calculations.

ANALYZING TCP/IP IN A MICROSOFT NETWORK

TCP/IP is the most widely used protocol and is considered the native protocol in NT because it is the default during installation. Usually, TCP establishes virtual circuits before each transfer of data and destroys the connection once the immediate transfer is accomplished. This function is performed by NetBIOS in a Microsoft network; therefore, only IP services are generally used.

IP contains routing information, and most information contained in the IP packet header is not important in a normal Microsoft network without routers. When IP routing is employed, many aspects of the IP protocol help you determine where packets have originated from, the route taken to arrive at the destination, how many routers the packet has transgressed, and so on. IP source and destination host addresses are contained at this layer and can be helpful in troubleshooting route establishment in an IP network with routers.

ANALYZING SMB

SMB is a proprietary Microsoft protocol that is the workhorse of Microsoft networking and used in all Microsoft network software. SMB provides access to a server's shared resources and exchanges messages between the client and the server. Every request for a file requires an exchange of protocol information to accomplish the request. Sending a print job to network printer is accomplished through an SMB session management between the client's print router and the server's printer device.

SMB is the payload that the transport protocols must deliver. Each NetBEUI, IPX/SPX, or TCP/IP packet contains an SMB packet to be delivered to its destination. As discussed previously, the transport protocol packet (containing the SMB packet) is encapsulated into the LAN frame for delivery on the LAN as shown in Figure 30.12.

Figure 30.12.
SMB packets being sent
in transport protocol
packets.

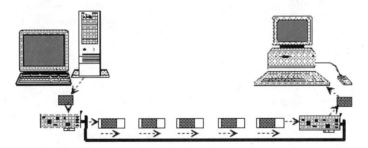

SMB packets may or may not contain data. In some cases, only SMB protocol information contained in the SMB packet header is needed to communicate with the receiver. In other cases, an SMB packet contains data, such as a file segment, that can be transported in the SMB packet data field. The packet header has the protocol information needed to tell the receiver what to do with the data; for example, to assemble it back into a message, this packet has a sequence number to make sure that the segments end up assembled in the correct order.

NetBIOS first establishes a virtual circuit, and then SMB can establish a session within the virtual circuit. A session transmits protocol information and sometimes transfers data in response to a client's request. Each session must be completed before another session can be initiated. In many cases, a session request kicks off a virtual circuit request and a series of NetBIOS broadcasts.

Figure 30.13 shows a simple file read request. An SMB request is sent (one packet with protocol information requesting a file read). The receiver (server, in this case) responds by segmenting the message (the file to be sent) into small enough segments to fit in the transport packets. It adds SMB protocol headers and then inserts the SMB packet (with the file segment) into the transport protocol header for delivery as shown in Figure 30.13. The transport protocol packet is then encapsulated into the LAN frame for delivery on the LAN.

Figure 30.13.
An SMB file
read request.

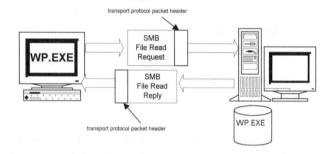

As you can see, the SMB packet is encapsulated into a transport packet (NetBEUI, IPX/SPX, or TCP/IP) which is in turn encapsulated into a LAN frame (Ethernet, Token ring, or other type of LAN frame) as shown in Figure 30.14.

Figure 30.14.
An SMB packet,
encapsulated into a
transport packet,
encapsulated into a
LAN frame.

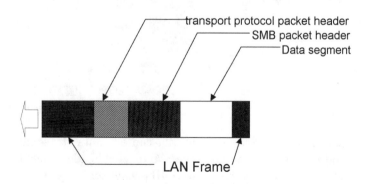

When there are problems, the search generally begins with the top layer. The absence of SMB packets in a file request generally indicates that NetBIOS has failed to set up a virtual circuit. If the connection has been established, SMB requests and replies can be traced to "listen in" on the conversation between the client and server. A plethora of problems can be related to SMB errors—too many to enumerate. However, SMB errors generally locate problems with software rather than lack of physical connectivity.

SMB analysis can turn up the following problems:

◆ Microsoft network software not configured properly (options set in the Network utility, including protocols and client services)

◆ System administration and domain problems

◆ Domain configuration and SAM corruption

◆ File access failures due to file corruption, file not found, insufficient permissions, and so on

◆ Server not responding

◆ Software bugs

Note

Microsoft has an excellent SMB help file on its Internet FTP server (`ftp.microsoft.com`). You will find SMB.ZIP, which contains SMB.HLP in the /developr/drg/SMB-info directory.

SMB is used between a computer that is using and a computer that is sharing a network resource. Upon connecting with the server, the client redirector and the server operating system negotiate the use of SMB and extensions. There are different extensions for MS-DOS, Windows 3.*x*, Windows for Workgroups, Windows 95, NT, and UNIX. As a result, SMB acts like several different protocols, having hundreds of different commands depending upon the client's and server's operating systems.

Note

In many of the technical documents about SMB, Microsoft refers to a client as a *consumer*.

30

LAN TROUBLESHOOTING

Within a NetBIOS connection, SMB creates a session, each session using a server process. For SMB to work, the following four criteria must be met:

Virtual Circuit Establishment—A virtual circuit (VC) must have been established by NetBIOS. The session uses the VC to transmit protocol information or data. The VC in use is identified in the SMB packet header.

Logon—The user account must be authenticated, and a logon presence must be established in the server (or domain controller's) logon process. During the logon, the server or domain controller issues a Tree Identification (TID). In each SMB packet header, the TID establishes that a logon has occurred, which makes the correspondence eligible for service per the limitations of the TID in the server's table.

Process—Each request for service is labeled with a Process ID (PID). This information is in the SMB packet header identifying what the nature of the request is. Processes are connection oriented; only when a process is completed can another request be issued. All process requests are issued a PID except the Negotiate request, which establishes a process. Each process is established with a client request and properly terminated with a Process Exit.

Tip

When analyzing SMB, watch client/server dialogues by tracing the establishment of a process, the dialogue between the client and server, and then the proper termination of the process.

File System—Any files that are opened are assigned a File Handle Identification (FID). This controls access to the file by referencing the file attributes, permissions, and so on. This permits sharing of files even though the client and server might have two different file systems (for example, client with a DOS FAT and server with an NTFS).

Tip

Because SMB must ensure completion of each process, if any one of these aspects fails, the VC is terminated and a VC must be reestablished. Look for this problem as an indication that one of the four processes is failing, causing loss of connection with the server.

Upon failure, you will often see a new round of NetBIOS broadcasts, a new VC, a background authentication (logon), and then a retry of the process that failed.

Summary

Troubleshooting your network can be simple or very complex. You can use simple trial-and-error methodology in locating problems, or you can use more definitive measures such as protocol analysis.

Troubleshooting your network requires you to look at the mechanics of how your network works in layers. Every type of network uses layer upon layer of protocol to move data from one computer to another transparently. A little insight about the protocol layers in your NT Server-based network helps narrow your search to the faulty component.

The protocol analysis approach to troubleshooting requires a good understanding of the protocols you are using and a good protocol analyzer. This chapter provides some simple clues about where to look for problems using protocol analysis.

- Using the Emergency Repair Disk

- Running CHKDSK

- Backing Up and Restoring the Registry and the BOOT.INI File

- Managing RAID Disk Subsystems

- RAID Levels

- NT Fault Tolerance Design

- Support for RAID Hardware Devices

- RAID Performance

CHAPTER 31

File System and Disk Subsystem Problems

Disk Adapter   A card inserted into the I/O slot of the computer that interfaces to one or more disks. It can also be referred to as a Host Bus Adapter.

Boot Partition   The disk partition that contains the NT system and utility files (that is, normally the \WINNT tree).

Controller   The electronic component attached to a disk to control the disk. SCSI disks have controllers installed on the disk.

Disk Array   Three or more partitions on separate disks used for striping, which creates a single logical drive. A disk array also contains parity data that is used to recover the data from one disk within the array if it fails. The use of multiple spindles also increases performance.

Duplexing   A mirroring technique in which each partition is on a disk attached to a different adapter.

Mirroring   Duplication of a partition on a second drive to form one redundant logical drive.

Parity Stripe   This is a stripe that contains the bit exclusive of the data on the stripes on the other disks in a disk array and is used for recovering data when there are I/O errors.

Partition   A set of sectors of a disk that are formatted to create a logical volume and assigned a driver letter.

Primary Partition   The first partition of the mirrored pair of drives. This is the partition that is created first, and the second partition is considered the mirror.

RAID   Redundant Array of Inexpensive Disks. RAID uses intelligent adapters and multiple disk drives to maximize data transfer rates.

Secondary Disk   The second partition of the mirrored pair of drives. This is the mirror of the primary partition.

Striping   Striping is a technique in which multiple partitions on separate disks are combined to create one logical disk.

System Partition   The partition that contains the files necessary to load NT (NTLDR, BOOT.INI, and so on). This partition can also be on an NTFT boot floppy.

Volume Set   This is the collection of physical partitions into a single logical drive.

Two of the worst problems you may encounter are file corruption and disk subsystem failure. File corruption can occur as a result of or independent from disk subsystem failure problems. Either or both problems are the system administrator's worst nightmare.

Disk subsystem failure may or may not be the most frequent problem you may encounter, but its repercussions are most significant. If the drive in which the operating system is installed fails, the operating system is down, and therefore the server is down. If the drive the data resides on is down, shared data is inaccessible, perhaps even lost. It may be necessary to restore backups to make the data accessible again. A restoration may cause workers to re-execute work done since the previous backup. At the very least, many hundreds of man-hours can be lost over such a small device.

File corruption occurs at the hands of malfunctioning hardware, because of user error, software errors, interruptions during update, or simply because the disk is full. File corruption renders the data inaccessible just as a failed hard drive does.

In many cases, you will be able to repair file system or Registry corruption using the Emergency Repair Disk made during installation. This disk allows you to return to the original configuration during reinstallation. The process is time-consuming, but it will restore your NT files if at all possible.

Note

The Emergency Repair Disk may help you reinstall your server without losing your device configuration or software installation and desktop.

This disk is not provided to restore your data or applications or to protect them in any way.

File corruption is most often a pretty damaging problem. When a file system becomes corrupted, repair may help save a few files. More often than not, you must reinstall NT, and then restore backups. If only a few files are corrupted, repairing them usually restores them as files—but more often than not, the files are not usable. At least they can be deleted so that a system restore can be successful.

Using the Emergency Repair Disk

The Emergency Repair Disk created during installation assists in restoring corrupted operating system files. It may be necessary to use this disk and procedure if your files have become corrupted as a result of hardware failure or software problems.

The Emergency Repair Disk is created during installation and is specific to your computer. Use only the Emergency Repair Disk that was created for the same computer, and update it whenever driver or configuration changes have been made.

The procedure may be necessary due to a file server hardware problem, but is treated like any other file damage problem.

When a disk problem occurs in a RAID disk subsystem, you will also use the Emergency Repair Disk to repair the damage. See the section of this chapter that discusses managing RAID subsystems for information about using the Emergency Repair Disk to restore a RAID subsystem.

PROCEDURE FOR USING THE EMERGENCY REPAIR DISK

You can restore your NT installation to the configuration as of the time the Emergency Repair Disk was made. To restore with this disk:

1. Start NT Setup (WINNT) the same way you did when you originally installed NT. If you used floppy disks, do so again; if you used CD-ROM, do so again.

2. The first character-based screen offers four options. Select "r" to start a restore of the installation.

3. Follow instructions as normal. You will reinstall files and have an opportunity to edit device configuration options (these options may vary with RISC-based computers).

4. When the procedure has finished, remove your Emergency Repair Disk, and reboot.

UPDATING THE EMERGENCY REPAIR DISK

You can update your Emergency Repair Disk using the RDISK.EXE utility. You can execute RDISK from the File Run menu option. The utility is shown in Figure 31.1.

Figure 31.1.
RDISK Emergency
Repair Disk utility.

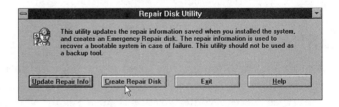

You should update this disk every time you make changes to the Registry or the BOOT.INI file. You should not write over the previous Emergency Repair Disk, as changes may corrupt the system—you may want to return to the last good configuration.

Running CHKDSK

The CHKDSK utility is normally pretty effective at fixing file and directory damage that you might encounter. Third-party utilities have not emerged yet, so hopefully CHKDSK will do the job.

CHKDSK works differently for different types of file systems. A CHKDSK run on a FAT file system works pretty much the same way that it did with DOS, but NTFS file systems get a far more thorough checkup. The following report is a typical CHKDSK screen output for an NTFS volume.

```
D:\>CHKDSK
The type of the file system is NTFS.
Warning!  F parameter not specified
Running CHKDSK in read-only mode.
CHKDSK is verifying files...
File verification completed.
CHKDSK is verifying indexes...
Index verification completed.
CHKDSK detected minor inconsistencies on the drive.
CHKDSK is verifying security descriptors...
Security descriptor verification completed.
CHKDSK discovered free space marked as allocated in the volume bitmap.

  412744 kilobytes total disk space.
  128083 kilobytes in 4078 user files.
     778 kilobytes in 70 indexes.
    8575 kilobytes in use by the system.
  275307 kilobytes available on disk.

     512 bytes in each allocation unit.
  825489 total allocation units on disk.
  550615 allocation units available on disk.
```

Note

NT does not have a SCANDISK utility. You cannot run your DOS SCANDISK on an NTFS file system. You can, however, run SCANDISK on a FAT file system by booting to DOS with a DOS disk, then running the DOS SCANDISK utility. This will not harm your file system, but if you have any Windows 95 long filenames on the volume, SCANDISK will remove the long filenames in favor of the system-substituted DOS filenames.

BACKING UP AND RESTORING THE REGISTRY AND THE BOOT.INI FILE

You should back up your Registry and other system configuration data frequently in case you need to restore it. A corrupted Registry prevents your system from working, thereby denying access to all data.

Not all tape drives back up critical NT files. A DOS backup is not capable of backing up NTFS file systems, or backing up critical NT files, such as the Registry. Your tape software and device must be compatible with NT's file system and file attributes.

You should use a backup device that is supported by Microsoft's Backup utility (in your Administrative Tools program group). This utility has an option for backing up the Registry, as shown in Figure 31.2.

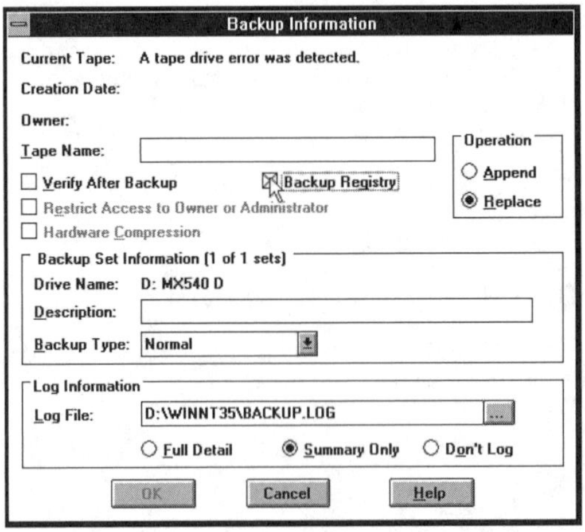

Figure 31.2.
The Microsoft Backup
utility.

Two critical file sets to back up are the BOOT.INI file, the Registry, and security-related files such as the Security Account Manager database.

THE BOOT.INI FILE

The BOOT.INI file contains configuration information that is used to run your boot menu. This file generally has the following options that appear in the boot menu:

```
Windows NT Server Version 3.51
Windows NT Server Version 3.51 w/VGA
MS-DOS
```

The BOOT.INI file is in the root of the bootable volume, normally C. A typical BOOT.INI file looks like this:

```
[boot loader]
timeout=30
default=multi(0)disk(0)rdisk(0)partition(1)\WINNT35
[operating systems]
multi(0)disk(0)rdisk(0)partition(1)\WINNT35="Windows NT Server Version 3.51"
multi(0)disk(0)rdisk(0)partition(1)\WINNT35="Windows NT Server Version 3.51 [VGA
mode]" /basevideo /sos
C:\="MS-DOS"
```

The BOOT.INI file normally does not change after the initial installation.

THE REGISTRY AND CONFIGURATION-RELATED FILES

Backing up the Registry and related security information is necessary. These files change every time you make a change to your hardware, desktop, network settings, passwords, and many more configuration options.

The user, computer, network, and configuration files are found in the \<WINROOT>\SYSTEM32\CONFIG directory. You should back up this directory regularly, especially when user or administrative changes are made. Always save the previous backup in case a later configuration proves unusable.

MANAGING RAID DISK SUBSYSTEMS

This section covers the most important hardware component of your NT Server, the disk subsystem. Besides the cooling fan in the computer's power supply, the only other moving parts in your computer are the disk drives. Because these are electromechanical devices, their mechanical components will eventually fail. Disk drive failure is the most drastic problem you can encounter. Drive failure can totally disable your system and require restoring and/or reinstalling your operating system and data.

NT provides several levels of protection against inevitable disk failure. The fault-tolerant disk system makes it possible to recover from disk failures. The NT Fault Tolerance system (NTFT) carries this out by fixing bad sectors dynamically. This is called sector sparing. Another method used by NTFT to provide fault tolerance is that it keeps copies of the data on alternate drives. Disk mirroring/duplexing and striping with parity are examples of redundancy.

In the event of a media failure, the downtime spent recovering data from backup storage could result in lost business opportunities and severe financial losses. Disk fault tolerance recognizes that media failure is unavoidable, and takes precautionary measures to ensure that media failure does not lead to system failure. Media errors are detected, identified, assessed, and recovered from, with a minimum of administrative interaction. The trade-off for increased availability is the additional costs of redundant media, which fortunately is getting less expensive. The cost of redundancy is determined by the degree of redundancy and the ease of recovery from failure.

RAID LEVELS

The methods used for achieving fault tolerance can be summarized in six levels of Redundant Arrays of Inexpensive Disks (RAID level 0 through level 5). Each method can provide various degrees of performance, reliability, and cost-effectiveness. Here is a list of the six levels of RAID:

Level 0:   Disk striping.

Level 1:   Disk mirroring.

Level 2:   Disk striping across drives, while keeping error correction codes across multiple drives.

Level 3:   Same as level 2 except that the error correction information is stored as parity information on one drive.

Level 4:   Uses striping data in larger blocks than level 2 and 3. Parity data is kept on a single drive.

Level 5:   Augments level 4 striping by storing parity data across multiple drives. This enhances performance and drive replacement ("hot-pluggable" drives can be replaced without system interruption).

RAID LEVEL 0

RAID level 0 or disk striping is not a common method of configuring disk subsystems because it actually reduces the reliability of a system. Suppose that you use two disks to create a stripe set. That means that each block of data will be split over these two disks. If even one of the drives fails, you will lose the data. In addition, there is very little likelihood of recovering even partial data. On the other hand, this is the easiest way of boosting performance. There is very little overhead, and you are spreading the load over multiple spindles.

RAID LEVEL 1

RAID Level 1 is disk mirroring. This implies that the data is written on two physical disks. There is no performance boost. On the other hand, there might be a slight overhead due to two streams of data going through the same channel. This is the most reliable configuration. The following rules apply to mirroring under NT Server:

◆ Mirrors are the only type of NT fault-tolerant (NTFT) partition that can be created from existing partitions. Volume sets, stripe sets, and stripe sets with parity must be created from free disk space.

◆ Only the NT Server Disk Administrator program can create and break mirror sets.

◆ Mirrors are not dependent on disk hardware configuration. The only requirement is that free disk space used to place the mirror on be equal to or greater than the size of the primary partition. Mirroring is not restricted to a partition of identical hardware configuration (size, number of heads, cylinders, tracks, sectors, and so on) nor is it restricted to a drive of the same type (IDE, ESDI, SCSI, and so on).

◆ Mirrors are file-system-independent. Any partition using a file system that NT Server recognizes or that is blank can be used to create a mirror.

◆ Primary and mirrored partitions must be on separate disk drives. They cannot be on the same physical disk drive.

◆ A single mirror set is limited to two hard disks only. Use disk striping with parity if fault tolerance over more than two disks is needed.

◆ Mirror sets are invisible to the user. When a mirror set is created, both partitions are assigned the same drive letter.

◆ Mirroring is the only NT fault-tolerant option available for use on boot and system partitions.

◆ NT does not allow the reuse of existing mirror sets for new installations. During setup, when you select the partition to install NT, setup identifies the mirror set as "NT Fault Tolerance." If you attempt to select this partition for installation, a message appears stating that NT does not recognize this partition, and it must be deleted for setup to continue.

◆ It does not make any difference if the two disk drives containing the primary and mirrored partitions are on the same or on different disk controllers. NT will define this as mirroring and make no distinction. Interfacing the disks with separate controllers is called disk duplexing.

◆ If the boot or system partition is mirrored and the primary partition is unavailable, the computer can boot off the secondary or mirror partition by using a fault-tolerant boot floppy disk.

◆ Only the NT Server installation that created the mirror set will usually recognize it. Other operating systems will not recognize the mirrored volume. DOS will identify the volume segments of the mirror as "Non-DOS" partitions. NT and other installations of NT Server identify the primary and mirror partitions as having an "Unknown" file system type when you look at them using the Disk Administrator program.

- The fault tolerance driver protects the applications from disruption by making the loss of one partition in a mirror set invisible. The applications will continue to read from and write to the remaining partition as if the mirror set were functional.

- The condition of a mirror set is shown in the status bar in Disk Administrator. When you click on one of the partitions of a mirror set, Disk Administrator displays information about the mirror set in the status bar.

- Status indicators in Disk Administrator include: [NEW], which appears immediately after the mirror set has been created in Disk Administrator, but before shutting down the system and actual generation of the mirror begins. The status [REGENERATING] is displayed when generation of the mirror set by the system has been started but is not yet complete. The status [RECOVERABLE] appears when either one of the partitions in the set has been lost but the other partition is undamaged. This message also appears when one partition loses synchronization with the other.

- No loss in performance occurs when a member of a mirror set fails.

- Disk mirroring has better write performance than striping with parity and better read performance when one of the partitions is lost. In some cases, parity rebuild can slow down the disk subsystem to such an extent that it is unusable during the loss of one of the stripe members.

RAID Levels 2,3, and 4

RAID levels 2, 3, and 4 are not available in NT Server. Of these technologies, only RAID 3 is commonly used. However, RAID 5 has several major advantages and is much more popular than RAID 3. RAID 5 performs better and is hot-pluggable.

RAID Level 5

RAID Level 5 uses striping and parity checksums to improve both performance and fault tolerance. It distributes the checksum data over all the drives in the set. The configuration of the parity checksum provides both performance and replaceability. If any drive in the system fails, the striped parity reconstructs data on the fly.

For example, sector 1 of disk 5 may store the checksum for sector 1 of the remaining data drives and so on. Because the checksum is just the exclusive OR of all the write data values for the corresponding sector on each of the data disks, as long as the previous sector data and the previous checksum values are known, the new checksum for a single sector write can be calculated without having to read the corresponding sectors from the other data disks. This way, only two disks are involved in a single-sector write operation: the target data disk and the corresponding disk that holds the check data for that sector.

RAID Level 5 disk subsystems allow data recovery when one of the stripes has been lost. When data is written to multiple disks, the exclusive OR of all the data values are written to the checksum disk. If any one disk fails, the missing data from that data disk can be recovered by taking the exclusive OR of the data values from the remaining data drives and the checksum disk. This operation is implemented in NT Server as Stripe Sets with Parity, which is a software implementation of RAID 5.

The main benefit of the RAID Level 5 distributed checksum method is that write operations take place concurrently. It also allows multiple reads to take place simultaneously and is efficient in handling small amounts of information. RAID 5 or stripe sets with parity is the recommended option when setting up fault tolerance in NT Server.

NT Fault Tolerance Design

The FTDISK.SYS driver provides the NTFT functions. It is only loaded on computers that are using volume sets, stripe sets (with or without parity), or mirroring. After initialization, all disk I/O requests go through the NTFT driver, FTDISK.SYS. It uses its internal structures to determine how to redirect requests in the most efficient way to the appropriate physical disks. In the case of writes, it creates additional requests.

NTFT Behavior

FTDISK.SYS uses the device object of the first member of each NTFT volume to make that volume available to the system. It intercepts all I/O to these volumes and directs them to the appropriate partitions on the physical disks. FTDISK.SYS hides the individual partitions making up the NTFT volumes from the disk driver above its level. FTDISK.SYS creates a new device object that is attached to the original device object created by the physical disk driver. The configuration of these FTDISK objects into NTFT volumes (that is, stripes, mirrors, volume sets) is a process of creating linked lists of FTDISK device objects.

FTDISK.SYS conceals the multiple partitions and shows only the NTFT volume. It makes the file systems think they are sending I/O to the actual disk object: however, the attached NTFT object intercepts the calls and creates physical I/O calls.

For example, if a mirror is created that includes partition 2 of disk 1 and partition 3 of disk 3, the file system will access the information through the device object for disk 1 partition 2. The FTDISK device object that is attached to the device object for disk 1 partition 2 will point to the device object for FTDISK.SYS that was attached to disk 3 partition 3. This way, FTDISK.SYS can create new I/O requests to operate on disk 3 partition 3 for writes and balance reads between the two devices. Volume sets and stripes are constructed in a similar manner.

FTDISK.SYS DRIVER DETAILS

The FTDISK.SYS driver is loaded and initialized immediately after the boot device drivers (start type 0) to attach to the device objects they create. It reads the configuration registry to create mirror relationships for the boot and system partitions. Then it registers itself with the I/O system to be invoked one more time after other disk device drivers have been initialized. When it is loading, the FTDISK.SYS driver also checks if a verification needs to be carried out on a mirror or stripe with parity subsystem by checking if the file system located on the NTFT volume is operational.

When the I/O manager loads, it also loads any disk drivers of start type 1. The I/O Manager then calls the NTFT driver, which attaches to each of the remaining disk device objects and reads the configuration registry to establish relationships between partitions making up additional NTFT volumes.

Note

> During the startup process, the NTFT driver performs all read operations from the primary partition of a mirrored pair or stripe. All write operations are performed to both components of the mirror or stripe.

FTDISK.SYS operates this way to address the situation in which the computer crashes during I/O. Because I/O might not have completed on all drives, the file system will recover and resynch the drives using CHKDSK. FTDISK.SYS makes sure that all write operations go to all the drives.

When all of the startup steps are completed, NTFT (or a cooperating file system such as NTFS) turns on the capability to read from both components of a mirror or stripe. NTFS will turn on this capability when it has determined volume integrity on its partitions.

NTFT VOLUME SECTOR SPARING

If an error occurs during an I/O request, then the request is suspended and sector sparing (remapping sectors) procedures are carried out. Most SCSI devices have the ability to remap a sector. If the NTFT driver accesses a faulty sector, it instructs the SCSI device to do the remapping, and the file system is never alerted. IDE and ESDI devices cannot carry out this function. If a sector needs to be remapped on an IDE or ESDI system, it is up to the hardware features of the device to react and repair.

Sector Sparing Failures

If remapping a read attempt fails, but the data was retrieved from the mirror or stripe parity, then the data is returned with the error read succeeded with retry to the file system. It is then the responsibility of the file system to determine if it should map the faulty sector from file system use.

If remapping a write request fails, the driver attempts to write the data to the mirror or parity stripe. If this succeeds, then the error write with retry is reported back to the file system. The file system may decide to map this faulty sector from use. If the write to the mirror or parity stripe also fails, then the error will be returned to the file system.

FTDISK.SYS Error Handling

When the primary disk fails, FTDISK.SYS shifts control to the mirrored disk. FTDISK.SYS hides all shifting of the primary from the user unless it is the boot partition or load partition that is being mirrored.

The FTDISK.SYS driver also logs the following errors to the system log:

FT_RECOVERY_ERROR: An error occurred while attempting to recover data from the FT set containing %1. Corrective action failed. Because the FT driver failed to get a correct copy of the data, the user should try to restore the data from an archived source such as a tape backup.

FT_MAP_FAILED: A warning was returned that the fault tolerance driver was unable to map a faulty sector from use by the system on %1. Corrective action is still working, but the bad sector cannot be removed by FT. The file systems are notified of the potential for data loss (that is, only one of the drives in the mirror or parity stripe now contains the correct data for this sector). NTFS reacts to this and attempts to find and remove this faulty sector.

FT_ORPHANING: An error was returned by the device driver for device %1, which is part of a fault tolerance set indicating that the device is not working properly. Fault tolerance has been disabled, and you now have only one copy of the data. Take corrective action by replacing the drive if bad, fixing faulty cables, and so on. Then use Disk Administrator to regenerate the parity stripe or mirror.

FT_SET_DISABLED: An error that the fault tolerance set containing device %1 has been disabled. Two members of a stripe with parity, both members of a mirror, one member of a stripe, or one member of a volume set have returned an error that says the device is no longer functioning correctly. The "set" has been disabled and no further reads or writes will be allowed until corrective action is taken (that is, replace drives, recable, and reboot). If you still have a problem, try rebooting. If the problem still persists, check the hardware.

FT_RECOVERY_NO_MEM: An error during the recovery process: The fault-tolerant driver was not able to allocate needed memory, resulting in low memory in the system. Increase the memory; if you do not, then fault tolerance features will not be available.

FT_DOUBLE_FAILURE: An error on a sector has occurred on both sides of the mirror. There is no redundant data. This can be caused by bad disks; all copies of the data are bad. That means both sides of a mirror or the stripe and parity data on a stripe with parity. NTFS will attempt a recovery in that it will remove the sector from use. There is no data recovery. New disks and restoring a backup might be a good idea.

FT_ORPHANED_MEMBER: This error indicates that a disk fault tolerance set member listed in the configuration information was missing. A volume segment was missing from a mirror or stripe set. There no longer is data protection on the mirror or stripe set with parity. Fix the disk and use Disk Administrator to regenerate the redundant copy (that is, remake the mirror or regenerate parity).

FT_MISSING_MEMBER: An error on a stripe set or volume that a set member listed in the configuration information was missing. A disk is powered off, removed from the system. Bad cabling.

FT_BAD_CONFIGURATION: An error about the fault-tolerant driver that the configuration information is corrupt. This can be caused by bad registry information. Try restoring from a restore disk (that is, the one you can create from Disk Administrator).

FT_CANT_USE_SET: This error indicates that the fault-tolerant set containing %1 cannot be used. Either configuration or missing members (that is, powered off) to any fault tolerant set. The set is disabled. No reads or writes will occur. Try to power on the disks, check cabling, and so on.

Support for RAID Hardware Devices

RAID devices are treated by FT as a single device. Because RAID devices provide fault tolerance at the hardware level, the RAID subsystem is "hidden" from software and appears to be one massive drive.

There is no protection from a system administrator setting up the NTFT form of mirroring or striping with parity on a RAID device. This configuration is not recommended.

Fault Tolerance Recovery

When a member of a mirror or stripe set with parity fails in a severe manner, the remaining member(s) of the set becomes an orphan. The fault-tolerant driver then determines that it can no longer use the failed device and directs all new reads and writes to the remaining members of the fault tolerance volume.

Identifying When a Set Is Broken

The process of error detection and recovery is very similar for both mirrored sets and parity striped sets. The exact system response to the problem depends on when the problem occurred.

A broken set is defined as any time one or the other partition in a mirrored or duplexed set cannot be written, or any time a stripe can no longer be written.

When an I/O error is first detected, the system performs some routines in an attempt to keep the set from breaking. The system's first priority is to try reassigning the sector that failed. This is done by issuing a command to remap the sector to the disk.

NT attempts remapping only if the disk is a SCSI device. SCSI devices are designed to support the concept of remapping. This is why SCSI devices work well as fault-tolerant devices.

If the disk does not support sector mapping, or if the other attempts to maintain the set fail, a high severity error is logged to the event log.

The partition that has failed is called an orphan. It is important to note that the process of orphaning a partition does not occur during a read, only during writes. This is because the read cannot possibly affect the data on the disks, so performing orphan processing would be superfluous.

During system initialization, if the system cannot locate each partition in a mirrored set, a severe error is recorded in the event log, and the remaining partition of the mirror is used. If the partition is part of a parity striped set, a severe error is recorded in the event log, and the partition is marked as an orphan. The system then continues to function using the fault-tolerant capabilities inherent in such sets.

If all of the partitions within a set cannot be located, the drive is not activated, but the partitions are not marked as orphans. This saves recovery time for simple problems like disconnecting the SCSI chain from the computer.

Restoring the Computer to its Normal State

1. Replace the bad disk.
2. Boot from the remaining partition (using an NTFT boot floppy if the boot drive has failed).
3. Within Disk Administrator, reconfigure the mirror or regenerate the stripe set.

Using an NTFT boot disk, the mirror partition can be easily configured as the boot partition. The BOOT.INI file on the boot partition or a floppy boot disk needs to have an entry that has an ARC path pointing to the mirror partition. NT boots from the mirror just like a normal partition.

When a mirror disk fails to the point that it is no longer usable, an error is logged. The mirror appears red in the Disk Administrator utility and is labeled "recoverable." At this point, the mirrored drive should be replaced and the mirror reset.

RECOVERING ORPHANS

When a partition is marked as an orphan, the system continues processing until a replacement disk or partition is available to recover from the problem and ensure fault tolerance again. A set with an orphan is not fault-tolerant. Another failure in the set can, and most likely will, cause the loss of data.

Recovery procedures should be performed as soon as the problem is discovered:

1. Break the mirror-set relationship using the Break Mirror option in the Disk Administrator utility.

2. This converts the remaining active partition of the set into a "normal" partition. This partition receives the drive letter of the set. The orphan partition receives the next available drive letter.

3. You can then create a new set relationship with existing free space on another disk in the local computer, or replace the orphan drive and re-establish the relationship with space from this disk.

4. Once the relationship is established, restart the computer.

5. During the system initialization, the data from the original good partition is copied over to the new mirrored partition.

When a member of a parity striped set is orphaned, it can be regenerated from the remaining data. This uses the same logic discussed earlier for the dynamic regeneration of data from the parity and remaining stripes. Select a new free space area that is as large as the other members in the set. Then choose the Regenerate command from the Fault Tolerance menu. When the system is restarted, the missing stripes are recalculated and written to the new space provided.

RAID PERFORMANCE

You can use Performance Monitor to see how various RAID and fault-tolerant disk configurations can improve performance. You need to perform these measurements on your own configurations and under real workloads to make your decision as to the right RAID configuration for you.

For this example, physical disk unit 0 is a hardware RAID array of 4 drives and 1 GB capacity. These are partitioned into drives C:, F:, and G:, which are 300MB each. There are also three other disk units with 500MB capacity each for reference checking. You need to create a 200MB file on a single partitioned drive D:, and another one on a mirrored partition on the other two disks, drive E:. After you have finished the experiments on drives D: and E:, you can rearrange those three spindles as a single striped partition for drive D: (no parity) and create a 200MB file on that.

There are two disk controllers, one for the hardware RAID array, and another for all three of the other disk units.

If you run a similar test, you will find that all the 200MB file creation times are about 450 seconds, except for the striped partition on drive D:, which created itself in 300 seconds.

Notice that the Avg. Disk sec/Write is 0.11 for the single unit and 0.06 for the striped set. This results in higher Disk Bytes/sec. Striping reduces disk drive seeks, and as a result, it improves performance.

The next step is to configure drive D: as striped across units 1, 2, and 3. When you check units 2 and 3, you will notice that 2 and 3 are not seen by DISKPERF.SYS. DISKPERF.SYS sees the stripe set as one unit because DISKPERF.SYS is located above the fault-tolerant disk driver FTDISK.SYS in the driver stacking order. The decision as to which spindle will get the data is made by FTDISK.SYS and therefore is invisible to DISKPERF.SYS. The only way to get visibility would be to add another measurement driver below FTDISK.SYS on the stack, but this configuration would increase overhead. Mirrors, stripes, and hardware RAID devices all share this Performance Monitor characteristic: Performance Monitor summarizes all Physical Disk statistics under the first unit assigned to the disk array.

You can check some more characteristics by reading 100 unbuffered (with no file system cache), normally distributed records of 8192 bytes from the file on each drive type. The hardware RAID is slower at this, for some reason—perhaps its physical drives are slower. The results show that the RAID device is more impressive at higher transfer sizes and increases linearly in performance as the transfer size goes up. The striped volume is not so consistent. It has spots where the performance degrades due to missed revolutions. This happens because you are rereading the same record over and over; only one spindle participates in this test.

Which of these two technologies is a better solution for you? To decide that, you need to understand the transfer size characteristics of your workload. For 4096- or 8192-byte transfers, the striped volume performs better; for transfers larger than five pages, the hardware RAID is better. Another factor to consider is the load that software-based RAID puts on your server. A hardware RAID subsystem offloads much of the I/O processing on its own controllers.

Another way to change the outcome is to try writing instead of reading. If we substitute writing for reading in the test example, we get 0.016 seconds per record for the striped volume, 0.030 for the single spindle, 0.032 for the hardware RAID, and 0.045 for the mirror. Writing is slower on the mirror because both spindles must be written. If you had another controller for one half of the mirrored pair, you would see an improvement. That will also give you a redundant hardware channel.

SUMMARY

There is one rule of thumb to remember—the more spindles there are, the better the performance. Where is the point of diminishing returns, when complexity and cost become unreasonable? Another rule of thumb: go with generic rather than proprietary solutions. Software RAID 5 under NT Server is a better way to go than a hardware RAID 5 solution.

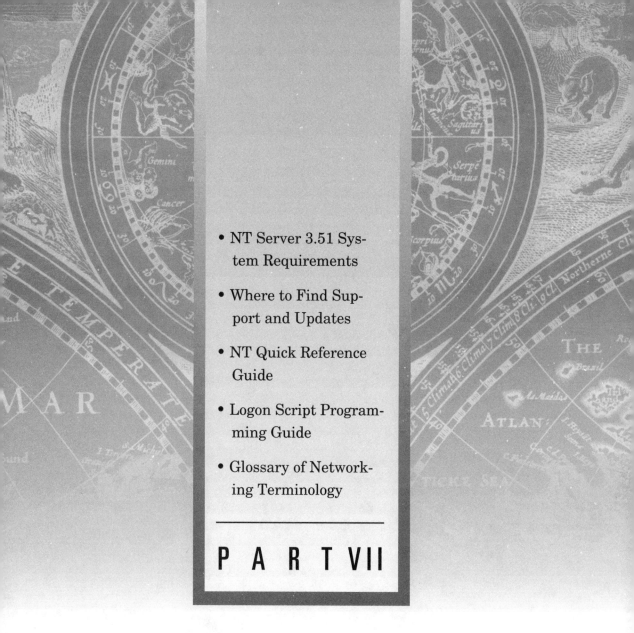

- NT Server 3.51 System Requirements

- Where to Find Support and Updates

- NT Quick Reference Guide

- Logon Script Programming Guide

- Glossary of Networking Terminology

PART VII

Appendixes

- NT Server/
  Workstation Features
  and Capacities

APPENDIX A

NT Server 3.51 System
Requirements

HARDWARE REQUIREMENTS

PROCESSORS

- Intel 386 or higher or compatible
- Digital Equipment Corporation Alpha AXP RISC
- MIPS R4000 RISC
- IBM Power PC (601 or 603)
- VGA or higher resolution, video display adapter

DISK STORAGE

- One or more hard disks
- 90 MB or more free hard disk space on the NT partition (110 MB for RISC systems)
- One high-density 3 1/2 or 5 1/4-inch floppy disk drive
- One CD-ROM drive (Computers with only one disk drive can install from a server's shared CD-ROM drive. RISC systems require a SCSI CD-ROM.)
- One or more network interface cards

MEMORY

16 MB RAM minimum (may require more for larger configurations)

OPTIONAL COMPONENTS (RECOMMENDED)

- Mouse or other pointing device
- One or more SCSI CD-ROM drives (required for RISC-based computers)

MULTIPROCESSING REQUIREMENTS

No modifications are required to support up to four Intel Pentium processors. Computers with more than four Intel processors or multiprocessor RISC systems require original equipment manufacturer's support.

Note

Check Microsoft's latest Hardware Compatibility Listing for computers and hardware that have been tested and known to be compatible with NT Server.

NT SERVER/WORKSTATION FEATURES AND CAPACITIES

Note

Many specifications are hardware specific. For example, although NT can support 408 TB of disk storage, Intel 386, 486, Pentium, and Pentium Pro processors can only support 32 TB of disk storage; therefore, NT on an Intel platform can only support up to 32 TB of disk storage.

Other specifications are theoretical; for example, there are currently no disk drives that have 17,000 TB of capacity, although that is the specification for NT's partition size limit.

SYSTEM ARCHITECTURE

Multiuser operating system
Preemptive multitasking
Processors—Intel, MIPS, DEC Alpha, IBM PPC
Symmetric multiprocessing: up to 32 processors (with OEM support)
Built-in support for up to 4 Pentium processors
Maximum RAM: up to 4 GB
Paged virtual memory
Dynamic memory cache
Unlimited user connections
Dynamic loading of services
Memory protection
Audit alerts
Structured exception handling
Micro-kernel based architecture
Protected subsystems
Hardware abstraction layer
Unicode support
Installable file systems

NETWORK INTERFACE CARD SUPPORT

16-bit Ethernet support
32-bit Ethernet support
16-bit Token ring support
32-bit Token ring support

NDIS support
ODI support
PCMCIA cards
Third-party driver support
Multiple network cards

Client Workstation Network Card Support

NDIS drivers

16-bit Ethernet
32-bit Ethernet
16-bit Token ring
32-bit Token ring
PCMCIA network cards

NetWare Open DataLink Interface (ODI)

NetWare Shells and Requesters (NETX and VLM)

Third-party drivers

Other Hardware Support

CD-ROM drives
SCSI adapters
Optical disk drives
Plotters
Scanners

Protocol Support

Novell's Internetwork Packet eXchange (IPX)
IPX Dial-in
Packet Burst NetWare Core Protocol compatibility
Large Internetwork Packet compatibility
AppleTalk protocols
NetBIOS
NetBEUI
TCP/IP (native)
Open System Interconnect protocols (in the Software Development Kit)
DECNet (Digital)
IBM's Data Link Control
Internal routing
Remote access service for NetBIOS, TCP, IPX, TCP/IP (native)

INTER-PROGRAM COMMUNICATION

Named Pipes (client side)
Named Pipes (server side)
Sockets
Transport Library Interface
DEC-compatible RPC
LU 6.2, LU 1, LU 0, LU 2, LU 3
HLLAPI
Local Procedure Calls (LPC)
Semaphores
Mutexes
Timers
Asynchronous Procedure Calls

FILE SYSTEM FEATURES

Unlimited number of file locks
Unlimited number of file opens
Maximum file size: 17 billion GB
Efficient subblock allocation: 512 bytes (NTFS only)
File compression (NTFS only)
Transaction-based file system
Support for DOS, Mac, and OS/2
Support for NFS (third party)
Total disk storage: 408 million TB
Up to 25 volumes per server
Unlimited physical drives per server
Maximum partition size: 17,000 TB
Maximum volume size: 17,000 TB
Disk quotas (third party)
High performance asynchronous I/O
Memory mapped file I/O
Length of filename: 255 characters
Long filenames are made visible to DOS programs

PERFORMANCE OPTIMIZATION FEATURES

Dynamic cache: 1 GB per process
Elevator seeking
Read-ahead caching
Background writes
Overlapped seeks

Split seeks
Directory hashing
File caching
Volume striping (RAID 0, 5)
Drive duplexing (RAID 1)
Virtual memory
Returnable memory

SECURITY FEATURES

U.S. C2 security (certified in September 1995)
European E3 security compliant
Designed to meet B2 security (third party)
Single logon to network
Single, secure logon and optional background authentication
Single logon compatibility for Microsoft client/server applications
Centralized security event auditing
Minimum password length restriction
Password encryption
Packet signing (secure authentication)
Password aging
Password history
Minimum time until password can be changed
Account lockout
Restrict logon to specific workstation
Replaceable client logon
Restrict logon by time and day
Set account expiration date
Disconnect when access time expires
Rekey password verify
Configurable administrative rights
Security event alert
File system auditing

NTFS DIRECTORY AND FILE PERMISSIONS

No Access
List
Read
Add
Add and Read
Change

Full Control
Special Directory Access
Special File Access
Take Ownership ()

User Rights

Access workstation from network
Log on locally
Back up files and directories
Restore files and directories
Change the system time
Shut down the system locally
Force system shutdown remotely
Load and unload device drivers
Manage audit and security logs
Take ownership of files or other objects

Security Auditing

Audit user security transactions
Audit user file transactions
Audit administrative transactions
Audit file-creation statistics
Audit volume statistics
Filter audit logs
Audit security policy changes
Audit restart or shutdown of system
Audit non-dedicated server activity

Printing

Remote printer port on workstation
Peer print services
Assign priorities to print queue
Multiple queues to a single printer
Multiple queues on multiple printers
Multiple printers on one queue
PostScript supported
Unlimited shared printers per server
Cross-platform printing to OS/2, UNIX, NetWare, and SNA
Remote queue management

Support for multiple forms
Network-attached printer support
User notification of job completion
Operator notification of print problem

PRINTER ALERTS

Out-of-paper
Printer request deleted
Printer request completed
Printer offline
Paper jam

NETWORK MANAGEMENT

Command-line utilities
GUI utilities
Remote administration and performance and event monitoring
Asynchronous remote administration
Remote installation
Remote upgrade
Remote corrective service
Remote session security
Remote modem callback
Dynamic Host Configuration Protocol (DHCP) support for TCP/IP
Windows Internet Name Service (WINS) support for TCP/IP

PERFORMANCE MONITORING

View total percent CPU use
View total privileged CPU use
View total user CPU use
View logical disk use
View physical disk use
View cache utilization
View packets/bytes sent
View page/faults per second
View number of active processes
View number of active threads
View processor time by process
View processor time by thread
Log performance statistics
Graphical remote performance monitoring

Delegating Administration Responsibility

Account operators
Backup operators
Directory administrator
Enterprise administrators
Print operators
Replication operators
Server operator

Alert Messages

Volume is getting full
Volume is full
Error log is full
Connection slots depleted
Disk utilization above threshold

Fault Tolerance

File system recovery log
Redundant directory structures
Directory verification during power-up
Read-after write verification
Hot-fix (sector sparing)
Uninterruptible Power Supply (UPS) support
Disk duplexing (RAID 1)
Disk mirroring (RAID 1)
Volume striping with parity (RAID 5)
Server mirroring (third party)
Dynamic volume sets

Backup Features

Backup/restore of server disk with security attributes intact
Online backup of account files
Backup utility shipped with product
Workstation backup (for NT Workstation, Windows 95, and Windows for Workgroups)
Automatic file replication service
Server job scheduling

- Before Calling
  Microsoft for Help

- Electronic Services

APPENDIX B

Where to Find Support
and Updates

BEFORE CALLING MICROSOFT FOR HELP

Many of the answers you need might be right on your desktop in Help and the NT Books Online software documentation included with your Microsoft product. You can get context-sensitive help to questions concerning product features and dialog boxes by pressing the F1 key at any time or by clicking the Help button on your application toolbar. You can also look in the user's guides and README files provided with program disks.

Microsoft provides extensive support in many forms. Third parties provide some services that are supported by Microsoft and some that are completely independent of Microsoft. This appendix provides a comprehensive listing of where to turn when you need support or information.

Note

Although this book provides information on many sources of support, please keep in mind that the services discussed in this appendix might change without notice. Phone numbers and contact information were current as of the publication date of this book.

MICROSOFT PHONE NUMBERS

Microsoft is a very large company. The following phone numbers will help you reach the resources you need quickly.

MAIN SWITCHBOARD (SALES AND INFORMATION)

Use the switchboard number for any inquires or calls to Microsoft. This phone line has an unattended voice mail system handling sales, service, automated services, and connections to internal extensions (no directory provided). There is no charge for any services provided on this line.

U.S. and Canada (800) 426-9400

MICROSOFT SUPPORT NETWORK SALES

Use the support number to find information and sales for Microsoft support products.

U.S. (800) 936-3500
Canada (800) 563-9048

WHERE TO FIND SUPPORT AND UPDATES   867

MICROSOFT SUPPORT CONSULTING

This support consulting phone number connects you with the sales line for paid consulting services from Microsoft factory engineers that goes beyond the boundaries of product support.

U.S. and Canada (800) 936-1565

MICROSOFT AUTHORIZED SUPPORT CENTERS (ASCs)

The ASC phone number provides referrals to Microsoft's most qualified third-party support vendors. Referrals are free; ASC services are provided on a fee basis.

U.S. (800) 936-3500

SOLUTION PROVIDER SALES AND INFORMATION

Use the Solution Provider line for referrals to Microsoft Solution Providers or information concerning the Solution Provider program.

U.S. (800) 426-9400
Canada (800) 536-9048

TECHNET ANNUAL SUBSCRIPTION SALES AND INFORMATION

TechNet is a CD-ROM-based technical library published regularly. Solution Providers receive this product at no cost. TechNet is available for an annual subscription fee. Call Microsoft for details.

U.S. and Canada (800) 344-2121

DEVELOPER NETWORK SALES AND INFORMATION

The developer line provides referrals to qualified Microsoft Certified Developers and information about the Developer program.

U.S. (800) 426-9400
Canada (800) 712-0333

MICROSOFT SOLUTION PROVIDER NETWORK

Microsoft's Solution Provider program bestows the title of Microsoft Solution Provider Network on business entities that have qualified and paid for the program. Currently, the program requires that the business have at least one Microsoft Product Specialist and one Microsoft Certified System Engineer on staff. The Solution Provider pays an annual fee to receive unlimited Microsoft support, product licenses as required, Microsoft TechNet, and other support tools and services.

WHERE TO FIND SUPPORT AND UPDATES

The Microsoft Solution Provider Network program was developed to equip those who provide and support Microsoft products in the marketplace. Solution Providers are resellers, consultants, developers, training firms, distributors, and other Microsoft business partners who have been given all the tools they need to support their clients. Of course, these businesses generally charge a fee for their services. In many cases, your purchase of Microsoft products or service might bring some value-added support along with the product you purchase. Keep in mind that Microsoft provides tools and support to officially registered Solution Providers and makes no warranty concerning a Solution Provider's services.

FastTips

Description: Automated, toll-free technical information on selected topics delivered via prerecorded voice mail, automated fax, or U.S. Mail.

Service hours: 24 hours/day, 7 days/week

Cost: Free

Contact: See Table B.1.

TABLE B.1. FREE STANDARD SUPPORT LINES.

Product	Time Period	U.S.	Canada
MS-DOS 6.0, 6.2	90 days	(206) 646-5104	(905) 568-3503
Windows, Windows for Workgroups	90 days	(206) 637-7098	(905) 568-3503
Windows 95	90 days	(206) 635-7000	(905) 568-3503

Service Hours:

U.S.: 6 a.m. to 6 p.m. Pacific time

Canada: 8 a.m. to 8 p.m. Eastern time

Holidays excluded

Cost: Free

Notes: For desktop application and development product support phone numbers, call (800) 426-9400 and follow the voice mail prompts for the product specific phone number. Also see the Note about limitations on Personal Operating System support.

BULLETIN BOARD SERVICE: MICROSOFT DOWNLOAD SERVICE (MSDL)

Description: Bulletin board service providing device drivers, patches, software updates, sample programs, and programming aids.

Service Hours: 24 hours/day, 7 days/week

Cost: Free (long distance charges at your expense)

Contact:

U.S. (206) 936-6735
Canada (905) 507-3022

STANDARD SUPPORT

Description: Product specific telephone support provided by Microsoft engineers per the terms of your Microsoft product. Free standard product support is provided according to the product you have purchased; however, most products include 30 days of technical support at no cost. The support period starts when the first technical support call is logged. Table B.2 shows phone numbers for some of the Personal Operating System product standard support phone numbers.

Note

Advanced Business products, including Windows NT, no longer receive free standard product support as of July 1, 1995.

Personal Operating Systems (MS-DOS, Windows, Windows for Workgroups, and Windows 95) receive 90 days free standard support from the time of your first support call. This service does not include support for network-related issues, such as setup and configuration of PCs used in a network environment, network interface card, protocols, e-mail, fax, Internet access from the operating system, or any other network-related issues (effective July 1, 1995).

PRIORITY SUPPORT

Description: Priority telephone support from Microsoft in-house support technicians trained and experienced in each specific application.

Service Hours:

U.S.: 24 hours a day, 7 days a week

Canada: 6 am to midnight Eastern time, 7 days a week

Excluding holidays (except for server down calls)

Cost: Various schedules based upon unlimited annual, 5 calls, 10 calls, or pay-as-you-call options and level of service.

Contact:

900 number support (charge per minute) (U.S. only)

Comprehensive (includes NT)	(900) 555-2100
Personal Operating Systems	(900) 555-2000
Development w/Desktop	(900) 555-2300
Desktop Applications	(900) 555-2000

Priority Credit Card Service (charge on Visa, Master Card, and American Express)

Comprehensive (includes NT)	(800) 936-5900
Personal Operating Systems	(800) 936-5700 (Canada (800) 668-7975)
Development w/Desktop	(800) 936-5700 (Canada (800) 668-7975)
Desktop Applications	(800) 936-5700

PREMIER SUPPORT AND PREMIER GLOBAL SUPPORT

Description: The premier service is provided for larger organizations where personalized support management and service is required. A support representative is assigned to your account. Premier Global Support is for multinational organizations.

Service Hours: 24 hours per day, 7 days a week

Cost: An annual support fee is negotiated, normally based upon site licenses and products purchased.

Contact: Microsoft Support Network Sales

U.S. (800) 936-3500
Canada (800) 536-9048

ELECTRONIC SERVICES

Electronic and online services are very convenient, and constitute the preferred method for support for many thousands of users. Microsoft support is available over many services, as outlined in this section.

INTERNET SERVICES

Microsoft's Internet services are visited by more than 100,000 Internet users every week. The Internet sites have the Microsoft Knowledge Base, the Microsoft Electronic Technical Library, and additional Microsoft information such as resource kits, white papers, and the latest information about Microsoft products. You can access these extensive databases at

> World Wide Web: `http:/www.microsoft.com`

The Web site contains the Knowledge Base (with full text-search capabilities), pointers to the Microsoft Software Library, various white papers (located, for example, in the Microsoft TechNet and Microsoft Developer Network areas), and other Microsoft product and service information.

> Gopher site: `gopher.microsoft.com`

The Gopher site provides the Microsoft Knowledge Base and Microsoft Software Library and takes advantage of the Gopher search capabilities.

> FTP server site: `ftp.microsoft.com`

The FTP site is a repository for the Microsoft Software Library, the Microsoft Knowledge Base, resource kit utility files, and other Microsoft product information files.

MICROSOFT KNOWLEDGE BASE

The Microsoft Knowledge Base is the same database that Microsoft support engineers use to provide answers over the phone from regional product support locations. It is a comprehensive collection of more than 50,000 detailed articles with technical information about Microsoft products, bug and fix lists, documentation errors, and answers to commonly asked technical support questions.

MICROSOFT ELECTRONIC TECHNICAL LIBRARY

The Microsoft Electronic Technical Library contains device drivers, patches, software updates, add-ons, sample programs, and programming aids. Use this library to keep your software up to date and in top working order and to be forewarned about technical problems encountered by Microsoft technical support personnel.

NEWSGROUPS

There are many independent newsgroups on all major topics related to Microsoft products. These privately operated services work much like a bulletin board service. You are free to join, enter discussions, and lurk in the shadows watching others' messages and replies.

WEB SITES

Many World Wide Web sites offer Microsoft and network-related services. See your favorite networking industry publications for a list of highly frequented Web sites.

ONLINE SERVICES

There are many online service providers. The largest include CompuServe, America Online, GEnie, Prodigy, and the Microsoft Network. Check with each service for Microsoft bulletin boards, libraries, round tables, and other electronic services. Most offer access to some Microsoft help facilities.

Access to the libraries are available from the online electronic service providers; however, Microsoft is most heavily vested in CompuServe where the most comprehensive services are available on the Microsoft Connection. Microsoft sysops operate 29 extremely active forums on CompuServe as of January 1996, including 7 foreign language forums.

CompuServe, America Online, GEnie, the Microsoft Network, and other providers offer many services, some of which are "free" and others that incur additional service charges. Each major provider charges a monthly service fee per account, which includes a given number of hours of connection time. Additional time and additional services incur additional charges. In all cases, you must have a service account, which is generally billed monthly on a major credit card or by other arrangement. Service charges and fees are subject to change (and do so on a regular basis). Most online service providers offer alternative programs for higher usage levels and corporate accounts. Check with your service provider's sales representative for more timely information.

Most of the online services are also Internet access providers. With a single online account you can access basic services, additional services (fees charged), and Internet access. Table B.2 shows various considerations for online service providers.

Note

Prices and services change frequently because this is a highly competitive area. Check with your online service representatives at the phone numbers shown in Table B.2 for current information.

The Microsoft Network (MSN) is primarily intended for Windows 95 support and information. MSN is very new, and services are not yet in full swing. As time goes on, this service will grow; as of January 1996, services were sadly lacking but were expected to grow rapidly.

Tip

You can try most of these services for a few hours without charge or obligation. Take advantage of "test drives" from at least two of the services. You should compare available Microsoft services, Internet access, and other criteria before committing. Be sure to compare CompuServe because Microsoft's forums on CompuServe are by far more extensive than other service providers' forums.

TABLE B.2. ONLINE SERVICE PROVIDERS EVALUATION GUIDE.

Service	CompuServe	America Online	GEnie	MS Network	Prodigy
Local access lines		14.4 Kbps	28.8 Kbps	14.4 Kbps	28.8-14.4
800 line avail/chgs		$6.00/hr	$4.80/hr	$6.00/hr	n/a-$6.00/hr
Free access software	DOS, Win, Mac	DOS, Win, Mac	DOS, Win, Mac	Win 95 only	Win
Internet access	Yes	Yes	Yes	Yes	Yes
Microsoft services	Best	Limited	Limited	Limited	Very Limited
NetWare services	Best	Limited	Limited	None	None
Monthly service fee	$9.95	$9.95	$8.95	$4.95	$9.95
Mo. fee includes hours	5 hrs	5 hrs	4 hrs	3 hrs	5 hrs
Contact 800 number	848-8199	827-6364	638-9636	386-5550	776-3449

NT Quick Reference Guide

This section lists commands that affect connectivity, operation, and will provide some diagnostics for Administrators to install, test, and diagnose potential problems between Windows for Workgroup 3.11 Workstations and NT Servers. In addition to common networking commands, you will find a complete list of TCP/IP commands. The TCP/IP utilities will provide you with complete diagnostic and connectivity tools to administrate your Windows NT.

Most of the commands covered in this section are DOS commands that can be initiated from the command (Virtual DOS Machine) prompt.

ACLCONV

Converts LANManager 2.x file and directory permissions to NTFS volumes.

For example, to restore the access permissions to files backed up on drive C to drive F using the LANManager backacc command, type

```
aclconv /datafile:c:\lanman\accounts\aclbakup.acl /log:d:\admin\aclcnv.log /
newdrive:f
```

APPEND

This command was not allowed in WFW 3.11, but it has been resurrected by NT. It allows programs to open data files in specified directories as if these files were in the current directory. These directories are referred to as appended directories.

Examples:

To allow programs to open data files in a directory named DOCS on the disk in drive E and in a directory named PROP on the disk in drive F as if the files were in the current directory, type the following command:

```
append e:\docs;f:\prop
```

To append the same directories and keep a copy of the list of appended directories in the Windows NT environment, type the following commands:

```
append /e append e:\docs;f:\prop
```

These must be the first append commands you use after starting your system.

Note

Do not use the file extension .EXE when typing the append command.

AT

The AT command schedules commands and programs to run on a computer at a specified time and date. The Schedule service must be running to use the AT command.

```
AT [\\computername] [ [id] [/DELETE] ¦ /DELETE [/YES]]

AT [\\computername] time [/INTERACTIVE]

    [ /EVERY:date[,...] ¦ /NEXT:date[,...]] "command"
```

\\computername specifies a remote computer. Commands are scheduled on the local computer if this parameter is omitted.

Id is an identification number assigned to a scheduled command.

/DELETE cancels a scheduled command. If id is omitted, all the scheduled commands on the computer are canceled.

/YES is used with the cancel all jobs command when no further confirmation is desired.

Time specifies the time when command is to run.

/INTERACTIVE allows the job to interact with the desktop of the user who is logged on at the time the job runs.

/EVERY:date[,...] runs the command on each specified day(s) of the week or month. If date is omitted, the current day of the month is assumed.

/NEXT:date[,...] runs the specified command on the next occurrence of the day (for example, next Thursday). If date is omitted, the current day of the month is assumed.

command is the Windows NT command or batch program to be run.

CACLS

Displays or modifies access control lists (ACLs).

CHKDSK

Displays a report for a disk based on the file system used. Chkdsk also corrects errors on the disk. If chkdsk cannot lock the drive it suggests to check it the next time the computer reboots.

Examples:

If you want to check the disk in drive D and have Windows NT fix any errors encountered, type the following command:

`chkdsk d: /f`

Chkdsk pauses and displays messages if it encounters errors. Chkdsk finishes by displaying a report showing the status of the disk. Also, no files can be open on the drive specified.

On a FAT disk, to check all files in the current directory for non-contiguous blocks, type

`chkdsk *.*`

Chkdsk displays a status report, then lists the files matching the file specification that have non-contiguous blocks.

CMD

This is the NT Command interpreter. This command initiates a Virtual DOS Machine (VDM) in which DOS applications can be run.

`CMD [/X] [/A ¦ /U] [[/C ¦ /K] [/Q] string]`

/C   Carries out the command specified by string and then terminates

/K   Carries out the command specified by string but remains

/Q   Silently carries out the command specified by string but remains

/A   Causes the output of internal commands to a pipe or file to be ANSI

/U   Causes the output of internal commands to a pipe or file to be UNICODE

/X   Enables the following extensions:

ASSOC is a new command for adding/displaying/changing file associations.

It may also enable extensions for all invocations of the command processor by setting the following value in the registry to 1.

`HKEY_CURRENT_USER\Software\MicroSoft\Command Processor\EnableExtensions`

If this is done, then the /X switch has the opposite effect; it disables the extensions for that invocation of the command processor.

Multiple commands separated by the command separator '&&' are accepted for string if surrounded by quotes.

COMPACT

Displays and alters the compression of files or directories.

Examples:

To compress the files in the current directory and all subdirectories and set the compressed attribute on the current directory and all subdirectories, type

```
compact /c /s
```

To compress all files ending in .BMP in the \TMP directory and all subdirectories of \TMP, but not modify the compressed attribute of these directories, type

```
compact /c /s:\tmp *.bmp
```

To force complete compression of the file EGYPT.BMP, which was partially compressed at the time of a system crash, type

```
compact /c /f EGYPT.bmp
```

To remove the compressed attribute from the directory C:\TMP, but not change the compression state of any files in that directory, type

```
compact /u c:\tmp
```

CONVERT

This converts a FAT file system or HPFS to NTFS. The conversion occurs when the server is brought back up after being shut down.

```
CONVERT drive: /FS:NTFS [/V] [/NAMETABLE:file-name]
```

drive	Specifies the drive to convert to NTFS. You cannot convert the current drive.
/FS:NTFS	Specifies to convert the volume to NTFS.
/V	Specifies that CONVERT should be run in verbose mode.
file-name	Specifies that CONVERT should construct a name-translation table and store it in the specified file in the root directory of the volume to be converted.

DISKPERF

Starts and stops system disk performance counters.

Examples:

To set the disk performance counters on the computer PRODUCTION to start at boot, type

```
diskperf -y \\production
```

To stop the disk performance counters from starting at boot on the local computer, type

```
diskperf -n
```

DOSONLY

Prevents starting applications other than MS-DOS-based applications from the COMMAND.COM prompt.

ECHOCONFIG

Echoes MS-DOS commands to the console during processing of the VDM command prompt. Place this command in the CONFIG.NT in the <winroot>\system32 directory.

FORCEDOS

Starts the specified program in the MS-DOS subsystem. This command is necessary only for those MS-DOS programs not recognized as such by Windows NT.

Examples:

To start the program THISPROG in the \DOSAPPS directory and use the \DOC directory, type

```
forcedos /d doc \dosapps\thisprog
```

IPXROUTE

Manages the source routing variables of the NWLink protocol on a Token ring network. This command is available only if the NWLink protocol has been installed.

LOADHIGH

DOS=UMB command is required. Before you can load a program into the upper memory area, you must install the HIMEM.SYS extended-memory manager. Use the device command in your CONFIG.NT or equivalent startup file to install HIMEM.SYS.

The most convenient way to use the `loadhigh` command is to include it in your AUTOEXEC.NT or equivalent startup file.

To load a driver into high memory, include the following line in your AUTOEXEC.NT or equivalent startup file:

```
lh %systemroot%\system32\dosx
```

NET ACCOUNTS

Updates the user accounts database and modifies password and logon requirements for all accounts. The Net Logon service must be running on the computer for which you want to change account parameters.

To set a minimum of seven characters for user-account passwords, type

```
net accounts /minpwlen:7
```

To specify that no password can be used more than every fifth time a password is changed, type

```
net accounts /uniquepw:5
```

To prevent users from changing passwords more often than every 7 days, to force users to change passwords every 30 days, and to force logoff after logon time expires and provide a 5-minute warning before forcing the user off, type

```
net accounts /minpwage:7 /maxpwage:30 /forcelogoff:5
```

To perform the preceding task on a Windows NT Workstation computer and ensure that the settings take effect for the Windows NT Server domain which the computer is logged on to, type

```
net accounts /minpwage:7 /maxpwage:30 /domain
```

To update the user accounts database of all member servers, type

```
net accounts /sync
```

NET COMPUTER

Adds or deletes computers from a domain database. This command is available only on computers running Windows NT Server. All computer additions and deletions are forwarded to the primary domain controller.

For example, to add the computer RICKS to the logged on domain, type

```
net computer \\RickS /add
```

NET CONFIG

Displays the configurable services that are running, or displays and changes settings for a service.

Examples:

To display information about the local server and prevent the display from scrolling, type

```
net config server ¦ more
```

To hide a server's computer name from the list of available servers, type

```
net config server /hidden:yes
```

To disconnect users after 15 minutes of inactivity, type

```
net config server /autodisconnect:15
```

NET CONFIG WORKSTATION

Displays or changes settings for the workstation service while the service is running.

Use the net config workstation command to change configurable workstation service parameters. The changes take effect immediately and are permanent.

Not all workstation service parameters can be changed using the net config workstation command. Other parameters can be changed in the configuration registry.

Examples:

To display the current configuration for the Workstation service, type

```
net config workstation
```

To set the number of milliseconds Windows NT waits before sending data to a communication device to 500 milliseconds, type

```
net config workstation /chartime:500
```

NET CONTINUE

Reactivates suspended services.

At a server and a client, use the net continue command to reactivate a service that has been paused. Pause a service before stopping the service to let users complete jobs or disconnect from resources. To make a minor correction to a resource, pausing the service or printer might be sufficient. Then use the net continue command to reactivate the service or printer, without canceling users' connections.

At a client, use the net pause and net continue commands to switch between network printers and a printer attached to your computer.

NET FILE

Displays the names of all open shared files on a server and the number of file locks, if any, on each file. This command also closes individual shared files and removes file locks.

Examples:

The display for the net file command is similar to the following:

```
File      Path              Username    #locks
------------------------------------------------
0         C:\A_FILE.TXT     NCHAGTAI      0
1         C:\DATABASE       RICKS       2
```

To view a display of information about shared files, type

net file

To close a file with identification number 1, type

net file 1 /close

NET GROUP

Adds, displays, or modifies global groups on Windows NT Server domains. This command is available for use only on Windows NT Server domains.

Use the net group command to group users who use the network in the same or similar ways. When you assign rights to a group, each member of the group automatically has those rights.

Examples:

A display of groups on the server is similar to the following:

```
Group Accounts for \\WORDPROC *Domain Admins *Domain Users
```

Notice that each group name is preceded by an asterisk (*). The asterisk distinguishes groups in displays including both users and groups.

C

To display a list of all the groups on the local server, type

`net group`

To add a group called exec to the local user accounts database, type

`net group exec /add`

To add a group called exec to a Windows NT Server domain user accounts database from a computer with Windows NT Workstation software installed, type

`net group exec /add /domain`

To add the existing user accounts NCHAGTAI, GRACE, and RICKS to the exec group on the local computer, type

`net group exec NCHAGTAI GRACE RICKS /add`

To add the existing user accounts NCHAGTAI, GRACE, and RICKS to the exec group of a Windows NT Server domain from a computer with Windows NT Workstation software installed, type

`net group exec NCHAGTAI GRACE RICKS /add /domain`

To display users in the exec group, type

`net group exec`

To add a comment to the exec group record, type

`net group exec /comment:"The executive staff."`

NET HELPMSG

Provides help with a Windows NT error message.

Examples:

When a network operation fails, you see a message similar to the following:

`NET 2182: The requested service has already been started.`

Windows NT error messages are preceded by the word net, but you don't have to type net with message#.

The net helpmsg command explains why an error occurred and tells you what action will solve the problem.

To get help with Windows NT error message NET 2182, type

`net helpmsg 2182`

The error message and help information appear.

NET LOCALGROUP

Adds, displays, or modifies local groups.

Use the `net localgroup` command to group users who use the computer or network in the same or similar ways. When you assign rights to a local group, each member of the local group automatically has those same rights.

To display a list of all the local groups on the local server, type

`net localgroup`

To add a local group called exec to the local user accounts database, type

`net localgroup exec /add`

To add a local group called exec to the Windows NT Server domain user accounts database, type

`net localgroup exec /add /domain`

To add the existing user accounts NCHAGTAI, GRACE (from the DOCS domain), and RICKS to the exec local group on the local computer, type

`net localgroup exec NCHAGTAI DOCS\GRACE RICKS /add`

To add the existing user accounts NCHAGTAI, GRACE, and RICKS to the exec group of a Windows NT Server domain, type

`net localgroup exec NCHAGTAI GRACE RICKS /add /domain`

To display users in the exec local group, type

`net localgroup exec`

To add a comment to the exec local group record, type

`net localgroup exec /comment:"The executive staff."`

NET NAME

Adds or deletes a messaging name (sometimes called an alias), or displays the list of names for which the computer will accept messages. The Messenger service must be running to use `net name`.

Use the `net name` command to specify a name for receiving messages. The Messenger service must be started to use the `net name` command. Each messaging name must be unique on the network. Names created with `net name` are strictly for messaging; names are not groups.

Windows NT uses three kinds of names:

◆ Any name for messaging, which is added with `net name`.

◆ The computer's computername, which is added when the Workstation service starts.

◆ Your username, which is added when you log on, provided your user name is not in use as a message name elsewhere on the network.

The computername cannot be deleted. The username can be deleted.

To view the list of names at your computer, type

`net name`

To add the name RICKS to your computer, type

`net name RICKS`

To remove the name RICKS from your computer, type

`net name RICKS /delete`

NET PAUSE

Pauses running services.

At a server, use the `net pause` command before stopping a service to let users complete jobs or disconnect from resources. Pausing a service puts it on hold but doesn't remove the software from memory. Users who already have a connection to the resource are able to finish their tasks, but new connections to the resource are prevented.

To reactivate a service that has been paused, use the `net continue` command.

At a client, use the `net pause` and `net continue` commands to switch between network printers and printers attached to your workstation.

Note

Not all services can be paused.

Pausing affects the Windows NT services in the following ways:

◆ Pausing the Net Logon service prevents the computer from processing logon requests. If the domain has other logon servers, users can still log on to the network.

◆ Pausing the Workstation service keeps the username, password, and connections defined, but directs requests for print devices to printers attached to the computer rather than to printers connected to the network.

Examples:

To pause the Server service, type

```
net pause server
```

To pause the Net Logon service, type

```
net pause "net logon"
```

NET PRINT

Displays or controls print jobs and printer queues.

You can display a particular queue by using `net print \\computername\sharename`.

To get information about job number 3 on the \\DOCS computer, type

```
net print \\DOCS 3
```

To hold job number 26 on the \\DOCS computer, type

```
net print \\DOCS 26 /hold
```

To release job number 26 on the \\DOCS computer, type

```
net print \\DOCS 26 /release
```

To list the contents of the LASER printer queue on the \\DOCS computer, type

```
net print \\DOCS\LASER
```

NET SEND

Sends messages to other users, computers, or messaging names on the network. The Messenger service must be running to receive messages.

Examples:

To send the message "Meeting changed to 3 p.m. Same place." to the user robertf, type

```
net send robertf Meeting changed to 3 p.m. Same place.
```

To send a message to all users connected to the server, type

```
net send /users This server will shut down in 5 minutes.
```

To send a message that includes a slash mark, type

`net send robertf "Format your disk with FORMAT /4"`

NET SESSION

Lists or disconnects the sessions between a local computer and the clients connected to it.

To display session information for the client with the computername RICKS, type

`net session \\RICKS`

To end all sessions between the server and the clients connected to it, type

`net session /delete`

NET SHARE

Creates, deletes, or displays shared resources.

To share a directory with a path containing a blank character, enclose the drive and the path of the directory in quotation marks (" ").

When you display all the shared resources on a computer, Windows NT reports the sharename of the resource, the devicename(s) or path associated with the resource, and a descriptive comment about the resource.

As you create shares on a server, they are saved. When you stop the Server service, all shares are disconnected, but they are reconnected automatically the next time the Server service is started or the computer is restarted.

Examples:

To display information about shared resources on the computer, type

`net share`

To share a computer's C:\docs directory with the sharename SECRETARY and include a remark, type

`net share secretary=c:\docs /remark:"For department 1."`

To stop sharing the docs directory, type

`net share secretary /delete`

To share a computer's C:\apps LST directory with the sharename LIST, type

`net share list="c:\apps lst"`

NET START

Starts a service, or displays a list of started services. Service names of two or more words, such as Net Logon or Computer Browser, must be enclosed in quotation marks (").

Use the `net start` service command to start Windows NT services.

You can also use the Services option in Control Panel to configure services to stop and start automatically. This Control Panel option also allows you to manually stop, start, pause, and continue network services.

Service names with two words, such as Net Logon or Computer Browser, must be enclosed in quotation marks (").

This command also starts network services that are not provided with Windows NT.

To list the services that are currently running, type

`net start`

NET START ALERTER

Starts the Alerter service. The Alerter service sends alert messages.

Alert messages are sent as Windows NT messages from the server to a user's computer. The Messenger service must be running on the user's computer for the user to receive the alert messages.

NET START BROWSER

Starts the Computer Browser service.

`net start "computer browser"`

NET START DHCP CLIENT

Starts the DHCP Client service. This command is available only if the TCP/IP protocol has been installed.

For example, `net start "dhcp client"`

NET START SNMP

Starts the SNMP service. The SNMP service allows a server to report its current status to an SNMP management system on a TCP/IP network. This command is available only if TCP/IP and SNMP have been installed.

For example, `net start "snmp"`

NET STATISTICS

Displays the statistics log for the local Workstation or Server service.

`net statistics [workstation ¦ server]`

Examples:

To display running services for which statistics are available, type

`net stats`

To display statistics for the Server service and prevent the display from scrolling, type

`net statistics server ¦ more`

NET STOP

Stops a Windows NT network service.

Stopping the Server service prevents users from accessing the computer's shared resources. If you stop the Server service when users are accessing resources, Windows NT displays a warning message, requesting confirmation that you want to cancel the connections. A "y" response cancels all connections to the computer.

Before stopping the Server service, you can pause the service (to disallow new connections), or send a message advising users to disconnect from the server's resources.

`net stop` can also stop network services not provided with Windows NT.

NET TIME

Synchronizes the computer's clock with that of another computer or domain. Used without the /set option, displays the time for another computer or domain.

NET USE

Connects a computer to or disconnects a computer from a shared resource, or displays information about computer connections. The command also controls persistent net connections.

Examples:

To assign the disk-drive devicename E: to the LETTERS shared directory on the \\FINANCIAL server, type

`net use e: \\financial\letters`

To assign (map) the disk-drive devicename M: to the directory MARIA within the LETTERS volume on the FINANCIAL NetWare server, type

`net use m: \\financial\letters\maria`

To assign the devicename LPT1: to the LASER2 shared-printer queue on the \\ACCOUNTING server, type

`net use lpt1: \\accounting\laser2`

To disconnect from the LPT1: printer queue, type

`net use lpt1: /delete`

To assign the disk-drive devicename H: to a home directory as the user mariel, type

`net use h: /home /user:mariel`

To assign the disk-drive devicename F: to \\FINANCIAL server's SCRATCH shared directory, which requires the password hctarcs, but not make the connection persistent, type

`net use f: \\financial\scratch hctarcs /persistent:no`

To disconnect from the \\FINANCIAL\SCRATCH directory, type

`net use f: \\financial\scratch /delete`

To connect to a resource shared on the FINANCIAL 2 server type

`net use k: "\\financial 2"\memos`

You must use quotation marks around a servername that includes a space. If you omit the quotation marks, Windows NT displays an error message.

To restore the current connections at each logon, regardless of future changes, type

`net use /persistent:yes`

NET USER

Adds or modifies user accounts or displays user-account information.

Type **net user** without parameters to view a list of the user accounts on the computer.

Examples:

To display a list of all user accounts for the local computer, type

`net user`

To view information about the user account nchagtai, type

`net user nchagtai`

To add a user account for Nadeem Chagtai, with logon rights from 8 A.M. to 5 P.M. Monday through Friday (no spaces in time designations), a mandatory password, and the user's full name, type

`net user nchagtai nchagtai /add /passwordreq:yes /times:monday-friday,8am-5pm/`
`fullname:"Nadeem Chagtai"`

The username (nchagtai) is entered the second time as the password.

`net user nchagtai /homedirnc:yes`

`/homedir \\SERVER\USERS\NCHAGTAI`

NET VIEW

Displays a list of domains, a list of computers, or the resources being shared by the specified computer.

Examples:

To see a list of the resources shared by the \\PRODUCTION computer, type

`net view \\production`

To see the resources available on the NetWare server \\MARKETING, type

`net view /network:nw \\marketing`

To see a list of the computers in the sales domain or workgroup, type

`net view /domain:sales`

To see all the servers in a NetWare network, type

`net view /network:nw`

NTCMDPROMPT

Runs the Windows NT command interpreter, CMD.EXE, rather than COMMAND.COM after running a TSR or after starting the command prompt from within an MS-DOS application.

`ntcmdprompt`

When COMMAND.COM is running, some features of the Windows NT command prompt, such as the Doskey display of command history, are not available. If you would prefer to run the Windows NT command interpreter after you have started a TSR or started the command prompt from within an MS-DOS-based application, you can use the `ntcmdprompt` command. However, keep in mind that the TSR may not be available for use when you are running CMD.EXE. You can include the `ntcmdprompt` command in your CONFIG.NT file or the equivalent custom startup file in an application's PIF.

Include `ntcmdprompt` in your CONFIG.NT file, or the Config startup file specified in the PIF.

PENTNT

Detects floating-point division error; when present in the Pentium chip, it disables floating-point hardware, and turns on floating-point emulation.

PRINT

Prints a text file while you are using other Windows NT commands.

For example, the following command prints the file REPORT.TXT on LPT1:

```
print /d:LPT1 report.txt
```

START

This command starts a separate VDM to run a specified program or command. Used for multitasking.

```
START ["title"] [/Dpath] [/I] [/MIN] [/MAX] [/SEPARATE ¦ /SHARED] [/LOW ¦ /NORMAL ¦
/HIGH ¦ /REALTIME] [/WAIT] [/B] [command/program] [parameters]
```

`"title"`	Title to display in window title bar.
`path`	Starting directory.
`I`	The new environment will be the original environment passed to the CMD.EXE and not the current environment.
`MIN`	Start window minimized.
`MAX`	Start window maximized.
`SEPARATE`	Start 16-bit Windows program in separate memory space.
`SHARED`	Start 16-bit Windows program in shared memory space.
`LOW`	Start application in the IDLE priority class.

C

NORMAL	Start application in the NORMAL priority class.
HIGH	Start application in the HIGH priority class.
REALTIME	Start application in the REALTIME priority class.
WAIT	Start application and wait for it to terminate.
B	Start application without creating a new window. The application has ^C handling ignored. Unless the application enables ^C processing, ^Break is the only way to interrupt the application command/program.
	If it is an internal cmd command or a batch file then the command processor is run with the /K switch to CMD.EXE.
	This means that the window will remain after the command has been run.
	If it is not an internal cmd command or batch file then it is a program and will run as either a windowed application or a console application.
parameters	These are the parameters passed to the command/program.

SWITCHES

Forces enhanced keyboards to emulate a standard keyboard when in a VDM window. This command is to be placed in the CONFIG.NT file located in the <winroot>\system32 directory.

TITLE

This command sets the title at the top of a VDM when using the CMD.EXE command interpreter.

TCP/IP Utilities Reference

ARP [-A INET_ADDR [-N [IF_ADDR]] [-D INET_ADDR] [-S INET_ADDR ETHER_ADDR [IF_ADDR]]

This command displays and allows you to modify the IP-to-Ethernet (or Token Ring) physical address tables. These tables are used by the ARP (Address Resolution Protocol).

a	Displays the current ARP entries. If the Inet_Addr is not specified, only the IP address and the physical addresses for the specified computer are listed.
n	Displays the ARP address for all the network interfaces specified by If_Addr.
d	Deletes the specified entry listed by Inet_Addr.
s	Adds an entry into the ARP cache table.
Ether_Addr	Specifies a single physical address.
If_Addr	Identifies, if it exists, the IP address of the interface whose address translation table will be modified. By default, if the IP address is not present, the first application available is used.
Inet_Addr.	Specifies the IP address in decimal notation.

FINGER [-L] [USER] @HOST [...]

The FINGER command displays information about a user on a specific system. The user must be using FINGER services and output may vary depending on configuration and type of remote system being accessed.

l	Displays all information in a long (verbose) fashion. This command is not supported on all systems.

Note

I have yet to see it function completely on any remote system.

User	Specifies which user you would like information on. By omitting the specific user parameter, the FINGER command will list information on all users attached to a specific HOST.
@HOST	Lists the host name (or the IP address) of the remote system whose users you want information about.

FTP [-V] [-N] [-I] [-D] [-G] [HOST] [-S:FILENAME]

FTP (File Transfer Protocol) is a command that transfers files between two computers. Each computer must be running the FTP service. While FTP may be used as a command-line connectivity utility, it may also be used interactively.

v	Does not show the responses from a remote server.
n	Forces a manual LOGON process every time the FTP command establishes an initial connection to a server.
i	Turns off the interactive prompting. This is especially helpful when you are transferring multiple files.
d	This parameter allows you to debug your FTP session. All commands that are passed between the client and the server are displayed for you to see.
g	This disables the use of wild-card option when transferring files between two servers (or a server and a client). Please see the GLOB command.
HOST	Specifies the host name of the remote server you wish to connect to. You may replace the host name with a decimal IP address.
s:Filename	The option activates a script file with FTP commands. The script file may be a simple ASCII text file with individual FTP command-lines. It is recommended to use the -S:Filename parameter instead of the redirection key (>).

The following table shows a series of FTP commands that are available when FTP services are activated on a Windows NT computer. If FTP services are not selected, then these commands will not be available to you, even if being accessed by a remote system with FTP services enabled.

Command	Description
!	Executes a specific command from the local computer.
?	Displays information for FTP commands. ? functions the same as HELP.
append	Adds a file, on the local computer, to a file on the remote computer using current file type settings.
ascii	Sets the file transfer type to ASCII. This is the default setting.
bell	This option signals every time a file is completely sent with a computer generated bell. By default, this option is turned off.
binary	Sets the file transfer type to BINARY.
bye	Ends the FTP session with the remote computer. It also exits the FTP program.
cd	Changes the working directory on the remote computer.

close	Ends the FTP session with the remote server and returns you to the command prompt.
debug	Toggles the debugging mode. When the debugging option is turned on, each command passed between the client and the server will be displayed for you. Each command is preceded by the '—>' string. By default, this option is turned off.
delete	Deletes files from the remote server.
dir	Displays a list of the remote computers' directories and files.
disconnect	Disconnects from the remote computer but does not exit the FTP session.
get	Copies a file (or files) from the remote server to the local computer using the current file transfer type.
glob	This toggle turns on/off file globbing. Globbing permits the use of wild-card characters during the selection phase of files to be transferred. By default, this option is on.
hash	Each block of transferred data (in 2048 blocks) can be represented by a hash mark #. As a file is transferred, a hash mark may be printed on the screen every 2048 bytes. By default, the hash mark is turned off.
help	Displays functional descriptions for FTP commands.
lcd	This option changes the working directory on the local computer. It is similar to the cd command.
literal	This option allows you to send multiple arguments to a remote FTP server. In response, the remote FTP server sends a single confirming reply code.
ls	Lists an abbreviated list of directories and files from the remote server.
mdelete	Deletes files on the remote computer.
mdir	Lists the directories and files from the remote server. The mdir command enables you to specify multiple files / directories.
mget	Copies a remote file to your local computer using the current file transfer file type settings.
mkdir	Creates a remote directory.

continues

Command	Description
mls	Lists for you an abbreviated list of directories and files from the local server.
mput	Copies files from the local computer to the remote computer using the current file transfer file type settings.
open	Connects to a specified FTP server.
prompt	During a multiple file transfer, FTP prompts you between each transferred file. This allows you to selectively choose files identified by the mget and mput commands. By default, this command is turned on.
put	Copies a local file from the local server to the remote computer using the file transfer file type settings.
pwd	Displays the current directory on the remote computer.
quit	This command ends the FTP session and exits from the FTP program.
quote	This option allows you to send multiple arguments to a remote FTP server. In response, the remote FTP server sends a single confirming reply code. This command is identical to the literal command.
recv	Copies a remote file to the computer using the current file transfer file type settings.
remotehelp	Lists the help screens for remote help commands.
rename	This option renames a file on the remote server.
rmdir	Deletes a remote directory.
send	Copies a local file on the local server to the remote computer using the file transfer file type settings.
status	This parameter displays the current status of the FTP session connections.
trace	This toggles the ability to trace individual packets, and shows their individual route, while running an FTP command.
type	Sets or displays the file type transfer settings.
user	This specifies a user to the remote server.
verbose	This toggles the verbose option. When it is on, all FTP commands and responses are displayed. As well, statistics regarding the file transfer rates and efficiency rates are displayed for other FTP functions. By default, this command option is turned on.

HOSTNAME

This diagnostic command prints the name of the current host.

IPCONFIG [/ALL | /RENEW [ADAPTER] | /RELEASE [ADAPTER]]

This diagnostic command lists all the current TCP/IP network configuration settings. When you are using DHCP, this command shows the user the settings that were set when the server was originally installed. Without any parameters, the IPCONFIG command displays TCP/IP, DHS, WINS, IP address, and Subnet mask values.

/All	Produces a complete display. Without this parameter, the IPCONFIG command displays only the IP address, Subnet mask, and the default gateway values for each network card.
/Renew [Adapter]	This command resets the DHCP configuration settings. If your client is not using DHCP services, this command will have no effect. To specify a specific Adapter, include the adapter name.
/Release [Adapter]	Releases the current DHCP settings. This option disables the TCP/IP services from the specified local host. To specify a specific Adapter, include the adapter name.

IPQ [-SSERVER | -PPRINTER] [-L]

The IPQ command is used to obtain information about a print queue running on a host computer. The host computer must be running the LPD services.

Sserver	Lists the name of the host computer that has the printer attached to it.
Pprinter	Specifies the name of the printer for the desired print queue.
l	This option lists a detailed status.

LPR [-SSERVER | -PPRINTER [-OOPTIONS] [-CCLASS] [-JJOBNAME] FILENAME

This connectivity utility is used to print a file to host computer running an LPD server.

C

If you plan to print a non-text file (PostScript for example), then use the LPR command with the -OL option flag. By using just the -L parameter, the file to be printed will be passed, as-is, directly to the print queue without first passing though and being processed by the LPDSVC services.

Sserver	Specifies the name of the host computer with a printer attached to it.
Pprinter	Specifies the name of the printer for the desired print queue.
ooptions	This option allows the LPR command to send values directly to the LPDSVC services in a host computer.
cclass	Lists the contents of the banner page for the class of print jobs going to the print queue.
jjobname	Specifies the name of the current print job.
Filename	The name of the file you are trying to print.

NBSTAT [-A REMOTENAME] [-A IPADDRESS] [-C] [-N] [-R] [-R] [-S] [-S] [INTERVAL]

This utility command displays all the protocol statistics and current TCP/IP connections when you are using NETBIOS over TCP/IP.

a Remotename	Lists the remote computers' name table while using the computer's name.
A IPaddress	Lists the remote computers' name table while using the computer's IP address.
c	Lists the contents of the NETBIOS name cache. It lists the IP address for each name listed.
n	Lists the local NETBIOS names.
R	Reloads the LMHOSTS file after purging all the name from the NETBIOS name cache.
r	This option lists the name resolution statistics for Windows networks. If your computer is using Windows for Workgroups, and you are on Windows NT, this option returns the number of names resolved and registered via a broadcast or via WINS.
S	This displays the workstation and the server session information. It lists the remote hosts by IP address only.
s	This option displays the workstation and the server session information. It attempts to resolve and convert remote host IP addresses to a name using the HOSTS database file.

Interval	Redisplays the specified information from the NBSTAT command every x seconds. You must press Control-C to stop the output. If you do not specify an Interval, the NBSTAT command displays information only once.

NETSTAT [-A] [-E] [N] [S] [-P PROTOCOL] [-R] [INTERVAL]

This diagnostic command displays the protocol statistics and the current TCP/IP network connections.

a	Displays all connections. Server connections are usually not listed with this command.
e	This option displays Ethernet statistics and may be combined with the -s option.
n	This parameter displays the addresses and port numbers in numerical form.
p Protocol	Shows connections for the specified protocol. The protocol may be TCP or UDP. If this command is combined with the -s option, then the protocol may be TCP, UDP, or IP.
r	Displays the contents of the routing table.
s	This displays per-protocol statistics. By default, the statistics are shown for TCP, UDP and IP. The -p option may be used as a subset for the above protocols.

PING REMOTE_COMPUTER [-T] [-A] [-N COUNT] [-L LENGTH] [-F] [-I TTL] [-V TOS] [-R COUNT] [-S COUNT] [[-J HOSTLINK] | [-K HOSTLINK]] [-W TIMEOUT] DESTINATION-LIST

The Ping utility is used to isolate and identify network hardware problems and incompatibilities. The PING command allows you to verify a physical connection to a remote computer, router, gateway or LAN.

Remote_Computer	The hostname or IP address of a remote computer.
t	This is the number of seconds that this node waits for an ICMP echo reply from a remote computer. The range is from 1 through 300 seconds; the default is 20 seconds.
a	This resolves addresses to Hostnames.

n Count	The n signifies the number of times the PING sends an echo request to the remote computer. Default is four echo requests. Each echo request is separated by one second.
l Length	Sends out ECHO packets containing the amount of data specified by the Length value. The default is 64 bytes and the maximum is 8192 bytes.
f	This option sends a DO NOT Fragment flag in the packet. The packet is not fragmented by any gateways enroute to its destination.
i ttl	Sets the Time To Live value in the TCP/IP packet.
v tos	Selects the type of service field value as specified by the tos type.
r Count	Records the route of outgoing packets and all returning packets in the Record Route field. A minimum of 1 to a maximum of 9 hosts must be specified by the count value.
s Count	This option determines the timestamp for the number of hops as specified by the Count value.
j Hostlist	Routes packets via the list of hosts as specified by the Hostlist. Consecutive hosts can be separated by intermediate gateways. This is also known as loose source routing. The maximum number allowed by IP is 9.
k Hostlist	Routes packets via the list of hosts as specified by the Hostlist. Consecutive hosts cannot be separated by intermediate gateways. This is also known as strict source routing. The maximum number allowed by IP is 9.
w Timeout	Specifies the timeout interval in milliseconds.
Destination-list	This option specifies the remote hosts to ping.

You can use the ping utility to test both the hostname and the host IP address. If the IP address is verified and the hostname is not, then you have a name resolution problem. In this case, be sure that the hostname you are querying is in either the local HOSTS file or is listed in the DNS database.

RCP [-A] [-B] [-H] [-R] SOURCE1 SOURCE2 ... DESTINATION

This connectivity command copies files between a Windows NT computer and another computer running RSHD (remote shell server) services. The RCP command may also be used to copy files from two computers (not Windows NT) if the command is issued from Windows NT and both other computers are running the RSHD remote shell server services.

a	Sets the file transfer mode to ASCII. This is the default file transfer file type setting. Also, all carriage return/linefeed characters are converted to carriage returns on all outgoing files. All incoming files will have carriage returns converted to line feeds/carriage returns.
b	Sets the file transfer mode to BINARY. In this case, no linefeed/carriage return conversion is completed.
h	This transfers source files marked with the hidden attribute on the Windows NT computer. Without this option, you would not be able to access a hidden file with the RCP command.
r	Recursively copies the contents of all subdirectories of the source to the destination. In this case, both the source and destination must be directories.
Source1 and Destination	Must be in the following form: [host[.user]:]Filename. If the [host[.user]:] is omitted, the host is assumed to be the local computer. If, however, the .user option is omitted, the currently logged on Windows NT username is used.

REXEC HOST [-L USERNAME] [-N] COMMAND

This utility command allows you to run a command on the remote host, only if the remote host(s) are running the REXECD services. REXEC authenticates the user name on the remote host by using a password before executing the specified command.

Host	Specifies the remote host on which you want to run the command.
l Username	Specifies the name of the user on the remote system.
n	Redirects the input of REXEC to NUL characters.
Command	Specifies the command that you wish to run.

ROUTE [-F] [COMMAND [DESTINATION] [MASK NETMASK] [GATEWAY]]

This diagnostic command enables you to manage and manipulate the network routing tables.

This option clears the routing tables of all gateway entries. If this parameter is used in conjunction with one of the following commands, the tables are cleared prior to executing the specified command.

Command	Description
print	Prints a route path.
add	Adds a route path.
delete	Deletes a route path.
change	Modifies an existing route path.
Destination	Specifies which host to send the Command to.
Mask	If present, this command specifies that the next parameter should be interpreted as the Netmask parameter.
Netmask	Specified, if present, the subnet mask value that should be associated with the current route entry. If the entry is not specified, the ROUTE command defaults to 255.255.255.255.
Gateway	Specifies the gateway to be used for all routing packets.

RSH HOST [-L USERNAME] [-N] COMMAND

This command runs commands on the remote host if the remote host is running RSH services.

Host	Specifies the remote host on which you want to run a command.
l Username	This option specifies the username to use on the remote host. If this option is omitted, the logged-on username is used.
n	This redirects the input of the RSH to NUL characters.
Command	Specifies the actual command you want to run.

Note

If you plan to use the RSH command from a Windows NT Server Domain, the Domain controller must be available to resolve the currently logged in user name. This is true because the logged-in username is not kept in the RAM cache on the local computer and must be re-created in the table as the user launches the RSH service.

TELNET [Host [Port]]

This commands starts a program that allows a user to emulate a terminal with a remote host system. The remote host must be running TELNET services. TELNET allows for the following terminals to be emulated; DEC VT100, VT52, or TTY. Each of these terminals will run in a *connection-based* mode within the services of the TCP protocol.

To provide terminal emulation from a Windows NT computer, the host must be configured with the TCP/IP program, the TELNET server program, and a user account for the Windows NT computer.

Host	This specifies the host name or the IP address of the remote system you wish to connect to. The system must be compliant with applications like Gopher and Mosaic.
Port	Specifies the remote port you wish to connect to. The default value for the PORT is specified in the SERVICES file. If there is no TELNET value listed within the SERVICES file, TELNET defaults the value of the connection port to decimal 23.

TFTP [-I] Host [get | put] Source[Destination]

This connectivity command transfers files to and from a remote computer running TFTP services. TFTP (Trivial File Transfer Protocol) service is similar to the FTP utility except that it does not check user authenticity. The TFTP commands do require adequate rights to READ and WRITE from within UNIX.

i	Specifies BINARY image transfer mode (also known as an octet). In this mode, a file is transferred byte by byte. If this parameter is not included, the file is transferred in an ASCII file transfer file type mode.
Host	Specifies the local or remote host.
get	Transfers the Destination on the remote computer to the Sources on the local computer. TFTP does not support user authentication.
put	Transfers the Source on the local computer to the Destination on the remote.
Source	Specifies the file to transfer.
Destination	Specifies where to transfer the file.

TRACERT [-D] [-H MAXIMUMHOPS] [-J HOSTLIST] [-W TIMEOUT] TARGETNAME

This diagnostic utility determines the route taken to a destination by sending an Internet Control Message Protocol (ICMP) echo packet with varying Time To Live values. Each router along the path that a packet takes is required to subtract 1 from the value of the Time To Live (TTL) value. When the TTL packet reaches 0, the router is supposed to send back an ICMP Time Exceeded message to the source sending computer. TRACERT continually sends out packets, starting with a value of 1 in the TTL setting, until the packet returns with an ICMP Time Exceeded message.

The TRACERT command determines exactly how many hops (routers) exist between the source computer and the destination computer.

d	Specifies the tracert command to omit resolving the address to hostnames.
h Maximumhops	Specifies the maximum number of hops to search for the target computer.
j Hostlist	This option specifies loose source routing along a predetermined list of host computers.
w Timeout	Waits the number of specified milliseconds for a timeout to occur.

- Logon Scripts

- Troubleshooting
  Logon Scripts

APPENDIX D

Logon Script
Programming Guide

LOGON SCRIPTS

A logon script is a .BAT, .CMD, or .EXE file that is run automatically when a user logs on at an NT network client running either NT Workstation, or DOS. A logon script can be used to set up the user's environment to perform such tasks as making network connections, running applications, and setting environment variables on startup.

NT User Profiles can do everything that logon scripts can do, plus a lot more. Here is a list of the differences between logon scripts and User Profiles.

◆ User profiles work only on NT Workstation and Windows 95 clients. Logon scripts can be used with DOS or DOS/Windows clients to manage the user desktop with a little creative configuration.

◆ Logon scripts are used if you only want to partially control the user's environment, such as network connections, without managing or dictating the entire Windows desktop.

◆ Logon scripts are used when you have decided not to use server-based User Profiles, and you want to create common network connections for multiple users.

◆ Logon scripts are easier to create and maintain than User Profiles.

You can assign a different logon script to each user or create logon scripts for use by multiple users. Whenever that user logs on, the logon script is downloaded and run. To assign a user a logon script, you designate the name of the logon script file in the user environment profile defined in User Manager on an NT Server computer. You need to specify only the filename, not the full pathname.

The default file extension for logon scripts is .BAT for all client computers other than OS/2 clients. You can define a different file type as the logon script by specifying the file extension. If the same logon script must run at both Intel-based and RISC-based workstations, it must be a .BAT file that runs the appropriate .EXE file or files on the workstation. Use the %processor% parameter in the logon script to run the appropriate .EXE file no matter which processor is being used.

You specify the path to the logon script using the Server option of Control Panel. By default, NT looks for logon scripts on the primary domain controller in the directory systemroot\SYSTEM32\REPL\IMPORT\SCRIPTS, where systemroot is the disk drive and directory in which NT Server was installed.

Logon scripts are not synchronized automatically from the PDC to the BDCs. You need to set up replication so that all servers in a domain can authorize logon requests. You need to make sure that the logon script for a user must be located on the server that approves the user's logon request.

Note

The filename for each user's logon script is defined with other user account information in User Manager for Domains. If you change the path to the logon scripts, this change is not replicated to the client workstations. The path must be updated manually in the Server option of Control Panel for each client computer.

NT Server creates a \SCRIPTS subdirectory under both the default import and export directories used for replication. If you replicate logon scripts, you must be sure to use the Server option of Control panel or Server Manager to change the logon script path to systemroot\SYSTEM32\REPL\IMPORT\SCRIPTS or systemroot\SYSTEM32\REPL\EXPORT\ SCRIPTS, as appropriate.

When you use replicated logon scripts, you identify the PDC as the export server and all the others as import servers.

Note

The export server for the logon scripts is usually the PDC, but does not have to be.

LOGON SCRIPT PATH

The path to your logon script is as follows:

```
\\<logon server>\<netlogon>\...\<logon script name>
```

The directory in which NT looks for your logon script depends on where Netlogon points to. If the path to your logon script is C:\SCRIPTS\ LOGON_SCRIPTS\CURRENT_SCRIPT.cmd, then you may either share C:\SCRIPTS as Netlogon and give the path to the script as LOGON_SCRIPTS\ CURRENT_SCRIPT.CMD, or you may share C:\SCRIPTS\LOGON_SCRIPTS as Netlogon and give the path as CURRENT_SCRIPT.CMD.

SPECIFYING HOME DIRECTORY

NT provides three environment parameters you can use in a logon script or other batch file to specify the location of the home directory, or in Program Manager to specify the working directory of an application. If a home directory has not been defined for the user, the default values are used as shown in the following table.

D

LOGON SCRIPT PROGRAMMING GUIDE

Parameter name	Definition
%homedrive%	Drive where the home directory is located
%homepath%	Pathname of the home directory\USERS\DEFAULT
%homeshare%	UNC name of the shared directory containing the home directory, or a local or redirected drive letter

If the \USERS\DEFAULT directory does not exist on the drive specified by the %homedrive% parameter, the value of the %homepath% parameter is set by default to the \USERS directory on that drive. If the \USERS directory does not exist, the %homepath% parameter is set to the root directory specified by the %homedrive% parameter.

When the user opens a Command Prompt window, the default directory is the equivalent of %homedrive%%homepath%. If a user's home directory is specified on a remote computer and that computer is not available, the default directory of the Command Prompt on an NT Workstation computer is the user's home directory on the local workstation.

You might also want to specify the working directory of each application as %homedrive%%homepath%. That way, all File Open and Save As dialog boxes default to the user's home directory.

TROUBLESHOOTING LOGON SCRIPTS

Use this list to troubleshoot the most common problems with logon scripts:

Make sure the logon script is in the directory specified in the Server option of Control Panel. When NT is installed, the logon script directory is as follows: systemroot\system32\repl\import\scripts. The only valid path option is a subdirectory of the default logon script directory. If the path is any other directory or it uses the environment variable %homepath%, the logon script will fail.

If the logon script is on an NTFS partition, make sure the user has Read permission for the logon script directory. If no permissions have been explicitly assigned, the logon script might fail without providing an error message.

Make sure the logon script has a filename extension of either .CMD or .BAT. The .EXE extension is also supported, but for executable programs only. If you use a nondefault file extension for your processor, be sure to specify it with the filename of the logon script. Attempting to use the .EXE extension for a script file results in the following error message: NTVDM CPU has encountered an illegal instruction. If this error message appears, close the window in which the logon script is running.

If the logon script is to run on a WFW computer, make sure the NT domain name is specified as a startup option in the Network option of Control Panel.

Make sure any new or modified logon scripts have been replicated to all domain controllers. Replication of logon scripts happens periodically, not immediately. To manually force replication, use Server Manager.

WRITING BATCH FILES FOR NT

Unlike NetWare, NT does not have a special scripting language for logon scripts. NT uses an enhanced version of the DOS command language. The following sections explain the most important NT commands.

AT

This command schedules commands, batch files, and programs to run on a computer at a specified time and date. This command requires you be a member of the local Administrator or Backup Operator group. See Appendix C, "NT Quick Reference Guide," for more information on how to use the AT command.

When you include the identification number for the command, the display provides information for a single entry and is similar to the following:

```
Task ID:      0
Status:       OK
Schedule:     Each  F
Time of Day:  04:30PM
Command:      net send group leads status due
```

Commands scheduled with the AT command run as background processes, so no output is displayed on the computer's screen. To redirect output to a file, use the redirection symbol (>). If you redirect output to a file, enclose the command name you are scheduling in quotation marks. The current directory for the executing command is the <winnt-root> directory.

When you change the System Time at a computer after scheduling a command to run with AT, synchronize the AT scheduler with the revised time by typing AT without options.

Scheduled commands are stored in the Registry, so scheduled tasks are not lost if you have to restart the Schedule service.

Scheduled jobs that access the network should not use redirected drives made by the user. The Schedule service may not be able to access these drives and they may not be present if a different user is logged on at the time the scheduled job runs. Instead, scheduled jobs should use UNC paths. If you schedule an AT command that uses a drive letter to connect to a shared directory, you should include an AT command to disconnect the drive when you are finished using it. If the drive is not disconnected, the drive letter assigned will not be available or seen at the command prompt. Examples of the AT command follow.

To display a list of commands scheduled on the server MARKETING, enter

```
at \\marketing
```

To check the status of a command with the identification number 3 on the server BNET, enter

```
at \\bnet 3
```

To schedule a net share command to run on the BNET server at 7:00 A.M., and redirect the listing to the server RICKS, shared directory REPORTS, and file BNET.TXT, enter

```
at \\bnet 07:00 "net share reports=d:\reports >> \\ricks\reports\bnet.txt"
```

To back up the BNET servers hard disk to a tape drive at midnight every five days, create a batch program (BUP.CMD) containing the backup commands. Then schedule the batch program to run by typing

```
at \\bnet 00:00 /every:5,10,15,20,25,30 bup
```

To cancel all commands scheduled on the current server, clear the AT schedule information by typing

```
at /delete
```

The Backup utility included with NT and NT Server does not include functionality for scheduling unattended backups. However, using the Schedule service in conjunction with the command line capabilities of the Backup utility, you can set up unattended backups.

1. Make sure that the Schedule service is started on the computer with the tape drive.

2. Execute the command BNET BACKUP FILES to backup the local Registry, and log all backup information to C:\BACKUP.LOG:

   ```
   ntbackup backup c: /D "BNET Backup Files" /B /L "c:\backup.log"
   ```

3. The following AT command schedules BUP.CMD to execute at 11:00 P.M. every Monday, Wednesday, and Friday:

   ```
   at 23:00 /every:M,W,F BUP.CMD
   ```

FOR

This command runs a specified command for each file in a set of files. You can use the FOR command within a batch program or directly from the command prompt.

```
for %%variable in (set) do command [command-parameters]
```

For example, suppose you want to use the type command to display the contents of all the files in the current directory with the extension .TXT or .LST. To do this, and to use the replaceable variable %f, type the following command at the command prompt:

```
for %f in (*.txt *.lst) do type %f
```

In this example, each file with the .TXT or .LST extension in the current directory is substituted for the %f variable until the contents of every file are displayed. To use this command in a batch file, you simply replace every occurrence of %f with %%f.

IF

The IF command performs conditional processing in batch programs. If the condition specified in an IF command is true, NT carries out the command that follows the condition. If the condition is false, NT ignores the command.

```
if [not] errorlevel number command
if [not] string1==string2 command
if [not] exist filename command
```

The following example displays the message "Can't find data file" if NT cannot find the file PRODUCT.DAT:

```
if not exist product.dat echo Can't find data file
```

IPCONFIG

This diagnostic command displays all current TCP/IP network configuration values. This command is of particular use on systems running DHCP, allowing users to determine which TCP/IP configuration values have been configured by DHCP.

```
ipconfig [/all ¦ /renew [adapter] ¦ /release [adapter]]
```

IPXROUTE

This manages the source routing variables of the NWLink protocol on a Token ring network. This command is available only if the NWLink protocol has been installed.

```
ipxroute board=n [clear] [def] [gbr] [mbr] [remove=xxxxx]
```

D

LOGON SCRIPT PROGRAMMING GUIDE

LPQ

This diagnostic utility is used to obtain status of a print queue on a host running the LPD server.

```
lpq -SServer  -PPrinter [-l]
```

NBSTAT

This diagnostic command displays protocol statistics and current TCP/IP connections using NBT (NetBIOS over TCP/IP). This command is available only if the TCP/IP protocol has been installed.

```
nbtstat [-a remotename] [-A IP address] [-c] [-n] [-R] [-r] [-S] [-s] [interval]
```

PING

ping verifies connections to a remote host or hosts. This command is available only if the TCP/IP protocol has been installed.

```
ping [-t] [-a] [-n count] [-l length] [-f] [-i ttl] [-v tos] [-r count] [-s count]
[[-j host-list] ¦ [-k host-list]] [-w timeout] destination-list
```

The following shows sample output for ping:

```
C:\>ping ds.internic.net
Pinging ds.internic.net [192.20.239.132] with 32 bytes of data:
Reply from 192.20.239.132: bytes=32 time=101ms TTL=243
Reply from 192.20.239.132: bytes=32 time=100ms TTL=243
Reply from 192.20.239.132: bytes=32 time=120ms TTL=243
Reply from 192.20.239.132: bytes=32 time=120ms TTL=243
```

RCP

This connectivity command copies files between an NT computer and a system running RSHD, the remote shell daemon. The RCP command can also be used for third-party transfer to copy files between two computers running RSHD when the command is issued from an NT computer. The RSHD daemon is available on UNIX computers, but not on NT, so the NT computer can only participate as the system from which the commands are issued. The remote computer must also provide the REP utility by running RSHD.

```
rcp [-a ¦ -b] [-h] [-r] source1 source2 ... sourceN destination
```

These examples show syntax for some common uses of RCP. To copy a local file to the logon directory of a remote computer, use

```
rcp filename remotecomputer:
```

To copy a local file to an existing directory and a new filename on a remote computer, use

```
rcp filename remotecomputer:/directory/newfilename
```

To copy multiple local files to a subdirectory of a remote logon directory, use

```
rcp file1 file2 file3 remotecomputer:subdirectory/filesdirectory
```

To copy from a remote source to the current directory of the local computer, use

```
rcp remotecomputer:filename .
```

To copy from multiple files from multiple remote sources to a remote destination with different usernames, use

```
rcp remote1.user1:file1 remote2.user2:file2 remotedest.destuser:directory
```

To copy from a remote system using an IP address to a local computer (where the username is mandatory because a period is used in the remote system name), use

```
rcp 11.101.12.1.user:filename filename
```

ROUTE

The ROUTE command is used to manipulate network routing tables. This command is available only if the TCP/IP protocol has been installed.

```
route [-f] [command [destination] [mask subnetmask] [gateway]]
```

START

This command starts a separate window to run a specified program or command.

```
start ["title"] [/dpath] [/i] [/min] [/max] [/separate] [/low] [/normal] [/high] [/
realtime] [/wait] [/b] [filename] [parameters]
```

Glossary of Networking Terminology

10Base-T   An IEEE 802.3 physical layer standard for Ethernet running on UTP cable at 10 Mbps.

100Base-TX   An IEEE 802.3 physical layer standard for running Ethernet on category 5 UTP at 100 Mbps.

100Base-T4   An IEEE 802.3 physical layer standard for running Ethernet on category 3 UTP at 100 Mbps.

100VG (100VG-AnyLAN)   An IEEE 802.12 LAN standard using Demand Priority access protocol over category 3 UTP at 100 Mbps. This standard also includes the capability of the hub to support Token ring and 10-Mbps Ethernet as well as 100VG switching between ports.

A

access protocol (access method, access scheme)   The method of communication used between network cards on a local area network. Frames of data that contain packets of data are exchanged between NICs. (See also *CSMA/CD*, *token-passing bus*, and *token-passing ring*.)

access token   Uniquely identifies the user and the groups to which that user belongs.

Access Control Entry (ACE)   An entry in an Access Control List (ACL). Each access control entry defines the protection or auditing to be applied to a file or other object for a specific user or group of users.

Access Control List (ACL)   A list of ACEs that control and record accesses to objects defined in the security account database. The owner of the object has discretionary control of the ACL and can control the level of user access to the object.

Address Resolution Protocol (ARP)   A network layer protocol used in TCP/IP networks to resolve names to IP addresses.

AppleTalk   Networking protocols and networking software proprietary to Apple Computers. (See also *OSI model*.)

application (application software)   Software program(s).

Arcnet (Attached Resource Computer Network)   A type of LAN that uses token-passing bus access protocol and (usually) 93 ohm coaxial cable. A trademark of Datapoint, Inc., Arcnet is proprietary, but it is widely licensed and used under various brand names. Standard Microsystems Corp. and Thomas-Conrad Corp. are the leading purveyors of Arcnet products, although many other Arcnet products are produced using SMC Arcnet chips.

Asynchronous Transfer Mode (ATM)   A set of networking standards that provide cell switching services with potentially very high bandwidths.

Attachment Unit Interface (AUI)   An IEEE term for a connector that connects an external transceiver to the AUI plug on an Ethernet network card.

attenuation   Signal wave form degradation.

authentication   The process of recognizing and granting access to a client. Security processes compare the user account against information contained in the server's (or domain controller's) security account database.

Auto-sense (auto detect)   A technique used by NT and Windows 95 to discover hardware devices and locate a driver to access each device during the setup program.

B

Backup Domain Controller (BDC)   A domain controller that contains a copy of the Primary Domain Controller's SAM and provides authentication service in place of the PDC when required. (See also *domain controller*.)

bandwidth   A measure of *capacity*, not of speed. Bandwidth measures how much time is occupied on the wire.

bandwidth utilization   The percentage of time the media (cable) is occupied with signaling.

BOOTP   An application used to boot and configure diskless workstations across the network. The bootstrap protocol BOOTP was originally defined in RFC 951. The latest BOOTP RFC is RFC 1542, which includes support for DHCP.

bridge   A device that joins two separate LANs but restricts LAN frame traffic to either side of the bridge unless forwarding is required. Bridges process LAN frames (not network packets) and are governed by IEEE standards. A bridge either filters or forwards frames by reading the node address in the frame header (MAC-layer bridge) or by reading the DSAP and SSAP in an 802.2 header (LLC bridge). A bridge should not be confused with a router, which uses an entirely different layer of protocol and information for forwarding packets (not frames). (See also *MAC-layer bridge*, *LLC bridge*, and *router*.)

brouter (bridging-router, routing-bridge)   A device that can perform both bridging and routing functions.

Btrieve   A client-server software product that is a LAN-based file system and record manager product. This product uses a B-tree internal file index structure to enhance file search speed and efficiency. Several network applications are Btrieve based due to Novell's previous ownership and promotion.

bus (computer)   The interface between devices in a computer. PCs incorporate bus designs that include ISA, EISA, MCA, and NuBus (Macintosh).

bus (network)   A network that includes one circuit on which data is sent and received. Bits of data are broadcast over a bus network; only one frame of data can occupy the bus at one time.

bus mastering   A function used to offload I/O processing to a processor on the interface card. Although some ISA boards use this technique for marginally improved performance, bus mastering is only truly effective when used with a bus design that is capable of controlling bus master access to the computer bus, as is the case in EISA, MCA, and PCI computers. Bus mastering alone does not fully realize the capabilities of the design unless it's implemented in conjunction with the 32-bit burst mode and streaming data modes of EISA, MCA, and PCI computer buses.

C

Carrier Sense Multiple Access with Collision Detection (CSMA/CD)   The access protocol used in Ethernet LANs. CSMA/CD is the foundation of IEEE 802.3 standards as well as Ethernet II standards developed by Digital, Intel, and Xerox. (See also *Ethernet* and *access protocol*.)

CD-ROM (Compact Disc Read-Only Memory)   Digital compact discs (CDs) contain read-only memory disk storage. CD-ROM drives provide over 600 MB of disk storage on one single CD. Data is generally formatted in ISO 9660 standard format and interpreted into various OS formats using CD Extensions (MSCDEX). Note: Macintosh computers use High Sierra format instead of ISO 9660.

centralized processing   In a minicomputer or mainframe environment, processing is conducted in one processor (or symmetrical multiprocessors). User devices are "terminals" that provide multiple user access to one centralized processing unit.

Central Processing Unit (CPU)   The processor that controls a computer. In an Intel-based computer, this is the 80x86 processor that runs the operating system and controls all internal devices. In a minicomputer or mainframe environment, this is the processor (or multiprocessor computer) where processing for all users takes place.

client   A computer configured with networking software to use another computer's resources.

cluster   A group of servers linked together to cooperatively process an application. Like SMP, this furthers the scalability of an operating system. Clustering is scheduled to be added to a future release of the NT Server operating system.

collaborative processing   A blend or combination of distributed and centralized processing.

Complex Instruction Set Computing (CISC)   A processor internal instruction set that uses more complex and explicit computing assembler code for processing. (See also *RISC*.)

connectionless protocol   A networking protocol that communicates in one direction only, not requiring an acknowledgment. (See also *IPX*, *connection-oriented protocol*, *NCP*, and *SPX*.)

connection-oriented protocol   A networking protocol that communicates in two directions, and each packet sent requires an acknowledgment packet. (See also *connectionless protocol*, *NCP*, and *SPX*.)

D

desktop   Windows' background screen. This term is used to discuss elements in and on the desktop that can be changed by the user.

distributed computing   Separate computers coprocessing a multiuser application over a network. In a distributed computing environment, each computer acts as a separate computer, sharing resources on the network. In some cases, the very same application is used on multiple computers at the same time. Distributed computing is the opposite of centralized computing, where a single CPU processes multiple user program execution and resource sharing as is done in a mainframe or minicomputer environment.

distributed processing   In a PC network, processing of data is conducted at each workstation instead of by one CPU. In some cases, some of the processing can be distributed to specialized application servers. The host computer is a server where file and print services are provided, but generally no centralized processing as in a minicomputer or mainframe.

distribution share (Share)   A directory shared for use on the network. (See also *Share*.)

domain   A grouping of file servers, computers, and user accounts.

domain controller   A primary (PDC) or backup (BDC) domain controller. These computers service a domain by providing the Security Account Manager (SAM) database against which logons and connections are authenticated.

Domain Name System (DNS)   A service that presents friendly names to users and resolves friendly computer names to IP addresses. This is sometimes referred to as the BIND service in BSD UNIX.

DOS (MS-DOS, PC-DOS, DR-DOS)   Used throughout this book to refer to any version of the DOS operating system that is used at a workstation.

drive array   A series of intelligent disk drives linked together for the purpose of spanning data across the drives or improving reliability. (See also *RAID*.)

Dynamic Host Control Protocol (DHCP)   A server protocol that dynamically assigns IP addresses. DHCP was designed by the IETF to reduce the amount of configuration required when using TCP/IP. DHCP is defined in RFCs 1533, 1534, 1541, and 1542.

E

Enhanced Small Device Interface (ESDI)   A drive controller type that utilizes a hard drive as a slave unit. ESDI controllers generally drive only two disk drives and have an on-board processor to translate drive geometry, manage I/O requests, and provide caching.

Ethernet   The term generally used to refer to CSMA/CD LANs based on 802.3 or Ethernet II standards. Although the term "Ethernet" is commonly used to refer to both Digital-Intel-Xerox Ethernet II and IEEE 10Base-5 standards, technical differences exist in terminology and frame formatting. The differences in frame formatting make Ethernet II and 802.3 LANs incompatible, even though they use the same cabling and physical specification. IEEE does not use the term Ethernet anywhere in their specifications. In this book, the term Ethernet is used as a synonym for both Ethernet II and 802.3 networks—to avoid confusion with common usage.

Ethernet II   The original Ethernet design developed by Digital, Intel, and Xerox in the late 70s. True Ethernet II design only includes thick Ethernet cabling with external transceivers, but today it is compatible with all IEEE 802.3 physical specifications and devices. Ethernet II frame formatting is not compatible with other Ethernet frame formats. Ethernet II frame formatting is commonly used in TCP/IP networks and networking vendors who have used Ethernet for many years. (See also *CSMA/CD* and *Ethernet*.)

Extended Industry Standard Architecture (EISA)   A computer, bus, and interface card design based on 32-bit bus mastering. EISA is an extension to ISA bus design and enables EISA and ISA interface cards to be used in a single type of bus interface slot. (See also *ISA* and *MCA*.)

F

Fast Ethernet   Ethernet (802.3) LANs that operate at 100 Mbps bandwidth.

fault tolerance   A system's capability to continue operating without interruption even when parts of the system have failed. Generally, this term is used in conjunction with hardware failures where a secondary device continues operation without interruption when a hardware device fails. A RAID 5 disk subsystem, for example, is fault tolerant.

File Transfer Protocol (FTP)   This is a TCP/IP client/server application used only to transfer files from one computer to another. However, FTP is not just for the Internet. You can also set up an FTP server on your local network to help users within your corporation find the information they need. Several versions of FTP clients are available, including both character-based and graphical-interface varieties. Software programs, such as Mosaic, can also provide a friendly client interface to the FTP server service.

firmware   Software that is programmed into a PROM chip to become part of the hardware function.

foreign domain   A domain other than the user's local domain.

frame   A unit of data that is exchanged on a LAN. Frame formatting implements an access protocol for the purpose of enabling communications between nodes on a LAN (Ethernet, Token ring, Arcnet, and so on). A frame should not be confused with a packet, which is encapsulated within a frame for transport across a LAN. The terms "frame" and "packet" often are interchanged in common usage but have distinctly different functions and use distinctly different layers of protocol. In this book, the terms are always used consistently to avoid confusion.

G-H

gateway   A logical component that connects two dissimilar protocols. The manner in which Microsoft uses the term also includes processes where clients are linked to network services even though protocol conversion might not apply. For example, Gateway Services for NetWare requires the use of NetWare native protocols (IPX or NWLink) to gain access to a NetWare server.

Hardware Abstraction Layer (HAL)   An object-oriented software layer that interfaces the computer hardware platform and devices to the NT operating system. This layer provides NT operability with different hardware platforms, including Intel x86, PowerPoint Computing, Alpha, and MIPS processors and devices.

High Performance File System (HPFS)   A file system used in an OS/2 environment to provide better performance and support for extended attributes.

hive   A subtree of the Registry that has been saved as a file. Because the hive is a file, it can be copied or moved to other systems and/or edited using the Registry Editor utility.

hub (active hub, passive hub)   A wiring concentrator or multiport repeater. (See also *wiring concentrator*.)

HyperText Transfer Protocol (HTTP)   Defines the commands used by the World Wide Web. Mosaic is a commonly used client software application on the World Wide Web. Often, the terms World Wide Web, HTTP, and Mosaic are used interchangeably. For example, the file name for the WWW server in the EMWAC resource kit is HTTPS.EXE for HTTP Server.

I-J

Industry Standard Architecture (ISA)   A term developed to describe the design of the 16-bit AT bus (sometimes called the classic bus) developed by IBM.

Institute of Electrical and Electronic Engineers (IEEE)   A U.S. trade association. The IEEE 802 committee was formed for the purpose of standardizing local area networks. They provide physical, medium access control, and logical link control standards for the purpose of interoperability between competing vendor devices.

Integrated Drive Electronics (IDE)   A drive design that incorporates an embedded controller on a smaller (3 1/2-inch) disk drive. IDE drives can be connected together, but the second drive must be a slave of the first, using the primary disk controller and not its own embedded controller. This type of drive is interfaced to a computer bus with an IDE host adapter, not a controller.

intelligent hub   A wiring concentrator, multiport repeater, multistation access unit, or other type of hub that includes a processor and logic to monitor the LAN. This type of hub has an embedded MAC (node) address and therefore populates a network segment.

International Standards Organization (ISO)   A worldwide standards organization based in Geneva, Switzerland. The United States has representation in ISO through ANSI, and ISO standards are sometimes included in international treaties or trade agreements to provide worldwide interoperability of computing and data communications systems. ISO often cites IEEE, ANSI, and CCITT standards for specifications. ISO is responsible for the OSI model. (See also *Open Systems Interconnection 7-layer model.*)

Internet Engineering Task Force (IETF)   An organization that manages Requests for Comments (RFCs) for Internet improvements and management.

Internet Protocol (IP)   A network protocol that provides routing services across multiple LANs and WANs that is used in the TCP/IP protocol stack. IP packet format is used to address packets of data from ultimate source and destination nodes (host) located on any LAN or WAN networked with TCP/IP protocol. IP provides routing services in conjunction with IP routers, which are incorporated into many computer systems and most versions of UNIX.

internetwork   A network of LANs and WANs linked together through bridges or routers.

Internetwork Packet Exchange (IPX)   A network protocol developed by Novell to address packets of data from ultimate source and destination nodes located on any LAN networked with NetWare and to provide routing services in conjunction with NetWare (and third-party) routers. IPX uses logical addressing to enable routing services in conjunction with routers and RIP and SAP protocols. The IPX packet has information fields that identify the network address, node address, and socket address of both the source and destination and provides the same functionality of the OSI network layer in the OSI model.

interoperability   Compatibility or the capability for equipment (usually manufactured by competing vendors) to work together. Industry standards (or *de facto* standards) are agreed upon or used by vendors to make their equipment work with other vendors' equipment. This factor has lead to wide implementation of LAN equipment.

Interprocess Communication (IPC)   Computing instructions between processes internal to the operating system.

K-L

key   The first major division of the Registry. Each key is shown in the title bar of a separate Registry Editor window. A basic installation yields four predefined keys. More keys can be added for specific purposes as necessary.

linear bus   A network topology consisting of connections strung over the length of a cable segment. Linear-bus topology can be used in Ethernet and Arcnet LANs.

Link Support Layer (LSL)   Novell application software that interfaces MLID network card drivers with ODI packet drivers dynamically in RAM. (See also *MLID* and *ODI*.)

LMHOSTS   A configuration file that maps names to MAC addresses. This file is commonly used on Microsoft networks to locate remote computers for network file, print, and remote procedure services and for domain services such as logons, browsing, replication, and so on.

Local Area Network (LAN)   A limited-distance, multipoint physical connectivity medium consisting of network interface cards, media, and repeating devices designed to transport frames of data between host computers at high speeds with low error rates. A LAN is a subsystem that is part of a network.

This book uses the term LAN differently from the way Microsoft uses the term in much of its training and documentation but is fully consistent with the way the term is used in operating system messages and screens. The use of the term LAN is also in full compliance with IEEE and ANSI standards, which specifically discuss technical aspects of LANs.

The term LAN is commonly used elsewhere to refer to an entire network of computers; however, in this book, the term LAN refers specifically to a single Ethernet, Token ring, or other type of LAN. It is important to accurately describe each LAN as a separate entity in a network where routable protocols are used, as is the case in a NetWare IPX network. (See also the Introduction of this book for more clarification.)

local domain   The domain local to a resource or user.

Local Procedure Calls (LPCs)   Procedure calls that are exchanged with processes internal to an operating system. LPCs are similar to remote procedure calls (RPCs), which are used over networks.

LocalTalk   A proprietary type of LAN developed by Apple Computer for Macintosh computers. LocalTalk uses flat telephone wire and AppleTalk network architecture for peer-to-peer access between nodes.

logical hop   The number of hops across routers. A router detects logical hops based on how many routers a packet must traverse to end up at its destination. If bridges exist, they constitute a physical hop, but no logical hop is detected because bridges do not work at the network protocol layer.

Logical Link Control (LLC)   IEEE's LLC (802.2) layer defines the protocol, frame header information, and methods of bridging similar and dissimilar types of LANs together. LLC includes spanning-tree and source-routing protocols and uses DSAP and SSAP addressing to determine specific bridge routes through an internetwork connected with LLC bridges.

logon   A user connection that is authenticated by a local server, a remote server, or a domain controller.

loss   Signal strength degradation.

M

MAC-layer bridge   A bridge that connect two similar LANs together. Each LAN must use the same frame formatting because a MAC-layer bridge reads the frame addresses, builds a table of which node addresses exist on either side of the bridge, and either filters or forwards each frame as necessary. This type of bridge is sometimes called a *transparent* or *learning* bridge. When a bridge joins two LANs together, they appear to be one single LAN; however, traffic on each side of the bridge is limited to that specific LAN—unless forwarding is required.

Management Information Database (MIB)   The database that SNMP notifications are saved in for later analysis.

mapping   A drive letter assignment to a shared directory.

Mbps (Megabits per second)   Signaling rates are shown in millions of bits per second. Although this is generally considered a data transfer rate, it is actually a measure of capacity. LANs are usually discussed in terms of this denomination. (See also *bandwidth* and *Mbytes/sec*.)

Mbytes/sec (Megabytes per second)   A million bytes per second. Data flow rates are most often discussed in terms of Mbytes/sec. Input/output ratings are normally discussed in this denomination. A byte is eight bits, and therefore a Mbyte/sec is eight times as much data flow as Mbps. (See also *Mbps*.)

media (medium)   Cabling, telecommunications medium, or electromagnetic wave medium used to transport bits of data from one node to another on a network. Generally, the term *medium* refers to whatever type of cable (or electromagnetic medium) is used in a LAN or WAN.

Medium Access Control (MAC)   The middle layer in IEEE's 802 model for LANs. The MAC layer specifies access protocol, frame formatting, node addressing, and error control mechanisms in a LAN. The MAC layer forms the basis for the type of LAN, whereas the physical layer adds various alternative physical media for transporting the LAN frames.

Medium Attachment Unit (MAU)   An IEEE term to describe the device that connects an external transceiver to the 15-pin connector on an Ethernet network card. The same device is described in Ethernet II vernacular as a DIX connector; there is no difference except in terminology.

messages   Data to be passed between nodes is first assembled as messages, which are further broken into packets appropriately sized to fit the specific frame type for the LAN. NCP provides this function, negotiating the appropriate packet size during a workstation connection request. NCP packet headers contain a sequence number that is used to reassemble the packetized data back into messages on the receiving end.

Micro Channel Architecture (MCA)   A proprietary 32-bit computer and bus architecture designed by IBM to improve bus bandwidth and facilitate bus mastering. MCA is not backward compatible with ISA and requires exclusive use of MCA devices.

microprocessor   A miniaturized processor. Previous processors were built on integrated circuit boards with many large components. Most processors today use high-tech, silicon-based technology that improves performance, reduces heat generation, and is more efficient. In this book, the term processor is used instead of microprocessor. (See also *processor*.)

Multiple Link Interface Driver (MLID)   A Novell specification for network card driver interface that provides concurrent support for multiple frame types and multiple packet types and therefore network protocols such as IP, OSI, and AppleTalk. MLID drivers are used with Link Support Layer (LSL.COM), the IPX ODI packet driver (IPXODI.COM), and other ODI-conforming packet drivers. (See also *IPX*, *IP*, *ODI*, *packet*, *frame*, and *network protocol*.)

multiport repeater   A repeater that has multiple in and out ports. (See also *wiring concentrator*.)

Multistation Access Unit (MAU)   A Token ring LAN device that implements star-wired ring topology. The MAU is a physical switching device that connects all nodes into a single serial circuit.

multitasking   The capability of an operating system to handle multiple processing tasks apparently at the same time. (See also *preemptive processing*.)

multiuser   The capability of an operating system (or NOS) to handle access from multiple users at the same time. A multiuser operating system must multitask to handle multiple user requests simultaneously. (See also *multitasking*.)

N

near end crosstalk (NeXT)   Signal bleed from one wire (or set of wires) to another.

NetBEUI (NetBIOS Extended User Interface)   Microsoft's proprietary simple network packet format and protocol. NetBEUI is non-routable and supports Microsoft-related networking products only. (See also *NetBEUI Frame*.)

NetBEUI Frame (NBF)   The implementation of the NetBIOS Extended User Interface (NetBEUI) protocol driver used in Windows NT.

NetBIOS   An IBM protocol (and packet structure) that provides several networking functions. NetBIOS was developed by IBM and Sytek to supplement and work with BIOS in PC-DOS-based, peer-to-peer networks. NetBIOS protocol provides transport, session, and presentation layer functions equivalent to layers 4, 5, and 6 of the OSI model. The NetBIOS software that is used to implement this protocol is the NetBIOS interface.

NetBIOS Naming Service (NBNS)   A protocol that assigns and broadcasts NetBIOS names over a network.

NetWare   A trademarked brand name for the networking operating system and other networking products developed and sold by Novell.

NetWare Core Protocol (NCP) A NetWare protocol that provides transport, session, and presentation layer functions equivalent to layers 4, 5, and 6 of the OSI model.

NetWare Loadable Modules (NLMs) Software applications that run on NetWare 3.*x* and 4.*x* server operating systems.

network A group of computers connected by a communications link that enables any device to interact with any other device on the network. The term "network" is derived from the term "network architecture" to describe an entire system of hosts, workstations, terminals, and other devices. Although the term network is often used in the industry to describe a LAN, LAN and network are used in this book as more specific terms to differentiate an entire system (network) from a LAN used specifically to describe one specific subsystem of a network. (See also *network architecture* and *LAN*.)

network architecture A "blueprint" or complete design of hardware and software layers of specifications, protocols, and functions that enable communications among hosts, workstations, and terminals on a network. Most notable of network architectures is the OSI model, which sets a standardized, layered model for network design. Every networked computer system has a formalized design for network architecture, including IBM's SNA, Digital's DECnet, Xerox's XNS, and others. (See also *network* and *OSI model*.)

network card, network adapter, network interface card (NIC) An interface card to be put in the bus of a computer (or other LAN device) to interface a LAN. Each network card represents a node, which is a source and destination for LAN frames, which in turn carry data between the NICs on the LAN.

Network Device Interface Specification (NDIS) A Microsoft specification for drivers that can concurrently support multiple frame formats and network protocols, such as NetBIOS, IP, AppleTalk, and IPX. This specification is equivalent to Novell's ODI and MLID specifications.

Network File System (NFS) A trademark of Sun Microsystems that comprises a set of presentation layer protocols providing operating system function calls. NFS provides a standardized interface between various UNIX and other operating systems.

network protocol A packet protocol that provides routing and other information for a network equivalent to layer 3 of the OSI model. NetWare's proprietary network protocol is IPX, which is very similar to IP.

network utilization The percentage of bandwidth in use on a LAN or WAN.

node An intelligent device connected to a network.

node address   An address assigned to each node on a LAN. IEEE-assigned "universal addresses" for Ethernet and Token ring are generally used for both the serial number of the network card and node address. Alternatively, a "local address" can be assigned. Arcnet NICs have locally assigned addresses that are configured with switch settings. This number is picked up by the network card driver as the node address for use in IPX protocol.

noise   Signal interference.

nonroutable protocol   A network protocol, such as NetBEUI, IBM's SNA, or NetBIOS protocols, that uses a name for the source and destination of packets and does not identify each LAN or WAN as a separate entity. These protocols do not work with traditional nonproprietary routers the way that routable protocols do, whereby network addresses (network numbers) and node addresses are used to locate the ultimate source and destination nodes (or hosts) for packets of data. Instead, the scheme for locating the ultimate destination and source of packets is contained in proprietary protocols that are part of the networking software. Therefore, "routing" usually occurs either by processing requests and re-packetizing them or by using intelligent bridging techniques, such as source-routing bridging (802.2 protocol). In the past, nonroutable protocols have restricted packet traffic to a specific physical LAN or WAN (network address), relying on bridges (as opposed to routers) to provide service across an internetwork. (See also *routable protocols*, *internetwork*, *bridges*, *routers*, *network address*, and *node address*.)

NT File System (NTFS)   A file system format used in NT to provide greater performance and support for extended attributes.

NWLink   Microsoft's emulation of Novell's IPX/SPX protocols.

O

object   Any user or resource-related network entity. Servers, users, printers, and groups are the most commonly used objects.

Open Data Link Interface (ODI)   A Novell specification that provides service for multiple network packet types and for network protocols such as IPX, IP, OSI, and AppleTalk with a single network card driver. Novell's MLID specification enables network card drivers to interface through Link Support Layer (LSL.COM) with IPX ODI (IPXODI.COM) and multiple ODI-conforming packet drivers. (See also *IPX*, *IP*, *ODI*, *packet*, *frame*, *network*, and *protocol*.)

Open Software Foundation (OSF)   A UNIX standards organization and set of standards for a UNIX operating system that is unified among several UNIX vendors. OSF-1, the first implementation of this UNIX version, is marketed by Digital Equipment Corporation.

Open Systems Interconnect (OSI) 7-layer model (OSI model)   A model developed by the International Standards Organization to establish a standardized set of protocols for interoperability between networked computer hosts. Each layer of the model consists of specifications or protocols that fulfill specific functions in a networking architecture. The OSI model parallels DECnet, SNA, XNS, and other networking models. The OSI model consists of specific protocols that are nonproprietary and offered in the hope of unifying networking protocols used in competing vendors' systems. In this book, the OSI model serves as a central model of traditional routable networking protocols, which helps clarify the functionality and equivalence of various network architectures.

P-Q

packet   A limited-length unit of data that is formed by the network, transport, presentation, or application layer (layers 3-7 of the OSI model) in a networked computer system. Packet headers contain information used by each corresponding layer of protocol in a network architecture. Packets may or may not contain data because their functions are often fulfilled by one of the codes in a field of the header or trailer. In all cases, data is transported over a network; larger amounts of data are broken into shorter units and placed into packets. Higher-layer packets are encapsulated into lower-layer packets for encapsulation into LAN frames (or in WAN frames or packets) for delivery to the ultimate host destination. The terms *packet* and *frame* should not be confused because each has different specific functions.

Microsoft often uses the term packet to describe frames, but this book makes a clear distinction and never uses the two terms interchangeably. NT uses several packet formats including NetBEUI, IPX with NetBIOS, and TCP/IP.

permissions   File and directory access privileges given to users or groups.

portability   Software capability to run on more than one hardware environment. An application can be ported to a different operating system or processor environment when various APIs and other types of function call libraries (such as Sun RPCs) are used in common in different platforms. (See also *Remote Procedure Calls*.)

PORTUAS   A utility that converts LAN manager accounts and security to an NT Security Account Manager database.

POSIX (Portable Operating System Interface for Computing Environments)   A set of standards drafted by the Institute of Electrical and Electronic Engineers (IEEE) that define various aspects of an operating system, including topics such as programming interface, security, networking, and graphical interface.

preemptive processing   In a multitasking operating system, multiple tasks (threads) are generally controlled by a scheduler that preempts, or interrupts, each process, granting processor time in the form of a time slice (about 1/18th of a second). This enables multiple tasks to *apparently* run at the same time. However, each task runs for a time slice and is then preempted by the scheduler, which then starts the next process and so on—rotating processor time among active threads. In most Intel-based, multitasking operating systems, the scheduler executes in ring 0, and threads execute in ring 3. (See also *ring*, and *time slice*.)

Primary Domain Controller (PDC)   A server that contains the SAM database for a domain and provides a central point of authentication within the domain. (See also *domain controller*.)

print device   The actual physical printer, such as HP LaserJet 4 or Epson FX-100, and the port on the computer, such as LPT1 or COM1.

print jobs   Each printing session submitted to the spooler is considered a print job. The spooler has to modify print streams according to the designated job type. For example, one print job might require no modification whatsoever, whereas another might require a form feed.

printer   The logical object to which print jobs are sent. The printer represents the print device (the physical printer itself).

printer pools   A group of print devices represented by one printer object. Printing to the printer object sends the print job to the first available printer device.

processor   The controlling device that interprets and executes instructions, performs computations, and otherwise controls the major functions of a computer. This book discusses Intel 80x86-series processors, which are miniaturized single-chip microprocessors that contain thousands to millions of transistors in a silicon-based, multilayered integrated circuit design.

processor utilization   The percentage of clock cycles that the processor is busy. When processor utilization reaches 100 percent, the processor cannot process more requests; it is fully saturated.

protocol   Rules of communication. In networks, several layers of protocols exist. Each layer of protocol needs to physically hand off or receive data only from the immediate layer above and beneath it, whereas virtual communications occur with the corresponding layer on another host computer. Layers between the two hosts are transparent. (See also *OSI model* and *access protocol*.)

protocol analyzer   A computer (or software module) that captures LAN frames for the purpose of disassembly, encoding, and analysis. Most protocol analyzers also include network statistical analysis, monitoring, and threshold notification.

R

recognizer Each time you start a computer running NT Server, the hardware recognizer updates hardware configuration data in the Registry.

redirector Microsoft's networking software module installed on a DOS or Windows computer that enables a computer (client) to connect to a server (computer sharing its resources). Microsoft also refers to NetWare shells and requesters as redirectors. (See also *requester* and *shell*.)

Reduced Instruction Set Computing (RISC) A processor instruction set that uses fewer assembler instructions in the interest of speeding up processing. (See also *CISC*.)

Redundant Array of Inexpensive Drives (RAID) A disk subsystem configuration in which logical volumes are mirrored, spanned, and/or parity checked over multiple disk drives. Recent University of California at Berkeley research white papers define five RAID levels. RAID 5 is most often used, in which data is spanned over multiple disk drives and a parity check retained on each drive is most commonly used for fault tolerant data protection with very high I/O performance. Some vendors have added additional RAID definitions. Most RAID disk subsystems implement RAID at a hardware level, while NT operating systems support RAID 0 (spanning data over multiple drives), RAID 1, (mirroring data on two drives), and RAID 5 at the software level.

Registry A database used by the operating system that contains computer hardware and software configuration data. When viewing data in the Registry with the Registry Editor, you see keys, subtrees, and subkeys in a hierarchical tree format on the left of the key window. Values (configuration parameters) for the subkeys appear on the right of the key window.

Remote Access Server (RAS) A software server module included in NT that provides dial in/dial out capability.

Remote Procedure Calls (RPC) Function calls exchanged between software applications running on separate computers over a network. NT uses Sun Microsystem's RPCs and network library to provide standard interoperability between NT software modules and software modules running on UNIX, NetWare, and other computing platforms.

rendering Modifying or processing the print job to produce printed output. Most graphics print jobs require rendering to translate complex print codes into printed graphics.

repeater A device that repeats or amplifies bits of data received at one port and sends each bit to another port. A repeater is a simple bus network device that connects two cabling segments and isolates electrical problems to either side. When used in a LAN, most repeaters take some role in reconstituting the digital signal that passes through it to extend the distances a signal can travel and reduce problems that occur over lengths of cable, such as attenuation.

requester   Novell's equivalent to the Microsoft redirector that redirects network function calls to a server.

Requests for Comment (RFC)   RFCs are submitted to the IETF for improvements or modifications to Internet operations. Once adopted by IETF, they become operating procedures and standards for use on the Internet or in products used with the Internet. For example, RFC-821 (SMTP) is about message exchange, RFC-822 is about message format, and RFC-1154 is about attachment support.

resources   Printers, disks, and any other physical devices that are shared on the network.

resource domain   The domain in which a resource is physically located.

RFC   See *Request for Comments*.

rights   Network activities (specific tasks) that a user or group can perform.

ring (processor ring)   Intel 80286 and higher processors execute threads in one of four rings. Ring 0 is termed the most favored ring, having priority over threads running in rings 1, 2, and 3. Each lower-numbered ring has priority over higher-numbered rings. Most multitasking operating systems execute code in ring 3, whereas a scheduler executes in ring 0, which has the capability to preempt the thread. Ring 3 has memory protection so that memory being utilized by each thread is protected from potential corruption from other threads that are concurrently running. (See also *preemptive processing*.)

ring (ring topology)   A network topology in which each node is a repeater and nodes are physically connected into a physical ring circuit. This topology can be used for Token ring and FDDI LANs, although star-wired ring is preferred. (See also *star-wired ring*.)

routable protocol   A network protocol that can work with nonproprietary routers. Traditional routers use the network packet header fields to identify network address (network numbers) and node addresses for ultimate source and destination nodes (or hosts) for packets of data. This scheme for routing packets across internetworks is used with OSI, NetWare (IPX), TCP/IP, and AppleTalk network protocols.

Conversely, other network protocols, such as NetBEUI, SNA, and NetBIOS protocols, use a name for the source and destination resource and do not identify each LAN or WAN as a separate entity. (See also *nonroutable protocols*, *internetworks*, *routers*, and *node address*.)

router   A device that reads network layer packet headers and receives or forwards each packet accordingly. A router does not in any way process LAN frames because the LAN frame is discarded once the LAN has delivered the frame to the network card driver. The destination logical address in the header is read and checked against the routing tables the router has learned; where necessary, the header hands off the packet to the network card driver for the destination network address.

Routers connect LANs and WANs into internetworks but must be able to process the network packets for a specific type of network protocol. Many routers process various packet types and are therefore termed multiprotocol routers. (See also *OSI model*.)

Routing Information Protocol (RIP)   A protocol used by routers to communicate network routing information. RIP or OSPF (Open Shortest Path First) is used to route IP and IPX packets between locally attached networks on multihomed systems (computers that are able to run more than one stack).

RSA   A software company and its C-2 compliant encryption algorithm used in NT as well as other software products.

S

scalability   Software's capability to run on small and large hardware platforms without modification. NT is scalable, meaning that it can run on a single Intel 386 or higher processor, multiple 486 or Pentium processors, or a few different RISC processors without modification. Virtually all NT applications can be considered scalable because the operating system it runs on is not hardware specific and is scalable.

security account database   A database of user account, password, and resource availability that is contained in each computer that shares access to its resources. In Windows for Workgroups, the security account database is called the password file; in NT, it is called the Security Account Manager.

Security Account Manager (SAM)   The security account database in an NT server or domain controller that controls network logons, authentication, and resource access. SAM contains a listing of user and resource objects and their related rights and permissions. SAM provides the mechanism for controlling authentication.

security database   See *security account database*.

Security Identifier (SID)   A value assigned to each object created in the SAM or local security databases. All names and other properties are related to this SID.

segment   An electrically isolated cabling section. LAN segments are connected with repeaters. A single Ethernet LAN can have as many as 1024 segments, but no more than four repeaters can be used in a series.

The term *segment* is sometimes used by industry writers to describe a LAN. To avoid confusion in this book, the term segment is never used in this manner. (See also *segmentation* and *repeater*.)

segmentation   A term used to describe separation of a LAN into multiple LANs using a bridge or a router. The term is often used in the industry in this manner (and is therefore used in this manner in this book).

This term is more accurately used to mean splitting a single LAN segment into multiple LAN segments for the purpose of isolating electrical problems on a cable segment to provide improved cabling reliability. This is the primary function of a wiring concentrator.

You should be certain when reading industry writing whether this term is meant to convey the first meaning or second meaning described here. In this book, the term *segmentation* is used only to describe separating a LAN into multiple LANs.

server   A computer that shares its devices with other network users. (See also *client* and *redirector*.)

Server Message Block (SMB)   The highest layer protocol universally used in all Microsoft networking products. This protocol defines a series of commands used to pass information between workstations and can be broken into four message types: session (connection) control, file, printer, and message. Session control consists of commands that start and end a redirector connection to a shared resource at the server. The redirector uses the file SMB messages to gain access to files at the server. The redirector uses the printer SMB messages to send data to a print queue at a server and to get status information about the print queue. The message SMB type enables an application to exchange messages between clients and servers.

Setup   The application program used to install all Windows operating systems. Windows 3.1, Windows for Workgroups, and Windows 95 use the SETUP.EXE application, whereas Windows NT uses WINNT.EXE. Microsoft refers to all of these applications as the Setup module.

Share   A shared directory or printer. (See also *distribution share.)*

shell   Novell workstation software that connects a DOS workstation with the file server and provides a DOS interface with the server operating system. The NETX.EXE software (or its equivalent) provides this function. Later NetWare installations use the NetWare requester.

shielded twisted-pair (STP)   Cable that contains wire twisted together into pairs and shielded with an outer conductive wrapping. STP is most often used in Token ring LANs. (See also *twisted-pair* and *unshielded twisted-pair*.)

Simple Network Management Protocol (SNMP)   A protocol, packet format, and set of standards used to relay network error notification. This is a network management protocol widely used in TCP/IP networks to communicate between a management program run by an administrator and the network management agent running on a host or gateway.

Small Computer System Interface (SCSI)   An ANSI standard bus design. SCSI host adapters are used to adapt an ISA, EISA, or MCA bus to a SCSI bus so that SCSI devices (such as disk drives) can be interfaced. A SCSI bus can accommodate up to eight devices; however, the bus adapter is labeled as one device, thereby enabling only seven usable devices to be interfaced on each SCSI adapter.

SCSI devices are intelligent devices. SCSI disk drives have embedded controllers and are interfaced to a SCSI bus adapter. A SCSI interface card is therefore a "bus adapter," not a "controller." (See also *SCSI-2*.)

Small Computer System Interface-2 (SCSI-2)   An ANSI standard that improves upon SCSI-1 standards for disk and other device interfaces. SCSI-2 bandwidth is 10 Mbytes/sec, whereas SCSI-1 is 5 Mbytes/sec. SCSI-2 also permits command-tag queuing, which enables up to 256 requests to be queued without waiting for completion of the first request. Another feature of SCSI-2 is the bus's capability to communicate with more than one type of device at the same time, where a single SCSI-1 host adapter could only support one type of device (that is, a disk drive or CD-ROM) to communicate on the bus. (See also *SCSI*.)

SMB   See *Server Message Block*.

socket address   An extension to the ultimate source and destination in an IPX combined address. The socket identifies the type of request and therefore where the request should be forwarded in a server operating system. Separate socket addresses are assigned to NCP, routing, printing, and other types of requests.

source-routing bridge/protocol   A type of LLC-bridge and protocol generally used with Token rings that use IEEE 802.2 source-routing protocol and frame header fields to identify the path a frame should take through a system of bridges. The protocol is termed "source-routing" because the source of the communications (the workstation) determines the path to be taken by a discovery process. The protocol and frame header fields identify SSAPs and DSAPs (entry and exit points) in the series of bridges. (See also *bridges*, *DSAP*, *LLC-bridges*, and *SSAP*.)

Source Service Access Point (SSAP)   The entry point bridge in an LLC-bridge that uses 802.2 protocol. (See also *bridges*, *DSAP*, *and LLC-bridges*.)

spanned volume   A volume that spans across more than one logical partition and therefore more than one disk drive.

spanning-tree bridge/protocol   A type of LLC-bridge and protocol, generally used with Ethernet, that provides service for more complex configurations of multiple bridges using one of IEEE's 802.2 spanning-tree protocols. When multiple bridges are employed, the possibility of frame traffic entering infinite loops exists, and complications such as determining the most efficient path develop. This protocol designates bridges as SSAPs and DSAPs (entry and exit points) in the series of bridges. (See also bridges, *DSAP*, *LLC-bridges*, and *SSAP*.)

spool file   Print jobs are actually sent to a spool file where they are queued up to be printed. In other systems, spool files are called queues. The spool files are controlled by the spooler.

spooler   The operating system process that directs print jobs and controls the mechanics of printing from the printer object to the print device.

spooling   The process of sending the print job over the network to be printed on the printer device.

star bus   A bus network topology configured into a star by introducing a wiring concentrator, sometimes called a *multiport repeater* or *hub*.

star-wired ring (star-ring)   A network topology where connections are strung along a cable that is configured as a ring but wired into a star. The ring is contained within a Multistation Access Unit (MAU) or Control Access Unit (CAU) with two pairs of wires extending to each connection. MAUs/CAUs can be connected together to form a larger ring.

This topology is the preferred method for configuring Token ring LANs because a break in a cable can be detected and corrected without losing the ring configuration and disabling the LAN.

streaming-data mode   A function of MCA and EISA bus architectures where four bytes are transferred at a time with only one address byte, instead of the normal one address byte per data byte. Devices that access this mode can increase data transfer rates up to four times for short bursts of data through the computer bus. This technique is used with 32-bit bus mastering devices.

striping   Blocks, sectors, or bytes of data that are recorded to separate disk drives can be striped across the drives. Striping can produce better performance by writing or reading data from or to multiple drives at the same time. When drives are spanned, NT automatically stripes sectors of blocks (of newly recorded data) across the drives, splitting seeks as it does and reducing access time. Data striping as implemented in NT is referred to as RAID 0.

subkey   A subkey is a Registry entry under a key or subtree that contains a value. Each subkey represents an object and the value represents configuration parameters.

subtree   Registry keys are organized or broken down into subtrees, each containing other subtrees or subkeys. Keys and subtrees are thus organized into a hierarchical tree format. Subtrees contain other subtrees or subkeys. Subtrees can also be subkeys, containing values as well as more subtrees or subkeys.

switching hub   A wiring concentrator that includes switches for separating LAN traffic into individualized channels. There are three different basic designs for switching hubs as implemented by various vendors. (See also Chapter 26, "Virtual LAN Capacity Allocation.")

Symmetrical Multi Processing (SMP)   A process where processor instructions are spread equally over multiple processors. SMP is built into the Pentium architecture, which NT takes advantage of without any integrator modifications.

Systems Network Architecture (SNA)   IBM's network architecture used in mainframe systems. (See also *network architecture*.)

T

task   Any kind of any internal operation performed by a software module (such as updating a record in a database).

terminal   An input/output device that is a slave of a CPU, such as is the case in a minicomputer or mainframe terminal. Terminals are not used in the distributed computing environment of a PC network. The term *terminal* is sometimes used to describe a workstation incorrectly. (See also *workstation*.)

time slice   A brief period of time in which a process is given access to the processor. Each second is divided into 18.3 time slices where multiple tasks can be scheduled for processing and outwardly appear to be occurring simultaneously. (See also *multitasking*.)

token-passing bus   An access protocol that employs a linear-bus or star-bus network but uses a logically configured ring to pass a token for exclusive access to the network. Arcnet uses this access protocol as does Thomas-Conrad's TCNS LAN and General Motors' MAP networks. The access protocol was described in IEEE 802.4 Medium Access Control specifications, which describe MAP. Arcnet and TCNS are proprietary and do not conform to IEEE 802.4 specifications.

token-passing ring   The access protocol used in Token ring networks. Token-passing ring uses a ring or star-wired ring topology to pass bits of data around a physically wired ring. Three frame types exist, the first of which is a token that grants exclusive use of the ring when received.

Token ring   A type of LAN that uses token-passing ring access protocol and a physical ring or a star-wired ring topology and twisted-pair or optical fiber cable. In this book, Token ring capitalized this way refers to a generic Token ring product.

Token-Ring   Token-Ring products produced by IBM are trademarked as Token-Ring (capitalized and hyphenated as shown).

topology   The layout or design of cabling on a network. Three basic topologies are used in LANs today: linear bus, star bus, and star-wired ring. Variations are used such as hierarchical star bus and distributed star-bus topologies. Although other topologies including mesh and tree topologies are used in networks, they are not commonly employed in LANs today and therefore are not discussed in this book.

The term *topology* is often misused by industry writers to identify a single physical LAN. This usage is vague, confusing, and inconsistent with industry standards. Moreover, it confounds clear and concise explanations of internetworking and is therefore not used in this manner in this book.

transceiver   An electrical LAN device that transmits and receives bits of data from a network. In an Ethernet LAN, the transceiver acts as a gate, closing the circuit to enable data to be transmitted when the cable is free and opening the circuit to disable transmissions when other activity is sensed on the cable. It also detects collisions (transmissions from other nodes during a transmission) and stops the transmission. Transceivers also introduce *jabber control* to prevent one node from dominating the network and Signal Quality Error (which is turned off in modern Ethernet LANs).

translating bridge   A type of LLC bridge that translates between different frame types or access protocols using 802.2 protocol. (See *LLC*, *bridges*, and *frames*.)

Transmission Control Protocol/Internet Protocol (TCP/IP)   A set of networking protocols developed in the 1970s and funded by the U.S. Government's Defense Advanced Research Projects Agency (DARPA). TCP/IP was the second generation of the previously established DARPANET, which had been developed for weapons research, development, and procurement by the Department of Defense. TCP/IP includes Transport Control Protocol, which is a connection-oriented transport protocol that includes transport, session, and presentation layer protocol functions equivalent to layers 4, 5, and 6 of the OSI model, and Internet Protocol, a widely used routable network protocol that corresponds to layer 3 of the OSI model. User Datagram Protocol (UDP) can be substituted in cases where connectionless datagram service is desired.

TCP/IP is more than these two protocols; it is an entire protocol stack that includes protocols for file transfers (FTP), terminal emulation services (Telnet), electronic mail (SMTP), address resolution (ARP and RARP), and error control and notification (ICMP and SNMP).

TCP/IP is used extensively in many computer systems because it is nonproprietary—free from royalties. Its use was mandated by the U. S. Congress in 1988 in computer systems for many government agencies and contract situations.

TCP/IP is used in the Internet, a huge government and research internetwork spanning North America and much of the world that was opened to commercial use in the summer of 1991. These factors have caused TCP/IP use to grow, making it the most commonly used set of network protocols.

transparent bridge   A MAC-layer bridge. (See also *bridge* and *MAC-layer bridge*.)

Transport Driver Interface (TDI)   A Microsoft interface provided to enable communication between two driver layers.

trust relationship   A relationship between domains where one domain is accessible from another domain.

twisted-pair   Cabling that consists of lightly insulated copper wire twisted into pairs and bundled into sets of pairs. The twists enhance the wire's capability to resist crosstalk (bleeding of signal from one wire to the next). Twisted-pair is used extensively in phone systems and LANs. (See also *unshielded twisted-pair* and *shielded twisted-pair*).

U-V

UAS   LAN Manager User Account System. (See also *user account database*.)

UNICODE   A new ANSI standard for character representation shared among different language character sets and keyboards.

Universal Naming Convention (UNC)   The name and path assigned to a resource includes the server to which it belongs.

unshielded twisted-pair (UTP)   Twisted-pair cabling that is not shielded. This is the most popular cabling type and is used most extensively in several types of LANs. UTP is graded into Category 3, 4, and 5, which designates suitability for various LAN installations.

user account database   See *security account database*.

User Datagram Protocol (UDP)   A connectionless transport layer protocol that is substituted for TCP when acknowledgments are not desired.

user domain   The domain in which the user account is defined.

user group   A group of users who are given resource permissions and user rights based upon common needs.

Virtual DOS Machine (VDM)   A DOS real-mode session opened as a window in NT. The CMD.EXE module provides a DOS emulation that provides an isolated platform for executing DOS applications and commands but still protects other VDMs and NT processes from corruption common in a DOS environment. VDMs can be configured to provide full or partial screen and backwards DOS compatibility and can extend other DOS options to the environment.

Virtual LAN (VLAN)   A LAN can be automatically divided into separate LANs with the use of a switching hub. Each separated LAN segment can at any time be combined with or separated from other LAN segments changing VLAN configuration to suit best performance.

Virtual Loading Modules (VLMs)   Novell NetWare requester support software modules that are dynamically loaded when VLM.EXE is loaded. These files are used with the DOS Requester.

W-Z

Wide Area Information Server (WAIS)   A server process that enables users to query full-content indexes of distributed databases and retrieve requested data. WAIS responds to client connections and queries, returning information on the files shared in the WAIS data directory.

Windows Internet Name Service (WINS)   A protocol that was designed to eliminate the need for broadcasts to resolve computer names to IP addresses and provide a dynamic database that maintains computer name to IP address mappings.

wiring concentrator   A multiple port repeating device used in Ethernet LANs to connect multiple cable segments into one LAN. Sometimes called a hub or multiport repeater, this device isolates cabling problems by separating each workstation connection on an isolated cabling segment. Wiring concentrators are a required component in 802.3 10Base-T (twisted-pair Ethernet) LANs and improve reliability on any type of Ethernet LAN. Wiring concentrators also link together different cable types, many incorporating AUI connectors for connection to thick coaxial (10Base-5), BNC connectors for thin coaxial (10Base-2), RJ-45 jacks for twisted-pair (10Base-T), and fiber optic connectors. Some token ring vendors also call their MAUs wiring concentrators.

workgroup   A group of computers networked together. In a workgroup, each computer that shares its resources also contains user accounts and functions as a server as well as a client. The term workgroup generally implies that computers are configured in a peer-to-peer relationship as opposed to a domain. (See also *domain*.)

working set   An NT-specific term referring to memory or RAM space allocated specifically to a running process.

E

workstation   A user computer. In the distributed computing environment on a PC network, workstations are user stations (not terminals) that are clients of one or more servers. A workstation has its own processor, processes applications locally, and may access data and resources located elsewhere on the network. In some cases, partial processing can be distributed back to a server such as a database server; however, a workstation always executes applications locally. (See also *terminal*.)

Xerox Network System (XNS)   Xerox's network architecture that provides the basis for Novell's protocols and packet formats.

Index

SYMBOLS

\\ (double backslashes), naming directories, 294
! (exclamation point), FTP command, 896
? (question mark), FTP command, 896
8-pin modular jacks, 801-802
10Base-2 Ethernet cabling, 116-117
10Base-T Ethernet cabling, 76, 626, 918
16-bit Windows applications, 7
32-bit data path, hardware selection, 57
100Base-T4 cable, 918
100Base-TX cable, 918
100Base-X (Fast Ethernet), 101, 105-106, 627, 922
  bandwidth comparison, 702
100VG (100VG-AnyLAN) standard, 918
100VG-AnyLAN, 108-109
  bandwidth comparisons, 702

A

AARP (AppleTalk Address Resolution Protocol), 476
Access Control Entry (ACE), 24, 28, 918
access control list (ACL), see ACL
access denial (networks), 739
access permissions (resources), 214-215
access protocols, 918, 920
access tokens, 286, 291, 918
  auditing, 318
  logon mechanics, 320-321

AccessAllowed ACE, 28
AccessDenied ACE, 28
accessing
  data pages, 650
  file resources (GSNW), 501-502
  objects, security process, 291-293
  printers (GSNW), 502
Accessories, user profiles, 339
Account Operators group, 267
account variables, 346
accounts, 301-308
  adding to domains, 216
  Administrator account, 303
  authentication, 248-255, 323-326
    local domain logons, 324-325
    MSV1_0 Authentication Package, 249
    pass-through authentication, 249-252
    SAM (Security Account Manager), 248-249
    share permissions (NTFS directories), 252-255
    SID (Security Identification), 324
    trusted domain logons, 325
    unknown domain name, 323-326
    untrusted domain logons, 326
    workgroup logons, 324
  caching usernames/passwords, 322
  creating, 301
  global accounts
    logon security, 310
    remote domain logons, 312-313

  Guest account, 304
  hidden accounts, 304-306
  initial user account, 303-304
  local accounts
    logon security, 310
    remote domain logons, 311-312
  logons
    local, compared to domain, 212
    security, 213-214, 308-313
  mapping to rights/permissions, 320-321
  remote domains, logon security, 311-313
  replicating (migration), 172
  SID (Security Identification), 302
ACE (Access Control Entry), 24, 28, 918
ACL (access control list), 24, 210, 286, 291, 918
aclconv command, 876
ACLCONV migration utility, 171
Active Monitor (Token ring)
  purge frames, 821
  ring polls, 820
  ring recovery counters, 821-822
adapters
  disk, 652-653, 836
  network, Setup, 140-141
  Registry subkeys, 420
  deleting, 736
  vendors, 179
Add & Read permission, 253
Add permission, 253
Address Resolution Protocol (ARP), 597, 918

addresses
frames, 79
I/O, 119
memory, 119
nodes, 79, 930
sockets, 937
virtual, 35
**Administration program
(SNA Server), 584-588**
**administration responsi-
bility, delegating (NT
Server features), 863**
**Administration User
Interface (RAS), 535**
**administrative installa-
tion (Microsoft Office),
459-460**
**Administrative Tools
program group (Registry
data), 408**
**Administrator account,
303**
**Administrator program
group (PerfectOffice),
469**
**Administrators group,
261, 266**
application servers, 244
managing rights, 274
**ADSP (AppleTalk Data
Stream Protocol), 476**
**Advanced Job Status
(Print Manager), 376**
**AEP (AppleTalk Echo
Protocol), 476**
**AFP (Apple Filing Proto-
col), 476**
accessing files, 479
configuring volumes, 479
creating volumes, 478
alerts, 863
counters, 672-673
disk space, 740-741
printers, 862
**alignment errors
(Ethernet), 816-817**
alpha testing, 53

answer files, 126
**API (application program
interface), 37**
RAS (Remote Access
Server), 534
append command, 876, 896
**Apple Filing Protocol
(AFP), 476**
AppleShare, 452, 474
**AppleTalk, 452, 474-475,
918**
phases, 475-476
printers, 481-482
*deleting destination,
763*
router configuration,
485-486
**AppleTalk Address Reso-
lution Protocol (AARP),
476**
**AppleTalk Data Stream
Protocol (ADSP), 476**
**AppleTalk Echo Protocol
(AEP), 476**
**AppleTalk Transport
Protocol (ATP), 476**
**Application Data Conver-
sion, migration, 174**
**application layer (OSI
model), 86**
**application log, auditing,
317-318**
**application servers, 243-
244**
application suites, 453-472
Microsoft Office, 456-468
*administrative installa-
tion, 459-460*
*client installation,
458-461*
*customizing setup script
files, 461-463*
*distributing setup script
files, 463-465*
installing, 457-459
MSAPPS files, 465-467

*troubleshooting,
467-468*
uninstalling, 461
versions, 457
PerfectOffice, 468-472
*Administrator program
group, 469*
*application integration,
469*
*Envoy (electronic
publishing), 470*
InfoCentral, 470
installing, 471-472
QuickTask, 470
*technical support,
470-471*
applications, 918
bandwidth demands,
699-700
BOOTP, 919
distributed computing, 31
DOS, printing from,
368-369, 398
executing, 663-665
foreground, prioritizing,
645-646
installing locally, com-
pared to centrally,
452, 454-456
Lotus Notes, 488-492
administration, 490
*configuring NWLink,
491-492*
definition, 488
*executing as DOS
application, 490-491*
*operating environment,
489-490*
printing, 490
replication, 488-489
monitoring, 634-638,
679-682
*average disk queue
time, 682*
Dr. Watson, 635-637
Event Viewer, 634-635
*processor bottlenecks,
681*

processor queue length, 681

service requests, 682

NetWare-aware, 503

network-aware, 455-456

printing, 380-383
 local applications, 380
 non-Windows-based applications, 382
 Windows-based applications, 380-382

Setup, 936

SMS (Systems Management Server)
 installing on clients, 522-523
 shared applications, 513-514, 521-522

Windows
 16-bit, 7
 availability in migration, 173
 printing from, 368

architectures, 74, 85-91
 ISA (Industry Standard Architecture), 924
 MCA (Micro Channel Architecture), 927
 network, 929
 operating system, 25-43
 SNA (Systems Network Architecture), 939
 streaming-data mode, 938
 system (NT Server features/capacities), 857
 XNS (Xerox Network System), 943

Arcnet (Attached Resource Computer Network), 918

ARP (Address Resolution Protocol), 597, 918

arp command , 894-895

arrays, disk, 836

AS/400 (SNA Server DOS clients), 592-593

ascii command , 896

ASCs (Authorized Support Centers), 867

assigning
 computer names, 139
 logon scripts, 344-345
 priorities, 644
 rights, 268-270, 276, 307-308

associations, file extensions (Macintosh), 480

AsyncMAC driver, 537-538

AsyncMAC parameters (Registry), 549-550

AT command, 877, 911-912

ATM (Asynchronous Transfer Mode), 109, 918

ATP (AppleTalk Transport Protocol), 476

Attachment Unit Interface (AUI), 919

attenuation, 792-793, 800, 919

auditing, 313-318
 event logs, 314-318
 mechanics, 318
 NT Server security, 861
 software, SMS (Systems Management Server), 518-519
 RAS security, 541

Auditor group, 270, 315-317

auditors (Security Administrator), 277

AUI (Attachment Unit Interface), 919

AuthenticateRetries (Registry parameter), 544

AuthenticateTime (Registry parameter), 544

authentication, 248-255, 286, 323-326, 919
 installing for Macintosh, 477-478
 local domain logons, 324-325

MSV1_0 Authentication Package, 249

pass-through authentication, 219, 249-252

RAS Server, 536

SAM (Security Account Manager), 248-249

share permissions (NTFS directories), 252-255

SID (Security ID), 324

trusted domain logons, 325

unknown domain name, 323-326

untrusted domain logons, 326

workgroup logons, 324

see also security

Authorized Support Centers (ASCs), 867

Auto Refresh option (Registry Editor), 411

auto-detect, 126

auto-sense, 126, 508, 919
 hardware devices, 60
 video cards, 127

AutoDisconnect (Registry parameter), 545

automating
 logons, 327-328
 printing to files, 374-375
 user disconnections, 740

average disk queue time, monitoring applications, 682

B

/B switch, 132

BACKACC migration utility, 170

backbone LANs (internetworks), 704

background processing, configuring, 351

backups
BOOT.INI file, 840-841
COM.CFG file (SNA Server), 586
devices, 726-727
open files, 727-728
Registry, 728-729, 840-841
SQL Server, 565-566
BackOffice, 13-14
backup (secondary) server, 776
backup domain controller (BDC), 154, 225-226, 286, 919
promoting, 227-229
synchronizing, 226
optimization, 229-233
Backup Operators group, 261, 266
Backup utility
NT Server features, 863
unattended backups, 912
bandwidth, 103, 626, 697-700, 919
baselining, 701, 813
bus design, 702-703
capacity, compared to speed, 697
Ethernet, 103-105
collisions, 810-815
troubleshooting, 631
high-capacity LANs, 702-703
monitoring, 700-701, 711-713
nodes, joining, 722-723
PCI bus, 63
theoretical, compared to usable, 698-699
Token ring, 103-105
transmission time, 697-698
upgrading considerations, 698
user demands, 699-700

baselining
bandwidth, 701
LAN capacity, 813
batch files (logon scripts), 45, 908
BDC (backup domain controller), 154, 225-226, 286, 919
promoting, 227-229
synchronizing, 226
beaconing (Token ring), 633, 822-823
bell command , 896
beta testing, 53
binary command , 896
BINDFIX utility, 497
binding network components (Registry), 447-448
BIOS shadowing, disabling, 658
boot floppies
creating, 744-745
fault-tolerant, 743-746
boot partition, 836
removing NT, 736-737
viruses, 737-738
BOOT.INI file
backing up, 840-841
editing, 734-736
booting
non-Setup failures, 745-746
server, troubleshooting, 780-781
Setup-related failures, 746
STOP messages, 781-782
troubleshooting, 752-753
BOOTP application, 919
bottlenecks, 662, 666, 673-679
cache, 677-678
disk, 675-676
LAN, 679
memory, 676-677
processor, 674-675
monitoring applications, 681

bridges, 74, 81-82, 100, 178, 919
compared to routers, 84-85, 707-708
frames (filters), 81
LLC (Logical Link Control), 624
MAC layer bridges, 705-706, 926
mixing with routers, 708
source-routing bridge/ protocol, 937
spanning-tree bridge/ protocol, 938
SSAP (Source Service Access Point), 937
switches, 716
translating, 940
transparent, 941
broadcast storms (NetBIOS), 598
broadcasts (NetWare), disabling, 498-499
brouters (bridging routers), 707, 919
BrowseMaster, conflicts, 757
browsers
disadvantages, 600-601
master browsers (domains), 246-248
disabling browsing, 248
elections, 246-248
TCP/IP, 601
Btrieve, 24, 919
built-in user groups, 261, 266-271
customizing rights, 275-276
global groups, 270-271
local groups, 266-268
assigning rights, 268-270
bulletin board service (technical support), 869
bundling cabling, 113

Burst 5 errors (Token ring), 823-824
burst mode, 59, 61
bus adapters (Registry subkeys), 420
bus mastering, 57-61, 710, 920
   network cards, 62
bus switching, 719-720
buses, 664
   bandwidth, 702-703
   computer, 919
   disk bottlenecks, 675
   EISA, 119
   LAN capacity, 709-711
   linear (network topology), 925
   local, 58
   network, 920
   streaming-data mode, 938
   token-passing, 939
   VESA, 58
   VL-bus, 58
bye command , 896

C

cable pin assignments (UPS), 748
cable testers, 805
cabling, 179
   10Base-2 Ethernet, installation, 116-117
   10Base-T Ethernet, 76, 626, 918
   100Base-T4 Ethernet, 918
   100Base-TX Ethernet, 918
   100VG-AnyLAN, 108-109, 918
      bandwidth comparisons, 702
   attenuation, 800
   breaks, 117
   bundling, 113
   category 5 unshielded twisted pair, 110, 112
   CAUs (Controlled Access

Units), 111
   CDDI (Copper Distributed Data Interface), 786
   certifying, 112
   coaxial (TV), 117
      troubleshooting, 792-794
   connectors, 114
   crossed pairs, 800
   EIA/TIA 568 cabling rules, 625
   Ethernet, monitoring, 626-627
   external transceivers, 117
   Fast Ethernet, 101, 105-106, 627, 922
      bandwidth comparison, 702
   FDDI (Fiber Distributed Data Interface), 786
      bandwidth comparisons, 702
   fluorescent lights, 113
   hubs, 117
   installation, 109-118
      twisted pair, 113-116
   layout, 110-112
   lengths, 77, 797
   monitoring, 625-626
   NeXT (near end crosstalk), 798-799
   noise, 797-798
   optical fiber, 77, 108, 118
   repeaters, 117
   segments, 936
   signal degradation, 797
   split pairs, 801-802
   STP (shielded twisted pair), 787, 937
   switching hubs, 716
   T-1 lines, 77
   terminations, 802
   testing, 112
   Token ring, monitoring, 632-634
   troubleshooting, 792
      attenuation, 792-793

   cable testers, 805
   certification tools, 806-807
   coaxial cabling, 792-794
   continuity testers, 804-805
   fiber optic cable, 804
   UTP (unshielded twisted pair), 795-802
   twisted pair, 941
      installation, 113-116
   UTP (unshielded twisted pair), 625, 787, 941
      installing, 802-804
cache
   bottlenecks, 677-678
   memory, 653-657, 664
   SERVER Service priority interaction, 646-647
cache manager, 39-40
caching
   disk controllers, 65
   usernames/passwords, 322
cacls command, 877
callbacks (RAS security), 542
CallbackTime (Registry parameter), 544
capacity
   allocation, planning, 718
   compared to speed, 697
   see also bandwidth
CAPTURE command (NetWare printing), 389
capturing
   AppleTalk printers, 481
   frames, protocol analyzer features, 789
   printers, 203
cards
   controller, 66
   EISA, 57
   moving data, 78-79
   multiple interface, 56
   network, 657, 929
      access protocols, 918
      adding, 151

bandwidth, 702-703
bus mastering, 62
drivers, 61, 120-123
hardware, 61-63
installation, 118-120
LAN capacity, 709-711
network interface
printers, 394
SMS network monitor-
ing, 527-528
sound cards, adding/
deleting, 152
video cards, auto-sensing,
127
**Carrier Sense Multiple
Access with Collision
Detection (CSMA/CD),
103, 920**
**category 5 unshielded
twisted pair cabling, 110,
112**
CATV cabling, 117
**CAUs (Controlled Access
Units), 111, 624**
cd command , 896
**CD-ROM (Compact Disc
Read-Only Memory), 126,
508, 920**
support, 61
**CDDI (Copper Distributed
Data Interface), 786**
**Central Processing Unit
(CPU), 920**
**centralized processing,
920**
**certifying cabling, 112,
806-807**
**Change permission, 46,
253**
channels (DMA), 119
**CHAP (Challenge Hand-
shake Authentication
Protocol), 540-541**
charting counters, 670
chatty nodes, 818
**CHKDSK utility, 640-641,
877-878**
running, 839

**circuits, comparing
virtual to physical, 78**
**CISC (Complex Instruc-
tion Set Computing), 24,
921**
Client Redirector, 27
**client/server computing,
26**
clients, 920
configuring Lotus Notes,
492
installation
IPX/SPX protocols, 75
LAN Manager disk set,
188
Microsoft Office,
458-461
ODI/MLID drivers, 75
SMS applications,
522-523
MS-DOS, bootable disks,
186-188
named pipes clients, SQL
Server configuration,
558-559
NetWare support, 92-95
NT Server network card
support, 858
NT workstations, connect-
ing to NetWare server,
92
printing, 365, 380-383
down level clients,
382-383
local applications, 380
Macintosh clients, 383
non-Windows-based
applications, 382
Print Manager as client,
383
remote workstations,
382
UNIX clients, 383
Windows-based applica-
tions, 366-367,
380-382

RAS (Remote Access
Server)
joining domains,
539-540
user interfaces, 534-535
reserving IP addresses
(DHCP), 606-607
setup, 180-189
filenames, 184-185
MS-DOS, 180-181,
189-190
peer-to-peer networks,
181
remote LAN segments,
182-184
utilities, 185-186
WFW (Windows For
Workgroups), 191-195
Windows 95, 195-204
Windows NT Worksta-
tion, 204
workgroups, compared
to domains, 182
SMS (Systems Manage-
ment Server), 515-521
Inventory Agent,
517-518
shared applications,
521-522
SNA Server
DOS clients, 592-593
TCP/IP clients, 589-590
WFW clients, 589
Windows-based clients,
588-589
SPX/IPX, SQL Server
configuration, 559-561
support, installation, 191
TCP/IP sockets, SQL
Server configuration,
561-562
upgrading to Windows NT
via SMS (Systems
Management Server),
525

WFW (Windows For Workgroups), installation disk set, 188
close command , 897
closing NT objects, 293
clustering technology, 30
clusters, 920
cmd command, 878
coaxial cable, 117
  troubleshooting, 792-794
collaborative processing, 920
collisions (Ethernet)
  bandwidth utilization, 810-813
  late collisions, 816-817
  local/remote collisions, 814-815
  SQE (Signal Quality Error), 815-816
  switching hubs, 717
  troubleshooting, 631
COM ports, deleting, 762
COM.CFG file (SNA Server), backing up, 586
Command prompt (user profiles), 339
command tag queuing, 65
commands
  ! (exclamation point), 896
  ? (question mark), 896
  aclconv, 876
  append, 876, 896
  arp, 894-895
  ascii , 896
  AT (logon scripts), 877, 911-912
  bell , 896
  binary, 896
  bye, 896
  cacls, 877
  CAPTURE (NetWare printing), 389
  cd, 896
  chkdsk, 877-878

close, 897
cmd, 878
compac, 879
debug, 897
delete, 897
dir, 897
disconnect, 897
diskperf, 879-880
dosonly, 880
echoconfig, 880
finger , 895
FOR (logon scripts), 913
forcedos, 880
ftp , 895-898
get , 897
glob , 897
hash , 897
help , 897
hostname , 899
IF (logon scripts), 913
ipconfig , 899, 913
ipq , 899
IPXROUTE (logon scripts), 880, 913
lcd , 897
literal , 897
Load Hive (Registry Editor), 412-413
loadhigh, 880-881
logon scripts, 911-915
LPQ (logon scripts), 914
lpr , 899-900
ls , 897
mdelete , 897
mdir , 897
mget , 897
mkdir , 897
mls , 898
mput , 898
NBSTAT (logon scripts), 914
net accounts, 881
net computer, 881
net config, 882
net config workstation, 882
net continue, 882-883

net file, 883
net group, 883-884
net helpmsg, 884
net localgroup, 885
net name, 885-886
net pause, 886-887
net print, 887
net send, 887-888
net session, 888
net share, 888
net start, 92, 889
net start alerter, 889
net start browser, 889
net start dhcp client, 889
net start snmp, 889-890
net statistics, 890
net stop, 890
net time, 245, 890
net use, 890-891
net user, 891-892
net view, 892
netstat, 901
ntcmdprompt, 892-893
open , 898
pentnt, 893
ping , 901-902, 914
print, 893
prompt , 898
put , 898
pwd , 898
quit , 898
quote , 898
rcp , 903, 914-915
recv , 898
remotehelp, 898
rename, 898
Restore Volatile (Registry Editor), 414
rexec, 903-904
rmdir, 898
route, 904, 915
rsh, 904-905
Save Key (Registry Editor), 413-415
scheduled commands, 911-912
send , 898

start, 893-894, 915
status , 898
switches, 894
telnet , 905
tftp , 905-906
title, 894
trace , 898
tracert , 906
type , 898
Unload Hive (Registry
   Editor), 413
user , 898
verbose , 898
communications, 76-85
compact command, 879
**Compact Disk Read-Only
   Memory,** *see* **CD-ROM**
compatibility, 7, 26-27
**Complete Trust Model,
   221**
**Complex Instruction Set
   Computing (CISC), 24,
   921**
**compressing data, RAS
   (Remote Access Server),
   533**
**Computer Profile Setup
   (CPS), 50**
**computers, restoring,
   849-850**
concurrency control, 43
**concurrent processing,
   58-59**
**CONFIG.SYS file, editing
   (Setup), 190**
configuration
   AFP volumes (Macintosh),
      479
   AppleTalk routers, 485-
      486
   devices, adding/editing,
      150
   DHCP servers, 605
   disk drives, 653-656
   Dr. Watson, 759-761
   Gopher servers, 614-617

GSNW (Gateway Service
   for NetWare), 496-498
hardware, 771-772
HTTP Server, 618-620
jumpers, 119
LMHOSTS configuration
   file, 925
migration, saving, 168
Migration Tool for
   NetWare, 159
network cards, drivers,
   95-96
NT Server for TCP/IP
   printing, 400-401
NWLink for Lotus Notes,
   491-492, 492
personal profiles, 336-337
post-installation, 150-152
protocols, 95-96
RAS (Remote Access
   Server), 538-540
Services for Macintosh,
   484
Setup, unattended, 148-
   150
SMS (Systems Manage-
   ment Server), 513-515
SQL Server, 555-562
   memory, 566-567
   *named pipes clients,
      558-559*
   reinstallation, 557-558
   SPX/IPX, 559-561
   *TCP/IP sockets,
      561-562*
   utilities, 557
switches, 119
UPS (Uninterrupted
   Power Supply), 747-748
user groups, 261-262
virtual memory, 144-145
WINS servers, 610-611
**configuration files, RAS
   security, 542-543**
**configuration manage-
   ment (Registry Editor),
   411-415**

Load Hive command,
   412-413
Save Key command, 413-
   415
Unload Hive command,
   413
viewing remote computer
   Registry, 411
conflicts
   BrowseMaster, 757
   hardware, 178
   RAS (Remote Access
      Server), 538-539
**congestion (Token ring),
   825**
**connection-oriented
   protocols, 921**
**connectionless protocols,
   921**
connections
   cabling (repeaters), 117
   dropped, 754-755
   permanent network (user
      profiles), 341
   shared printers, 371
   shared resources, 298-300
   WFW RAS connections,
      538
connectors (cabling), 114
**conservative migration
   strategies, 154-157**
continuity testers, 804-805
Control Panel
   COM ports, 762
   components, 763-764
   Device applet, 779
   Registry data, 408
   user environment vari-
      ables, changing, 348-349
   user profiles, 339
   viewing environment
      variables, 345
**control sets, SYSTEM
   subtree (Registry),
   427-432**
**Control subtree (Regis-
   try), 429-432**

Controlled Access Units (CAUs), 111, 624
controllers, 63-64
  cards, 66
  disk, 653, 836
    caching, 65
controlling
  environment, centralized
    control, 43-46
  hardware, program
    execution, 7
conversion utilities (PORTUAS), 210
CONVERT migration utility, 171
Copper Distributed Data Interface (CDDI), 786
counters
  alerts, 672-673
  charting, 670
  Current Commands, 689-690
  graphing log data, 673
  hierarchy, 669-670
  logs, 671
  monitoring
    applications, 679-682
    networks, 682-684
  Network Errors/sec, 690
  performance tuning, 666-667
  Reads Denied/sec, 690
  reports, 672
  Writes Denied/sec, 690
CPS (Computer Profile Setup), 50
CPU (Central Processing Unit), 920
CRC, late collisions, 816-817
CreateWindow( ) stub function, 37
creating
  AFP volumes (Macintosh), 478
  bootable disks, 186-188
  DHCP Scopes, 605-606

  fault-tolerant boot floppies, 744
  logon scripts, 344-345
  NTFS boot floppies, 744-745
  printer pools, 395-396
  server-based profiles, 337-341
  Shares, 294-295
  SMS packages, 519-520
  TCP/IP printers, 401-402
  trust relationships (domains), 312-313
  user accounts, 301
CREATOR OWNER account, 306
Creator Owner group, 270-271
cross-platform printing, 393
crossed pairs (cabling), 800
CSMA/CD (Carrier Sense Multiple Access with Collison Detection), 103, 920
Current Commands counter, 689-690
custom separator page files (printing), 372-373
Custom Setup, 134, 146-150
customizing
  rights for built-in user groups, 275-276
  setup script files (Microsoft Office), 461-463

D

DARPANET, 940
data
  auditing, 313-318
    event logs, 314-318
    mechanics of, 318

  compression, RAS (Remote Access Server), 533
  encryption, RAS (Remote Access Server), 533
  flushing (Registry), 441-442
Data Communication Exchange (DCE), 24
data communications, 76-85
Data Link Control (DLC), 41, 91, 494
Data Link layer (OSI Model), 86
data pages, accessing, 650
data storage, moving to another server, 774-775
data types
  print processors, 384-386
    Macintosh, 386
    Windows, 385-386
  Registry subkey value entries, 440
  system-defined, 34
databases
  Lotus Notes, 488-492
    administration, 490
    configuring NWLink, 491-492
    definition, 488
    executing as DOS application, 490-491
    operating environment, 489-490
    printing, 490
    replication, 488-489
  security account databases, 210, 286, 935
  SQL Server
    backup/recovery, 565-566
    devices/databases, 564-566
    normalization, 569-570
Datagram Delivery Protocol (DDP), 476
date, Setup, 145

DCE (Data Communication Exchange), 24
DDP (Datagram Delivery Protocol), 476
debug command , 897
debugger, 782-783
debugging printers (JetDirect), 755-757
default printer spool directory, changing, 691-692
default profiles, 337
definitions, user groups, 261-262
delete command , 897
deleting
   adapters, 736
   COM ports, 762
   Control Panel components, 763-764
   Gopher servers, 614
   NT from boot partition, 736-737
   primary NTFS partitions, 737
   print jobs from queues, 376
   printers, 762-763
   protocols (Windows 95 setup), 199
   Shares, 295-296
   sound cards, 152
   tape drives, 152
demand paging, 35
demoting PDCs (Primary Domain Controllers), 229
dependencies, GSNW (Gateway Service for NetWare), 499
dependency handling, network components (Registry), 448-449
designing
   internetworks, 704
   NTFT (NT Fault Tolerance system), 845-848

desktop (Windows), 286, 330, 921
   profiles, 331-341
Developer program (Microsoft) phone number, 867
Device applet (Control Panel), 779
device drivers, 122
   hardware, 40-41
   RASHub, 537
   Registry data, 408
   Registry subkeys, 420-422
   replacement, 38
   Services subtree (Registry), 432-438
   storage, loading, 135
devices
   backup devices, 726-727
   configuration, 150
   editing, 151-152
   hardware, auto-sensing, 60, 508
   inserting, 151-152
   ISA, 119
   nodes, 929
   Plug-and-Play, 127
   print devices, 360, 362, 932
   repeaters, 933
   routers, 935
   SCSI peripherals, 654
   SQL Server devices/ databases, 564-566
   storage, adding/editing, 151
   transceivers, 940
   wiring concentrators, 942
DHCP (Dynamic Host Control Protocol), 508, 597, 604-608, 922
   configuring servers, 605
   creating Scopes, 605-606
   IP address leases, 607-608
   reserving client IP addresses, 606-607
Diagnostics utility, 778

dialog boxes
   Printing Notification network dialog boxes, disabling, 375
   Services (Gopher servers), 617
   User and Group Options, 162
   Welcome Dialog Box (logons), 319
dir command , 897
directories
   BackOffice, 13
   default printer spool directory, changing, 691-692
   distribution share directory, 921
   home directories, 351-354
     logon scripts, 351, 909-910
     permissions, 353-354
   mapping, 286, 330
   MSAPPS directory, 521-522
   NTFS share permissions, 252-255
   ownership, 274-275
   permissions, 279-282
     editing, 281-282
   printing, 378
   replication, 233-236, 354-357
   sharing, 286, 293-296, 452, 936
     connecting to Shares, 298-300
     creating Shares, 294-295
     deleting Shares, 295-296
     disconnecting from Shares, 300
     UNC (Universal Naming Convention), 294

directory objects, 34
DisableMcastFwd (Registry parameter), 546
disabling
  browsing (domains), 248
  Dr. Watson, 759
  messages (printers), 764-765
  print job logging, 692
  Printing Notification network dialog boxes, 375
  Shutdown button, 765
disconnect command, 897
disconnecting
  from Shares, 300
  users
    automatically, 740
    RAS security, 541
discovery (pass-through authentication), 250-251
disk arrays, 836
disk channel, 66
disk drives
  configuration, 653-656
  connecting, 64
  drive arrays, 922
  fault tolerance, 741
  mapping, 286, 330
  monitoring, 639-641
    CHKDSK utility, 640-641
    physical defects, 641
    viewing partitions, 639
  partitions, creating on RISC-based computers, 734-735
  performance tuning, 686-688
    linear memory addressing, 686
    paging files, 687-688
  striping, 686, 938
  testing, 780
  viruses, 737-738
disk monitoring, activating, 667

disk queue time, monitoring applications, 682
disk space (installation), 131
disk space alert message, 740-741
disk storage, NT Server hardware requirements, 856
diskperf command, 879-880
disks
  adapters, 836
    SCSI, 63
  bootable (MS-DOS clients), 186-188
  bottlenecks, 675-676
  CD-ROM (Compact Disc Read-Only Memory), 126, 508, 920
    support, 61
  configurations, 66-67
  controllers, 836
    caches, 65, 653
  emergency repair, 146
  hard disks, 63-65
    adapters, 652-653
    corruption, scanning, 138
    partitioning, 131
  restoring NT system volume to different disks, 730-731
  secondary, 836
  subsystem failure, 837
display (Setup), 145
distributed computing, 31-32, 921
  applications, 31
  environments, 452
distributed processing, 921
distributing
  setup script files (Microsoft Office), 463-465
  SMS packages, 519-520

distribution share (Setup), 149
distribution share directory, 921
DLC (Data Link Control), 41, 91, 494
DLL (dynamic link library), 32
DMA channels, 119
DNS (Domain Name System), 921
Domain Admins group, 270
domain controllers, 286, 921
Domain Guests group, 270
domain logon, compared to local logon, 212
Domain Users group, 270
domain-local groups, 265
domains, 210, 258, 286, 330, 921
  account authentication, 248-255
    MSV1_0 Authentication Package, 249
    pass-through authentication, 249-252
    SAM (Security Account Manager), 248-249
    share permissions (NTFS directories), 252-255
  adding user accounts, 216
  application servers, 243-244
  BDC (Backup Domain Controller), 225-226, 919
    promoting, 227-229
    synchronizing, 226, 229-233
  browsers, 246-248
    disabling browsing, 248
    disadvantages, 600-601
    elections, 246-248
    TCP/IP, 601

built-in global user groups, 270-271
changing, 765-767
compared to workgroups, 182, 211-212
definition, 215
directory replication, 233-236
domain rules, 217
foreign domains, 210, 923
  trust relationships, 216
joining via RAS (Remote Access Server), 539-540
local, 210, 926
  logon authentication, 324-325
logon security, 213-214
  NT servers, 322-323
NT Workstation servers, 236
PDC (Primary Domain Controller), 932
  replication, 225-226
reconfiguring, 236-242
  during installation, 237-238
  recombining split domains, 239-241
  renaming computers, 241-242
  via Server Manager, 237
  workstations joining domains, 238-239
remote domains
  logon security, 311-313
  overriding cached usernames/passwords, 322
resource domains, 210, 934
rights for user groups, 307-308
setting time, 245
settings (Setup), 143-144
trust relationships, 210, 216-225, 941

creating, 312-313
domain models, 220-221
one-way trusts, 218
pass-through authentication, 219
routes for passing validations, 222-225
setting up, 221-222
trusted compared to trusting domains, 217-218
two-way trusts, 218
trusted, logon authentication, 325
unknown domain name, authentication, 323-326
untrusted
  access denial, 739
  logon authentication, 326
user domains, 210, 941
user group definitions, 262
Domino network analyzer, 712
DOS (disk operating system), 921
applications, printing from, 368-369, 398
clients
  bootable disks, 186-188
  setup, 180-181, 189-190
compatibility, 7
executing Lotus Notes as, 490-491
print drivers, 361
SMS clients, 516
SNA Server clients, 592-593
VDM (Virtual DOS Machine), 7, 360, 942
dosonly command, 880
double backslashes (\\) in naming directories, 294
down level printing, 367-368, 382-383

Dr. Watson (monitoring tool), 635-637, 759-761
drive arrays, 922
drive letters, mapping to a share, 202
drivers, 127-128
AsyncMAC, 537-538
communications, 38
device drivers, 122
  hardware, 40-41
  RASHub, 537
  Registry data, 408
  Registry subkeys, 420-422
  replacement, 38
  Services subtree (Registry), 432-438
  storage, loading, 135
file system, 40
  replacement, 38
FTDISK.SYS., 845-846
  error handling, 847-848
  read operations, 846
IPXODI client support, 92-94
mini-drivers (printing), 392-393
MLID (Multiple Link Interface Driver), 928
NDIS (Network Device Interface Specification), 11, 94-95
  32-bit, 94
network, 41-42
network adapters, 179
network cards, 61, 120-123
  configuration, 95-96
printer drivers, 392
  cross-platform printing, 393
  directories, 378
  DOS, 361
  installing, 369-370
  Windows, 360
Setup, 193
vendors, 128
video (Setup), 145

**dropped connections,
754-755**

duplexing, 66, 836

**Dynamic Host Control
Protocol (DHCP), 508,
597, 604-608, 922**

configuring servers, 605

creating Scopes, 605-606

IP address leases, 607-608

reserving client IP ad-
dresses, 606-607

**dynamic link library
(DLL), 32**

E

**ECC (error checking and
correcting) memory, 55**

echoconfig command, 880

**edge triggered interrupts,
402**

editing

BOOT.INI parameters,
734-736

CONFIG.SYS file (Setup),
190

configuration (devices),
150

devices, 151-152

file access permissions,
281-282

options (protocols), 151

print processor functions
(Print Manager), 387-388

Registry, 407

RAS security, 543-550

rights for user groups, 301

**EIA (Electronic Industry
Association), 786**

**EIA/TIA 568 cabling rules,
625, 795-797**

**EISA (Extended Industry
Standard Architecture),
50, 57, 922**

32-bit features, 56

bus mastering, 57

buses, 119

ISA comparison, 59-61

**elections, master brows-
ers (domains), 246-248**

emergency repair, 733-734

**emergency repair disk,
146, 837-838**

procedure for using, 838

RISC, 70

updating, 838

**EMFs (enhanced
metafiles), printing, 367**

**EMI (electromagnetic
interference), 787,
797-798**

**EnableAudit (Registry
parameter), 544**

**EnableBroadcast (Regis-
try parameter), 546**

enabling

Dr. Watson, 759

Shutdown button, 765

**encapsulation, NetBIOS
into TCP/IP, 600**

encrypting

data

*CHAP (Challenge
Handshake Authenti-
cation Protocol), 540-
541*

*RAS (Remote Access
Server), 533*

passwords, SAM (Security
Account Manager),
248-249

**enforcing password
policy, 279**

**enhanced metafiles
(EMFs), printing, 367**

**Enhanced Small Device
Interface (ESDI), 922**

**envelopes, printing,
376-377**

**environment, centralized
control, 43-46**

**environment variables,
345-351**

account variables, 346

recovery options, 350

system environment
variables, 346-348

tasking options, 351

user environment vari-
ables, 348-349

virtual memory, 349-350

**Envoy (electronic publish-
ing), PerfectOffice, 470**

ERROR.LOG file, 170

errors

FTDISK.SYS

*FT_BAD_CONFIGURATION,
848*

*FT_CANT_USE_SET,
848*

*FT_DOUBLE_FAILURE,
848*

FT_MAP_FAILED, 847

*FT_MISSING_MEMBER,
848*

*FT_ORPHANED_MEMBER,
848*

FT_ORPHANING, 847

*FT_RECOVERY_ERROR,
847*

*FT_RECOVERY_NO_MEM,
848*

*FT_SET_DISABLED,
847*

handling (FTDISK.SYS.
driver), 847-848

logging, migration, 163,
164

messages (NT Messages
database), 637-638

Setup, 773

**escape codes, separator
page files (printing), 373**

**ESDI (Enhanced Small
Device Interface), 922**

Ethernet, 74, 922

10Base-2 cable, 116-117

10Base-T cable, 76, 626,
918

100Base-T4 cable, 918

100Base-TX cable, 918

802.2 frame format, 809

802.3 frame format, 809
bandwidth, 103-105
collisions
bandwidth utilization, 810-813
late collisions, 816-817
local/remote collisions, 814-815
SQE (Signal Quality Error), 815-816
CSMA/CD (Carrier Sense Multiple Access with Collison Detection), 920
distance, 77
Fast Ethernet, 101, 105-106, 627, 922
bandwidth comparison, 702
frame error types, 818
frame formats, 808-810
monitoring, 626-632
networks, 76
SNAP frame format, 809
Thinnet, 116
troubleshooting, 630-632, 807-828
usable bandwidth, 698-699
Ethernet II, 808, 922
Event ID 2013 (disk space alert), 740-741
event logs, 777
auditing, 314-318
counters, 671
graphing data, 673
Event Viewer, 635
print job logging, disabling, 692
truncating, 657
event objects, 34
Event Viewer (monitoring tool), 634-635
Everyone group, 267, 306
exclamation point (!), FTP command, 896
.EXE file extension (logon scripts), 908
Execute-only file attribute

(NetWare), 501
executing
applications, 663-665
CHKDSK utility, 839
Lotus Notes as DOS application, 490-491
Registry Editor, 410
SCANDISK utility, 839
SNA Server, 585-586
SQL Server, 562-564
remotely, 572-573
exiting Windows, 335
export directories, replication, 354-357
Express Setup, 134
Extended Industry Standard Architecture, see EISA
external transceivers (cabling), 117

F

failover, 30
Fast Ethernet, 101, 105-106, 627, 922
bandwidth comparison, 702
fast SCSI, 656
FastTips, 868
FAT (file allocation table), 26
compared to NTFS security, 254-255
fault domains (Token ring), 822
fault tolerance, 24, 42-43, 290, 741, 922
BDC (Backup Domain Controller), 225-226
directory replication, 233-236
FDDI (Fiber Distributed Data Interface), 108
NT Server features, 863
NTFS, 742-746
boot floppies, 743-746
hot-fixing, 743

RAID
identifying broken sets, 849
levels, 842
RAID 0 (striping), 842
RAID 1 (mirroring/duplexing), 842-844
RAID 5 (striping with parity), 844-845
recovery, 848-849
sector sparing, 841
faults (page), resolving, 650
FDDI (Fiber Distributed Data Interface), 101, 107-108, 786
bandwidth comparisons, 702
FDDI on Twisted Pair (TP-DDI), 107-108
fiber optic cable, 77, 108, 118
troubleshooting, 804
file access permissions, 279-282
editing, 281-282
file allocation table, see FAT
File and Print Services for NetWare (FPSN), 504
file attributes, Execute-only (NetWare), 501
file extensions
associations (Macintosh), 480
logon scripts, 908
file locks (NetWare), 501-502
File Manager
creating Shares, 294-295
deleting Shares, 295-296
editing permissions, 281-282
user profiles, 338
file mapping (Gopher servers), 615-617
file objects, 34

file systems
   CHKDSK utility, 640-641
   drivers, 40
      replacement, 38
   HPFS (High Performance
      File System), 923
   NetWare, restoring to NT
      drive, 156
   NFS (Network File
      System), 929
   NT Server features/
      capacities, 859
   NTFS (NT File System),
      930
      directory / file permis-
      sions, 860-861
      hidden accounts, 304-
      306
   Setup, 136-137
File Transfer Protocol ,
   see FTP
filenames
   client setup, 184-185
   translating (Macintosh),
      480
files
   accessing
      via AFP volumes
      (Macintosh), 479
      GSNW (Gateway
      Service for NetWare),
      501-502
   adding filenames to
      Registry, 374
   answer files, 126
   automatically printing to,
      374-375
   batch files (logon scripts),
      45
   BOOT.INI, backing up,
      840-841
   corruption, 836-837
      CHKDSK, 839
      Emergency Repair Disk,
      837-838
   ERROR.LOG, 170

hives (Registry), 406, 415-
   416
INF, 50
INI, compared to Registry,
   408-409
LMHOSTS configuration
   file, 925
LOGFILE.LOG, 170
MSAPPS files (Microsoft
   Office), 465-467
NTFS system files, 742
open files, backups, 727-
   728
ownership, 274-275, 307
paging, 647-648
   performance tuning,
   687-688
RAS configuration files,
   542-543
replication, 354-357
   migration, 172
security, GSNW (Gateway
   Service for NetWare),
   500-501
selecting for migration,
   166-168
separator page files
   (printing), 372-373
sharing, 187
SMSLS.INI file, 515
SNA Server, third-party
   emulators, 591-592
storing on Macintosh, 480
SUMMARY.LOG, 170
transparent file sharing,
   472-473
filters, frames (bridges),
   81
finger command , 895
firewalls, RAS security,
   541
firmware, 923
floppy disks
   boot floppies
      creating, 744-745
      fault-tolerant, 743-746

installing from, 133
fluorescent light fixtures
   and cabling, 113
flushing data (Registry),
   441-442
FOR command (logon
   scripts), 913
forcedos command, 880
foreground processing,
   configuring, 351
foreign domains, 210, 923
   trust relationships, 216
FPSN (File and Print
   Services for NetWare),
   504
fragmented frames, 817
frames, 74, 78-79, 100, 706,
   786, 814, 923
   addresses, 79
   capturing (protocol
      analyzer features), 789
   compared to packets, 596
   Ethernet frames
      error types, 818
      formats, 808-810
   filtering (bridges), 81
   fragmented frames, 817
   illegal length frames, 817-
      818
   MAC frames, monitoring
      Token ring, 632-633
   purge frames (Token ring),
      821
   Ring Change frames
      (Token ring), 820-821
   Token ring, 633-634
   transmission time, 697-
      698
   troubleshooting Ethernet,
      630-631
FramesPerPort (Registry
   parameter), 549
FT_BAD_CONFIGURATION,
   848
FT_CANT_USE_SET, 848

FT_DOUBLE_FAILURE, 848
FT_MAP_FAILED, 847
FT_MISSING_MEMBER, 848
FT_ORPHANED_MEMBER, 848
FT_ORPHANING, 847
FT_RECOVERY_ERROR, 847
FT_RECOVERY_NO_MEM, 848
FT_SET_DISABLED, 847
FtDisk (fault tolerance), 741
FTDISK.SYS. driver, 845-846
    error handling, 847-848
    read operations, 846
FTP (File Transfer Protocol), 597, 923
    commands, 896-898
    technical support sites, 871
ftp command , 895-898
Full Access permission, 46
Full Control permission, 253
functional stations (Token ring), 819-820
functions
    CreateWindow( ), 37
    stub, 37
    VirtualLock( ), 648, 652

G

Gateway Service for NetWare (GSNW), 9, 96, 494-504
    accessing
        file resources, 501-502
        printers, 502
    configuring, 496-498
    dependencies, 499
    FPSN (File and Print Services for NetWare),

504
    installing, 495-496
    NetWare-aware applications, 503
    NWLink, 495
    performance tuning, 499-500
    RIP/SAP broadcasts, disabling, 498-499
    security, 500, 500-501
    system utilities, 502-503
gateways, 530, 923
    NetBIOS Gateway (RAS), 536
    SNA Server, 578-593
        Administration program, 584-588
        capacities, 581
        COM.CFG file backups, 586
        DOS clients, 592-593
        executing, 585-586
        features, 578-580
        installing, 582-583
        NT Server integration, 580-581
        renaming servers, 584
        system requirements, 581-582
        TCP/IP clients, 589-590
        third-party emulators, 591-592
        WFW clients, 589
        Windows-based clients, 588-589
GDI (Graphics Device Interface), 366, 380-382
general remote access parameters (Registry), 544-545
GEnie, 872
get command , 897
glob command , 897
global groups, 286, 330
    built-in, 270-271
    compared to local groups, 259-260

group dynamics, 300-301
    mechanics, 263
    membership, 265
    rules, 264-265
global user accounts
    logon security, 310
    remote domain logons, 312-313
Gopher servers, 611-617
    configuring, 614-617
    deleting, 614
    file mapping, 615-617
    installing, 612-613
    Services dialog box, 617
    technical support sites, 871
granting/revoking system access, 278
Graphics Device Interface (GDI), 366, 380-382
graphing counter log data, 673
group dependencies, 449
groups, 258-261, 941
    assigning rights, 268-270, 276, 307-308
    built-in, 261, 266-271
        customizing rights, 275-276
        global groups, 270-271
        local groups, 266-268
    configurations/definitions, 261-262
    domain-local groups, 265
    global groups, 286, 330
    local, 286, 330
        compared to global, 259-260
    security, 262-263
    setting up, 300-301
    strategies, 261-265
        global group mechanics, 263
        global group rules, 264-265

groups as members of
groups, 265
local group mechanics,
263-264
**GSNW (Gateway Service
for NetWare), 9, 96,
494-504**
accessing
file resources, 501-502
printers, 502
configuring, 496-498
dependencies, 499
FPSN (File and Print
Services for NetWare),
504
installing, 495-496
NetWare-aware applica-
tions, 503
NWLink, 495
performance tuning,
499-500
RIP/SAP broadcasts,
disabling, 498-499
security, 500, 500-501
system utilities, 502-503
Guest account, 304, 309
Guests group, 261

H

**HAL (Hardware Abstrac-
tion Layer), 29, 50, 923**
handle ID, auditing, 318
handles (objects), 34
hard disks, 63-65
adapters, 652-653
corruption, scanning, 138
partitioning, 131
hardware, 14
bridges, 74, 81-82, 100,
178, 919
compared to routers,
84-85, 707-708
frames (filters), 81
LLC (Logical Link
Control), 624

MAC layer bridges,
705-706, 926
mixing with routers,
708
source-routing bridge/
protocol, 937
spanning-tree bridge/
protocol, 938
SSAP (Source Service
Access Point), 937
switches, 716
translating, 940
transparent, 941
brouter (bridging-router),
707, 919
compatibility, 25, 54
configuration, 771-772
conflicts, 120, 178
controlling program
execution, 7
devices
auto-sensing, 60, 508
backup devices, 726-727
configuration, 150
editing, 151-152
inserting, 151-152
ISA, 119
nodes, 929
Plug-and-Play, 127
print devices, 360, 362,
932
repeaters, 933
routers, 935
SCSI peripherals, 654
SQL Server devices/
databases, 564-566
storage, adding/editing,
151
transceivers, 940
wiring concentrators,
942
disk interface card prob-
lems, 773-774
failure signs, 772-774
incompatibilities, 771-772
interrupts, troubleshoot-
ing printing problems,
402-403

isolating components,
776-784
LAN hardware perfor-
mance tuning, 688-689
network cards, 61-63, 657,
929
access protocols, 918
adding, 151
bandwidth, 702-703
bus mastering, 62
drivers, 61, 120-123
installation, 118-120
LAN capacity, 709-711
NT Server hardware
support, 858
problem identification,
770-776
RAID 5 implementation,
67
recognizers, 933
repeaters, 74, 117, 933
disabling SQE (Signal
Quality Error), 816
multiport repeaters, 928
requirements
NT Server, 856
RAS (Remote Access
Server), 538
routers, 74-75, 82-83, 100,
178, 706-707, 935
AppleTalk, router
configuration, 485-486
brouters (bridging
routers), 707, 919
compared to bridges,
84-85, 707-708
DDP (Datagram
Delivery Protocol), 476
internetworks, 184
logical hops, 926
mixing with bridges,
708
Multi Protocol Router,
605
NetBIOS, 87, 599
NT routing support,
601-602

packets, 83
print routers, 360, 365, 384
selection, x86-based computers, 55-67
Setup, 136
errors, 773
switching hubs, 939
symmetric multiprocessing (SMP), 30
transceivers, 940
wiring concentrators, 942
see also cabling
Hardware Abstraction Layer (HAL), 29, 50, 923
HARDWARE subtree (Registry), 417-422
hardware-based monitors, 629-630
hash command , 897
HCT (Hardware Compatibility Test) kit, 53
heartbeat periods (Inventory Agent), 518
help command , 897
help (technical support), 866-873
bulletin board service, 869
FastTips, 868
Internet services, 871-872
Microsoft Electronic Technical Library, 871
Microsoft Knowledge Base, 871
Microsoft phone numbers, 866-867
Microsoft Solution Provider Network, 867-868
newsgroups, 871
online services, 872-873
PerfectOffice, 470-471
premier support, 870
priority support, 869-870
standard product support, 869

Hewlett-Packard JetDirect cards, clearing print jobs from queues, 376
Hewlett-Packard printers, deleting network destination, 762
Hewlett-Packard UNIX (HP/UX), 24
hidden accounts, 304-306
hierarchy, counters, 669-670
High Performance File System (HPFS), 178, 923
access, client setup, 184
compared to NTFS security, 254-255
history of MS-Networks, 287-288
hives (Registry), 406, 415-416, 923
backing up, 728-729
flushing data, 441-442
Load Hive command, 412-413
restoring, 414-415, 729-730
Save Key command, 413-415
security, 449
Unload Hive command, 413
HKEY_CLASSES_ROOT key, 438
HKEY_LOCAL_MACHINE key, 417-438
HARDWARE subtree, 417-422
SAM subtree, 418, 422-423
SECURITY subtree, 418, 423
SOFTWARE subtree, 418, 423-427
SYSTEM subtree, 418, 427-438

HKEY_USERS key, 439
home directories, 351-354
installing logon scripts, 351
permissions, 353-354
specifying for logon scripts, 909-910
hop counts, mixing bridges with routers, 708
hops, logical, 926
hostname command , 899
hot-fixing sectors, 743
HP/UX (Hewlett-Packard UNIX), 24
HPFS (High Performance File System), 178, 923
access, client setup, 184
compared to NTFS security, 254-255
HTML (HyperText Markup Language), 597
HTTP (HyperText Transfer Protocol), 924
HTTP Server, 617-620
configuring, 618-620
installing, 618
hubs, 74, 100, 923
10Base-2 Ethernet, 116
cabling, 117
intelligent, 117, 924
switching, 83, 939

I

I/O (input/output)
addresses, 119
request packets, 38
I/O Manager, 38-39
IBM PC Support/400 (SNA Server DOS clients), 592-593
ICMP (Internet Control Message Protocol), 597
IDE (Integrated Drive Electronics), 924

IEEE (Institute of Electrical and Electronic Engineers), 786, 924

IETF (Internet Engineering Task Force), 924

IF command (logon scripts), 913

illegal length frames, 817-818

impedance mismatches (cabling), 794

import directories, replication, 354-357

incremental migration, 174

independent auditing, 315

indexes (SQL Server), performance tuning, 568-569

Industry Standard Architecture, see ISA

INF file, 50

InfoCentral (PerfectOffice), 470

INI files, compared to Registry, 408-409

initial logons, 321-322

initial user account, 303-304

inserting
  devices, 151-152
    configuration, 150
    storage, 151
  sound cards, 152
  tape drives, 152

Inspect Boot Sector (repair option), 733

Inspect Configuration Registry Files (repair option), 733

Inspect Startup environment (repair option), 733

installation, 129-130
  authentication for
    Macintosh, 477-478
  cabling, 109-118

10Base-2 Ethernet,
  116-117
twisted pair, 113-116
checklist, 130-131
clients
  IPX/SPX protocols, 75
  ODI/MLID drivers, 75
  support, 191
Custom Setup, 134
disk sets, 188
disk space, 131
Dr. Watson (monitoring
  tool), 636
Express Setup, 134
failure, 131
file system, 136-137
floppy disks, 133
Gopher servers, 612-613
GSNW (Gateway Service
  for NetWare), 495-496
hardware, 136
HTTP Server, 618
local, compared to central,
  452, 454-456
lockups, 120
Microsoft Access via SMS
  (Systems Management
  Server), 524
Microsoft Office, 457-459
  administrative installa-
    tion, 459-460
  client installation,
    458-461
  via SMS (Systems
    Management Server),
    523-524
Microsoft Word via SMS
  (Systems Management
  Server), 524
Microsoft Works via SMS
  (Systems Management
  Server), 524
network cards, 118-120
Network Monitoring Agent
  Service (SMS), 527-528
non-native printer drivers,
  393

NT, restoring with emer-
  gency disk repair, 838
options, 132
path, 132-133
PerfectOffice, 471-472
post-installation configuration, 150-152
print drivers, 369-370
procedures, 131-146
RAS (Remote Access
  Server), 538-540
reconfiguring domains,
  237-238
servers, 62
  IPX/SPX protocols, 75
  ODI/MLID drivers, 75
  preparation, 102
  RISC-based, 69-70
Services for Macintosh,
  477
Setup, 130-146
shared CD-ROM, 132
SMS (Systems Manage-
  ment Server), 511-512
  applications on clients,
    522-523
SNA Server, 582-583
SQL Server, 555-562
  named pipes clients,
    558-559
  reinstallation, 557-558
  SPX/IPX, 559-561
  TCP/IP sockets,
    561-562
  utilities, 557
target directory, 137
TCP/IP, 399-400, 602-604
UTP (unshielded twisted
  pair) cabling, 802-804
Welcome screen, 134
WINS servers, 608-610

Institute of Electrical and Electronic Engineers (IEEE), 786, 924

Integrated Drive Electronics (IDE), 924

Integrated Services Digital Network (ISDN), 534
intelligent hubs, 117, 924
Intelligent Token ring, CAU (Control Access Unit), 624
inter-program communication features (NT Server), 859
INTERACTIVE account, 306
Interactive group, 267
interference (cabling), 797-798
International Standards Organization (ISO), 924
Internet
  RAS Internet support, 533
  technical support services, 871-872
  WINS (Windows Internet Name Service), 210, 597, 608-611, 942
    advantages, 608
    configuring servers, 610-611
    disadvantages, 600-601
    installing servers, 608-610
Internet Control Message Protocol (ICMP), 597
Internet Engineering Task Force (IETF), 924
Internet Protocol (IP), 924
Internetwork Packet Exchange (IPX), 88, 925
internetworks, 178, 596, 925
  bridges, compared to routers, 707-708
  LAN capacity, 704-708
    backbone LANs, 704
    bridges, 705-706
    brouters, 707
    designing, 704
    routers, 706-707
  routers, 184

interoperability, 925
Interprocess Communication (IPC), 24, 925
Interprocess Control (IPC$) resource, 210
interrupt requests, 119
interrupts
  edge triggered, 402
  level triggered, 402
  troubleshooting printing problems, 402-403
Inventory Agent, SMS (Systems Management Server), 517-518
IP (Internet Protocol) addresses, 924
  DHCP (Dynamic Host Control Protocol), 604-608
IPC (Interprocess Communication), 24, 925
IPC$ (Interprocess Control resource), 210
ipconfig command , 899, 913
ipq command , 899
IPX (Internetwork Packet Exchange), 88, 925
IPX/SPX protocol, 88-89
  client installation, 75
  compatible transport, 94-95
  server installation, 75
  SQL Server, 559-561
  troubleshooting, 828
IPXODI client support, drivers, 92-94
ipxroute command, 880, 913
IrpStackSize (Registry parameter), 550
ISA (Industry Standard Architecture), 924
  devices, 119
  EISA comparison, 59-61
ISDN (Integrated Services Digital Network), 534

ISO (International Standards Organization), 924

J-K

jabbers, 817-818
jamming, 816
JetDirect printers, 755-757
journal files, printing, 382
jumpers, 119

keys (Registry), 406, 409-410, 925
  HKEY_CLASSES_ROOT key, 438
  HKEY_LOCAL_MACHINE key, 417-438
    HARDWARE subtree, 417, 418-422
    SAM subtree, 418, 422-423
    SECURITY subtree, 418, 423
    SOFTWARE subtree, 418, 423-427
    SYSTEM subtree, 418, 427-438
  HKEY_USERS key, 439
  referential integrity, 441
  Save Key command, 413-415
  see also subkeys

L

LAN bottlenecks, 679
LAN capacity, 696-714
  bandwidth, 697-700
    baselining, 701, 813
    bus design, 702-703
    capacity, compared to speed, 697
    high-capacity LANs, 702-703
    monitoring, 700-701, 711-713

theoretical, compared to usable, 698-699
transmission time, 697-698
upgrading considerations, 698
user demands, 699-700
internetworks, 704-708
  backbone LANs, 704
  bridges, 705-706
  brouters, 707
  designing, 704
  routers, 706-707
network cards, 709-711
LAN layer, troubleshooting, 790, 807-826
  Ethernet, 807-818
  Token ring, 819-826
LAN Manager, 4
  clients, installation disk set, 188
  integrating with NT Server, 171
  limitations on NT Server, 171
  UAS (User Account System), 210
  upgrading from, 170-172
LAN segment, 178
LANalyzer (monitoring tool)
  for NetWare, 628-629
  for Windows, 713
LANDesk Manager (monitoring tool), 628
language (Setup), 139
LANs (local area networks), 50, 74, 76-77, 100, 126, 925-926
  frames, 596, 786, 814, 923
    Ethernet frame error types, 818
    fragmented frames, 817
    illegal length frames, 817-818
    purge frames (Token ring), 821
    Ring Change frames (Token ring), 820-821
  hardware performance tuning, 688-689
  internetworks, 596
  LocalTalk, 926
  MAC-layer bridges, 926
  monitoring, 624-634
    cabling, 625-626
    Ethernet, 626-632
    Token ring, 632-634
  packets, 786, 814
  segments, 936
    client setup, 182
    remote, 183
  subnetworks, 596
  switching hubs, 708-709
  technologies, 102-109
  troubleshooting
    LAN layer, 790, 807-826
    physical layer, 788-807
    protocol analyzers, 787-791
    SMB protocol layer, 790-791, 829-832
    transport layer, 790, 827-829
    virtual circuit management layer, 790, 826-827
  VLANs (Virtual LANs), 708-709, 942
  see also networks
LargeSystemCache subkey, 651
late collisions (Ethernet), 816-817
layers
  OSI model, 86
  troubleshooting
    LAN layer, 790, 807-826
    physical layer, 788-807
    SMB protocol layer, 790-791, 829-832
    transport layer, 790, 827-829
    virtual circuit management layer, 790, 826-827
lcd command , 897
leases (IP addresses), DHCP servers, 607-608
Legal Notice warning screen, displaying, 283-284
level triggered interrupts, 402
licensing information, 139
Line Printer Remote (LPR), 494
linear bus (network topology), 925
  breaks at segment, 117
linear memory addressing, 686
Link Support Layer (LSL), 925
List permission, 254
literal command , 897
LLAP (LocalTalk Link Access Protocol), 476
LLC (Logical Link Control), 624, 926
LMHOSTS configuration file, 210, 597, 925
  disadvantages, 600-601
Load Hive command (Registry Editor), 412-413
loadhigh command, 880-881
loading device drivers, storage, 135
local accounts
  logon security, 310
  remote domain logons, 311-312
  trust relationships, 251-252
local applications, printing, 380

local area networks (LANs), 50, 74, 76-77, 100, 126, 925-926
  frames, 596, 786, 814, 923
    Ethernet frame error types, 818
    fragmented frames, 817
    illegal length frames, 817-818
    purge frames (Token ring), 821
    Ring Change frames (Token ring), 820-821
  hardware performance tuning, 688-689
  internetworks, 596
  LocalTalk, 926
  MAC-layer bridges, 926
  monitoring, 624-634
    cabling, 625-626
    Ethernet, 626-632
    Token ring, 632-634
  packets, 786, 814
  segments, 936
    client setup, 182
    remote, 183
  subnetworks, 596
  switching hubs, 708-709
  technologies, 102-109
  troubleshooting
    LAN layer, 790, 807-826
    physical layer, 788-807
    protocol analyzers, 787-791
    SMB protocol layer, 790-791, 829-832
    transport layer, 790, 827-829
    virtual circuit management layer, 790, 826-827
  VLANs (Virtual LANs), 708-709, 942
local bus, 58
local collisions (Ethernet), 814-815
local domains, 210, 926

logon authentication, 324-325
local groups, 286, 330
  built-in, 266-268
    assigning rights, 268-270
  compared to global groups, 259-260
  group dynamics, 300-301
  mechanics, 263-264
  membership, 265
local logon, compared to domain logon, 212
local print providers, 365, 387-388
local printers (Setup), 140
Local Procedure Calls (LPCs), 24, 37, 926
local profiles, 335-336
Local Security Authority (LSA), 210, 308
LocalTalk, 452, 474-475, 926
LocalTalk Link Access Protocol (LLAP), 476
locks, file (NetWare), 501-502
LOGFILE.LOG file, 170
logging (migration)
  errors, 163-164
  options, 169-170
logical hops, 926
Logical Link Control (LLC), 624, 926
logical ports, 362
logon scripts, 44-45, 341-345, 908-915
  advantages, 342-343
  assigning home directories, 351
  compared to User Profiles, 908
  creating/assigning, 344-345
  file extensions, 908
  home directory, specifying, 909-910

  mechanics of, 343
  migration, 158
  NT commands, 911-915
  parameters, 344
  paths, 909
  PUTINENV utility, 345
  replicating, 908-909
  SMS (Systems Management Server), 526
  troubleshooting, 753-754, 910-911
logons, 926
  automating, 327-328
  initial logons, 321-322
  local domain authentication, 324-325
  local logon, compared to domain logon, 212
  Macintosh, 483-484
  mechanics of, 319-321
  non-interactive logons (local accounts), trust relationships, 251-252
  NT servers, 322-323
  NT Workstations, 327
  pass-through authentication, 219
  RAS security, 542
  security, 213-214, 308-313
    global user accounts, 310
    local user accounts, 310
    remote domains, 311-313
  settings (Setup), 192
  trusted domain authentication, 325
  unknown domain name, 326
  untrusted domain authentication, 326
  Welcome Dialog Box, 319
  WFW (Windows for Workgroups), 327
  workgroup authentication, 324

logs
auditing, 314-318
counters, 671
graphing data, 673
Event Viewer, 635
events, 777
truncating, 657
print job logging, disabling, 692
loss of signal strength, 926
Lotus Notes, 488-492
administration, 490
configuring NWLink, 491-492
definition, 488
executing as DOS application, 490-491
operating environment, 489-490
printing, 490
replication, 488-489
LPCs (Local Procedure Calls), 24, 37, 926
LPQ command (logon scripts), 914
LPR (Line Printer Remote), 494
lpr command , 899-900
ls command , 897
LSA (Local Security Authority), 210, 308
LSA Secret Object, renaming NT Servers, 242
LSL (Link Support Layer), 925

M

MAC (Medium Access Control) layer, 530, 927
bridges, 705-706, 926
frames, monitoring Token ring, 632-633
Macintosh, 472-488
AARP (AppleTalk Address Resolution Protocol), 476
AFP volumes

accessing files, 479
configuring, 479
creating, 478
AppleShare, 452, 474
AppleTalk, 452, 474-475
phases, 475-476
printers, 481, 482
router configuration, 485-486
Chooser, 477
clients, printing, 383
connections to NT Server printers, 481
DDP (Datagram Delivery Protocol), 476
file extension associations, 480
higher-layer protocols, 476-477
installing authentication, 477-478
LLAP (LocalTalk Link Access Protocol), 476
LocalTalk, 452, 474-475
logons, 483-484
PostScript printing, 473
print monitor, 482
print processors, 386
Print server for Macintosh, 481
printer sharing, 473
Services for Macintosh, 473
configuring, 484
disadvantages, 487-488
installing, 477
Registry entries, 486-487
setting permissions, 483
SFMPSPRT.DLL (printing), 482
SMS clients, 516-517
storing files, 480
translating
filenames, 480
permissions, 482-483

transparent file sharing, 472-473
mailslots, 31
Management Information Database (MIB), 927
monitoring Ethernet, 627
mapped file I/O, paging, 36
mapping, 286, 330, 927
drive letters to shares, 202
Gopher server files, 615-617
user accounts to rights/permissions, 320-321
master browsers (domains), 246-248
disabling browsing, 248
elections, 246-248
Master Domain Model, 220
matrix switching, 720-721
MAU (Medium Attachment Unit), 927
MAU (Multistation Access Unit), 624, 928
MaxBcastDgBuffered (Registry parameter), 546
MaxDgBufferedPer (Registry parameter), 546
MaxDynMem (Registry parameter), 546
MaxFrameSize (Registry parameter), 550
MaxNames (Registry parameter), 546
MaxSessions (Registry parameter), 547
Mbps (mega bits per second), 50, 927
Mbytes (mega bytes per second), 50, 927
MCA (Microchannel Architecture), 50, 927
mdelete command , 897
mdir command , 897
media (networks), 927

Medium Access Control (MAC) layer, 530, 927
bridges, 705-706, 926
frames, monitoring Token ring, 632-633
Medium Attachment Unit (MAU), 927
membership, groups as members of groups, 265
memory
addresses, 119
bottlenecks, 662, 666, 676-677
caches, 653-657, 664
ECC (error checking and correcting), 55
leaks, 676-677
linear memory addressing, 686
NT Server hardware requirements, 856
optimization, 647-652
paging, 664
pools, 649-651
SQL Server, configuration, 566-567
virtual memory, 349-350, 647-648
configuration, 144-145
manager, 34-36
working sets, 942
messages, 927
printers, disabling, 764-765
reassembly, 79-81
segmentation, 79-81
metafiles, printing, 381
mget command , 897
MIB (Management Information Database), 927
monitoring Ethernet, 627
Microchannel Architecture (MCA), 50, 927
microprocessors, 927
Microsoft
operating systems, limitations, 180-185

phone numbers, 866-867
priority support, 869-870
TCP/IP, 89-90
Microsoft Access, installing via SMS (Systems Management Server), 524
Microsoft Authorized Support Centers (ASCs), 867
Microsoft Certified Developers phone number, 867
Microsoft Download Service (MSDL), 869
Microsoft Electronic Technical Library, 871
Microsoft Hardware Compatibility List, 52
Microsoft Knowledge Base, 871
Microsoft Mail, distributing script files, 464-465
Microsoft Network, 872
Microsoft Office, 456-468
administrative installation, 459-460
client installation, 458-461
customizing setup script files, 461-463
distributing setup script files, 463-465
installing, 457-459
via SMS (Systems Management Server), 523-524
MSAPPS files, 465-467
troubleshooting, 467-468
uninstalling, 461
versions, 457
Microsoft Solution Provider Network, 867-868
Microsoft Word, installing via SMS (Systems Management Server), 524
Microsoft Works, installing via SMS (Systems Management Server), 524
migration, 11, 172-173

account replication, 172
Application Data Conversion, 174
configuration, saving, 168
conservative strategies, 154-157
errors, logging, 163, 164
file replication, 172
file selection, 166-168
incremental, 174
LAN Manager, 171
logging options, 169-170
login scripts, 158
minicomputers, 173-175
NDS-related information, 158
Network Management tools, 173
options, 160-165
overwriting information, 163
peer-to-peer networks, 173
phased, 174
planning, 155-160
printer queue information, 158
rebuilding NT Server, 160
servers, selecting, 160
starting, 168
supervisor defaults, 164
UNIX system, 173-175
user group managers, 159
user-defined objects, 159
username conflicts, 159
utilities, 170-171
ACLCONV, 171
BACKACC, 170
CONVERT, 171
PORTUAS, 171
Windows applications, 173
workgroups, 159
Migration Tool for NetWare, 157-170
passwords, 162
mini-drivers (printing), 392-393

minicomputers, migration, 173-175
mirroring, 66, 836
mkdir command , 897
MLID (Multiple Link Interface Driver), 88, 928
mls command , 898
models, domain models (trust relationships), 220-221
MODEM.INF (RAS configuration file), 542
modular 8-pin jacks, 801-802
monitoring
  activating disk monitoring, 667
  applications, 679-682
    average disk queue time, 682
    processor bottlenecks, 681
    processor queue length, 681
    service requests, 682
  bandwidth, 700-701
  disk drives, 639-641
    CHKDSK utility, 640-641
    physical defects, 641
    viewing partitions, 639
  hardware-based monitors, 629-630
  LANs, 624-634
    cabling, 625-626
    capacity, 711-713
    Ethernet, 626-632
    Token ring, 632-634
  networks, 682-684
  non-vendor-specific monitoring tools, 628
  NT Messages database, 637-638
  NT Server usage, 638-639
  operating system, 634-638
    Dr. Watson, 635-637
    Event Viewer, 634-635

out-of-band monitoring, 628
protocol analyzers, 628-629
see also auditing; performance tuning
moving
  data between network cards, 78-79
  traffic, printing, 88
mput command , 898
MS-DOS, 921
  applications, printing from, 368-369, 398
  clients
    bootable disks, 186-188
    setup, 180-181, 189-190
  compatibility, 7
  executing Lotus Notes as, 490-491
  print drivers, 361
  SMS clients, 516
  SNA Server clients, 592-593
  VDM (Virtual DOS Machine), 7, 360, 942
MS-Networks, history, 287-288
MSAPPS directory, 521-522
  Microsoft Office, 465-467
MSDL (Microsoft Download Service), 869
MSV1_0 Authentication Package, 249
Multi Protocol Router, 605
multi-users, 10
MultiCast (Registry parameter), 547
multiple interface cards, 56
Multiple Link Interface Driver (MLID), 88, 928
Multiple Master Domain Model, 220
multiport repeaters, 74, 928

multiprocessing requirements
  NT Server, 856
multiprocessor-based computers, 658-659
Multistation Access Unit (MAU), 624, 928
multitasking, 10, 928
multiuser operating systems, 928

N

NADN (Nearest Active Downstream Neighbor), 633
Name Binding Protocol (NBP), 476
named pipes, 31
  SQL Server configuration, 558-559
naming
  computer (Setup), 139
  NetBIOS name resolution, 601
  objects, 34
  Shares, 294
  UNC (Universal Naming Convention), 210, 214, 941
NBF (NetBEUI Frame), 928
NBNS (NetBIOS Naming Service), 597, 928
NBP (Name Binding Protocol), 476
NBSTAT command (logon scripts), 914
NCP (NetWare Core Protocol), 494, 929
NDIS (Network Device Interface Specification), 24, 74, 90, 100, 929
  drivers, 11, 94-95
    32-bit, 94
near end crosstalk (NeXT), 798-799, 928

Nearest Active Downstream Neighbor (NADN), 633
net accounts command, 881
net computer command, 881
net config command, 882
net config workstation command, 882
net continue command, 882-883
net file command, 883
net group command, 883-884
net helpmsg command, 884
net localgroup command, 885
net name command, 885-886
net pause command, 886-887
net print command, 887
net send command, 887-888
net session command, 888
net share command, 888
net start alerter command, 889
net start browser command, 889
net start command, 92, 889
net start dhcp client command, 889
net start snmp command, 889-890
net statistics command, 890
net stop command, 890
net time command, 245, 890
net use command, 890-891
net user command, 891-892
net view command, 892

NetBEUI (NetBIOS Extended User Interface), 75, 87-88, 928
  troubleshooting, 828
NetBEUI Frame (NBF), 928
NetBIOS (Network Basic Input/Output System), 24, 87, 598-599, 928
  broadcast storms, 598
  disadvantages, 598-599
  name resolution, 601
  routers, 87
  TCP/IP encapsulation, 600
  troubleshooting, 790, 826-827
  WINS (Windows Internet Name Service), 608-611
    advantages, 608
    configuring servers, 610-611
    installing servers, 608-610
NetBIOS Gateway (RAS), 536
  parameters (Registry), 545-549
NetBIOS Naming Service (NBNS), 597, 928
NetbiosGatewayEnabled (Registry parameter), 545
NetLogon Service
  pass-through authentication, 249-251
  synchronizing domain controllers, 230-233
netstat command , 901
NetWare, 928
  CAPTURE command (printing), 389
  clients, support, 92-95
  compared to NT, 289
  configuring SMS (Systems Management Server), 515

file systems, restoring to NT drive, 156
  GSNW (Gateway Service for NetWare), 96, 494-504
    accessing file resources, 501-502
    accessing printers, 502
    configuring, 496-498
    dependencies, 499
    FPSN (File and Print Services for NetWare), 504
    installing, 495-496
    NetWare-aware applications, 503
    NWLink, 495
    performance tuning, 499-500
    RIP/SAP broadcasts, disabling, 498-499
    security, 500, 500-501
    system utilities, 502-503
  LANalyzer for NetWare (monitoring tool), 628-629
  migration utility, 157-170
  NT similarities, 8
  print providers, 390
  printing, compared to NT printing, 363
  RAS (Remote Access Server), 533
  WFW SQL Server clients, 560-561
NetWare Core Protocol (NCP), 494, 929
NetWare Loadable Modules (NLMs), 13, 50, 929
NetWare Requester for NT, 157
NETWORK account, 306
network adapters
  drivers, 179
  Setup, 140-141
  vendors, 179
  see also network cards

network architecture, 100, 929
- data link control (DLC), 91
- IPX/SPX, 88-89
- NDIS, 90
- NetBEUI, 87-88
- NetBIOS, 87
- OSI model, 86
- TCP/IP (Microsoft), 89-90

Network Basic Input/ Output System (NetBIOS), 24, 87, 598-599, 928
- broadcast storms, 598
- disadvantages, 598-599
- name resolution, 601
- routers, 87
- TCP/IP encapsulation, 600
- troubleshooting, 790, 826-827
- WINS (Windows Internet Name Service), 608-611
  - *advantages, 608*
  - *configuring servers, 610-611*
  - *installing servers, 608-610*

network cards, 657, 929
- access protocols, 918
- adding, 151
- bandwidth, 702-703
- bus mastering, 62
- drivers, 61, 120-123
  - *configuration, 95-96*
  - *MLID (Multiple Link Interface Driver), 928*
- hardware, 61-63
- installation, 118-120
- LAN capacity, 709-711

Network Client Administrator utility, 185-186

network components (Registry), 443-449
- binding, 447-448
- dependency handling, 448-449

service-registration information, 446
software-registration information, 445-446, 447-448
subkeys, 443-444

Network Device Interface Specification, see NDIS

network drive share, 149

network drivers, 41-42

Network Errors/sec counter, 690

Network File System (NFS), 929

Network group, 267

Network Interface Card (NIC), 929
- NT Server support, 857-858
- SMS network monitoring, 527-528

network interface printers, 394

Network layer (OSI Model), 86

network management (NT Server features), 862

network operating systems (NOS), 4
- integrating, 6

Network Setup utility, 191

network transport protocols, SQL Server, 553-555

network utilization, 929

network-aware applications, 455-456

NetworkAddress (Registry parameter), 550

networks, 596, 929
- access denial, 739
- architecture, 74, 85-91
- BackOffice, 14
- bridges, 919
- connection-oriented protocols, 921
- connectionless protocols, 921

domain rules, 217
history of MS-Networks, 287-288
media, 927
monitoring, 682-684
  SMS (Systems Management Server), 526-528
NetBIOS, 598-599
  broadcast storms, 598
  disadvantages, 598-599
nodes, 929
NT overview, 288-289
permanent network connections, user profiles, 341
printers, 296-298
protocols, 929
resources, 210
restricted access, RAS security, 541
services, Windows 95 setup, 197-202
setting time on domains, 245
Setup settings, 142-143
topologies, 940
  linear bus, 925
  ring, 934
  star bus, 938
  star-wired ring, 938
workgroups compared to domains, 211-212

newsgroups, technical support, 871

NeXT (near end crosstalk), 798-799, 928

NFS (Network File System), 929

NIC (Network Interface Card), 929
- NT Server support, 857-858
- SMS network monitoring, 527-528

NLMs (NetWare Loadable Modules), 13, 50, 929

No Access permission, 46, 254

nodes, 74, 76, 100, 929
addresses, 79, 930
bandwidth, joining,
722-723
WANs (wide area networks), 77
noise, 797-798, 930
**Nominal Velocity of
Propagation, 103**
**non-interactive logons
(local accounts), trust
relationships, 251-252**
non-native printer drivers, installing, 393
**non-vendor-specific
monitoring tools, 628**
**non-Windows-based
applications, printing,
382**
nondedicated servers, 10
**nonpaged memory pools,
649-651**
**nonroutable protocols,
596, 930**
**normalized databases
(SQL Server), performance tuning, 569-570**
**NOS (network operating
systems), 4**
integrating, 6
**Not_Enough_Quota
subkey, 652**
Notes, 488-492
administration, 490
configuring NWLink,
491-492
definition, 488
executing as DOS application, 490-491
operating environment,
489-490
printing, 490
replication, 488-489
NT
commands (logon scripts),
911-915

compared to NetWare, 8,
289
deleting from boot partition, 736-737
features, 6
installation, restoring with
Emergency Disk Repair,
838
networking overview, 288-289
object-oriented features,
289-293
*ACL (access control
list), 291*
closing objects, 293
security, 291-293
optimizing, 663
reinstalling, 732-733
*editing BOOT.INI
parameters, 734-736*
routing support, 601-602
upgrading clients via SMS
(Systems Management
Server), 525
**NT Fault Tolerance
system (NTFT), 841**
behavior, 845
design, 845-848
FTDISK.SYS. driver,
845-846
error handling, 847-848
volume sector sparing, 846
failures, 847
**NT File System (NTFS),
24, 178, 930**
access, client setup,
184-185
compared to FAT/HPFS
security, 254-255
directories, share permissions, 252-255, 860-861
fault tolerance, 742-746
boot floppies, 743-746
hot-fixing, 743
hidden accounts, 304-306
primary partitions,
deleting, 737

system files, 742
**NT Kernel (Registry data),
408**
**NT Messages database,
637-638**
NT Server
adding TCP/IP, 604
alert messages, 863
backup features, 863
client workstation network
card support, 858
configuring for TCP/IP
printing, 400-401
delegating administration
responsibility features,
863
fault tolerance, 863
file access permissions,
279
file system features/
capacities, 859
hardware
requirements, 856
support, 858
inter-program communication features, 859
monitoring usage, 638-639
multiprocessing requirements, 856
Network Interface Card
(NIC) support, 857-858
network management
features, 862
non-native printer drivers,
installing, 393
NTFS directory/file
permissions, 860-861
performance monitoring,
862
performance optimization
features, 859-860
print spooling components,
363-365
printer alerts, 862
printers, Macintosh
connections, 481

printing features/capabilities, 861-862
protocol support, 858
renaming, 241-242
security auditing, 861
security features, 860
SNA Server integration, 580-581
system architecture, 857
user rights, 861
workgroup logon authentication, 324

NT servers, logons, 322-323

NT system volume, restoring, 730-731

NT Workstations, 126
clients, connecting to NetWare server, 92
file access permissions, 279
logons, 327
renaming, 242
as servers, 236
user profiles, 439-440

ntcmdprompt command, 892-893

NTFS (NT File System), 24, 178, 930
access, client setup, 184-185
compared to FAT/HPFS security, 254-255
directories, share permissions, 252-255, 860-861
fault tolerance, 742-746
boot floppies, 743-746
hot-fixing, 743
hidden accounts, 304-306
primary partitions, deleting, 737
system files, 742

NTFT (NT Fault Tolerance system), 841
behavior, 845
design, 845-848
FTDISK.SYS. driver, 845-846

error handling, 847-848
volume sector sparing, 846
failures, 847

null sessions, printer security, 398-399

NumRecvQueryIndications (Registry parameter), 545

NWLink, 9, 41, 94-95, 154, 495, 930
configuring for Lotus Notes, 491-492
packets, size adjustment, 757-758

O

Object Manager, 33-34
object type objects, 34
objects, 24, 930
counter hierarchy, 669-670
directory objects, 34
event, 34
file, 34
handles, 34
names, 34
NT object mechanics, 289-293
ACL (access control list), 291
closing objects, 293
security, 291-293
object type, 34
port, 34
printer pools, 360, 363, 395-396
creating, 395-396
managing, 396
printers, 360-363, 932
security, 396-399
sharing, 369-371
process, 34
section and segment, 34
semaphore, 34
symbolic link, 34
thread, 34
types, 34
user-defined, 159

ODI (Open Datalink Interface), 88, 930
ODI/MLID drivers, client/server installation, 75
OEM (original equipment manufactured), 52
one-way trusts (domains), 218
Online Help, user profiles, 339
online services, technical support, 872-873
open command , 898
Open Data Services, 554
open files, backups, 727-728
Open Software Foundation (OSF), 24, 930
Open Systems Interconnect (OSI) model, 931
layers, 86
OpenGL standard software, 69
OpenView (monitoring tool), 628
operating environment, Lotus Notes, 489-490
operating systems (OS), 4, 33-43
architecture, 25-43
integrating, 6
Microsoft, limitations, 180-185
monitoring, 634-638
Dr. Watson, 635-637
Event Viewer, 634-635
multiuser operating systems, 928
Setup, 936
Operators group, 266
optical fiber cable, 77, 108, 118
troubleshooting, 804
optimizing
domain synchronization, 229-233
memory, 647-659
NT, 663, 859-860

options
installation, 132
logon (migration), 169-170
migration, 160-165
protocols, editing, 151
Setup, 189
orphans, 849-850
OS (operating systems), 4, 33-43
architecture, 25-43
integrating, 6
Microsoft, limitations, 180-185
monitoring, 634-638
Dr. Watson, 635-637
Event Viewer, 634-635
multiuser operating systems, 928
Setup, 936
OS/2, executing Lotus Notes, 490-491
OSF (Open Software Foundation), 24, 930
OSI (Open Systems Interconnect) model, 931
layers, 86
out-of-band monitoring, 628
overriding cached usernames/passwords, 322
ownership
files, 307
resources, 274-275

P

Package Definition Files (PDF), 508
package rule files (SMS audited software), 518-519
packages (SMS), creating/ distributing, 519-520
packet switching, 78
packets, 74, 81, 100, 706, 786, 814, 931

compared to frames, 596
headers, 82
NWLink, size adjustment, 757-758
routers, 83
SMB packets, 829-832
PAD.INF (RAS configuration file), 543
page faults, resolving, 650
page states, 35
paged memory pools, 649-651
pagefiles, 144-145, 647-648
virtual memory, 349-350
pages
data pages, accessing, 650
memory, 664
paging
demand-based, 35
mapped file I/O, 36
performance tuning, 687-688
placement, 36
replacement, 36
virtual memory, 687
PAP (Printer Access Protocol), 476
PAPI (Password Authentication Protocol), 541
parameters
AsyncMAC (Registry), 549-550
general remote access (Registry), 544-545
logon scripts, 344
NetBIOS Gateway (Registry), 545-549
RASHub (Registry), 550
parity stripes, 67, 836
partitions
boot partition, deleting NT, 736-737
creating on RISC-based computers, 734-735
defined, 836
duplexing, 836
mirroring, 836

orphans, 849
recovering, 850
primary, 836
deleting, 737
system partition, 836
viewing, 639
volume sets, 836
pass-through authentication, 219, 249-252
passing validations, trust relationships, 222-225
Password Authentication Protocol (PAPI), 541
passwords, 278
caching usernames/ passwords, 322
enforcing password policy, 279
Migration Tool for NetWare, 162
SAM (Security Account Manager), 248-249
Setup, 144
suggested policies, 278
trust relationships (domains), routes for passing validations, 222-225
paths
installing from, 132-133
logon scripts, 909
PCI (Peripheral Component Interface), 50
buses
32-bit features, 56
bandwidth, 63
bus mastering, 57
VL-bus comparison, 59-61
network cards, 711
PDCs (Primary Domain Controllers), 154, 215, 286, 932
promoting BDCs (Backup Domain Controllers) to, 227-229
replication, 225-226

PDF (Package Definition Files), 508
peer-to-peer networks, 178
  migration, 173
  setup, 181
Pentium processors, 55
pentnt command, 893
PerfectOffice, 468-472
  Administrator program group, 469
  application integration, 469
  Envoy (electronic publishing), 470
  InfoCentral, 470
  installing, 471-472
  QuickTask, 470
  technical support, 470-471
performance
  monitoring (NT Server features), 862
  RAID, 850-852
Performance Monitor, 665-673
  activating disk monitoring, 667
  counters
    alerts, 672-673
    charting, 670
    graphing log data, 673
    hierarchy, 669-670
    logs, 671
    reports, 672
  monitoring applications, 679-682
    average disk queue time, 682
    processor bottlenecks, 681
    processor queue length, 681
    service requests, 682
  monitoring networks, 682-684
  performance improvements, RAID, 850-852

security, 667-668
workstation tuning, 689-690
performance tuning, 685-693
  bottlenecks, 673-679
    cache, 677-678
    disk, 675-676
    LAN, 679
    memory, 676-677
    processor, 674-675
  counters, 666-667
  default printer spool directory, changing, 691-692
  disabling print job logging, 692
  disk drives, 686-688
    linear memory addressing, 686
    paging (virtual memory), 687
    paging files, 687-688
  GSNW (Gateway Service for NetWare), 499-500
  LAN hardware, 688-689
  NT Server features, 859-860
  overview, 662-665
  RAW mode read/writes, 693
  remote servers, 690
  servers, 685-686, 690-691
  SQL Server, 568-572
    indexes, 568-569
    normalized databases, 569-570
    query design, 570, 571-572
  transactions, 665
  workstations, 689-690
  see also monitoring
Peripheral Component Interface (PCI), 50
  buses
    32-bit features, 56
    bandwidth, 63

    bus mastering, 57
    VL-bus comparison, 59-61
  network cards, 711
permanent network connections, user profiles, 341
permissions, 45-46, 258, 279-282, 286, 330, 931
  access permissions (resources), 214-215
  ACL (access control list), 291
  editing, 281-282
  file ownership, 307
  GSNW (Gateway Service for NetWare), 500-501
  home directories, 353-354
  mapping user accounts to, 320-321
  network printers, 298
  NTFS directory/file permissions, 252-255, 860-861
  printers, 396-399
  setting Macintosh permissions, 483
  translating Macintosh permissions, 482-483
  see also rights
personal information managers, InfoCentral (PerfectOffice), 470
personal profiles, 336-337
PGC (Program Group Controller), 508
phased migration, 174
phases (AppleTalk), 475-476
phone numbers
  FastTips, 868
  Microsoft technical support, 866-867
  priority support, 869-870
physical circuits, 78
physical defects in disk drives, monitoring, 641

physical layer, trouble-shooting, 86, 788-807
physical ports, 362
pin assignments (UPS), 748
ping command , 901-902, 914
pipes, named, 31
placement, paging, 36
planning security, 282-284
Plug-and-Play devices, 127, 196
Point-to-Point Protocol (PPP), 532
port objects, 34
portability, 24-30, 931
ports
    COM, deleting, 762
    logical, 362
    physical, 362
PORTUAS utility, 171, 210, 931
POSIX (Portable Operating System Interface for Computing Environments), 931
POST (Power On Self Test), 772
post-installation configuration, 150-152
PostScript printer description (PPD), 393
PostScript printer drivers, 393
PostScript printing, 383, 386, 473
power supply (UPS), 747-748
Power Users group, 261, 266
PPP (Point-to-Point Protocol), 532
preemptive processing, 932
premier support, 870
Presentation layer (OSI model), 86

preventing total system failure, 290
Primary Domain Controllers (PDCs), 154, 215, 286, 932
    promoting BDCs (Backup Domain Controllers) to, 227-229
    replication, 225-226
primary NTFS partitions, 836
    deleting, 737
print command, 893
print devices, 360, 362, 932
print drivers
    DOS, 361
    installing, 369-370
    Windows, 360
print jobs, 360, 932
    clearing from queues, 376
    disabling logging, 692
    rendering, 360, 933
    spool files, 938
    spoolers, 938
    spooling, 360, 938
Print Manager, 296-298, 362
    Advanced Job Status, 376
    as client, 383
    editing print processor functions, 387-388
    printing to files without prompting, 374
    remote printer administration, 377
    separator page files, 372-373
    user profiles, 339
print monitors, 365, 391-392
    Macintosh, 482
Print Operators group, 267, 267-268
print processors, 365, 384-386
    Macintosh, 386
    Windows, 385-386

print providers, 387-390
    local print providers, 365, 387-388
    NetWare CAPTURE command, 389
    NetWare print providers, 390
    remote print providers, 365, 389
    spool/shadow files, 388-389
    Windows print providers, 389
print routers, 360, 365, 384
Print Server for Macintosh, 481
Printer Access Protocol (PAP), 476
printer alerts (NT Server), 862
printer drivers, 392
    cross-platform printing, 393
    directories, 378
    non-native printer drivers, installing, 393
printer pools, 360, 363, 932
    creating, 395-396
    managing, 396
printers, 360-363, 932
    AppleTalk, 481-482
        deleting destination, 763
    capturing, 203
    deleting, 762-763
    GSNW (Gateway Service for NetWare), accessing via, 502
    Hewlett-Packard, deleting destination, 762
    JetDirect, debugging, 755-757
    local, setup, 140
    Macintosh, 473
        connections to NT Server printers, 481
    messages, disabling, 764-765

network interface printers, 394

ownership, 274-275

queue information, migration, 158

remote printers, administering, 377

security, 396-399

sharing, 296-298, 369-371

printing

adding filenames to Registry, 374

automatically to files, 374-375

clients, 365, 380-383

down level clients, 382-383

local applications, 380

Macintosh clients, 383

non-Windows-based applications, 382

Print Manager as client, 383

remote workstations, 382

UNIX clients, 383

Windows-based applications, 366-367, 380-382

default printer spool directory, changing, 691-692

directories, 378

from DOS applications, 368-369, 398

down level printing, 367-368

EMFs (enhanced metafiles), 367

envelopes, 376-377

FPSN (File and Print Services for NetWare), 504

journal files, 382

from Lotus Notes, 490

metafiles, 381

mini-drivers, 392-393

NetWare, compared to NT printing, 363

NT Server features/capabilities, 861-862

Registry entries, 378-380

rendering, 384-385

separator page files, 372-373

servers, 360

SFMPSPRT.DLL (Macintosh printing), 482

spool files, 360, 363

spoolers, 360

spooling, 360, 938

components of, 363-365

TCP/IP, 399-402

configuring NT Server, 400-401

creating TCP/IP printers, 401-402

traffic, moving, 88

troubleshooting, 402-403

from Windows applications, 368

workstations, 360

Printing Notification network dialog boxes, disabling, 375

priorities

assigning, 644

foreground applications, 645-646

server performance, 645-646

SERVER service priority, 645

priority support, 869-870

problem-solving

backing up

BOOT.INI file, 840-841

Registry, 840-841

cabling, 792

attenuation, 792-793

cable testers, 805

certification tools, 806-807

coaxial, 792-794

continuity testers, 804-805

fiber optic, 804

UTP (unshielded twisted pair), 795-802

CHKDSK utility, 839

Emergency Repair Disk, 837-838

Ethernet, 630-632

intermittent problems, 779

LAN layer, 790, 807-826

Ethernet, 807-828

Token ring, 819-826

logon scripts, 910-911

Microsoft Office Setup, 467-468

non-Setup boot failures, 745-746

NT Messages database, 637-638

partitions, recovering orphans, 850

physical layer, 788-807

printing problems, 402-403

protocol analyzers, 787-791

features, 788-789

RAID, 841-842

restoring computers, 849-850

Setup-related boot failures, 746

SMB protocol layer, 790-791, 829-832

transport layer, 790, 827-829

IPX/SPX, 828

NetBEUI, 828

TCP/IP, 829

virtual circuit management layer, 790, 826-827

procedure calls, LPCs (Local Procedure Calls), 926

process ID, auditing, 318

Process Manager, 36-38

process objects, 34

processing
centralized processing, 920
collaborative processing, 920
distributed processing, 921
multiprocessing, NT Server requirements, 856
preemptive processing, 932
SMP (Symmetrical Multi Processing), 939
time slices, 939
processor queue length, monitoring applications, 681
processors, 55, 644, 932
bottlenecks, 674-675
monitoring applications, 681
CPU (Central Processing Unit), 920
microprocessors, 927
multitasking, 928
NT Server hardware requirements, 856
rings, 934
RISC (Reduced Instruction Set Computing), 933
testing (Setup), 145-146
utilization, 932
Prodigy, 872
profiles, 43-44, 331-341
advantages, 333-334
compared to logon scripts, 908
default profiles, 337
local profiles, 335-336
mandatory profiles, 337
mechanics of, 334-335
overview, 332-333
permanent network connections, 341
personal profiles, 336-337
Registry, 439-440
server-based profiles, creating, 337-341
settings, 338-339

Program Group Control, SMS (Systems Management Server), 520-521
Program Group Controller (PGC), 508
Program Manager, profiles, 334-335, 338
promoting BDCs (Backup Domain Controllers), 227-229
prompt command , 898
propagation rate, 103
protocol analyzers, 76, 628-629, 787-791, 932
features, 788-789
troubleshooting Ethernet, 807-828
protocol decodes (protocol analyzer features), 788
protocol stacks, 74
protocols, 74-85, 100, 103, 184, 932
AARP (AppleTalk Address Resolution Protocol), 476
access protocols, 918
ADSP (AppleTalk Data Stream Protocol), 476
AEP (AppleTalk Echo Protocol), 476
AFP (Apple Filing Protocol), 476
AppleTalk, 452, 474-475, 918
phases, 475-476
printers, 481-482
router configuration, 485-486
ARP (Address Resolution Protocol), 597, 918
ATP (AppleTalk Transport Protocol), 476
CHAP (Challenge Handshake Authentication Protocol), 540-541
configuration, 95-96
connection-oriented, 921
connectionless, 921

CSMA/CD (Carrier Sense Multiple Access with Collison Detection), 920
DDP (Datagram Delivery Protocol), 476
deleting, Windows 95 setup, 199
DHCP (Dynamic Host Configuration Protocol), 508, 597, 604-608, 922
configuring servers, 605
creating Scopes, 605-606
IP address leases, 607-608
reserving client IP addresses, 606-607
frames, 74
FTP (File Transfer Protocol), 597, 923
commands, 896-898
technical support sites, 871
gateways, 923
higher-layer protocols (Macintosh), 476-477
HTTP (HyperText Transfer Protocol), 924
ICMP (Internet Control Message Protocol), 597
IP (Internet Protocol), 924
IPX/SPX, 88-89, 925
client installation, 75
server installation, 75
SQL Server, 559-561
troubleshooting, 828
layers, 81-82
LLAP (LocalTalk Link Access Protocol), 476
LLC (Logical Link Control), 624
migration, 11
NBNS (NetBIOS Naming Service), 928
NBP (Name Binding Protocol), 476
NCP (NetWare Core Protocol), 494

NetBEUI (NetBIOS
  Extended User Inter-
  face), 75, 87-88, 928
  troubleshooting, 828
NetBIOS (Network Basic
  Input/Output System),
  24, 87, 598-599, 928
  broadcast storms, 598
  disadvantages, 598-599
  name resolution, 601
  routers, 87
  TCP/IP encapsulation,
  600
  troubleshooting, 790,
  826-827
  WINS (Windows
  Internet Name Ser-
  vice), 608-611
network, 929
nonroutable, 596, 930
NT routing support,
  601-602
NT Server protocol
  support, 858
NWLink, 9, 930
options, editing, 151
packets, 74
PAP (Printer Access
  Protocol), 476
PAPI (Password Authenti-
  cation Protocol), 541
PPP (Point-to-Point
  Protocol), 532
RIP (Router Information
  Protocol), 494, 597, 935
  disabling broadcasts,
  498-499
routable, 75, 934
SAP (Service Advertising
  Protocol), 494
  disabling broadcasts,
  498-499
selecting at setup, 141-142
SLIP (Serial Line Internet
  Protocol), 532
SMB (Server Message
  Block), 597, 936

troubleshooting,
  790-791, 829-832
SMTP (Simple Mail
  Transfer Protocol), 597
SNAP (Subnetwork Access
  Protocol), 624, 809
SNMP (Simple Network
  Management Protocol),
  508, 597, 937
  monitoring Ethernet,
  627
source-routing bridge/
  protocol, 937
spanning-tree bridge/
  protocol, 938
SPAP (Shiva Password
  Authentication Protocol),
  541
SQL Server networking
  protocols, 553-555
stacks, OSI Model, 86
TCP/IP (Transmission
  Control Protocol/Internet
  Protocol), 597-620,
  940-941
  adding to installed NT
  Servers, 604
  advantages, 599
  browsers, 600-601
  HTTP Server, 617-620
  installing, 399-400,
  602-604
  NetBIOS encapsulation,
  600
  NetBIOS name resolu-
  tion, 601
  printing, 399-402
  SNA Server clients,
  589-590
  SQL Server clients,
  561-562
  troubleshooting, 829
  utilities reference,
  894-906
  WINS (Windows
  Internet Name Ser-
  vice), 608-611

token-passing bus, 939
token-passing rings, 939
transport, NetBEUI, 75
UDP (User Datagram
  Protocol), 597, 941
WINS (Windows Internet
  Name Service), 942
**Pulse (Registry param-
  eter), 232**
**PulseConcurrency (Regis-
  try parameter), 232**
**PulseMaximum (Registry
  parameter), 232**
**PulseTimeout1 (Registry
  parameter), 232**
**PulseTimeout2 (Registry
  parameter), 232**
**purge frames (Token
  ring), 821**
put command , 898
Putinenv Utility, 45, 345
pwd command , 898

Q

**queries (SQL Server),
  performance tuning,
  570-572**
question mark (?), 896
queues, 644
  average disk queue time,
    monitoring applications,
    682
  printers, information, 158
  processor queue length,
    monitoring applications,
    681
  tagged command queuing
    (SCSI), 656-657
  see also spool files
**QuickTask
  (PerfectOffice), 470**
quit command , 898
quote command , 898

R

RAID (Redundant Array of Inexpensive Disks), 836, 841-842, 933
fault tolerance
identifying broken sets, 849
levels, 842
recovery, 848-849
NTFT (NT Fault Tolerance system), 841
behavior, 845
design, 845-848
FTDISK.SYS. driver, 845-848
sector sparing, 841, 846
volume sector sparing failures, 847
performance, 850-852
support for hardware devices, 848-850
RAID 0 (striping), 66, 933
fault tolerance, 842
RAID 1 (mirroring/duplexing), 66, 933
fault tolerance, 842-844
RAID 5 (striping with parity), 67, 933
fault tolerance, 844-845
implementation, 67
RAM (random access memory), testing, 780
Randomize (Registry parameter), 233
RAS (Remote Access Server), 494, 530-550, 933
APIs, 534
AsyncMAC driver, 537-538
capabilities, 530-534
data compression, 533
data encryption, 533
hardware requirements, 538
installing/configuring, 538-540
Internet support, 533

joining domains, 539-540
NetWare networks, 533
potential conflicts, 538-539
PPP (Point-to-Point Protocol), 532
RAS Server, 536
RAS Subsystem, 536-538
RASHub device driver, 537
security, 540-550
auditing, 541
callbacks, 542
CHAP (Challenge Handshake Authentication Protocol), 540-541
configuration files, 542-543
disconnecting users, 541
editing Registry values, 543-550
firewalls, 541
logons, 542
restricted network access, 541
SLIP (Serial Line Internet Protocol), 532
SNA Server, 581
user interface, 534-535
WFW connections, 538
X.25 networks, 534
RASHub device driver, 537
parameters (Registry), 550
RASPHONE.PBK (RAS configuration file), 543
raster printer drivers, 392
RAW mode read/writes, 693
rcp command, 903, 914-915
RcvDgSubmitted (Registry parameter), 547
RDISK.EXE utility, updating Emergency Repair Disk, 838
re-initialization (Token ring), 633

Read permission, 46, 253
Reads Denied/sec counter, 690
reassembling messages, 79-81
rebuilding NT Server (migration), 160
Recognizer, 406, 933
Registry data, 408
recombining split domains, 239-241
reconfiguring domains, 236-242
during installation, 237-238
recombining split domains, 239-241
renaming computers, 241-242
via Server Manager, 237
workstations joining domains, 238-239
recovery
non-Setup boot failures, 745-746
options, configuring, 350
SAM (Security Access Manager), 738-739
Setup-related boot failures, 746
SQL Server, 565-566
recv command , 898
redirectors, 24, 933
Reduced Instruction Set Computing (RISC), 658-659, 933
editing BOOT.INI file, 734-735
emergency repair disk, 70, 734
platform, 68-70
server installation, 69-70
Redundant Array of Inexpensive Disks (RAID), 836, 841-842, 933
fault tolerance
identifying broken sets, 849

levels, 842
recovery, 848-849
NTFT (NT Fault Toler-
ance system), 841
behavior, 845
design, 845-848
FTDISK.SYS. driver,
845-848
sector sparing, 841, 846
volume sector sparing
failures, 847
performance, 850-852
support for hardware
devices, 848-850
**redundant paths, mixing
bridges with routers, 708**
referential integrity, 42
Registry, 440-449
flushing data, 441-442
keys, 441
size limits, 442-443
Registry, 406-449, 933
adding filenames for
printing to, 374
AsyncMAC parameters,
549-550
automating logons,
327-328
backing up, 728-729,
840-841
compared to INI files,
408-409
editing, 407
RAS security, 543-550
general remote access
parameters, 544-545
hives, 406, 415-416, 923
restoring, 414-415
HKEY_CLASSES_ROOT
key, 438
HKEY_LOCAL_MACHINE
key, 417-438
HARDWARE subtree,
417, 418-422
SAM subtree, 418,
422-423
SECURITY subtree,
418, 423

SOFTWARE subtree,
418, 423-427
SYSTEM subtree, 418,
427-438
HKEY_USERS key, 439
keys, 406, 409-410, 925
NetBIOS Gateway param-
eters, 545-549
network components,
443-449
binding, 447-448
dependency handling,
448-449
service-registration
information, 446
software-registration
information, 445-446
subkeys, 443-444
overview, 407-410
printing entries, 378-380
RASHub parameters, 550
referential integrity,
440-449
flushing data, 441-442
keys, 441
size limits, 442-443
restoring, 729-730
security, 449
Services for Macintosh
entries, 486-487
SQL Server entries,
574-575
structure, 415
subkeys, 406, 415-416, 939
value entries, 439-440
subtrees, 406, 939
saving as hives, 414
thread priority, 403
user profiles, 439-440
viewing for remote com-
puters, 411
Registry Editor, 407
Auto Refresh option, 411
configuration manage-
ment, 411-415
Load Hive command,
412-413

Save Key command,
413-415
Unload Hive command,
413
viewing remote com-
puter Registry, 411
executing, 410
Restore Volatile command,
414
reinstallation
NT, 732-733
editing BOOT.INI
parameters, 734-736
SQL Server, 557-558
**relationships, trust (do-
mains), 210, 216-225, 941**
creating, 312-313
domain models, 220-221
logging in without, 311
one-way trusts, 218
pass-through authentica-
tion, 219, 249-252
routes for passing validations, 222-225
setting up, 221-222
trusted compared to
trusting domains,
217-218
two-way trusts, 218
**remirroring fault-tolerant
file systems, 743-746**
**remote LAN segments,
client setup, 182-184**
**Remote Access Server, see
RAS**
APIs, 534
AsyncMAC driver, 537-538
capabilities, 530-534
data compression, 533
data encryption, 533
hardware requirements,
538
installing/configuring,
538-540
Internet support, 533
joining domains, 539-540
NetWare networks, 533

potential conflicts, 538-539
PPP (Point-to-Point Protocol), 532
RAS Server, 536
RAS Subsystem, 536-538
RASHub device driver, 537
security, 540-550
  auditing, 541
  callbacks, 542
  CHAP (Challenge Handshake Authentication Protocol), 540-541
  configuration files, 542-543
  disconnecting users, 541
  editing Registry values, 543-550
  firewalls, 541
  logons, 542
  restricted network access, 541
SLIP (Serial Line Internet Protocol), 532
SNA Server, 581
user interface, 534-535
WFW connections, 538
X.25 networks, 534
remote collisions (Ethernet), 814-815
remote computers, viewing Registry for, 411
remote domains
  logon security, 311-313
  overriding cached usernames/passwords, 322
remote print providers, 365, 389
remote printers, administering, 377
Remote Procedure Calls (RPC), 31, 210, 933
remote servers, 178
  performance tuning, 690
remote workstations, printing, 382

remotehelp command , 898
RemoteListen (Registry parameter), 548
remotely executing SQL Server, 572-573
rename command , 898
renaming
  computers in domains, 241-242
  SNA Server servers, 584
rendering, 360, 384-385, 933
repair process, 733-734
repeaters, 74, 117, 933
  disabling SQE (Signal Quality Error), 816
  multiport repeaters, 928
replacing components, 783
replication, 354-357
  accounts (migration), 172
  directories, 233-236
  files (migration), 172
  logon scripts, 908-909
  Lotus Notes databases, 488-489
  PDC (Primary Domain Controller), 225-226
ReplicationGovernor parameter, synchronizing domain controllers, 230-231
Replicator account, 306
Replicator group, 261, 266
reports (counters), 672
requesters, 934
Requests for Comment (RFC), 934
reserving client IP addresses (DHCP), 606-607
resource domains, 210, 934
  trust relationships, 217-218
Resource Kit Upgrade utility, 659

Resource Kit WEB Server (Gopher servers), 611-617
  configuring, 614-617
  deleting, 614
  file mapping, 615-617
  installing, 612-613
  Services dialog box, 617
  technical support sites, 871
resources, 210, 215, 934
  access permissions, 214-215
  connecting to shared, 298-300
  domain rules, 217
  GSNW (Gateway Service for NetWare), accessing file resources, 501-502
  local groups, compared to global groups, 259-260
  logon security, 308-313
    global user accounts, 310
    local user accounts, 310
    remote domains, 311-313
  ownership, 274-275
  sharing, history of MS-Networks, 287-288
  UNC (Universal Naming Convention), 210, 214, 941
Restore Volatile command (Registry Editor), 414
restoring
  computers, 849-850
  hives (Registry), 414-415, 729-730
  NT installation with Emergency Disk Repair, 838
  NT system volume, 730-731
restricted network access, 278
  RAS security, 541
restricting users, 44

rexec command , 903-904
RFC (Requests for Comment), 934
rights, 258, 271-279, 286, 330, 934
    assigning to user groups, 268-270, 276, 307-308
    customizing for built-in user groups, 275-276
    editing for user groups, 301
    managing via Administrators group, 274
    mapping user accounts to, 320-321
    mechanics of, 271-274
    NT Server user rights, 861
    resource ownership, 274-275
    Security Administrator, 277
    setting up user groups, 300-301
    see also permissions
rights masks, 45
Ring Change frames (Token ring), 820-821
ring polls (Token ring), 820
ring re-initialization, 633
ring recovery counters, 821-822
ring topology, 934
rings
    processors, 934
    token-passing rings, 939
RIP (Router Information Protocol), 494, 597, 935
    disabling broadcasts, 498-499
RISC (Reduced Instruction Set Computing), 658-659, 933
    editing BOOT.INI file, 734-735
    emergency repair disk, 70, 734

platform, 68-70
    server installation, 69-70
rmdir command , 898
routable protocols, 75, 934
route command , 904, 915
routers, 74-75, 82-83, 100, 178, 706-707, 935
    AppleTalk, router configuration, 485-486
    brouters (bridging routers), 707, 919
    compared to bridges, 84-85, 707-708
    DDP (Datagram Delivery Protocol), 476
    internetworks, 184
    logical hops, 926
    mixing with bridges, 708
    Multi Protocol Router, 605
    NetBIOS, 87, 599
    NT routing support, 601-602
    packets, 83
    print routers, 360, 365, 384
RPCs (Remote Procedure Calls), 31, 210, 933
RSA software company, 210, 935
RSAPPCTL.EXE utility, 522
rsh command , 904-905
rules, global groups, 264-265
running, *see* **executing**

S

SAM (Security Account Manager), 24, 210, 286, 330, 406, 935
    media corruption, 738-739
    password authentication, 248-249
SAM subtree (Registry), 418, 422-423
SAP (Service Advertising Protocol), 494

disabling broadcasts, 498-499
Save Key command (Registry Editor), 413-415
saving configuration (migration), 168
scalability, 12, 24, 26, 30-31, 935
SCANDISK utility, executing, 839
scheduled commands, 911-912
Scopes (DHCP), creating, 605-606
scripts
    customizing setup (Microsoft Office), 461-463
    distributing setup (Microsoft Office), 463-465
    installing Microsoft Office, 461
    logon, 44-45, 341-345, 908-915
        advantages, 342-343
        assigning home directories, 351, 909-910
        compared to User Profiles, 908
        creating/assigning, 344-345
        file extensions, 908
        mechanics of, 343
        NT commands, 911-915
        parameters, 344
        paths, 909
        PUTINENV utility, 345
        replicating, 908-909
        SMS (Systems Management Server), 526
        troubleshooting, 910-911
SCSI (Small Computer System Interface), 50, 126, 508, 937

disk adapters, 63
drives, 653-656
fast SCSI, 656
performance characteris-
tics, 655
tagged command queuing,
656-657
**SCSI-2 (Small Computer
System Interface-2),
64-67, 937**
secondary disks, 836
**section and segment
objects, 34**
sector sparing, 841
NTFT (NT Fault Toler-
ance system), 846
failures, 847
sectors, hot-fixing, 743
security, 26-28, 138-139
auditing, 318
authentication, 248-255,
286, 323-326, 919
*installing for
Macintosh, 477-478*
*local domain logons,
324-325*
*MSV1_0 Authentication
Package, 249*
*pass-through authenti-
cation, 219, 249-252*
RAS Server, 536
*SAM (Security Account
Manager), 248-249*
*share permissions
(NTFS directories),
252-255*
SID (Security ID), 324
*trusted domain logons,
325*
*unknown domain name,
323-326*
*untrusted domain
logons, 326*
workgroup logons, 324
file access permissions,
279-282
editing, 281-282
granting/revoking system
access, 278

GSNW (Gateway Service
for NetWare), 500-501
logons, 213-214, 308-313
automating, 327-328
*global user accounts,
310*
initial logons, 321-322
local user accounts, 310
mechanics of, 319-321
NT servers, 322-323
*remote domains,
311-313*
*Welcome Dialog Box,
319*
LSA Secret Object, renam-
ing NT Servers, 242
NT objects, 291-293
NT Server features, 860
NTFS, compared to FAT/
HPFS security, 254-255
ownership (files), 307
passwords, 278
*caching usernames/
passwords, 322*
*enforcing password
policy, 279*
*Migration Tool for
NetWare, 162*
*SAM (Security Account
Manager), 248-249*
Setup, 144
suggested policies, 278
*trust relationships
(domains), routes for
passing validations,
222-225, 278*
Performance Monitor,
667-668
planning, 282-284
printers, 396-399
profiles, 333-334
RAS (Remote Access
Server), 540-550
auditing, 541
callbacks, 542
*CHAP (Challenge
Handshake Authenti-
cation Protocol),
540-541*

*configuration files,
542-543*
disconnecting users, 541
*editing Registry values,
543-550*
firewalls, 541
logons, 542
*restricted network
access, 541*
Registry, 449
rights, 271-279
*customizing for built-in
user groups, 275-276*
*managing via Adminis-
trators group, 274*
mechanics of, 271-274
*resource ownership,
274-275*
SMS (Systems Manage-
ment Server), 512
user groups, 262-263
viruses, 737-738
**security account data-
bases, 210, 286, 935**
**Security Account Man-
ager (SAM), 24, 210, 286,
330, 406, 935**
media corruption, 738-739
password authentication,
248-249
**Security Administrator,
277**
**security auditing, NT
Server, 861**
**Security Identification
(SID), 213, 286, 302, 308,
935**
auditing, 318
authentication, 324
**security log, auditing,
315-317**
**security model
(BackOffice), 13**
**SECURITY subtree (Reg-
istry), 418, 423**
**seed routers (AppleTalk),
configuring, 485-486**

segmentation, 936
messages, 79-81
segments, 80
cabling, 936
LANs
client setup, 182-184
remote, 183
selecting
files for migration,
166-168
hardware, x86-based
computers, 55-67
protocols (Setup), 141-142
servers for migration, 160
semaphore objects, 34
send command , 898
**separator page files
(printing), 372-373**
**Sequenced Packet Ex-
change (SPX), 88**
**Serial Line Internet
Protocol (SLIP), 532**
**SERIAL.INI (RAS configu-
ration file), 543**
Server, 126
Server Manager
promoting BDCs, 227-229
reconfiguring domains,
237
**Server Message Block
(SMB), 91, 494, 597, 936**
RAW mode read/writes,
693
**Server Operators group,
266-267**
**SERVER service priority,
645**
cache interaction, 646-647
server-based profiles
creating, 337-341
mandatory profiles, 337
personal profiles, 336-337
servers, 936
adding to domains during
installation, 237-238
application servers,
243-244
backup (secondary), 776

booting, troubleshooting,
780-781
clusters, 920
configuring
DHCP servers, 605
WINS servers, 610-611
domain rules, 217
durability testing, 774
Gopher servers, 611-617
configuring, 614-617
deleting, 614
file mapping, 615-617
installing, 612-613
Services dialog box, 617
installation, 62
IPX/SPX protocols, 75
ODI/MLID drivers, 75
preparation, 102
RISC-based, 69-70
WINS servers, 608-610
LAN capacity, 696
logons, 322-323
moving data to another,
774-775
network cards, 657
nondedicated, 10
NT Workstation servers,
236
performance, prioritizing,
645-646
performance tuning,
685-686, 690-691
printers, migration, 158
printing, 360
RAS (Remote Access
Server), 536, 933
remote, 178
performance tuning, 690
replacing, 51, 776
selecting, 51
for migration, 160
superservers, 51
WAIS (Wide Area Infor-
mation Server), 942
**Service Advertising
Protocol (SAP), 494**
**service requests, monitor-
ing applications, 682**

**service-registration
information, network
components (Registry),
446**
**Services dialog box
(Gopher servers), 617**
**Services for Macintosh,
473**
configuring, 484
disadvantages, 487-488
installing, 477
logons, 483-484
Registry entries, 486-487
translating filenames, 480
**Services subtree (Regis-
try), 432-438**
**Session layer (OSI model),
86**
setting up
trust relationships (do-
mains), 221-222
user groups, 300-301
settings
domains (Setup), 143-144
user profiles, 338-339
workgroups (Setup),
143-144
**Setup, 67-68, 102, 126,
129-130, 508, 936**
assigning computer
names, 139
auto-sense, 919
BackOffice, 13
boot disk, 133-134
boot failures, 746
clients, 180-189
filenames, 184-185
MS-DOS, 180, 189-190
*peer-to-peer services,
181*
*remote LAN segments,
182-184*
utilities, 185-186
*WFW (Windows for
Workgroups), 191-195*
Windows 95, 195-204
*Windows NT Worksta-
tion, 204*

workgroups, compared to domains, 182
Custom, 134, 146-150
customizing script files (Microsoft Office), 461-463
date, 145
distributing script files (Microsoft Office), 463-465
distribution share, 149
domain settings, 143-144
emergency repair disk, 146, 733-734
equipment options, 136
errors, 773
Express, 134
file system, 136-137
installation
    Microsoft Office, 460-461
    NT 3.51, 130-146
language, 139
licensing information, 139
listing items, 139
network settings, 142-143
options, 189
password, 144
printers, 140
processor testing, 145-146
protocols, selecting, 141-142
Registry data, 408
RISC-based servers, 69
scanning hard disk for corruption, 138
security, 138-139
settings, workgroups, 143-144
starting, 132
switches, 464
target directory, 137
time, 145
troubleshooting Microsoft Office, 467-468
unattended, 146-150
    configuration, 148-150
video drivers, 145

Welcome screen, 134
Windows 95
    capturing printers, 203
    troubleshooting, 203-204
Workstation Setup (Microsoft Office), MSAPPS files, 465-467
Setup subkey (Registry), 438
SFMMON.DLL (Macintosh print monitor), 482
SFMPSPRT.DLL (Macintosh printing), 482
shadow files (printing), 388-389
shadowing (BIOS), 658
shared application startup, SMS (Systems Management Server), 513-514
shared applications, SMS (Systems Management Server), 521-522
Shares, 286, 293-296, 330, 452
    connecting to, 298-300
    creating, 294-295
    deleting, 295-296
    directories, 45, 178, 279-282, 936
    disconnecting from, 300
    drive letters, mapping to, 202
    permissions, 45, 214-215
        NTFS directories, 252-255
    UNC (Universal Naming Convention), 294
sharing
    files, 187
        distributed computing environments, 452
        transparent file sharing, 472-473
    objects, history of MS-Networks, 287-288
    printers, 296-298, 369-371

shells, 936
shielded twisted-pair (STP) cabling, 787, 937
Shiva Password Authentication Protocol (SPAP), 541
Shutdown button, 765
SID (Security Identification), 213, 286, 302, 308, 935
    auditing, 318
    authentication, 324
Signal Quality Error (SQE), 815-816
signals
    degradation (cabling), 797
    loss, 926
    NeXT (near end crosstalk), 928
    noise, 930
silent installation (Microsoft Office), 461
Simple Mail Transfer Protocol (SMTP), 597
Simple Network Management Protocol (SNMP), 508, 597, 937
    monitoring Ethernet, 627
Single Domain Model, 220
size limits (Registry), 442-443
SizWorkBufs (Registry parameter), 548
SLIP (Serial Line Internet Protocol), 532
Small Computer System Interface (SCSI), 50, 126, 508, 937
    disk adapters, 63
    drives, 653-656
    fast SCSI, 656
    performance characteristics, 655
    tagged command queuing, 656-657
Small Computer System Interface-2 (SCSI-2), 64-67, 937

SMB (Server Message Block), 91, 494, 597, 936
protocol layer, trouble-shooting, 790-791, 829-832
RAW mode read/writes, 693
SMP (Symmetrical Multi-processing), 674, 939
support, 68
SMS (Systems Management Server), 508-528
applying updates, 514
audited software, 518-519
capabilities, 508-509
clients, 515-521
components, 509-510
configuring, 513-515
for NetWare, 515
creating/distributing packages, 519-520
installing, 511-512
applications on clients, 522-523
Microsoft Access, 524
Microsoft Office, 523-524
Microsoft Word, 524
Microsoft Works, 524
Inventory Agent, 517-518
logon scripts, 526
network monitoring, 526-528
Program Group Control, 520-521
security, 512
shared applications, 521-522
startup, 513-514
SMSLS.INI file, 515
structure (levels), 510-511
system requirements, 511
upgrading clients to Windows NT, 525
SMSLS.INI file, 515
SMTP (Simple Mail Transfer Protocol), 597

SNA (Systems Network Architecture), 24, 210, 939
SNA Server, 578-593
Administration program, 584-588
capacities, 581
COM.CFG file backups, 586
DOS clients, 592-593
executing, 585-586
features, 578-580
installing, 582-583
NT Server integration, 580-581
renaming servers, 584
system requirements, 581-582
TCP/IP clients, 589-590
third-party emulators, 591-592
WFW clients, 589
Windows-based clients, 588-589
SNAP (Subnetwork Access Protocol), 624, 809
SNMP (Simple Network Management Protocol), 508, 597, 937
monitoring Ethernet, 627
socket addresses, 937
soft errors (Token ring), 823-825
soft switches, 721-722
software
backup software packages, 726-727
Btrieve, 919
compatibility, 25
development, 11
network components (Registry), binding, 447-448
non-vendor-specific monitoring tools, 628
OpenGL, 69
portability, 931

RAID 5 implementation, 67
RAS (Remote Access Server), 530-550
APIs, 534
AsyncMAC driver, 537-538
capabilities, 530-534
data compression, 533
data encryption, 533
hardware requirements, 538
installing/configuring, 538-540
Internet support, 533
joining domains, 539-540
NetWare networks, 533
potential conflicts, 538-539
PPP (Point-to-Point Protocol), 532
RAS Server, 536
RAS Subsystem, 536-538
RASHub device driver, 537
security, 540-550
SLIP (Serial Line Internet Protocol), 532
user interface, 534-535
WFW connections, 538
X.25 networks, 534
redirectors, 933
scalability, 935
shells, 936
SMS (Systems Management Server)
applications, installing on clients, 522-523
audited software, 518-519
capabilities, 508-509
clients, 515-521
components, 509-510
configuration, 513-515
installation, 511-512
Inventory Agent, 517-518

logon scripts, 526
Microsoft Access, installing, 524
Microsoft Office, installing, 523-524
Microsoft Word, installing, 524
Microsoft Works, installing, 524
network monitoring, 526-528
package creation / distribution, 519-520
Program Group Control, 520-521
security, 512
shared applications, 513-514, 521-522
SMSLS.INI file, 515
structure (levels), 510-511
system requirements, 511
updates, 514
upgrading clients to Windows NT, 525
tasks, 939
see also applications
SOFTWARE subtree (Registry), 418, 423-427
software-registration information, network components (Registry), 445-448
Solution Providers (Microsoft Solution Provider Network), 867-868
sound cards, adding, 152
Source Service Access Point (SSAP), 937
source-routing bridge/ protocol, 937
spanned volumes, 938
spanning-tree bridge/ protocol, 938

SPAP (Shiva Password Authentication Protocol), 541
specific dependencies, 448-449
speed (bandwidth), compared to capacity, 697
split domains, recombining, 239-241
split pairs (cabling), 801-802
spool files, 360, 363, 388-389, 938
clearing print jobs from, 376
directories, 378
spoolers, 360, 363-365, 938
spooling (print jobs), 360, 938
components of, 363-365
default printer spool directory, changing, 691-692
SPX (Sequenced Packet Exchange), 88
SQL Server configuration, 559-561
SQE (Signal Quality Error), 815-816
SQL Bridge, 555
SQL Server, 552-575
backup/recovery, 565-566
devices/databases, 564-566
executing, 562-564
remotely, 572-573
features, 552-553
installing/configuring, 555-562
named pipes clients, 558-559
reinstallation, 557-558
SPX/IPX, 559-561
TCP/IP sockets, 561-562
utilities, 557
memory configuration, 566-567

networking protocols, 553-555
Open Data Services, 554
performance tuning, 568-572
indexes, 568-569
normalized databases, 569-570
query design, 570-572
Registry entries, 574-575
SQL Bridge, 555
truncating transaction logs, 573-574
SSAP (Source Service Access Point), 937
stacks, protocols (OSI Model), 86
standard product support, 869
star bus (network topology), 938
star-wired ring (network topology), 938
start command, 893-894, 915
starting
migration, 168
Network Monitoring Agent Service (SMS), 527-528
shared application startup (SMS), 513-514
see also executing
startup data, SYSTEM subtree (Registry), 427-429, 429-432
static dependencies, 449
status command , 898
storage
devices
adding/editing, 151
drivers, loading, 135
files on Macintosh, 480
STP (shielded twisted-pair) cabling, 787, 937
streaming data mode, 59, 61, 938
striping, 66, 836

disk drives, 686, 938
with parity, 67, 836
stub functions, 37
**subkeys (Registry), 406,
415-416, 939**
Control subtree, 429-432
LargeSystemCache, 651
network components,
443-444
Not_Enough_Quota, 652
Services subtree, 432-438
Setup subkey, 438
value entries, 439-440
**Subnetwork Access
Protocol (SNAP), 624, 809**
subnetworks, 596
Subsystem (RAS), 536-538
**subtrees (Registry), 406,
939**
HARDWARE, 417-422
SAM, 418, 422-423
saving as hives, 414
SECURITY, 418, 423
SOFTWARE, 418, 423-427
SYSTEM, 418, 427-438
suites, 453-454
Microsoft Office, 456-468
*administrative installa-
tion, 459-460*
*client installation,
458-461*
*customizing setup script
files, 461-463*
*distributing setup script
files, 463-465*
installing, 457-459
MSAPPS files, 465-467
*troubleshooting,
467-468*
uninstalling, 461
versions, 457
PerfectOffice, 468-472
*Administrator program
group, 469*
*application integration,
469*
*Envoy (electronic
publishing), 470*

InfoCentral, 470
installing, 471-472
QuickTask, 470
*technical support,
470-471*
SUMMARY.LOG file, 170
**SunNet Manager (moni-
toring tool), 628**
superservers, 51
Supervisor (RAS), 536
support, 53
CD-ROMs, 61
clients, installation, 191
IPXODI clients, drivers,
92-94
Microsoft, 867
NetWare clients, 92-95
SMP, 68
workstations, 91
**SWITCH.INF (RAS con-
figuration file), 543**
**switchboard (Microsoft)
phone number, 866**
switches, 119, 716
/B, 132
bus switching, 719-720
design, 719-722
matrix switching, 720-721
Setup, 464
/T:path_name, 132
switches command, 894
**switching hubs, 83,
708-709, 716-718, 939**
collisions, 717
selection, 718
soft switches, 721-722
symbolic link objects, 34
**Symmetrical Multipro-
cessing (SMP), 30, 674,
939**
**synchronizing domain
controllers, 226**
optimization, 229-233
**system access, granting/
revoking, 278**
SYSTEM account, 306
**system administration,
10-11**

**system architecture, NT
Server features/capaci-
ties, 857**
**system environment
variables, 346-348**
**system failure, preven-
tion, 290**
system files (NTFS), 742
system logs, auditing, 315
system requirements
NT Server, 856
SMS (Systems Manage-
ment Server), 511
SNA Server, 581-582
**SYSTEM subtree (Regis-
try), 418, 427-438**
**system utilities, GSNW
(Gateway Service for
NetWare), 502-503**
**system-defined data
types, 34**
SystemAudit ACE, 28
**Systems Management
Server (SMS), 508-528**
applying updates, 514
audited software, 518-519
capabilities, 508-509
clients, 515-521
components, 509-510
configuring, 513-515
for NetWare, 515
creating/distributing
packages, 519-520
installing, 511-512
*applications on clients,
522-523*
Microsoft Access, 524
*Microsoft Office,
523-524*
Microsoft Word, 524
Microsoft Works, 524
Inventory Agent, 517-518
logon scripts, 526
network monitoring,
526-528
Program Group Control,
520-521
security, 512

shared applications,
521-522
startup, 513-514
SMSLS.INI file, 515
structure (levels), 510-511
system requirements, 511
upgrading clients to
Windows NT, 525
**Systems Network Archi-
tecture (SNA), 24, 210,
939**

T

T-1 lines, 77
**tagged command queuing
(SCSI), 656-657**
**Take Ownership right,
274-275**
tape drives, 152
**tasking options, configur-
ing, 351**
tasks (software), 939, 662
**TCP/IP (Transmission
Control Protocol/
Internet Protocol), 41,
597-620, 940-941**
adding to installed NT
Servers, 604
advantages, 599
browsers, 600-601
DHCP (Dynamic Host
Control Protocol),
604-608
HTTP Server, 617-620
installing, 399-400,
602-604
Microsoft, 89-90
NetBIOS
encapsulation, 600
name resolution, 601
printing, 399-402
*configuring NT Server,
400-401*
*creating TCP/IP
printers, 401-402*
SNA Server clients,
589-590

sockets, SQL Server
configuration, 561-562
support, 9
troubleshooting, 829
utilities reference, 894-906
WINS (Windows Internet
Name Service), 608-611
**TDI (Transport Driver
Interface), 24, 941**
**TDR (Time Domain
Reflectometry), 792-793**
TechNet, 867
technical support, 866-873
bulletin board service, 869
FastTips, 868
Internet services, 871-872
Microsoft Electronic
Technical Library, 871
Microsoft Knowledge Base,
871
Microsoft phone numbers,
866-867
Microsoft Solution Pro-
vider Network, 867-868
newsgroups, 871
online services, 872-873
PerfectOffice, 470-471
premier support, 870
priority support, 869-870
standard product support,
869
**technologies, LANs,
102-109**
**Telecommunications
Industry Association
(TIA), 786**
telnet command , 905
**templates, creating user
profiles, 340-341**
terminals, 939
**Terminate and Stay
Resident (TSR), 178, 494**
**terminations (cabling),
118, 794, 802**
testing
cabling, 112
disk drives, 780
processor (Setup), 145-146

RAM (random access
memory), 780
tftp command , 905-906
**theoretical bandwidth,
compared to usable,
698-699**
Thinnet, 116
**third-party emulators
(SNA Server), 591-592**
thread objects, 34
**thread priority (Registry),
403**
threads, 644
**TIA (Telecommunications
Industry Association),
786**
time
setting for domains, 245
Setup, 145
**Time Domain Reflectom-
etry (TDR), 792-793**
time slices, 939
title command, 894
**Token ring, 74, 106-107,
940**
bandwidth, 103-105,
698-699
beaconing, 633, 822-823
congestion, 825
distance, 77
frames, 633-634
functional stations,
819-820
Intelligent Token ring,
CAU (Control Access
Unit), 624
MAU (Multistation Access
Unit), 624
monitoring, 632-634
networks, 76
purge frames, 821
Ring Change frames,
820-821
ring polls, 820
ring re-initialization, 633
ring recovery counters,
821-822
soft errors, 823-825

token rotation time,
825-826
troubleshooting, 819-826
**token rotation time,
825-826**
token-passing bus, 939
token-passing rings, 939
Token-Ring, 940
topologies, 940
linear bus, 925
ring, 934
star bus, 938
star-wired ring, 938
**TP-DDI (FDDI on Twisted
Pair), 107-108**
trace command , 898
tracert command , 906
traffic
bridges, 81
printing, moving, 88
**transaction logs (SQL
Server), truncating,
573-574**
**transactions, performance
tuning, 665**
transceivers, 940
translating
bridges, 940
Macintosh filenames, 480
Macintosh permissions,
482-483
**Transmission Control
Protocol/Internet Proto-
col,** *see* **TCP/IP**
**transmission time, band-
width, 697-698**
transparent bridges, 941
**transparent file sharing,
472-473**
**Transport Driver Inter-
face (TDI), 24, 941**
transport layer, 86
troubleshooting, 790,
827-829
IPX/SPX, 828
NetBEUI, 828
TCP/IP, 829

**transport protocols
(NetBEUI), 75**
**transports, IPX/SPX
compatible, 94-95**
**trend analysis, bandwidth
monitoring, 700-701**
troubleshooting
backing up
BOOT.INI file, 840-841
Registry, 840-841
cabling, 792
attenuation, 792-793
cable testers, 805
*certification tools,
806-807*
coaxial, 792-794
*continuity testers,
804-805*
fiber optic, 804
*UTP (unshielded
twisted pair), 795-802*
CHKDSK utility, 839
Emergency Repair Disk,
837-838
Ethernet, 630-632
intermittent problems, 779
LAN layer, 790, 807-826
Ethernet, 807-828
Token ring, 819-826
logon scripts, 910-911
Microsoft Office Setup,
467-468
non-Setup boot failures,
745-746
NT Messages database,
637-638
partitions, recovering
orphans, 850
physical layer, 788-807
printing problems,
402-403
protocol analyzers,
787-791
features, 788-789
RAID, 841-842
restoring computers,
849-850

Setup-related boot fail-
ures, 746
SMB protocol layer,
790-791, 829-832
transport layer, 790,
827-829
IPX/SPX, 828
NetBEUI, 828
TCP/IP, 829
virtual circuit manage-
ment layer, 790, 826-827
truncating
transaction logs (SQL
Server), 573-574
event logs, 657
**trust relationships (do-
mains), 210, 216-225, 941**
creating, 312-313
domain models, 220-221
logging in without, 311
one-way trusts, 218
pass-through authentica-
tion, 219, 249-252
routes for passing validations, 222-225
setting up, 221-222
trusted compared to
trusting domains,
217-218
two-way trusts, 218
trusted domains
compared to trusting
domains, 217-218
logon authentication, 325
**trusting domains, com-
pared to trusted do-
mains, 217-218**
**TSR (Terminate and Stay
Resident), 178, 494**
tuning, 685-693
bottlenecks, 673-679
cache, 677-678
disk, 675-676
LAN, 679
memory, 676-677
processor, 674-675
counters, 666-667

default printer spool directory, changing, 691-692

disabling print job logging, 692

disk drives, 686-688
   linear memory addressing, 686
   paging (virtual memory), 687
   paging files, 687-688
GSNW (Gateway Service for NetWare), 499-500
LAN hardware, 688-689
NT Server features, 859-860
overview, 662-665
RAW mode read/writes, 693
remote servers, 690
servers, 685-686, 690-691
SQL Server, 568-572
   indexes, 568-569
   normalized databases, 569-570
   query design, 570-572
transactions, 665
workstations, 689-690
see also monitoring

twisted pair cabling, 941
installation, 113-116
troubleshooting, 795-802

two-way trusts (domains), 218

Type 1 errors (Token ring), 823

Type 2 errors (Token ring), 823-824

Type 3 errors (Token ring), 824

Type 4 errors (Token ring), 825

type command , 898

U

UAS (User Account System), 941

LAN Manager, 210

UDP (User Datagram Protocol), 597, 941

unattended backups, 912

unattended Setup, 146-150
configuration, 148-150

UNC (Universal Naming Convention), 210, 214, 941
Shares, 294

UNICODE (character representation), 24, 941

uninstalling Microsoft Office, 461

uninterruptible power supplies (UPSs), 747-748
cable pin assignments, 748
configuring, 747-748

UNIX
clients, printing, 383
systems, migration, 173-175

unknown domain name, authentication, 323-326

Unload Hive command (Registry Editor), 413

unshielded twisted pair (UTP) cabling, 625, 787, 941
installing, 802-804
troubleshooting, 795-802

untrusted domains
access denial, 739
logon authentication, 326

updates
emergency repair disk, 838
SMS (Systems Management Server), applying to, 514

upgrading
bandwidth, 698
clients to Windows NT via SMS (Systems Management Server), 525
LAN Manager 2.x, 170-172
see also migrating

UPSs (uninterruptible power supplies), 747-748

cable pin assignments, 748
configuring, 747-748

uptime (fault tolerance), 42

UpToMP utility, 68

usable bandwidth, compared to theoretical, 698-699

user account databases, 210, 286, 935

user account information, 302

User Account System (UAS), 941
LAN Manager, 210

user accounts, 301-308
adding to domains, 216
Administrator account, 303
authentication, 248-255, 323-326
   local domain logons, 324-325
   MSV1_0 Authentication Package, 249
   pass-through authentication, 249-252
   SAM (Security Account Manager), 248-249
   share permissions (NTFS directories), 252-255
   SID (Security Identification), 324
   trusted domain logons, 325
   unknown domain name, 323-326
   untrusted domain logons, 326
   workgroup logons, 324
caching usernames/ passwords, 322
creating, 301
global accounts
   logon security, 310
   remote domain logons, 312-313

Guest account, 304
hidden accounts, 304-306
initial user account,
  303-304
local accounts
  logon security, 310
  remote domain logons,
    311-312
logons
  local, compared to
    domain, 212
  security, 213-214,
    308-313
mapping to rights/permis-
  sions, 320-321
remote domains, logon
  security, 311-313
replicating (migration),
  172
SID (Security Identifica-
  tion), 302
User and Group Options
dialog box, 162
user command , 898
User Datagram Protocol
(UDP), 597, 941
user disconnection, RAS
security, 541
user domains, 210, 941
trust relationships,
  217-218
user environment vari-
ables, 348-349
user groups, 258-261, 941
assigning rights, 268-270,
  276, 307-308
built-in, 261, 266-271
  customizing rights,
    275-276
  global groups, 270-271
  local groups, 266-268
configurations/definitions,
  261-262
domain-local groups, 265
global groups, 286, 330
local, 286, 330
  compared to global,
    259-260

security, 262-263
setting up, 300-301
strategies, 261-265
  global group mechanics,
    263
  global group rules,
    264-265
  groups as members of
    groups, 265
  local group mechanics,
    263-264
user interfaces
protocol analyzers, 789
RAS (Remote Access
  Server), 534-535
User Manager for Do-
mains, 216
assigning
  profiles, 334-335
  rights, 276
creating
  trust relationships, 313
  user accounts, 301
editing rights, 301
managing rights, 271-274
user profiles, 43-44,
331-341
advantages, 333-334
compared to logon scripts,
  908
default profiles, 337
local profiles, 335-336
mandatory profiles, 337
mechanics of, 334-335
overview, 332-333
permanent network
  connections, 341
personal profiles, 336-337
Registry, 439-440
server-based profiles,
  creating, 337-341
settings, 338-339
user rights, 258, 271-279,
286, 330, 934
assigning to user groups,
  268-270, 276, 307-308
customizing for built-in

user groups, 275-276
editing for user groups,
  301
managing via Administra-
  tors group, 274
mapping user accounts to,
  320-321
mechanics of, 271-274
NT Server, 861
resource ownership,
  274-275
Security Administrator,
  277
setting up user groups,
  300-301
see also permissions
user sessions, disconnect-
ing automatically, 740
user-defined objects, 159
usergroup managers,
migration, 159
usernames, conflicts, 159
users, restricting, 44
Users group, 261
utilities
Backup
  NT Server features, 863
  unattended backups,
    912
BINDFIX, 497
CHKDSK, 640-641
  executing, 839
Diagnostics, 778
installing SQL Server
  utilities, 557
migration, 170-171
  ACLCONV, 171
  BACKACC, 170
  CONVERT, 171
  PORTUAS, 171
NetWare
  migration, 157-170
  system utilities, 502-503
network adapter diagnos-
  tics, 179
Network Client Adminis-
  trator, 185-186

Network Setup, 191
PORTUAS conversion
  utility, 210, 931
Putinenv, 45, 345
RDISK.EXE, updating
  Emergency Repair Disk,
  838
Registry Editor, 407
  configuration manage-
  ment, 411-415
  executing, 410
Resource Kit, 659
RSAPPCTL.EXE, 522
SCANDISK, executing,
  839
TCP/IP utilities reference,
  894-906
UpToMP, 68
User Manager for Do-
  mains, 216
UTP (unshielded twisted
pair) cabling, 787, 941
  installing, 802-804
  troubleshooting, 795-802

V

validations, routes for
passing (trust relation-
ships), 222-225
value entries (Registry),
439-440
variables, environment,
345-351
  account variables, 346
  recovery options, 350
  system environment
    variables, 346-348
  tasking options, 351
  user environment vari-
    ables, 348-349
  virtual memory, 349-350
VDM (Virtual DOS Ma-
chine), 7, 24, 360, 942
verbose command , 898
Verify NT System Files
(repair option), 733

VESA (Video Electronics
Standards Association),
58
video cards, auto-sensing,
127
video driver (Setup), 145
viewing
  hidden accounts, 305
  partitions (disk drives),
    639
virtual circuit manage-
ment layer, troubleshoot-
ing, 790, 826-827
virtual circuits, 78
virtual memory, 349-350,
647-648
  configuration, 144-145
  paging, 687
virtual memory manager,
34-36
VirtualLock( ) function,
648, 652
viruses, 737-738
VL-bus, 58
  PCI comparison, 59-61
VLANs (Virtual LANs),
708-709, 716-717, 942
VLMs (Virtual Loading
Modules), 942
volumes (AFP)
  accessing files, 479
  configuring, 479
  creating, 478
  sets, 836
  spanned, 938

W

WAIS (Wide Area Informa-
tion Server), 942
WANs (Wide Area Net-
works), 24, 50
  nodes, 77
warranties, 53
Watchdog (monitoring
tool), 629-630
Welcome Dialog Box
(logons), 319

Welcome screen (Setup),
134
WFW (Windows for
Workgroups), 50
  clients
    installation disk set,
    188
    setup, 191-195
  configuring SQL Server
    clients, 560-561
  file access permissions,
    280
  logons, 327
  RAS connections, 538
  similarities to NT, 8
  SMS clients, 516
  SNA Server clients, 589
Wide Area Information
Server (WAIS), 942
Windows
  applications
    16-bit, 7
    availability in migra-
    tion, 173
    printing, 368, 380-382
  clients, printing from,
    366-367
  desktop, 286, 330, 921
    profiles, 331-341
  exiting, 335
  LANalyzer (monitoring
    tool), 713
  print drivers, 360
  print processors, 385-386
  print providers, 389
  Setup, 936
  SNA Server
    clients, 588-589
    third-party emulators,
    591-592
windows, multiple, 9
Windows 3.1, similarities
to NT, 8
Windows 3.x TCP/IP
clients, configuring for
SNA Server, 590
Windows 95, 179

clients, setup, 195-204
file permissions, 280-281
setup
  capturing printers, 203
  network services,
    197-202
  troubleshooting,
    203-204
SMS clients, 516
Windows for Workgroups,
see WFW
Windows Internet Name
Service (WINS), 210, 597,
608-611, 942
advantages, 608
configuring servers,
  610-611
disadvantages, 600-601
installing servers, 608-610
Windows NT
commands (logon scripts),
  911-915
compared to NetWare, 8,
  289
deleting from boot parti-
  tion, 736-737
features, 6
installation, restoring with
  emergency disk repair,
  838
networking overview, 288-
  289
object-oriented features,
  289-293
  ACL (access control
    list), 291
  closing objects, 293
  security, 291-293
optimizing, 663
reinstalling, 732-733
  editing BOOT.INI
    parameters, 734-736
routing support, 601-602
upgrading clients via SMS
  (Systems Management
  Server), 525
Windows NT Work-
station, 4

client setup, 204
WINS (Windows Internet
Name Service), 210, 597,
608-611, 942
advantages, 608
configuring servers,
  610-611
disadvantages, 600-601
installing servers, 608-610
wiring concentrators, 74,
111, 812, 942
Word, installing via SMS
(Systems Management
Server), 524
workgroups, 258, 942
compared to domains,
  211-212
  client setup, 182
logons
  authentication, 324
  security, 213-214
migration, 159
settings (Setup), 143-144
user group definitions, 262
working sets, 648-649, 662,
942
Workstation, 126
clients, connecting to
  NetWare server, 92
file access permissions,
  279
logons, 327
renaming, 242
as servers, 236
user profiles, 439-440
Workstation Setup
(Microsoft Office),
MSAPPS files, 465-467
workstations, 943
joining domains, 238-239
NT Server network card
  support, 858
NT Workstations
  renaming, 242
  as servers, 236
performance tuning,
  689-690
printing, 360

remote workstations,
  382
support, 91
World Wide Web (WWW)
Gopher servers, 611-617
  configuring, 614-617
  deleting, 614
  file mapping, 615-617
  installing, 612-613
  Services dialog box, 617
technical support sites,
  871
Writes Denied/sec
counter, 690

X-Y-Z

X.25 networks, RAS
(Remote Access Server),
534
x86-based computers,
54-67
hardware selection, 55-67
Xerox Network System
(XNS), 943